For

Bill Peter – Masterful Teacher and Friend

And

Michael Murray and Ann Fitzgibbon Friends and Mentors

FOREWORD

Little acorns grow big and when Trinity College's first Educational Management outreach centre under Professor Heywood was established in Portlaoise Vocational School almost 20 years ago, little did Principal, Michael Parsons, think that 20 years later in his role as President of the National Association of Principals and Deputy Principals (**NAPD**) a plea to enable principals to be the instructional leaders in their schools would be the genesis of this wonderful book.

Professor Heywood's seminal work on Instructional and Curriculum Leadership sits easily with key objectives of **NAPD**
- To show leadership in the formulation of education policy
- To promote the professional and personal development of principals and deputy principals
- To adopt a proactive and dynamic approach to developing the international and European dimension in schools
- To promote strategies for the development of research.

NAPD has consistently called for the necessary supports to be put in place to enable the school principal to be the leader of instruction in the school. By publishing Instructional and Curriculum Leadership, **NAPD** hopes to initiate a debate within Irish education and beyond in an attempt to bring instructional leadership centre stage.

Recent OECD Studies have emphasised school leadership as being high on policy agendas throughout the world. Equally the role of the school leader has changed as countries demand that the education system prepare young people to function in a world of economic globalisation.

While acknowledging the functions and tasks set out for school leaders in the OECD studies, **NAPD** believes that the primary role of each principal is to be the leader of learning in their school.

While **NAPD** continues to campaign to enable leaders to undertake this onerous task, the Association jumped at the opportunity to engage with Professor Heywood on a topic so central to our concerns.

Many Trinity graduates who are principals and deputy principals will be familiar with Professor Heywood's work. Indeed, many may well have taken part in some of the research leading to the publication of this work as Higher Diploma or as students on Masters and Ph.D. courses.

This impressive work succeeds at different levels. It makes clear that successful instructional leaders may have to delegate the actual task to middle management with a cascading effect to subject departments and individual teachers.

This will prove to be a greater challenge in the context of inclusivity, diversity and the requirement on schools to cater for pupils with specific learning difficulties and disabilities.

This work will provide a framework for practitioners at every layer in the system to engage the relevant issues within the "assumptional dialogues" process envisaged in the text.

NAPD hopes that the publication of Prof Heywood's work will act as a catalyst towards inquiry oriented schools with learning and curriculum at their heart.

The National Association of Principals and Deputy Principals (NAPD) is proud to be Associated with Professor Heywood and with the publication of his study on Instructional and Curriculum Leadership.

Clive Byrne

Director, National Association of Principals and Deputy Principals (**NAPD**)

PREFACE

In 2005 the President of the National Association of Principals and Deputies of Ireland (NAPD) Mr Michael Parsons led a delegation to the Department of Education and Science (DES). The delegation asked the Minister for Education to change the role of Principal from that of being just an administrator to that of being an instructional leader. The association's written statement said that *"there is a continuing need for curriculum development and this will require a cultural change in many schools. The provision of instructional leadership crucially involves freeing up the Principal to exercise this responsibility."*

Recently Mr Parsons and his colleagues received a lot of support from a study carried out McKinsey and Company the international business consultants for the Organization for Economic and Cultural Development (OECD). They found that *"the only way to improve outcomes is to improve instruction"* (p26). They argued that principals should be instructional leaders. *"Once the school system has identified and developed the right people with the right skills, it then needs to structure the roles, expectations, and incentives to ensure that its principals focus on instructional leadership and not on school administration [. . .] the systems which seek to use their principals as drivers of reform expect them to be excellent instructors who spent most of their time coaching teachers [. . .] Being a teacher is about helping children to learn. Being a principal is about helping adults to learn."* (pp 30/31).

It is argued here that often student learning can be influenced as much by the curriculum as it is by instruction. This requires that principals should exercise a leadership role in respect of both instruction and the curriculum. To achieve this schools have to have curricular subsidiarity as well as administrative subsidiarity. .Ireland provides some good examples of curricular subsidiarity in both primary (elementary) and post-primary education, as for example the Transition Year between the end of the junior cycle and the beginning of the senior cycle of post-primary education.

The Christian Brothers Development Project that investigated instructional leadership concluded that Principals neither had the time or the resources to be instructional leaders. In this text it is taken as axiomatic that Principals should be trained in the principles of instructional leadership but so should every other teacher. It is recognized that within schools there is nevertheless a role for instructional and curriculum leaders. Strangely for a company that purports to know about management the McKinsey authors did not conclude that the

Instructional and Curriculum Leadership

Towards Inquiry Oriented Schools

by

John Heywood

ORIGINAL WRITING

for the National Association of Principals and Deputy Principals (NAPD)

© J. Heywood, 2008.

All rights reserved. No part of this publication may be reproduced in any form or by any means—graphic, electronic or mechanical, including photocopying, recording, taping or information storage and retrieval systems—without the prior written permission of the author.

ISBN: 978-1-906018-75-7

A CIP catalogue for this book is available from the National Library.

Published by Original Writing Ltd
for the National Association of Principals and Deputies, Ireland

Original Writing, Spade Enterprise Centre, North King Street, Smithfield, Dublin, 1.

National Association of Principals and Deputy Principals (NAPD), 40 Lower Leeson St. Dublin, 1.

Printed by Cahills, Dublin.

Principal's task is to create an organization for learning. That it is, is a primary assumption of this text.

Learning is achieved by inquiry so schools should be inquiry oriented. Schools should engage in what Argyris and Schön have called "assumptional dialogues." A rather ugly phrase to say the least that is intended to indicate that a school should question what it does regularly not on the basis of teacher opinion and experience but on the basis of acquired knowledge especially that from research and the experience of others. Such dialogues should be the basis of the whole school planning which should be the source of renewal. Throughout this text examples are given of assumptions that should be questioned.

One of the problems that the report from the McKinsey Company does not discuss is the usage of the term "instruction" in different cultures yet this is important. In the British Isles, for example, the term "instruction" is connotative with "training" and "training" is connotative with teaching by rote. "Instruction" in the report could be construed as "training" for examinations. Teachers in these countries would rightly object that that is not "education," a term that for them is connotative with the development of the whole person and something that cannot be measured by tests of achievement alone. In the United States the term is understood to be connotative with teaching and to the classroom experience of that teaching. It is that connotation that is used in this text.

What surprises experienced teachers who attend my courses in Curriculum and Instructional leadership is that the curriculum either across the whole school or within subjects is not sacrosanct. It can and should be challenged from time to time. The belief that they should accept the curriculum as handed down by the Government is deeply ingrained. Teachers cannot claim to be professional if they are not prepared to acquire a framework of knowledge that will enable them to make their own judgements about the validity or otherwise of a curriculum. Neither are they professional if they allow others to check their performance without reflecting on it themselves prior to such inspection. Effective accountability begins with self-accountability. The view taken in this text is that on the one hand governments have progressively de-professionalized teaching, and on the other hand teachers can redress this situation if, like scientists, they use their classrooms as laboratories for research into their own teaching. That is self-accountability and should be linked to positive within-school systems of appraisal. This text is focused on the knowledge required for such professionalism, and thus, the provision of a "technical pedagogy" with which to discuss schooling, assessment, curriculum and instruction. These points are developed in the introduction and summary that follows.

John Heywood
Dublin. September 2008

Acknowledgements

The publication of this book has been made possible by the support of the National Association of Principals and Deputies. I am very grateful to Mr Michael Parsons former President and Mr Clive Byrne Director of the Association for their support throughout this venture. It goes without saying that the opinions expressed in this study are mine and mine alone. Nevertheless I am grateful to all those who have challenged those opinions over the years and hope the study is the better for them. I number Michael Parsons as one of those critics. Like John Cowan, whose profound studies were published after many years of gestation so to with this text which has had a long gestation. During this period which covered the years John was at Heriot-Watt and The Open Universities he painstakingly waded through many iterations and helped me to bring it to a size suitable for today rather than yesterday. I am grateful to him for all that work and to my American friend and critic Dr Glen Rogers of Alverno College who gave me a US perspective on my advocacy.

The formal attempt to develop a framework for the study of Instructional and Curriculum Leadership began when I introduced a course of this title into our programme for the continuing professional development of experienced teachers. Jimmy Fitzmaurice the Principal of small primary (elementary) school evaluated his role as an instructional leader in an action research for a dissertation. He showed just how chaotic and confused thinking was about this topic and I determined to bring some order to this chaos. Two opportunities were given me to achieve this goal. The first came from Dr Michael Murray of the Christian Brothers who asked me to Direct a project in which principals and teachers would be trained in the design, implementation and evaluation of a curriculum in the Irish Transition Year. I am grateful to him for that opportunity and continuing support.

The second opportunity came when the Education Research and Methods Division of the American Society for Engineering Education asked its chairman Professor Barbara Olds, Professor Richard Culver of Binghamton University and myself to make proposals to the Division for future work in this area. Together we developed the idea of levels of leadership in instruction and the curriculum. It led to seminars on the topic and a book that helped me to focus on the issue as it related to post primary education. I am grateful to them both.

ACKNOWLEDGEMENTS

During the same period Dr Karen Mayo then of Stephen F. Austin University in Texas set me on the path of comparing the differences between the roles of principals in Texas and in Ireland. This confirmed the need to bring some order to the field. That particular aspect of this work has been continued and broadened by Ms Verity Swan as part of her doctoral study. I am grateful to Dr Mayo for her help and Ms Swan for her continuing help and criticism in the development of these ideas. I am indebted to Ms Ann Fitzgibbon who suggested the exercises on imagery and learning styles.

Finally are the students of the Higher Diploma Course for graduates training to be post-primary teachers, B.Ed students in their final year and the experienced teachers in the professional development courses who responded in one way or another to the ideas presented. In particular during the 1980's and 1990's were the Higher Diploma Students who undertook very detailed investigations into their teaching. The results of their work are used to illustrate chapters 5 through 9. Their reports gave me many insights into the issues and great deal of pleasure in reading. Each of the three thousand odd reports I read had something of interest to say but in the final analysis only a few illustrations could be used. So my heartfelt thanks go first to those who allowed us to publish full copies of their reports in Departmental Monographs – Charlotte, L. Callaghan, Paula Carroll, Ian Donovan and Peter Lydon, and second those whose illustrations were taken from these reports- Niamh Clarke, Ruadhan Hayes, Mariele Hesper, Graham Hewston, Deidre Power, Catherine Roche, Phyllis Stefenazi and Kate Willis. And for illustrations from their reports- Fiona Anderson, Michael Ashmore, Valerie Bistany, Edel Byrne, Linda Campbell, Niamh Casey, Audrey Clarke, David Clarke, Caroline Cleary, Alan Coad, Niamh Collins, Evelyn Cosgrave, Alan Cox, John Davis, Margaret Fegan, Samantha Fox, Georgina FitzPatrick, Ann FitzSimmons, Berbhile Gallagher, Ann Geraghty, Mary Greene, Terri Harris, Gilian Harte, Katrina Hegarty, Antonia Hegarty, Martina Jones, Antonia Kelly, Julie Kelly, Mary Killen, Sinead Lambe, Catherine McAndrew, Jeanne McKeever, Susan Maguire, Ann Moynan, Elizabeth Murphy, Ursula O'Brien, Michael O'Loughlin, Elizabeth O'Neil, Paulette O'Riordan, Wynne Oliver, Lucinda Packham, Linda Prendergast, Tanja Putz, Grace Reddington, Kevin Reilly, Carmel Ring Catherine Roche, Maria Stack, Ciara Vaughan, Thomas Walshe, Rosemary Waugh, Helen O'Connor Watson, Suzanne Wilde. I wish to thank Diarmuid Doyle for his help with the text.

I am very grateful to Aoife Lyons for help in the preparation of the manuscript.

Summary and Introduction
to the Text

Why the focus on Instructional and Curriculum Leadership

A study carried out by McKinsey and Company the international business consultants for the Organization for Economic and Cultural Development (OECD) explains the importance of instructional and curriculum leadership. Its investigators found that *"the only way to improve outcomes is to improve instruction"* (p26). They argued that principals should be instructional leaders. *"Once the school system has identified and developed the right people with the right skills, it then needs to structure the roles, expectations, and incentives to ensure that its principals focus on instructional leadership and not on school administration [. . .] the systems which seek to use their principals as drivers of reform expect them to be excellent instructors who spend most of their time coaching teachers [. . .] Being a teacher is about helping children to learn. Being a principal is about helping adults to learn."* (pp 30/31).

In this text it is taken as axiomatic that Principals should be trained in the principles of instructional leadership but so should every other teacher. It is recognized that within schools there is nevertheless a role for instructional leaders. Strangely for a company that purports to know about management the McKinsey authors did not conclude that the Principal's task is to create an organization for learning. That it is, is a primary assumption of this text.

Defining Instructional and Curriculum Leadership.

It is very difficult to pin-point clear definitions of instructional and/or curriculum leadership in the literature. Sometimes they are confused with educational leadership and at other times educational leadership embraces both dimensions. Books on these topics tend to be about either instructional or curriculum leadership and not about both. One book of several hundred pages on curriculum leadership mentions instruction on only one page. The picture is further confused by the notion of teacher leadership an idea that includes helping teachers make curriculum decisions, plan instruction and teach effectively.

The definition offered here is that curriculum and instructional leadership are those aspects of educational leadership that contribute to the attainment of the curriculum. The curriculum is defined as the formal mechanism through which educational aims are intended to be achieved, and as such, it embraces those factors that contribute to its attainment, namely content, assessment, evaluation, instruction and learning.

In this context curriculum leadership is a sub-set of educational leadership and is concerned with the aggregate of the formal teaching activities in an institution (whole curriculum) as well as with the individual components (subjects, knowledge areas) that make up this whole school curriculum. Instructional leadership is a sub-set of curriculum leadership specifically concerned with the effectiveness and delivery of instruction within the context of learning.

The need for Instructional and Curriculum Leaders.

During the last twenty years legislatures have become involved in the assessment, teaching and learning process in a way that was previously inconceivable. They have done this in the name of accountability, and often the mechanism for its attainment has been a form of total quality management that specifies the outcomes and standards that schools have to meet. Politicians have gone so far as to indicate the methods of instruction that teachers should use and recently in the UK the style of question that should be asked in written public examinations. They have taken away curricular subsidiarity. If teaching is a profession capable of making right decisions about assessment, teaching and learning then it has been deprofessionalized, and in political debate the teachers' voice is not heard. Teachers are ciphers whose task is to implement reforms and if the reforms are not successful teachers are unfairly held responsible.

Part of the problem is in the way intending teachers are professionalized into teaching. They enter school, go to university, and return to school during which time they learn from role models. The only knowledge beyond that of the subject matter of teaching that is thought relevant is the "practical" which can be gained from experience and a little help with the 'nuts and bolts' during training. This is often reinforced by policy makers who see a combination of experience mentored by good role models as the essence of effective training. In these circumstances theory is rejected as irrelevant and a gulf between theory and practice quickly emerges not always helped by the practitioners of research. Furthermore training compared with other professions, as for example medicine, is severely limited. After relatively short "practicums" teachers are dumped in classrooms and relatively few subsequently pursue programmes of professional development.

The problem is acerbated by the fact that teachers are regarded as ciphers whose function is to instil in children the content prescribed by policy makers. They have no role in curriculum making and in training they perceive this to be the case and in consequence reject or find difficult courses in curriculum theory and practice. In all they emerge from training without a pedagogy that derives from a "common technical culture" and teaching decisions are made largely on personal grounds. If teachers want their voice to be heard then they will have to speak with an authority that has as its basis pedagogy rooted in a common technical culture. They will have to claim curricular subsidiarity. Such a culture is not "out there" for the asking. It will have to be built. Thus the need for a cadre of teachers who on the one hand can lead the building of a common technical culture and on the other hand represent the voice of teachers. Those are the functions of curriculum and instructional leaders. They will not be able to achieve such goals without the active support of educational leaders.

Creating a "common technical culture."

A "technical culture" is a "professional culture" and a characteristic of a profession is that its members should accept responsibility for their actions. They accept the necessity for accountability and they hold that self-accountability is the basis of public accountability. Teachers, therefore, should evaluate their instruction. At its most simple this means the use of classroom assessment techniques (some of which they probably use (but not necessarily for this purpose) on a regular basis. A next but much more difficult task is to ask a colleague to participate in the assessment by observation. A further step is to subject one's teaching to more formalised research, a step that requires an extension of knowledge through reading and consultation and professional development. It is a characteristic of professionals that they are open to professional development. In sum, classrooms become laboratories and teaching becomes research.

Teachers require the support of their school community to purse these goals, ambitious as they are by today's standards. The community has to be a learning community. This cannot be done without the active encouragement of the educational leader whose task it is to create the conditions for the organization to learn. Such an institution might be described as an inquiry-oriented school. In an inquiry-oriented school, building on their own self-assessments teachers share their concerns about their teaching in dialogue with the community that both affirms and questions assumptions about what is done in classrooms and in school. An educational leader will not be able to do this without the active involvement of curriculum and instructional leaders.

Inquiry oriented schools, the curriculum and the community

An inquiry-oriented school will necessarily consider the curriculum and involve its teachers in curriculum making. Subject curricula do not remain static and reform movements respond to the need for change but often the sponsors of these movements view the teacher as a cipher for the implementation of their views about curriculum and instruction. The teacher is not seen as a professional who has a major contribution to make to curriculum debates. Teachers, nevertheless, take the blame when reforms fail. Teachers have therefore to bring the community with them if they are to be listened to in curriculum debates. School based curriculum development increases the professionalism of teachers. But for it to be successful teachers require a substantial knowledge base and need to develop defensible theories of philosophy (epistemology, and values), and psychology (development and learning). They need to understand the historical development of the education system and the culture (history and sociology) in which the system functions. They will have to arrive at a view of effective teaching. For many that means taking much more seriously these subjects during their training than they did before, it means taking a first step toward instructional and curriculum leadership. It also means a response to continuing professional development in which curriculum and instructional leaders have a major role to play.

Origins, organisation and purposes of this book

In a document submitted to the Minister for Education and Science in 2005 the National Association of Principals and Deputies of Ireland (NAPD) said *"there is a continuing need for curriculum development and this will require a cultural change in many schools. The provision of instructional leadership crucially involves freeing up the Principal to exercise this responsibility."* Statements like this would apply to other education jurisdictions. While principals can help change the culture of schools so as to foster an inquiring organisation they cannot hope to achieve this on their own without the help of considerable expertise. The instructional and curriculum leader is taken to be this consultant. It is the instructional and curriculum leader who advises and assists the teaching community and mentors beginning teachers into their professional roles. Thus principals have to have the range of knowledge that instructional and curriculum leaders have. This book has its immediate origins in the wish of NAPD expressed through its President at the time (Mr. Michael Parsons) for a detailed study of the knowledge base required for instructional and curriculum leadership and more generally reflective practice. Its purpose, therefore, is to explore the concepts of professionalism, instructional and curriculum leadership and to outline the scope of the pedagogy required.

The book is organised in four parts. Building on the idea of inquiry oriented schools each chapter contains issues that should be a matter for whole school dialogue in which assumptions are challenged (assumptional dialogues). These are noted.

The first two chapters comprise the Introduction. They set out in more detail the arguments offered above. Instructional and curriculum leadership is perceived to function at four levels. The first two are at the level of the individual and describe increasing skill and personal knowledge in the evaluation of instruction which they are the able to share with others and at the same time acquire skill in curriculum making (third level). A fourth level is reached when they engage with the external community in debates about instruction and curriculum. An example of reflective practice through action research (third level) is given.

Part 2 might be called preparing for teaching. The boundaries of educational and instructional leadership meet in the area of discipline (chapter 3). Effective instruction is dependent on good discipline. Discipline is the subject of much discussion in schools but very often some of the assumptions made go unchallenged. Contrasting theories of masterful teaching that embrace motivation and discipline are presented as a catalyst for "assumptional-dialogue." Chapters 4 and 5 discuss the planning and implementation of lessons. Techniques that can be used to get lessons off to a good start are considered in chapter 4 as is the acquisition of study skills.

Part 3 explores the potential of different teaching strategies to develop higher order thinking skills, (an important goal of education,) through the eyes of graduate student teachers who undertook to evaluate them in their classrooms during their *practicum*. In these chapters the focus is on the teacher as researcher.

Part 4 rests on the assumption that changes in instruction impact on the curriculum. Even if it is only at a micro-level teachers are involved in curriculum making. Thus it is that the design of the curriculum mirrors that of instruction. Both necessarily begin with the determination of aims and objectives. The first chapter (10) in this section is, therefore, concerned with the meaning of aims and objectives and their derivation within the context of the curriculum. In the second chapter (11) the role of the curriculum leader in integrating the components of the curriculum to bring about the learning necessary to be achieved the declared goals and the knowledge base required for this task is considered.

Chapter 12 is an extension of chapter 11. It focuses on models of assessment led and interdisciplinary and integrated curricula, and issues related to the curriculum and education for work and life.

The final chapter begins with a discussion of the balanced-curriculum and how it relates to practical, reflective, social and emotional intelligence.

Two theories of development that have been used to describe the process of higher education are discussed. They focus on the role of higher order thinking and the development of reflective judgement. Their relevance to schooling and the design of curriculum and instruction is considered and the idea of philosophy for children considered. This section is followed by a brief discussion of religious and moral development.

The chapter concludes with the view that success with curriculum and instructional projects in school provides examples of the strategies that can be used in whole school improvement. The role of curriculum and instructional leaders is self-evident.

Contents

Foreword IV

Preface VI

Acknowledgements VIII

Summary and Introduction to the Text X

Part I. Introduction.

Chapter 1.
Toward Instructional and Curriculum Leadership. 2

Chapter 2.
*Toward Inquiry-Oriented Schools: Classroom Assessment
and Classroom Research* 26

Part II Toward Masterful Teaching

Chapter 3.
Toward Masterful Teaching 56

Chapter 4.
Disciplined Learning: Confidence, Cognition and Empathy 86

Chapter 5.
Planning, Implementation and Evaluation of Lessons 123

Part III. Instruction. Toward Higher Order Thinking.

Chapter 6.
Toward Transfer. The Learning of Concepts and Principles 156

Chapter 7.
Learning from the Outside, Learning from the Inside 187

Chapter 8.
Learning Styles and Strategies 207

Chapter 9.
Problem Solving, Decision Making and Heuristics 240

Part IV. Curriculum Theory and Practice

Chapter 10.
Aims, Objectives and Outcomes 270

Chapter 11.
Concepts of the Curriculum:
The Curriculum Leaders Knowledge Base 297

Chapter 12.
Models of the Curriculum and Other Issues 321

Chapter 13. Toward Human Growth,
Moral Development, and Intelligent Behaviour 349

Retrospect and Prospect 382

Subject Index 388

Name Index 396

Part 1
Introduction

1
Toward Instructional and Curriculum Leadership

Summary

The curriculum is defined as the formal mechanism through which educational aims are intended to be achieved, and as such, it embraces those factors that contribute to its attainment, namely content, assessment, evaluation, instruction and learning.

In this context curriculum leadership is a sub-set of educational leadership and is concerned with the aggregate of the formal teaching activities in an institution (whole curriculum) as well as with the individual components (subjects and knowledge areas) that make up the whole curriculum.

Instructional Leadership is a sub-set of curriculum leadership specifically concerned with the effectiveness and delivery of instruction within the context of learning.

A Curriculum leader will necessarily have experienced instructional leadership. Four levels of instructional and curriculum leadership are defined together with the knowledge and skills base required for work in this area of educational management. Given that every teacher should aspire to be an extended professional they should all function at level 1. In that sense every teacher should be an instructional leader since level 1 requires a willingness to assess their own teaching. Level 2 is activated when teachers do more formal research into their own instruction and student learning. Level 3 is activated when this knowledge is used for advocacy and advice. Instructional and curriculum leaders who function at this level will have developed defensible theories of knowledge and learning together with an informed philosophy of education so that existing assumptions may be challenged.

A fourth level is reached when the instructional and curriculum leader engages in public debate on these issues and ensures that existing assumptions are challenged among all the educational partners..

In this approach technical pedagogy is acquired through increasing expertise in research, development, and design in curriculum and instruction. Leadership skills are acquired from increasing advice and advocacy among colleagues and the outside world.
Since assessment and evaluation of any kind generally cause new learning, teachers contribute to the school as a learning system The principal's (educational leader's)

task is to develop an inquiry-centred school so as to give coherence to that learning. One way of starting the process of developing an inquiry oriented school is through "assumptional-dialogues". The Instructional and curriculum leaders role is to support the educational leader in that task.

The chapter begins with the argument that too much experience can be inhibitive of learning. The training of teachers based on experience denies them the professionalism needed to lead and adapt to substantial change. Cognitive dissonance may be created if that value system is challenged. The training of teachers is greatly influenced by their socialisation into teaching. It begins at a very early age, and during formal training the demand is for "nuts and bolts" that will help the new entrant teach. Theoretical frameworks are rejected and the possibility of a technical pedagogy is not admitted. The situation is exacerbated by the fact that teachers have to teach to a prescribed curriculum and because they do not possess a technical pedagogy they are only able to enter discussions about the curriculum in a naïve way. They become in Hoyle's terminology "restricted" professionals. A few "extend" their professionality and begin to acquire a technical pedagogy. Teachers extend their professionalism if they become involved in "making" aspects of the curriculum. For this reason there needs to be some curriculum subsidiarity as has been the case with tht Transition year in ireland. A prime purpose of inquiry oriented schools is to help teachers extend their professionalism and instructional and curriculum leaders have a major role to play in this task. All professionals have an obligation to assist new entrants to develop extended professionalism.

A little about learning and experience

Some years ago a team of investigators analyzed the jobs that engineers in a highly innovative company did.[1] The company made components and systems for aircraft and in this case a particular group of engineers were developing a system for an aeroplane that was as yet on the drawing board. The investigators found that the engineers had considerable difficulty in making large jumps in the general pattern of the development of an artefact. The investigators observed that well trained engineers, accustomed to designing gear boxes in a 250 mm x 250 mm x 250 mm cube to encompass a well-defined mesh system in a transmission line, could not apparently without considerable difficulty, design a gearbox of cubic dimensions that was several magnitudes greater, if such gearboxes had not been part of their previous experience. They had to go through a new learning experience for which they were not adequately prepared. The procedure adopted was to search for past developments that might help them with the present. No attempt, seemingly, was made to apply the principles of science supposedly learnt in their education and training.

"*A crucial problem for human development is that we have to be aware of the discrepancy between our perception and the incoming information from our environment, and the impact of our own subjective experiences upon our per-*

ceptual world...Applied to [this example] *it means that special experience in the same organisation provides an individual with such frames of reference. The very existence of these frames of reference or schemata determines the meaning of our perceptions. It shortens the time before reaching a percept and reduces the ambiguity of the situation. Specialism fosters autistic tendencies because one tends to define each situation as fitting one's own schemata*"[2]

To put it in another way too much reliance on experience can ultimately be inhibitive of change (innovation).

Accompanying this specialism is the development of its own language thus research engineers speak one language, designers another, manufacturing engineers another and so forth and one of the reasons some firms find it difficult to innovate is because no one wants to speak different languages. Hesseling, a Dutch authority whose interpretation is given above concluded that persons operating in such environments have to be administered a '*chocs des opinions*'.

The lesson of this study is that in spite of all that is said about experiential learning and the value of learning through experience, too much experience can be inhibitive of learning. Indeed it can be argued that the problems with British manufacturing after the second world war arose from a too easy reliance on persons trained by experience, and by extension it may be argued that training teachers by experience denies them the professionalism needed. Moreover, the development of a specialism will be accompanied by the development of a language system that expresses and defines the value system of the specialism. It is the challenges to that value system and the possibility that they may create 'cognitive dissonance' that change agents have to address. This applies to the management of schools and the curriculum as much as it does to any other private or public sector organisation. How then does it come about?

Learning to teach

Learning to teach begins at a very young age. Three-year olds try to direct the activities of their one year old siblings. They are very authoritarian. Some children set up a classroom with their dolls. I taught my Teddy Bear. In those days teachers in grammar and public grammar and public schools in Britain and Ireland still wore academic gowns. Somehow I knew this, so I put my dressing gown over my shoulders. Again it was very authoritarian, all about control, all about not being naughty. The curriculum was received by the Teddy Bear; his mind was a *tabula rasa*. Only occasionally was he told that he was good. And all this could happen in spite of attendance at a play- group. The next step is primary school, then post-primary school and then if we don't gamble some form of appropriate third level education. All the time we are learning about teaching but I doubt if we are learning much about learning. We are socialised into attitudes and beliefs about teaching from a very early age and it has a profound effect on the assumptions we make about teaching and learning and apparently they differ little between cultures.

Nowhere has this problem been more examined than in the United States. Cohn and Kottkamp (1993)[3] who repeated with some adaptation a study of teachers that had been undertaken twenty years earlier by Lortie (1975)[4] found a remarkable degree of consistency between the results of these two studies of teacher behaviour. They affirm Lortie's view that stability, and thus a reluctance to change stems in part from the way that teachers are *"recruited, and socialized into the occupation and rewarded for their efforts."* They write:

"In the domain of socialization, Lortie maintained that although prospective teachers are required to have a certain amount of formal preparation, they are not expected to complete a highly demanding program. All teachers must have at least a college degree, and their formal schooling includes both general special schooling. One unique feature of the general schooling of teachers is that it actually functions in Lortie's terms as an "apprenticeship of observation", in that those who become teachers have as students, already had at least sixteen years of contact with teachers. This apprenticeship encourages the observers to internalize traditional patterns and leads to a widely accepted belief that "we teach as we were taught."[5] The special schooling, moreover, is relatively short and citing Lortie is *"neither intellectually nor organizationally as complex as that found in the established professions". It includes a mini-apprenticeship in the form of student teaching, which can be as short as six to eight weeks, and which is highly dependent for its quality on the skill of the supervising classroom teacher. Once hired, a beginning teacher is given the same full load of responsibilities that experienced teachers have and is expected to "learn by doing". The novice typically seeks advice from more experienced colleagues but is disposed to accept or reject suggestions largely on personal grounds. The criteria for acceptance appear to be that if they fit one's situation or style that they "work"."*

"This process of socialization leads, in Lortie's words to an "emergence and reinforcement of idiosyncratic experience and personal synthesis" and to the absence of "a common technical culture". The inability to draw on an accepted body of knowledge in turn affects status and contributes to the individualistic and conservative outlooks of the occupation."[6]

But there is more to it than this for this process of socialization gives rise to contradictory expectations. On the one hand the intending teacher expects that they are being socialized as a professional but, on the other hand, the expectation of training is that it will provide them with the nuts and bolts that will enable them survive in the classroom. It is viewed as tips that will help them control the class: it is not viewed as the systematic acquisition and development of a professional pedagogy of teaching. For example, in Ireland, there is among many entrants to the Higher Diploma course in Education, (a one-year pre-service course for university graduates) a view that it is not very practical. But it has to be put up with because that is the only way to get registered as a secondary teacher. And politicians have been known to criticise it for the same reason. Similarly with an undergraduate programme for training primary teachers where students had great difficulty in appreciating the value a course in curriculum studies. It is not merely the inability to draw on an accepted body of knowledge, but an unwillingness to appreciate its value or to see that teaching can be something more than a matter of nuts and bolts. My experience was that this situation is not largely dissimilar to the different systems of education in the British Isles. It certainly is similar to that found by Cohn and Kottkamp.

Since everyone is taught then every one is socialized into the same set of attitudes and beliefs. Everyone knows how to teach. And in these circumstances whether they are politicians, civil servants, inspectors or parents they are entitled to an equal opinion. Moreover, it is not in their interests to admit the possibility of a technical pedagogy. Teachers are there to act as purveyors of knowledge in ways determined by others.

In the absence of a 'technical pedagogy' it is no wonder that *"teachers do not feel confident to speak as a group or to respond to the demands of others from an authoritative knowledge base"*. As Cohn and Kottkamp write, *"the overall weakness and brevity of the formal socialization simply cannot counteract the tendencies to absorb and use the ideas and approaches of one's prior personal experience"*. As we have seen it is well documented that over reliance on experience inhibits change and innovation and encourages professional autism.[7]

The situation is exacerbated by the fact that they have to teach to a prescribed curriculum (a *received curriculum* as Eggleston, describes this paradigm).[8] Which means that they and many teacher trainers do not see the need to study the curriculum as defined here, *per se*. They soon find that when they are dissatisfied with the curriculum that the authorities are not prepared to consult them on curriculum matters.[9] In these circumstances they are not in a position, except in a naive way, to argue about the curriculum because they have rejected access to the knowledge base on which they could build their criticism. In any event many of them see no reason why the curriculum should change. So they affirm the divorce between the curriculum and teaching that was created in the nineteenth century. Clandinin and Connelly who charted the history of the curriculum reported that the term "teacher" did not feature early in the curriculum literature. *"The development of an association of "teacher" with "curriculum" appears to have been mostly a consequence of a working distinction between ends and means, which presumed that teachers and teaching mediate between the curriculum and its object, students."* [...] The teacher acts as a conduit. Later they write *"it is we think fair to say that the conceptual histories of the teacher and the curriculum as seen in the research literature have been more or less independent."*[10] It is contended here that this has been detrimental to the development of teaching as a profession. This is because teachers are treated as ciphers whose job is to transmit the intentions of the curriculum authorities to the students without any consideration of what they are asked to teach. Clandinin and Connelly cite studies from many countries to show that this divorce (they call it "functional split"}, is alive and well. One might argue that often there is also a functional split between teaching and learning.

Referring to the many curriculum projects reported in the international literature[11] they note that even when teachers are involved in project development an underlying purpose of their participation is conversion to the values of the reform. Moreover they believe that this applies to school based staff and curriculum development.[12]

They also conclude that the *"view of curriculum development as a form of imposed teacher development [...] if teacher development did not occur, student development in the direction specified by the reformers would not follow. Teachers in this view are as much the target of reform as are students."*[13] Thus reform projects typically develop materials for teachers and some reformers try *"to limit the teacher's role either by constructing materials in such a way that teachers' screening influence between materials and students was minimized or by devising implementation strategies to ensure materials were used as intended."*[14] Teachers reinforce this philosophy because they neither have the wish or the knowledge to develop their own materials or curriculum. Thus they are happy for the authorities to change curriculum content (which is what is normally meant by curriculum reform) provided they are given training and some would demand in school-time. In this they concede their authority, they confirm an idea prevalent among politicians and journalists that if reforms fail it is due to the teacher and they allow themselves to be put in the position where they are told how to teach and recently in the UK how to examine. In a nutshell they are not allowed or encouraged to be very professional.

Many years ago, working from an English perspective Hoyle defined the kind of professionalism that is inherent in teachers of the kind described in the American studies as "restricted". He contrasted it with "extended" professionalism. The differences between the two are shown in exhibit 1.1. Hoyle argued that one of the reasons why it was so difficult to change the curriculum was because of the restricted professionality of teachers. We would probably want to make some changes to the categories because of an increased understanding about extended professionalism. In the first place we would want to assert the ethical dimension of responsibility as it relates to performance and accountability. If there is to be sensible accountability in schools then it has to begin with professional accountability. That is, with the accountability that a teacher owes their identity as a professional. Such accountability arises from what is currently termed "reflective practice" or "educational connoisseurship". The "value" of whole school evaluation depends on such practice.

Clearly Cohn and Kottkamp are seeking the attitudes among teachers of the *extended* professional. However, they also argue, and Hoyle would not disagree, that if meaningful learning is to be made the norm that *"the system itself as well as the teachers in it must undergo substantial change, and that such change must be grounded in a more meaningful conception of learning."* To which I would add *"and curriculum."* We might expect the extended professional to have developed defensible theories of learning and instruction and defensible positions in the philosophy and sociology of education and to embrace school based curriculum development. We would expect those teachers who find security in prescribed syllabuses to resist school based curriculum development and to demonstrate the characteristics of a restricted professional

Restricted Professionality.	Extended Professionality.
Skills derived from experience.	Skills derived from a mediation between experience and theory.
Perspective limited to the Immediate time and place.	Perspective embracing the broader Social context of education.
Classroom events perceived in isolation.	Classroom events perceived in relation to institution policies and goals.
Introspective with regard to methods.	Methods compared with those of colleagues and with reports of practice.
Value placed on autonomy.	Value placed on professional collaboration.
Limited involvement in non-teaching Professional activities.	High involvement in non-teaching Professional activities (e.g. subject associations)
Infrequent reading of professional Literature.	Regular reading of professional Literature.
Involvement in in-service work Limited and confined to Practical courses	Involvement in in-service work considerable and includes courses of a theoretical nature.
Teaching seen as an intuitive activity.	Teaching seen as a rational activity.

Exhibit 1.1. Hoyle's characterisation of the dimensions of *restricted* and *extended* professionalism among teachers.[15] (The term institution is a substitute for school in the original since the argument applies equally to third level education. (see Warren Piper, 1994[16]).

For such change to take place new knowledge is required and that knowledge is contained, perhaps not satisfactorily, in knowledge areas in teacher education that are commonly rejected by student teachers whether graduate or undergraduate. Given this situation such changes will not come about unless those entrusted with educational leadership see it as a primary function of their task to develop a common technical culture and make use of it in their schools. In such cultures teachers need to be given the experience of "making the curriculum" Thus instructional and curriculum leaders need to develop defensible theories of learning and instruction as well as defensible positions in respect of the philosophy and sociology of education as they apply to curriculum making.[17] In this context "curriculum making" ranges from a positive view of the interpretations and modifications made to the formal or legislated curriculum in order to assist student learning to the design of substantial components of a curriculum that they can teach. The latter requires a degree of curricular subsidiarity. This is to be found in certain aspects of the Irish curriculum in both primary and post primary education as for example in civics in both sectors and the Transition Year in post-primary.[18] It seems too that the authorities in England and Wales are trying to reverse the widely held view that schools are constrained to follow national schemes and some schools are already taking advantage of this change. The more teachers can "make" the curriculum the more professional they are likely to become.[19] This has implications for the education and training of teachers and this text sets down basic parameters for the study of instruction and the curriculum.

Instructional and Curriculum leaders have a major contribution to make to the pursuit of this goal. Clearly the role of the Principal is to facilitate the development of a common technical culture in which an agreed pedagogy can function within the school. It is a function more generally for the system to provide areas in which the curriculum can be made.

A little about management and leadership

One of the findings of the task analysis of engineers mentioned at the beginning of this chapter was that the term engineer was used in a very loose fashion. It could imply a very highly qualified person acting in a senior capacity or it could imply someone working in what might be described as a clerical task. When the investigators attempted to describe a taxonomy of engineering objectives they found that nearly everyone in the firm, however high, however lowly performed some kind of managerial task. Everyone exerted some form of direction and control over themselves and their job and sometimes over others.[20] As was pointed out at the time there is nothing very new in this finding. After all we have to manage ourselves from the time we get up in the morning to the time we go to bed. What was different was the assertion that every person was a manager and that this had implications for organisational behaviour as well as the organisational structure of the firm.

One of the investigators subsequently developed this point in respect of education. Teachers want to have a greater say in the running of their schools. In so far as teachers are concerned they want the schools to be democratic and they want principals to respond to that democracy. They want administrative subsidiarity. But many of them want consensus and it takes but one teacher to exert her/himself to bring change to a halt. Neither do they necessarily want to engage in public accountability. At some stage it becomes an act of management by the teachers to allow the principal to act on their behalf. We do not want to explore this route here. Suffice it to say that once we wish to exert direction and control on proceedings we are managing, and suffice it to say that in this respect the management of a classroom is no different to that of management anywhere else.[21]

The same is true of leadership. Far too much time is spent trying to make distinctions between management and leadership. Just as every one is a manager so everyone is a leader. Leading implies following. To the extent that we set ourselves goals, and to the extent that we set about obtaining those goals, we both lead and follow. In this sense every individual is a leader. Because this is the case, each individual has within him or herself the attributes of leadership. What distinguishes one person from another as a leader is the use to which they put the attributes of leadership in the varying situations in which they find themselves.[22] To acknowledge the findings of educational research and not to do anything about them is a neglect of professional responsibility. It is also a denial of the professional's responsibility to lead.

Evaluations of teacher expectations of principals show teachers expect principals to be leaders even if they find it difficult to say what they mean by leadership. Quite simply on the one hand this might be about leading the school toward a vision or on the other hand in the "way" a teacher is asked or empowered to do a particular task. Suffice it to say that once we wish to lead proceedings we are leading, and suffice it to say that in this respect leadership in the classroom is no different to leadership anywhere else.

We deduce from this that the development of a culture that will support extended professionalism will depend not only on the managerial and leadership qualities of the principal but on those of his/her colleagues as well. As we have seen opportunities for such exercises in the context of the curriculum differ as between one educational system and another. But before this discussion of leadership can be extended to curriculum and instruction it is necessary to define the curriculum.

Educational, instructional and curriculum leadership

In order to define the roles of a instructional and curriculum leaders it is necessary to define curriculum.[23]

Here, it is defined as the *formal mechanism through which educational aims are intended to be achieved, and as such, it embraces all the factors that contribute to content, assessment and evaluation, instruction and learning.*

Instructional leadership is a sub-set of curriculum leadership in that it focuses on assessment, evaluation and learning within the context of the classroom.[24] Clearly curriculum leadership is a sub-set of educational leadership which is an overarching concept that embraces a concern to ensure that the aims of the school are met (see exhibit 1.2). It is, therefore, the responsibility of the Principal, but given all the things that a principal is expected to do he/she could hardly undertake the leadership at the shop floor level necessary to introduce a new curriculum, as for example the transition year in Ireland. At the same time, it is equally clear that the responsibility for the task is the Principal's. Thus the Principal has to have a knowledge first of "Change" models (i.e how to bring about and maintain change)[25] and, second of the technical pedagogy required to bring about change. If that technical pedagogy does not exist the principal is obligated to facilitate its acquisition among those whose task is curriculum change and/or development. Neither can the Principal escape responsibility for the instruction given in the school and in the event of weaknesses being detected to take appropriate action even to the extent of helping teachers in instructional difficulty.

1. Professional leadership
2. Shared vision and goals.
3. A learning environment.
4. Concentration on teaching and learning.
5. Purposeful teaching.
6. High expectations.
7. Positive reinforcement.
8. Monitoring progress.
9. Students rights and responsibilities.
10. Home-school partnership.
11. School based development.

Exhibit 1.2. The Eleven Characteristics that contribute to an effective school.[26]
Mortimore defined an effective school as one in which students' progress further than might be expected from its intake of students. An effective school thus adds value to its students' outcomes in comparison with other schools serving similar intakes.

Recent research in Ireland and the United States suggests that the task of the principal is so multi-faceted that the principal would have to delegate the task of instructional and curriculum leadership to others. In Texas, however, Principals see themselves as primarily instructional leaders and they have a particular responsibility for teachers who are failing. They are required to help them bring their instruction up to scratch and this may involve them in having to send the teacher on a refresher course.[27]

Exhibit 1.3 shows the results of a study in the United States that found that Principals' had 21 responsibilities that could influence student performance. Clearly the items could be clustered in different ways. However, teachers in Ireland would have expectations that principals would take responsibilities in all of the areas except items 11, 12, 13 and 14. The NAPD (National Association of Principals and Deputies) in Ireland, however, has clearly come to a view that they should be part of the principal's role. At the moment they posses some administrative subsidiarity but little curricular subsidiarity. While the practice of 12 and 13 may be delegated, the practice of 15, (inspire and lead new and challenging innovations), in the curriculum area would remain essential. For this the principal would have to have a "technical pedagogy" since its understanding is imperative if curriculum leadership is to function within the schools at all levels. It would require principals to have a defensible theory of learning as well as defensible epistemology. In any case, without that, how could the principal practice item 11- "intellectual stimulation." So what should instructional and curriculum leaders do?

One answer to this question has been provided by Fitzmaurice who as part of a research for a higher degree investigated his own role as an instructional leader in a four teacher rural primary (elementary) school.

At the time when he undertook the study (circa 1995) the term curriculum leader had hardly entered the vocabulary but the term instructional leader had. Its worth noting that in the same year that he published his thesis a book was published in America with the title *"A Handbook for Teacher Leaders."*[28] Fitzmaurice did not have access to that book but he examined a considerable volume of material on educational and instructional leadership, mostly from the United States and found that the terms were very confused.[29] From this review he deduced an operational description of the instructional leader thus:

1. *The instructional leader leads others in the process of change through school planning which involves*
    -Identification of instructional or curriculum areas that need change/improvement/innovation.
    -Preparation of and planning processes that prepare the ground by pooling resources, selection through consensus, and designing a plan.
    -the implementation of change in the classroom.
    -Review and assessment.

2. *The instructional leader energises and encourages others to focus on the two main concerns of schools- teaching and learning. This is used as the bottom line reference whenever there is controversy or indecision*

3. *The instructional leader uses reports, test results, feedback from parents, management, inspectors and pupils to identify areas for instructional improvement.*

4. *The instructional leader provides resources from a variety of sources to support,*

maintain or initiate change, improvement and reflection. This may include reports, studies articles, advice, teacher-centres, fellow professionals, support groups, in-service courses and new technology.

5. *The instructional leader speaks to and questions teachers about children, teaching, subject areas, problems, projects, concerns and difficulties in their teaching and classrooms. This can be done both formally and informally.*

6. *The instructional leader supports teachers in their efforts in classrooms by being available to offer advice, opinion, praise, judgement and encouragement to their work and the efforts of children. He/she might encourage the display of projects and provide a public area for this. He/she might check copies or essays on classroom visits.*

7 *The instructional leader is a reflective practitioner who continually seeks to improve the teaching/learning process in his/her class and throughout the school by constantly asking- what and how can we improve? He/ she must also lead and train others in this process of reflection so that it becomes school-wide and automatic."*[30]

In the book too which he did not have access Pellicer and Anderson in the United States at around the same time wrote about "teacher leaders". They considered that they should help teachers plan instruction, teach effectively and learn from their students. They also suggested that teacher leaders should help teachers to grow professionally, and help teachers develop a system of peer coaching. [31]

Fitzmaurice who was a teaching Principal in a four teacher national (elementary) school in rural Ireland wanted to find out if it was possible to carry out the duties of a Principal who had to teach through the day, and at the same time, be an instructional leader. The occasion was a good report from an inspection but that carried with it a recommendation that the school should do much more science in its curriculum. He described how he persuaded his colleagues over a period of months to design a new curriculum, and found that up to that stage it had been possible for him to be an instructional leader. He was clearly providing curriculum leadership rather than instructional leadership, and that accords with the more precise definitions given here.

INSTRUCTIONAL AND CURRICULUM LEADERSHIP

Responsibility	Extent to which Principal
1. Affirmation	Recognises and celebrates accomplishments and acknowledges failures
2. Change Agent	Is willing to challenge and actively challenges status quo
3. Contingent Rewards	Recognizes and rewards individual accomplishments
4. Communication	Establishes strong lines of communication with and among students
5. Culture	Fosters shared beliefs and a sense of community and cooperation
6. Discipline	Protects teachers from issues and influences that would detract from their teaching time or focus
7. Flexibility	Adapts his or her leadership behavior to the needs of the current situation and is comfortable with dissent
8. Focus	Establishes clear goals and keeps those goals in the forefront of the school's attention.
9. Ideals/Beliefs	Communicates and operates from strong ideals and beliefs about schooling
10. Input	Involves teachers in the design and implementation of important decisions and policies
11. Intellectual stimulation	Ensures faculty and staff are aware of the most current theories and practices and makes the discussion of these a regular aspect of school culture.
12. Involvement in curriculum, instruction and assessment	Is directly involved in the design and implementation of curriculum, instruction and assessment practices
13. Knowledge of curriculum, instruction, and assessment	Is knowledgeable about current curriculum and instruction, and assessment practices.
14. Monitoring/evaluating	Monitors the effectiveness of school practices and their impact on student learning.
15. Optimizer	Inspires and leads new and challenging innovations
16. Order	Establishes a set of standard operating procedures and routines.
17. Outreach	Is an advocate and spokesperson for the school and to all stakeholders
18. Relationships	Demonstrates an awareness of the personal aspects of teachers and staff
19. Resources	Provides teachers with materials and professional development necessary for the successful execution of their jobs.
20. Situational awareness	Is aware of the details and undercurrents in the running of the school and uses this information to address current and potential problems.
21. Visibility	Has quality contact and interactions with teachers and students.

Exhibit 1.3. 21 Responsibilities of Principals derived from a meta-analysis of researches on principal leadership in schools in the United States. Marzano, J., Waters, T and B. A. McNulty (2005). *School Leadership that Works. From Research to Results.* Association for Supervision and Curriculum Development (ASCD), Alexandria, VA.

It is not too difficult to read the same into Pellicer and Anderson's definition of instructional leadership, that is *"the initiation and implementation of planned change in a school's instructional program, supported by various constituencies in the school, that results in substantial and sustained improvement in student learning."* [32]

Guidance about the abilities required of curriculum/instructional leaders can be obtained from Joseph Schwab who believed that the university-based curriculum specialist should be an educator of school-based curriculum specialists.[33] This was the purpose of the course for which Fitzmaurice undertook his assignment, and its view of the abilities required by a curriculum specialist in schools differed little from that of Schwab as Philip Jackson's summary of outcomes shows.[34] The apparent differences (i.e my additions) are shown in italics.

-Skilful use of the rhetoric of persuasion (which includes knowing how to elicit participation in small group settings and person to person encounters). *(A knowledge of the factors influencing change in educational organisations).*

-Experience in deliberation *(and causing people to deliberate at greater levels than they have before).*

-Ability to read learned journals and the habit of doing so.

-Ability to guide colleagues to the use of the journals, *and to encourage them to believe that their classrooms are laboratories for valid research.*

-Knowledge of curricular practices *(their design and improvement, including instruction and assessment).*

-Knowledge of the behavioural sciences which contribute to the guidance of educational *policy and* practice *e.g. branches of psychology and sociology.*

-Knowledge of the humanities which contribute to the guidance of educational policy and practice e.g. philosophy, and history.

-Defensible theories of learning and instruction

-Defensible positions in respect of the philosophy and sociology of education.

-"nodding" acquaintance with the academic fields from which school curricula are drawn.

-Assist teachers preparing for accountability.

There are difficulties with this list. For example, the first item would pre-suppose that the person is a propagandist for a particular model of the curriculum or instruction. In the case of the latter there may well be empirical evidence to back up the argument. In the case of the former the advocate should be prepared to summarise research in terms of the advantages and disadvantages of a particular curriculum model, as for example when a department or school is considering a change to a problem-based learning programme. It presupposes a desire to promote a professional pedagogy as a professional activity, and it takes into account the need to have an understanding of the factors that enhance or impede change.

To summarise, both instructional and curriculum leaders require to function in a common technical culture with an accepted body of knowledge (pedagogy) as is the case in other professions like medicine. There are levels of knowledge and practice that distinguish instructional from curriculum leadership. The view taken here is that instructional leadership relates to the performance of individual teachers in delivering the programmes for which they are responsible in the classroom. Curriculum leadership relates to the total curriculum of the school and the design, implementation and evaluation of new programmes. Like Pellicer and Anderson the view is taken that *"instructional (/curriculum) leadership does not necessarily begin and end with the principal. Rather, instructional (/curriculum) leadership must come from teachers if schools are to improve and if teaching is to achieve professional status."*[35] But the principal has overall responsibility for instructional and curriculum leadership, the professional development of teachers, and facilitation of a culture in which such leadership can flower at different levels throughout the school.

Levels of instructional and curriculum expertise: The school as an organisation for learning

Teachers are accountable for what they do to numerous stakeholders of whom the pupil is the most important. Because pupils do not have the knowledge to judge the merits of teachers, the profession has probably a more important role in this respect than do, say the professional organisations that represent medical practitioners. The profession has to act on behalf of pupils. Although it is disputed teachers claim to be professionals. Therefore, like any other expert profession they have an obligation to ensure that beginning teachers have an adequate training that projects them on to the road of curriculum leadership. They also have an obligation to be aware of the pedagogical knowledge that is available to inform the curriculum process in which they are partners.

Given that this is the case it is surprising that the notion that teaching and learning should be informed by research is not high in the minds of teachers. Mostly pedagogical knowledge, if it is perceived to be pedagogical knowledge, is gained from the vagaries of experience. Even then there is little reflective practice. K. Patricia Cross has argued in respect of university teaching, that such teaching will not become a respectable activity until teachers treat their classrooms as laboratories for research.[36] This applies as much to school teachers as it does to university teachers.

To encourage the development of this idea Tom Angelo and Patricia Cross worked with teachers to develop and evaluate fifty techniques of classroom assessment. They are intended to help *"individual teachers obtain useful feedback on what, how much and how well their students are learning. Faculty (teachers) can then use this information to refocus their teaching to help students make their learning more efficient and more effective"*[37] Many of these tasks can be used in post primary education, as for example, the minute paper and concept mapping. The minute paper with its half sheet response *"provides a quick and extremely simple way to collect written feedback on student learning. To use the minute paper, an instructor stops the class two or three minutes early and asks students to respond briefly to some variation on the following two questions: what was the most important thing you learned during the class? And what important question remains unanswered?"* Answers are written on half a sheet of paper.[38] Twenty-four similar, (not all of them identical), techniques for formative evaluation have been described by George and Cowan.[39] The techniques described by Angelo and Cross cover the following domains- The assessment of course related knowledge and skills. The next domain relates to the assessment of learner attitudes, values and self-awareness. Finally there is the domain of the assessment of learner reactions to instruction. Much more recently Phillips and Carr have written specifically on *Becoming a Teacher through Action Research.*[40] It includes specific ideas for beginning teachers during their first year. It is accompanied by a CD and self-study activities.

This is a first level of instructional/curriculum expertise. It is a level at which the teacher exercises self-accountability. It assumes that a teacher is relatively "effective" and that the purpose of these exercises is to check that effectiveness. It is a level of self-leadership.[41] As such it is the Level when the ability to reflect on one's performance and educational beliefs comes into play. A major step is taken if the teacher asks a colleague into his classroom to observe him at work with a view to helping his development. In short it is not too much to ask that teachers who consider themselves to be professional to function at this level. Culver (private communication) considers that most teachers operate at a level 0- a point that should be self-explanatory.

A second level is reached when a teacher tries to learn through more formal research into one's classroom practices, and even more generally into other dimensions of the curriculum process. Patricia Cross and Mimi Steadman followed up the earlier Angelo and Cross study to show how this might be done.[42] In Ireland this writer required his post-graduate students in a course described later to undertake such research (chapters 2 and 6 – 9)). He had two purposes in mind. The first was that the students should purposefully evaluate the theories they learnt about in lectures and texts. The second was that they would learn some skills that would lead them to treat their classrooms as laboratories of research for the improvement of their teaching through better understanding of student learning. He wished to promote the idea of teaching as research. As with level 1 a major step is taken when two or more teachers agree to undertake such research.

Classroom assessment and classroom research require different levels of expertise. Classroom research requires more knowledge before one can begin. This might be related to a specialist topic (e.g. cooperative learning, teaching mixed-ability classes, concept learning, motivation, and other instructional theories) or, it may be of a more general kind (e.g. the redesign of a curriculum).

Teachers who, in an ethos that values experience above research, spend time on classroom assessment strategies are leading themselves, and by example others. If they try to persuade others that such activities are worthwhile and lead to better practice, they are leading in the traditional understanding of leadership. The same is true of classroom research, the second level of expertise.

More generally part of the role of the professional teacher is to lead beginning teachers into the pedagogy of education. In Ralph Tyler's words, they have the goal of *"helping practitioners who want to improve the curriculum of the schools in which they work."*[43]

There will be those who have acquired the capability to do this at the first level of expertise. There will be others who can do it at the second level of expertise. Those who take on these leadership roles can help create a climate of cultural change from the bottom up. By themselves such activities cannot be expected to maintain cultural change since they are often due to the initiatives of individuals. In any event those individuals also need support from the top, and this means that those at the top will have to have an understanding of the professional pedagogy. While they may wish to act as instructional and curriculum leaders themselves, given the scope of the knowledge required there would seem to be a requirement to recognise the need for curriculum leaders and leadership in schools who have a third level of expertise. That is the ability to use knowledge at the second level to persuade others to improve their instruction and engage in curriculum activities. Such persuasion requires that change is *"perceived to be intelligible, beneficial, plausible and feasible."*[44] The ability to stand up in front of one's colleagues and suggest that things can be done better is no mean skill, and a sub-skill is to recognize the expertise that others have.[45] It also requires a developed skill in "curriculum making" over and above the micro-making that takes place during instruction. The Texas Principal's functioned at this level but Swan did not elicit the details of the training they had to perform this task.

At the same time there is other testimony to the fact that while principals may sanction "experiments" if they do not give the teacher(s) continuing support such "experiments" may come to grief. Northfield points out that principals', not only have to sanction an "experiment," but they have to continually support it through the provision of resources, reinforcement and encouragement. They also have to push and nudge.[46] *"For the principal, as for any educative leader, the key features are the leader (as a learner) providing opportunities for participants to develop personal understanding and encouraging the conditions for reflection and practice."*[47] This point is reiterated time and again in the curriculum.[48]

A key role for the principal is the selection of persons to undertake curriculum responsibilities at this level. For example the cordinators for the Transition year and Leaving Certificate Applied in Ireland.[49] High level skills in the so-called affective domain will be required for such work by both principal and those appointed. A principal might through her/his instructional and curriculum leaders initiate school wide curriculum and instructional policies and evaluations in order to extend the professionality of her/his teachers. Indeed if they do not lessons of the kind described in part 2 of this text may have much less of an impact on the students than might be desired. This point is reinforced by the evaluation of an attempt to develop a Learning-how-to-Learn module for the transition year in a network of schools. It would have been more successful had it have been made part of a whole school policy so that all the teachers involved in teaching these students reinforced the learning about learning in the main core of the course.[50]

The implications of this view are quite profound. They imply that teaching (and the teachers' role) should be viewed from the perspective of a learning organisation. Extended professionalism begins with a commitment to learning. This entails the acquisition of a technical pedagogy. The leaders first task is to assist teachers acquire that pedagogy within the framework of a commitment to the school as a learning organization. All professionals have a responsibility for the mentoring of new comers to the profession.

Cohn and Kottkamp argued that if learning is to be made more meaningful then the assumptions and structures of the prevailing educational system will have to be changed. There is no reason to believe that the performance of educational systems has changed for the better in the period since their book was written. To provide this challenge they proposed that a certain number of schools be established as centres of inquiry into the teaching learning process and the structures that support it in a contemporary context. They find a rationale for this in the writings of Schaefer who in 1967 wrote *"we can no longer afford to conceive of schools simply as distribution centers for dispensing cultural orientations, information, and knowledge developed by other social units. The complexities of teaching and learning in formal classrooms have become so formidable and the intellectual demands upon the system so enormous that the school must be much more than a place of instruction. It must be also a center of inquiry-a producer as well as a transmitter of knowledge. One basic fact is our ignorance of teaching. We simply do not know how to master the abstract knowledge and the analytical skills modern society demands. It seems necessary to transform at least some schools into centers for the production of knowledge about how to carry out the job.*"[51] But should not all schools be centres of inquiry about learning for the essence of learning is inquiry?

While I do not disagree with these sentiments realism dictates that change has to begin within systems that are publicly controlled by those who have little regard for pedagogy and where teachers and controllers collude to produce systems that are primarily information giving. Some teachers will see that as an impossible task as they did of the Public Examinations Evaluation Project in Ireland.[52] But they were shown through involvement in "experiments" that teacher involvement in the design of public examinations was feasible. It will also be argued that very much more is known about instruction and learning and that much more can be learnt about learning and instruction than teachers have cared to accept.

In the United States one of the few substantial investigations into inquiry based learning funded by the Wallace Foundation provides evidence and illustrations that support this view although the procedures used differ from those discussed in this text. They affirm that it is a *"step toward reclaiming a degree of professionalism and responsibility that is lacking in far too many schools.*[53] In the three approaches they describe the issues of accountability loom large. Those involved, including a single classroom teacher, engaged themselves in trying to answer the questions "Why do we do what we do? Why do we do it in the way that we do it? How might we do it better? It is with these questions that this text is concerned. Reason and Reason argue that *"when teachers come together to answer tough questions about instruction in their school they take teacher leadership to the next level."*[54] And in respect of inquiry they note that whether or not they are aware of it all schools have an inquiry agenda. Perhaps their most important point that the emotional relevance of each inquiry topic has to be established and taken into account. This seldom if ever happens when decision is bureaucratically centralised.

Their view of teachers and teaching at a time when there is a *lack "of respect for both students and teachers, for the subject matter, and for the processes of learning and teaching"* is no different to the view taken here. They write (p 155) that a *"central premise of this [work] and of the inclination to establish collaborative inquiry among teachers in schools is that teachers are fully capable and, in many ways, uniquely situated to achieve these new understandings and invent more effective teaching practices. They need all the help they can get of course. But they don't need someone else to do all of the work for them. In the end, no one can do the work of understanding and invention for anyone else, though we all benefit from the insights of others and can, through collaboration, often solve problems and design new practices that we could barely approach on our own."* It is argued here that the development of a culture of collaboration is a major task for the educational leader who will require the support of one or more instructional and curriculum leaders. Where subsidiarity exists and schools are allowed to make their own curriculum within a general framework as is the case with the Transition Year in Ireland collaboration with other schools is likely to be beneficial.[55] But forums for shared learning can only be maintained through strong leadership and the support of all the principals in the participating schools otherwise they can wither and die.[56]

Part II will attempt to show that relatively simple inquiries in the classroom can have major implications for the curriculum and the way that it is assessed, and for the "theory-in-use" that teachers have.[57] It is shown that much can be done to improve instruction and facilitate learning even within the constraints of a public examination system. The argument is that teacher "theories-in –use" can only be changed through the acquisition of new knowledge. This may for example, be achieved through action research that evaluates the explicit theories and practice made available in the literature. It may be accompanied by *"assumptional dialogues"* that provide *"opportunities to raise awareness and examine largely unrecognized assumptions that currently underlie [the] educational structures and practices [in a school, institution or system] and to generate alternatives to them."*[58] Assumption digging suggest Cohn and Kottkamp often provides the potential to motivate teachers. Thus it is that Cohn and Kottkamp envisioned *"schools as communities of scholar- teachers, where everyone including principals collaborate on action research projects that have the capacity to change the very structure of schools or significant elements within them."*[59] Those schools will of necessity extend the professionalism of the teachers within them and these teachers will take responsibility for beginning teachers. Each of the chapters in this book raises issues of concern for the whole school that could be the subject of such "assumptional-dialogues."

Leadership skills will also be required for a fourth level of curriculum leadership that requires engagement with the "authorities" responsible for the curriculum and structures, that is, with the external debate that goes on in public outside the school, as for example, the education and training of teachers. Such an engagement would challenge existing assumptions on the basis of research. This view has implications for the type of person selected by organisations such as managerial bodies and trade unions to represent them on organisations that control the curriculum and structures. At levels three and four those who would seek to implement change need also to have knowledge of the factors that inhibit or enhance change.[60]

In this approach technical pedagogy is obtained through increased expertise in research, development and design in curriculum and instruction. Leadership skills are acquired from increasing advice and advocacy among ones colleagues and in the outside world.

It is clear in the prevailing climate that a curriculum leader will have to be a missionary as well as a mentor. So what knowledge does a curriculum leader require to perform this role? Given that a curriculum leader should have experience of instructional leadership then the knowledge base will develop from an understanding and experience of effective teaching. The purpose of this text is to focus on this knowledge base and how this technical pedagogy may be acquired and developed.

The chapters on instruction (6, 7, 8, and 9) are seen through the eyes of student teachers and their needs. Within each chapter are themes that could form the basis of "assumptional dialogues." Some themes are often the subject of discussion in schools as for example discipline. But often they are based totally on the experience within the school and lack insights from other sources especially those of research and development. They, therefore, indicate the range of knowledge that instructional and curriculum leaders can bring to such dialogues. Sometimes, as is the case with the matter of this and the next chapter issues surrounding accountability and professionalism are seldom discussed or for that matter issues surrounding the nature of schools as for example "Should we become and inquiry oriented school?" The discussion of professionalism is continued in chapter 2 and issues surrounding accountability raised, and the idea of an inquiry-oriented school is considered in more detail.

Notes and references

[1] Youngman, M. B., Oxtoby, R., Monk, J. D., and J. Heywood (1978). *Analysing Jobs.* Gower, Aldershot. P 95.
[2] Hesseling, P. (1966). *A Strategy for Evaluation Research.* Van Gorcum, Aassen.
[3] Cohn, M. M. and R. B. Kottkamp (1993). *Teachers. The Missing Voice in Education,* State University of New York Press, Albany, NY
[4] Lortie, D. C. (1975*). Schoolteacher: A Sociological Study.* Chicago University Press, Chicago
[5] *loc.cit* pp 21
[6] *loc.cit* pp 22
[7] See for example Hesseling, P. (1966). *A Strategy for Evaluation Research.* Van Gorcum, Aassen. Or, Heywood, J. (1989). *Learning, Adaptability and Change.* Paul Chapman/Sage, London
[8] Eggleston, J (1977). *The Sociology of the School Curriculum.* Routledge, London.
[9] Helsby, G (1999). *Changing Teachers Work.* Open University Books, Buckingham.
[10] Clandinin, D. J and F. M. Connelly (1992). The Teacher as Curriculum Maker in P. W. Jackson (ed). *Handbook of Research on Curriculum.* Macmillan, New York. p 365
[11] They refer to large reform oriented projects in the US and the UK. They note that Canada, Australia and Israel adopted previously developed projects and that the OECD carried out curriculum adaptation projects in Ireland and Scotland. Projects conducted in Austria, Germany and Sweden are also discussed. In their discussion of the UK they use the example of the Humanities Project to illustrate some of their points. They do not, however refer to the evaluation of some of the major mainstream examination syllabus projects e.g Waring, M (1979) *Social Pressures and Curriculum Innovation. A Study of the Nuffield Foundation Science Teaching* Project. Methuen, London.
[12] *ibid* p377. "*The literature suggests an alliance between reformers and researchers with policy makers and school administrators-that somehow if these groups work together more closely, they would be able to force reform through the conduit of the classrooms*".
[13] *ibid* pp 373. Anyone who is asked to participate in a project is "involved" in the project but the degree of involvement may be peripheral. There is in these conditions no guarantee that the teacher will do what the centre expects. See Munro, R. G. (1977). *Innovation. Success and Failure.* Hodder and Stoughton, London. Clandinin and Connelly suggest that the UK Geography 14 – 18 Project, The Austrian Learning Objectives

for Vocational Schools Projects and the German Mathematics Projects represent a continuum that expresses the degree of teacher responsibility for the ideas and materials developed. They cite Garry, R. F., Connelly, F. M. and E. Dittan (1975) Interpretative Case-Study of Selected Projects in P. Dalin (ed) *Handbook on Curriculum Development*. OECD, Paris p 105.

[14] *ibid* p 374

[15] See Hoyle, E and A. McMahon (1976). In Hoyle, E (1984). The professionalism of teachers. A paradox. In P. Gordon (ed) *Is Teaching A Profession?*. Bedford Way papers No. 15. London. University of London Institute of Education

[16] Warren Piper, D (1994). *Are Professors Professional? The Organisation of University Examinations*. Jessica Kingsley, London.

[17] *loc. cit* ref 10.

[18] Subsidiarity is discussed by Blyth W.A.L (1993). Subsidiarity in education: The example of British primary humanities. *The Curriculum Journal* 4, (2), 283 – 294. Blyth makes a distinction between administrative and curricular subsidiarity. He makes the point that even though in the Irish system there is little administrative subsidiarity there is a certain amount of curricular subsidiarity and he cites primary humanities at the time. The transition year is another case in point. Subsidiarity is a medieval concept that is built in to church law. *"The Church has elaborated the principle of subsidiarity according to which ' a community of a higher order should not interfere in the internal life of a community of a lower order depriving the latter of its functions, but rather should support it in case of need and help to coordinate its activity within the activities of the rest of society with a view to the common good."* Paragraph 1883. *The Catechism of the Catholic Church* (1994). Veritas, Dublin. In catholic teaching it has special relevance to the resposibilities of families and social institutions including government to the family (paragrapph 2209) Recently it has become important because the relations ships between the European Union and the States that make up that union. Blyth argues that "subsidiarity appears relevant to education, both as an interpretative concept and a principal procedure." I argue that the deprofessionalisation of teachers has taken away many of their legitimate functions.

[19] Feasey, R.(2007).Starting from scratch. *Managing Schools Today* (2007) April/May, 25 – 28.Describes a primary school that set aside the national curriculum in favour of a skills based curriculum. The author cites the QCA website as stating *"Curriculum development is not about waiting for the next initiative or toolkit to hit. It is about taking ownership of, and responsibility for the curriculum that young people experience. It involves disciplined innovation, making informed decisions and taking intelligent risks. It means rejecting the notion that a 'one –size- fits-all' approach and tailoring the curriculum so that it meats the needs and interest of your learners.*"

[20] *loc.cit* pp 113 – 115.

[21] Heywood, J (1989). *Learning, Adaptability and Change*. Paul Chapman, London.

[22] *ibid*

[23] I am conscious of the fact that there is no escape from colloquial usage of the term curriculum. Outside of this text the term is used as a function of the context in which it is employed. At one level it is used to describe all subjects (contents) that comprise the course of studies that an individual pursues. Thus, we speak of the school curriculum and in this context the engineering curriculum. Sometimes the term programme is used instead of curriculum. In the case of degree courses in the British Isles we speak of the subjects (or subjects when it is a two-subject degree) studied. In this sense subject is being used instead of curriculum. But within these subjects numerous other subjects may be taken that are often called courses. Thus, in engineering there will be a requirement for mathematics. Teachers in higher education tend to specialise and teach a particular subject or course within a programme. Sometimes the term curriculum means for them the subject they teach. Broadly speaking they mean the content of what is taught even though the notion of content is problematic. More often than not they mean a detailed list of topics that will be covered. In Britain that list is sometimes called the syllabus. A syllabus is not the same thing as the two or three line description that appears in a college catalogue. The point is that we know what we mean when we are talking to colleagues and we know that we are talking about something that is formal. In higher education the most common usage appears to relate to the list of topics. In this paper it refers to the total process of curriculum design, implementation, assessment and evaluation, and this is not about listing topics

[24] In the British Isles the term 'instruction' is often associated with training, and is not used as an alternative to 'teaching'

[25] It is not part of the purpose of this book to consider in any detail the management of change but there are two points worth noting. If the general theory of firms as learning organizations is correct then a school is no different. While that may seem obvious it is not always clear that the management of schools understand this to be so. It follows that if schools are learning organizations (or organizations for learning) then the

same factors that enhance and impede learning in the classroom will enhance or impede the organizations capability to learn. See Heywood, J (2006) Factors in the adoption of change; identity, plausibility and power in promoting educational change. *Proceedings Frontiers in Education Conference* T1B- 9 to 14. The second point relates to the reason why educational innovations fail to persist see p 267.

[26] Beginning some thirty years ago the school effectiveness movement spawned numerous research studies in the UK (a), and the US(b). These studies sought to establish the influence of schools, teachers and the education they provide on student achievement. They arose in response to studies in the United States that schools had a relatively small effect on performance (c). Since then the majority of studies in the UK and the US, although sometimes with different goals have been on inner city schools (d). It is only recently that studies have been undertaken that control (statistically) for the intake of students (e). This is important when, as in the UK, performance tables of schools are published in the national press.

It needs to be understood that definitions of effectiveness are dependent on a number of factors including the sample of schools evaluated, the choice of outcome measures, and control for the differences between institutions, methodology, and time scale i.e. i.e. longitudinal versus snapshots (f) [...]

A critical review of school effectiveness research (d) to pointed out that there were problems (not withstanding the above) in relation to its definition. There were also problems in relation to the type of evidence collected, methodology of analysis, and the transferability of data concluded that there is a core consistency to be found across a variety of studies conducted in different settings in different countries (g)

(a) Rutter, M., Maughan, P., and J. Ouston (1979). Fifteen Thousand Hours: Secondary Schools and their Effects on Children.
Open Books, London.
(b) Goodlad, J (1984). A Place Called School. Prospects for the Future. McGraw Hill, New York
Coleman, J. S. et al (1966). Equality of Educational Achievement. US Government Printing Office, Washington, DC
Jencks, C. et al (1972). Inequality: A Reassessment of the Effects of Family and Schooling in America. Basic Books, New York.
(d) Sammons, P., Hillman, J., and P. Mortimore (1995) Key Characteristics of Effective Schools. A Review of School Effectiveness Research. Institute of Education, University of London, London
(e) Mortimore, P., Sammons, P and S. Thomas (1995). School effectiveness. Assessment in Education. Principles, Policy and Practice, 1, (3), 315-352.
(f) Sammons, P (1994). Findings from school effectiveness research. Some applications for improving the Quality of Schools in P. Ribbins and E. Burridge (eds). Improving Education. The Issue of Quality. Cassell, London.
(g) ibid (d)

[27] Swan, V., Heywood, J and K. Mayo (2005) A comparative study of the factors influencing the retention of teachers in the Republic of Ireland and Texas in *Bulletins of the EFEA* (European Forum on Educational Administration) No 8 117 – 126.

[28] Pellicer, L. O. and L. W. Anderson (1995). *A Handbook for Teacher Leaders*. Thousand Oaks, CA. Corwin Press.

[29] The July 2001 issue (Volume 29 No 3) of *Educational Management and Administration* is devoted to leadership although it is focused on problems in Britain. It was published at a time when the National College for School Leadership established by the British government was getting under way.

[30] Fitzmaurice, J (1996). MSt Thesis University of Dublin, Dublin.

[31] *loc.cit*

[32] *ibid*

[33] Schwab, J. J. (1978) *Science, Curriculum and Liberal Education. Selected Essays, Joseph J. Schwab*. Ed by I, Westbury and N. J. Wilkof Chicago University Press, Chicago

[34] Schwab, J. J. (1983). The Practical 4. Something for curriculum professors to do. *Curriculum Inquiry*, 13, (3), 239-265

[35] *loc.cit*

[36] Cross, K. P. (1986). A proposal to improve teaching or "what taking teaching seriously should mean. *AAHE Bulletin*, September pp 9-14.

[37] Angelo, T and P. Cross (1993) *Classroom Assessment Techniques*. 2nd edition. Jossey Bass, San Fransisco.

[38] *ibid* p 148.

[39] George, J and J. Cowan (1999). *A Handbook of Techniques for Formative Evaluation*. Kogan Page, London.

[40] Phillips, D. K and K. Carr (2006). *Becoming a Teacher through Action Research*. Routledge, New York.

[41] In many ways this is a combination of what Gardener calls intra-personal and inter-personal intelligence. The first relates to understanding of one's self and the second to the reading of the intentions and desires of the student's' in the teacher's class. Gardener, H (1985) *Frames of Mind. The Theory of Multiple Intelligences.* Basic Books, New York. P 239.

[42] Cross, K. P. and M. Steadman (1996). *Classroom Research.* San Fransisco, Jossey Bass.

[43] Tyler, R. W. (1949). *Basic Principles of Curriculum and Instruction.* Chicago University PressChicago

[44] Northfield, J (1992) Leadership to promote quality in learning in P. A. Duignan and R. J. S. Macpherson (eds) *Educative Leadership. A Practical Theory for New Administrators and Managers.* Falmer Press, London p 90.

[45] Lieberman, A and L. Friedrich (2007). Teachers, writers, leaders. *Educational Leadership*, 65, (1), 42 –47. They give a quotation from Paul Epstein who evidently worked with the project they describe.

[46] *loc.cit* pp 99 –100. Northfield lists the activities required under each of these headings.

[47] *ibid* p 100.

[48] For a recent example see Johnson, S. M and M. L Donaldson (2007). Overcoming the obstacles to leadership. *Educational Leadership* 65, (1), 8 – 13.

[49] This is a year between the formal ending of compulsory post primary education at 15+ years (or thereabouts) and the beginning of senior cycle education to the age of 18 or thereabouts in post-primary schools. The students are expected to pursue a programme designed by the school that will enable them to learn life skills. They continue with about 20% or so of the time devoted to traditional studies. The ending of compulsory education is accompanied by a public examination set by the State called the Junior Certificate. Separate examinations are set for each subject of the curriculum. The students may take as many subjects as they wish (i.e. perceived to be capable of). Some subjects (eg mathematics) are set at three levels so as to cater for the whole population. A similar examination is set at the end of the senior cycle called the Leaving Certificate. This is set at two levels Honours and Ordinary. Points are awarded according to the level taken and the grade awarded at that level in each subject. The aggregate of the points taken for all subjects is the basis of selection to university. In order to encourage students from the whole range of ability to continue their education in senior cycle a Leaving Certificate Applied Examination was introduced with a somewhat different content and subject basis and with grades determined from a considerable component of coursework assessment. Teachers were given much more responsibility for the design, implementation and assessment of the course.

[50] Keane, D (1999). *A Study of a learning to Learn Module in a Community School.* M.St Thesis, University of Dublin, Dublin. Summarised in Heywood, J and M. Murray (2005). Curriculum Led Staff development: Towards Curriculum and Instructional Leadership in Ireland. *Bulletins of the European Foundation of Educational Administration* No 4. ISBN 1 84357 121 4. 93

[51] *loc. cit* Cohn and Kottkamp pp 363-364 citing Schaefer, R. J. (1967). *The School as a Center of Inquiry.* Harper and Row, New York. p 2.

[52] Heywood, J., McGuinness, S., and D. E. Murphy (1980). Final Report of the Public Examinations Evaluation Project. University of Dublin, Dublin.

[53] Weinbaum, A et al (2004) *Teaching as Inquiry. Asking hard Questions to Improve Practice and Achievement.* Teachers College, Columbia University, New York and National Staff Development Council, Oxford, Ohio.

[54] Reason, G and L. Reason (2007). Asking the right questions. *Educational Leadership* 65, (1), 36 – 40. They suggest the following steps to develop strategic inquiry in a school. 1. Identify the questions that are being asked and answered in your school. 2. Choose strategic inquiry pursuits that directly relate to teaching and learning. 3. Identify the emotional relevance of each inquiry topic. 4.Work as a team and task ownership of inquiry pursuits. 5. Take the inquiry public.

[55] Heywood, J and M. Murray (2005). Curriculum-Led staff development. Towards curriculum and instructional leadership. *Bulletins of the EFEA* (European Forum on Educational Administration) No 4, 3 – 97.

[56] *loc.cit* ref 47.

[57] Cohn and Kottkamp draw on work by Argyris and Schön on organizational learning who point out that it is the "theory in use" that determines the behaviour of individual or organizational action. In this case it relates to teachers theories of discipline, learning, knowledge and the curriculum. Cohn and Kottkamp point out that these theories –in-use are deeply embedded and the assumptions on which they are based are not easily articulated. What matters in this text is that it is understood that many teachers reject the theories of curriculum, instruction and learning taught in their education courses in favour of models that fit the prevailing climate of instruction in schools.

[58] *ibid.* Cohn and Kottkamp p 266

[59] *ibid* p 283.

[60] A point that is both illustrated and supported by Cohn and Kottkamp as well as in many other studies.

2
Toward Inquiry-Oriented Schools. Classroom Assessment and Classroom Research.

Summary

It was argued in chapter 1 that if there is to be sensible accountability in schools then it has to begin with professional accountability. When teachers ask "how well am I doing?" and "what do I need to do to improve? And use some techniques of assessment to answer these questions as objectively as possible they become professionally accountable and act at the first level of instructional and curriculum leadership. The techniques available for such exercises are summarised.

Such techniques necessarily involve teachers in reflection and in this sense level 1 is indicative of a reflective practitioner. Teachers have continually to ask epistemological questions such as "How do I know what I know?" and question their own assumptions. In so doing they develop defensible epistemological theories and belief/value systems about teaching.

Extended professionalism develops when teachers have sufficient confidence to engage with their colleagues in the evaluation of their instructional practices.

Success at level 1 is likely to motivate the teacher to undertake more profound research with the accompanying reading that is necessary for such research. Such research brings the teacher to level 2 of instructional and curriculum leadership. The remainder of the chapter is devoted to various aspects of such research and especially its evaluation.

Reflective practice and educational criticism require skill in evaluation. As these skills are developed so the teacher develops Eisner's skill of educational connoisseurship. "As one learns how to look at educational phenomena, as one ceases using stock responses to educational habits of perceptual exploration the ability to experience qualities and their relationships increases." But such reflective behaviour requires action. At the level of the school such behaviour might be helped by the introduction of "assumptional dialogues" and these might begin with a rigorous discussion of accountability and professionalism.

Skill in educational criticism requires an adequate theoretical base. The provision of such a base is one of the functions of initial training. If such training is linked to the planning and implementation of lessons reflective judgements become a necessary facet of their evaluation. Extended professionals are characterised by those who value and practice research, development and evaluation. The practice of evaluation leads to self-actualisation.

The particular approach to training teachers to be researchers' discussed is but one of several that are categorised as action research. Some aspects of action research are discussed and the application of Elliott's model is described. A school whose teacher's are involved in research, development and innovation is, if it is coherently organised an "inquiry-oriented" school.

The implications of the foregoing for the role of the principal and middle management are considered. The Principal's task is to lead an inquiry-oriented school in which middle management are together involved in the task of instructional and curriculum leadership.

The issue of critical thinking and reflective judgement as goals of schooling are dealt with in chapter 13. Some aspects of that chapter are relevant in this context.

Instructional leadership, professional responsibility and self-accountability

It was argued in chapter 1 that if there is to be sensible accountability in schools then it has to begin with professional accountability. That is, with the accountability that a teacher owes their identity as a professional. Such accountability arises from what is currently termed "reflective practice" or "educational connoisseurship." It requires the teacher to undertake a purposeful and continuing process of responding to the question "How well am I doing, and what do I need to improve?" When the teacher conducts this with fairly simple exercises and an equally elementary knowledge base that teacher is self-managing or self-leading her or himself. That teacher is setting him/herself targets to be met. Such teachers function at a first level of instructional and curriculum leadership with the focus on the classroom and instruction. The teacher functioning at this level was described as one who would use classroom assessment exercises of the kind described by Angelo and Cross[1] or some equivalent activity.

What technique is chosen will depend on the goal that the teacher wishes to achieve. Clearly if the goal is to measure student learning outcomes then some kind of test will be required. But there are good alternatives such as concept mapping, and on an individual basis talk-aloud protocols.[2] If, however the teacher wishes to examine the effects of her/his performance on the class then some other means of assessment is going to be required as for example a focus group or an interview. Other investigators have gone so far as to suggest the Delphi-technique. Attitudes and values might be established by the use of an everyday ethical dilemma, a course related self-confidence survey, or a classroom opinion poll. The self-awareness of a learner might be established through a focused autobiographical sketch, or a self-assessment of ways of learning.

In these examples the term assessment has been used in preference to evaluation. This is because the term assessment has come to be a substitute for evaluation. So whether you use 'evaluation' or 'assessment' in this context they both amount to the same thing except the 'phenomenon' to be assessed (evaluated) are very different. The terms 'test' and 'tested' have been avoided because this type of assessment (evaluation) is not achieved by traditional testing except when the teacher wishes to test knowledge and skills. Even in those circumstances it might be possible to use some other technique than a traditional test. The supposition here is that while there maybe an overall improvement in class performance arising from the steps that might be taken as a result of an assessment it is not essential, for assessments are as much about helping the teacher to be at ease with her/himself. Such assessments necessarily require the teacher to reflect on what he/she finds. It was argued in chapter 1 that "reflective practice" is the hallmark of the extended professional. To critically reflect is to accept that teaching is a process of continuing formation. "*When understood as a critically reflective process, good teaching becomes synonymous with a continuous and critical study of our reasoning processes and pedagogic actions. We study their origins and their consequences. We also study the extent to which these processes and actions are embedded in investigated experience, as opposed to some external source of authority from which they have been uncritically assimilated. At no time do we ever consider the possibilities for learning and change to be fully closed.*" [3] Thus all teachers who think of themselves as professionals should function at the first level of instructional leadership described in chapter 1. So what is meant by reflective practice.

Reflective practice

Elliott argued that.

" *If teacher education is to prepare students or experienced teachers for accountability then it must be concerned with developing their ability to reflect on classroom situations. By "practical reflections" I mean reflection with a view to action. This involves identifying those practical problems which exist for the teacher in his situation and deciding on strategies for resolving them. The view of accountability which I have outlined, with its emphasis on the right of the teacher to evaluate his own moral agency, assumes that teachers are capable of identifying and diagnosing their practical problems with some degree of objectivity. It implies that the teacher is able to identify a discrepancy between what he in fact brings about in the classroom and his responsibilities to foster and prevent certain consequences. If he cannot do this he is unable to assess whether or not he is obliged to. I believe that being plunged into a context where outsiders evaluate their moral agency without this kind of developmental preparation would be self-defeating since the anxiety generated would render the achievement of an objective attitude at any of these levels extremely difficult."*[4]

Brookfield, an American scholar offers similar sentiments in his study of reflective teaching.[5] In Ireland an experienced teacher wrote "*While outside inspections that take a look at the teacher in one or two classes cannot possibly give a true picture of a teacher's performance it is surely right that they should be made because society needs to know that its schools are run by competent teachers. In any event the prospect of inspections might cause among teachers who don't normally reflect such reflection.*"[6] They have an obligation to defend their practices. This means that they "*need not only understand that something is so; the teacher must further understand why it is so, on what grounds its warrant can be asserted, and under what circumstance our belief in its justification can be weakened or even denied.*" (From Shulman[7] cited by La Boskey [8]). La Boskey went on to point out that while this view applied to subject content it also applied to pedagogy. Elsewhere, Shulman writes that teachers have to continually *ask, "How do I know what I know? How do I know the reasons for what I do? Why do I ask my students to perform or think in different ways?"* [9] Add to these Cowan's What if . . . . ? And other questions that prompt reflection.[10] Shulman's questions are epistemological and as teachers begin to answer them so they begin to develop a defensible epistemology. It is instructive to note La Boskey's comment that reflective teachers ask "why" questions whereas non-reflective teachers seldom do[11] Of such are the questions of epistemology but also of accountability for they imply that if there is to be change then we have to know what that change is and whether or not we have achieved it. Some call this target setting. The answers may be uncomfortable to policy makers as well as teachers because they must question educational practices and assumptions that may be dearly held even by those who expect them to be accountable.

Clearly the intention of self-accountability is to maintain and improve where necessary teacher competence. Such questions begin to be asked the more one explores ones own situation and tests it against what is written as well as the views of others.

Extended professionalism begins with self-accountability. A teacher gains confidence when a colleague is invited to contribute to that self-assessment. A person who is comfortable in a room with a colleague is likely to be well prepared for subject review by an inspector. That person is also more likely to make an informed contribution to whole school planning and evaluation. But those who fear being found out are unlikely to benefit. As Brookfield shows they may put on a performance that is at odds with what they normally do.[12] He gives the example of a performance put on by a teacher that was spotted by the students who seemed to feel it was not for their benefit.

Training with these points in mind should also foster a willingness to go beyond level 1. It should enable the teacher to *"see his work in the wider context of the community and society, ensuring that his work is informed by theory, research and current exemplars of good practice, being willing to collaborate with other teachers in teaching, curriculum development and the formation of school policy, and having a commitment to keep himself professionally informed."*[13] Level 1, is therefore, a pre-requisite to level 2 but success at level 1 is likely to create a want to achieve at level 2. Instructional leadership and self-accountability are mutually entwined. They are the beginning of teacher wisdom.

Teaching as research: toward educational connoisseurship

Unfortunately the capability of educators to change terms and leave semantic muddles is unbounded. The terms' assessment, evaluation and reflection come within this mix. In this text the focus is on techniques of formative assessment that can enlighten teachers about the student learning in their classes and how that information may influence their teaching. Their purpose is to ask "How well am I doing?" This is an evaluative question because it inevitably infers answers to the question "Would there have been a better way of doing what I did?" The teachers in the Public Examinations Evaluation Project wanted the pupils who had undertaken projects in history to evaluate them. Their rubric for evaluation was: *"The student applies a standard of reasoning and judgement which leads him to assess consequences and to distinguish between fact and opinion; history and legend. The project should have some form of conclusion in which the candidate is expected to explain his findings and/or opinions having taken into account different view points and values."*[14] While there was no direction to review what had been done, some of the activities required were evaluative. That is they asked the pupil to judge between fact and opinion, and in this way it was hoped that the student would gain the skill of evaluation as stated by the examiners.

A more direct requirement is to be found in the assessment rubric for project work in the Engineering Science A level examination of the Joint Matriculation Board. Under the heading of critical review appeared the statement- *"In comparing the final product or outcome with the original specification the candidate has produced a thorough and objective discussion in which consideration has been given to all major aspects of the work including suggestions for further development and a critical appraisal of the conduct of the project with a clear indication of lessons learnt."*[15] Here, yet another similar term is introduced "appraisal." Clearly what was wanted was that the student should evaluate such things as the design of the project, the design of the artefact. Were there other ways of achieving the same goals that might have been more effective? This looking back is what Schön called *reflection-on-action*. Its purpose is to obtain generalizations that will be of future use. In the first example these would be about the value of the processes used in the study. In the second example they would be about project planning and design in the same area. In both cases because it was a summative assessment the students could not take it further and trigger action. This looking back and looking forward to the immediate Schön calls *reflection-in-action*.[16] Cowan has suggested that when a person reflects on types of problem which he/she hopes to resolve more effectively in the future than in the past, this is anticipatory and, therefore *reflection-for-action*.[17] I take it that this is the kind of activity I underwent as I tried to work out the schema for chapters 1 and 2 of this text both at the beginning and in response to the reviewers comments.

Before Schön published his first study in 1993 an American educator Elliot Eisner in a text with the main title "*The Educational Imagination*" had written about the teacher as an educational connoisseur. Like Elliot he was fiercely critical of the scientific approach to evaluation that stemmed from a particular version of behavioural psychology. There was, he argued, a need for educators to develop a technique of evaluation similar to the kind of criticism used in art that he calls educational connoisseurship. He described the difference between educational connoisseurship and educational criticism thus:

"*The consequence of using educational criticism to perceive educational objects and events is the development of educational connoisseurship. As one learns how to look at educational phenomena, as one ceases using stock responses to educational situations and develops habits of perceptual exploration, the ability to experience qualities and their relationships increases. This phenomenon occurs in virtually every arena in which connoisseurship has developed. The orchid grower learns to look at orchids in a way that expands his or her perception of their qualities. The makers of cabinets pay special attention to finish, to types of wood and grains, to forms of joining, to the treatment of edges. The football fan learns how to look at plays, defence patterns, and game strategies. Once one develops a perceptual foothold in an arena of activity- orchid growing, cabinet making and football watching the skills used in that arena, one does not need the continual expertise of the critic to negotiate new works, or games or situations. One generalizes the skills developed earlier and expands them through further application.*" [18]

In doing this, and they all do it subconsciously or otherwise how could teachers develop a vocabulary about classrooms? The problem is that it is not formalised or developed. It remains at a naïve level and as such is open to all sorts of prejudice and misperception. Hence the need to have a grasp of perceptual learning theory of the kind discussed briefly in chapter 1 in relation to experience, and later in chapter 4. Educational criticism is the art of looking at our work and Eisner was the first to admit that not only was the idea in its infancy but that it had room for several models including the scientific model.

Skills in educational criticism require an adequate theoretical base, and subsequent chapters are partly concerned with aspects of what that theoretical base might be. We have to be clear about the role of theory and Eisner clarifies this when he relates it to reflective thinking that he regards as the base for curriculum planning. He calls the reflective moments that a teacher has *'preactive teaching'* a term due to Philip W. Jackson who first identified the hidden curriculum. It would seem to have some similarities with Cowan's reflection-for-action. Eisner wrote:

"Prior to actual teaching planning at home reflecting on what has occurred during a particular class session, and discussing in groups ways to organize a program. Theory here sophisticates personal reflection and group deliberation. Insofar as theory suggests consequences from particular circumstances, it enables those who understand the theory to take those circumstances into account when planning. Any theory is but part of the total picture . . . In one sense all teachers operate with theory, if we take theory to mean a general set of ideas through which we make sense of the world. All teachers whether they are aware of it or not, use theories in their work. Tacit beliefs about the nature of human intelligence, about the factors that motivate children, and about the conditions that foster learning influence teacher's actions in the classrooms. These ideas not only influence their actions, they also influence what they attend to in the classroom: that is, the concepts that are salient in theories concerning pedagogical matters also tend to guide perception. Thus theory inevitably operates in the conduct of teaching as it does in other aspects of educational deliberation. The major need is to be able to view situations from varied perspectives that different theories provide and thus to be in a position to avoid the limited vision of a single view." [19]

Substitute school for classroom and school management for school teaching and the same applies. Indeed in a powerful text Heirs argued that most management suffers from the failure of managers to think reflectively.[20] An example of a principal's reflection following an assignment for a management in education course is shown in exhibit 2.1. A common problem for both principals and teachers is discipline. The implication of Eisner's view is that both principals and teachers should take cognisance of other's views. There is no better challenge to traditional approaches to discipline (and in consequence motivation) than those proposed by Kohn in his *"Punished by Rewards"*[21] and Peter's concept of masterful teaching.[22] These are considered in detail in chapter 3 where Kohn's views on discipline will be described and Peter's concept of the masterful teacher presented. They are controversial theories that might be used to start what Cohn and Kottkamp call an "assumptional dialogue" to help teachers develop theories of discipline and motivation (see above and chapter 1)

Herein is (or should be) the purpose of initial training to provide a range of theories on the one hand, and on the other hand to help teachers begin to reflect on the classroom situation. For example, it was with this in mind that post-graduate teachers training for post primary teaching were asked to design, implement and evaluate lessons. Part of the process was to critically reflect on a lesson on the evening after it had been given. They were asked to approach the problem as educational connoisseurs and the analogy of examining a picture with many people on it was given. What they see is a picture of young people in the classroom. These student teachers were asked to say what had happened to themselves as well as what had happened to their pupils. Inevitably the young teachers reports showed they concentrated more on what had happened to them than on what had happened to their

---

I am six on the Enneagram Personality test, my need for affiliation was high. I agree with the statement that "A person who has a strong need for affiliation
is unlikely to adopt behaviours that would lead the group to exclude him or her from membership"

If I am honest enough with myself I realise that it is very true of me. I avoid embarrassing situations and to do this I use ego-defense mechanisms. These I have learned from experience. They are mental devises that help me to cope with the mental stress arising from conflicting needs. I think the ego-defense mechanism I use most frequently as Principal is sublimation. It is the redirection of a motive from a relatively unacceptable goal to a more acceptable one. It helps me to control my behaviour. I over control myself and try to over control others because of my fear.
I cannot cope with being out of control.

I realise that role analysis is a very important tool for examining an organisation. If I am to shape the school environment I need to understand how I perceive and develop and adapt my role as a Principal to meet the differing circumstances with which I am continually faced. My adaptability depends on my dispositions. I can be helped to develop this skill. To be able to adapt within a school I need to learn how my skills can contribute to the school and to understand how the skills of my staff will be utilised. Jobs need to be redesigned, to serve better both the individual staff member and the school.

Exhibit 2.1. Extract from a reflection at the end of a post-graduate assignment by a Principal. Other parts of the Reflection deal with Conflict, Power and Facing up to change. The list of ego-defense mechanisms too which reference is made is in Heywood, J. (1982) Ch on Motivation. *Pitfalls and Planning in Student Teaching*. Kogan Page, London.

pupils. Thus part of training has to be to get student teachers to think more about their pupils than themselves. A colleague Ann FitzGibbon required these students to write a journal to develop their powers of self-knowledge and awareness in order to help them with the reflective components of these exercises. She found some relationship between personality type and willingness to complete the journal.[23] Her finding is a reminder that personality and learning styles should be taken into account. To help students learn to see themselves through the eyes of their students Brookfield suggests a series of questions to help them write their journals. Guidelines he says are necessary but it is also necessary to convince the students that it is in their best interests to keep a journal.[24] But first students have to learn about themselves and their emotional responses to learning. The practice of self-criticism should lead a teacher to self-actualization.

Another way of achieving this goal is suggested by recent work reported by Ryan who argues the case for structured reflection and shows its value with a group of experienced primary (elementary) teachers.[25] Her study was based on the view that *"effective teacher development is premised upon the practitioners ability to reflectively access meaningful 'tacit knowledge' of professional practice contained in thought and to address the manner in which it impacts on their work."* Expressed in terms of the opening section of chapter 1 its purpose is to evaluate the constructs that have been developed from their experience and to see if the theories they have are found wanting. Ryan argues that because *"understanding in personal and professional life is constructed through an essentially metaphorical process the unknown with what is known,"* that to bring about change, teachers have to reflect on professional self and practice. Through such reflection, come if possible, to identify and evaluate actual theories that lend coherence to their practice. In so doing they may unravel conflicts in their practice that require adjustment, as for example, the teacher who *" highlighted concerns about balancing a commitment to 'traditional' curricular principles with a desired 'lightness' of approach. As she concluded by reconstructing self as 'theatre director' in the classroom she might more successfully incorporate both responses, and thereby satisfy her own pupils requirements."*[26]

That teacher's finding resulted from structured reflection. Ryan had received questionnaires from more than one hundred Irish primary (elementary school) teachers, mostly over the age of 40 and mostly female. They had responded to a sentence completion questionnaire in which a list of words or images were given for the respondent to complete a statement like *"Being a teacher is like being a . . ."* They were also asked to draw a picture of people at work on a supplied sheet of paper. From an analysis of the responses ten individuals were asked to expand on their responses and drawings in a semi-structured interview, and then to keep a reflective journal for a five-day period. These respondents found this structured process rewarding and valuable. *"They seldom had the 'time' or 'a chance' to 'step back' and 'actually think about their roles [. . .] there was consensus that the process [. . .] of reflecting on their work "through metaphor and image helped to reduce the complexity and indeed confusion of thought associated with their daily activities."* For most [. . .] *"the reflective practice saw them identify a degree of disequilibrium in their practices. They both undertook the generation of further images with a view to reconstructing some of their professional situations and responses, and thereby improving teaching and learning in their classrooms."*[27]

While Ryan's work was with experienced teachers it does provide another method that could be used by teachers in their training. Both FitzGibbon and Ryan and Ryan show the importance of developing reflective practice during initial training. FitzGibbon has also focused on the development of reflective skills in her professional development courses (private communication) and would support and be supported by Ryan's conclusions. What is required is that experienced teachers take for granted the need for self-reflection structured or otherwise as part of their continuing professional obligation rather than something that is once off in a professional development course. An inquiry-oriented school should encourage such reflection.

Finally to return to the initial theme from the perspective of initial training, the writing of lesson plans that are not implemented and reflected on, is in my view a waste of time, a view that is supported by research in the United States.[28] A lesson plan should be implemented, it should be the vehicle for testing out a range of theories about instruction and the skills of teaching and classroom management. The development of skill in educational criticism should be at the heart of the work of beginning teachers. It should be the focus of the mentoring given by the Principal or, delegated instructional leader. Lesson planning and implementation should be the vehicle for the development of skill in educational criticism. Because the view is taken that lesson planning mirrors the strategies for curriculum planning, implementation and evaluation and vice versa, it is argued that curriculum improvement will stem from lesson improvement. For this reason and the reason that there are still so many criticisms of educational programmes that they encourage rote learning rather than the development of higher order thinking skills part II illustrates these activities in detail. It is argued that through such activities curriculum and instructional leaders can develop "assumptional dialogues." Educational connoisseurship begins in the classroom. The focus of Angelo and Cross, and Elliott is at this level.

Practical educational criticism

Elliott wrote at a time when technology was not very advanced. Nevertheless he recommended that teachers could learn about themselves by recording what they did in their classes. This would have required a relatively large reel to reel tape recorder. Nowadays very small instruments with very powerful yet small microphones can catch the voices of teacher and pupils quite easily. This makes the recording of self, practical. Even listening without a checklist is a learning exercise for most people. The evidence from micro-teaching where a trainee teacher is televised while teaching a small number of pupils (half or dozen or so) is that it helps even experienced teachers who undertake it. It is more difficult to self-televise because it restricts movement but one can arrange for one's self to be televised in front of a full class. Brookfield recounts what he learnt from watching himself teaching. "*I have been shocked at my own defensiveness when faced with strong women and intrigued at my reluctance to challenge contributions from people of color, as compared with my readiness to "take on" Anglo students.*" But Brookfield reminds us of the obvious that video taping does not necessarily tell us what to do when we find a fault that seems to need rectification. Neither is there support for the view that knowledge of ones behaviour will necessarily improve it.[29] But as I have argued elsewhere at the very least knowledge of our behaviour in managerial situations is better than no knowledge. I found that making an instructional video gave me insights not only into my own behaviour but into learning *per se*.[30]

When a teacher has confidence in self-criticism he/she will feel confident enough to invite a colleague into his/her classroom to observe him/her at work and an advantage will accrue if the visit is reciprocated the exercise.

It has been argued that discussion is the most effective way to generate reflection.[31] While it is arguable that reading scholarly literature as opposed to tips about teaching is an equally good generator of reflection Argyris and Schon's reflective seminars are likely to be more successful. Teachers tend to work in isolation and are used to monologues rather than dialogues. Dialogues among teachers on a round table basis bring together all the different levels of power, and that can only be to the good.[32]

The question arises as too how formal such an evaluation should be. Lesson assessment schedules tend to cover all the things that should be looked at. (see for example exhibit 2.2). They are useful guides that focus on the areas where issues arise. Moreover they can help organize strategies for self-evaluation. The purpose of the schedule in exhibit 2. 2- is self-evaluation. It would be difficult to improve it.

The more experienced the teacher the more challenging the evaluation should be. The check-list in exhibit 2.2 asks the teacher if having answered all these questions the teacher would have adopted a different approach. Student teachers may be helped to answer such questions by providing them with some reading on alternative approaches to instruction that they might have used.

Teachers, depending on where they are at in their careers, may want to focus on particular aspects of their teaching. It is likely, for example, that a beginning teacher will want to be concerned with their planning and performance. In that case the teacher or mentor or teacher working with the mentor might draw up a simple list of questions derived from the literature that might be asked in a particular area such as, for example, classroom routines, discipline, motivation and questioning. Nevertheless, holistic observation followed by a reflective discussion can be a valuable aid to any teacher. An individual who draws up a schedule on the basis of the literature will almost of necessity become involved in reflective thinking.[33] One simple form of self- criticism is for the teacher to write her/himself a letter that takes into account her/his performance over a period of time against those headings.

Classroom research

Exhibit 2.3 shows the outline of a scheme for classroom research that was in the course on instructional theory mentioned in chapter 1 and above.[34] It has also been used in in-service education courses in curriculum and instructional leadership.

Planning
(i) Were the most appropriate objectives identified?
(ii) How accurate was my assessment of the children's background knowledge, interests and abilities?
(iii) Were the most appropriate resources prepared and made available beforehand?
(iv) Was a proper balance of activities planned to allow for active participation by the children and a variety of activities during the longer periods?
(v) Did I choose the best method or approach?
(vi) Did I have adequate knowledge of the subject matter.

Introduction
(i) Was the introduction suited to the subject matter?
(ii) Was it too long or not long enough?
(iii) Was the purpose of the lesson made clear to the children?
(iv) Did all the children understand what to do, what to read, how they should record their work and what standards to achieve?
(v) Would a demonstration have helped the development along by improving understanding of what was expected of it?

Control
(i) How successful was I in winning the children's Cooperation and in establishing good work habits?
(ii) Were the routine duties and activities carried out with the minimum of supervision?
(iii) How effective was I in dealing promptly, promptly quietly and firmly with misconduct?

Personal qualities
(i) Was I relaxed, tense, or nervous?
(ii) Was my voice suitably loud, properly pitched, and did it have suitable inflexion?
(iii) Was the rate of speech satisfactory, and did it very according to circumstances?
(iv) Was my vocabulary suited to the children's understanding? Did I talk down to them?
(v) Did I listen to the children?
(vi) Did I show a sense of humour while still maintaining control?

Development
(i) Was the content suited to the intellectual development and experience of the child?
(ii) Was the lesson material well organized and, if necessary, prepared beforehand?
(iii) Was appropriate emphasis placed upon meaning and the important details of the lesson?
(iv) How effectively were correlations made with other subjects?
(v) Were the blackboard ,work card, text and reference books, used to the best advantage?
(vi) Was the appropriate IT/visual aids used—and how effectively?
(vii) Did all groups/individuals get a fair share of attention and guidance-by helping children to help themselves, by diagnosing group/individual weaknesses, and by applying the most appropriate remedial measures?
(viii) Were the children allowed to participate actively in the lesson or were they passively receptive?
(ix) Was any discussion guided so that every one got some satisfaction from it?
(x) Were questions well worded, well distributed, in logical sequence?
(xi) How successful was I in dealing with incorrect or partial answers?
(xii) Was interest maintained throughout the activity or was restlessness and boredom obvious? Was the noise excessive in view of the type of work being carried out?

Conclusion
(i) Was the work involved related to the development or given merely to occupy the children? Was it specific, or vague and general?
(ii) Was sufficient time allowed for the children to complete the set work?
(iii) Was suitable provision made for those children who completed their work well within the allotted period?
(iv) Was the stage set for further learning? How much revision will be necessary, who will need it, how will it be carried out?
(v) What will be the next stage? Were the children interested or knowledgeable enough to continue with the activity with understanding or will a change of method and/or subject matter be necessary?

Exhibit 2.2. A Scheme for Self-Evaluation by R. F. Roberts (1982) Preparing for Teaching Practice. City of Liverpool College of Higher Education, Liverpool. Reproduced with his permission in my *Pitfalls and Planning in Student Teaching*, Kogan Page, London. (1982). The purpose of the scheme is to determine how much the behaviour of the children has changed at the completion of the activity. To be effective it needs to be continuous and an integral part of the teacher-learning process. It means critically examining not only the educational outcome of a lesson or series of lessons but comparing them with the expected outcomes and then judging whether, how and where changes should be made?

As indicated the purposes of the programme were first to help trainees and teachers test the relationship between theory and practice, and second to acquire skill in using their classrooms of laboratories for research into student learning. It was introduced because other attempts to better relate theory to practice by the same teacher were deemed not to have been very successful.[35] Inherent in the plan of the exercise is training in reflection (called evaluation in the schedule), and the promotion of the professionalism of teachers through the concept of the teacher as researcher. In the training course six exercises all following the same pattern were required to be completed during the year's training. (These are described in detail in part 2).

---

1 Student preparation
   (a) Read the literature on the designated topic.
   (b) Select a small topic from the literature for investigation.
       (This may replicate one of the studies reported in the literature)
   (c) Design a lesson to test the hypothesis shown in b.
       (This to include the entering characteristics of the pupils, a statement of aims and objectives, the instructional procedures showing how they will test the hypothesis etc).
   (d) Design a test of knowledge and skill which is directly related to the objectives of the lesson.

2 Student implementation
   (a) Implement the class as designed.
   (b) Immediate evaluation
            What happened in the class?
            What happened to me?
            What have I learned about myself?
            What have I learned about my pupils?

3 Evaluation
   One week (or so) later
   (a) Test students.
   (b) Analyse test data.
   (c) Substantive evaluation.
            How does what I have done relate to the theory that I set out to evaluate?
            How, if at all, will this influence my teaching in the future?

4 Complete Report

Exhibit 2.3. Lesson plan assessment schedule used in post-graduate course for training post primary teachers at the University of Dublin. (adapted from Heywood, J (1992) Student teachers as researchers of instruction in the classroom in J.H.C. Vonk and H. J. van Helden (eds) *New Prospects for Teacher Education in Europe*. Association for Teacher Education in Europe, Brussels)

Each exercise required the students to test out a theory or strategy of instruction and evaluate its usefulness for themselves. For this purpose readings were provided for each exercise. The student had to summarise them and where a theory was to be tested show how they proposed to test the theory, or evaluate a strategy. A lesson plan had to be designed that would not only test the theory but would continue with the pupils' normal classwork. Student teachers in this programme had their teaching practice classes throughout the school year.[36]

The lesson plan had to contain a statement of objectives and a description of instructional procedures that would achieve the research and course objectives. A list of content was not required although the key concepts should have been apparent. It would also be accompanied with a description of a mechanism for testing the outcomes. (The design of tests proved to be quite difficult).

After the lesson had been given the students were asked to provide an immediate evaluation or reflection.[37] Eisners concepts of connoisseurship and criticism were discussed with the class prior to beginning the exercises. As indicated previously they were also required to keep a journal in another course that had the purpose of developing skill in reflective thinking. The students found this first evaluation quite difficult and, as might be expected, they tended to concentrate on what happened to them rather than on what happened to their pupils.

A week or so later the students were required to test the students, and as indicated above, this test had to check both the value of the theory, and coursework taught. When this analysis, which was expected to include descriptive statistics, was completed the student was asked to complete a substantive evaluation. This evaluation would answer questions such as "How does what I have done relate to the theory which I set out to evaluate?" and "How, if at all, will this influence my teaching in the future?" There was considerable variation in the quality of the evaluations submitted showing the need for training in reflection. Provided that students get immediate feedback on each of the exercises the fact that they have to do five or six does provide an element of training in reflective thinking.

The transfer of skill proved to be very difficult. The students were given an examination question at the beginning of the academic year that would have to be answered in a one-hour session at the end of the year. It was found that performance improved if the students were shown examples of the kind of response that was expected. Transfer of skill cannot be left to chance.[38]

This exercised mixed the approach of an approximately scientific model of research with the qualitative- the reflective-dimension. The implementation of the programme did depend on a certain skills at level three of curriculum and instructional leadership because it required a considerable effort from the student that might have conflicted with their work for the other subjects in the course. Changes were made to try and reduce the load. One of them is of some significance. When the exercises were first introduced the students also had to take a three-hour examination at the end of the academic year that was supported by weekly lectures. This examination was dropped in favour of the test of transfer described above. The lecture programme was reduced to a few introductory lectures related to the implementation of lessons and classroom management. The majority of the lectures were devoted to discussions about the lesson plans. It was felt that the readings that the students had to do for the exercises more than covered the course. This approach raises all sorts of questions about the nature of the curriculum even in subjects where there is a specified content. Reorganizing the curriculum in this way seemed to help student learning.

One of the weaknesses of the programme put by Seamus McGuiness was that it did not help the student-teachers learn to work in teams. More and more schools require teamwork. He cited the post-primary school in a disadvantaged area where the students had poor literacy skills. This meant that in the first year all teachers had to take responsibility for that aspect of English that their subjects required (e.g. in science- report writing, in English—creative writing; in history—narrative).

One of the objections by some critics was that the students should do such exercises when they have had some experience. In this way positive attitudes to teamwork could have been developed, and so forth. But that was not possible for once students are trained, they are trained. They have no obligation to undertake further training. There was a case for extending the whole training by another year and those who would campaign for this would be demonstrating level 4 of instructional and curriculum leadership.[39]

It is not the only way to learn about theory and practice. In China in each of its secondary schools (some 90, 000) there is a mathematics research group. *"As part of the activities of these groups, individuals prepare experimental lessons developed around new ideas or methods. These experimental lessons are observed in classrooms by fellow teachers, followed by seminars in which what has been observed is discussed in considerable detail, with the teacher providing appropriate background to what has been presented."*[40] Excellent lessons that have been evaluated by researchers according to agreed criteria are shared among teachers and prizes may be awarded. The same writers report that there is systematic attempt to pass down the accumulated wisdom to beginning teachers in Japan. They draw attention to the fact that roughly forty percent of a teachers time in elementary schools was spent in joint planning and sharing whereas only one hour was typically available in the US.[41] In Australia promising mathematics lessons that focused on mathematical and pedagogical teams were trialled and at the end of a four year period 114 exemplary lessons summarised 'snapshots' of innovative teaching.[42] The purpose was to encourage teachers to innovative. The danger is that teachers would see them as a package for practical use. At the same time there is a very real sense in these projects of the teacher making the curriculum once they begin to experiment. The Australian experiment shows [43] that curriculum development takes time a fact that is not often appreciated by policy makers.

The approach described above is a hybrid of the so-called scientific approach and the qualitative. Many authorities argue for a solely qualitative approach. The arguments for this have been set out by Cross and Steadman in their book on *Classroom Research*[44] but they look at it from an American perspective. Within educational research there has been a long tradition of qualitative research often associated in the UK with Parlett and Hamilton's challenge to the "agricultural-botany" model in favour of what they called the "illuminative model"[45] It aims to evaluate an innovatory programme, how it operates, how it is influenced by the situation, its merits, demerits as seen by participants, and how students' intellectual tasks and experiences are affected.[46] It is a research model that can be applied *in situ* that is in action research of the kind defined and described by Elliott for his model of school based accountability.[47]

Another example of action research in teacher training that has a little similarity with the student teacher investigations described above has been called *implicit personal research* by Hatch and Shiu.[48] Final year students are asked to keep a reflective file about an explicit action research project they have been set. It focused on a question they had identified in their teaching practice. The notes on their observations are recorded in their files. At the University of Sydney students training to be elementary school teachers worked in small groups where they took the role of action researchers of applied education. *"They work in small goups and each group has a responsibility to make decisions, try out new ideas, explain strategies and choices in educational terms, review their practice and reflect on and evaluate their solutions. Later they use their own experiences as a basis for further analysis, reflection, theory building and theory testing."*[49] There are several other reports of teachers undertaking research into their own classroom practice.[50] And several innovations have had the intention of finding connections between teacher education in the field and the research community.[51] Krainer's study led him to recommend the building of learners and co-learners.[52] In terms of developing inquiry-oriented schools my approach may be criticised because it did not encourage the development of such communities and that there was no time set aside for the students to discuss their studies together. There was plenty of evidence that this was done outside the lecture room. It could be argued that because they were asked to develop skills in inquiry they would understand the concept of an inquiry-oriented school but the argument is weak.

Cross and Steadman in their approach to classroom research used many of the Classroom Assessment Techniques discussed earlier. The basis of Cross and Steadman's approach is a series of case studies which they use to illustrate the approach of classroom research. The last case study which is about the problems experienced by two teachers teaching a "History and its Methods" course. These teachers wanted to know if the course was working. Cross and Steadman point out that this is really two questions "First, are the students learning what the instructors are trying to teach? Second, how are the students responding to the teaching methods that the instructors are using? The instructors were using small group methods and one of their main aims was to teach skills commonly grouped together under the heading "critical thinking." The teachers were concerned that the students should be able to distinguish between narrative and analytical descriptions of history. Cross and Steadman pointed out that one approach would be to use a minute paper mid-way through the term to find out what was happening in the class (see chapter 1). They suggested an evaluation of what was happening on a day to day basis could be achieved by use of the *Defining Features Matrix*. It gives information about the differences between analytical thinking and narrative thinking, and group work evaluation would give information about the effectiveness of the small groups. The purpose of the *Defining Issues Matrix* is to establish how well a student can distinguish between the similarities and differences among two or more concepts. Essentially it is a rubric of N items (depending on the topic) in which the items are categorised as analytical or narrative. Among the items given were *"Aims to capture the uniqueness of a historical even,"* and *"Aims to draw conclusions or formulate hypotheses about cause and effect."* The former is narrative, the latter analytical. This rubric is very similar to those used in the history project of the Public Examinations Evaluation Project on the Intermediate Certificate Examination (see exhibit 10.6). There are plenty of evaluation schedules for group work but Angelo and Cross suggested two questions that are of importance. These were *"Give one specific example of something you learned from the group that you probably would not have learned working alone, and Give one specific example of something other group members learned from you that they probably would not have learned otherwise?"*[53]

Any programme of the kind described in the case study is hoping that some intellectual development will accrue as a result. The problem is that intellectual development is difficult to assess. The teachers involved need to have an understanding of theories of intellectual development (see chapter 13). Without this understanding teachers would not know what to look for. Cross and Steadman suggest that collaboration with other teachers may help. They suggest that over the period of a term a small group would study the literature with a view to answering such questions as *"How closely does what we observe in our classes conform to what the literature says?* [. . .]*Do colleagues from different disciplines find different example, or do the observations support the theory of common patterns or stages of intellectual development?* [. . .]*How do students at various levels of intellectual development react to such various types of situations as ambiguity, and ill-defined problems, ethical issues, taking responsibility for coming to a reasoned conclusion, and dealing with complexity and uncertainty?"*[54] These questions are from among a long list that relates to the final years of high school and third level education. But they can be re-written specifically for schooling at its various levels. It is interesting to note that Cross and Steadman do not mention the possibility of using instruments that purport to assess level of intellectual development.

Cross and Steadman do not advocate the use of generic measures of critical thinking to assess whether critical thinking took place in the course. They cite Cromwell of Alverno College who believes that teachers know what critical thinking is in their disciplines and should measure it continuously in their own assignments and tests.[55] Cross and Steadman suggest that many classroom tests simply measure factual knowledge, and that it is somewhat more difficult to assess critical thinking. This was our experience in the Public Examinations Evaluation Project where this was an issue for teachers of both history and maths in respect of problem solving. It was also an issue in a more recently published project on the transition year.[56] Even with training experienced teachers found it difficult to design tests that would measure higher order thinking skills. Yet schools wish to develop higher order thinking skills and many "imagine" that they do even if it is by osmosis.

1. Formulate a question about the learning of students in your class that is important to you in your teaching.
2. Keep your question simple, realistic, and focused on your own experience. Follow your hunches; predict what might happen.
3. Inform yourself about what is known about the learning issue you have selected. Read-with focus-not necessarily exhaustively or exhaustingly. Form a study group to share the load.
4. Reformulate your question into a researchable question. What do you want to know?
5. Work with other faculty to discuss, design, cooperate on, and interpret your classroom research projects.
6. Think through how students will benefit; how they can be included in the research; what issues are too sensitive for the student-teacher relationship
7. Decide how you will investigate your question. (Avoid the temptation to use an instrument because it is there or to collect data that have no clear purpose).
8. Conduct a pilot study, with yourself and colleagues as respondents
9. Estimate the time needed for student response and for analysis of the data.
10. Write up your results to clarify for yourself what you have learned- about doing research, about learning, about your teaching

Exhibit 2. 4 Things to keep in mind when planning a classroom research project from Cross, K. P and M. Steadman. (1996). *Classroom Research*. Jossey Bass, San Fransisco. P 226.

Instructional /curriculum leadership at Levels 3 and 4 is illustrated by a Principal who engages the teachers in an exploration of the effects they have on the development of higher order thinking skills. Whole school Evaluation will be of value if it promotes such enquiries. Cross and Steadman show that a qualitative approach of the kind described above can be effective but they accept that it might need the help, on occasion, of external expertise. The issue of teaching these skills will be considered again in Ch 9. Exhibit 2.4 is Cross and Steadman's list of things to keep in mind when planning classroom research.

The classroom investigations described above belong to the category of action research. They have the possibility of entertaining change. Elliott defined action research as *"The study of a social situation with a view to improving the quality of action within it."*[57] Prior set out to establish the validity of Elliott's model in an Irish primary school with the support of the Principal and his colleagues on the staff.[58] The start of any research is to clarify the problem and this is often by no means easy. In the first place Prior used, as did Elliott the Nominal Group Technique. This is an extension of brainstorming. It has 6 stages 1. Question setting; 2. reflection; 3, pooling; 4.clarification; 5, evaluation; and 6. review. It is quite an extensive procedure[59] and Prior found that in order to clarify the problem he required more than one session.

One effect is that it requires teachers to publicly declare problems they have and in so doing they have to try and separate self-esteem from classroom practice, and that exemplifies the beginning of an "assumptional-dialogue." Elliott had found that teachers found this difficult to do. Exercises like this also demonstrate that the problems that teachers face in isolation are likely to be the case in other classrooms. Prior's study found that this was no exception.

Prior circulated a summary of the first meeting with his colleagues. Before the next meeting he also circulated a document that set down the aims and guidelines for future meetings. At this stage the purpose was seen to be *"to make a largely academic curriculum more meaningful for the development of the whole student."*[60]

He also recorded the inability of the project to alter the academic emphasis of the curriculum. The principal said that nothing could be done about it. *"Efforts should be made to make the academic curriculum more attractive to academically less able students."*[61] Nevertheless, Prior reported that the variety of issues that had been raised offered scope for classroom research. The teachers had to learn to focus. To get this focusing Prior decided to intervene during the third meeting with the teachers through means of a statement and a question. As a result comparison between the records of the earlier meetings and this meeting suggested to Prior that at last the teachers had begun to focus.[62]

The next stage in the Elliott model is reconnaissance. It has two components -description and explanation of the problem. The problem now became that (1) some pupils were not fully occupied in the class, and (2) how can this situation be improved? The first would be for research the second would be for discussion meetings. Teachers were now asked to observe and record what happened in their classrooms in respect of time wasting. Prior's guidelines for observation are shown in exhibit 2.5. The written results ranged from the diary type listing of events to holistic reflections. Prior recorded that *"the general feeling was that the problem of pupils wasting time in class might be rooted in the quality of tasks they are asked to engage in. Such quality depended on the willingness of the teacher to develop suitable programmes of learning, rather than performing better in present ones. Also important are methods of teaching and learning."*[63]

More generally it was found that lessons aimed at the average group and that those above or below this range were neglected. Such problems have not gone away.

At this stage Prior began to look at the instructional issues. The teachers were asked to keep diaries and also to shadow study a single pupil. More interestingly the teachers were asked to invite a colleague to observe them in their rooms (triangulation). Tape recorders were also provided. The Principal assisted by supervising the class of a teacher who was observing. But at this stage Prior records that a crisis occurred because what was happening was not leading to change. He, therefore, decided to continue at a lower level and to concentrate on change in classrooms rather than at school/staff level.

Ten hypotheses had emerged as a result of classroom observation. It was accepted that there was a serious problem that centred on teacher's problems in dealing with students of all ability levels. It was proposed that there should be an inservice but for a number of reasons including the failure of the university (this writer) to come up with a facilitator it never ran. There were now only 5 weeks left. So Prior decided to ask teachers to become researchers in their own classrooms and to devise, implement and evaluate a lesson that took into account the earlier findings and the hypotheses they generated. The results were of some interest. One teacher whose study is fully recorded was very successful but found the exercise exhausting.

Teachers were also asked to submit any aspect of learning that interested them, and an interview with the Principal was also conducted.

Prior points out that while many teachers said that change was not possible because of class size one teacher had actually achieved such change.

This is by no means all but that is not for this text. While the project met with many vicissitudes there is no way that it can be regarded as a failure. It may not have achieved its goals but like any action research it achieved many things enroute. First, it showed that many teachers find it difficult to reflect and have to be helped if they want to achieve a new level of thinking. Second, the whole process is lengthy. Prior felt that if he were to do it again he would shorten the process of finding the problem. Perhaps, however, teachers should go through that lengthy process. Third, at the time he wrote he did not see a direct connection with the whole school plan. When he undertook the project whole school planning was in its infancy. Similarly research on TQM in management in education was only beginning to appear in books and journals. It seems clear from this research that a school that concentrates on a project like this over a year is likely to achieve much more than the engagement of different small groups in small projects. Here the whole school was involved in a problem of teaching mixed ability groups. This is still a problem for teachers. But now in several countries there is a drive to focus on the needs of individual children and design curricula that meet the needs of each child.[64] It is in this sense that we begin to understand the concept of teamwork in schools. Fourth, the project indicates, as does the recently published project on the Transition Year[65] that there is much more to the design of instruction than is currently thought to be the case. Fifth, the conduct of the project provided a *chocs des opinions* and began to get the teachers thinking outside of their normal frames of reference. Instructional leaders will find the maintenance of such attitudes difficult unless agreed changes are built into the curriculum. Sixth, although teachers believed they were constrained by a *received* curriculum and large class sizes they nevertheless, were able to undertake developments within these constraints. In all, during this period the school was of the kind described by Cohn and Kottkamp[64] as inquiry-oriented and the teachers were acting as extended professionals.

Aim
To gather evidence from classrooms which is relevant to the following problem; There are some pupils who are not fully occupied in class. How can this situation be improved?

Guidelines
Teachers are asked to observe and describe the fact of the situation, using the following suggestions:

Which pupils are not adequately occupied in class?
What are such pupils doing when they should be working?
Do pupils so behave during a particular type of class or teaching or at certain times of the day?
Any other instance and circumstances of time-wasting noticed.

Exhibit 2.5. Prior's Guidelines for his colleagues for observation of their classes.

Implications for curriculum and instructional leadership

Prior pointed out that some of his problems arose from the fact that he had had no training for this task. There were things he could not change like the curriculum and class size although he pointed out that as teachers made changes so little changes were made in the curriculum. He was fortunate to have a supportive Principal. It is now possible from this example to see the role of a Principal as an Instructional Leader. First, it is clear that the Principal would not have had time to undertake the task. Therefore there was a need for an instructional leader within the school. Second, the Principal should have the necessary knowledge to be able to formulate problems for the staff to consider in "assumptional-dialogues" or to undertake and to provide the resources for the task to be implemented and the results to be evaluated. Morale is lowered when things are agreed but not acted on in schools. Essentially the Principal's task is to lead an inquiry-oriented school. Principals have to understand the tasks of instructional and curriculum leadership in order both to delegate and lead. The support of the principal in such activities is a prerequisite of their success. Equally middle management has to recognize that it has a key role to play in instructional and curriculum leadership.

The issue of critical thinking, reflective judgement, and development as goals of schooling are dealt with in chapter 13. Some aspects of that chapter are relevant in this context.

Notes and references

[1] Angelo, T and K. P. Cross (1993). *Classroom Assessment Techniques.* Jossey Bass, San Fransisco.
[2] George, J and J. Cowan (1999) *A Handbook of Techniques for Formative Evaluation.* Kogan Page, London. See also McKernan, J (1996) *Curriculum Action Research. A Handbook of Methods and Resources for the Reflective Practitioner.* Kogan Page, London
[3] Brookfield, D.(1995). *Becoming a Critically Reflective Teacher.* Jossey-Bass, San Fransisco p42. This view of the professional teacher being a reflective practitioner is also taken by McKernan *ibid..*
[4] Elliott, J (1976) Preparing teachers for classroom accountability. *Education for Teaching*, 100. Pp49 – 71. Cited by Heywood, (1984). *Considering the Curriculum during Student Teaching.* Kogan Page, London. p160
[5] *loc.cit*
[6] Tobin, K (2007). MSt Thesis. University of Dublin, Dublin. Inspections by Government appointed inspectors are the norm in the five education systems in the countries of the British Isles
[7] Shulman, L. S. (1986a). Paradigms and research programs in the study of teaching: A contemporary perspective in M. C. Wittrock (ed) *Handbook of Research on Teaching.* 3rd Edition. Macmillan, New York.
[8] LaBoskey, V. K (1994) *Development of Reflective Practice. A Study of Preservice Teachers.* Teachers College Press, Columbia University, New York. p115.
[9] Also cited by LaBoskey ref 6, p 124. Shulman, L. S (1988). The dangers of dichotomous thinking in education. In P. P. Grimmett and G. L. Erickson (eds). *Reflection on Teacher Education.* Teachers College Press, Columbia University, New York.
[10] Cowan, J (1998). *On Becoming an Innovative University Teacher. Reflection in Action.* Open University Press, SRHE, Buckingham. Pp 54-56 and other pages.
[11] *loc.cit.* ref 8
[12] *loc.cit* ref 3 p 232
[13] Hoyle, E (1973) Strategies for curriculum change in Watkins, R (ed) *Inservice Training Structure and Context.* Ward Lock, London. also cited in Heywood (1984) p 160
[14] Heywood, J., McGuinness, S and D. E. Murphy (1980) *Final Report of the Public Examinations Evaluation Project to the Minister for Education.* School of Education, University of Dublin. Cited in Heywood, J (1989). *Assessment in Higher Education.* Wiley, New York. P 273. The project was an evaluation of the Intermediate Certificate Examination. This examination was taken by 14/15 year olds at the end of their compulsory education in the subjects they studied at school. These were listed by the Department of Education who also defined the content and set the examination nationally. This examination has since been replaced by the Junior Certificate. See note 42 Chapter 1.
[15] Also cited in Heywood, 1989. P 263. *Ibid.* 'A' level examination is the Advanced Level of the General Certificate of Education (GCE). At the time this examination was set in England, Wales and Northern Ireland by Matriculation Boards that were independent of Government. Some were owned and managed by Universities. These examinations were set in subjects of the curriculum and students usually took 3 or 4 subjects at the end of a period two years study after the age of compulsory schooling (i.e. 16 to 18 years)

[16] Schön, D (1983). *The Reflective Practitioner. How professionals Think in Action*. Basic Books, New York. Schön also describes single and double loop learning. Single loop learning is when a person or an organization evaluates a process with a view to determining if there have been deviations from the norm. It does not question the basic assumptions of the organization. Sometimes change requires an institution to discard assumptions and policies and this will involve a second loop of learning –hence double loop learning. See Pettit, D and I. Hind (1(92) Reorganizing the delivery of educational services and educative leadership in P. A Duignan and R. J. S. Macpherson (eds) *Educative Leadership. A Practical Theory for New Administrators and Managers*. Falmer Press, London.
[17] loc.cit ref 10
[18] Eisner, E (1979). *The Educational Imagination: On the Design and Evaluation of School Programs*. Collier-MacMillan, New York. The Eisner quotations will also be found in Heywood, J (1984). *Considering the Curriculum during Student Teaching*. Kogan Page, London.
[19] ibid
[20] Hiers, B (1989). *The Professional Decision Thinker: Our New Management Priority*.. Grafton Books (Collins), London.
[21] Kohn, A (1993). *Punished by Rewards. The Trouble with Gold Stars. Incentive plans as Praise, and other Bribes*. Houghton Mifflin, Boston
[22] Holliday, C. B (2001) *Learning to Motivate Students. An Evaluation of Dr William Peter's Theory of Masterful Teaching*. M.Ed. Thesis. University of Dublin, Dublin.
[23] FitzGibbon, A (1994). Self-evaluation exercises in initial teacher education. *Irish Journal of Educational Studies* 13, 145 – 164.
[24] loc.cit ref 3 ch 5.
[25] Ryan, A (2005) Teacher development and educational change: empowerment through structured reflection. *Irish Educational Studies* 24, (2-3), 179 – 198.
[26] ibid
[27] ibid
[28] Bellon, J. J., Bellon, E. C. and M. A. Blank (1992) *Teaching from a Research Knowledge Base: A Development and Renewal Process*. Macmillan (Merrill), New York. p 44
[29] loc.cit ref 3 p 81
[30] Heywood, J and H. Montagu Pollock (1976). *Science for Arts Students. A Case Study in Curriculum Development*. Society for Research into Higher Education, London
[31] Hunt, M. P. and L. P. Metcalf (1955) *Teaching High School Social Studies*. Harper and Row, New York p21 cited by Gunter, M. A, Estes, T. H., and J. Schwab (1999) *Instruction. A Models Approach*. 3rd edition. Allyn and Bacon, Boston
[32] See chapter 1. Cohn and Kottkamp make the case for reflective seminars of the type described by Argyris and Schön (1974- *Theory in Practice: Increasing Professional Effectiveness*. Jossey Bass, San Fransisco). The idea of a round table where the different levels of power sit next to each other comes from D. Perkins (2003). *King Arthur's Round Table. How collaborative Conversations create Smart Organizations*, Wiley, New York.
[33] There are such scales, as for example those for classroom routines and motivation in Cohen, Manion and Morrison but the point is to read literature that is not a summary but dealing with these conceptual areas in depth. Cohen, L., Manion, L and K. Morrison (1996) *A Guide to Teaching Practice*. 4th edition Routledge, London.
[34] Heywood, J (1992) Student teachers as researchers of instruction in the classroom in J.H.C. Vonk and H. J. van Helden (eds) *New Prospects for Teacher Education Europe*. Free University of Amsterdam, Association of Teacher Education in Europe, Brussels.
[35] See for example, Heywood, J (1982). *Pitfalls and Planning in Student Teaching*. Kogan Page, London.
[36] Two and a half days were spent in the school and two and half days in the university during the academic terms. In between times the students continued to teach in schools.
[37] Immediate taken to mean the same evening.
[38] In round 1 it was found that only about 35% of the students understood the issue. In round 2 after examples were given over 60% demonstrated understanding of the issue.
[39] The writer made a submission to a committee on the training of post-primary teachers but this committee's report has never been made public. The research part of this submission will be found in Heywood, J (2007) Theory into practice in teacher education in A. Rupp (ed) *Moderne Konzepte in der betrieblichen und universitären Aus-und Weiterbiding*. Dgvt Verlag, Tubingen.
[40] Wang, Lin Quian (1992). Chinese advancements in mathematical education. *Educational Studies*

in Mathematics 23, 287 – 298 cited by Clarke, B., Clarke, D and P. Sullivan (1996) The mathematics teacher and curriculum development in A. J. Bishop et al (eds*). International Handbook of Mathematics Education*. Part 2. Kluwer, Dordrecht.

[41] *ibid*. They cite Stigler, J. W and H. W. Stevenson (1991) How Asian teachers polish each lesson to perfection. *American Educator* , 15, (1), 12 – 47.

[42] *ibid*. They cite Lovitt, C. J. and D. M. Clarke (1988, 1989)*Mathematics Curriculum and Teaching Program Activity Bank* Vols 1 and 2. Curriculum Corporation, Carlton Victoria, Australia.

[43] See for example Murphy, D. E (1980) M.Ed Thesis University of Dublin. He showed that a minimum of two cycles was required for teachers to internalise the thinking behind what they had been asked to evaluate through their own development and trial.

[44] Cross, P. K and M. Steadman (1996). *Classroom Research*. Jossey Bass, San Fransisco.

[45] Parlett, M and D. Hamilton (1972). *Evaluation as Illumination*. Centre for Educational Sciences, University of Edinburgh.See also Parlett, M and D. Hamilton (1977) Evaluation as illumination: a new approach to the study of innovatory programmes in D. Hamilton et al eds. *Beyond the Numbers Game*. Macmillan, London. McKernan who has taught college student teachers in both Ireland and the US has written a substantive treatise on action research. It includes a large section on its philosophical and historical foundations. These are rooted in the work of Kurt Lewin. McKernan, J (1996) *Curriculum Action Research. A Handbook of Methods and Resources for the Reflective Practitioner* 2nd edition. Kogan Page, London.

[46] Prior, P (1985) *Teacher self-evaluation using classroom action-research. A Case study*. M.Ed Thesis. University of Dublin, Dublin p 100 ff. See also Heywood ref 19 p144 ff.

[47] Elliott, J.(1991) *Action Research for Educational Change*. Open University Press, Buckingham. 2001 printing.

[48] Unfortunately Breen who cites this study does not describe the action research in any detail Breen, C (2003). Mathematics teachers as researchers. Living on the Edge? In A. J. Bishop et al (eds). *Second International Handbook of Mathematics Education*. Kluwer, Dordrecht. Hatch, G and Shiiu (1998). Practtioner Research and the construction of knowledge in mathematics in A. Sierpinska and J. Kilpatrick (eds). *Mathematics Education as a Research Domain*. Book 2. Kluwer, Dordrecht.

[49] cited by Crawford, K and J. Adler (1996). Teachers as researchers in mathematics education. In A. J. Bishop et al (eds). *International Handbook of Mathematics Education*. Part 2. Kluwer, Dordrecht. See Crawford, K. P. and C. E. Deer (1993) Do we practice what we preach? Putting Policy into Practice into teacher education. *Journal of South Pacific Association of Teacher Education*, 21, (2), 111 –112.

[50] *ibid* Breen cites studies in Jaworski, B., Wood, T., and S. Dawson (eds). *Mathematics Teacher Education. Critical International Perspectives*. Falmer, London.

[51] *ibid* Breen. Notes initiatives in the Netherlands, Portugal, Hungary, Israel, The UK and Austria reported by Krainer, K (2000) *Teacher education as research; A trend in European mathematics teaching*. Paper presented at to working group for action 7 at the Ninth International Congress on Mathematical Education, Tokyo.

[52] *ibid*.

[53] *loc.cit* p 197

[54] *loc.cit* p 201

[55] Cromwell, L (1992). Assessing critical thinking in C. A. Barnes (ed*). Critical Thinking: Educational Imperative*. New Directions for Community Colleges No 77. Jossey Bass, San Fransisco

[56] Heywood, J., McGuiness, S. and D. E. Murphy (1980). *Final Report of the Public Examinations Evaluation Project to the Minister for Education*. School of Education, University of Dublin.
Heywood, J and M. Murray (2005) Curriculum-Led Staff Development: Towards Curriculum and Instructional Leadership in Ireland. *Bulletins of the European Forum on Educational Administration* (EFEA) No 4.

[57] *loc.cit* and Elliott, J (1981). *Action-research: a framework for self-evaluation in schools*. Mimeo. Cambridge

[58] Prior, P (1985) *Teacher self-evaluation using classroom action-research. A Case study*. M.Ed Thesis. University of Dublin, Dublin

[59] *loc.cit.* George, J and J. Cowan ref 2 p 93 and 94. Also O'Neil, M. J. and L. Jackson (1983). Nominal Group Technique; a technique for initiating curriculum development in higher education. *Studies in Higher Education*, 8, (2), 129 – 138.

[60] *loc.cit.* Prior p 47

[61] *ibid*

[62] *ibid*

[63] *loc cit* Prior

[64] see note 19 chapter 1 for the approach of a primary school in England.

[65] *loc.cit.* note 56

Part 11
Toward masterful teaching

INTRODUCTION
CHAPTERS 3, 4 AND 5

Instructional leaders require a concept of masterful teaching particularly in their role as mentors to beginning teachers and advisers to educational leaders on the problems that are sometimes faced by experienced teachers. Three of the dimensions that contribute to masterful teaching form the themes of these three chapters. It should be made clear from the outset that they are not to do with the improvement of the test performances of students although this might come out of improvements in the use of different approaches to pedagogy. Behind the structure of these chapters is the hypothesis that the thoughts of beginning teachers are often focused on discipline, the fear of not being able to keep control of a class, and fear of the community of their colleagues. Coupled with this hypothesis is the often reported assertion that the changing school population has brought with it changes in attitudes toward discipline that have made the task of some teachers much less bearable than in the past. Whatever else is clear from research it is that teachers should be seen to fair and consistent.

Discipline is a much talked about topic in schools. It is a subject that can benefit very much from "assumptional-dialogues" where exchanges about experiences can help teachers develop a theory of action about pupils, and where the findings of research can contribute by challenging convictions that are sometimes deeply held. It is assumed that students who are motivated are less likely to be troublesome than those students who are not. Much of the challenge of teaching today, not only for beginning teachers, is to try to motivate the unmotivated. Getting lessons off to a good start is an imperative. Some teachers may need to change deeply held beliefs and one of the tasks of the instructional leader is to work with them to change those beliefs if it is thought their existing beliefs are creating problems for them.

Finally pupils want teachers to plan lessons well and they want to trust their knowledge. If these are absent students are likely to be troublesome in any level of education including universities.

It is taken as axiomatic that the purpose of discipline is to enhance learning, and that the school and classroom climate (or culture) should be conducive to learning. No textbook can tell a teacher how to react in class but it can provide teachers with a theoretical framework for action based on both research and reported practice. Teachers should then be in a position to judge their own theories for all us have theories of why people do this and don't do that. Chapter 3 begins with a brief discussion of some of these theories. Learning and its relation to motivation are discussed. The chapter ends with contrasting theories of motivation and learning, behaviourist and non-behaviourist. It includes a brief *resumé* of William Peter's theory of masterful teaching.

The first concern of chapter 4 is with study skills since if pupils do not have adequate study skills they are likely to misbehave. The second concern or theme of this chapter arises from the axiom that if a teacher does not get a class off to a good start he/she will be in trouble. It is argued that often students do not learn because the cognitive structures appropriate to that learning have not been developed. The value of advanced organizers and imagery in getting a class off to a good start is considered. The chapter ends with a discussion of the value of cooperative learning for motivation and the development of social skills.

Chapter 5, is more generally about the planning, implementation and evaluation of lessons. Students respond to teachers who are well planned, perceived to be knowledgeable and fair in discipline, hence the importance of planning. Examples of planning are given, This chapter summarises the descriptive statistics that should be in any instructional leader's toolkit. The reliability and validity of various modes of assessment are considered.

3
TOWARD MASTERFUL TEACHING

Summary and introduction

The boundaries of educational and instructional leadership meet in the area of discipline. During the last fifteen to twenty years or so teachers have had to accustom themselves too increasingly disruptive behaviour accompanied very occasionally by violence. At a very minimum children have become much more precocious and teachers have to deal with what has been called the 'me' generation. Such behaviour has been and is a source of stress since undisciplined behaviour is likely to have both cognitive and social consequences for children the problem of discipline is as much a problem for an instructional leader as it is an educational leader. Nevertheless it is the educational leader, the Principal, who has to take overall responsibility. Ultimately, however it is teachers who have to act, and teachers can only learn to act in the light of experience and the shared experience of their colleagues. Nevertheless advice, research, and particularly "assumptional-dialogues" can help them construct frames of reference against which they can judge their actions. Therefore, educational and instructional leaders have to have defensible theories of discipline based on the testing of the assumptions gained from experience and belief. Such testing should not only be on the basis of experience but against a theoretical framework.

It is taken as axiomatic that if the purpose of discipline is to enhance learning that teachers, instructional and educational leaders have to provide an environment or climate for learning in their classrooms and schools. No textbook can tell a teacher how to react in class. It can provide teachers with a theoretical framework based on both research and practice against which a teacher can judge their own theories and actions for we all have theories about why some people do this and why others do that.

The framework taken in this chapter seeks not to ask why do pupils misbehave in that way or this way but to ask why are some pupils motivated to learn and others not for on the opposite side of the discipline coin is motivation. What is it that turns people on to learn? In chapters 1 and 2 the case for schools to be "inquiry oriented" was made. It was suggested that an "inquiry oriented" school" would provide a forum where long established assumptions and structures could be challenged by means of reflective seminars. The term "assumptional-dialogue" was used. The latter part of this chapter contrasts two ideolo-

gies of discipline and motivation and is intended to provide the material for an "assumptional dialogue" on discipline and motivation. One of these theories by an American educator (William Peter) sought to answer the question what is a Masterful teacher. His theory runs against the grain of much teacher practice. Based on intrinsic as opposed to extrinsic motivation it provides the challenge that an "assumptional-dialogue" needs. A question that schools and teachers can ask is where does their school stand on the continuum of extrinsic-intrinsic motivation and does this position affect discipline, if at all.

The chapter begins with an outline of the importance of the school's culture in discipline. It concludes that the beliefs we have about what motivates individuals to work and learn are of paramount importance in our interactions with other people. This point is taken up in the next section that examines the effects of two "thought models" on our behaviour in organizational systems. These are the well known Theory X and Theory Y. The assumptions we make about how individuals and groups are motivated clearly influence a school's climate. For this reason instructional leaders should determine from time to time what the stakeholders perceive the climate to be.

Knowledge of attribution and expectancy theories of motivation throws some light on the behaviour of individuals. These aspects are discussed in the next section. This is followed by a discussion of behaviourist and non-behaviourist theories of motivation stemming from Theory X and Y in terms of extrinsic versus intrinsic motivation. Kohn's advocacy of intrinsic rewards is summarised.

Discipline and instructional leadership

The boundaries of educational and instructional leadership meet in the area of discipline. During the last fifteen years or so teachers have had to accustom themselves' to increasingly disruptive behaviour accompanied occasionally by violence. Such behaviour has been and is a source of stress.[1] Governments and others responsible for education, including Trade Unions have become increasingly concerned with the problem. Committees of enquiry have been established, codes of behaviour have been suggested and much printed and spoken advice given.[2] Ultimately, however it is teachers who have to act, and teachers can only learn to act in the light of experience and the shared experience of their colleagues. Nevertheless advice and research can help them construct frames of reference against which they can judge their actions.

It is into this ethos that beginning teachers find themselves and it is no wonder that they should be worried about their ability to "manage," some think of it as "control," and motivate their classes of students. They worry much more about such matters than they do about the best strategies for developing cognitive skills and understanding of the subject they teach. If they do not want the principal to advise them about their classroom work they certainly want the principal to foster a learning environment that is free of the problems of discipline. In this sense they want the school to become a learning organisation.

What they sometimes find is a culture that conflicts with this laudable aim. They may find that although the school has a formal code of discipline known to both students and their parents that it breaks down. Sometimes, for example, a Principal does not consult with parents when a misdemeanour is sufficiently serious to merit the attention of parents. Occasionally Parents bypass the school and go straight to the Chairperson of the Board of Management (Governors). Sometimes teachers do not follow the procedures and in serious cases this can have consequences if litigation is taken against the school. A major difficulty is that different teachers and parents place different interpretations on what they regard as a serious misdemeanour. So there can be conflict between schools and parents. Among teachers there are different views about the role of year heads. Some teachers want to off-load onto year heads every misdemeanour such as the failure to bring in homework, a matter that they could easily deal with themselves. So care has to be taken in drawing up a code of practice to ensure everyone takes exactly the same understanding away from it.

Principals often get landed in very difficult situations when judgements about a child's behaviour may cause them to side with the parents against a teacher and such actions can damage teacher morale throughout a school irrespective of the rights or wrongs of the case. In schools where discipline is effective morale is likely to be high. The visitor to a school soon gets messages about the extent to which it is happy and disciplined or unhappy and undisciplined to draw two extremes. In other words the culture of the school, as reflected in the picture it presents of discipline may impact on teachers and the discipline regimes they operate in their classrooms.

Level 3 of the Principal's instructional leadership role requires the Principal to ensure an environment where the pursuit of learning is free of interruption. The Principal's attitudes and dispositions to discipline and organisation are, thus, of paramount importance. Since our beliefs about what motivates a student to learn or misbehave determine our reactions to the student it is important that we should have a self-understanding of what our belief models are. But a Principal cannot do all of this on her/his own and in particular beginning teachers need to have an instructional leader delegated to guide (mentor) them through any problems of discipline they may have. This text, however, is primarily with the understandings that principals must have if they are to create an environment in which everyone is free to learn. In this respect a little management theory is likely to be helpful. Since motivated learners are likely to be disciplined learners, the motivation to work (learn) is considered first.

A little management theory

The view we take of why individuals are motivated to work underpins the judgements we make about organizational structure, the role of the Principal and thus the meaning given to service in the managerial role. The same applies to teachers and their evaluations of why students learn. Teachers are managers of learning.

Historically views about the reasons why students and workers work well or badly are rooted in the assembly line approach to manufacture and education. Such views in their extreme may be summarised as follows.[3]

1. *A student (individual) is inherently lazy and must therefore be motivated by outside incentives.*
2. *The student's (individual's) goals run counter to those of the organization, hence the pupil (individual) must be controlled by external forces to ensure his working toward organizational goals.*
3. *Because of his/her irrational feelings, a student (individual) is basically incapable of self-discipline and self-control.*

Translate this model into one that is controlled by a system of public examinations (and/or tests) thus:

1. *The student is primarily motivated by academic incentives and will do whatever gets him or her, the greatest academic gain.*
2. *Since academic incentives are under the control of the institution, the student is essentially a passive agent to be manipulated, motivated and controlled by the organization.*
3. *The student's feelings are essentially irrational and must be prevented from interfering with his or her rational calculation of self-interest.*
4. *Institutions and their organizational (curriculum) arrangements can and must be designed in such a way as to neutralise and control the students' feelings and therefore, their unpredictable traits.*

Beliefs like that may cause extrinsic incentives, such as regular testing, to encourage students. Chalk-and-talk methods of teaching will probably be employed.

Views such as these imply an authoritarian style of teaching and management that believes extrinsic incentives are the primary causes of motivation. They are a picture of a rational-economic person and were enshrined in the literature of management by McGregor who called it Theory X. This model presents a depressing view of student and worker attitudes and potential. Clearly there are circumstances when students and workers respond in this way to teachers and managers. It is equally clear that some teachers and managers have a disposition to behave in this way. This is not surprising because there is a tendency to model what one has experienced. One has only to observe children teaching their teddy bears and dolls. They "tell" them what to do: their understanding is of the need to "control."

In schools it is the psychology of human behaviour inherent in such judgements that is worrying. It can for example reinforce the isolation of teachers in their classrooms to the detriment of a corporate mission to educate children. Such dispositions can reinforce "them" and "us" attitudes.

Other research in organizations suggested that when organizations showed an interest in their workers they were likely to work hard. Coupled with developments in humanistic psychology a new model of what motivates individuals to work that contrasted with Theory X emerged. McGregor called it Theory Y. Theory Y assumes that:

1. *The expenditure of physical and mental effort in work is as natural as play or rest.*
2. *External control and the threat of punishment are not the only means for bringing about effort toward organizational objectives. A student (person) will exercise self-direction and self-control in the service of the objectives to which he is committed.*
3. *Commitment to objectives is a function of the rewards associated with their achievement.*
4. *The average person (student) learns, under proper conditions, not only to accept but, to seek responsibility.*
5. *The capacity to exercise a relatively high degree of imagination, ingenuity and creativity in the solution of organizational problems is widely, not narrowly, distributed among the population.*
6. *Under the conditions of modern classrooms (industrial life), the intellectual potentialities of the average student (human being) are only partially utilized.* [4]

A Principal on a management course as part of an assignment gave a rating scale to some students in his school. The scale was designed to distinguish between Theory X and Theory Y teacher behaviour. He asked them to rate their teachers and themselves. Surprise, Surprise! They rated their teachers as Theory X and themselves as Theory Y. Of course there may be some truth in this if these perceptions are based solely on the classroom behaviour of teachers. But it needs to be remembered that the organisation can cause theory X teacher behaviour as well as a Theory X response from students. For example, the belief that examinations test rote knowledge leads to the belief that the classroom is best arranged for children to learn by rote. And, this implies teacher-centred as opposed to so-called student-centred learning. The differences between autocratic and democratic teachers are summarised in exhibit 3.4 at the end of this chapter.

Clearly the assumptions that managers make about the reasons for the behaviour of others influence their own behaviour which, in its turn, influences the climate of the organization in which they work. But these reasons should be influenced by the goals that they have for the organization. It is quite clear in the case of schools that they are learning organisations and that the purpose of discipline is to ensure that learning takes place at an optimal level. Much depends on the example that the Principal gives to pupils and their parents as well as teachers.

The findings of Rutter and his colleagues remain relevant:"*The 'atmosphere' of any particular school will be greatly influenced by the degree to which it func-*

tions as a coherent whole, with agreed ways of doing things which are consistent throughout the school and which have the general support of all the staff"[. . .]. For obvious reasons, school values and norms are likely to be more effective if it is clear to all that they have widespread support. Discipline will be easier to maintain if the pupils appreciate that it relates to generally accepted approaches and does not simply represent the whims of the individual teacher. The particular rules which are set and the specific disciplinary techniques which are used are probably much less important than the establishment of some principles and guidelines which are both clearly recognisable and acceptable by the school as a whole." That is, students and staff should see that the school has a clear direction in all matters.[5]*

An instructional leader should know how the stakeholders perceive the 'climate' of the school.[6] He may wish to establish what it is through more formal methods and one way of doing this has been described by McBeath.[7] A recent meta-analysis of research on school leadership in the United States found that an effective leader builds a culture that influences teachers,' who, in turn positively influences students.[8] However, if a substantial change (innovation) is undertaken the team spirit that is so important in creating a cohesive culture and therefore climate has to be present.[9]

"Leaders act through and with other people. Leaders sometimes do things, through words or actions, that have a direct effect on the primary goals of the collective, but more often their agency consists of influencing the thoughts and actions of other persons and establishing policies that enable others to be effective"[10] Peter argues that "the most practical knowledge for the professional is theory but the theory must be effectively translatable into practice if it is to have any value." [. . .]. Motivation theory is more valuable in the hands of an intelligent teacher than a bag of motivational tricks. In fact, a bag of motivational tricks can be downright dangerous in the hands of a practitioner who does not fully understand the theory and philosophy supporting them."[11]

A little more about learning

The Acquisition of information: attribution, expectancy and gossip

Related to the human desire to investigate is the idea that persons seek to attribute causes to what they see in the actions of others.[12] Once again this is a matter of everyday experience. It derives from the fact that we impose meaning on the objects of knowledge. *"An attribution is an inference about why an event occurred or about a person's dispositions."* [13]

Quite clearly the tendency (temptation) to *attribute* is a powerful factor in interpersonal relationships. Gossip is so often attributive, so is much journalism. Our attributions often result in other persons obtaining erroneous perceptions of other people.

One of the purposes of stating aims and objectives at both school (organization) and classroom levels (departmental) is to remove ambiguity from the rules required for schools and classrooms to function. If the criteria for discipline are inadequately defined they can create problems throughout the school. For example, as we have seen, teachers by no means agree among themselves as to what constitutes disruptive behaviour or what constitutes an appropriate punishment.[14] Even when they are agreed about principles they may disagree about the significance of an incident and therefore about the manner of retribution. It is the function of the Principal to ensure there is agreement about the level of action.

Children too may have their own ideas about what constitutes disruptive behaviour. They may also perceive some teachers to be less fair than others. Much of the hidden curriculum involves students in learning what behaviours are acceptable.[15] It is for these reasons that some authorities advise teachers to establish learning contracts with their students. In that way everyone in a class is clear about what is tolerable and what is not.[16] However, these contracts should derive from a whole school policy otherwise there can be differences between teachers that can be exploited by their students. It is no bad thing to engage pupils in the design of such contracts.

An important aspect of attribution theory is self-attribution. When things go wrong we tend to blame other people.[17] And, because we are confident that something or someone else is to blame we do not evaluate our attributions.[18] Politicians often demonstrate such behaviour. But it happens in schools among principals, parents, teachers and pupils. The other party is always to blame. Parents always rightly or wrongly believe their child is in the right. Their beliefs may be a form of cognitive dissonance (see below).

For example, our own failures in examinations, or not to do as well as we expected, rather than outright failure, are blamed on factors other than those created by ourselves.[19] Teachers may ascribe to students characteristics that they do not possess in order to account for their failure in tests or to carry out successfully work set by the teacher. Such students can be described as 'odd,' 'disturbed' or 'peculiar.'[20] Some self-attributions can effect our behaviour so, for example, if we believe we are hard working this will stimulate further effort.

Understanding such behaviour is important if we are to develop objectivity, not only in the classroom but in respect of all activities involving interpersonal relationships, as well as in our understanding of others. As Johnson[21] says attribution research signals *"a need for open communication within faculties, staff rooms, and classrooms and help in understanding educator's and stake holders' explanations for organizational and personal successes, failures and behaviour."* Attribution and expectations are closely related.

Expectancy and Expectations

Expectancy as used by de Cecco and Crawford, is a momentary belief that a particular outcome will follow a particular act. In relation to classroom teaching, it is useful to think of the expectations which pupils have of what will happen in class, as well as the ability of the teacher to create expectations within the class. But this is to lose the "momentary" aspect of the definition. The "momentary" relates our instantaneous behaviour to what we are. If there is discrepancy between what we see, we may become angry. For instance if we enter a classroom and find pupils jumping on desks when we expected to see them sitting and reading, then there is a discrepancy between perception and expectation that could cause anger. Such discrepancies are causes of arousal. It has been suggested that a small discrepancy may cause us to feel pleasant while a large discrepancy may cause unpleasant feelings.

The expectancy theory of perception suggests that we perceive more readily and more clearly those events that we expect. Our expectations are maps of the future that we have constructed on the basis of past experience. This is also one of the reasons why teachers sometimes tell their students what the objectives of the lesson are. Allport used the term 'set' to describe this stage of expectancy[22]. 'Set' in this sense refers to the way that people receive information in that, generally, information is received more quickly and understood when it has either been brought to their attention or is of interest to them. Formal education becomes difficult for some students and impossible for others because one of its tasks is to bring uninteresting information thought to be of general importance into the perceptual frameworks of the recipients. Expectancy theory has profound implications for the curriculum not least because it questions the value of some programmes for some students.

According to expectancy theory it is only by developing expectation frameworks that we can effectively sample the available information, and cope with the events with which we are faced. This is how individuals and organisations socialize each other. Both try to shape expectations by creating their own perceptions for us to perceive. In the classroom a concept map can be used to help students understand what is expected of them (see chapter 6).

In education students have expectations of examinations and tests. They attempt, as their teachers do to predict the questions that will be set. They also prepare for examinations by creating model answers they hope will meet their expectations.[23] If the questions are set in such a way that they do not perceive their expectations to have been met they may be unable to cope because they allow their first impressions to dominate their thinking process.

Expectancy is also accompanied by estimates of the level of satisfaction attained. Psychologists call this valence. This is not the same as enjoying the outcome when we have it. De Cecco and Crawford illustrate valance with the example of under-achievers. A student who has the ability to achieve academically has a high expectancy of success. If he or she does not get any satisfaction from academic success (low valency), he or she, may not do as well as their potential suggests. Such persons are called under-achievers: they are not motivated to achieve, nor do they expect to succeed. Even the prospect of failure will not produce a higher level of drive.[24]

Rist[25] in a study of teacher expectation and achievement found that a kindergarten teacher classified students into slow and fast learners from her initial impressions of physical appearance, forthrightness of behaviour and language usage. This was done by relating the impression to an ideal type which was a social-class based model of the successful child i.e. middle class. The two groups were managed in different ways. Those thought to be "fast" were encouraged whereas those viewed as "slow" students were controlled. Thus the teacher's expectations came to be fulfilled and at succeeding grade levels. In its turn this fuelled the self-fulfilling prophecy which had arisen from these initial impressions. Other writers explain findings such as these by pointing out that student perceptions of their teachers' expectations could influence their self-image in such a way that it is reflected in their level of achievement.[26]

McClelland argued that teachers have to inspire students with the desire to achieve[27] It is easy to see in the speeches of politicians in the UK and the US that this is what they expect teachers to do. The problems arise with many pupils from the lower socio-economic and minority groups who for one reason or another do not desire to achieve, at least within the framework of the traditional academic curriculum.

McClelland's propositions for teaching achievement motivation are[28]

1. *An individual must believe that he/she should develop a motive. (One of the problems which teachers have in dealing with children caught in the poverty trap is that the children have no perception that there might be a way out of the trap and that this "sense" is reinforced by similar parental views)*
2. *Therefore motives have to be realistic, reasonable, and attainable.*
3. *This means that an individual must be able to describe for him or herself the attributes and values of the motive*
4. *To ensure action the motive should be linked to related actions*
5. *Thus the most chance of success will occur when individuals perceive the motive to be related to everyday life.*
6. *If the adoption of a new motive is seen to improve a person's self-image then the thoughts and actions of the individual are likely to be influenced (Teachers working with deprived children often report that it is lack of self-esteem (self-concept) which inhibits their motivation).*
7. *When individuals see and experience the new motive as an improvement on prevailing cultural values. (This implies that teachers have to demonstrate that it is possible to become like someone else in a different sub-system of society if they are working with deprived children [see below]. In its turn,*

the attempt to do this might imply a radically different curriculum to what exists.)
8. *If an individual sets concrete goals in life related to the motive then the motive is likely to influence thought and action*
9. *Individuals who record their progress toward the attainment of new goals are more likely to be influenced by the motive*
10. *Persons who wish to change their motives need to feel that they have the support of others and to be respected by them for what they can do. (A reminder of the importance of peer groups to learning—see 12 below).*
11. *If new motives are worked out in an environment which lifts them out of the routine of everyday life then more changes are likely to occur. (This may be observed among people who relentlessly pursue hobbies, e.g. stamp collecting, railway enthusiasts).*
12. *If a new motive brings with it a new and desirable reference group this will reinforce the change in motive (One of the problems which teachers have in helping children from the lower socio-economic groups is that their reference groups cannot readily be changed. It is for this reason, among others, that vocational preparation courses prior to the students leaving school are important. It is also one of the reasons for the use of co-operative learning with such groups).*

Achievement Motivation is therefore the expectancy of finding satisfaction in mastering challenging and difficult performances. McClelland's propositions are not extraordinary and most of us would agree that they are necessary for achievement. There is every reason why these axioms should be applied to those children who find discipline difficult.

Several important studies have been made of teacher attitudes to gender. Thus in a nursery school boys misdemeanours were more likely to be noticed than girls misbehaviours. Teachers assumed that the girls would be better behaved. Adults expect children to fit in with their gender role expectations and in consequence are more alert to those behaviours. Gender role typing in the very early years has a powerful influence on the attitudes, behaviour and, values of children as they grow older.[29] In high school in England it has been found that teachers are more attached to those students they expect to pass the final public examination (A Level). Even so boys were much more likely to receive this concern than girls. This applied to teachers' of either sex.[30]

Suffice it to say that at this stage our expectations of what and why students achieve and why workers are motivated to work are functions of the models or stereotypes we have created that inform our perceptions.[31] In any event principals need to be aware of these problems since they have a bearing on the effectiveness of the school, and this implies careful monitoring of student performance.

The teacher has to maintain the students in a state of willingness to learn. This is achieved through teaching strategies that range from simple questioning to complex projects. The teacher achieves the expectancy function by first defining what is expected of the students and then modifying the students' expectations in such a way that they are encouraged to pursue the teacher's objectives. This activity is related to the incentive function, for pupils often value their achievements in terms of their success and failure. It is for this reason it is argued that students should be told where they are going either through a properly designed advanced organizer or a statement of objectives.

Although much of what has been said relates to the single lesson it is clear that students also have expectations of the curriculum and this has a bearing on what is taught as well as on how it is taught.

Expectancy and first impressions of individuals

Objectivity in managing is the ability to stand back from first impressions. This is because of the dominance they exert over subsequent perceptions.[32] First impressions are often difficult to shift and many individuals find it difficult to adapt to new circumstances. Clearly part of management (teacher) development is to get managers (teachers) to reflect on their practice and to come to understand their own stereotypical behaviour. When we see the power of advertising and the media on our perceptions it is easy to argue that an understanding of the factors which influence our behaviour and in particular our objectivity should be a necessary component of the curriculum at all levels of education.

At the level of personal interaction between principals and teachers, and teachers and students, we need constantly to be reminded that appearances do count. For example it seems that the facial expressions which demonstrate our emotions may be culturally influenced[33] and if not understood therefore, a source of misunderstandings in society, and especially in school. Unfortunate though it may be body language (dress, expression, stance, etc) sends powerful and immediate signals that we can and often do misread. How often have you been told that you conveyed the wrong impression? The trouble is that these impressions last and we do not seem to learn from our own experience of the impressions that people have of us.

Expectancy and cognitive dissonance

An important characteristic of memory and perception is the tendency to remember our successes and forget our failures.[34] At the same time we tend also to be very consistent in our attitudes and opinions.[35] Apart from the fact that this makes it more difficult to adapt, we try to adapt, by accommodating new perceptions that possess values within our own value maps. We tend to use sets that have served us well in the past. The same is true of problem solving: we tend to use the same heuristic whatever the problem[36] (See also chapter 9). Bruner has called this persistence *forecasting* and it can in a new situation prevent us from using more efficient strategies. We tend to believe in the advantages of what we already possess. Dissonance or downshifting arises when we have to accommodate a new value system with which we have no empathy. Discipline problems may arise when there is a conflict of value systems between pupil and teacher.

For example when a subject that we have to learn is cognitively complex and where values are involved, such as in political studies, a student may be in disagreement with the views held by the teacher. In these circumstances there may be considerable resistance to learning, and apparently this is particularly likely to be the case if the students are only mildly critical of the teacher's standpoint. Such students may become alienated from the political and economic system. However, as Marshall [37] shows, a teacher can cause learning through his teaching style, even if his or her rating with the students deteriorates during the course.

Since we impose meaning on the objects of knowledge it should come as no surprise to find that a pupil can deliberately impose misunderstanding in order to achieve consistency between the message and his feelings. If there is consistency, a pupil can change his attitude to a teacher from like to dislike if the teacher's messages appear to be untenable. This can happen in university when first-year students have to cope with certain value propositions in the social and behavioural sciences: anything that is contrary to the student views can create such dissonance. For this reason as a Catholic, I found the study of some aspects of sociology most difficult. In management and politics groups often distort their perceptions of the policies of opposing groups the result of which is a general misunderstanding of the other group's intention, and in consequence mistrust and suspicion.[38]

Challenges to values may be perceived as threatening. More generally in situations perceived to be threatening we narrow our perceptual field and return to the safety of our beliefs.[39] Behaviour in which we revert to tried and trusted ways can affect the higher order cognitive functions and thus the ability to solve new problems. Downshifting of this kind it is argued is one of the reasons why students fail to apply the higher levels of the Bloom *Taxonomy*.[40]

Cognitive dissonance theory accounts for the behaviour of institutions and politicians. For example politicians become so committed to the values expressed in their slogans that they become unable to entertain reasoned arguments against their points of view even from some of their own supporters! And of course it is necessary for the dynamic of political parties that the workers should not deviate from their beliefs and beliefs are easily entrenched.

It is both a fortunate and worrying aspect of life that we can change our ideas, and learning is possible as a result of reasoning. It is worrying when we change with the crowd and fail to think things through, for in those situations propaganda finds a powerful ally. It is fortunate when we apply reason to our behaviour. These ideas apply as much to the experience of taste and touch as they do to vision.

The acquisition of Information: Attention

The importance of attention has already been alluded to in reference to dual task performance. The attention required to drive a motor car is considerable and our perceptions are subject to a whole range of stimuli. Very many objects in the environment are competing for our attention, and in the classroom it is the instructors task to focus attention on that which is to be learnt. The television producer's task is to manipulate our attention to her/his programme just as it is the advertisers job to draw a positive response from the material presented. Thus the control of focus is an important area of study in psychology.

Hesseling[41] has made the point that attention is an integrating mechanism. Using the example of the car once again, he cites the case of the person who while driving is listening to a friend on a quiet road. So long as the situation is quiet the driver can attend to his friend but as soon as an unfamiliar (i.e. within the context of the driving) situation occurs the driver's attention has to shift and he or she is only vaguely aware of what has been said. Hesseling uses this example to illustrate the point that anyone who specialises in a functional role learns to give a different kind of attention to detail to those whose occupations are generalists. Then if a person is appointed to a general management function from a job that entailed a high level of highly focussed detail they not only have to change the focus of their attention but have to attend in quite a different way (e.g. consider generalisations rather than specifics). This applies in particular to the teacher, albeit a post-holder, who becomes a principal. Such persons require to acquire new skills and some find these difficult to obtain. It will be seen that such a transfer is required of many of those individuals who volunteer to become governors or managers of schools especially if they have no experience of management.

Receiving

Once we have decided to attend we receive. That again is a matter of common sense. It is this that creates the new experience (learning), and it is now that we have to allocate our limited capacities. As we have seen it is often difficult to undertake more than one task at once. Other factors come into play, and it has been shown that perception of task difficulty is a significant factor in task performance. The task must neither be too easy or too difficult.[42]

Our personality contributes to performance and is a partial determinant of our learning capacity. As we have seen one of the major problems is the fact that we are easily wedded to our previous dispositions. These tend to be very stable and contribute to the difficulty we have in the transfer of knowledge and skill to other domains. As Hesseling[43] suggests if a general manager is to be appointed from among functional specialists it is necessary to determine that they are able to master more general perceptual strategies. This is a problem for appointing committees in Ireland. For historical reasons numerous principalships became available to secondary school teachers. In the past this group of teachers had not been able to obtain principalships because they were the prerogative of the Religious Orders that owned the schools. Some of the teachers appointed to these posts found it extremely difficult to adjust to being alone and not be part of the 'staff room.' Situations like this create stress, and it is important to be reminded of the obvious, namely that some stress either physiological or psychological may effect perception.

One effect of our limited experience that applies to job perception is rather like a societal self-fulfilling prophecy. We come to believe that a person in a job is only capable of doing that job in other situations. We do not believe that he or she either has other skills, or has the skill to be able to transfer to different jobs. This is a serious limitation in societies where there are manpower shortages.[44] The structures of educational systems tend to reinforce this view.

In both attending to and receiving information we can become immune to repeated stimuli. The media and in particular the radio and TV have, so some would argue, reduced generally, our time span of attention. We need to be continually stimulated by new things. There are time limits for situation comedies, documentaries and the like and for classroom instruction! If my interpretation of criticisms of teaching by journalists is correct then it seems they would want instruction to be of the highly disciplined chalk and talk variety. That such an approach is to the detriment of learning can easily be demonstrated (see later chapters).

Hesseling draws our attention to the effects on people of repeated stimuli. Management can become insensitive to situations such as interpersonal rivalries to the detriment of performance. The same is true of students who continually cause minor disruptions in the classroom. Hesseling suggests that the prior experience of social workers may make them insensitive to the human problems that they daily encounter.

Trial and check

This component of perception has also been called hypothesis testing[45] This activity is part of a matching process to which reference has already been made. *'The trial phase is a tentative reading of a sign, a tentative decipherment of a puzzle, a tentative characterisation of the object; and the check phase is an acceptance or rejection, a positive or negative reinforcement of the tentative perception.'*[46] The process continues until the percept is assimilated into our existing frames of reference or rejected. We often have to proceed by trial and error because we do not always have the information available to make an objective decision. It is a regular feature of classrooms when pupils 'test' their teachers to see what they will do. And, as we saw in the activity of receiving it is possible to have a situation where we become unable to decide because of our being swamped by information. It is this component of the perceptual process that is related to risk taking. Clearly it is important in the development of the tacit knowledge required for effective performance.

It is clear that important lessons for discipline and the management of lessons are to be found in understanding the processes of perception. By themselves they do not provide an adequate theory of discipline and motivation. Understanding what motivates a child is probably the best approach to take to discipline. But even this is difficult because there are several contrasting theories of motivation. However Principals and instructional leaders might use these as the basis for reflective practice in which the assumptions made are dug-out. "Assumptional-dialogues" write Cohn and Kottkamp have the *"potential for motivating people to act. When the assumptions that lie within the tacit theory-in-use are extrapolated so that they may be compared with what the individual or organization espouses, the incongruence can provide a strong jolt for change."*[47] One way of getting an "assumptional dialogue" underway is for the educational or curriculum leader to provide the participants with contrasting theories. For this reason the remainder of chapter considers two contrasting ideologies of discipline and motivation

Two ideologies

Earlier it was suggested that the models that people describe what motivates a person to study or work can usefully be thought of in terms of McGregor's theory X on the one hand, and on the other hand Theory Y. X leads us to think that extrinsic rewards will motivate pupils. Y leads us to take a contrary view in the belief that intrinsic rewards should be the major source of motivation. X has been associated with behaviourist theories of motivation, and Y with humanistic theories. Both have their protagonists.

Lee Canter is on the X side. He and his wife proposed an "assertive discipline" that was designed to be a classroom discipline plan based on rules, consequences, and positive recognition. They acknowledged that the ideas were not new and that what they did was to systematize them. Clear rules should be set at the beginning of the year. Pupils should be consistently rewarded for good behaviour; consequences should be imposed promptly for misconduct; and, rewards and consequences should be incremental and designed for speedy application.[48] The idea is that it will promote student growth because it requires students to choose to behave or suffer the negative consequences. Canter cited 23 studies that purported to support assertive discipline. Holliday points out that while they support the theory they do not dispute the criticism that it can have negative side effects.

Canter later developed the theory to take into account students who think the rules are meaningless. Therefore, before assertive discipline can function the teacher has to have earned the respect of his/her students. Included in his new recommendations were:

- *Motivate and excite students to learn-active teaching methods with more meaning than facts; active learning and cooperative learning strategies that appeal to the students' natural desire to interact with other people and things (bored students are disruptive; motivated students aren't). .*
- *Establish a discipline plan-essential; children need structure, boundaries and behaviour limits; they need praise and recognition.*
- *Make a sharper distinction between rules and directions-rules are in effect all the time, directions are only in effect for the duration of an activity.*
- *Distinguish between disruptive and non-disruptive off-task behaviour- in the case of the latter re-direct.*
- *Emphasise positive strategies for keeping students on task—focus on students who are helping to create a positive environment.*
- *Keep consequences minimal- the key to effective consequences is not severity but consistency.*
-

According to Holliday Canter's stance as evidenced in these axioms is less harsh than it was. His intention remains the effective management of a class and pupils have to be shown and by implications controlled. It is not as hard over to the X end of the spectrum as the boss manager painted by Glasser[49] who

- *has impulses vested largely in assignments, management of the classroom and control of the students*
- *Tends to establish rules arbitrarily, often with a corresponding list of consequences.*
- *Tends to assume the role of keeper-of-the-rules . . . tends to police his/her room for breakage of the rules.*
- *Typically meets out punishment for infraction of the rules.*
- *Tends to model a reactive mode, looking for and reacting in ways designed to control/manage learning and behaviour.*
- *Generally sets the task, the rubrics, the assessment standards, and the completion time for what the students are to do.*
- *Tends not to compromise-the students have to adjust to the assignments as the teacher defines them.*
- *Inspects and evaluates all student work (accuracy in objective; though pleasing to him or her is often the hidden agenda)* [50].
-

The teacher is autocratic and the class is centred on him/her. The opposite is the democratic teacher whose orientation is student-centred. It is a useful exercise in reflection to complete the list for the democratic teacher and work out where one stands on the scale.

Perhaps the most famous challenge to the X model came from Kohn in 1993 in his *Punished by Rewards*[51]

Kohn argued that rewards are by no means as effective as we are led to think they should be. Rewards are effective in the short term and many parents will be familiar with the situation where their children will not undertake tasks when offered a reward. As Kohn says, most of the behaviours that are rewarded are behaviours that parents would want the children to perform in the absence of reward. Giving a reward may therefore inhibit the performance of this behaviour in future situations. Systems in schools where good marks can be redeemed for privileges (token reinforcement) do not it seems cause the behavioural gains made to be retained. Kohn quotes work by Kazdin[52] in support of this view that does not find much to favour in programmes of behavioural modification. Perhaps his most devastating conclusion is *"that people who are trying to earn a reward end up doing a poorer job on many tasks than people who are not."* He suggests five reasons for this behaviour.

The first of these is that rewards and punishments are not opposites rather they are two sides of the same coin. Their use arises from a particular view of human behaviour. It is a theory of control. Even if you prefer rewards to punishment *"the do this and you'll get that"* has a punishment dimension to it particularly if the person involved has good reason not to want what is suggested. In the classroom situation those who are not rewarded may feel punished. There is also the problem that expectations are created which may not be met.

It is easy to see that in the classroom rewards are discriminating and wherever there is discrimination there is the possibility that relationships can be ruptured. This is one reason why Kohn objects to rewards being given for the highest score in a test. Tests can set up students as rivals. In cultures where public examinations are important there will also be a competitive element and many politicians believe that such competition is good if overall it can raise standards. Failure or relative failure in tests is not a pleasant thing and can have a strongly demotivating effect. Unfortunately, teachers soon learn to judge students and place them in neo-normal distributions and they come to expect this distribution. The question for both teachers and schools is what should they do about the children in the lower end of the distribution? By and large rewards says Kohn ignore reasons. The teacher is not required to understand the reasons for student performance. Tests should have diagnostic as well as an achievement function.

Kohn's fourth reason for opposing rewards is that they discourage risk taking because the task stands in the way and has to be done as quickly as possible in order to obtain the reward. This can prevent students from *"taking risks, thinking creatively, and challenging themselves."* People who are working for rewards will do that which is required to gain the reward. This is one of the problems with public examinations in the British Isles. By and large they test for knowledge and comprehension. This is why there is so much interest in portfolio assessment although written examinations can be designed to provide challenges through testing conceptual understanding. It must be remembered, however, that attention must be paid to standards and in particular quality. Education should not remove itself too far from the realities of life. We do live in a competitive world and we have to be prepared for its eventualities. The issue is how we should prepare children for this world while motivating them to learn.

This 'how' applies to the administration of praise in the classroom. Kohn makes four points. Following from the above he advises teachers to avoid praise that creates competition. Second, avoid phony praise. Third, make praise as specific as possible that is by relating it to specific aspects of the work done. That means amplifying the 'good' that so often appears by itself at the end of or beside a part of a report. Finally and related to this is the importance of praising what it is that is done rather than the person. In these remarks Kohn is following research reported Brophy.[53]

A study reported by Boyle[54] of 99 pupils (F=46:M=43) in the senior grades of an Irish Primary School gives one food for thought and lends some support to Kohn's view of the value of praise. Asked to comment on the role of rewards in learning, only 30 pupils said, *"since I like rewards I try to do my homework well."* The majority said *"sometimes."* Only 20 said that they behaved well because they liked to please the teacher. In response, as it were, only 14 believed the teacher rewarded them when they did well but 17 reported that the teacher never rewarded them when they did well. 42 said they knew the teacher meant it when they were praised. That 48 should say *"sometimes"* should give teachers' food for thought.

Boyle found that the rewards perceived to be received from the teacher were almost inversely related to the rewards the pupils favoured.

It is often difficult to know when intrinsic motivation takes over from the extrinsic. We think and act at such a rate. Extrinsic motivation describes motivation of the kind experienced in a stimulus-response learning situation or from the action of physiological drives. An extrinsic reward is something promised in return for an action. In a student teachers example it is a 5p piece (dime) or Yorkie Bar (Hershey). Intrinsic motivation is something that happens within us that makes us seek a goal for its own sake. And with that description it is best left, since a little reflection should draw out the difference. In any case Kohn points out that there is a difficulty in both defining and measuring it. He suggests that it may be enough to define intrinsic motivation as the desire to engage in an activity for its own sake. Newman believed that it was the purpose of liberal education to encourage learning for its own sake. Following Maslow we might argue that it is the experience of self-actualisation. Clearly neither can be separated from our emotions and intrinsic motivation or at least what motivates us intrinsically will be related in some way to our personality. Thus, it is that the way in which our temperament interacts with our learning is of considerable importance to the outcomes of that learning.[55]

In the renewed research on intrinsic motivation in the early 1970s Deci[56] found that when individuals were given physical rewards like money and Yorkie (Hershey) bars they lost interest in the activities for which they were given a reward more quickly than when they were not given a reward. These findings led him and other workers to investigate the factors that influenced autonomy and self-determination and one study observed the reward structures and their effects on children at play.[57]

Csikszentmihalyi and Nakamura[58] summarised the position thus:- First, individuals are moved by curiosity and novelty; second, individuals need to feel in charge of their actions; and finally, autonomy and self-determination will lead individuals to act in ways that often override the instructions built into their nervous systems by their genes and prior learning. It is argued that some self-esteem is necessary if individuals are to assume responsibility for their own actions. There are, say Csikszentmihalyi and Nakamura, two systems at work, a genetic system and a self-system.

Intrinsic motivation occurs when an individual gets a reward directly from doing the activity itself. It is a direct experience within the consciousness of the individual: it is internally generated. This notion of an action having a goal within itself that creates intrinsic motivation is termed autotelic. Autotelic experiences are necessary for survival but so too are extrinsic rewards.

Social life, say Csikszentmihalyi and Nakamura *"would be unimaginable if people were not motivated also by extrinsic rewards."* And therefore, we do things because we have to without necessarily receiving autotelic experiences. It seems that few adolescent (teenage) students claim to have had autotelic experiences while studying. And many workers undertake instrumental work and get their satisfaction elsewhere.[59] In this way our psychic motivation becomes redirected which may have implications for overall performance.

Csikszentmihalyi and Nakamura list seven conditions of being which individuals have told them that they are in when they are doing something which they enjoy. Pause a minute, they suggest, before you read on and set down how you feel when you are enjoying something. Your answer is likely to be among the following:

1. Mind and body completely involved in the activity
2. Deep concentration
3. Knowing what you want to do
4. Knowing how well you are doing
5. Not worried about failing
6. Time passes quickly
7. Loss of any sense of self-consciousness.

There is plenty of evidence among published bibliographies, without reference to these studies, to testify to this description of the autotelic state. This they call *"flow experience." "Flow is what people enjoy when they are doing, when they would not want to do anything else."* It is an everyday experience that anger may erupt or frustration felt when that flow is interrupted and this can happen when a project activity is brought to a halt at the end of a class. However, the reality is that like self-actualisation which is a somewhat different dimension, flow is not experienced very often because there is seldom a fit between an individual's capacity to act and the opportunities for such action provided by the environment. Flow would seem to be necessary for any form of writing.

In the classroom students have to be provided with challenges which match their skills. The quality of the experience depends on the perceptions of the recipient and is related to the importance attached to the individual by the activity, and this relationship is central. Flow is important because of its effect on experience and such experience might be the cause of growth if there is a *"Eureka effect."* To have the experience of finding something new is to grow. At a more elementary level the activity, as for example of mountain climbing or tennis, may require us to continually improve our skills. An inability to master an activity would stop the flow.

At a more practical level Kohn offers advice for managers that could equally well be applied to teachers. Adapted for students and learning he says: *"Watch. Don't put students under surveillance: look for problems that need to be solved and help people to solve them.*
Listen. Attend seriously and respectfully to the concerns of students and try to imagine how various situations look after their point of view,
Talk. Provide plenty of informational feedback. Students need a chance to reflect on what they are doing right, to learn what needs improvement, and to discuss how to change."
Think. About one's teaching style and its influence on teaching

These are the conditions for what Kohn calls authentic motivation. Kohn believes that all rewards should be removed and, in particular, grades. In the American context he argues that the number of possible grades should be reduced to two plus "incomplete": that students should not be graded: grades should not be awarded against a normal distribution and involve students in the evaluation. Kohn is evidently influenced by Bruner and advocates active learning with appropriate content in a collaborative context. *"We can,"* he argues, *"get children hooked on learning—if that is really what we are determined to do."* And this is what Peter found masterful teachers did.

Unlike Kohn whose polemic is based on the evaluation of other research William Peter undertook research to find out what a masterful teachers do. He linked that research to the courses he gave in teacher education at the Central Missouri State University (Warrensberg). As a result he developed a theory of Non-Assertive Motivation Effectiveness (NAME). Contrary to Canter it focuses on intrinsic motivation and the avoidance of extrinsic incentives. In many respects it is similar to Kohn's theory with the difference that it is based on personal research.[60] Holliday points out that Peter allows that sometimes students will require extrinsic incentives to learn material that is not otherwise intrinsically interesting but the goal of education should be to make the curriculum as intrinsically interesting as possible. His results contradict Brophy's view that while intrinsic motivation is a useful concept it is unrealistic in practice. It is not the purpose of these remarks to describe the strategies Peter commends for the development of intrinsic motivation but to elaborate on his definition of masterful teaching.

The data for his theory was derived from observations of some three hundred teachers about a third of whom were post-primary and, two thirds elementary. He found no differences in his results between the two groups. The teachers were identified by their instructional supervisors as those who consistently *"get kids turned-on and tuned into learning and very likely to continue learning after the interaction with the teacher had ceased."* The supervisors were asked to identify *"that one special teacher in your building who gets kids enthused without resorting to all sorts of behavioural manipulation"* [61]

Peter makes a sharp distinction between effective teaching and masterful teaching. He argues that *"while masterful teachers are generally skilled instructors, there are masterful teachers who are rather average when it comes to instructional techniques."* [62] But they can cope with today's classes of unmotivated students and get those students learning intrinsically. He had seen skilled teachers fall apart when confronted with such classes.

He was led to define a masterful teacher as one who
- *is highly effective in the general teaching/learning and management processes*
- *fosters self-discipline and a love of learning in his/her students.*
- *Motivates and manages kids non-assertively- i.e without resorting to coercion, bribery, or other forms of extrinsic motivation.*
- *Awakens that intrinsic motivation that lies sleeping within many students, especially ones who have emotionally and intellectually dropped out and who might, without intervention, actually drop-out.* [63]

He found that there was a relationship between getting the children turned on and the fostering of the goals of education in their intellectual, psychological and moral dimensions. Coupled to this masterful teachers see things from the individual pupil's point of view.

"The masterful teacher doesn't have a set of skills, per se, that the teacher needs to master . . . It's more a matter of their becoming aware of the importance of the way things look from the students' point of view, number one . . . and it plays up on the feelings . . . In other words, how do things appear from the point of view of the student and how does that make the student feel, in respect to his her own belief system? How does that affect them and then what do they believe about themselves? And then, and only then . . . are the intellectual processes affected." [64]

As reported earlier this writer found that getting graduate student teachers to see things from the pupil's point of view is easier said than done. A few students were able to do it quite naturally so one wonders if everyone can be a masterful teacher? Yet the reports of the teachers who attended Peter's courses tend to be very positive. That is, of the kind- Why weren't we told about this before? Masterful teachers foster certain feelings, perceptions, and sensations in their pupils that are loosely related to Maslow's hierarchy. Holliday's synthesis of Peter's work in this respect is shown in exhibit 3.1.

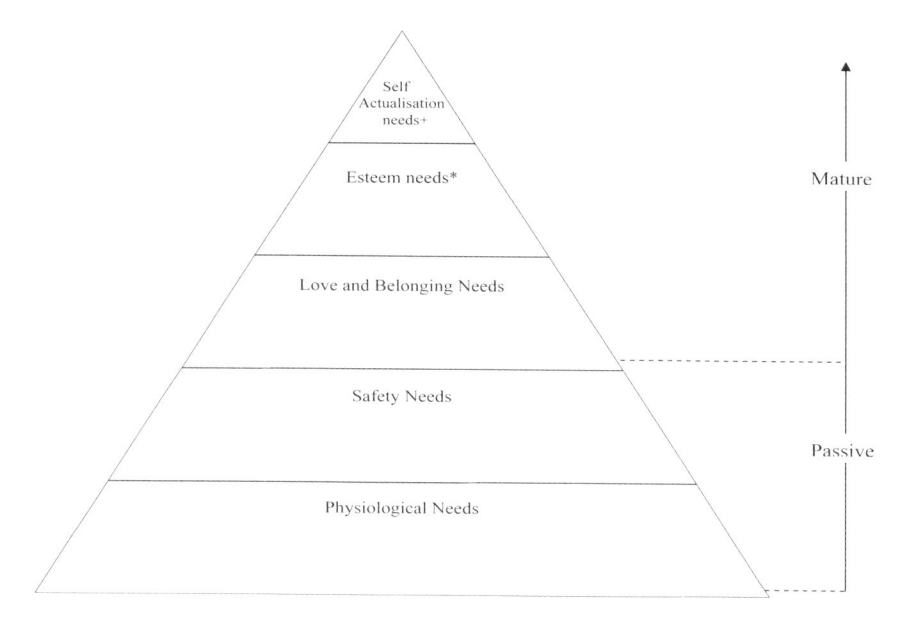

```
          /\
         /Self\
        /Actualisation\
       /  needs+  \
      /─────────\
     /  Esteem needs*  \              Mature
    /─────────────\
   / Love and Belonging Needs \
  /─────────────────\
 /      Safety Needs       \
/─────────────────────\
/      Physiological Needs      \         Passive
/─────────────────────────\
```

+ Desires to know and understand
* Desires for achievement recognition

Figure 3.1 Maslow's hierarchy of needs

Human need	Classroom need	Feeling that is fostered by Masterful Teachers
Physical and spiritual safety, freedom	Stability, knowledge that there is a leader in charge who will not allow anyone to be attacked, physically or spiritually	Sense of stability, psychological support, spiritual and physical safety
Recognition by others as a worthy person; validation.	Especially important that the teacher as a significant person in the child's life, recognize each child as a person of worth and individual merit	Sense of identity, autonomy and feelings of personhood.

Inner need to feel belonging to a social entity, particularly the social venue in which the day is spent	Every child must feel he or she somehow belongs in the social context of the classroom.	Sense of belonging
Sense of power over the rest of the world; sense that what one does matter in their surrounding world; feeling of self-determination and ability to survive one's own problems.	Developing confidence in students' minds, abilities and decision making; students' measure of control over students' own destinies and the world around them.	Sense of adequacy, competency, self-sufficiency, and self-direction.
Fun and enjoyment	Sense of joy in learning and in delayed gratification	Sense of enjoyment, comfort, fun, and humour.
Feeling of growth and maturation, self direction	Increasing sense of self-direction, self-responsibility due to increasing maturity and growth, to be spoken to in a way which conveys respect, without condescension, maturity modeled by teachers.	Sense of maturation; self-direction, growth, self-sufficiency.
Feeling of ownership in the on-going activity in which they are immersed	Each student feels the class is not something he comes to that belongs to the school or the teacher, but him/her, as a part owner or partner/stakeholder in learning objectives, as well as social and teaching processes	Feeling of ownership
Feeling that one is a meaningful contributor in one's world, or the world at large.	Opportunities for volunteer activity that is selfless and considerate of others; ability to discover the 'natural high that can result from doing something unselfishly for someone else by connecting it with learning activities.'	Sense of altruism, value and purpose in the world beyond self, no will to do harm.

Exhibit 3.1 Needs Met/feelings fostered by Masterful Teachers. Synthesis due to Holliday.[65]

Peter considers that the classroom environment is very important and is of the opinion that it can help to overcome student apathy. His description of the masterful teaching environment is shown in exhibit 3.2. It is possible to see the essential principles of Non Assertive Motivation Effectiveness (NAME) in the feelings fostered by masterful teachers. First, it is based on a view of motivation rather that a view of discipline. Second, practice of NAME should lead to an intrinsic drive to learn. Third, it depends on both the classroom and school climates. Fourth, it is a cooperative endeavor with the students. The ten essentials of NAME are

1. A positive and involving environment
2. Relationships that are humanistic and personalized.
3. A sense of ownership, enjoyment from cooperative activity or altruism.
4. Interesting content.
5. Clear and acceptable intended outcomes.
6. Appropriate time and place for focussing on objectives.
7. Challenging but achievable tasks.
8. Positive, realistic teacher expectations.
9. Appropriate recognition of efforts and accomplishments.
10. Encouragement to participate.

It is an environment
- wherein all students feel accepted, respected, capable and worthy
- which facilitates each student's discovery of the personal meaning of ideas
- which encourages involvement and active participation and includes considerable choice of activity
- which recognizes the uniquely personal and subjective aspects of learning and classroom social processes
- which encourages and facilitates openness, genuineness and depth
- where many truly important questions have no absolute "right" answers
- wherein individual differences are truly valued and their development is encouraged
- which not only permits, but encourages confrontation through diplomatic, thoughtful, honest dissent as a skill to be developed
- where students are encouraged to trust in themselves and others
- wherein it is not only acceptable to make mistakes, but desirable, as they are signs of venturesome and creative endeavor
- wherein evaluation is a formative and cooperative process which includes a good deal of ever increasingly mature self-evaluation
- where the authoritarian function, both instructional and social, is increasingly surrendered to the growing maturation and self-direction of each student.

Exhibit 3.2 The Masterful Teaching Environment. [66]

For each of these elements Peter lists a set of prescribed actions. These are shown for dimension 7 in exhibit 3.3. He also provides guides on "Right ways to say you are wrong)" and how to administer praise. Peter would not expect masterful teachers to possess facility in all the dimensions he discovered.

- Use set objectives that are challenging but not threatening. True success in this may dictate that objectives and instruction may be individualized.
- Where a task appears intimidating to one or more student(s), break tasks down into logical non-intimidating steps.
- Utilise student team learning, peer coaching and goal setting.
- Encourage team competition rather than individual competition
- "Fix" the game to equalise the chances, or better fix it so all will succeed.
- Create an "I can" curriculum.
- Have a "success curriculum" and practice "no fault teaching".
- Success orientation
- Let students know that every student is successful if he or she grows.
- Teach children how to succeed Show them how to play the school game-how to take tests, how to remember information and how to organize and be organized. Show them how to play the game called life (i.e. how to win friends and influence people and how to prepare for getting a good job).

Exhibit 3.3 Prescribed action for "Challenging but Achievable Tasks"

Peter's model is clearly a theory Y model of teaching. It is derived from an investigation that set out *"to assay the effect of teaching practices on the development of democratic attitudes and skills in teachers of sharing thought provoking idea and effective methods that can (to varying degrees) be replicated by other teachers and taught to intending and practicing teachers by teacher educators."*[67] To put it in another way while the concern was with the teaching practices that contributed to civic-democratic and civic-moral education they applied across the spectrum of the curriculum.

His differentiation between the theory X (autocratic) and theory Y (democratic) teacher is shown in exhibit 3.4. He notes that in many respects a good deal of frustration comes from the attempt by many teachers to play in both ball parks simultaneously. I suspect that many teachers occupy mid-way positions and this can lead to difficulty if they are not consistent and know precisely where they stand on the continuum for each item. It might also be argued that the data was obtained from teachers in schools in the mid-west and rural communities. But Holliday reports that his summer courses based on this theory evidently had an influence on subsequent teacher behaviour in the direction sought.

Some teachers may aspire to these ideals. Others may say "yes but in our circumstances……." They may offer an argument that schools in Missouri are very different to those in Dublin that is to argue that Peter's teachers' function in a different culture where it is easier for them to achieve motivation and discipline in this way. They might note that in particular the culture in the British Isles is public examination dominated. But there is no absence of testing in the United States. In any case examinations can be improved a hundred-fold and made more challenging. And that does not mean substituting tests with reams of coursework. That can be just as demotivating. Nevertheless, it is difficult if not impossible to challenge most of the aims that are inherent in this theory. That said, they are very challenging and suggest a climate that is worth working for even if some extrinsic pressures are called for, and it is against such parameters that a school climate and the effectiveness of its discipline in enhancing learning may be judged. One would hope that judged on the extrinsic/intrinsic continuum a school would tend to the intrinsic.

Implications for Educational, Curriculum and Instructional Leadership

Discipline and motivation occupy much of a teacher's life. There is considerable variation among teachers' assumptions about the reasons for good and poor discipline and good and poor motivation. Often these assumptions are based on myths. Often teachers come to dialogue about discipline but the dialogues are often based on their own experience in the school and untested against theory. Instructional and curriculum leaders can bring different perspectives of theory and relevant outside experience to such dialogues. Young teachers are likely to need advice and curriculum and instructional leaders have an important role in mentoring beginning teachers. Sometimes for a whole variety of reasons experienced teachers lose their grip. They need to know that there are leaders to whom they can turn in confidence for help.

Tendencies of teachers
The Autocratic teacher

1. has impulses vested largely in management of the class-room and control of the children.
   tends to establish rules arbitrarily, often with corresponding list of consequences.

2. tends to assume the role of keeper of the rules...tends to police his/her room for breakage of the rules.
   typically meters out punishment for infractions of the rules.

3. tends to model a reactive mode, looking for and reacting in ways designed to control/manage learning and behaviour.

4. generally sets the task and the standards for what the students are to do.

5. tends not to compromise; the students have to adjust to the assignments as the teacher defines them.

6. inspects and evaluates student work. (Right answers is the objective. Though pleasing him or her is often the hidden agenda).

7. often uses strategies vested in extrinsic rewards to motivate students to participate in the assigned learning activities and do quality work.
   *typically uses praise and positive reinforcement to manipulate students.
   *metes out rewards for what pleases him or her.

8. when students resist the above, tends to use psychological coercion (generally vested in fear) to try to make them do as they are told. creates an adversarial relationship.

9. uses incidental language that focuses on his or her needs rather than that of the student.
   *sets up a please the teacher atmosphere-roadblock to self-actualization.

10. tends to arrest student autonomy...uses methods engages in teacher/student teacher interactions that tend to inhibit student's growth toward independent thought and action.
    *does this in may ways: asks loaded questions. Reinforces conformity. Defines acting responsibly as doing what I want when I want it.

The Democratic teacher

1. has impulses vested foremostly in nurturing student intellectual, psycho-spiritual, and philosophical growth.
   *tends to engage students in the co-development of behaviour codes and discussions of responsible behaviour.

2. initiates or makes possible democratic class meetings in which infractions of the behaviour codes are discussed.
   *draws the main focus to solution and growth rather than wrongs committed, blame or consequences.

3. typically models a reflective mode, reflective problem solving rather than knee-jerk reaction.

4. typically engages the students in discussion of the objectives, their rationale, the quality of the work to be done and the time needed to do it-invites their input.

5. Makes a constant effort to fit assignments to the skills and needs of the students.

6. asks the students to evaluate their own work for quality. (Accomplishment and growth are the objectives).

7. typically uses non-assertive strategies, ones vested in intrinsic values, to stimulate interest and effort.
   *tends to offer feedback rather than subjective praise, on student accomplishment.
   *celebrates individual students' accomplishments.

8. when a student does not respond to the above, generally initiates a personal problem solving venture for ways to reach the student.
    *creates an atmosphere of mutual respect.

9. uses incidental language that focuses on the student and the learning objective at hand.
    *establishes an atmosphere in which autonomy is valued.

10. tends to stimulate philosophical maturation and autonomy... engages students in discussions about issues, teaches them how to discuss, cooperatively solve problems detect hype, analyze, and be intellectually courageous.
    *does this in almost every teacher/student teacher interaction. Asks stimulating questions, extends answers with meta questions, reinforces quality thinking.

Exhibit 3.4 William Peter's comparison of autocratic with democratic teachers taken from his lecture handout which ends with "and several more, of course".

Notes and references

[1] Wheldall, K and F. Merrett (1988). Which classroom behaviours do primary teachers say they find most troublesome. *Educational Review* 40, (1), 14 – 27. For a short review of this and other papers on this topic and related to this paragraph see Cohen, L, Manion, L and K. Morrison (1996). *A Guide to Teaching Practice*. 4th edition. Routledge, London.
[2] For example Elton, Lord (1989). *Discipline in Schools*. Department of Education and Science, HMSO, London.
[3] The models of what motivates individuals to work will be found in Schein, E. H. (1965). *Organizational Psychology*. Prentice Hall, Englewood Cliffs, NJ. Their adaptation to take into account students and teachers will be found in Heywood, J (1989). *Learning, Adaptability and Change*. Paul Chapman, London. Ch 4.
[4] *ibid*
[5] Rutter, M et al (1979) *Fifteen Thousand Hours. Secondary Schools and their effects on Children*. (Paul Chapman Publishing re-issue), London.
[6] Halpin, A (1966). *Theory and Research in Administration*. MacMillan, London.
[7] A more recent study supports this view McBeath, J (1999). *Schools Must Speak for Themselves. The Case for School Self-Evaluation*. Routledge, London. On whole school organization and disruptive behaviour see Badger, B (1992). In D. Reynolds and P. Cuttance (eds) *School Effectiveness. Research, Policy and Practice*. Cassell, London.
[8] Marzano, R. J., Waters, T., and B. A. McNulty (2005). *School Leadership that Works. From Research to Results*. Association for Supervision and Curriculum Development, Alexandria, VA. p 47
[9] *ibid* p 74
[10] Leithwood, K. A and C. Riehl (2003). *What do we already know about successful school leadership?* Paper presented at the annual meeting of the American Educational Research Association, Chicago quoted by Marzano, Waters and McNulty *ibid* p 47.
[11] Peter is cited by Holliday, C. B (2001). Learning to Motivate Students. An Evaluation of Dr William Peter's Theory of Masterful Teaching. M.Ed Thesis. University of Dublin, Dublin. P 36.
[12] for a brief history of attribution theory see Jones, E. E. (1998) Major developments in five decades of social psychology in Gilbert, D. T, Fiske, K. E., and G. Lindzey (eds). *The Handbook of Social Psychology*. McGraw Hill, New York. More generally this book also contains a review of developments in motivation research. Ch 12 by T. S. Pittman.

[13] Harvey, J. H. and G.Weary (1981). *Perspectives in Attributional Processes*. Brown. Duberque, IL

[14] Galloway, D., Ball, T., Blomfield, D and R. Seyd (1982) *Schools and Disruptive Pupils*. Longmans, London.

[15] Eggleston, J (1979). *The Sociology of the School Curriculum*. Routledge, London.

[16] Coulby, D and T. Harper, (1985) *Preventing Classroom Disruption. Policy, Practice and Evaluation in Urban Schools*. Croom Helm, London.

[17] Jones, E. E and R. E. Nesbitt, (1971). *The Actor and the Observer. Divergent Perceptions of the causes of Behaviour*. Gneral Learning Press: Moristown, NJ..

[18] Olson, J. M and M. Ross (1985).Attribution Research. Past contributions, current trends and future prospects in J. H. Harvey and G. Weary (Eds). *Attribution., Basic Issues and Applications*. Academic Press, Orlando, Fl.

[19] Shaver, K. G (1981) *Principles of Social Psychology* (2nd edition). Winthrop, Cambridge, MA

[20] Rogers, C. G (1982). The contribution of attribution theory to educational research in C. Antaki and G. Brown (eds) *Attributions and Psychological Change*. Academic Press, London.

[21] Johnson, N. A (1987). The pervasive, persuasive power of perceptions. *Alberta Journal of Educational Research*. 33, (3), 206 – 228.

[22] Allport, F. H (1955). *Theories of Perception and and the concept of Structure*. Wiley, New York. See also note 24

[23] Heywood, J (2000) *Assessment in Higher Education. Student learning, Teaching, Programmes and Institutions*. Jessica Kingsley, London.

[24] De Cecco, J and W. R. Crawford (1974). *The Psychology of Learning and Instruction*. Prentice Hall, Englewood Cliffs, NJ

[25] Rist (1970) *Social Class and Teacher Expectations*. The self-fulfilling phrophecy in ghetto education. Harvard Educational Review 40, (2), 411-415.

[26] Good, T. L and J. E. Brophy (1973) *Looking in Classrooms*. Harper and Row, London. (see 5th edition)

[27] McClelland, D. C. et al (1963) *The Achievement Motive*. Appleton-Century-Crofts, New York.

[28] *ibid*

[29] Davies, D (1984). Sex role stereotyping in childrens imaginative writing in H. Cowie (ed). *The Development of Childrens Imaginative Writing*. Croom Helm, London.

[30] Stanworth, M (1982). *Gender and Schooling: A Study of Sexual Divisions in the Classroom*. Hutchinson, London.

[31] Schein, E (1985). *Organizational Psychology*. Prentice Hall, Englewood Cliffs, NJ. see also Heywood, J (1989*). Learning, Adaptability and Change*. Paul Chapman, London.

[32] Krech, D., Crutchfield, R. S. Livson, N., and A..Parducci (1982). *Elements of Psychology*. (4th edition) Knopf, New York.

[33] Taguiri, R (1969). Person perception in G. Lindzey and E. Aronson (eds). *The Handbook of Social Psychology*. Vol 3. (3rd edition) Addison Wesley, Reading, MA. The 1998 edition contains a review of perception research to that date pp 38-40.

[34] Bruner, J Goodnow, J. J. and G.A. Austin (1956). *A Study of Thinking*. Wiley, New York.

[35] Festinger, L (1959). *A Theory of Cognitive Dissonance*. Stanford University Press, Stanford. CA

[36] Luchins, A. S. (1942) Mechanisation in problem solving: the effect of "einstellung". *Psychological Mongraphs*, No 248. See also Gagné, R (1976). *The Conditions of Learning*. 3rd Edition. Holt, Rinehart and Winston, New York.

[37] Marshall , S (1980) Cognitive affective dissonance in the classroom. *Teaching Political Science*, 8, (1), 111 - 117

[38] French, W. L., Kast, F. E., and J. E. Rosenzweig (1985). *Understanding Human Behaviour in Organizations*. Harper and Row, New York. Thouless, R. H (1974). *Straight and Crooked Thinking*. Pan Books, London.

[39] Combs, A. W and D. Snygg (1949) *Individual behaviour: A Perceptual Approach to Behaviour*. Harper and Row, New York.

[40] Caine, R. N and G. Caine (1991) *Teaching and the Human Brain*, Association for Supervision and Curriculum Development, Alexandria, VA

[41] Hesseling, P (1966) *A Strategy of Evaluation Research*. Van Gorcum, Aassen

[42] Jaques, E (1970) *Work Creativity and Social Justice*. Heinemann, London.

[43] *loc. cit.*

[44] Thomas, B and C. Madigan (1974) Strategy and job choice after redundancy: a case study in the aircraft industry, *Sociological Review,* 22, 83 – 102. Yougman, M., Oxtoby, R., Monk, J. D. and J. Heywood (1978).

Analysing Jobs, Gower Press, Aldershot

[45] Allport, F. H. *loc. cit.* See also Bruner, J. S.(1951) Personailty dynamics and the process of perceiving in R. R. Blake and G. B Ramsey (eds). *Perception. An Approach to Personality*. Ronald Press, New York.

[46] Solley and Murphy cited by Hesseling *loc.cit*

[47] Cohn, M. M. and R. B. Kottkamp (1993) *Teachers. The Missing Voice in Education*. State University of New York Press, Albany, NY. P 269. Pp 266 – 271 deal with assumptional-dialogues and reflective seminars the latter derive from the work of Argyris, C and D. Schön (1974). *Theory in Practice. Increasing Professional Effectiveness*. Jossey Bass, San Fransisco.

[48] Canter, L (1989). Assertive Discipline. A Response *Teachers College Record*, 90, 631. Canter, L (1996). First, the rapport – then the rules. Learning, 24, 12. For a recent commentary that takes in both Canter and Kohn see Marzano, R. J., Marzano, J. S., and D. J. Pickering (2003). *Classroom management that Works. Research-Based Strategies for Every Teacher*. Association for Supervision and Curriculum Development, AlexandriA, VA. Canter's work is reviewed Holliday, C (2001). *Learning to Motivate Students. An Evaluation of Dr William Peter's Theory of Masterful Teaching..* Thesis. School of Education, University of Dublin, Dublin.

[49] Cited by Holliday from Glasser . W (1998) *The Quality School: Managing Students without Coercion*. Rev. Ed. Harper Collins, New York

[50] *ibid*

[51] Kohn, A (1993) *Punished by Rewards. The Trouble with Gold Stars, Incentive Plans, A's, Praise and other Bribes*. Houghton Mifflin Boston. MA

[52] Kazdin, A. E. (1982). *The Token Economy*. Plenum, New York.

[53] Brophy, J. E. (1998). *Motivating Students to Learn*. McGraw Hill, New York.

[54] Boyle, (1997). *Discipline as a Learning Process*. MSt Thesis, University of Dublin, Dublin.

[55] Goleman, D. (1995) *Emotional Intelligence*. Bantam Books, New York.

[56] Deci, E. L (1971) Effects of externally mediated rewards on intrinsic motivation *Journal of Personality and Social Psychology*. 18, 105 – 115. and (1978) Applications of research on the effects of rewards in M. Lepper and D. Greene (eds) *The Hidden Costs of Rewards*. Lawrence Erlbaum, Hillsdale, NJ.

[57] Lepper, M and D. Greene (1978) (eds). *The Hidden Costs of Rewards. New Perspectives on the Psychology of Motivation*. Lawrence Erlbaum, Hillsdale, NJ

[58] Csikszentmihalyi, M and J.Nakamura (1989),The Dynamics of intrinsic motivation in C. Ames and R. Ames (eds) *Research on Motivation in Education*. Vol 3. Academic Press, New York.

[59] Goldthorpe, J et al (1970) *The Affluent Worker*. Cambridge University Press, Cambridge UK

[60] Peter never published the theory although he gave papers on it at conferences of the Association of Teacher Educators , The National Rural Education Association, Association of Teacher Educators in Europe and other conferences. The work is recorded in a number of unpublished documents. These were made available to Christine Holliday who made a detailed study of them as well as his course literature and the responses of teachers to his work and concluded that he had made an important contribution to knowledge. Holliday, C (2001). *Learning to Motivate Students. An Evaluation of Dr William Peter's Theory of Masterful Teaching..* Thesis. School of Education, University of Dublin, Dublin. The remarks here are derived from her study.

[61] *ibid*

[62] *ibid* p 18.

[63] *ibid* p 19.

[64] *ibid* p 24.

[65] Taken from Peter's lecture notes. The population from which this data was derived was 100 teachers in thirty two p-12 school districts in the service-area of Central Missouri State University at Warrensburrg. The teachers were identified by their supervisors as being ones who typically excel in teaching and especially in getting students intrinsically turned on and tuned in to learning.

4
DISCIPLINED LEARNING: CONFIDENCE, COGNITION AND EMPATHY

Summary

Undisciplined behaviour is likely to have both cognitive and social consequences for the child. It has become increasingly common and occupies much time of educational, instructional and curriculum leaders. Among its outcomes may be poor study habits and poor social behaviour. One response has been the development of programmes of personal and social education that aim among other things to promote values of mutual respect, self-discipline and social responsibility. The role of individual subject teachers in providing a solution for these problems should be a matter for whole school planning and, therefore, teamwork. It is a major responsibility of educational, instructional and curriculum leaders and an ideal topic for "assumptional-dialogue" that should lead to action.

Research on effective teaching emphasises the importance of planning, variety of instructional techniques, detailed knowledge of the students being taught and attention to the needs of each student. A high level of skill is required and instructional leaders can help beginning teachers acquire these skills and aid experienced teachers renew them. They are a concern for continuing professional development. This chapter is concerned with four aspects of the planning and implementation of lessons and the curriculum particularly in its social dimension.

Many minor misdemeanours arise from a lack of ability to cope and the consequent loss of confidence this may incur. Some children will already come to school lacking in confidence or, self-esteem. Very often failure to master subject matter is due to a lack of specific study skills. If skills cannot be mastered lack of confidence will more than likely ensue. Examples of lessons devoted to the development of specific study skills are given but if these are to be maintained there needs to be a school policy which integrates the work of individual teachers teaching a particular year group as well as across the years. Such activities need to be persistent and the support of the whole school as well as parents is essential. It is the function of the educational leader with the assistance of the instructional and curriculum leader(s) to achieve these goals.

Therefore it goes without saying that if a lesson gets off to a bad start a teacher can be wrong-footed and remain on the wrong foot for the rest of the lesson and this may influence student behaviour in future lessons.The second part of the chapter considers the role of cognitive organizers in preparing students for learning. Often teachers confuse their preparatory statements with advanced organizers. By and large students like to know where they are going and advanced organizers seem to be an effective way of linking prior to future knowledge.

Some evidence suggests that if a lesson begins with a fantasy or imagery exercise it will have a calming effect on the class. Evidence in support of this view is presented. It is also shown that imagery exercises can have positive effects on cognition. It is noted that the development of skill in imagery can be helpful to creativity and the reduction of stress particularly when approaching and during examinations and tests.

Finally, co-operative (collaborative and group) learning may promote values of mutual respect, self-discipline and social responsibility without detriment to cognition that it can also enhance.

For many teachers the giving of an imagery exercise or the conduct of cooperative learning groups is a challenge to adopt unfamiliar roles. Some teachers approach such change with trepidation. One of the functions of instructional and curriculum leaders is to support teachers when they trying to adapt to change.

Research and practice is reviewed. The illustrations given are taken from the work of beginning teachers or from investigations conducted by experienced teachers. The implications for curriculum and instructional leadership are considered.

Study discipline

It is often said, and with a considerable amount of justification, that low achievers fail because they do not have disciplined study skills. However, it is equally true that high achievers can benefit from understanding learning and how they learn (meta-cognition).

Sometimes schools make provisions for "how to study programmes." More often than not it is left to individual teachers. Many believe these skills are unconsciously acquired as part of the activity of schooling; but there are others who make special provision for them within their lessons.[1]

It goes without saying that if a low achieving student can learn to use a study skill that that student will gain in confidence provided he/she persists. These skills may be categorised as follows:

1. Those relating to the planning and implementation of study e.g. homework; revision; note taking, use of dictionaries.
2. Those relating to the particular processes of study within subject e.g. historiography, experimental science).
3. Genuine Cognitive Skills that relate to all or many subjects.

These categories are interdependent and as such there is much overlap. They embrace the following general abilities:

1. To identify the problem and plan a solution to solve the problem.
2. To identify the available sources of information.
3. To locate individual sources.
4. To examine, locate and reject or conserve what is found.
5. To evaluate this material through interpretation, analysis and synthesis.
6. To present and communicate the results in an organized way.
7. To evaluate personal performance with a view to improving future performance. Commonly called self-assessment.

Some writers call 5 and 6 stages of interrogation and review.

It will be appreciated that the performance of a project or a personal topic should involve the student in the development of all these skills. They are skills associated with the acquisition and use of information in the search for knowledge.[2] Learning how to use these skills is a prime function of education. In such learning other important skills and emotional traits may also be acquired. A project, for example, will necessitate skill in formulation, planning and self-assessment but, at the same time it will demand persistence; moreover the choice of project will involve the student in coming to terms with what he/she is capable of. It is found that the formulation of a problem is a high level skill. It will reveal for example whether the student is likely to complete the proposed project or not.

Much, if not most of life, is not about the pursuit of big projects, but about a sequence of little activities that while semi-automatic involve the use of such skills. It is held that the more we understand the processes of problem solving and decision making the better will be our performance.[3] (See also chapter 9). For the moment our attention will be focused on the skills listed in category 1. First, homework.

Homework

Increasing attention is being paid to homework. I found as long ago as 1960 that among relatively low achieving students taking technology subjects those who had experience of homework at school more chance of passing their examinations.[4] Some evidently had not done any homework in their post-primary education and, therefore, had no idea how to apply themselves. This is not to say that effort can always compensate for lack of ability in a particular subject but it is an important and cultural influence at work. The positive effects of homework have been reported in a number of American studies.[5]

Other studies have shown that low achievers do much less homework than high achievers.[6] In these studies the high achievers were found to enjoy the challenge presented by homework while the low achievers preferred to socialise.

Schools can be to blame if they do not set homework. It is reported that some American schools do not set homework. It is noted that if they do not involve parents in that activity then it is not surprising that some white students do not do as well as they might.[7]

Clearly while there are cultural differences among the nations effort does count. One cannot be a sportsman or a musician or an actor without lots of practise. The challenge is to motivate low achievers with homework that creates "flow" i.e. makes it interesting and absorbing. In this context McBeath in the UK investigated homework in the late 1980's. He and his colleagues' ideas about homework were changed because of the different home contexts in which learning took place.[8] McBeath found among many other things that there was often a hiatus between class work and homework. Teachers and schools did not think through what the relationship might be and they paid little attention to the nature of children's learning out of school. McBeath's comments showed that they thought the learning at home should be the same as that in schools. Thus, children are instructed to plan for a week, find a quiet place, sit in an upright chair and so on. But as McBeath reminds us this is far from reality. Half the pupils in his sample worked against a background of loud music. *"The young people in our sample persuaded initially sceptical researchers that music actually helped them concentrate."* It created a sound-barrier against other interventions such as the TV. Much of this text was written against a background of classical music.

A large proportion of students reported that they did not get helpful comments on their homework from their teachers. As children grow older it would appear that fewer parents comment on their children's work. Could it be that they are no longer asked?

In some schools no homework was given and some pupils were resentful because it was not given. Again some children with learning difficulties *"benefited most conspicuously from tasks set them to do alone or with the support of parents."* Parents also complained that they were not involved.

An altogether confused picture emerges. The same seems to be true in Ireland. One of my student-teachers found as long ago as 1985 that among a class of 13–14 year olds in Ireland.[9]

-*"The majority of students normally do homework in their bedroom or other private place.*

-The range of time spent on homework varied from 1/2 hr—3 hours. It appeared that the average time was 2—2 1/2 hrs.
-Most of them said they worked best in silence.
-A minority do homework in front of T.V. or with radio on, but admitted this to be a distraction.
-A very small no. (4 out of 26) said they made out a plan of study.
-Most pupils admitted to feeling tense and worried about exams."

Whether or not the same pattern would be repeated today is a matter of conjecture. This student teacher used the results for class discussion and reported that

"Once again the students participated in a very fruitful discussion. They now began to recognize their own study habits and to discuss those factors which helped one study effectively (correct atmosphere, organization etc) and those factors which hindered effective study (disorganization, noise etc). I was pleased to notice an atmosphere of co-operation in the class as people exchanged ideas and hints about what works for them.
e.g." One person said she found it useful to make notes on scraps of paper. Another said she finds it good to tape herself in French, German and then give a dictation test. Others stressed the need to take short breaks."

In music practise is essential if one is to learn a musical instrument. Another student teacher reported of her music students that

"None had any kind of a timetable system—most practised when they felt like it, varied the time of day and became more diligent as the lesson approached. All but one picked up the recorder without any thought and began playing. All aimed to get through everything in one session but usually didn't and left the same work 'till last each time with the result that their scales were quite good and their pieces slapdash. All practised most what they were good at, paid little attention to detail and made no attempt to monitor their progress."

She introduced the idea of practise logs and these came to be *"proudly displayed at each lesson."*

Students are particularly reluctant to make self-study plans even when they are preparing for public examinations. To my disappointment wrote a student-teacher of mathematics about her 15 to 16 year olds, *"many in the class thought that revision was a matter of looking over the book the night before. A structured time-table did not appeal to them."*

Another science teacher designed a guide for reading in the form of a worksheet because she found that her 13 to 14 year-olds *"while usually quite bright, were having considerable difficulties in revising. They tended to reread a chapter in their text book and science notebook without even making an attempt to note the main points. When I pointed this out to them, the ensuing discussion made clear that they found it very difficult to decide what the main points were."*

The American experience is very similar. Bellon and his colleagues consider homework to be a form of independent practice.[10] This writer is of the opinion that not enough is made of the notion of independent learning and the ability to "transfer" knowledge so that one can learn on ones own. These are key aims of education and seen in this light students may see the benefits. This is not to deny the reinforcement of lessons' value of homework. It is to say that the objectives of homework need to be made clear to students and that it needs to be set with those objectives in mind.[11]

Homework should be a matter for school policy and it is a function of the instructional leader to ensure such a policy exists and functions to help teachers clarify their objectives and see that what is set is likely to achieve those objectives.

Note taking and revision

Schools do not pay as much attention to note taking as they might. For example, in science, note taking during experiments is of extreme importance since these notes contain the evidence on which the final report will depend. In a science experiment the student is very much involved in the activity whereas in a lecture the student is very much a passive listener. Some teachers hold that the act of note taking involves the student in lessons of the chalk and talk variety. However, note taking can cause loss of attention and key points can be missed. One way to overcome this is to prepare a handout of key points in which there are blanks that have to be filled in during the class. Such is the cultural press that students, in higher education in particular, expect to take notes; they become very frustrated if they are told to stop taking notes and listen. Therefore it is of some consequence that students should be given help and practise in note taking. In school students often have the notes dictated to them by the teacher. One outcome of making the students take their own notes is that it should help them become more autonomous and self-reliant in their learning. Teachers also argue that note-taking helps recall. It should be remembered that the success or otherwise of notes will depend on the students comprehension of the lesson. Notes will not be able to recompense poor understanding.

The need for help with note taking is illustrated by a student-teacher who decided to teach her 15–16 year olds skills in note taking. She found a substantial difference between the high and low achievers in her class. Notice in her example (below) how it is necessary to get low achievers to persist. This means that the teacher has to ensure that the students will not stop after the specific lesson(s) have been given.

"I found that the pupils who usually score well in tests i.e. Grade C upwards, took the best notes. These students were able to isolate the relevant points and

disregard the less important infrastructure. Their note-taking therefore, was structured and so easily understood and revised. The less able students were inclined to copy out complete sentences—some of which were not relevant, and they overlooked some important points. Extra time spent on the acquisition of this skill helped to improve their ability—by homework to take notes on paragraphs in their text book. This persistence actually helped to improve the students answers in some exam questions."

In helping students to appreciate the value of note taking it is useful to employ some kind of "before-and-after-technique" and also to involve the students in examining each other's notes, and perhaps the teacher's notes. This can be followed by a discussion. It is important not to impose a uniform structure since student approaches to note taking and revision vary in many ways. If they can explain their approaches to each other students will learn from each other. Equally, it is necessary for teachers to continue to look at student notes so that the value of the exercise can be maintained. A teacher of history to 15–16 year olds wrote:

"with my direction—in the form of questions and insisting that they compress the material down we got together 3/4 page of notes—on the OHP, I felt that they could see "how" to go about making notes, but this was a beginning. Since this class, I check their 'notes' every two weeks and have spent 15 minutes of the odd class going over this ground again, in order to promote this skill. I am also trying to get them to take their own notes in class, if they wish to, rather than being dependent on what I write on the blackboard or OHP"

The same applies to comprehension; students will learn from each other if allowed.

Comprehension Skills Including Listening and Writing

The need to develop comprehension skills has been found in all age groups including those in higher education. Youngsters of the age of 12 had, to quote a student teacher of a mixed ability class learning English Literature,

" developed the habit of frantically and unthinkingly seeking out the answers to Comprehension questions in the main text of the passage. On finding a word which had appeared in the question they then copied out large chunks of mostly irrelevant material, even if the answer required only a short precise sentence. They had no confidence whatever in attempting an answer based on what they remembered from the passage or based on what they considered a sensible reply."

In particular she was concerned that the children did not understand what might loosely be called speculation.

"The pupils were under the impression that all questions required "right" or "wrong" answers, and these answers could be found only in the passage. Speculation, suggestion, personal opinion, initiative or common sense were seldom included in their efforts. Constant searching of the written word for solutions to a question was the order of the day. Attempts to elicit answers from the pupils without reference to the text left them insecure and hesitant."

To resolve this situation she also helped students develop their listening ability as an important skill in its own right

"having access to a tape-recorder and blank tapes, I recorded the extract I wished to teach; and I rewrote the questions (differently from those in the text-book) and photocopied them. Our text-books were rendered temporarily redundant"

"Our Comprehension lesson now consisted of an Aural exercise in the first stage—pupils listening to a short extract on the tape. After the tape was played through photocopied sheets containing questions on the passage were distributed to the pupils. The pupils in groups of four now discussed, analysed and argued among themselves the relevancy (not the correctness or incorrectness) of their replies to the questions."

"I now led a discussion on each question listed on the pupils' sheet. Great care was taken to elicit suggestions and analysis from the more introverted pupils. Pupils now individually or as a group argued and assessed the merits or demerits of the answers put forward by the various groups."

"As the discussion proceeded it was clear that the attitude and confidence of the pupils towards their own opinions were more positive and constructive. They appeared to realise that their own opinions, their own perceptions, their own analysis mattered and were important. They began to listen more carefully to each other, they were more willing to offer suggestions and soon showed that they understood that learning could be more than passive acceptance of bookish opinions and lists of "correct" or "incorrect" answers to questions."

"They were capable and willing to abandon a negative learning style and adopt a positive one in conjunction with the teaching style they obviously found sympathetic. I like to think they had picked up a critical thinking skill while adopting the new learning style. Active learning had replaced passive acceptance."

Associated with comprehension is the skill of précis. That is the ability to perceive the main ideas in and the structure of a text. A text may be given and the students invited to compare each other's summaries. This can be the basis of a teacher-chaired summary. As the students develop this skill so they can be taught a variety of reading skills (e.g. skimming, scanning etc). In a modification of this approach 15–16 year old students in a German class were able to choose the article they wished to summarise. The teacher felt that this helped their motivation but she pointed out that it was part of a series of activities to help to develop reading skills. Yet another reminder of the fact that the development of such skills cannot be done on a one off basis.

Comprehension skills could be developed by asking students to summarise passages in newspapers. In the nineteen seventies the Southern Regional Examinations Board in England built a public examination in general studies around a newspaper. Students had to read carefully a purpose designed newspaper and answer questions on its content. These would include interpretations of graphs etc so that numerical comprehension was covered. A news paper- *Authentik-* has been published for many years in several languages at Trinity College Dublin with one of its purposes the development of comprehension skills in those languages

Unfortunately very little attention has been paid to the design of textbooks. In Ireland textbooks influence the examinations. An American commentary suggests that *"too many textbooks are guilty of a fault that is sometimes called "mentioning," the awful tendency to say very little about very much. A lot has to be covered, and so the textbook must make mention of many facts. But the root of the word cover has the meaning "to conceal, or hide." The effect of textbook coverage results in the tendency to neutralize by objectification. Perhaps the reason so many people learn to despise what they are taught in school is for precisely for the reason that the facts of the subjects taught in school tend to devalue human beings."*[12]

Gunter and his colleagues were writing primarily about the humanities. In countries where there are national public examinations the syllabus and questions often affirm the approach of textbook writers. Much of the difficulty that some students have in learning mathematics lies in the presentation of text books. Students also have difficulty in understanding the questions. A student teacher of mathematics built a lesson around comprehension of a maths textbook. Having discussed with them the importance of reading comprehension before the exercise she reported that

"It did take a while for them to adapt to the new teaching style. At the start many pupils could not distinguish the major points of a section. After a while however they began to learn more through reading the textbook. All the pupils agreed that in mathematics, one of the best ways of learning and remembering something was to actually do some examples. Therefore doing sums after each section was read, reinforced the ideas in their minds and also encouraged them in the sense that they could answer most questions correctly [. . .] Finally I can only deduce that these classes have helped my class in some important ways. I find now the pupils accept the textbook being used in class more readily. They are now prepared to use the book, before, they felt they could not use it. I also think the pupils confidence in their own ability increased and they came to real-

ize that they themselves had a responsibility towards their own learning, that they could learn by themselves."

And once students have confidence so discipline might improve.

Comprehension is extremely important in secretarial work. Comprehension often requires the use of dictionaries and therefore dictionary skills. Very often students are asked to purchase dictionaries. Having done so they don't use them because no systematic effort is made to get them to use them. Again this requires class time. It needs to be followed up to see that the students incorporate them into their repertoire of study skills.

As indicated above the skill of listening is important in all walks of life (in addition to modern language). We are so easily distracted from paying attention, not only by others but, by our own thoughts. A student teacher of French had her class talking to each other in pairs about their families. They found it more difficult to listen than to talk.

"The nature of their difficulties was internal, i.e. lack of concentration, rather than external such as noise or interference. In trying to explain to me what they meant by 'lack of concentration,' every pair said that they had a tendency to 'wander off'/'to dream,' if even for a couple of seconds while their partner was talking. However, when I asked each one if they could recall what their partner said, only the very weak pupils in the class failed to do this successfully—this being mainly due to their poor knowledge of French."

She attributed some of the success of the class to the fact that she gave them a clear statement of objectives. Five weeks on she said

"to my amazement they are still very aware of this study skill. They are no longer happy to sit back and let me repeat everything on the tape. They now listen and repeat the sentences themselves. Of course this is of great benefit to them, for not only are they improving their listening skills, but they are getting very accustomed to the various notations and sounds of the French language."

With the advent of project work at all ages research skills, in particular those associated with the library, have become important. The behavioural objectives (outcomes) of a science class and project for twelve-year olds are listed below.

"At the end of this lesson the pupils will be able:
1. To list some sources which may be consulted for information on the lives of scientists.
2. To explain how to use the reference section in the local library and how to consult an encyclopaedia.
3. To state the information they want to collect, and the information they can ignore.
4. To explain how they will record the information collected and how they intend to present this to the other members of the class.

At the end of the project the pupils will be able:
1. *To describe the contributions made to science by the particular scientist they have studied.*
2. *To indicate the time during his/her work when imagination played a role in a discovery or invention."*

To achieve these objectives the students were given a lesson on finding out information in a library. They were then asked to do a project the terms of which were to write a story about a scientist of their choice. The student teacher concerned said this involved them in learning a whole range of skills. She reported that:

"On reading through their work at a later stage, most children, it appeared, had been able to ascertain relevant information. Some, though, had obviously transcribed sections of text which they probably did not understand. (Perhaps this particular study skill might be developed in greater detail at a later stage). One or two pupils had indeed carried home many library books and went to great lengths to present their work. All pupils produced pictures or diagrams and all had taken into account that the final work was for public presentation, as judged by the size of their writing, the use of coloured felt-tip pens, large headings and attractive pictures. When the projects were applied each pupil, or a representative of each group was asked to relate to the other members of the class, a brief account of the life and work of the scientist they had studied. They were also asked to point out what they thought was imaginative about their ideas. As they crowded around the display board for a recheck on their particular scientist, it appeared that they were quickly scanning the pages for what was appropriate. I had not thought of this as a study skill previously, but as each child stood up and in a few short sentences described their scientist's work, it was obvious that I had inadvertently provided an opportunity for scanning and synopsis. Many pupils performed this task very well although some needed help in identifying the imaginative thinking episode. I believe that this group possesses several study skills already. Perhaps I could encourage the development of these in more detail"

Finally one student teacher wrote;

"I have a strong impression that secondary teachers look down on this kind of basic activity. Many feel that the primary school is where writing must be learned and that once children come to secondary school it can be ignored. The simple fact is, however, that many of these students cannot write at all and unless they get the opportunity to practise and have individual corrective attention, they will manage to go all the way through school without learning to write properly—as many do."

Rather than looking on it as a remedial activity it should be looked on as developmental and provision for its development should be made throughout school and this applies to the development of all the other study skills. It should be evident that inherent in such activities are the development of skills in problem solving. In any event to simply give only one activity of this kind and not to follow it up is to defeat the purpose of the endeavour particularly if students view it as a one off and not permanently relevant to what they have to do.

The student-teachers whose comments have been given had been asked to read Hamblin and Irvine[14] and then give a lesson with the purpose of teaching a study skill The idea of specifically teaching study skills was not in their repertoire of things to be done. Some argued that although they had not recognised what they were doing as such was teaching study skills. So they may have done; but if a systematic approach is not taken to the teaching of study skills learning will be haphazard if at all. This is not to imply that there should be separate courses for study skills. It does imply there should be a whole school policy for their development. Each subject has something specific to offer. However, it is clear that time is required for preparation and evaluation of the pupils' work. It is also clear that their teaching takes time from the normal programme. This has implications for the size of the syllabus (content) and the design of public examinations and class tests. However, instruction in any subject can easily be designed to encourage the development of such skills. More often than not it seems they are not used for this purpose.

Advanced Organisation : Getting Lessons off to a good start

Most student teachers recognise the need to get a lesson off to a good start. They recognise the need for students to be calm and sometimes this is particularly hard especially after students have been playing games or been involved in physical education. They also recognise that it is not simply a matter of calming the students down but of focusing their attention. Good humour is essential at this stage of the lesson and sometimes the teacher will tell a joke bearing in mind that sometimes it is only the joke that will be remembered!

It takes student teachers somewhat more time to learn that it is useful to tell the students where they are going, that is, to tell the students the objectives of the lesson. While there are instances when there might be good reason for not stating objectives it seems that learning is enhanced if students know where they are going. This is particularly so when the teacher relates it to specific instructions on how to organize specific information.[15] It is the first stage of building a scaffold on which the students can then build their concepts.

Some teachers begin the lesson with a description or survey of what they intend to cover. Others try to use an advance organizer. An idea suggested by Ausubel[16] the advanced organizer is intended to link past knowledge with future work so as to begin new work that has no past in terms of previous lessons. The organizer surveys the concepts and principles in the new work. Advanced organizers are difficult to design.

The general idea can be got from this response to an examination question on advanced organizers by a student teacher.

"Ausubel also postulates advance organizers: a theory I tested with my fourth class history lessons on St. Colmcille. After a brief introduction half the class read the account of his life in the history book, with a view to answering questions on it. The other half had to write the answers to four key questions on the life of Colmcille. Thus while reading they were searching for the answers to these questions which were keys to his life-story. They acted as sorting categories into which they could fit the rest of the information, and this task was a preparation for the major learning task: ability to reproduce eight facts on St. Colmcille's life. Those guided by the written questions retained significantly more." (quoted by Heywood, 1982 [17]*)*

In this example, the second group of pupils undertook the advanced organizer in that student teacher's understanding of the Ausubelian principles.[18] It is, in essence, a mini-lesson in which the principles to be learnt are highlighted. This, it is argued, facilitates meaningful learning. They also provide 'readiness' for what is to be learnt as well as structure.

Ausubel was also influenced by Piagetian ideas in that he accepted the ideas of accommodation and assimilation. He did not however accept the more general theory and some of his ideas were closer to that of Gagné. A person became ready to learn when they had a knowledge structure on which new learning could be built.

Readiness is dependent on prior knowledge.[19] But *"to Ausubel even if the child was not ready all was not lost. There was the possibility of using an advance organizer to bridge the gap"*[20] As we shall see advance organizers were rigorously defined and to quote Ausubel *"more general, more abstract and more inclusive."*

Many of my student teachers used the idea of advanced organization but the examples I have collected suggest they have not fully assimilated the complexity of the idea. Indeed what they do is commonly practised, and they find the term "advanced organizer" is useful in explaining the 'what' and 'why' of their actions. In this respect, Scandura and Wells[21] definition that an advance organizer is *'a general, non-technical overview or outline in which the non-essentials of the to-be-learned material are ignored"*[22] seems to describe teachers' understanding of this technique. It may be argued that a clear statement of terminal objectives fills this need. In respect of mathematics, Orton said that the concept of the advanced organizer is valuable even though there are few occasions when new knowledge cannot readily be linked to existing knowledge.[23] Such is the nature of linearity in the subject of mathematics.

Most textbooks cite two examples from early papers by Ausubel. The first relates to the teaching of the metallurgical properties of plain carbon steel and the second to Buddhism and Zen Buddhism. In both cases experimental and control groups were used and pre- and post-tests given. The differences in the treatment between the experimental and control groups were in the type of advanced organizer they were given. Exhibit 4.1(a) shows my interpretation of the arrangement of the experiment in the traditional form of a scientific experiment. The same post-test was, of course, set to both groups. The more successful of the two was the experimental group in which the advanced organizer contained the basic principles.

One way in which to learn both complex and simple things is by similarity and differences. If we want to remember the differences between two theories we try to understand the ways in which their basic parameters differ. The degree of contrast may be important. This is illustrated by Ausubel's experiment with Buddhism where the respondents were asked to distinguish between Buddhist and Zen Buddhist doctrines. Once again, a pre-test for prior knowledge was given. The experimental technique is illustrated in Exhibit 4.1(b).

Although the experimental group did better than the control group in respect of Buddhism; neither group did so well on Zen Buddhism. Ausubel has suggested that there were difficulties in discriminating between the two forms of Buddhism. The questions in the post-test were multiple choice. We know little of how people respond in these situations to different types of test, for example; if they had to write an essay on the two forms of Buddhism, their understanding of the differences might have been judged differently.

The advanced organizer can take the form of a question but the question has to be set in a way that extracts the mediating structure. The activity that the first group (half) of the students were asked to do is unlikely to achieve this goal. That advanced organizers can be used in any subject is illustrated by another student teacher's response.

"I have used advanced organizers in my own class of third year pupils. (14 to 15 yrs) They were introduced to new words in Irish before being presented with one of the stories on the Intermediate Certificate course that they were required to read. On a subsequent occasion my class was split because of Christmas examinations. One group received instruction by means of the 'advance organizers.' The other group did not. Instead they were given a brief summary of the story. The group using the 'advance organizers' were superior to the other group when tested on the contents of the story." [24]

This example relating to the teaching of languages more especially vocabulary is a reminder of the importance in learning of prior—knowledge especially of vocabulary and other relations.[25] One student teacher explained the problem thus

INSTRUCTIONAL AND CURRICULUM LEADERSHIP

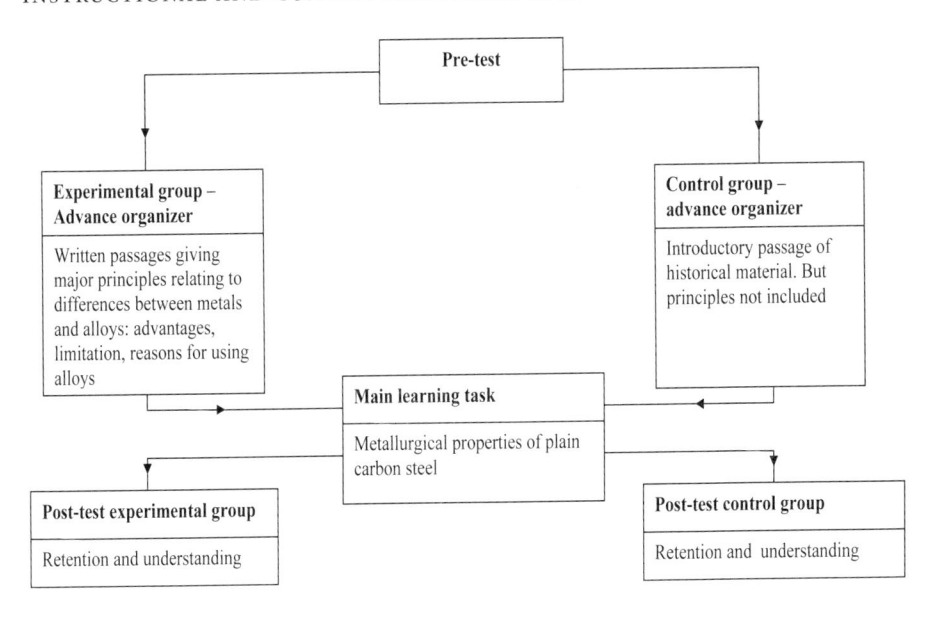

```
                          ┌──────────┐
                          │ Pre-test │
                          └──────────┘
                         ↙            ↘
┌─────────────────────────┐          ┌─────────────────────────┐
│ Experimental group –    │          │ Control group –         │
│ Advance organizer       │          │ advance organizer       │
├─────────────────────────┤          ├─────────────────────────┤
│ Written passages giving │          │ Introductory passage of │
│ major principles        │          │ historical material. But│
│ relating to differences │          │ principles not included │
│ between metals and      │          │                         │
│ alloys: advantages,     │          │                         │
│ limitation, reasons for │          │                         │
│ using alloys            │          │                         │
└─────────────────────────┘          └─────────────────────────┘
              ↘    ┌─────────────────────────┐    ↙
                   │ Main learning task      │
                   ├─────────────────────────┤
                   │ Metallurgical properties│
                   │ of plain carbon steel   │
                   └─────────────────────────┘
              ↙                                   ↘
┌─────────────────────────┐          ┌─────────────────────────┐
│ Post-test experimental  │          │ Post-test control group │
│ group                   │          ├─────────────────────────┤
├─────────────────────────┤          │ Retention and           │
│ Retention and           │          │ understanding           │
│ understanding           │          │                         │
└─────────────────────────┘          └─────────────────────────┘
```

Exhibit 4.1.(a)

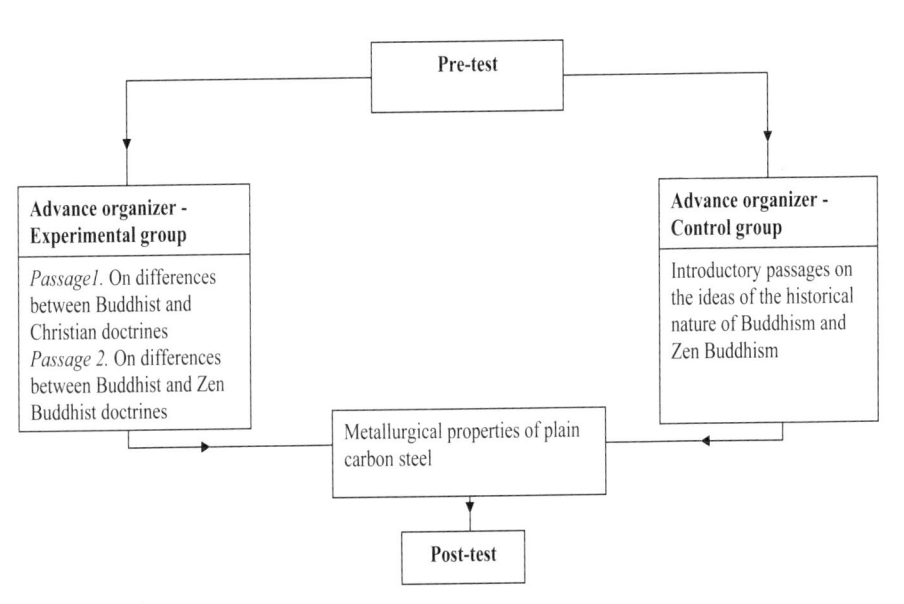

```
                          ┌──────────┐
                          │ Pre-test │
                          └──────────┘
                         ↙            ↘
┌─────────────────────────┐          ┌─────────────────────────┐
│ Advance organizer -     │          │ Advance organizer -     │
│ Experimental group      │          │ Control group           │
├─────────────────────────┤          ├─────────────────────────┤
│ Passage1. On differences│          │ Introductory passages on│
│ between Buddhist and    │          │ the ideas of the        │
│ Christian doctrines     │          │ historical nature of    │
│ Passage 2. On           │          │ Buddhism and Zen        │
│ differences between     │          │ Buddhism                │
│ Buddhist and Zen        │          │                         │
│ Buddhist doctrines      │          │                         │
└─────────────────────────┘          └─────────────────────────┘
              ↘    ┌─────────────────────────┐    ↙
                   │ Metallurgical properties│
                   │ of plain carbon steel   │
                   └─────────────────────────┘
                              ↓
                       ┌──────────┐
                       │ Post-test│
                       └──────────┘
```

Exhibit 4.1.(b)

Exhibit 4.1.(a) and (b) Arrangement of Ausubel's experiments

"I had begun human (reproduction) biology and was about to teach the digestive system. I realized that all the books would be using terms like enzymes and starch, proteins and vitamins. Before introducing digestion we had a lesson on diet and the seven types of food used in daily diet. This was a form of advance organizer and I used it to facilitate the learning of the digestive system. It was a stepping stone to digestion.' [26]

As you see this student teacher argued that the first lesson was itself an advance organizer. One way of linking prior knowledge with new learning is to get the pupils to talk about their strategies for learning so that they are brought to an awareness of the implicit information they already possess. This can be achieved in both co-operative groups and whole class discussion.[27]

Sometimes even the connecting stimuli we employ have to be used with care since learning is that process by which experience develops new responses and reorganizes old ones. There is, therefore, a connection between that which is already learned and that which it is intended should be learned. At the same time, we need some stimuli to learn.

Without any knowledge of educational psychology, teachers use these principles to aid learning, through the association of one idea with another. To do this they use a mediating response, i.e a term in the form:
- is like,
- is different from.

Using statements that include these terms, new phenomena or things can be related to the experience of the pupil. However, mediating responses have to be used with care: otherwise they may cause ambiguity, or may not be understood. For example, McDonald points out that teachers sometimes use the word familiar instead of experience.[28] They also use familiarity in two different senses. Great care must be exercised in the choice of such terms to ensure that they are clearly understood by the students in the context in which they are to be used. Mediating responses like 'is different from' may also cause the teacher considerable problems since the pupils may not grasp the significant differences.

Prawat has pointed out that the use which students make of prior knowledge is dependent on the way that knowledge is organised in their memory systems.[29] This has implications for the planning of courses for it is evident that an advance organizer cannot be used in isolation of previous work. Thus, lessons have to be designed together in sequence if students are to construct an adequate scaffold. In these circumstances the advance organizer facilitates the memory because it draws attention to the specific ideas and principles to be considered[30] hence the importance of key concepts both for instruction and curriculum design.

Just as a prior lesson may be used as an organizer so too may prior reading. The student-teacher examples evidently involved the students in learning. In the first example they were expected to look for information and organize it in particular ways. Moreover, the advance organizer should help them do this during the remainder of the class.[31]

As we have seen there are other ways of organizing knowledge that will assist the development of higher order thinking. These and advanced organizers are sometimes grouped under the generic heading of cognitive organization (or organizers). For example in my 1982 book the chapters were organized around examination questions. They were designed to draw out significant principles Studying examination questions is valuable since they can help students preparing for public examinations to construct scaffolds and prevent them from memorising answers to questions they think might appear on the paper. In this way students learn to integrate the disparate knowledge put before them in their courses. Students can also be asked to design questions that should elicit principles. They could even be asked to design mark schemes.

However, just as question setting for a class is an art, so too is question setting for an examination. Contrast the two examples that follow:

"Describe two kinds of advance organizer for use in learning the same material in the subject which you teach. Indicate the characteristics of those advance organizers and say why you think they will facilitate the acquisition of new information."

"Construct at least two kinds of advance organizers for use in learning the same material. Indicate the characteristics of the advance organizers and why you think they will facilitate acquiring new information."

The former insists that respondents give examples from their own teaching, whereas responses to the latter could come from examples in a textbook.

In project work it is found that students who can clearly define what it is they want to do have a much better chance of completing a project than those students whose focus is ill-defined at the beginning.[32] In other words those who perform well are able to create their own advance organizers. Those in difficulty require much help which is consistent with the finding that mature students derive greater benefits from exposure to new information and experience than immature students who are unable to apply rules and are inhibited by a limited knowledge base.[33]

When children are given problem-solving tasks it seems they are able to accomplish them when they have a sufficient knowledge base.[34] This is consistent with the experiences of our student teachers.

Chi found a four and half year old who knew the names of 40 dinosaurs. They played a game with this boy in which information was given about the proportions of each known dinosaur. They then divided the Dinosaurs into familiar and unfamiliar groupings and examined his recall. It was found to be consistently better for those judged familiar. A year later after the boy had lost interest in dinosaurs he was asked to name the 40 again. He achieved 11 familiar and 3 unfamiliar. The proportions of the dinosaurs were examined and Chi and Koeske argued that the boy's recall and retention was due to the extensive and integrated knowledge base that he had about the familiar dinosaurs.[35]

Cognitive Organization in relation to discipline.

Cognitive organizers of whatever kind help students to alter and to focus on what is to be learnt. They mediate between what has been learnt and what is to be learnt. They are knowledge dependent in two ways—first, if the students do not have prior knowledge they will be "out of their depth." It is the experience of beginning teachers that getting the level of instruction right is sometimes difficult. If it is not aligned with prior knowledge it may cause minor disruptive behaviour. Sometimes, however, a class may ramble along quite cheerfully for several weeks before the beginning teacher finds out that the principles have not been understood. Difficulties can be profound in mixed ability classes if they are not organized with this problem in mind. Second, cognitive tasks that demand the active transformation of knowledge are very demanding[36] thus while the low achievers will learn only what they themselves do[37] it is necessary to set tasks that are within their capability otherwise depression will set in. Thus, cognitive organizers should not only take into account level of maturity but contain ways of capturing the interest of the class for lack of interest is so often a cause of minor misbehaviour. It is argued here that appropriately designed advance organizers should assist the confidence with which students approach their learning and enhance the self-esteem of those in need of such enhancement. If they do not then their design needs to be reconsidered. But there are more fundamental cognitive structures and ensuring that students have them.

Cognitive structures and reluctant learners

There are reluctant learners at all levels of education. The cognitive structures referred to here are often assumed by teachers in post-primary education to have been developed in primary (elementary) school. However, given the difficulties that many students have in post-primary education this may not be the case.

There are three cognitive structures—Comparative, symbolic representation and logical reasoning. These structures relate to the general abilities listed earlier. In the United States Garner found that many middle and high school students had not developed these structures.[38] Garner's case studies were derived from questions and interactive assessment tasks based on the theories of Piaget and Feuerstein.[39] She found that many students lacked adequate comparative cognitive structures. For example, skill in recognition defined here as the ability to identify a match or fit between two pieces of information was lacking.

Related to this is the ability to classify so that information becomes more accessible. Garner also found that students also had difficulties with memorization. *"Teachers can help students strengthen (and others) by encouraging children to reflect on how they make connections, identify patterns, formulate rules, and pull out abstract principles to create meaning. Too often they confuse imitation, a preliminary form of memorization, with learning. Instead of processing information, they depend on short-term memory and simply imitate what they are modeled."* Assessment systems very often encourage rote memorization and this disadvantages not only the low achieving student but the high achieving student as well. It will be evident that both the ability to recognize and the ability to memorize require the ability to reflect. Garner suggests that although student teachers study Piaget they rarely understand just how important conservation of constancy is. If a student cannot understand that while some characteristics of a thing can change others remain the same their ability to use higher order thinking skills will be impeded. Garner also showed that some students had limited spatial orientation. (See below for further discussion and chapter 8). She also drew attention to the importance of temporal orientation and metaphorical thinking.

Clearly post-primary schools should engage in assumptional-dialogues about what they need to know about students when they transfer from primary to post-primary education. Such dialogues might lead to different teaching methods and different curriculum content that should take into account its imaginative and emotional features. Egan and Judson argue that to engage students in learning teachers have to bring out the imaginative and emotional features of the curriculum. This applies as much to mathematics as it does to any other subject in the curriculum.[40] One of several activities that might help students with their imagination and emotion is imagery.

Imagery and discipline

Student teachers as part of their teaching practice have been asked to design, implement and evaluate an imaginary exercise with one of the classes they teach. It is undertaken at the beginning of the class and is intended to influence both cognition and behaviour. It can be designed to obey the principles of advanced organization. This has been done with each group of graduate trainees over an eight-year period. Apart from a small amount of formal instruction the student teachers gained their information on lesson design from papers by Galyean and practical instructions on the conduct of imagery exercises from Hall, Hall and Leech.[41] These authors describe how the room should be prepared and some student-teachers went so far as to find a room where the students could lie down which is to take a big risk in the school situation. They are then given instruction on the intellectual, emotional and physical preparation. Should students be allowed to open their eyes or not? How should they sit? How much time should be spent on the activity and so on? The examples of some of the classes conducted by some of the student teachers will serve to answer these and other questions

Attention is paid to processing which is regarded as integral to the fantasy experience. Its purpose is to enable the students to make sense of and reflect on their immediate experience. When it is appropriate after the activity has finished the students may be invited to talk about their fantasies in pairs but the task should be clearly defined. Hall, Hall and Leech suggest that this activity can be used to enhance listening.

Curwin and Mendler have described a number of strategies that can help teachers reduce stress.[42] These include breathing relaxation exercises (because under stress breathing may become shallow and irregular), private retreats for 5 or 10 minutes at some time prior to an anticipated stressful situation, one retreats from the realities which one faces in order to face them with new energy and freshness.Breathing exercises can also help in the examination room as can a clenched fist. Teachers can also benefit from group exercises but these, suggest Curwin and Mendler, are unlikely to be available to teachers unless some teacher takes an initiative. If such exercises can help reduce stress among adults why shouldn't they work with pupils? Another way of processing is to ask students to draw their feelings or write about them.

The issue of confidentiality is sometimes raised. Hall,Hall and Leech have firm views on this matter and say,"*We would argue that the expression of feeling and other forms of self-disclosure have a legitimate place in the school curriculum, as legitimate as maths, French, computer science and so on. In this way, confidentiality becomes an issue not to be avoided, but to be placed in its correct perspective. It is possible for teachers to create problems by over-emphasising confidentiality. It is as if talking about feelings were so unusual in schools that we have to have strict rules to handle it. Thus confidentiality may be re-interpreted by students and other teaching colleagues as secrecy, and secret activities often carry connotations of guilt, embarrassment or even shame. Students and their teachers have a right to confidentiality if that is what is required to help them to begin the process of talking about themselves and their experiences in a real way. Enforcing or policing this right emerges not out of teacher edict but out of an awareness of what it means to respect the needs of each other. It is a group issue and can profitably be presented as such by the classroom teacher.*"

In 1990, 1991 and 1995 questionnaires were administered to the student teachers, who undertook the exercise, to obtain their attitudes to the activity.[43] Around three-quarters of the classes were said to be normally well behaved in-spite of the novelty of the exercise. However, about eleven per cent of the 1991 group (N=79) said it made the class more naughty while 38% said there was no change in discipline among those who are generally naughty. But in the 1995 group (N=91) 42% considered the imagery exercise to have calmed the students down. Only 5% and 3% reported that the class had become more boisterous or and behaved badly as a result of the exercise. In contrast 67% reported that it had enhanced the interest of their pupils and 59% said the exercise had focused their attention. Evidently their classes influenced the students in a positive way. In only 5% of the classes did the pupils behave in an unusual way and in 74% the perception was that the students were more motivated. Some students responding to the 1991 questionnaire pointed out this might be because of the novelty of the exercise (16%) and there were comments to this effect in the 1995 responses. Overall, there is not much difference in the response profiles for the two years cited. Imagery it seemed was likely to influence behaviour in a positive direction.

However, this exercise was not set to assist student-teachers evaluate another method for improving the behaviour of their students it was set primarily to see if imagery would improve the performance of their students.

Before designing the exercise student teachers were asked to read the aforementioned paper by Galyean which argued the case for imagery.[44] They were also given a short, but unpublished research report, by Galyean on the teaching of remedial English. The main paper distinguished between 4 types of imagery—Guided Cognitive, Guided Affective, Guided Transpersonal and Confluent. Confluent is an amalgam of any two of the three. The purpose of guided cognitive imagery is to improve cognitive performance and to help develop thinking skills. It is argued that it also assists memory and that pupils may learn to write more imaginative essays, and letter writing. Instances of improvement in drawing had also been reported. In guided cognitive imagery the students relate their subjective images to the cognitive material. It can also be used to refine psycho-motor skills. She claims that by expanding holistic modes of learning such as art, music, movement, and drama immersed in imagery that our mental activity is sharpened.

The purpose of guided affective imagery is to help our general awareness and acceptance of self and others. It is about the development of self-worth. Information -processing theory suggests that the brain acts similarly to a computer[45] and applied to the problem of "affect" we programme ourselves with images of ways of being and acting. So students with low self-esteem programme themselves with negative learning images. The problem is to reverse these images and it is held that guided affective imagery can help them accomplish such a reversal. It, to quote Galyean, "*enables students to develop healthy self-concepts by owning their own power, recognizing latent capabilities, and enlarging those that are already working for them.*"

In undertaking guided affective imagery, students learn to recognize their needs and wants, and identify and transform self-defeating images and become comfortable with introspection and self-disclosure. Such exercises are accompanied by cognitive development and have been shown to improve language development. They can also contribute to moral education for example in the study of discipline. Galyean argues that such imagery should be conducted in a secure environment for which reason teachers sometimes group their students and place them in a circle.

Guided Transpersonal Imagery is intended to help the student recognize as valid the mystical, psychic and spiritual dimensions of life. It is concerned with *"optimum psychological health and well being."*[46] One has both to believe in and be comfortable with such activities in order to conduct them. It is controversial and teachers are bound by the regulations of the State (Country) in which they teach. Where it is allowed then it requires the support of school and parents.

Most of the student teachers in these studies undertook guided cognitive imagery but it seems to be difficult to hold the view that there is no affective dimension in such an activity and of course vice-versa.

Over half the teachers in both samples said the imagery exercise was more successful than their expectations had led them to believe and similar proportions were surprised by the impact that the imagery had on their students.

Heywood reported that 70% said that it improved cognitive performance.[47] Given that this view is very often based on tests given a week or so afterward it might be inferred that there was some improvement in memory; however, this is a matter that requires further and more detailed investigation.

Many student teachers were surprised by the impact of the exercise on the low achievers. 82% said that it improved their performance. Startling demonstrations of this point were given, as, for example, changes in creative writing technique and drawing ability. 66% reported an improved performance among their average students. However, a disturbing feature, was that only 15% felt the lesson improved the performance of the high achievers. To put it in another way, 74% reported that the high achievers performed as they usually do. This is a matter that needs to be further investigated. It should be noted, however, that it is very difficult to improve on good performances.[48] The lesson may have helped motivate some students to maintain their performance. It is also possible that the student-teachers are deceived by this point, since few believe that imagery will work with all pupils or adults: 15% believe that it will work with some adults. There are in each year, reports of work with adults who have come back to school to try to pass the Leaving Certificate. In some cases the imagery has been surprisingly successful but in others this was not so. In contrast to the 16% who said it would work with all pupils in senior cycle (15 to 18 years), 42% said that it would work with all pupils in the Junior Cycle. It seems from the replies to the previous question that the response of the high-achieving pupils to the lesson may have influenced this perception.

If these student teachers use imagery in the future 85% will use it to provide variety in their teaching and 63% will use it to enhance motivation. But 64% and

22% respectively will use it to try to enhance cognitive performance and/or creativity. Overall Galyean's thesis for guided cognitive imagery is well supported.

The question arises as to whether it is possible to make imagery more attractive particularly to the older adolescents, because teacher's beliefs about older adolescent behaviour may lead them to dismiss imagery as an irrelevant exercise with that group.

First, this cannot be because the evidence is that some of the most eminent mathematicians and scientists think first in images. They demonstrate high levels of spatial ability.[49] Therefore one approach might be to discuss with the students at some length thinking in these terms and invite them to indicate how they themselves visualize. Perhaps a whole lesson could be devoted to this activity at the end of which they might be invited to collaborate in an imagery activity in the next lesson. If this could be done in collaboration with other teachers so that the student experienced imagery in science and literary subjects the student would therefore be in a better position judge its value to him /her.

Second, in systems with public examinations the students might be shown how imagery could help them to reduce stress during public examinations. Given the annual hype and the consequent self-fulfilling prophecy that examinations cause unnecessary stress this could prove valuable. Put simply it can help to redirect attention from the arousal that causes the anxiety to the task and so integrate this arousal into the task.[50] Understanding how affect can cause stress and how a relaxation exercise and/or imagery can help alleviate stress might be a sufficient stimulus for students to be willing to experiment with imagery.

Some of the examples given by Galyean relate to the teaching of mathematics. However, mathematics students may not see the immediate relevance of imagery. But as Skemp points out visual representations are to be found in diagrams of all kinds where as algebraic symbols have much in common with verbal symbols.[51]

He argues that while the verbal algebraic system predominates whenever we need to describe an overall structure we resort to visual representation as for example in flow diagrams and organization charts. The visual superimposes itself on the algebraic.

"We may look quickly at the beginning and conclusion of an argument, before examining details. We may recapitulate whenever we wish, and this becomes necessary more often as the argument becomes more involved. In other words, a verbal-algebraic exposition, once written down, shows the over-all structure in addition to the logical-sequential implications within the structure; and may be scanned in other ways besides the conventional left to right, top to bottom order."

It now becomes possible to account for the use of spatial/visual thinking by scientists. Mathematics provides them with the thinking and insights that enable them to integrate and synthesize whereas verbal representation provides analysis, logical argument and socialized thinking.

In summary, it seems clear that imagery can not only contribute to a reduction in minor misbehaviour it can also enhance learning particularly of low achieving students. The student-teacher case studies confirm that this is generally the case.

Co-operative learning

Another teaching strategy for developing positive social skills is co-operative learning. While the claims for co-operative learning do not include discipline among them there are specific forms of it that have as their goal the development of social skills and high self-esteem. Since lack of social skill and lack of self-esteem may be contributory factors to minor misbehaviour co-operative learning is a technique that should be investigated by teachers as a device for both cognitive learning and control. The US Department of Education and American sociologists like Oakes[52] had drawn attention to the successes that co-operative learning has had with low achievers and those needing remedial treatment in elementary schools. Co-operative learning has been used in middle and high schools as well as higher education.

In the United States where it is most widely used there are two main schools of thought about how it should be run and at times there seems to have been acrimonious debate between them about differences that some may think are minor. These schools are centred on Slavin at The Johns Hopkins University and Johnson and Johnson at the University of Minnesota. Slavin seems to have had a hand in six of the eight or so variations of co-operative learning.[53] In this context, the concern is with Johnson and Johnson's formal co-operative learning groups.[54]

Although there is more than one definition of co-operative learning they are very similar as the three that follow show. In Johnson, Johnson and Holubec it is defined as *"the instructional use of small groups so that students work together to maximise their own and each others' learning."*[55]

Slavin defines it as *"instructional methods in which students of all performance levels work together in small groups toward a group goal"*[56] and Kagan as *"a set of instructional strategies which include co-operative student-student interaction over subject matter as an integral part of the learning process."*[57]

American educators have been determined to promote methods that will involve each member of a heterogeneous group and overcome the difficulty that low achievers won't contribute and high achievers will get bored. Everyone has to contribute if the team is to do well. It is not the assignment of pupils to groups but a very sophisticated way of getting groups to work that avoids the general complaints that teachers make about group work. It may be accompanied by individualized instruction. A group may be as small as two individuals.

Formal co-operative learning groups may be of the order of one class session or last over a period or groups. Students work together to ensure that the objectives of the lesson(s) are obtained. Johnson and Johnson's *"learning together mode"* differs from other approaches in that it involves the specific learning of social skills. Also the work is continuously monitored and the groups only submit one activity i.e. from the group as opposed to individuals. Generally these variations are characterised by their systematic approach to the design of instruction. Kirk has suggested the following differences between co-operative groups and other kinds of small group work.[58]

Co-operative groups	*Small group activities*
Positive interdependence	No necessary interdependence
We sink or swim together	Students often work on their own
Carefully structured	Lacking structure, often incidental may be haphazard
Individual accountability	
Emphasis on face to face inter-personal skills	Social skills not explicitly developed
Group processing	No group processing
Peer tutoring	No systematic peer tutoring

Of course small group work can be carefully designed as the Inspectors' report of practice in comprehensive schools in England showed.[59] There is also much systematic small group work in both America and the UK that involves the students in collaborative learning.

In England and Ireland small group work has sometimes been called mixed ability teaching. Its intention is to mix groups from the range of abilities but as the Inspectors (HMI) report showed very often it is the average student in the middle of the range who benefit (see below). Teachers have undoubtedly practised group processing in these countries but not under the name of co-operative learning. Group processing as in imagery is the activity of reflecting on what happened in the group and this takes place for all age levels.

These variations in co-operative learning however, generally include the following dimensions.

(i) Positive Interdependence
(ii) Individual and group accountability
(iii) Promotive interaction, preferably face to face
(iv) Interpersonal and small group social skill development
(v) Reflection on the activity in the group (as in the imagery exercise described in the previous section it is group processing)
(vi) Describing the helpful and unhelpful actions of the group members
(vii) Deciding what to do in the future

The failures of group work have been highlighted in England and this is one of the reasons why there is a demand for whole class teaching of a more traditional kind. Often this, sadly, expresses a concern for the high achiever than the low achiever. This concern has been echoed in the US where one investigation based, unfortunately, on a very small sample of gifted children suggests they do not like it. For example, they cannot understand why other children can't grasp the material. They also resent the time taken away from their own learning since they do not learn any better this way. Sometimes the other students lazed around while the gifted child did all the work to get a D grade, because the others in the group did nothing. They would rather work in homogenous groups and some teachers see this as an advantage.[60] The author of this small scale study suggested that working with others at the same level of achievement might have positive effects on their self-esteem.[61] She did not, however, argue that for these reasons gifted children should not be involved in co-operative learning but suggested that they should be allowed to work in homogeneous groups for some of the time. Matthews cites Kulik and Kulik in support of this view.[62] They found that when gifted students work together for all or part of a school day their achievement surpasses that of gifted students who are not grouped together for instruction.

Advocates of streaming (tracking) would take this view. Since attitudes are formed early some form of heterogeneous collaborative work would seem to be essential if 'all' are to be prepared for the work place where 'all' have a say in management.[63] The view that high achievers have the necessary social skills to work in teams has no foundation. Indeed it is a widespread criticism of industrialists that young graduates do not possess the interpersonal skills required for industry or the ability to work in teams.[64] One has only to look around a university to see that this is by no means the case. It may be that adolescent gifted students can be given an understanding of these issues prior to their introduction to heterogeneous groups, or would this make them more arrogant?

Given that these children are likely to go to university teachers should note that the overwhelming evidence favours cooperative /collaborative techniques over traditional methods for effective performance.[65]

The problem seems to be very similar to that found with imagery. That is, that the handling of high achievers is a major problem. It also seems that low achieving students benefit from co-operative learning and small group work. However, that teacher said that the process took a considerable amount of time to initiate, orchestrate and maintain and this problem of the work-load created for teachers is taken up in the English Inspectorate's report.[66] If collaborative learning is to be taken up it has to be well prepared and researched and time must be made available for its planning. Of such was the programme developed and evaluated by Kirk in a primary school in Ireland.[67]

The class with whom the experiment was conducted had exhibited passive learning styles throughout their previous four/five years in primary school. A general apathy toward school was openly expressed. The students generally had a record of poor attendance poor punctuality and consistent behavioural and attitude problems. They were all females aged between 12 and 13.

They were a class no one wished to teach. Since Kirk had expressed an interest in theories of learning as well as an interest in seeking an 'alternative' approach in the belief that 'there's got to be a better way,' she was invited to try out her theories with this particular class.

In pre-tests, in terms of literacy and numeracy skills, the data indicated a broad mix of ability ranges varying from very poor to average ability with more than fifty per cent of students with poor mathematical ability. *"Arising out of the literature as described above, I determined to institute collaborative learning strategies based on grouping students of dissimilar levels, embracing the range of abilities in each group. While this was a foreign concept to students whose self-esteem and motivation was very low, I was determined to pursue the project with a view to sparking the urge to learn and exploring strategies that might work."*

"By assisting students—through questioning, discussion, critical debate and analysis, sharing ideas and evaluation—to identify attainable targets within the context of the group, students of all levels experienced immediate success."

"I observed that the more able students, unknown to themselves, adapted a tutorial role within the group but were sensitive to the inadequacies felt by some of the fellow students, and in the context of the group, had to satisfy the learning needs of all members in the group. Another observation being the role of the teacher changed from a didactic form of teaching to one of coaching and motivating students. A spirit of interdependence was generated between groups. This was manifested in their desire to achieve targets which they themselves had agreed and in their ability to set simple tests to evaluate other groups' performances. Again the teacher's role as coach and tutor, assisted groups in identifying specific learning targets and evaluation benchmarks."

"This method I employed in all aspects of English and Mathematics. It soon naturally spilled over into other subject areas with equal success."

"The results of this process became manifest towards the end of year one, when so many students had raised their literacy and numeracy levels above certain grades, as follows":
* All but ten per cent of students had reached or surpassed their chronological age scores in reading and mathematics.
* Fifteen per cent increased their scores to twelve months above the chronological age.
* Five per cent increased their scores to eighteen months above the chronological age.

Such marked improvement in core subjects had a domino effect on all other subjects such as history, geography, social and environmental studies, civics, etc."

"The principal was so impressed by the results, particularly in relation to improved behaviour, that he broke with tradition and requested me to retain the class for a second year, thus working with the same students from fifth through sixth class."[68]

In the school concerned, it was the practice for teachers to change classes each year. In this case the Principal asked the teacher to take the final year group again and she reported that this enabled her to consolidate her work. *"Thus, through exposure to methodologies of inviting and expecting students to participate in curriculum design and adaptation, the overwhelming successful outcomes— not only in terms of educational achievement as identified in post-test scores but also in terms of behaviour modification—were encouraging. The latter was measured in terms of decreased acts of indiscipline and suspensions, decreased referrals to school principal and parents, and an encouragingly higher attendance of parents at parent teacher meetings."*

So how does a co-operative group work? To explain we shall examine the classroom experiment carried out by this teacher, with this group of 32 eleven and twelve year old girls in their final year of primary school in Galway. She set out to experiment with an adaptation of Johnson and Johnson's Learning Together Model in Mathematics by dividing her class into two and using one half as a control. Because the control group received traditional tuition during the whole of the three-week period of the experiment, and because they were excluded from the novel approach to learning they were switched with the other group at the end of the three-week period. The control group then did co-operative learning in spelling for three weeks. Measurements were made prior to the first three weeks and at the end of it, and again at the end of second activity. While the results of the first experiment might be considered safe the second experiment's results might suffer from interference and account for some of the curiosities found. Since this is teacher-led inquiry the final judgement must be the teacher's for if it worked for her then she/he can add the method to her repertoire of techniques and this is what happened in this case.

As already indicated the Principal of the school acted as an independent observer throughout and was provided with structured observation forms designed by Kirk.

Triangulation[69] was achieved because the students' views were taken into account. Various instruments were used to obtain measures of change between input and output. These included a mathematics achievement test designed by the investigator, Young's[70] parallel spelling test, Miller's[71] adaptation of Coopersmith's self-esteem inventory, Barker-Lunns Academic Self-Image Scale.

Kirk also designed questionnaires for the co-operative and control groups. Having selected her students, Kirk initiated them into co-operative learning with a brief training scheme in which the groups chose their names and made flags, logos and mobiles to signify their identities. They were also briefed on what was expected from individuals in the group and the group itself.

Small groups of 4 and 5 were selected. They are likely to be more successful than larger groups[72] for the reason that they are easier to monitor. Difficulties that students have in working with each other can be identified easily. Moreover, classroom organisation is simplified and if monitors are charged with the distribution of materials the groups can be at work very quickly.

Group members have to be helped to the view that membership of the group is something that is quite positive[73] and so in training, some team building activities are desirable. Kirk used some handouts that had been prepared by Johnson and Johnson for this purpose. These were headed 'Knowing Myself'; 'Recognising my Worth'; 'In touch with Myself'; 'Forming Groups'; 'Building a bridge among Group Members'; 'Meeting my Group'; 'Making a Group Mobile'; 'Communication Skills'; 'Body Talk'; 'Disagree with Ideas, not People,' &c. A formidable array of simple reflective exercises which ended with one titled 'How can I Help?

Co-operative learning specialists take on the criticism that both high and low achievers are disadvantaged and set out to ensure there is group interdependence. They insist therefore on heterogeneous groups. Kirk, therefore, followed procedures suggested by Johnson and Johnson[74] and Slavin[75] for the selection of the groups. The results of a mathematics Sigma T standardised test and Schonell Graded Spelling Test were available and the class was ranked, ordered, and divided into high, medium and low scoring groups from which the students were randomly assigned to triads. There being four co-operative groups, two students remained. They were assigned to two of the triads to make these two groups of four.

In order to assure group interdependence—that is, to ensure that each member of the group contributed—Kirk followed the rules set out in exhibit 4.2. The groups were located so that each had its own space. Environmental interdependence was created by ensuring eye to eye contact, near enough knee to knee contact, &c. Materials interdependence was created by giving them only one worksheet or one maths book to be shared.

Each student was given a role and the roles were rotated after each problem had been solved. For the triads the roles were (1) reader and recorder; (2) Explainer of ideas and (3) checker of understanding and encourager of participation. These last two became separate roles in the quadrupeds. In the spelling co-operatives additional roles were necessary for asking, spelling and checking and encouraging.

---

1. Keep the size of the groups small (three and four member to a group).

2. Give weekly tests to each student following a revision of the week's work

3. Randomly check individual students ability to explain how to solve problem or to spell a word.

4. Assign roles (and rotation of roles) of explainer and checker of understanding to each cooperative group.

5. Observe each group member and record the frequency with which each member explained the assigned material and checks other group members for understanding. This data to be monitored by the observer present in the classroom.

6. Require signatures to be signed on every group product daily. Although this does not guarantee that everyone would participate, it gives students the message that they are expected to take responsibility for their behaviour in the group.

7. Each student to write out the computations required for the solution for each problem.

Exhibit 4.2 Actions to be taken to ensure individual as well as group accountability.

Role cards were provided and instruction was given in the roles with the aid of charts that were also affixed to the wall. The other skills were listening and checking. The checker helps the students formulate what they are learning. Role interdependence was encouraged though instructions that told the students to stay with their groups, use quiet voices, and take turns.

Co-operative learning took place in one lesson per day over a three-week period at which time the groups were changed. The lesson began with an explanation of the assignment. The objectives were then stated in terms of what it was the students would be able to do as a result of the lesson. The key concepts, principles and strategies were outlined and related to their prior experience and the rules and procedures for the group work were explained. They were:

1. To solve each of the problems on the worksheet correctly

2. To understand the strategies required to do so and

3. To discover alternate ways of solving problems and to be able to show they got the answer.

Emphasis was placed on specific expected behaviours that would be monitored by both the observer and teacher/researcher. Such social skills practised during the experiment included:

Saying so when you think someone's idea helps.
Saying so when you do not understand a question or answer.
Making sure that all students get a chance to share their ideas.
Sticking to your roles.
No interrupting.
Pleasant encouraging words and gesture.
Good eye-to-eye contact
Calling each other by Christian names.

It will be noticed that practice in these skills contributes to the development of emotional intelligence. The more this is developed the more disciplined a person is likely to become.[76] As the students learned about group work so the time devoted to instructions was reduced. Meanwhile the control group learnt the same material in the normal way.

A complex system of rewards was introduced. Student work in the control group was recognised on the basis of competitive achievement and students in this group were awarded certificates if they had demonstrated outstanding achievement. Two kinds of certificate were awarded for group work. The first was called the social skills certificate. This was awarded each week to the members of the group who had achieved the highest points for collaborative skill. The second was called the co-operative award certificate and was given in the second and third weeks to those who had improved scores in social skill. The academic scores were tallied daily and the overall performance for each was displayed. An American approach to scoring was used in which the top range of marks of the normal curve was used.

Suggestions from the students that were taken on board for teacher recognition of the work done. These included: no homework for one night in one subject; each member of the most successful group to design a poster on the computer; group members to select activities for Physical Education; and a certificate of achievement to be awarded to each successful group member. There was an emphasis on 'celebrating' what had been achieved throughout the course.

Group processing took place during the last fifteen minutes of the class. This was assisted by the preparation of sheets that enabled the children to reflect on how helpful they had been (adapted from Kagan)."[77] Group Processing asked: did everyone contribute ideas? Did we share our materials? Did we ask for everyone's ideas? Did we make sure everyone in the group understood? Did we help, encourage and finish our work? Answers had to be given on a three-point-scale as were the answers to a questionnaire on how well did our group do? In summary they had to write short notes in answer to the questions what needs improvement? And, how can the group improve the way it works together?

During the lessons the independent observer did not intervene. She completed a daily observation form for each group on social skill development and simple sociograms to indicate frequency of communication patterns within the groups. The teacher only intervened as a consultant.

The previous paragraphs can only give some idea of the flavour of the exercise and in analysing the results Kirk is well aware that the novelty of the exercise and the interest shown it by the principal and a special visit by myself might well have influenced student behaviour. Yet this will always be the case for if the teacher finds that a method is successful she will try it again with a new class for whom it will also be a novelty unless there is a school policy which ensures that co-operative learning is undertaken in earlier years. The paradox is that too much of anything leads to boredom whereas too little may not bring about desired changes in attitude. It is a problem that bedevils the design of instruction within and across the years.

Little can be said about discipline other than that it confirms previous work that children become interested in what they have to do if they are involved in it and it is well planned. It also confirmed that if lessons are to be well planned a great deal of time has to be allowed for such planning. But it is not unreasonable to suppose that if social skills improve so to will behaviour.

I could not see a "Principal" effect when I observed the class but I was of the impression that the class was normally well behaved.

To take one of the major criticisms of co-operative learning first, that is, its potential to reduce achievement levels. In this case there was a considerable increase in mathematics achievement by the co-operative learners when compared with the control group. By contrast the control group did better in the spellings than the co-operative group. Thus whereas other research is supported by the maths findings it is not in regard to the spellings. Kirk suggests this may be due to the fact that she could not find reported work on spelling among co-operative groups for practical advice on how to plan her lessons. Could it be that the particular topic was not suitable for co-op groups? Might it be that skill in short story writing (or something like that) would have been more appropriate? Mathematics is a notoriously difficult subject to learn and may gain from the cross-fertilisation.

The Academic Self Image scale shows that there was an increase between the mean pre and post -scores of both the co-op and control groups in mathematics whereas in the spellings there was a "huge increase" in the mean score of the co-op group when compared with the control. However, for the self-esteem inventory the co-op group yielded twice the improvement of that of the control group in mathematics and a more or less similar outcome was found for the spellings groups. This suggests that if there had been interference between the two groups it would seem to have been in favour of the co-operative groups. It does seem therefore that co-operative learning can greatly improve self-esteem and this can help both high and low-achievers because in both groups persons with low self-esteem can be found. Moreover this does not seem to have been done at the expense of achievement.

In respect of friendship patterns it seems that whereas these remained fairly constant throughout the experimental period there were greater changes in helpful working relationships (i.e. with persons they would like to work with to solve problems). The investigator came to support Johnson and Johnson's[78] belief that self-esteem played a role in this respect. The higher one's self-esteem the greater one's acceptance and liking of others tends to be and thus one is less prejudiced against others. There is of course the danger that high self-esteem can give a student an unrealistic view of their potential.[79]

Student questionnaires, other teacher's comments and parental views added to the information gained. Taken together it was concluded that there was a greater awareness of social skills as for example " *a greater frequency in the use of overt social behaviours, such as listening to others, appropriate reactions to other's comments, appropriate body language, more responsible behaviour and more positive attitudes displayed towards work and towards others.*"

This was due in no small way to the investigator's development of group processing.

Affirmation of the value of the course came from student responses to an essay that they had to write three months after the experiment was over on "Co-operative Learning. Some of the observations shared by the Sixth Class participants in these essays included.

"I owe a lot to co-operative learning as my attitude towards school and teachers has improved greatly. I accept criticism and I show more respect for my teachers, family and friends." *"My mom said I changed in ways. I am more responsible, helpful and I encourage my friends a lot more. I improved in doing housework."* *"I gained a lot of confidence and am not afraid to be wrong any more. I think about how to do the sums much more."* *"In my group I learnt to be helpful and have more patience. I learnt to listen to people without interrupting every second word. I enjoyed co-operative learning immensely and I think it is a wonderful method of learning."* *"I really enjoyed co-operative learning*

and it was the best programme I ever undertook (sic)." "I had three weeks of fun learning and that's three weeks of primary I'll never forget."

Many post-primary schools conduct rather rigorous and rather limited whole class teaching. Will this cause a loss of self-esteem? Or, will the self-esteem remain so that the students can more readily enter into helpful working relationships. The problem as with so many of these techniques is to maintain the experience of them in such a way that the students continue to learn and develop through them. If this inquiry had been conducted in the United States there is the chance that students would come up against co-operative learning in higher education.

One problem with the study that has since been repeated with another group with roughly similar results is that it is difficult to determine if both control and experimental groups received the same treatment in planning. It is however difficult to concede that they did not since both were asked to learn the same things. By its very nature cooperative learning requires careful planning. Whenever the graduate student teachers whose work is described in these chapters had to undertake an experimental exercise they pointed out that preparation took a great deal of time. Too little attention is paid to this dimension of the teacher's work and too little time is allowed in the working day for such planning.

One of the criticisms of co-operative learning is that the principal investigations have failed to take into account the effect of individual differences on performance.[80] There is a need to find out how children respond to different instructional treatments and to see if some perform better in one situation as opposed to another. It is open to the teacher to find answers to these problems in his/her classroom. So long as particular children are not disadvantaged it is desirable that they are exposed to a range of learning strategies and they should certainly learn to collaborate. However, single exercises will be of little avail. Students have to return to such activities throughout their educational careers and curriculum planning should take this into account. Sometimes students experience much group work in primary school and little in post-primary only to come across it again in higher education. Curriculum planning needs to embrace all three sectors in the design of the learning sequences through which students should be taken in order that they should make the best use of them when they occur and it needs to be undertaken on a whole school basis.

Implications for curriculum and instructional leadership

Very often it is assumed that pupils can learn to study by osmosis. This cannot be true for how else would so many students have failed to achieve high grades, or why do we write on essays, "could do better." Time spent on helping pupils to learn basic study skills is likely to be time well spent. Provision for the development of study skills should be on a whole school basis. It is the function of the educational leader with the assistance of the instructional and curriculum leader(s) to ensure this goal is achieved.

Students welcome planned lessons with fair discipline that encourages learning from knowledgeable teachers. Beginning teachers are likely to need help with the implementation and planning of lessons. A mentor skilled in instructional and curriculum leadership should be able to give such help.

Group work like imagery can influence behaviour in classrooms for good or ill. Taken together with the discussion on advanced and other cognitive organizers it is clear that disciplined learning will take place when lessons are carefully constructed and implemented effectively. The idea that there should be variety in teaching is reinforced. There is no evidence in the studies that illustrated the comment that the student teachers could not overcome the fear of implementing strategies that for most of them were outside their plausibility. Indeed many of them found the experience of imagery rewarding.

Co-operative (collaborative and group) learning has been shown to promote values of mutual respect, self-discipline and social responsibility without detriment to cognition which it can also enhance.

When teachers especially beginning teachers are challenged to try a technique of instruction with which they are unfamiliar some may do so with fear and trepidation. Instructional and curriculum leaders should provide the support and encouragement that some teachers need to experiment with the new. Interpersonal skills in this respect are backed up by knowledge of research that has established what has worked and what has not worked.

Notes and references

[1] Gall, M. D., Gall, J. P., Jacobsen, D. R. and T. L. Bullock (1990). *Tools for learning. A Guide for Teaching Study Skills.* Association for Supervision and Curriculum Development, Alexandria, VA. Hobson, B and M. Scally (1981) *Lifeskills Teaching*. McGraw Hill, London. Elias, M. J et al (1997). *Promoting Social and Emotional Learning. Guidelines for Educators*. Association for Supervision and Curriculum Development. Alexandria, VA.
[2] See for example Heywood, J (1970) *Examining in Second Level Education*. ASTI, Dublin for details of Research on history projects.
[3] Saupe, J. L (1961). in P. Dressel (ed) *Evaluation in Higher Education*. Houghton Miflin, Boston. Bruner, J (1960) *The Process of Education*. Harvard U. P. Camb Ma
[4] Heywood, J (1961) Part-Time Courses in Further Education. *Nature*
[5] Summarised in Bellon, J. J., Bellon, E. C. and M. A. Blank (1992). *Teaching from a Research Knowledge Base. A Development and Renewal Process.*, Merrill (MacMillan), New York.
[6] Csikszentmihalyi, M and I. Csikszentmihalyi, (1988) (eds) *Experience: Psychological Studies of Flow in Consciousness.* Cambridge U. P., Cambridge. Nakamura, J (1988) in Csikszentmihalyi and I. Csiksentmihalyi
[7] Wynne, E. A. and K. Ryan (1993)*Reclaiming Our Schools. A Handbook on Teaching Character, Academics and Discipline*. Merrill/Prentice Hall, Englewood Cliffs, NJ
[8] McBeath, J (1996) The homework question. *Managing Schools Today*, 5, (7), 20 – 22.
[9] Boyle, T. (1997). *Discipline as a Learning Process*. MSt Thesis. University of Dublin, Dublin.
[10] *loc.cit* ref 5 pp 369 – 373.
[11] *ibid*. In this respect Bellon et al cite Jackson, L and W. Pruitt (1983-84). Homework assignments. Classroom games or teacher tools in D. Strother (ed). *Time and Learning*. Phi Delta Kappa, Bloomington, Il. Pp 211 - 215
[12] Gunter, M. A., Estes, T. H. and J. Schwab (1999). *Instruction. A models Approach*. 3rd edition. Allyn and

Bacon, Boston, MA. P 261.

[13] Robitaille, D. F. and K. J. Travers (1992) International studies of achievement in mathematics in D. A. Grouws (ed). *Handbook of Research on Mathematics Teaching and Learning.* Macmillan, New York

[14] Hamblin and Irvine (1982)

[15] Corno, L (1981) Cognitive Organizing in Classrooms. *Curriculum Inquiry*, 11, 359 – 377

[16] Ausubel, D. P (1960) The use of Advanced Organizers in the learning and retention of meaningful verbal material. *Journal of Educational Psychology*, 51, 267 – 272.

[17] Heywood, J (1982). *Pitfalls and Planning in Student Teaching.* Kogan Page, London.

[18] Ausubel, D. P. (1963). *The Psychology of Meaningful Learning.* Grune and Stratton, New York, and (1968) *Educational Psychology a Cognitive View.* Holt, Rinehart and Winston, New York.

[19] Shulman, L. S. (1970). Psychology and Mathematics in E. Begle (ed). *Mathematics Education.* NSSE 69th Yearbook. Chicago University Press, Chicago. He compares and contrasts Ausubel, Bruner and Gagné

[20] Orton, A (1992). *Learning Mathematics. Issues Theory and Practice* (2nd Edition). Cassell, London.

[21] Scandura, J. M. and J. M. Wells (1967) Advanced organizers in learning abstract mathematics. *American Educational Research Journal* 4, 295 - 301

[22] Cited by Orton *loc.cit*

[23] *ibid*

[24] Quoted by Heywood, J (1982) in *Pitfalls and Planning in Student Teaching.* Kogan Page, London

[25] Henry, J (1990) *Enriching Prior Knowledge.* Enhancing mature literacy in higher education. Journal of Higher Education 61, (4), 425-477.

[26] Quoted by Heywood, J (1982) in *Pitfalls and Planning in Student Teaching.* Kogan Page, London

[27] Hiebert, J and T. P. Carpenter (1992). Learning and teaching with Understanding. In D. Grouws (ed) *Handbook of Research on Mathematics Teaching and Learning.* Macmillan, New York.

[28] McDonald, F. J (1969). *Educational Psychology.* Wadsworth, Belmont, CA

[29] Prawat, R. S (1989). Teaching for understanding. Three key attribute. *Teaching and Teacher Education,* 5, 315 – 328.

[30] Gage, N. L. and D. C. Berliner (1988) *Educational Psychology.* 4th edition. Houghton Mifflin, Boston.

[31] Joyce, B and M. Weil (1986). *Models of Teaching.* Prentice Hall, Englewood Cliffs, NJ.

[32] Carter, G., Heywood, J., and D. T. Kelly (1986). *A Case Study in Curriculum Assessment. GCE Engineering Science Advanced.* Roundthorn, Manchester.

[33] Brown, A. L., Campione, J. C and J. C. Day (1981). Learning to learn. On training students to learn from texts. *Educational Researcher*, 10, (2), 14 –21.

[34] Chi. M (1986). Can little children think big? *ASCD Update* 28, (2), 2 – 3.

[35] Chi, M and R. D. Koeske (1983). Network representation of child's dinosaur knowledge. *Developmental Psychology.* 19, 29 – 39.

[36] Corno, L (1986). Self regulated learning and classroom teaching. Paper at annual meeting of the American Educational research Association cited by Bellon et al (1992) *loc cit*.

[37] Saupe, J. L (1961) Learning. In P. Dressell (ed). *Evaluation in Higher Education.* Houghton Mifflin, Boston, MA.

[38] Garner, B. K (2008). When students seem stalled. *Educational Leadership*, 65, (6), 32 – 38.

[39] Piaget, J (1951). *The Psychology of Intelligence.* Basic Books, New York. Feuerstein, R (1980) *Instrumental Enrichment: An Intervention Program for Cognitive Modifiability.* Scott Foreman, Glenview. Il.

[40] Egan, K and G. Judson (2008). Of whales and wonder. *Educational Leadership.* 65, (6), 20 – 25.

[41] Galyean, B. C (1982). Guided imagery in the curriculum. *Educational Leadership*, 40, (6), 54 –58. Hall, E. C., Hall, and A. Leech (1990). *Scripted Fantasy in the Classroom.* Routledge, London.

[42] Curwin, R. L. and A.N. Mendler (1988). *Discipline with Dignity.* Association for Supervision and Curriculum Development, Alexandria, VA

[43] Heywood, J (1996) Theory into practice through replication of research in student-teaching practice: a partial evaluation of a course, Association of Teacher Educators Conference, St Louis *in Resources in Education (RIE) (ERIC)* ED 394 926/SP 036 607.

[44] *loc. cit*

[45] Hart, L (1975). *How the Brain Works.* Basic Books, New York. since these activities were undertaken much work has been done on brain based learning. See for example Wolfe, P (2001). *Brain Matters. Translating Research into Classroom Practice.* Association for Supervision and Curriculum Development, Alexandria, VA.

[46] Walsh, R. N. and F. Vaughan (1980). *Beyond Ego.* Tarcher, Los Angeles.

[47] *loc.cit*

[48] Carter, G and J. Heywood (1991). The value-added performance of electrical engineering students in a British University. *International Journal of Technology and Design Education* 2, (1), 4 –15.
[49] MacFarlane Smith, I (1964). *Spatial Ability*, University of London Press, London.
[50] Aylwin S (1988) Imagery and affect. Big questions, little answers in P. J. Hampson, D. F. Marks and J. T. E. Richardson (eds). *Imagery. Current Developments*. Routledge, London.
[51] Skemp, R. R. (1979). *Intelligence, Learning and Action*. Wiley, Chichester (see also 1971: *The Psychology of Learning Mathematics*. Penguin, Harmondsworth)
[52] Oakes, J (1985). *Keeping Tracks. How Schools Structure Inequality*. Yale University Press, Newhaven, CT.
[53] Slavin, R. E. (1987) *Cooperative Learning Student Teams*. 2nd Edition. National Education Association, Washington, DC
[54] Johnson, D. W. Johnson, R. W. and E. J. Holubec (1983) *Circles of learning. Cooperation in the Classroom*. Association of Supervision and Curriculum Development, Alexandria, VA
[55] *ibid*
[56] *loc.cit*
[57] Kagan, S (1994) *Cooperative Learning*. Kagan Cooperative Learning, California.
[58] Kirk, T (1997). The Effectiveness of Cooperative Learning in Primary Classes in Ireland. Doctoral Thesis, University of Dublin, Dublin.
[59] HMI (1978) *Mixed Ability Work in Comprehensive Schools*, Department of Education and Science, HMSO, London
[60] Willis, S (1990) Cooperative learning fall out. *ASCD Update* 6, 8.
[61] Matthews, M (1992) Gifted students talk about cooperative learning. *Educational Leadership*, 50, (2), 48 – 50.
[62] Kulik, J and C, Kulik (1987) Effects of ability grouping on student achievement. *Equity and Excellence* 23, (1-2) 22 – 30.
[63] Beckman, M (1990) Coolaborative learning for the workplace and democracy. *College Teaching* 28, (4), 128 – 132.
[64] See ch 2 of Heywood, J (2005). *Engineering Education. Research and Development in Curriculum and Instruction*. IEEE/Wiley, New York and Smith, K. A (2004) *Teamwork and Project Management* 2nd edition. McGraw Hill, New York.
[65] Springer, L., Stanne, M. E. and S. S. Donovan (1999) Effects of small group learning on undergraduates in science, mathematics, engineering technology: a meta analysis. *Review of Educational Research*, 69, 21 – 51. In the liberal arts Astin, A. W (1967) *What Matters in College. Four Critical Years Revisited*. Jossey Bass, San Fransisco
[66] *loc. cit*
[67] *loc.cit* Kirk
[68] *ibid*
[69] . Elliott, J and C. Adelman (1976) *Innovation at the Classroom Level. A Case Study of the Ford Teaching Project. Course* CE203. Open University, Milton Keynes.
[70] Young, D (1983). *Parallel Spelling Tests*. Hodder and Stoughton, London.
[71] Miller, T. C. G. (1993). Effects of cooperative with challenge education on social skill development and self concept. Doctoral thesis. Bell State University cited by Kirk.
[72] Dishon, D and D. W. Leary (1994*). A Guide for Cooperative Learning. A Technique for Creating More Effective Schools*. 2nd ed. Learning Publications Inc. FL.
[73] Rosenberg, M (1989) Citation. Classic determinants of self-esteem. *Current Contents –Social and Behavioural Sciences* 21, (11), 16. Cited by Kirk.
[74] loc.cit
[75] *loc.cit*.
[76] Goleman, D. (1994). *Emotional Intelligence. Why it can matter more than IQ*. Bantam Books, New York
[77] *loc.cit*. Kagan
[78] following Johnson, D. W. and R. W. Johnson (1991) Conflict in the classroom. Contoversey and learning. *Review of Educational Research* 49, 51 - 70. Also Johnson, D. W. and R. W. Johnson (1989*) Cooperative Learning Lesson Structures*. Interaction Book Co. Minneapolis, Minnesota
[79] Murray, M (1992). *An Evaluation of an Introductory Programme in Management Studies for Schools*. Doctoral thesis. University of Dublin, Dublin
[80] Dunn, R., Dunn, K., and J. Perrin (1994) *Teaching Young Children through their Individual Learning Styles. Practical Approches for Grade 2*. Allyn and Bacon, Boston. MA.

5
Planning, Implementation, and Evaluation of Lessons

Summary

All the evidence shows that students respond to teachers who are both well ordered and competent. This chapter continues the discussion begun in chapter 4 but is more generally concerned with the planning, implementation and evaluation of lessons. It continues with the primary philosophy that each teacher should be a researcher of her/his own instruction and instructional behaviour. Teaching is a process of inquiry and teachers who accept this view lead themselves and are as such instructional leaders. Much of this chapter is an expansion of the discussion begun in chapter 2. The model of the curriculum, assessment, teaching, learning process on which it is based is presented. This model integrates assessment into that process. The objectives of assessment and instruction are the same. Instructional/learning techniques and the materials they require are the means of achieving those objectives. A lesson plan or series of lesson plans, therefore, comprise a statement of objectives, a description of the instructional techniques for obtaining those objectives, and a test designed to ascertain that the objectives have been obtained some time later after the lesson or lessons. These points are illustrated by the work of graduate student teachers who investigated the merits of certain techniques of instruction. But for initial training to shape what student teachers subsequently do requires a commitment by the school community to inquiry. Instructional leaders have a major role to play in the mentoring of beginning teachers and the support of experienced teachers in the maintenance of the spirit of inquiry.

Various methods of testing are discussed but the focus is on objective tests and essays. It is acknowledged that there are many possibilities. Issues of validity and reliability and their importance in classroom testing are considered. The chapter ends with some comments on the descriptive statistics that can be used for classroom measurement. Instructional leaders should be fluent in the use of descriptive statistics and their interpretation.

A model of the curriculum-assessment-teaching-learning process

Figures 5.1 and 5.2 show alternative views of the curriculum learning process. They are in effect identical. They are presented here because some persons prefer the schematic presentation of figure 5.1 to the circular presentation of exhibit 5.1.[1] Figure 5.1 is derived from an American model of the curriculum. It did not include assessment but that is necessary in educational systems that are dominated by public examinations such as those in Britain and Ireland. Both are derivations of Tyler's model of the curriculum that begins with a statement of objectives.[2] Figure 5.2 was drawn in that form to indicate the complexity of the system of learning and teaching whether it be a single lesson or a whole or part of a curriculum. The same model applies in all three cases. The chief differences between planning for lessons and planning for a curriculum lie in the aims and objectives and the procedures for their determination. There will also be differences in the scale of assessment and evaluation. The curriculum will be considered in chapter 10 and the chapters that follow. This chapter is concerned with the planning of a lesson or series of lessons within a curriculum.

The discussion of advanced organizers in chapter 4 showed quite clearly the dependence of a lesson's success on the prior knowledge of the students. This is part of the baggage that the pupils bring with them to the lesson. They also bring their own ways of learning to the class as well as their personalities. The diagrams bring all these things together under the heading of "entering characteristics". At the very least the teacher should know what the prior knowledge of the pupils is. The question is whether or not the teacher should know something more about the learning potential of the students other than their prior knowledge, as for example their possession of the cognitive structures briefly discussed in chapter 4. In addition in chapter 8 it will be argued that it is of value for the teacher not only to know her/his learning style but for her/him to know the learning styles of her/his pupils. In any case the lesson plan and objectives will have to take into account the prior knowledge and cognitive development of the pupils.

Questions for the design of lessons and curriculum and the role of the teacher

A lesson planner or a curriculum designer will want to answer the following questions:

1. What change will there be in a pupil's performance at the end of the lesson (s) or course?
2. How will the pupil apply the knowledge from this lesson (s) or course?
3. What major insight will develop in the pupil as a result of this lesson(s) or course?
4. What do the pupils need to know?
5. What do the pupils need to do?

6. What do the pupils need to think?
7. What attitudes should pupils have?[3]

From these the implications for the role of the teacher should be clear. It is to

1. Determine the aims and objectives which the curriculum, course or lesson should seek to obtain.
2. Select the learning experiences that will help to bring about the attainment of these aims and objectives.
3. Organize those learning experiences so as to provide continuity and sequence for the pupil and to help the pupil integrate what might otherwise appear as isolated experiences.
4. Evaluate the extent to which these aims and objectives are being attained.[4]

Preparing lessons

Traditionally student teachers have been asked to prepare lesson plans. These more often than not comprised a statement of sequenced content that would be transmitted in a lesson. Very often they engendered a transmission of learning model in which the pupil was a passive recipient of information. Moreover they were often returned to the tutor without having been implemented. Thus an opportunity to better relate theory to practice was lost. It is a challenge for some teachers to go beyond the "transmission model" of learning yet that is what the model described above demands. The premise on which it stands is that for each objective that is to be obtained, there will be an appropriate teaching and learning strategy. In the same way there will be an appropriate technique of assessment. Objectives are not declarations of content but declarations of the cognitive skill levels that the content is intended to develop. They may of course be about the development of skills in the affective domain as might be appropriate in a course concerned with the development of social skills. Or they may be about the development of skills in the psychomotor domain, as for example in physical education or craft-work of some kind or another.

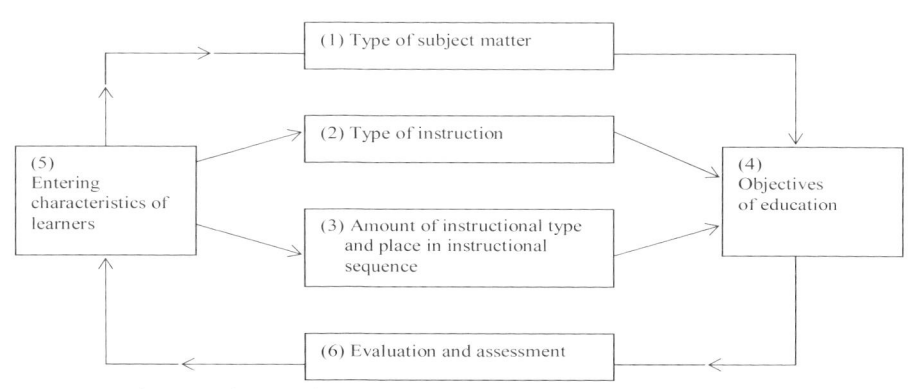

Figure 5.1 Theoretical generalisation about the nature of instruction. Shulman's (1970)[5] generalization of Cronbach's view of the nature of instruction. Block 6 has been added by this writer

INSTRUCTIONAL AND CURRICULUM LEADERSHIP

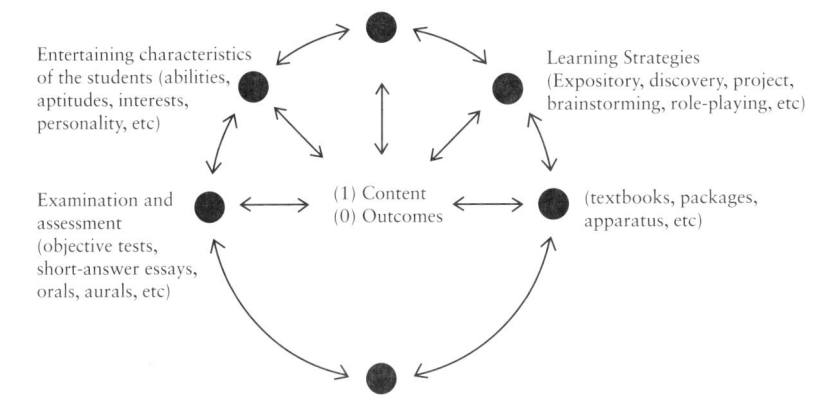

Figure 5.2. A development of figure 1.3 to show the dynamic nature of the process. A model of the assessment-curriculum-learning-teaching process (1) the first phase in which the structure of the syllabus content is derived and (2) how the intended learning outcomes are a function of a complex interaction between all the parameters and allowing that there will also be unintended outcomes. The original model in Enterprise Learning and Its Assessment in Higher Education (Technical Report No. 20, Employment Department, Sheffield) referred only to the design of the syllabus while indicating that evaluation took care of the dynamic nature of the model. Professor Georgine Loacker of Alverno College suggested that this dynamism would be better expressed if the model also recorded the outcomes of the on going activity in the centre

Sometimes it is impossible to separate the cognitive from the affective or for that matter from the psychomotor. In any case the purpose of expressing an objective to is to provide a measurable focus to a lesson or to a series of lessons. Such objectives are sometimes called "behavioural objectives" or "learning outcomes". This model presupposes a different approach to lesson planning and a schematic that illustrates the model in practice is shown in exhibit 5.1,[6] in addition to a column for the objectives there are columns for the phases of the lesson content and learning-strategies. In an actual lesson plan these would be aligned. The lesson phases do not have to follow those suggested; there are other models. The intent of the content column is that it should only emphasise the concepts and principles to be understood for it is the understanding of these that is the key requirement in building scaffolds, solving problems and critical thinking. They have equal standing with objectives. The strategies are those most appropriate for the task in hand, that is, the objectives to be achieved. An earlier version of this schema included a statement of the ability range but as the argument in chapter 8 will show a more detailed entry relating to the entering characteristics of each student is to be preferred.

In these days when the portfolio is regarded as a useful means of teacher

Knowledge, learning Skills, Values (expressed appropriately for the level i.e. mission statement - goals, course aims and objectives, intended and expressive outcomes, key concepts and principles)

Learning Strategies

Exploration, discovery, project, brainstorming, role playing etc)

(textbooks, packages, apparatus etc)

(i) Content
(o) Outcomes

Entering characteristics of the students (abilities, aptitudes, interests, personality etc)

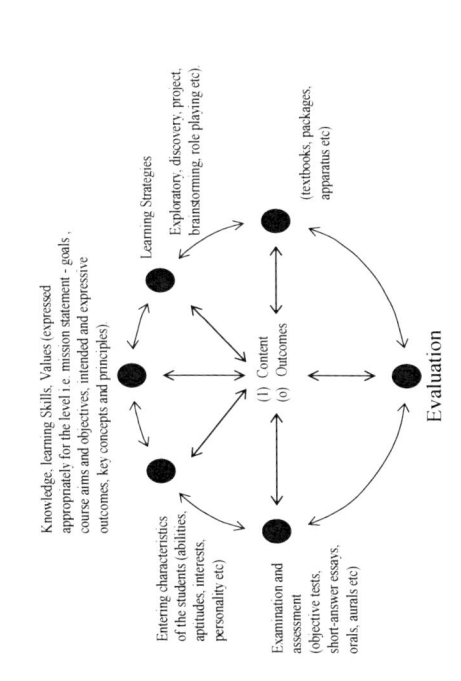

Examination and assessment (objective tests, short-answer essays, orals, aurals etc)

Evaluation

Corrected Version of Figure 5.2

appraisal the lesson plans might be part of a portfolio that includes the entering characteristics of the class. It is also useful to plan some questions for the class. Even if they are not used they might form the basis of a test to be administered sometime after the lesson. They may have to be changed if the lesson goes skew which is a reminder that a major role of the teacher is to decide when to allow a lesson to go skew. These plans should not be interpreted rigidly. Teachers have to assume that things may go wrong during a lesson and sometimes for the better. It is important however that the teacher evaluates why things went wrong. The plan makes no provision for the reflections required of the student teachers undertaking the research studies described in chapter 2 and to be illustrated in the chapters that follow. Neither is it the intention that every lesson should be a research study of that kind, but reflection is, as was argued in chapter 2, a necessary activity of all professional teaching. Examples of lesson plans are shown in exhibit 5.2 and 5.3. It is not intended that such plans should be developed for every lesson but that beginning teachers should use them to develop a portfolio that ensures the key areas are covered, and through their use develop a spirit of inquiry. Other plans will be shown in later chapters. Preparing lesson plans of this kind is a considerable challenge and there is little doubt that graduate student teachers benefit from such exercises. However, there is no evidence that the ideas acquired will be carried out in practice for beginning teachers soon adapt

Aim	Lesson phases	Content	Learning strategies	Questions
Non-behavioural objective	Introduction	Facts	e.g	e.g.
	Presentation		Large group Small group Individualised	questioning in class
Behavioural objectives.	Application	Concepts	Discovery Guided Discovery Expository	Questions for test
		Principles	Role Playing Case study Project work Laboratory work	
(problem to be solved)	Conclusion	(problem to be solved)		

Exhibit 5.1 A Scheme for a lesson plan

to the culture of the staff room and school in which they find themselves. At the same time experienced teachers on professional development courses have found the conduct of the same experiments beneficial. For whatever reason they were not aware of the instructional theories or strategies they support. In Ireland the post-primary education system is dominated by examinations and many teachers believe that a good memory will get the students through these examinations, and this some believe merits a degree of rote learning and chalk and talk.

But as was argued in the previous chapter such an approach while immediately helpful has no long-term benefits. However, it is seems clear as the chapters that follow will demonstrate that it is possible to approach teaching in such a system using a variety of techniques. For these to be successful the institution needs a whole school policy and the educational leader will require the support of its instructional leader(s) to develop that policy. But public systems of examination of this kind have an obligation to design examinations that test for higher order thinking skills as well as basic knowledge.

The remainder of this chapter will be devoted to problems related to the derivation of objectives and their assessment (testing). It should be noted that the term "objective" is one of those terms that many teachers and policy makers have been unwilling to adopt. They prefer "outcome." In this text "outcomes" and "objectives" have the same meaning.

Stating objectives (outcomes)

In the mini-research projects that my student teachers had to undertake they were asked to follow a formula recommended by Cohen and Mannion.[7] They had suggested that each lesson plan should begin with a statement of aim(s), non-behavioural objective(s), and behavioural objectives. They represent different levels of focusing on a problem area or topic. Similarly each level is of increasing specificity. We can distinguish between behavioural and non-behavioural by the instructional verb used at the beginning of the statement. A behavioural objective is always an action statement about what a pupil should be able to do. In contrast, terms like know, understand, appreciate are non-behavioural. Most of us feel it necessary to use such terms. We know what they mean even if they are not measurable as such. But we don't know whether we teach them and that is the problem. Twenty five years on Cohen and Mannion (now with Morrison)[8] in the latest edition of their book still use the same formula although they have dropped the aim. This is consistent with the experience of my students.[9] Sometimes it was very difficult to tell the difference between the aim and the non-behavioural objective but statements of aims can be useful in planning as the illustration in exhibit 5.4 demonstrates. The skills mentioned by this student teacher come from *The Taxonomy* described below.[10] They can also be useful in planning work for a year as the example in exhibit 5.5 shows. It is easy to imagine this student's lessons structured by behavioural objectives. Cohen, Mannion and Morrison retain aims for schools and curriculum moreover they have substantially extended the sections on planning. Examples of aims, non-behavioural and behavioural objectives are given in exhibit 5.6.

The idea from which behavioural objectives originate came from the publication in the British Isles in 1964 of *The Taxonomy of Educational Objectives in the CognitiveDomain*. The many authors of this work attempted to state a universal set of learning outcomes that would apply in most circumstances. They were ordered hierarchically. Each category was divided into a number of sub-categories. The authors showed test questions on the subjects of the curriculum for each of the abilities. The Taxonomy has been popular with some teachers, and also controversial. It will be considered in more detail in chapter 10. For the moment it is of interest to list the action verbs that go with each category. These are shown in exhibit 5.7. The skills of analysis, synthesis and evaluation (judgement) are some times called higher order thinking skills (HOTS) and the relation between them and problem solving and critical thinking should be apparent. These are the skills on which the ability to learn for one's self in unfamiliar circumstances (transfer of learning) depend.

Lesson Phases	Content	Learning Strategies
Introduction Students to name noticeable features of poetry-rhyme. Introduce assonance as another form of rhyme. Tell students what they will be able to do at the end of the class.	Concept of assonance	
Presentation Ask if they know what assonance might be. Write the definition on the board. Verbally say "How now Brown Cow" which they will be familiar with from the elocution class. Ask them to note the sound. What sound is being repeated? Which vowel sound is it? Describe the main features of assonance-which the students will write down. This will be followed by the illustration of the concept via the simultaneous presentation of positive and /or non-examples.	Positive examples taken from Ode on a Graecian Urn- John Keats Fight – Barrie Wade Personal Helicon- Seamus Heaney The Blackbird of Derrycairn- Austin Clarke. Non-examples taken from Hymn – Eavan Boland The Swan- Richard Bell The Wild Swans at Coole- W. B. Yeats	Encourage students to say the examples out loud- this is important as the same vowels in a line of poetry need not necessarily sound the same. Thus the verbalising of written examples is a key strategy in this lesson. Identification strategy -Assonance uses vowel sounds that usually number three or more. These vowel sounds occur quite close to each other. It is used in poetry to create effect.
Application. Demonstrate examples on the board using different colour markers to highlight relevant vowel sounds. Invite comments and observations after all examples have been shown.		
Conclusion To check understanding students will be asked to invent their own examples of assonance. The identifying marks on the board will be rubbed out and individual students will be asked to re-mark the assonance. Conclude with a brief review of the lesson.		

Exhibit 5.2 Slightly adapted from a lesson plan by a graduate student-teacher for 12 – 13 year-old students in English. The aims and objectives are shown in Exhibit 5.5.

Finally, stating behavioural objectives (outcomes) should help teachers plan their lessons when at the same time they take into account the learning capabilities of their students. Many student-teachers and for that matter teachers often feel the need to rush through content to meet the official requirements of the curriculum. This leads some of them to state many objectives rather than to concentrate on a few that will lead to meaningful learning. We will return to this issue in the chapters that follow.

Lesson phases	Content	Learning Strategies
Introduction	Explain to students about there being four types of learning and that today's class is investigating this theory	
Phase one: Concrete experience	Guided imagery exercise. Students take part in this exercise centred on the area of shape with irregular boundaries.	Students participate individually. Speaking to entire class.
Phase two: Reflective observation	1. Students asked to write down the shapes they saw etc as a result of the imagery exercise 1. Discuss what each person experienced 2. Discuss in same groups why they think, in everyday life, it would be necessary to know the area of such shapes and where it would be useful Each group presents their opinions which are all written down onto the OHP	In groups of 2/3 (During this time circulate and listen to the group discussions)
Phase three: Abstract conceptualisation	1. Draw shape with irregular boundary on the board. 2. Divide into strips of equal width and assign y etc to lengths. 3. Give formula for Simpson's rule. 4. Explain basis for this formula 5. Give easy method for remembering the formula. 6. Sample problems solved on the board and then by individuals.	Students work individually and are given time to ask questions. (circulate and deal with problems)
Phase four: Active experimentation	1. Students are asked to recall what they pictured in the imagery exercise (and later drew). They are each given a piece of cardboard and asked to make the shape. 2. Students have then to first predict its area by calculating the area of the shape it most resembles (if circular use πr^2) 3. Then divide into strips and apply Simpson's rule 4. Compare actual result with estimate. 5. Ensure all using the correct units.	Students work individually
Conclusion	1. reinforcement of lesson using questions to test behavioural objectives. 1. Collect written descriptions and cardboard shapes.	Questioning.

Exhibit 5.3. A lesson plan (slightly adapted) by a Graduate Student Teacher in Mathematics for the Transition Year (15 – 16 year olds). The aims and objectives are shown in exhibit 5. 5(b). the lesson used imagery and was designed to get students to assess the value of learning styles (see chapter 8)

Questioning in Classrooms.

Assessment depends on the ability to ask questions that will produce valid answers. Not every question achieves this aim. Most of us have asked and are aware that we have asked bad questions. This often happens when we are put on the spot. It is an everyday hazard for teachers. Bad questions are generally characterized by ambiguity, or vagueness, or multiple purposes, or are set at a level that is beyond the level at which the student is. If one is not sure why one is asking a question difficulties may arise.[11] Good questions are set in simple clear language. For these reasons students have to be asked if they have understood the question.

Every question asked in a classroom is a form of assessment. It is, therefore, no wonder that a great deal of research has been done on questioning the results of which have become embedded in the literature on teaching. Several general findings may be drawn from this research.[12]

I take from my own experience the example of teaching a fifth year class of 16 year-old girls for English. The text used was George Orwell's 1984. I set the general aim of "Reading the book critically". Achievement of this objective involved planning a learning strategy towards helping the girls develop and use the skills necessary to read critically; evaluation by questioning and homework exercises provided feedback to me and to the pupils to enable us to modify our techniques as necessary.

Simple understanding of the narrative and plot involved the skill of comprehension. This was easily checked by questioning. Picking out the significant elements in the story and connecting them to make a coherent pattern involved using analytic and synthesizing skills. Thus, the overall pattern of the totalitarian society was identified by bringing together the threads of Thought Police, Newspeak, Doublethink etc. Extrapolation of the events and scenes in the book to contemporary times led on to the process of evaluation. The girls were required to consider not just whether the story was convincing but the role of propaganda and whether in fact the book itself was a piece of propaganda.

Towards the achievement of this general aim, the learning strategy concentrated on directing the students' minds to the text itself for evidence to support any assertion they might make. The questioning in class moved from the lower order "what" and "where" questions to the higher order ones of "why". Emphasis was placed on pupil-pupil interaction with me as catalyst. This was done through getting a different student to produce a short essay for each class period, and having the class discuss it. The content of the essay was determined by me and thus I exercised control over the learning experience for that period.

Exhibit 5.4 From a Graduate Student Teacher's report on a series of lesson on a topic in English.[13]

> A general objective for the year may be planned and presented to the class eg "This year we shall be studying every day life in France. We shall be discovering how and where the French live, how they go shopping, how they go to work and what type of work they do, what they do at weekends and during the holidays etc"
>
> This single objective covers a vast range of material: vocabulary, dealing with houses, flats, shops and shopping, travel, work, sports, leisure, hobbies; grammar- presenting new verbs, syntax, adjectives. The objective is clear: after stating the objective, the teacher should add what the class will achieve by the end of the year/term: so, at the end of this year/term you will be able to describe where you live in French, what you do at the weekends and during the holidays, what hobbies you have. You will know a lot more about French life and, if you go to France, you will be able to talk about your home, your interests, you will be able to go shopping and order food in a café or restaurant.

Exhibit 5.5. Illustrating the use of a general aim (objective) in the planning of a course. From a Graduate Student Teacher's assignment. [14]

Perhaps the most important of these relates to the intensity of usage and type of question asked. Classroom observations suggest that up to 80% of classroom time can be used for questioning. During this time the majority of questions when classified against *The Taxonomy of Educational Objectives* are found to belong to the lower order classifications of knowledge and comprehension. Such questions encourage recall and in so doing encourage memory skills at the expense of higher order thinking skills. There are several reasons why this might be so. Of these two may be singled out.

First, it may be due to a lack of training and lack of preparation. It may be that teachers think that it is easy to ask questions and do not, therefore, consider it necessary to work out the questions they intend to ask beforehand. This is not to argue that a class should be governed by those questions. The teacher has to decide what routes to follow as a function of class progress.

> **Aims and objectives for a class of 13 – 13 year olds in English**
>
> Aim
> -To enable students to note and identify assonance as a literary function in poetry.
>
> Non-behavioural objectives
> - To assist students' awareness and understanding of the concept of "assonance"
> - To facilitate their understanding by defining the concept and making them aware of the main features (dominant attributes and values) of assonance.
> - To assist their appreciation of the literary effects of assonance in poetry.
>
> Terminal objectives of the subject component of the lesson
> By the end of the lesson the students will be able to:
> - Define the concept of assonance.
> - Name the main features (dominant attributes) of assonance
> - Identify examples of assonance in poetry with reasons for identification.

Exhibit 5. 6(a). An example of aim, non-behavioural and behavioural (terminal) objectives for the lesson plan shown in exhibit 5.2

PLANNING, IMPLEMENTATION AND EVALUATION OF LESSONS

Aims and objectives for a Transition Year Class in Mathematics
Aims 1. To extend the students understanding of area. 2. To introduce four different learning and hence, teaching styles. Non-behavioural objectives 1. To introduce the concept of Simpson's rule. 2. To illustrate the use of guided imagery in mathematics. Behavioural objectives. By the end of the lesson the students should be able to 1. Describe in own words what is meant by area. 2. State the purpose of Simpson' rule. 3. Give examples where Simpson's rule can be applied. 4. Apply Simpson's rule mathematically.

Exhibit 5.6 (b) Example of aims, non-behavioural and behavioural objectives in mathematics for the lesson plan shown in exhibit 5.3

Taxonomy Category	Command words and question type.
Knowledge	Arrange, define, describe, match, order, memorize, name, note, order, repeat. Who? What? When Where? Questions
Comprehension.	Alter, change, classify define in your own words, discuss, explain, extend. Give examples, translate.
Application	Apply, calculate, compute, construct, operate, practice. How many? Which? Write an example question.
Analysis.	Analyse, appraise, categorize, compare, conclude, contrast, criticize, diagnose, differentiate etc. Why? Questions.
Synthesis	Assemble, compile, compose, create, improve synthesize. What if ? How can we improve? What would happen if? How can we solve? Questions.
Evaluate	Appraise, argue, choose, certify, criticize, decide, deduce, defend, discriminate, estimate, evaluate, recommend etc.

Exhihibit 5.7. The categroires of the *Taxonomy of Educational Objectives* showing command words that begin statements. (After Batanov, Dimmitt and Chookittikul (2000)[15]

Second, it may be due to classroom culture. There is always a pressure to get on with teaching (perceived as talking) so the teacher may ask short questions that demand brief answers. Questions that seek recall may well answer that need. Teachers very often do not wait for students to answer questions. One consequence of this is that teachers may tend to select those students who readily answer questions at the expense of those who do not. This has implications for classroom relationships as between peers and students and their teachers. Somehow teachers have to help the less able for it is these students that are so often disadvantaged by the techniques of questioning.

Both students and teachers benefit when the wait time between questions and even repeated questions is relatively long. Rowe[16] argued that the space between questions and answers should be at least three seconds and when they want a thinking response at least fifteen seconds should be allowed. This is an "enormous" period relative to the rate at which teachers conduct their classes. Neither pupils nor teachers are used to such lengths of silence.

When time allows questions can be designed which lead to longer responses that may contain argument based on evidence. Students may also be encouraged to speculate. If students become used to this kind of questioning they may also become more confident in their answers. Longer answers may be asked to help teachers learn about the effectiveness of their teaching. We may be surprised to find that student understanding is somewhat different to that which we expected.

Teachers have to learn ways of asking higher order questions. One way of doing this is for them to be aware of the way interrogatives may be used. For example a question which begins with "What if......" is likely to lead to a higher order response than one which begins with "What was......" Similarly "Explain" or "How" questions are likely to lead to higher order thinking provided what is asked is not something that can be easily recalled (see exhibit 5.6).

In the development of higher order thinking skills it is for the teacher to be clear about what answers they are prepared to accept. If the questions are relatively open then hopefully there will be a diversity of answers that may lead to discussion. One of the reasons for declaring objectives in the lesson plan is that they should lead to good questions, that is, items that have validity. Those questions should be reflected in subsequent tests on that area of knowledge and skill.

Taba who proposed the idea of key concepts (see chapter 6) also proposed questioning strategies to help students form concepts.[17] It is a hierarchical approach and Ornstein[18] says that it may take several lessons to complete the strategy. When linked to key concepts (as objectives) it could also provide a strategy for the design of a sequence of lessons. The strategy follows this sequence

A Concept Formation	(i)	Enumerate and List.
	(ii)	Group together.
	(iii)	Label Categories.
B Generalizing and Inferring	(i)	Identify points (or information).
	(ii)	Explain items of information that have been identified.
	(iii)	Make generalizations and inferences.
C Application of Principles	(i)	Produce consequences, explain familiar phenomena, hypothesis.
	(ii)	Explain and support predictions and hypotheses.
	(iii)	Verify predictions and hypotheses.

The reader may like to relate this to De Cecco and Crawford's seven-point plan for teaching concepts described in Chapter 6. Taba considered that quite a long time is required to understand concepts and their applications.

Questions may be used to help good behaviour in the classroom by gaining attention, controlling behaviour, maintaining and encouraging participation and motivation. They may help to elicit whether students understand what is being taught may lead students to new thinking. The principles of classroom questioning are no different to those applied to the design of formal tests.

Finally, although questioning is a life skill seldom are students explicitly taught to ask questions. There is no evidence, it would be surprising if there were, that there is a correlation between the ability to answer questions and the ability to ask questions. They are different skills. All testing is about questioning. Whenever we set ourselves, or someone else a question we are in fact testing ourselves or that person and that is particularly true of teacher questioning in the classroom. Setting questions in whatever context is a high level skill.

Classroom tests and testing

There are, as was shown in chapter 2, many techniques for classroom assessment. Much has been written about formative assessment (evaluation). This section is only concerned with the use of objective tests, short answer questions and essays when used in a norm-referenced as opposed to mastery or criterion referenced situation. Mastery or criterion-referenced tests indicate whether or not a person can perform a task. The criteria against which tests are judged are their reliability and validity.

Reliability (especially of essay and objective tests) [19]

Most of us have taken tests at some time or another. We would assume that two markers assessing our essay or other answers would give the same mark. Unfortunately that has not been found to be the case. There can be a considerable discrepancy between the two marks. When this result is obtained the test is said to have low reliability. Similarly, if we repeated the test after a month and gave exactly the same answers we would expect to get the same mark. Not so, there might be a discrepancy. This has been established by asking markers to remark test papers after some time has elapsed. Reliability is expressed as a co-efficient of correlation.

It is findings such as these that are the root of the objections to essay examinations in particular, since they can have quite low reliabilities. In contrast, an objective test in which each question (item) has one right answer should in theory have a reliability of 1. This is because in theory there is no room for error since no judgments have to be made. In practice the best designed standardised[20] objective tests by organizations such as the Educational Testing Service and the American College Testing Program only approximate to 1 with correlations around 0.9. For most of us this performance would be more than satisfactory. One would not expect teacher designed tests to produce high reliabilities but this is not to argue that they should not be used in classroom situations; on the contrary.

When questions are set which require equal weighting (e.g. one mark for each answer correct in multiple choice questions, or say 20 marks for a 40 minute essay answer) we expect the test to be internally consistent. We expect each answer to be marked in exactly the same way. One simple way of assessing the internal consistency of a test is to divide it in half and see if the results produce a high correlation between the two halves.

It is quite clearly the view of teachers in Britain and Ireland that some degree of unreliability is tolerable because of the valuable information that essay and problem solving answers provide over and above that which would have been provided from an objective test. Likewise there is a trade-off and this trade-off is also made with the assessment of coursework such as projects since it is considered that the information obtained is different to that which could have been got from a written examination. It should be noted that even in science, engineering and mathematics examinations of the problem solving kind a degree of unreliability has been found.

In America and Britain the drive toward authentic assessment and outcomes/performance-based measures has brought with it many changes in attitude toward reliability and validity.[21] Whereas in the past the concentration was on reliability there is now much more interest in the problem of validity. Nevertheless many teachers in America continue to use standardized tests and object to the essay tests because it is difficult if not impossible to standardize them.

Validity

Simply put validity is the measurement of whether a test achieves what it sets out to achieve. Unfortunately like all things connected with the assessment of human behaviour it is not as simple as it seems to create a valid test. In any case there are several types of validity. One that is important for selection procedures is the extent to which a test will predict future behaviour as for example at university or in graduate school (*predictive or criterion validity*). Classroom tests will want to predict performance in public examinations in the countries of the British Isles. Hence there is a premium on knowledge of content in each of the examinations for which candidates present themselves. In such examinations we need to know the extent to which an assessment does measure the content, aptitude, attitude, skill it is intended to measure, and at the same time predict results on other measures of content, aptitude, attitude and skill. This measure is called the *construct validity*.

There are two other types of validity that are of importance. These are

Face Validity : The extent to which an assessment appears to be measuring the variable it is intended to test (for example visual inspection of the items or questions in comparison with the declared objectives). Face validity is extremely unreliable as a measure. However, as outcomes and competency-based measures have developed it seems that in certain circumstances it may be reasonably reliable to use ones own judgement

Concurrent Validity: That is, the comparison of an assessment designed to evaluate performance in a task with an alternative evaluation (e.g. a test designed to predict bus driver performance compared with actual observations by a skilled judge).

Objective Tests.

Objective tests are comprised of items (questions) which have only one answer. They can be machine scored and may have high reliability and validity. The language of objective testing is not particularly well known on the European side of the Atlantic where they are commonly known as multiple choice questions. Four types commonly in use are shown in exhibit 5. 8. True/False tests are objective tests.

Macintosh[22] listed the strengths and weaknesses of objective tests as follows:

Objective tests - weaknesses

1. An Objective Test cannot test written expression or a candidate's ability to develop an argument.
2. An Objective Test can all too easily test only factual recall or simple understanding of fact.

3. An Objective Test may encourage candidates to guess the answers to questions.
4. An Objective Test is difficult and expensive to construct.

Objective tests - strengths

1. An Objective Test can pose a whole series of precise problems which can be clearly stated and quickly answered.
2. An Objective Test can provide a wide content of coverage. Moreover, because of the comparative precision of each item, the danger of overlap is reduced. The number of items also reduces the possibility of question spotting.
3. An Objective Test can be speedily and accurately marked.
4. An Objective Test can be tried out in advance (pre-tested) and on the basis of the evidence obtained, tests of differing levels of difficulty can be constructed.
5.

It is often objected that objective items only test good memory and at best only test the lower order thinking skills. But, it has been shown elsewhere that they can be used to test diagnosis, as for example in engineering and medicine. But this may not be achieved within the time constraints of a few seconds for which objective items are usually designed.[23] Not-with-standing the fact that objective items can test some higher order thinking skills it is clear they are no panacea. They cannot assess a person's ability for connected and informed discourse in their own language neither can they reveal the outstanding student who knows more than the teachers suspect. Nevertheless they do have the advantage of being able to give a fair coverage of the syllabus which a few essay questions cannot. One should not, as most critics do, undervalue the skill of recall since in diagnostic work (e.g. Medicine-Engineering) the ability to recall a large number of facts quickly is essential. Clearly objective tests can enhance this skill provided they are properly designed. Graduate student teachers who tried to write 10 item tests for use during their student teaching found them a valuable aid to their teaching. But they thought they should be used with other forms of testing. Some of their items are shown in exhibit 5. 9.

The other principal criticism of objective tests is that they encourage guessing. This may be countered in three ways. First, the better the question the more likely it is to inhibit guessing. Second an equivalent game of guessing is played in essay answers i.e. fudging - the ability to deceive examiners by the answer. Third, rather than argue that one can statistically correct for guessing it may be argued that those who guess (apart from not guessing correctly) may well represent a particular group of examinees in the population who resort to guessing in all sorts of situations as a whole. Some evidence supporting this view has been found in Ireland.[25] Whatever else may be said about them, they can be invaluable as classroom tests of immediately prior knowledge within a course even when relatively few items are used (e.g. 10). In formal examinations such a length would seriously reduce reliability.

One of the advantages of objective tests is that statistical analyses can lead to both the improvement and rejection of items. A good multiple choice question will be designed so that all the options appear equally likely to give the right answer. Some students will be drawn to each option but in a norm-referenced test only between 50% and 60% should get the correct option. If there are no responses to one option then it isn't working as a distractor and needs to be replaced. Although very sophisticated item analyses are undertaken for public examinations to determine the levels of discrimination between the options and the facility of the items (relative ease or difficulty) there are methods of item analysis that can be done by the classroom teacher.

---

1. **Multiple choice question.**
Stem. Which one of the following was the primary purpose for which the craft guilds were formed in the middle ages?
A. The regulation of production.   The **Key** (correct answer)
B. The distribution of goods.   First **distractor**
C. The control of town governments.   Second **distractor.**
D. The training of new workers.   Third **distractor.**

A, B, C and D are the **options.**

2. **Multiple completion question (more than one correct answer)**
Stem Which one of the following contributed to bringing about the rebellion in Ireland in 1916?
A.   Arthur Griffith's leadership of Sinn Fein.
B   The reorganization of the Irish Republican Brotherhood by Tom Clark.
C   The outbreak of the first World War.
D   The help sent from Germany.

(i)   A and B only
(ii)   A, B, C and D.
(iii)   B only.
(iv)   B and C only.

3. **Assertion-Reason Question**

Assertion. Ireland declined as a spoken language in the 19th Century. *Reason* because the Gaelic league was not founded until 1893.
A   If the assertion is true, the reason is true and the reason is a correct explanation of the assertion.
Or
B.   If the assertion is true and the reason is an incorrect explanation of the assertion.
Or
C   If the assertion is true and the reason is false.
Or
B.   If the assertion is false

4. **Classification Sets (matching pairs)**
Candidates are given two lists of items and asked to match an item in the first against an item in the second.

Statement Sets.
A series of items relating to a common situation.

5. **Multi-facet.**
Single question in which a group of objective responses are required as for example the completion of empty boxes in a matrix of data.

Exhibit 5.8. The Jargon and types of objective questions. The example questions are taken from teacher designed tests.[24]

For example, the simplest measure of discrimination is to divide the class into two groups (i.e. below and above average) and compare their performance on the options in each item. Another method separates the candidates into three groups according to their scores. The facility value (correct answers) is calculated for each group thus:

F1 = Facility of Above Average Group
F2 = Facility of Average Group
F3 = Facility of Below Average

The index of discrimination is given by F1 - F3 . Fraser and Gillam[26] suggest that this value should not fall below 0.3. They also say that F1 - F2 and F2 - F3 should not fall below 0.1. If the number of correct responses in the top 27% of the pupils is called H, and the number of correct responses in the bottom 27% of the pupils is called L then:

Discrimination = H – L / M

M is the number of candidates in each of the groups. (i.e. the number who make up 27%)

Many teachers use objective items as instructional aids. Although they are difficult to design students may learn much from having to construct tests for themselves.

They may also be used to help teachers understand the thought processes through which students go especially in the solution of mathematical problems. Mathematics teachers in Ireland objected to multiple choice questions on the grounds that students would be encouraged to work backwards from the answer. This would seem to me to be perfectly proper and to show some understanding of mathematics. Irrespective of the subject taught many teachers learn a lot about student learning if they ask students to explain how they arrive at the answer.

Short Answer Questions

It is sometimes said that short answer questions would be better set as multiple-choice questions. Maybe so, but there are short answers and short answers as practice in Britain and Ireland shows. For example sometimes the total problem is set in such a way that a series of short answers are generated. Sometimes there is a series of questions requiring two or three line answers. In England the term "short-answer" sometimes arises from the comparison which is made with the more traditional 30-40 minute essay required by some questions. Short answer questions should have greater reliability than essay questions, although this may not be true if a very simple grading system is used (e.g. A, B, and C). One investigation suggests that the greater reliability in marking short answers is achieved at the expense of examiners' time, and is reported to demand more concentration.[27] This was certainly the writer's experience in marking comprehension tests in Engineering Science at 'A' level. We did try to design multiple choice questions for this paper but found it exceptionally difficult.[28]

From the point of view of classroom tests the same strictures apply to their design as to questioning in the classroom. The designer needs to consider what skill is to be assessed.

Essays

Essays whether used for homework or in tests should be marked in the same way and students should be given helpful rather than trivial comments. The problem with impression marking is that it is unreliable. The problem stems in part from the fact that the *"grader is creating the essay in much the same way as the writer."* [29] If the two do not match the grader wins. It is for this reason that tightly prescribed rubrics have been used to solve this problem. But the problems with such schedules are that they can easily degenerate into a check-list and that check-list or not they are time consuming to mark. The advantage is that they can be used to help students write essays. They can help with grammar[30] on the one hand and on the other hand with the development of criticism.[31] Problems arise in different genre such as narrative and story writing where creativity and originality might be the key characteristics that are sought. In so far as criticism is concerned one alternative is to have a simplified scheme which concentrates on the characteristics that provide a quality essay. I have used both of the above and find the tightly structured rubric time consuming. The scheme I have favoured is to mark holistically and check the result against criteria stated for each mark band.

An alternative is to write model answers for good, average and failing essays. Model answers can show the student what counts and does not count for quality. For example Thompson and Rentz of the University of Georgia described four levels of skill in the assessment of English essays against which assessors marked large number of essays.[32] They wrote of the high quality essay that:-

"The '4' theme clearly and effectively states a thesis that relates directly to the assigned topic. The theme concentrates on this central idea and has a clear overall organizational plan. The theme should reveal the writer's ability to select effective, appropriate words and phrases, to careful use of effective transitional devices, and to maintain a consistent appropriate tone. The theme should also be free from mechanical errors".

Gronlund includes the following principles among a list of principles for marking essay examinations:[33]

> " -Use essay questions to measure complex learning outcomes only.
> -Relate the questions as directly as possible to the learning outcomes being measured.
> -Formulate questions which present a clear, definite task to the student.
> -Do not permit students choice of questions unless the learning outcome requires it.

-Provide ample time for answering and give suggested time limits for each question.
-Evaluate answers to essay questions in terms of the learning outcomes being measured.
-Evaluate all of the students answers to one question before proceeding to the next question"

Teachers should not be under the illusion that writing questions is a simple task. It is not as the previous discussion of questioning indicates.

Time for Designing and Marking Tests

If classroom testing is to be improved in line with the improvements advocated by the promoters of performance based testing it is clear that teachers will need more time for preparation and scoring. Moreover, if a number of different types of objectives are to be tested a variety of techniques will have to be used, and this will complicate the design.

Classroom Statistics

Simple classroom statistics are too easily dismissed on the basis that the samples are too small. This has not been found to be true of the case studies on which this book is based. Mean scores by themselves are not very helpful but they do focus on the notion of standard. In neo - norm referenced systems of grading the mean score may be of some guidance to teachers since mean scores of over, say about 65%, might be considered to be on the easy side and therefore not very discriminatory. There is a tendency for critics of teaching to take this point of view rather than admit that the results might be due to effective teaching. As indicated previously, there is some evidence that in public examining systems teachers are more generous markers than moderators.[34] The Standard Deviation is a valuable descriptor since it describes the distribution of marks and forces the teacher to look at individuals in the class. It also enables a teacher to compare his/her judgement of the merits of different methods of teaching against another standard. One worry that emerged in the analysis of the case studies presented by the graduate student teachers is that when a new strategy of instruction produced scores similar to those obtained in normal classes the student teacher was happy enough with that situation. He/she did not ask what they could do to raise the performance of students at the tail-end of the distribution.

PLANNING, IMPLEMENTATION AND EVALUATION OF LESSONS

Year	Item	Analysis
1st year. Maths. High Ability. (Two classes)	What money will earn £ 25.20 interest if invested for one year at 3% per annum? A. 325. 20. B 640. 00 C.75.60. D 814. 80	N =56. Set to test technique Key = B. Discrimination (Disc). 0.67 Facility (Fac). A= 7% B= 50% C= 36% D = 4%
5th year Business studies (Two classes)	Which of the following statements is false with regard to delayering? A Delayeriing simplifies the structuring of an organisation and reduces confusion. B. Eliminating staff levels reduces the number of highly paid managers and reduces labour costs. C. Fewer layers in an organisation can improve the speed and accuracy of internal communications. D. Delayering reduces the span of control of managers and thus reduces their stress levels.	N = 41. Set to test understanding of delayering. Key. D. Disc 0.64 Fac. A = 4.8%. B= 19.51% C= 19.51%. D = 56.10% Group 1. N = 11. No Correct = 10. %Correct = 90.91 Group 2. N = 19. No Correct = 10 %Correct = 52.63 Group 3 N = 11. No Correct = 3 %Correct = 27.27 Options answered. A B C D Group 1 0 1 0 10 Group 2 1 4 4 10 Group 3. 1 3 4 3
1st Year English. Average ability.	Which of the following refers to tone? A. Saying one thing but meaning something else. B. A reflection of the mood. C. The main topic or subject. D. A clever or witty expression?	N = 25. Set to test retention. Key. B. Disc. 0.42 Fac. A = 20% B= 52.1% C = 20% D = 8%
5th Year Physics. Mixed ability.	Which of the following is a scalar? A. Acceleration. B. Energy. C. Force. D. Momentum.	N = 17. Set to test knowledge of recall. Key B. Disc 0.8 Fac. A = 17.6% B = 64.7% C =0 D= 17.6%
2nd Year Geography. High ability.	Which mineral is washed from the soil by acid rain? A. Magnesium B. Zinc C. Iron D. Calcium	N = 22. Key C. Disc 0.33 Fac. A = 2 B= 1 C = 12 D = 7. C = 54.54%
2nd Year Music	Which group of the following letters can be used to structure the second movement of 'spring' from the Four Seasons? A. A-E B. G C. F D. A-G	N = 18. Examined for knowledge of structure. Key C. Disc. 0.6 Fac. A = 4. B = 2. C = 9 D = 3. C = 50%
1st Year French	'Le' and 'La' are replaced by 'L' before which of the following? A. All words beginning with a vowel. B. All words beginning with a vowel and 'h'. C. All words beginning with 'h' only D. All words beginning with a vowel, 'h' and 'y'.	N = 20. Key B. Disc. 0. 6. Fac. A = 4. B = 13 C = 1 D = 2 B = 65%.

Exhibit 5.9. Examples of items taken from tests administered by graduate student teachers. They are selected to illustrate relatively good items. When norm-referencing items need to have a facility of between 50 and 60%. Using the simple formula given in the text the discrimination needs to be above 0. 3. With small samples the facilities can be given as the numbers responding to each option. A good item will draw some candidates to respond to each option. If there are no responses to one or more options, with the exception of small samples the item is not working very well and the options should be changed. For example the designer of the fourth item thought that option C could be changed to displacement. The analysis of a good item may suggest changes to options that are apparently working well. A simple item analysis is given for the second item. This can be

extended by an examination the responses from each participant. Some of these student teachers were surprised to find that it was not always their best students who performed well in the test. There was a tendency among this group of teachers to design items that were too easy. A test of mastery would require high success rates.

One final point: marks are not absolute. There is always some error and this may be calculated (The Standard Error). Objective tests have the least error.

Mean Marks and their Display.

The mean mark (average) is the sum of all the scores divided by the number of scores. It does not tell the teacher very much other than whether the particular test was relatively difficult or easy. It cannot tell the teacher if it was more or less difficult than previous tests unless the teacher has good reason to make that judgement. To make classroom judgements about changes in performance the teacher has to design tests that are of equal difficulty and this is not an easy task.

While the teacher is interested in the distribution of marks there is no reason why they should follow a normal distribution. More often than not classroom tests are likely to be skewed away from the norm. The simplest way to establish what is happening is to plot the frequency distribution in the form of a histogram. Sometimes it might be considered useful to plot the data in the form of a Pie Chart (Fig 5.3). The histogram suggests that the test is relatively easy (assuming that ease or difficulty is measured against an average score of 50).

From the classroom perspective it may be considered a good test because the weak candidates are getting around 50% and this may help motivation. However, results should not mislead students to believe they are more able than they are. Students need to be encouraged to achieve. If it represented a test of mastery then only a few students would have achieved mastery if the minimum score for mastery is set at 80%.[35]

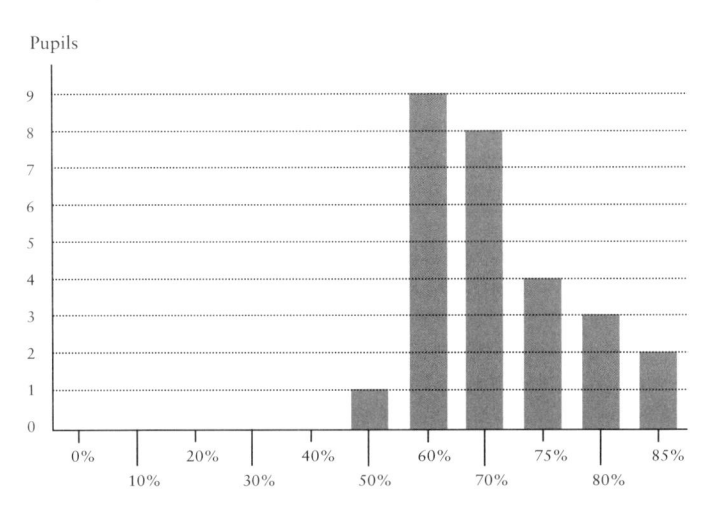

Test Results

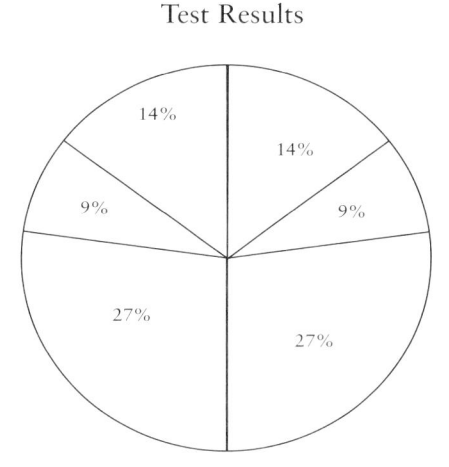

Figure 5.3. Histogam and Pie chart of the results in a test in German for 13 – 14 year olds from a lesson plan by a graduate student teacher.

Question by Question Analysis

As with the analysis of objective items it is often useful to analyse tests question by question. This will yield the relative difficulty of items. In the learning styles activity described in chapter 8 this is an essential part of the analysis.

One of the things to look for is the weighting applied to each question. Sometimes an easy question will be assigned quite high maximum marks and this will distort the overall result. It is preferable, particularly in tests for learning styles to try and design questions that are of equal difficulty.

Other Descriptive Statistics

Fig 5.4 describes the results of a maths test and includes the mode, median and standard deviation. The mode is the score achieved by the most number of persons. The Median is the middle score in a distribution or the point between two middle scores. The Standard deviation is a measure of the variability of the distribution (see below).

It is often useful to know how the scores vary between two tests. This, as has been shown, can be achieved by inspection of the histograms of the two tests. Another way is to plot cumulative frequency curves. This is shown in fig 5.5.

The standard deviation describes the way in which scores are distributed and is probably the most important measure of variability. It is based on all the scores and may be used to compare different tests. When the standard deviation is low relative to the numbers of scores these scores will be clustering about the mean.

INSTRUCTIONAL AND CURRICULUM LEADERSHIP

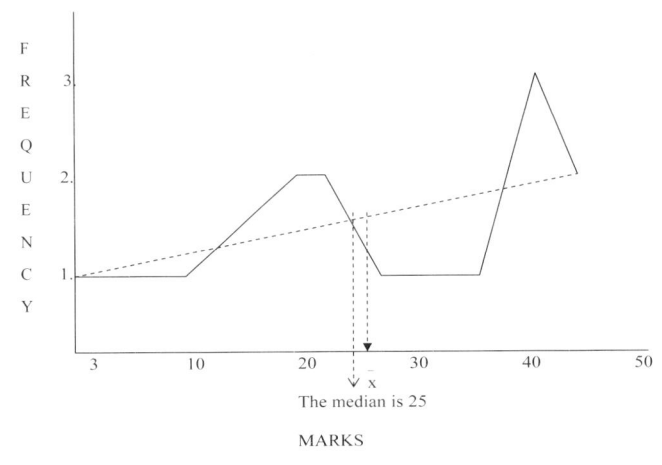

The Modal mark is 40%
The Mean is 26.55%
The Median is 25%
The Standard Deviation is 10.45

Figure 5.4. Illustrating mean, mode and median scores.

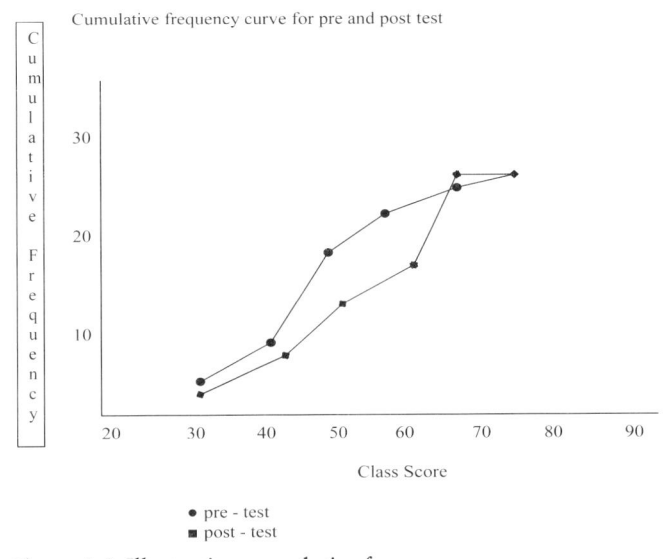

Figure 5.5. Illustrating cumulative frequency.

A large standard deviation indicates high variability or wide dispersion. One standard deviation accounts for approximately 68% of the area under the normal curve (i.e. 34% on either side of the mean).

Standard Deviation = $\sum x^2/N$

Where $\sum$ = the sum and x = the deviation of each score from the arithmetic mean.

Unfortunately it is a bit of lengthy calculation and one has to ensure that the individual figures are programmed in correctly. An example of the calculation of standard deviation is shown exhibit 5.6. In Exhibit 5.7 the data is shown for two tests one before and the other after the experimental treatment. In this case all the candidates improved their scores. While there were some dramatic increases in scores but the standard deviation does not change very much.

One of the reasons for comparing scores of two is to establish if, for example 8/10 has the same meaning in each of the tests. This cannot be done by direct comparison. It is necessary to convert the scores on the tests to the same mean and distribution using either t or z scores.

Samples and Significance

The samples in these illustrations are very small and this is likely to be the case for all classroom research. Much will depend on the way the experiment is set up. It is possible in certain circumstances to replicate research. By and large the value of doing the statistics is that it forces the teacher to focus in detail on what is happening in his/her class.

Often teachers will see a substantial increase in scores between previous performance and the performance obtained from a new instructional treatment. This they will report as being significant but this is to use the term in its colloquial sense. Such scores may not be statistically significant.

What matters for the teacher is whether or not the new scores are likely to reflect subsequent performance in a standardised test or public examination. The teacher is likely to know this from previous experience. In the case of a public examination which is graded such that there is a ten-point difference between grades, viz.50 D 59; 60 C 69; 70 B 79; 80 A 100, then when a candidate's whole score jumps from 57 to 61 which may not be statistically significant it nevertheless improves his/her performance by a grade and for that candidate the improvement is "significant" especially if the teacher's tests are regarded as good predictors of performance.

Nevertheless, in studies of the long term effects of teaching it will be useful to undertake tests of significance and perhaps correlations.

Authentic asssessment

Finally there is increasing interest in authentic assessment. Authentic assessment is an umbrella term. According to Fischer and King it is an inclusive term for alternative assessment methods (i.e., to the traditional normed referenced tests) *"that examine student's ability to perform tasks that closely resemble authentic situations."*[36] Authentic implies "real". Given a broad interpretation of the term "real" to mean what is real to the student, authentic assessment would embrace portfolios and journals and in terms of instruction such things as projects and other practical activities. Whereas there has been much research on the assessment of laboratory activities and projects research on portfolios is only in its infancy. In Ireland there has been much interest in the use of portfolios in the transition year. A study of their use showed that teachers require substantial training if portfolios are to be effective tools for learning and assessment.[37]

Some claim that authentic assessment is superior to traditional assessment but the same principles of assessment apply to authentic assessment as they do to traditional forms of measurement.[38] The advantage of project work and other activities is that carefully designed assessments can assess skills that traditional examinations cannot but not always with ease, as for example, attempts to measure creativity.

Implications for curriculum and instructional leaders

It is important that teachers understand where they want to go and plan how to get there. While this should ultimately be a disposition, teachers need to be prepared for change either as a result of their own evaluations or the demands of the school or policy makers. This disposition can be fostered among beginning teachers if they prepare a substantial portfolio of exercises that have been well planned, implemented and evaluated. The instructional and curriculum leaders role is to help them with planning and evaluation.

A teaching career spans a long period of time and teachers like any other worker can go through phases when their performance is poor. Sometimes poor performance by students is found to be related to lack of planning and loss of interest by the teacher. Instructional and curriculum leaders have a role in supporting experienced teachers.

At the fourth level instructional and curriculum leaders need to continually remind policy makers especially those concerned with the content of the curriculum that very often the performance and understanding that children have is not what it should be because insufficient time is allowed for learning basic concepts. In consequence there is much misunderstanding. Moreover since the understanding of concepts is necessary for higher order thinking it is essential they are understood. Problems associated with the learning of concepts are discussed in chapters 6 and 7 that follow.

PLANNING, IMPLEMENTATION AND EVALUATION OF LESSONS

Score (x) %	Frequency (x)	F(x)	Deviance (d) x-m	d^2	$F(d^2)$
10	3	30	-48.5	2352.25	7056.75
30	1	30	-28.5	812.25	812.5
40	1	40	-18.5	342.5	342.25
50	3	150	-8.5	72.25	216.75
60	5	300	1.5	2.25	11.25
70	2	140	11.5	132.25	264.5
80	1	80	21.5	462.25	462.25
90	0	0	31.5	992.25	0
100	4	400	41.5	1722.25	6889
Total 430	20	1170			16055

Mean (m) = 58.5 Standard deviation 28.3

Exhibit 5.6. the Standard Deviation. The mean score for the class is 58.5 and the Standard Deviation 28.3. This indicates that although the average result is reasonable there is wide divergence between the scores of the high and low achievers.

Candidate	Test 1	Test 2
1	47.5	62.5
2	72.5	82.5
3	40	57.5
4	55	72.5
5	47.5	70
6	40	72.5
7	57.5	62.5
8	52.5	67.5
9	42.5	72.5
10	57.5	70
11	55	67.5
12	72.5	87.5
13	55	72.5
14	57.5	77.5
15	42.5	55
16	55	62.5
17	67.7	72.5
18	62.5	77.5
Mean score	54%	70%

Test 1					Test 2				
x	f	d	d^2	$F(d^2)$	x	f	d	d^2	$F(d^2)$
47.5	2	6.5	42.25	84.5	62.5	3	7.5	516.25	168.75
72.5	2	18.5	342.25	684.5	82.5	1	12.5	156.25	156.25
40	2	14	196	392	57.5	1	12.5	156.25	156.25
55	4	1	1	4	72.5	5	2.5	6.25	31.25
57.5	3	3.5	12.25	36.75	70	2	0	0	0
52.5	1	1.5	2.25	2.25	67.5	2	2.5	6.25	12.5
42.5	2	11.5	132.25	264.5	87.5	1	17.5	306.25	306.25
67.5	1	13.5	182.25	182.25	77.5	2	7.5	56.25	112.5
62.5	1	8.5	72.25	72.25	55	1	15	225	225

Standard deviation test 1 = 4.8   Standard deviation test 2 = 8

Standard deviation $\sigma = \sqrt{\Sigma fd^2 / \Sigma f}$

Notes and references

[1] see ch 1 of Heywood, J (2005). *Engineering Education Research and Development in Curriculum and Instruction*. IEEE/Wiley, New York. for a detailed discussion of these models.

[2] Tyler was not the first educator to believe that the curriculum should be defined by objectives. Bobbitt (1924) devised a model that was in many respects similar to Tyler's. He derived his objectives from human experience. As described by Jackson (1992) Bobbitt's first step was to analyse the broad range of human experience into major fields The second step was to take these fields, one after the other, and analyse them into their specific activities.. In the activities once discovered one can see the objectives of education (Jackson, P. W.(1992) *A Handbook of Research on Curriculum* AERA/Macmillan, New York).

[3] Adapted from Cone, W. F (1972) A Teaching technique to increase teacher productivity. *Engineering Education*, 63, 180 – 181.

[4] Adapted from Tyler, R. W. (1949). *Basic Principles of Curriculum and Instruction*. University of Chicago Press, Chicago. See also Furst, E. J. (1960) *The Construction of Evaluation Instruments*. McKay, New York.

[5] Shulman, L. S (1970) Psychology and mathematics education in E. Begle (ed). *Mathematics Education*. Year Book of the National Society for the Study of Education. University of Chicago Press. Chicago.

[6] Adapted from Heywood, J (1982). *Pitfalls and Planning in Student Teaching*. Kogan Page, London p 152.

[7] Cohen, L and L. Mannion (1971) *A Student's Guide to Teaching Practice*. Methuen, London.

[8] Cohen, L., Mannion, L., and K. Morrison (1996). *A Guide to Teaching Practice*. Routledge, London

[9] Between 1984 and 1996 my students completed over 5000 lesson plans using this formula in all the subjects of the curriculum.

[10] Bloom, B et al (1964). *The Taxonomy of Educational Objectives. Volume 1. Cognitive Domain*. Longmans Green, London. Krathwohl, D et al (1965) *The Taxonomy of Educational Objectives. Volume 2. Affective Domain*. Longmans Green, London.

[11] Borich, G. D (1992). *Effective Teaching Methods*. Merrill/Macmillan, New York.

[12] Bellon, J. J.., and Bellon, E. C.., and M. A. Blank (1992). *Teaching from a Research Knowledge Base. A Development and Renewal Process*. Merrill/MacMillan, New York.

[13] cited in Heywood, J (1982) note 6.

[14] *ibid*

[15] Batanov, D. M, Dimmit, N. J and W. Chookittikul (2000). Q and A teaching/learning model as a new basis for developing educational software. *Proceedings Frontiers in Education Conference* 1, F2B – 12 to 17. IEEE, New Jersey. Also cited in Heywood note 1.

[16] Cited by Bellon, Bellon and Blank note 9. Rowe, M. B. (1974). Wait-time and rewards as instructional variables: their influence on language, logic and fate control. Part 1. Wait time. *Journal of Research in Science Teaching*, 11, 263 – 279. Rowe, M. B. (1986) Wait times: slowing down may be a way of speeding up! *Journal of Teacher Education*, 37, (1), 43 –50.

[17] Taba, H (1966) Teaching strategies and cognitive functions in elementary school children. Cooperative Research Project No 2404. San Fransisco State College, San Fransisco Cited by Bellon, Bellon and Blank ref 9.

[18] Ornstein, A. C. (1987) Questioning: the essence of good teaching. *NASSP Bulletin*, 71, (499), 71 – 79 Ornstein, A. C (1988). Questioning: The essence of good teaching- part 2. *NASSP Bulletin*, 72, (505), 72 – 78. Both cited by Bellon and Bellon and Blank ref 9.

[19] For a detailed discussion of reliability and validity and other issues associated with formative and summative evaluation see Wood. R (1993). *Assessment and Testing. A Survey of Research*. Cambridge University Press, Cambridge. Heywood, J. (2000) *Assessment in Higher Education. Student learning, Teaching, Programmes and Institutions*. Jessica Kingsley, London. Pellegrino, J et al (2001) *Knowing what Students Know. The Science and Design of Educational Assessment*. National Academy Press, Washington, DC.

[20] Standardised tests enable a testee to be compared with the performance of large numbers of testees having a similar characteristic or characteristics. A Standardised test is one for which *norms* have been established. Each item is tested for its reliability and validity. The items are tested on a representative sample that is as large as possible. The scores are calibrated against a normal curve (bell shaped)

[21] A large vocabulary has developed for performance based assessment but the key terms as defined by R. E. Blum and J. A. Arter (eds) (1996*) Handbook of Student Performance Assessment in an Era of Restructuring*. ASCD, Alexandria, VA., are:

1. Performance Assessment: Direct observation of student performance or student work and professional judgment of the quality of that performance. Good quality performance assessment meets/satisfies pre-established performance criteria.

2. Outcome Assessments: Assessment of specified desired knowledge, skills or processes, and attitudes to be developed as a result of educational experiences.

3. Authentic Assessment: Assessment tasks that elicit demonstrations of knowledge and skills in ways that resemble "real life" as closely as possible. An authentic assessment also engages students in the activity and reflects best instructional activities. Thus, teaching to the authentic assessment is desirable.

4. Analytical Trait Scoring: A scoring procedure in which performances are evaluated for selected dimensions or traits, with each trait receiving a separate score. For example, a piece of writing may be evaluated according to organization, use of details, attention to audience, and language usage/mechanics. Trait scores may be weighted and /or totalled.

5. Primary Trait Scoring: A scoring procedure by which products or performances are evaluated by limiting attention to a single criterion or a few selected criteria. These criteria are typically based on the trait or traits that are most essential to a good performance.

[22] MacIntosh, H. G (1974) *Techniques and Problems of Assessment*. Arnold, London.
[23] See for example Heywood, J. (2000) Assessment in Higher Education. Student Learning, Teaching, Programmes and Institutions. Jessica Kingsley, London.
[24] For the Intermediate Certificate Examination syllabus. See Heywood, J. (1977). *Examining in Second Level Education*. Association of Secondary Teachers Ireland, Dublin.
[25] Youngman, M. B and J. Heywood (1981). Pupil's reactions to multiple choice items in mathematics. *Educational Research* 23, (3), 228 – 229.
[26] Fraser, W. J. and J. N. Gillan (1972). *The Principles of Objective Testing in Mathematics*. Heinemann, London.
[27] Mowbray, R. M and B. M. Davies (1967) Short note and essay examinations. *British Journal of Medical Education*. 1, 356 –358.
[28] Carter, G., Heywood, J and D. T. Kelly (1986).*A Case Study in Curriculum Assessment. Engineering Science at A Level*. Roundthorn, Manchester
[29] Hake, R. and D. Andrich. *The Ubiquitous Essay*. Reproduced in Heywood, J (1977) *Assessment in Higher Education*. 1st Edition, Wiley, Chichester pp 36 – 38.
[30] *Ibid* Hake and Andrich in Heywood p 37
[31] See chapter 9 for a scheme due to FitzGibbons
[32] Thompson, D. J and D. R. Rentz (1973). Large scale essay testing implications for test construction. Mineo. International Symposium on testing. The Hague, Holland. Such criteria are fairly easily designed.
[33] Gronlund, N.E (1968) *Constructing Achievement Tests*. Prentice Hall, Englewood Cliffs, NJ.
[34] *loc. cit*. Carter, Heywood and Kelly (1986)
[35] See Heywood, J (1989). *Assessment in Higher Education*. 2nd edition Wiley, Chichester for a discussion of competency based assessment and learning pp 149- 156
[36] Fischer, C. F. and R. M. King (1995) *Authentic Assessment. A Guide to Implementation*. Sage, Thousand Oaks, CA.
[37] Clarke, A, R. (2005*). An Evaluation of Portfolio Assessment in Transition Year*. MSt Thesis. University of Dublin, Dublin.
[38] Heywood, J (2000) *Assessment in Higher Education. Student Learning, Teaching, Programmes and Institutions*. Jessica Kingsley, London.

Part III
Instruction: toward higher order thinking

Introduction
Chapters 6, 7, 8 and 9

These chapters have as their intention the creation of an "assumptional dialogue" on the issue "Should schools educate for higher order thinking", that is skill in problem solving, critical thinking and more generally the transfer of knowledge and learning to unfamiliar situations? Schools are often criticised for not doing this and retort that covering the required syllabus (content) causes them to adopt traditional transmission teaching which does not facilitate the development of these skills except by osmosis. Each of chapters provides material for sub "assumptional dialogues" that contribute to the overall theme. Each chapter concludes with a summary of implications for instructional and curriculum leaders.

These chapters also illustrate the idea of "teaching as research." The examples are taken from graduate student teacher evaluations of their teaching.

These chapters are concerned with specific strategies of instruction that help students understand basic concepts and principles and some simple strategies for teaching problem solving and decision making skills. Chapter 6 in addition to pointing out that students often misunderstand basic concepts and principles with consequent effects for future learning also considers the importance of examples in learning concepts and approaches for using them in teaching. Chapter 7 looks at the merits of discovery (inquiry) learning in contrast to expository learning in learning concepts and principles. Chapter 8 asks the question, What do we need to know about our students for effective learning and teaching? More specifically should student learning styles be matched to teaching styles? Finally in chapter 9 the debate about teaching critical thinking is summarised and the value of heuristics in teaching decision making and problem solving considered. Each chapter is illustrated by evaluation studies undertaken by graduate student teachers.

Instructional and curriculum leaders have a major role in supporting (mentoring) beginning teachers. If beginning teachers are to make effective use of their training they need to work in a culture that encourages them to use a variety of teaching learning and assessment strategies. They need to be in a school that emphasises inquiry. Instructional and curriculum leaders should seek to create such a learning culture in order to attend to the particular issues of teaching. This means that teachers have to be persuaded that much can be done toward the development of critical thinking within the framework of preordained syllabuses (content) and examinations (tests). It is argued that these chapters demonstrate that possibility.

At the policy level curriculum and instructional leaders need take up with policy makers issues relating to the learning of concepts. Namely that there is much misunderstanding of concepts and principles and such misunderstandings are carried forward. Care needs to be taken in teaching concepts and assessing their acquisition. The pressure to cover a large amount of content is self-defeating and time needs to be allowed their teaching. This demands a new approach to the construction of curricula with careful attention to aims and objectives and the "key" concepts that have to be covered. Further the assessment strategies have to be carefully designed to meet those aims and objectives and test the higher levels of thinking.

It should be stressed that the approach used for the evaluation of classroom instruction is by no means the only method available to teachers as the work Cross and Stedman[1], and Wienbaum[2] and her colleagues show. What is behind these different approaches is the development of *"the power of teacher learning to ask questions in a specific context with the ability to follow through by answering them for him/herself and changing his/her practice."*[3]

---

[1] Cross, K. P. and M. Steadman (1996). *Classroom Research*. Jossey Bass, San Fransisco.

[2] Weinbaum, A et al (2004) *Teaching as Inquiry. Asking Hard Questions to Improve Practice and Achievement.* Teachers College Press, New York. National Staff Development Council, Oxford, Ohio.

[3] *ibid.* p 65. From a chapter that describes a single teacher's inquiry.

6
TOWARD TRANSFER: THE LEARNING OF CONCEPTS AND PRINCIPLES.

Summary

Many conventional curricular emphasise the learning of facts, and in consequence value memory of information over understanding and high level thinking. One remedy is to design curricular around key concepts. But for this to occur, radical changes in curricular and the means by which it is assessed will have to be made. An obligation on instructional and curriculum leaders is to make the case for and facilitate such change.

By learning is meant that process through which experience develops new and reorganizes old frames of reference. One of the principles of learning cited by Saupe[1] is that learning proceeds much more rapidly and is retained much longer when that which has to be learned possesses meaning, organization and structure. The means by which this organization is achieved are concepts and principles. Concepts are classifications of stimuli that have common characteristics. Concepts are the practical outcomes of the schema we acquire. We may like to think of them as frames of reference or simply as organizations of concepts upon which we can call. It has been well established that for one reason and another we easily misunderstand concepts and principles and that unless corrective action is taken those misunderstandings persist even to the extent of overriding the learnt correction. The epistemology of constructivism has been used to explain this problem but the teaching methods proposed by those who take this view are for most part those that would be used by any good teacher irrespective of epistemology. Whatever epistemological position we take, and it should be defensible, the fact such misunderstandings easily occur places a burden on teachers to ensure that the students in their care understand the concepts and principles to be learnt. It also places an obligation on those responsible for the syllabus (content) and assessment to ensure they function in a way that encourages learning. In these circumstances instructional and curriculum leaders have an obligation to ensure that all the stakeholders in the teaching enterprise understand these learning needs.

This chapter establishes the significance of concept learning. This is followed by definitions of concepts and principles and uses Gagné's theory of instruction to illustrate the points made. Next the obligations that a teacher has to determine and correct the misunderstandings that students have is discussed. This is followed by a discussion of strategies for teaching concepts in which the focus of attention is on the use of examples and instructional steps that might be taken to teach a concept. At the same time several different types of concept are considered. As concepts become more complex and fuzzy other teaching strategies are invoked. The chapter ends with a brief consideration of how key concepts may be used to design a curriculum framework. The illustrations come from graduate student teachers asked to evaluate the relevance of some reported researches on examples and concept learning to their own teaching.

Transfer and the learning of Concepts and Principles.

By learning is meant that process through which experience develops new and reorganizes old frames of reference. One of the principles of learning cited by Saupe[2] is that learning proceeds much more rapidly and is retained much longer when that which has to be learned possesses meaning, organization and structure. This principle is fundamental to Ausubel's theory of cognition and is the reason for advanced organizers and mediating responses[3] (see chapter 4). Meaning, organization and structure is given to learning by the concepts and principles that are to be reorganized. Without an understanding of concepts and principles there can be little transfer of knowledge and skill. Development of skill in transfer, that is the ability to solve unfamiliar problems, together with the ability to think critically is at the heart of the educational enterprise. Key to the attainment of these goals is the learning of concepts and principles: therefore, they should be the principal focus of teaching.

These rules apply to teachers and teaching as much as they do to students. Clarke, Clarke and Sullivan use points made by Shulman and Brophy to illustrate this point. Shulman they write *"claimed that thinking properly about content knowledge 'requires understanding the variety of ways in which the basic concepts and principles of a discipline are organised to incorporate its facts'. This organisation is important for as Brophy indicated "where (teachers') knowledge is more explicit, better connected, and more integrated they will tend to teach the subject more dynamically, and encourage and respond to student comments and questions. Where their knowledge is limited, they will tend to depend on the text for content, de-emphasize interactive discourse in favor of seatwork assignments, and in general, portray the subject as a collection of static, factual knowledge'. In their everyday understanding "It seems essential that teachers be thoroughly prepared for their work, in order that their involvement in curriculum development and implementation demonstrate the kind of dynamic described by Brophy."*[4] That dynamic is another way of expressing the characteristics of the masterful teacher described by Peter (chapter 3). It is the chance to think properly about concepts that teachers need to give students and much research suggests that teachers do not give students this chance.

There is a considerable body of research that supports the view that concept formation is the foundation for higher order thinking.[5] At the same time another mountain of research during the last thirty years has demonstrated that the learning of concepts and principles is easier said than done even at elementary levels and several textbooks on instruction devote much space to this topic,[6] and some are solely devoted to it.[7] Children from a very early age learn their own principles of science and while they may help these children they may be somewhat different from those derived from scientific research, and not much help, therefore, in learning science. Worse still these personal models tend to persist. Research on concept learning has been and continues to be of considerable importance. Unfortunately it seems that many teachers, especially graduate student teachers fail to understand the significance of concept learning. They ignore research both ancient and modern that could help them with their teaching.[8] More significantly if they do not understand the ease with which students can misunderstand it is likely that these misunderstandings will persist. At the same time if they do not understand the importance of concepts and key concepts they have no basis on which to challenge curricula which to them seem to emphasise facts and the value of memory over understanding. Thus in terms of instructional content as opposed to the management of classes for effective learning the instructional and curriculum leader's knowledge base should be founded on an understanding of the significance of concepts and how they may be formed.

In order to demonstrate these points in more detail this chapter begins with definitions of concepts and principles and uses Gagné's theory of instruction as a means of illustration.

Concepts and principles (rules)

Concepts are classifications of stimuli that have common characteristics. Concepts are the practical outcomes of the schema we acquire. We may like to think of frames of reference as simple organizations of concepts upon which we can call. Without concepts we would be unable to handle all the knowledge that is available to us. They are the means by which we discriminate between one thing and another. Their functions are therefore to help us reduce the complexity of the environment through the identification of objects in the world around us. With them we build networks (semantic maps and trees or scaffolds) with which we examine the world, as well as appraise the new knowledge that 'comes' at us all the time. However, this examination would be impossible without the application of principles. *"Knowledge of things is not produced in us through knowledge of signs, but through knowledge of things more certain, namely principles. For knowledge of principles produces in us knowledge of conclusions; knowledge of signs does not."* [9]

In other words, we have to relate concepts one with another to form principles that can be tested by experiment in the case of science or criticism in the case of the humanities.

TOWARD TRANSFER: THE LEARNING OF CONCEPTS AND PRINCIPLES

Unfortunately, not everyone uses the term in the same way. This arises from the fact that some concepts are very large in every sense of the word and therefore abstract, as for example 'democracy' or, 'learning-how-to-learn' and are thus open to more than one interpretation. One rather apt word that is used to describe them is 'fuzzy'.

In 1965 Gagné[10] proposed a model of instruction that encapsulated the importance of concepts in learning. That model, in particular, showed the importance of concept learning for principle learning, and problem solving. It is hierarchically ordered, and the understanding of concepts precedes that of the understanding of principles, and understanding of principles-precedes the solving of problems. In this theory a principle is the linking together of two concepts. The example he gave was, *"birds fly"*. Unfortunately, it is somewhat more complex than this for some concepts embrace principles and they become fuzzy when there is debate about the principles that contribute to their structure. Again the concept of 'democracy' serves to illustrate this point.

In Gagné's model, irrespective of this complexity problem-solving can only be accomplished when the principles have been learnt and understood. In later work when he revised the model he distinguished between 'concrete' and 'defined' concepts. *"Learners have acquired concrete concepts when they can identify previously unencountered instances of a class of objects, class of object properties, or class of events by instant recognition."*[...]*"Learners have acquired a defined concept when they use a definition to put something they have not previously encountered or put some things into classes"*... Using the term rule rather than principle, learners have understood the rule *"when they can demonstrate its application to previously unencountered instances."* This is what is meant by -"transfer of learning." Principles or rules derive from relationships between concepts. *"Higher order rules"* as Gagné now calls problem solving, *"are obtained when two or three more previously learned rules are used to answer a question about an unfamiliar situation."*[11] Gagné's five categories of human learned capabilities are shown in exhibit 6.1.

The transfer of knowledge is not possible without an understanding of the concepts involved. The ways that individuals construct their schema distinguishes the "expert" from the "novice". This has consequences for teaching and learning. Novices have to acquire a basic conceptual knowledge before they can move to strategic levels of understanding and skill.[12]

Applied to teaching Gagné's model is hierarchical. It begins with a statement of terminal behaviour. He gives the example of parallel parking a car. To arrive at the required terminal behaviour the driver has to demonstrate motor skills (eg to move the vehicle in reverse at a low speed in a chosen direction). Concepts used to identify the position of alignment with the other car, and component rules such as to put the vehicle in the correct starting position. In Gagné's example there are four motor skills, four concepts and four component rules.

Each motor skill and concept relate to one of the four component rules in the hierarchy.

Terminal Behaviour

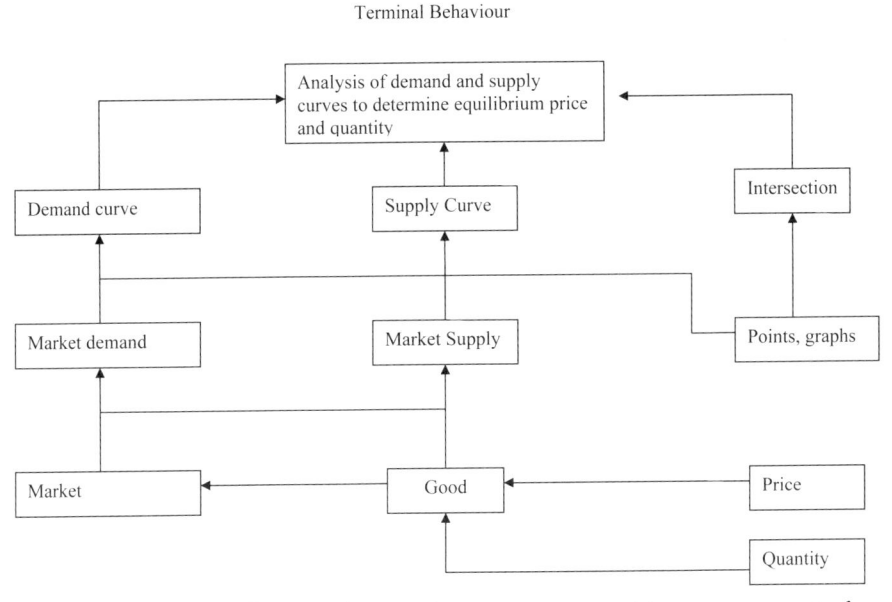

```
                    ┌─────────────────────────────┐
                    │ Analysis of demand and supply│
                    │ curves to determine          │
                    │ equilibrium price and quantity│
                    └─────────────────────────────┘
```

[Concept tree diagram with boxes: Demand curve, Supply Curve, Intersection; Market demand, Market Supply, Points, graphs; Market, Good, Price, Quantity]

Figure 6.1. From a graduate student teachers report on teaching a component of economics structured by means of a concept tree. (From Heywood, J. (1982). *Pitfalls and Planning in Student Teaching*. Kogan Page, London.

A student teacher used the early version of Gagné's theory to design a lesson in economics. His schematic of the lesson is shown in figure 6.1. It will be understood that at this level a substantial level of prior-knowledge is required. Other examples are shown in figures 6.2 and exhibit 6.2.

One difficulty with Gagné's theory is that it is the language of science and not the humanities. Teachers in the humanities are more likely to use terms like 'understanding', 'concepts' (in the abstract and fuzzy sense), and 'critical thinking' even though in their debates they may be seeking a 'principle (rule), as for example when one country should make a political intervention in another country. The important point is that teachers in the humanities should be able to explain their mental processes in learning to their students.

Gagné's approach as set out in the model may be taught by either expository or guided discovery methods. There is some evidence that guided discovery approaches have a more dynamic effect on student motivation, and that students are more likely to have a better understanding of the concept or principle involved (see chapter 7). In either case teachers need to be cognisant of the difficulties that students have in learning concepts, and the alternatives available, as for example, the exploration of student understanding of concepts through verbal protocols

TOWARD TRANSFER: THE LEARNING OF CONCEPTS AND PRINCIPLES

and specifically designed tests. This means they have to be aware of the misperceptions that students have and the instructional strategies most likely to reduce the possibility of misconception.

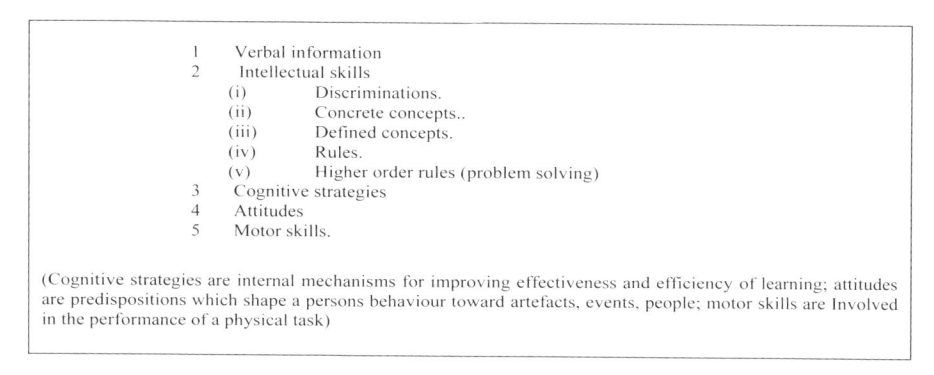

---

1 Verbal information
2 Intellectual skills
    (i) Discriminations.
    (ii) Concrete concepts..
    (iii) Defined concepts.
    (iv) Rules.
    (v) Higher order rules (problem solving)
3 Cognitive strategies
4 Attitudes
5 Motor skills.

(Cognitive strategies are internal mechanisms for improving effectiveness and efficiency of learning; attitudes are predispositions which shape a persons behaviour toward artefacts, events, people; motor skills are Involved in the performance of a physical task)

Exhibit 6.1. Gagné's five categories of human learned capabilities

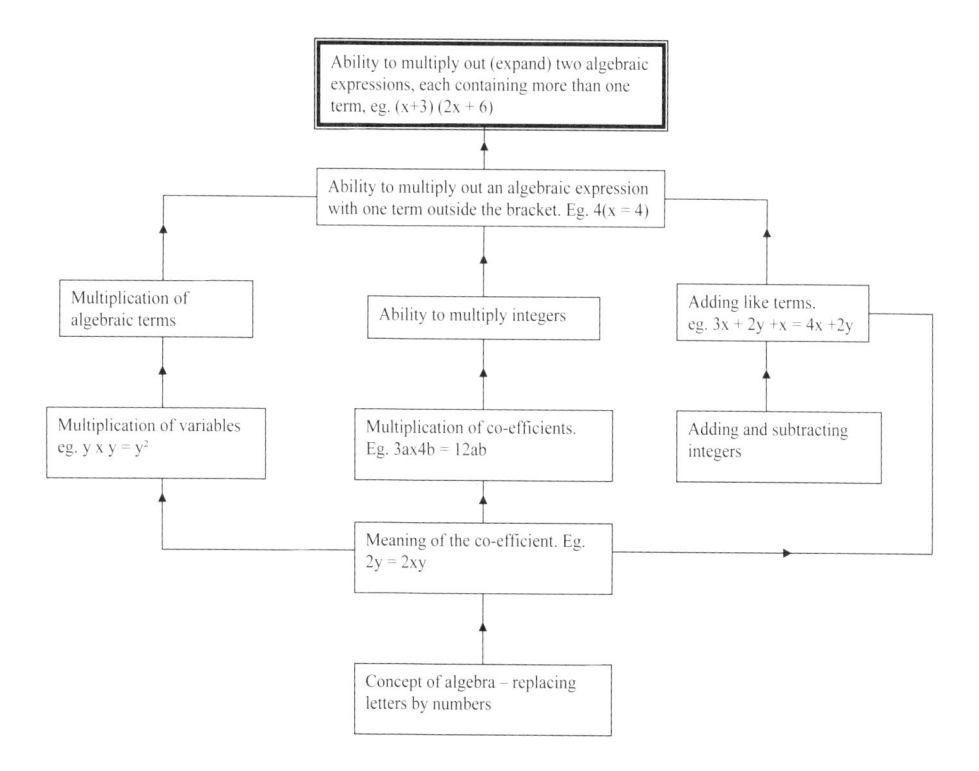

Figure 6.2 A model of Gagné's early approach to learning prepared by a student teacher (Algebra for 12 year olds)

INSTRUCTIONAL AND CURRICULUM LEADERSHIP

Facts and associations	Concepts	Principles	Problem
How tourists get to Ireland	Infrastructure		
Number and source of tourists	Aesthetic value	Tourist areas need high tertiary industry levels to increase accessibility	
Development of the Irish tourist industry	Recreational value	Tourists prefer areas of high aesthetic and recreational value	
Bord Failte. List of functions	Tourist		Make case for the development of any Irish county as a major tourist centre.
Why tourism has increased in importance	Tertiary industry		
Where tourists go in Ireland	Multiplier effect	The multiplier effect spreads the value of tourism and has greater impact in underdeveloped areas	
	Social need	In Ireland many areas of high aesthetic value have a high social need but low infrastructure development.	

Exhibit 6.2. An alternative way of showing the hierarchical structure illustrated by a problem in tourism prepared by a graduate student teacher.

Misconceptions and the obligation of the teacher

Unfortunately much of the research that has been done on misconceptions, and it is voluminous, has focused with good reason on the problems of learning science. In physics, for example, it is found that some students focus on the formula and while they can do the maths they don't understand the physics. Clement[13] gave detailed accounts of two interviews (verbal protocols) in which a student was to asked to explain his problem solving processes. The first interview related to the concept of acceleration. As explained by him, it seemed that Jim the student had demonstrated an understanding of the concept because he had successfully obtained the acceleration of an object as a function of time. However, when Jim was asked to draw a qualitative graph for the acceleration of a bicycle going through a valley between two hills he confounded the concept of acceleration with concepts of speed and distance. It appeared, wrote Clement that while *"Jim can use a symbol manipulation algorithm, his understanding of the underlying concept of acceleration is weak. The student has a procedure for getting the right answer in special cases but demonstrates little understanding of the concept when asked to apply it in the practical situation. We may describe such a student as having a 'formula centred view of the concept"*

This formula centred view would appear to be a general problem for many students[14]. But there are other problems. Some students, for example, choose inappropriate formulae with which to solve problems. Many school teachers were alerted to this issue by Driver[15] and her colleagues. They showed that many misconceptions are already present in the thinking of young children. Moreover if McElwee[16] is correct then it is a universal problem. He had studied the misconceptions that grade 8 students had in Ireland and the United States and found that there were few differences between them. Bruner was of the view that if something is to be discovered the first step is for the learner to experience incongruity or contrast. Davis had the child learn a principle and its application until the child was confident that it really understood. Then to quote Shulman, he provided the "… child with a whopper of a counter example"[17] thereby forcing the child to reorganise its understanding. As a result of the disequilibrium that occurs the child is forced to escape if it wishes to continue to learn. At the same time, a new rule may have to be learnt at a higher level of abstraction. In this respect motivation might be described as helping the child to want to escape from present difficulties or knowledge constraints.

Although the balance of research has been done in the sciences, it stands to reason that in the humanities where the concepts are often abstract and fuzzy, that there should be misconceptions (see exhibit 6.3). Much research in the social sciences shows our understanding of why people 'do this' and 'do that' is often without foundation.

The study of misconceptions was instrumental in the development of constructivism as an explanation of why they happened. Constructivism postulates that we are the constructors of our own knowledge. Further knowledge is relative to the learner. It has its educational basis in the work of Piaget who held that children are active and not passive agents in understanding the world. The mind has to make sense of what it perceives (in all dimensions of perception). The child responds to and tries to make sense and shape his/her environment. Schema are built up and changed and adapted with learning. Schema are assimilated and accommodated (changed). Without this ability to accommodate new knowledge we would not be able to adapt. In order to act in the world we necessarily learn our own science and technology. It may not be the same as the science and technology that has been derived by experiment. As such our understandings are often misperceptions even though they enable us to get by. Constructivist theory holds that they are phenomena and there is not a real world to observe. It leads to a 'notional' view of science. Hernstein Smith would dispute this view but the opposite view of constructivists is widely held.[18] In contrast the realist view holds that there is an objective world that is independent of the learner. The world is learner independent and it is possible to seek truths (universals) about that world, as they are currently understood.

Constructivism leads to an inductive approach to teaching. Students are trained or, because of the mode of instruction learn to induce a general law from particular methods in which generally reasoning operates from the general to the particular. A moment's reflection will show this has implications for the way in which subjects are approached and materials (including textbooks) are designed.

I learned that although the students seemed to have grasped the concept of 'solution', they had not learned the appropriate words to describe the concept and it's values. In reviewing my lesson plan I realised that I had not paid sufficient attention to the learning of the words 'solution', 'solute', 'solvent' and more emphasis on these words would have improved learning. I could have gotten the students to write them out for each of the samples they tested and the repetition might have considerably improved answers to wuaestion1 (of the test)

(a) **Comment by a graduate student teacher on a chemistry lesson for 12 – 13 year old girls.**

The majority of the children saw a revolution as a major revolt aimed at the overthrow of government. They cited the French revolution as one such example. I replied that the French Revolution was indeed an example of a revolt against a government. I then asked the class if the Industrial Revolution was similar to the French Revolution. The children were immediately struck by the obvious differences between the two revolutions. I asked them if they thought the word 'revolution' was an appropriate word to describe the events of the Industrial Revolution Some of the children replied that the word revolution was the correct word to use in this context, as the Industrial Revolution involved major political and social change and therefore qualified as a revolution. This as I had hoped had led the class to think about the complexities involved in the concept of a revolution. Those who saw a revolution as the stereotyped image of a violent political revolt were forced to question their preconceptions The children began to see that a revolution could also mean a slow progressional change in the way people lived and worked.

(b) **From a report on the teaching of the industrial revolution. Although the teacher concerned had anticipated the difficulties in her lesson plan we are not because of the nature of exercise told what happened to long term understanding.**

I had difficulty in convincing the students that 'implicit costs' should be included as most of them had a stereotype that 'costs' were comprised solely of 'explicit costs' such as rent, wages etc…Implicit costs include an item known as 'normal profit', and the students were extremely reluctant to allow this to be classed as a cost of production. Until they overcame their original and slightly imperfect view of the concept of profit they were unable to appreciate the existence of these implicit costs. Thus, concepts are highly influential as the student develops an understanding of his environment and all it entails. They can be important facilitators of education and instruction and allow generalisations to be made. However, if the child enters the salesroom bearing a subjective idea of a concept that is not quite correct, then it can serve as extremely harmful hindrance to effective learning. I found it very difficult to get them to appreciate that normal profit should be included. They had come armed with a stereotype that 'profit' and 'costs' should be entirely estranged.

(c) **Difficulties in the teaching of the concept of 'production costs' to sixteen year old students experienced by a graduate student teacher.**

Exhibit 6.3. Difficulties experienced in the teaching concepts.

While it is not the purpose of this chapter to discuss constructivism it has to be mentioned because it has had a profound influence on teaching. However, the point has been made that any good teacher is likely to use the principles of teaching it advocates and they are not the prerogative of constructivists (see exhibit 6.4). Matthews has pointed out that *"much of the best constructivist technique- with its emphasis on actively engaging the learner in their own learning and paying attention to prior beliefs and conceptualizations of students is at least as old as Socrates' interrogation of the slave boy in the Meno."*[19] In any event given the dictum that curriculum and instructional leaders should have a defensible epistemology it is a matter of some significance that they should be aware of this debate and not merely at a superficial level.

> (1) **Orientation**. Where pupils are given the opportunity to develop a sense of purpose and motivation for learning.
> (2) **Elicitation**. During which pupils make their current ideas on the topic of the lesson clear. This can be achieved by a variety of activities, such as group discussion, designing posters or writing.
> (3) **Restsructuring of ideas**. This is the heart of the constructivist lesson sequence. It consists of a number of stages including: **Clarification and exchange** of ideas during which pupils' meanings and language may be sharpened up by contrast with other, and possibly conflicting points of view held by other students or contributed by the teacher. **Construction of new ideas** in the light of the above discussions and demonstrations. Students her can see that there are a variety of ways of interpreting phenomena or evidence. **Evaluation of the new ideas** either experimentally or by thinking through their implications. Students should try to figure out the best ways of testing alternative ideas. Students may at this stage feel dissatisfied with their existing conceptions.
> (4) **Application** of ideas, where pupils are given the opportunity to use their developed ideas in a variety of situations, both familiar and novel.
> (5) **Review** is the final stage in which students are invited to reflect back on how their ideas have changed by drawing comparisons between their thinking at the start of the lesson sequence, and their thinking at the end.

Exhibit 6.4. Driver and Oldham's summary of the principles of constructivist thinking. Cited by Matthews[29]

Whatever ones philosophical beliefs the fact that students easily learn misperceptions places an obligation on teachers to ensure that their pupils understand the concepts being taught and if there are misunderstandings to find out why. In the first place tests have to be designed that distinguish between factual information and the concepts to be learnt. In the case of physics, tests of conceptual understanding have been developed in the United States.[20] However, Wittrock[21] pointed out that it is not sufficient to find out what is wrong and try to change the student's view by teaching the difference. It is much more difficult than that for it involves the student in relearning something that may be deeply held. One way of finding out how they think is to use verbal protocols. They are likely to reveal 'rich' information.

Verbal protocols in which students talk through their problem solving processes aloud can yield much more about learning than misconceptions. They have been shown to reveal valuable information about student learning in computer assisted situations irrespective of subject.[22] They have been used in the evaluation of computer assisted language learning (CALL) in Spanish that used a text based approach to develop reading comprehension, lexis and terminology, grammar, text analysis and text construction. The course designers found from protocol sessions that it was a very valuable technique. The students used *"the material in unexpected ways, for example, they may give nonsense answers just to access the feedback. They react spontaneously to technical aspects of the software. Some aspects of the presentation irritate them, others capture their attention. It becomes immediately obvious when there is lack of clarity in the instructions or lack of comprehension of certain points. They also state clearly the limitations of the materials, and what they would have liked to be able to do with them and cannot. Some of these findings would never have been perceived by simply asking them to fill in questionnaires [ ]"*[23]

Good teachers when helping pupils to solve problems try to understand the mental processes that they are using to solve problems. Protocols formalise the activity and provide more data but they are a tool for classroom assessment rather than an everyday tool because their analysis can be time consuming. However the problem is approached, its purpose is to find out what the students have actually learnt and how they came to learn it.

Strategies for teaching concepts

Probably the most common approach to the teaching of concepts is to use examples. They are important because as Cowan[24] wrote conceptual understanding usually begins with examples. He had been convinced that this was the case by Skemp[25] who was a specialist in mathematics education. Skemp believed *"that it is essential that a concept is first encountered in the form of examples which establish the beginning of understanding. And he maintained that it is only when an initial understanding has been acquired, through the use and consideration of examples, that any abstract generalization or refinement of definition is possible or meaningful. For only at that point, he asserted has the learner developed sufficient understanding of the underlying concept on which to build theories and understanding which use and consolidate the concept."* [26]

Cowan went on to describe how he had seen an elegant demonstration of this technique at an international conference in a keynote address on the acquisition of concepts. The lecturer *"taught her audience as she had taught her research subjects, the grammatical concept of the morpheme. First, she provided an assortment of examples, all of which were undoubtedly morphemes- and so this concept was established in the minds of her listeners- including me, who had not hitherto encountered it. Then she quickly tabled a set of examples, all of which were not morphemes- although I might have a little earlier have so classified them, while I was still uncertain about what a morpheme is. Thus the concept was yet more firmly concreted in the minds of the learners like me in the audience, as it had been in her research study. As her next step, and in refinement of our understanding, she gave us some borderline examples of morphemes and no more; and, finally, other borderline examples which were marginally not morphemes. By this point we had well and truly mastered the concept of the morpheme from examples"* [27]

There is ample research to show the value of teaching by examples and using non-examples in a supporting role. De Cecco and Crawford[28] have described a scheme for teaching concepts that uses examples and non-examples (exhibit 6.5). Stage 1 requires that the teachers are not only clear about what their terminal objectives are but that their pupils are equally clear. Concepts may be identified by their 'attributes' and 'values.' Their attributes are dimensions like colour, form and size. Each attribute has a value. For example the colour of an object is usually inadequately described by the primary colour – red can vary from scarlet to crimson.

> 1. Describe the performances expected of the student after the concept has been learned.
> 2. Reduce the number of attributes to be learned in complex concepts and make important attributes dominant.
> 3. Provide the student with useful verbal mediators.
> 4. Provide positive and negative examples of the concept in terms of appropriate number and realism.
> 5. Present the examples in close succession or simultaneously.
> 6. Provide occasions for student-response and reinforcement of those responses.
> 7. Assess the learning of the concept.

Exhibit 6.5. de Cecco and Crawford's seven instructional steps for concept learning.

These variations show the *value* of the attribute, and some attributes are more dominant than others. Concept learning is at its most difficult when the attributes are not obvious. For this reason at stage 2 of the model the teacher has to reduce the number of attributes to be learned and make the important attributes dominant.[30] (See exhibits 6.6 and 6.7 for examples of attributes and values). At any age when learning a new concept the learner is likely to try and simplify the concept.

Science concepts can be very difficult. For example, if clouds are to be taught to twelve to thirteen year olds then difficult attributes such as structure, moisture content, and electrical charge should be ignored in favour of attributes such as height, shape and colour.[31]

Two of the concepts that confuse people of all ages are primary sources of evidence and primary causes of events, be they in history, the politics of the present or, a court of law. The debates which range among experts about the desirability or otherwise of American intervention in Europe (the Balkans), the Persian Gulf, Korea and Vietnam are littered with primary causes. (Of such stuff is revisionist history made). *"In so far as twelve and thirteen year old students are concerned to try and deal with both would lead to confusion. Thus one deals with 'secondary sources' on another occasion"*.

Graduate student teachers find it difficult to define attributes and values but the evidence is that when they are forced to think about the dominant features of a concept they find it be an aid in the planning and implementation of a lesson. It is also evident that part of the confusion pupils have in learning concepts is that many tutors do not take a step-by-step approach that ensures that the pupils understand the dominant attributes first. But this takes time and often tutors are unwilling to give that time because of beliefs about the need to cover the syllabus.

There is some evidence to support the view that pupil learning is enhanced if teachers help them to distinguish between different types of concept. De Cecco and Crawford distinguish between conjunctive, disjunctive and relational concepts. A conjunctive concept is one in which the values are added together. For example, car as compared with motor cycle and bicycle. A disjunctive concept is probably the most difficult to learn. In a disjunctive concept the attributes and values are substituted one for another. Sometimes they are 'culture bound'. For example, individuals from other cultures often have difficulty in understanding the games that are particular to a culture as for example, Cricket, Gaelic and American football.

Relational concepts such as distance and direction are important in geography in everyday life. That they can be difficult to learn is illustrated by the difficulty that some drivers have in following directions. Culture is also important in such learning. Witness the difficulty that Americans, the British, Irish and continental Europeans have in converting imperial units to metric units and vice-versa.[32]

A typical disjunctive concept is that of neighbour. It has two attributes that can be substituted for each other or be related. The "and/or" construction needs to be carefully explained by the teacher as it may be difficult to understand.[33]

Attributes	Values
Financial value	Variable
Security	Crossings
Convenience	Cashless
Record/stub	Details
Transferable	Endorsement

(a) Attributes and values of a cheque as listed for a class of twelve to thirteen-year olds in Business Studies by a student teacher.

Attributes	Values
Pitch	Range of pitch
Interval of notes	Large or small intervals
Rythm	Rhythmic pattern

(b) The attribute and values of the concept "melody" as defined for a class of twelve-year olds by a student teacher.

Attributes	Values
Conjugation	Given expression to personal pronouns
Changeability	Can be used as present/past participle
Tense	Can be singular or plural
Definition of behaviour	Can express past, present, future
Linkage	Offer assertion
Regularity/irregularity within fixed range	Join words into sentence/phrase. Change in conjugation

(c) The dominant attributes of the conjunctive concept "verb" by a student teacher of modern languages.

Attributes	Values
Time	Contemporaneous (business) documents
Form	Remains. Eye-witness accounts
Meaning	Innate. Not creative

(d) Attributes and values of the concept of "primary sources" in history by a student teacher.

Exhibit 6.6. Attributes and values of concepts as taught in the twelve to fourteen year old age range.

Although the de Cecco and Crawford model does not call for these definitions the evidence from the student teacher case studies is that they do provide a useful grammar and could usefully be included in stage 2.

Stage 3 of the model requires the use of verbal and visual mediation. According to Jensen *"verbal mediation is talking to yourself in relevant ways when faced with something to be learned or a problem to be solved."*[34] We do talk to ourselves. Fortunately most of it is inaudible. We often see people talking to themselves while driving their cars. At least we used to before the mobile phone. They blush if they are found out, as I do in the same situation. Arising from naturalistic studies of individual children in classrooms in New Zealand, Nuthall and Alton-Lee[35] reported that the second most frequent type of utterance in the classroom was talking to self. The comments *"consisted of answering or repeating the teachers questions, repeating the answer given by another student, making associations with the public content, referring to related personal experience or making puns or wordplays"*[ ]. *"Sometimes "public content would cue quiet singing and humming."*[36]Private talk and peer-talk are important components of learning.

As long ago as 1935 Miller[37]demonstrated how what we say to ourselves can act as internal stimulus to a public act. It is a matter of reflection to observe that we think before we act, and Luria and Yudovitch[38]have demonstrated the power of internal speech in the control of behaviour.

Teachers can help students to mediate by interventions in the learning process. These can be oral, aural, and visual. Gagné[39]shows for example, how teachers can intervene in the process of learning modern languages. The English equivalent of 'terre' in French is the 'earth' for which the verbal mediator is 'terrestial'. Mediation can also be made from the English language into the grammar of the language to be learnt. The implication is that sometimes we understand even though we cannot articulate that understanding.

This student found that when the attribute of size and shape were important for recognising the concept, and obvious, the mastery of the concept was easy. Mastery of the concept was most difficult when the attributes were not obvious. I have found that emphasising three of the seven characteristics (I mentioned above), guided the students to a better understanding of the use of pronouns, namely
(a)   Size- all monosyllabic words –usually two or three letters.
(b)   Position- before the verb in the sentence.
(c)   Meaning – replace nouns and give specific information about those nouns.

I have found that, as de Cecco and Crawford mention that students more easily attend to some parts than others, and in the order I have listed them. The most common mistake is to position them correctly and then to mix up gender. Therefore, I have put extra emphasis on highlighting these attributes.
(a)   **A graduate student teacher reporting on the teaching of 'pronoun' to a a group of seventeen year old Hotel and Catering students learning French**.

" I found that pointing out its dominant attributes and giving positive and negative examples quickened up the learning process and greater progress was possible……this is especially so when the students grasp the concept correctly and can modify all their interpretative frameworks via this concept. Thus for example, with the concept 'trawler' further progress will be made in discussing fishing and the fishing industry and more knowledge can be added to the concept.
(b)**A graduate student teacher reporting on the teaching of derrick, the trawl derrick and trawl net in a geography lesson**

I found that introducing the students to the concept *Genes* and *also being forced to restrict the number of major points* made in the class provided a good starting point to give a fundamental but clear understanding of the topic. It made me see that no matter how complex and involved the topic is, it is always possible to simplify it for clarity and yet get the main points across.
(c)**A graduate student teacher commenting on the teaching of the concept genes in a biology lesson**.

Exhibit 6.7 Comments by graduate student teachers on the use of attributes in teaching and learning concepts.

A graduate student teaching the idea of unconditional loops in programming reported that *"I had analysed the concept 'loop'. It is a relational concept because it has the effect of changing the flow of programme execution. The dominant attributes of the concept 'loop' I take to be purpose, direction, number and size. Its purpose is repetition, its direction is forward until the end of the loop, then start again, its number varies and continues to rise until there is a break in the programme (the user presses the 'break' key or the power is cut-off), its size also varies. Considerable evidence indicates labels (as verbal mediators) facilitate the students learning of a concept. I wrote down the word 'loop' on the board together with other words which help give an understanding of the concept; 'jump', 'repetition', 'unconditional' and 'infinite'.*

The evidence suggests that verbal mediators have a role to play at all levels of education especially when students have to deal with abstract concepts. Many post-graduate students who train as teachers find the language of 'education' difficult even though they are high achievers.[40] Other examples are given in exhibit 6.8.

Visual (pictorial) mediation is a major mechanism for learning used by the media. It is equally valuable in the classroom. Teachers of modern languages use 'flash cards'. Teachers in primary schools use pictures of non-examples and examples to aid children's learning. An experiment conducted by Stern[41] showed that children learnt new concepts better when they were given categories as opposed to specific examples (tree as opposed to Christmas tree). Thus the examples we choose to use in the classroom when new materials are introduced may help or hinder generalisation. Too much specificity, it seems, may hinder generalisation.

We should not, in this age underrate the significance of the visual. In science subjects concept learning has been achieved with concept cartoons[42] and animation, and science fiction film[43] although it has been reported that too much animation can be inhibitive of learning.[44] This stage of the de Cecco and Crawford model is a reminder that teachers need to understand the entering characteristics of their students if meaningful learning is to take place. This is particularly important when students transfer from school to another educational setting- (Junior to Senior Primary (elementary), Primary to Post-primary, and Post-Primary to university. In England and Wales many university programmes depended on the teachers being able to rely on what had been taught at school if these degree programmes (especially in the science) were to be completed in three years. Similarly, post-primary teachers require a certain level of mathematical attainment to have been achieved in the primary school. Teachers often misunderstand the level at which the students are at and such misunderstandings occur particularly at times of transition and they cause difficulty for them as well for their students.[45] (See also chapter 4 on cognitive structures).

> For me stage 3 meant that I was required to ascertain the student's knowledge of the words used as attributes, attribute values and the relational words necessary. I had to ensure that the students had acquired the concept of Active Voice and understood the term transitive verb. Up to now each student had only dealt with active verbs but they might not be aware of the practice of applying the terms active or passive depending on whether the subject performs the action of the verb or receives it. By looking at these two aspects in English we can then proceed to look at the passive voice in Latin. Proceeding from English and Latin should help contextualise the lesson with regard to our own language and then with regard to a classical language. Any verb used in the passive voice must be transitive. Each student has already used verbs taking direct objects but they may not be familiar with the term transitive which applies to such verbs. This must be reinforced at the outset because in the passive voice what had been the object of the transitive verb, now becomes the subject of the passive verb (still receiving the action of the verb).
> (a) **From a graduate student teachers report on the teaching of Latin to 13 year olds.**
>
> Did I provide the class with verbal mediators? At the beginning of the class, we recalled the necessary preliminary concepts to be used as building blocks for the learning of the concept (Gagné). In our discussion of the 5 attributes I questioned the students on the meaning of any complex words or concepts. Fortunately these students are capable of operating at the symbolic level of concept learning (Bruner). An example of a helpful suggestion from a student relates to the understanding of the concept of totalitarianism, one of the attributes we had listed fascism. His advice to his fellow students to focus in on the element 'total' to jog the memory was recalled by another student some weeks later in our study of nazi Germany in response to a need to define totalitarianism again.
> (b) **Teaching the concept of fascism in history to 17 – 18 year olds.**

Exhibit 6. 8. Comments from graduate student teachers on stage 3 of the de Cecco and Crawford model.

Stages 4 and 5 of the model require the provision of examples and non-examples (similar and dissimilar if you like).[46] At the time that de Cecco and Crawford were writing their book research workers had attempted to answer such questions as "do students learn a concept better if they are only presented with examples than when they are presented with a mix of examples and non-examples? How many examples should be used in concept learning? Can students learn from the use of non-examples only?"

The graduate student teachers were asked to read up the research and to replicate one or other of the investigations in their classroom teaching. A typical lesson plan for this exercise is shown in exhibit 6.9. Their findings showed considerable agreement with the findings of research.[47] At the same time the results gave indirect affirmation of the view obtained from earlier classes that many graduates do not fully understand the role of concepts and their associated frameworks in their own subjects.[48] The students' case studies seem to confirm McDonald's view that students differ in their ability to profit from examples but "*more students prefer a mix of positive and negative instances.*"[49] De Cecco and Crawford take this view but recommend the simultaneous presentation of examples and non-examples. When they wrote they suggested that this could be done on the blackboard or with the aid of a work sheet. Modern technology gets round such difficulties. It was thought that simultaneous presentation was successful because it placed less stress on the learner. The first example is always positive but the second example may be positive or negative.

The problem for the teacher, is that if learning concepts by examples is a matter of individual preference, without some detailed research in his or her own classroom she or he will not know which students learn best by the different techniques. One way of achieving this goal is to try and replicate some of the early investigations or to put it in a more appropriate way to behave as a level 2 instructional leader.

Three of these investigations led to the view that a mix of positive and non-examples should be used.[50] Another student teacher concluded that non-examples only help learning when they are accompanied by positive examples[51] while another concluded that the understanding of the positive example had to be relatively strong before the negative examples could help develop powers of discrimination.[52] One graduate student teacher expressed the view that the pupils might get bored if only positive examples were used. Moreover, the provision of negative examples alone places a great deal of stress on the learner. Evidently the examples that students use has a powerful influence on their learning.[53]

An important reason for learning through the use of both positive and negative examples is that the students may not have understood a concept if it is learnt solely through positive examples. Similarly while identifying the concepts they may not be able to define them correctly.[54] Inclusion of negative examples helps them to discriminate and this discrimination should assist their understanding. (See exhibit 6.10) This has implications for the way understanding is tested.[55]

Step 6 requires that occasions are provided for student responses and the reinforcement of these responses, while step 7 requires the assessment of what has been learnt both at the end of the lesson and subsequently. Exhibit 6.11 illustrates these stages with extracts from a report of a graduate student teacher.

TOWARD TRANSFER: THE LEARNING OF CONCEPTS AND PRINCIPLES

Content	Method	Content	Method
Stage 1. Introduction			
Simulation of interest in clouds	Introduce a discussion on rain. Its relevance to the Irish climate. Is there any chance of a predicting rain?	The use of non-examples	1. As the slides are shown a kettle is allowed to boil so that when the lights are turned on a layer of steam occurs in the upper layers of the classroom. 2. Breaking the new laws on smoking in public places a cigar is then lit. 3. A picture of Dublin smog is passed around. 4. The pupils are asked to look at a picture in the text books which show industrial pollution.
Give a definition of clouds	A succinct and straightforward definition of the concept is given and written on the board.	Discussion of non-examples	A discussion is initiated to find out why these non-examples cannot be included in our concept.
Ascertain any previous knowledge and understanding of the terms to be used	One must use verbal questioning to find out what they know to see if they have any misconceptions, and to see if they have understood the previously related classes including the terms, condensation, saturation, precipitation.	**Stage 3. Application**	
The concept of the hydrological cycle	Revise verbally the concept of the hydrological cycle (dealt with in previous lesson) and hand out a copy to which they must assign labels.	Diagrams are drawn in books	A copy of diagram (ii) is taken down in the copy books as a visual reminder of the height shape and attributes of the clouds.
Stage 2 presentation		**Stage 4. Conclusion**	
An explanation of the attributes of clouds	The discussion is initiated by a review of their previous observations on the attributes of height and colour. This is reinforced by a discussion on other attributes such as formations and shape.	A summary and reinforcement programme is used	The class reviewed by discussion with the essential information being highlighted by writing on the blackboard.
Classification of clouds	Using a diagram shown on an OHP to indicate height (diagram (ii)). Shown permanently, a number of slides of cloud types are shown. (examples)		

Exhibit 6.9. A lesson plan on clouds showing the use of examples and non-examples.

The use of negative examples in learning and other aspects of teaching concepts.

Comment (a) The usefulness of negative examples was something which gave the pupil an opportunity to develop their powers of discrimination as negative examples omitted certain attributes and consequently a range of values. The ability of a pupil to recognize negative examples placed him or her firmly on the road to learning the concept (concept to be learnt 'archaeology')

Comment (b) The negative examples help the pupils see where they are going wrong themselves. Any of the examples I gave, I picked out from their essays. So they were in fact applying the concept to their own work (concept to be learnt 'collective noun' in English)

Comment (c). The presentation of non-examples is fundamental to the teaching and the learning of the concept of 'negatives'. Thus for every example of a negative word/sentence that I will present to the class, I will follow it by a non-example of a positive sentence in Spanish. No Tengo Nada Amora (I don't have anything now). Tengo Algo Alora (I have something now).

Choosing negative (non-) examples.
Comment (d). The choice of an example that has no meaning for the student is misleading. In teaching the concept of 'insect' the negative example of 'tick' was used. It was a mistake because only two of the girls had ever actually seen one. I drew a tick on the board and explained what it was and where it could be found, but I felt that this diversion was distracting for them. After explaining what a tick is, I had to turn round and get back to the point of what an insect is and what it is not.

Sometimes it is difficult to find appropriate non-examples as for example when teaching the earthworm.
Comment (e). As you can imagine, I experienced tremendous problems at Stage 4 of the de Cecco and Crawford model because the earthworm was in fact my only positive example. My negative examples were far too diverse and removed from the concept to be meaningful and complicated matters. Perhaps what I have actually shown is the difficulty involved when learning a concept based on purely negative examples.

And sometimes they can create confusion.
Comment (f). My negative examples of 'digestion' were harder then expected to explain and as a result created some confusion within the pupil's mind.

The effects of 'noise' on the teaching of concepts: information overload.
Comment (g).[He was disappointed with the response to a test designed to elicit understanding of archaeological evidence associated with ancient Egypt because his thirteen year old students could only list at most five objects] I may have complicated the concept by giving such a detailed description of each example in the presentation. While this made the class more enjoyable for the students they lost sight of the importance of the concept. In addition more time should have been spent reinforcing the pupils responses with positive and negative examples. I realise now that the best course of action would have been to give general examples and non examples of archaeological evidence e.g. tools, weapons, ornaments etc from both the past and present.

The need for care with diagrams
Comment (h). [Diagrams were used to teach the concept of a 'flowering plant' But on inspecting students drawings of a flowering plant it was found that] The definition of the internode appeared to be understood until I checked at the end of the class. Some children thought it was in the middle of a stem. I think this idea may have embedded itself because the diagram in the book and my diagram showed an internode at the middle of the stem. I should have marked in more than one internode, perhaps on the top and side branch also to show that an internode can occur anywhere.

Problems in the selection of examples
Comment (I). I think my examples may have been too alike to develop a real sense of the range of 'living things' (.eg dog, plant, bird, fish and tree)

Comment (j). [Students were found to confuse metaphor and simile during the teaching of metaphor] Since metaphor is a super ordinate students have to have a prior knowledge of what an image is. Therefore it would have been better if I had encouraged the students more directly to visualise sentences when they were trying to create, using imagery, I think they may have understood the concept better.

An alternative to using examples and non-examples. Let the students generate them.
(comment (k). The concept being taught was the 'comet' during the year when Halley's comet was seen. Instead of using examples and non-examples the class was divided into groups each with a leader and they were asked to generate ideas about what a concept is. To explain what is required an example is given 'what is rocklike?' answer 'cheese'. After writing down their answers the leader will give one answer to the question 'what is a comet like?' and the list of analogies is written on the blackboard. Prior to this the student had to read an article in a newspaper on comets. Each group then listed reasons why a comet is like the list of analogies written on the board. The groups also listed reasons why the comet is unlike the list of analogies given and in both cases reasons had to be given. These were all written on the board.

Exhibit 6. 10

Step 3. Provide the students with verbal mediators
[…] In the lesson I started out by using the words "mix into" in relation to what they do with sugar in their tea and proceeded from there to ascertain that they were familiar with the word "dissolve". With these verbal mediators I formed a bridge to the general term "soluble". Asking them what they thought the opposite of soluble elicited the guess "unsoluble" and from that I proceeded to "insoluble". I also ascertained that they knew the word "solution" from mathematics classes and went from there to explain that we attached a special meaning to the word in science.
"Solvent" and "solute" were not words they had come across before so I had to specially explain them, drawing attention to the similarity in sound between the words and the concept we were discussing.

Step 4. Provide positive and negative examples of the concept.
[…] After introducing the concept with the example of sugar in tea, I drew diagrams of the process of a solid going into solution so that the children would have a means of representing in pictorial form what occurred when a substance dissolves in a liquid. Following on the work with verbal mediators I wrote the formula - Solute + Solvent ---→ Solution under the appropriate diagram. Under this I wrote out as I presented them the positive examples of sugar in teas, and coffee in water, and the negative examples of marbles in tea, and paper in water. In a final column was written SOLUBLE or INSOLUBLE for each example. […] I did not consider it useful to present the negative example of suspension at this time, nor the attribute of concentration. With older children capable of taking in more in a lesson one could almost certainly have introduced these without fear of confusing the issue.

Step 5. Present the examples in close succession or simultaneously.
[…] Presenting all the examples simultaneously on the board met the recommendation for maximum contiguity.

Step 6. Provide occasions for the student responses and the reinforcement of these responses.
[…] Contrary to the advice for step 4 on the use of realistic examples I felt that direct experience in this case would be very useful for fixing the concept and that it was unlikely to overload the brains of the children as warned against in de Cecco and Crawford. […] I requested the children to draw up a table of substances they were to test in the lab and start it off with four examples I had presented marking down after each one if it was soluble or insoluble. Then as they tested substances themselves they would add to them to the list and mark them as soluble or insoluble in the same way. […]

Step 7 Assess the learning of the concept.
[…] this step emphasises generalization or the ability of the student to make the conceptual response to a new but similar pattern of stimuli. The teacher should present several new positive and negative examples of the concept and ask the student to select only positive ones. Reinforcement is provided by informing the student about the accuracy of his/her response.[…] At the end of the class I demonstrated test-tubes of Potassium Permanganate, Sodium Acetate, Iron Filings and Sulphur mixed with water and asked them to tell me which ones were soluble and had formed a solution. […]

Extracts from the evaluation
Immediately after the lesson.
[…] The technique of illustrating the concept with several examples and non-examples felt like it was really driving the point home by repetition and contrast. In previous lessons I had used examples of a concept but had tended to ignore or underplay non-examples possibly fearing they would complicate the issue for the students. During this exercise I realized that non-examples could highlight a point instead of confusing it.… I also realized that one could teach something else by use of non-examples-not only information about the concept and its examples but also information about the non-examples. This could allow for greater connectedness between ideas and students could have more of their pre-existent knowledge brought to bear on the learning situation. […]
What I learned about my pupils was that they seemed to enjoy being able to correctly identify examples and non-examples. I had felt that in the past that too many examples of a concept would bore them, but during the exercise I noticed that they were interested in practising the concept once they had acquired it. It seemed to give them a feeling of power that they were keen to exercise and display to me and to each other. This is referred to in the literature as 'reinforcement', and I realized that providing them with the opportunities for this reinforcement, with its attendant gratification of their desire for a sense of achievement, was a very important factor. It not only boosted their self-esteem but it also helped them to learn the concept better through repetition.[…]
After the subsequent test
In the light of evidence from question 1 of the test I learned that although the students seemed to have grasped the concept of solution, they had not learned the appropriate words to describe the concept and its values. In reviewing my lesson plan I realised that I had not paid sufficient attention to the learning of the words 'solution', 'solute' and 'solvent' and more emphasis on these words would have improved learning. I could have gotten the students to write them out for each of the samples they tested and the repetition and writing practice might have considerably improved the answers to question 1. The keyword technique and concept mapping discussed in Howard could have been useful in this instance. I don't think de Cecco and Crawford dealt adequately with the teaching of new words for the concepts. My students had learned the concepts but not the words.

Exhibit 6. 11. Illustrations of Stages 3, 4, 5, 6 and 7 of de Cecco and Crawford's model for teaching a concept (Solution) in practice extracted from the report of a graduate student teacher together with extracts from the evaluations. For an example of a lesson plan in English see Exhibits 5.2 and 5.5)

Coping with complexity

Three quarters of the students who read a chapter on modern approaches to concept learning[56] said that they would not have changed their approach to the teaching of concepts. Of the remainder 18% would have used concept maps and a few would have used metaphors. But many of them were teaching children at the younger end of the age range (12 to 18 years). Even so children are faced with increasingly abstract concepts. Moreover some concepts are fuzzy in that they do not have clearly defined boundaries. Not every domain of knowledge can be cut up into clearly defined basic concepts. Students particularly in the social sciences and humanities sometimes have difficulty in their first dealings with these subjects because they are looking for black and white definitions the effect of which is to restrict their understanding. *"If you initially conceptualise an issue in an over restrictive way, this can prevent later insights from developing, committing you to a single track of thinking."*[57]

Dunleavy[58] recommended a five-step approach to the clarification of concepts. They are

1. Place the concept in its universe.
2. Search antonyms to the concept within this universe.
3. Look for antonyms of potential antonyms.
4. Look for unstated 'partner' words.
5. Explicitly examine different forms of the concept.

Like other authors he uses the concept of 'democracy' to illustrate his point. Thus for step 1 democracy is placed in the universe of 'political system'. For step 2 the student has to ask what is the opposite of democracy. Some of the dichotomies proposed will be appropriate and others inappropriate. It is as Dunleavy shows easy to fall into the inappropriate thus *"for example, the familiar contrast between 'democracy' and 'totalitarianism' is a false dichotomy because totalitarian regimes are a very small sub-class of non-democratic regimes…but most non-democratic regimes do not go this far."*[59] False dichotomies can arise from or be stereotypes.

The third step is a further check. The student asks what is the antonym of the antonym selected. By generating the antonyms of totalitarianism, fascism, communism and dictatorship it will be found that the correct antonym of dictatorship is democracy. Dunleavy warns against precision in the search for definitions that might be brought about by a single substitute. *"If you initially conceptualise an issue in an over restrictive way, this can prevent later insights from developing, committing you to a single track of thinking."*[60]

Similar complexities will be met in science. Howard[61] makes the point that some stimuli are hard to classify as 'exemplars' and cites the example of a teacher who used the example of 'species' in a course on evolution only to pull the notion itself apart at the end of the course. Yet 'species' is a concept in the post-primary curriculum and is often considered with the aid of examples and non-examples. What, may we ask, is the point of doing this if it is to be contradicted at a later stage? The answer lies in the concept of cognitive development. We begin in the concrete and develop our ideas. As our cognitive capacities develop so we become capable of greater understanding and abstraction. If this is correct then we should as Bruner suggests design the curriculum as a spiral so as to develop at appropriate intervals the students understanding of concepts.[62]

A development of traditional procedures uses a "best-example" or "prototype". A prototype is the most typical case among a category of members. A stimulus exemplifies a category as a function of its resemblance to the prototype.[63] One approach is to define the concept, present the learners with one or two typical exemplars with the instruction to remember them by forming a visual image or to memorise their features. The learners are then presented with a series of examples and non-examples among which is a best example. They categorise the examples and non-examples by reference to the best example or prototype and in so doing learn how to generalise and discriminate against the prototype. They can also define the dimensions along which the examples vary from the best example.[64] In the social sciences and humanities concepts may be taught by reference to an ideal. It is the ideal that becomes the prototype. Such a concept is "victimisation". Howard is of the opinion that great care has to be taken with the selection of examples. It has also been pointed out that care has to be taken with the phrasing of the definition.[65] While the best example procedure helps adults and older students to understand fuzzy concepts the studies by the graduate student teachers would seem to suggest that the best-example approach with younger students will work best when the concept is clearly defined.

Analogy and metaphor are techniques that are commonly used in teaching both easy and difficult concepts. *"Sound waves can be likened to ripples in a pond. An amoeba's behaviour can be likened to the advance of an army. The nucleus corresponds to the general, the false foot to the advance guard, and the creature's method of 'eating' (surrounding its food) is like an enemy surrounding its enemy."* [66] Analogies with water systems are often used by teachers to explain electrical circuits.

Gordon distinguishes between three types of metaphor, direct analogy, personal analogy and compressed conflict. The first involves comparison of two concepts (X is like Y). The second asks the learner to put themselves in the position of someone / thing. "What would it be like if I were...?" the third is the combination of two contradictory concepts.[67]

Metaphors can cause confusion and misunderstanding. There is a danger that if the incorrect features are transferred considerable misunderstanding will ensue. For this reason it is important that students are familiar with one of the domains. It is, therefore, important to check that the metaphor has been understood (See exhibit 6. 10 comment j).

The favoured alternative of the student teachers for teaching concepts was the concept or semantic map. Concept maps are frames of reference that organize the essential information into a visual framework that displays the attributes and values of the concept to be learned. They are techniques to facilitate meaningful learning.[68] Such maps may be used to design and evaluate instruction and to diagnose what students know. They may be used as advanced organizers. In their turn students can use them to help plan their learning as well as to learn in class. There are a variety of such 'maps' ranging from the very formal 'trees' to 'sketches' and 'doodles.'[69] (See figures, 6.3, 4 and 5) The form should be chosen to reflect content. When learning a concept the concept may be presented at the centre of a diagram with its attributes surrounding it in a spider's web. Other arrangements include 'chains'- useful in describing a historical theme- Venn diagrams, multiple cause and stem diagrams as for example the underground train routes in London and New York. Student teachers have found the kind of map used to describe a Gagné type lesson (figure 6.1) useful. Their value in learning is enhanced if students are helped to use them to construct frames of reference that will help them deal with new situations. This skill is the basis of both synthesis and systems thinking. Training requires persistence and repetition. Students have to be shown how to apply the maps, and to summarise and reflect on what has been learnt, and how to apply them to new situations. One approach to this is to show them how to use them in the planning of answers to essay questions.

Concepts and Curriculum

A curriculum may be designed around concepts, some of which are more central to the curriculum than others. These have been called key concepts. They are procedural devices that have as their purpose the design of the structure and content of their courses. Taba who is credited with the invention of the term uses difference, multiple causation, interdependence and democracy as examples. In regard to the American social science curriculum, she writes: *"These types of concepts are usually in the background and therefore often relegated to incidental teaching. In a sound curriculum development they should constitute (what some have called) recurrent themes, the threads which run throughout the centre curriculum in a cumulative and overarching pattern."*[70] The term 'key' is not introduced, although the significance of concepts as organizing elements in the design of the curriculum should be readily apparent.

A curriculum project undertaken for middle school children in England uses key concepts as the basis of its design (exhibit 6. 12).[71] The purpose of the 'key concepts' is to help teachers choose, and organize, actual topics for work. The interpretation of a syllabus in terms of its concepts is an essential task for it helps teachers concentrate on those tasks necessary for understanding and the transfer of learning. They are therefore, objectives to be achieved and are as important as behavioural objectives. Moreover given the understanding that often teaching is carried out at too fast a pace linking concepts to objectives should ensure a focused and coherent curriculum that will bring about higher order thinking.

TOWARD TRANSFER: THE LEARNING OF CONCEPTS AND PRINCIPLES

Exhibit 6.13 gives part of a student-teachers design for a curriculum in geography for the first three years of the post-primary curriculum.

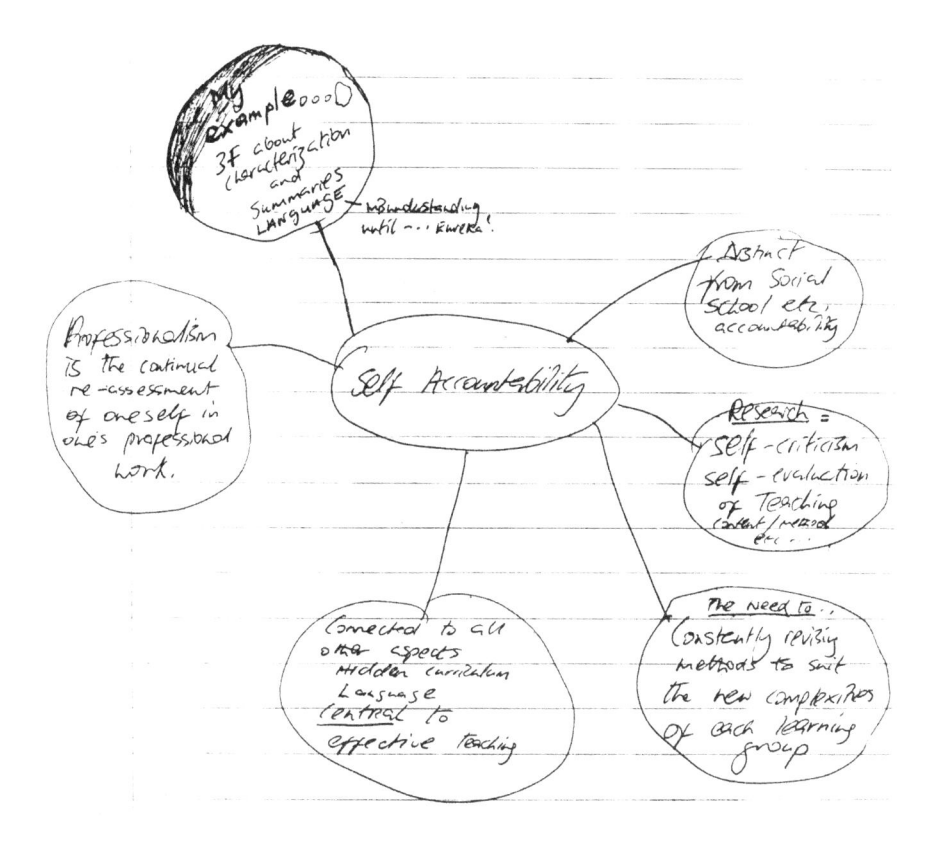

Figure 6.3. A concept map drawn by a graduate student in teacher education prior to writing a 1 hour answer to a question on self-accountability in education in a university examination.

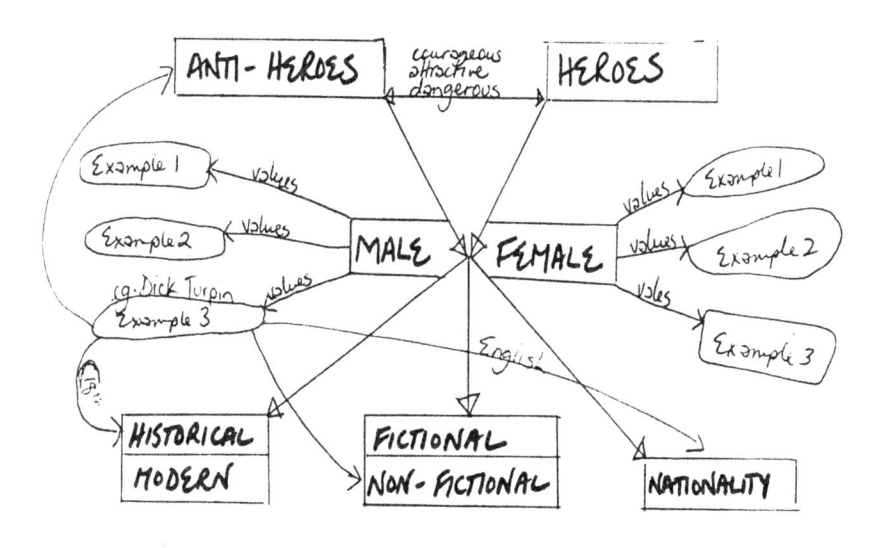

Figure 6.4. A spiders map for the concept of 'hero' in a drama lesson for fourteen year olds by a graduate student teacher.

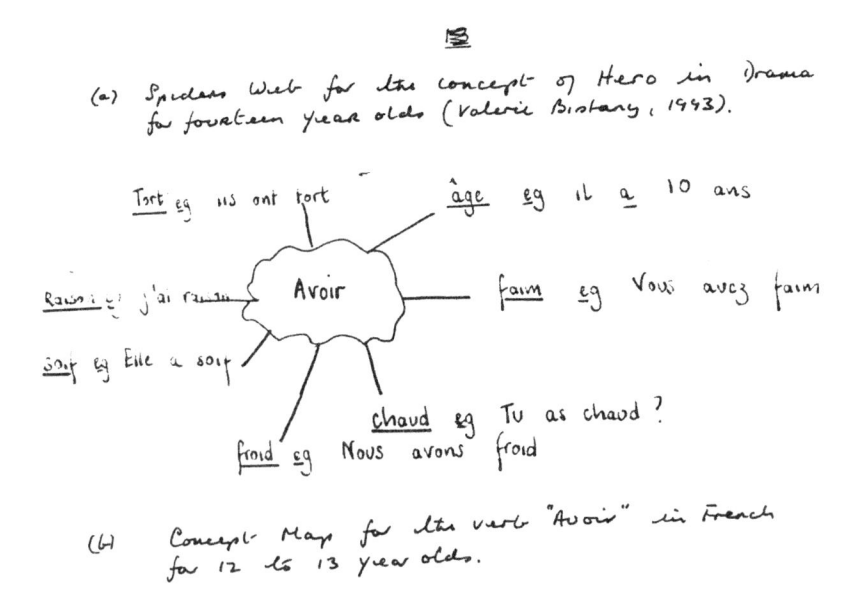

Figure 6.5. Concept map for the verb 'avoir' in French for 12 to 13 year olds by a graduate student teacher.

1. Communication.	The significant movement of individuals, groups or resources or, the transmission of significant information.
2. Power.	The purposive exercises of power over individuals and society's resources.
3. Values and Beliefs	The conscious or unconscious systems by which individuals and societies organize their response to natural social and supernatural disorders.
4. Conflict/Consensus.	The ways in which individuals and groups adjust their behaviour to natural and social circumstances.
5. Similarity/Difference	Classification of phenomena according to relevant criteria.
6. Continuity/Change	Distinction of phenomena along this essentially historical dimension.
7. Causes and consequences.	The notion that change in a state of affairs can be contributed to the phenomena preceding.

Exhibit 6.12. Key concepts in the University of Liverpool's History, Geography and Social Sciences Middle Schools project.

In the United States Erickson[72] has questioned the 'standards' movements ability to raise the level of conceptual thinking. *"Does raising 'standards' mean learning more content, which is delineated through 'objectives'? Or does it mean using critical content as a tool to understanding key concepts and principles of a discipline, and applying, and applying understanding in the context of a complex performance? From a review of national standards, it is clear that most disciplines favor the latter goal. Certainly, knowing (and often memorizing) a body of critical content knowledge is important for an educated person. But conventional models of curriculum design have focused so heavily on the information level that most teachers lack training for teaching beyond the facts. Yet the standards and newer assessments assume that students will demonstrate complex thinking, deeper understanding, and sophisticated performance"* Erickson believes that national standards have to be looked at through concepts so that thinking can be taken beyond facts so as to facilitate deep understanding.

In Ireland the Committee on the Form and Function of the Intermediate Certificate Examination wanted its research unit to design assessments (examinations) that would test the higher order thinking skills of the *Taxonomy of Educational Objectives*. (See chapter 10).[73] Its research unit trained teachers to design procedures for assessment that would test the higher order skills. Looking back, while they were relatively successful in achieving this objective the model examinations could have been improved had they placed it within a framework of 'key concepts.'

Objectives	Key concepts	Specific content	Learning experiences
1. The fostering of willingness to explore personal attitudes and values and to relate these to other people. 2. To understand how other people interact with their particular environments. 3. To make connections between concepts and percepts which have been learned in previous lessons to the present analyses. 4. The encouraging of an openness to the possibility of change in attitudes and values.	ENVIRONMENTS (similarity and difference).	1. Tropical lands. 2. Temperate lands 3. Cold lands	Group work. Various groups make a study of these three environments. Work could be divided into (a) physical environments (b) social environments (c) cultural environments. Overview.
1. To develop in the students an ability to plan. 2. To apply theories to new situations and to evaluate the result. 3. To develop and test hypotheses. 4. To work in a group and to coordinate efforts and delegate tasks.	URBANIZATION (continuity and change)	1. Urbanization on a global scale (a) process over time (b) third world cities (problems of growth). 2. Economic development. (a) Agriculture to industry. (b) Stages of development and the third world. (c) Theories- Growth centres v decentralisation 3. Planning city growth. (a) Urban sprawl and decay. (b) Renovation and renewal. (c) Rehousing and new town 4. Shannon development 5. Dublin.	Application of Rostow's stages of development. Evaluation of theories. Group project 1. Fieldwork around Dublin collecting information. 2. An urban study of Dublin emphasizing problems associated with growth and proposing possible solutions.

Exhibit 6.13. Extract from a curriculum for geography developed by Gina Plunkett a graduate student teacher. Part of the third year reprinted from Heywood, J. (1982). *Pitfalls and Planning in Student Teaching*. Kogan Page, London. It includes the programme for all three years of the junior cycle. (The other key concepts were communications, resources and landforms which were described in similar fashion. The terminology was that of the period. Now days instead of third world the term developing nations is used. At that time an Intermediate Certificate Examination was taken in Ireland by 15 year olds after a three-year cycle in post-primary education).

The committee and its research unit considered that the examinations primarily tested knowledge of facts and that this encouraged rote memorization and teaching to suit. The research unit found that substantial training involving the implementation of assessments was required if the teachers were to internalise a new approach to assessment. The problem was confounded by the fact that the unit was not allowed to consider the syllabus yet the assessment designs clearly required new approaches to teaching and a reduction in the amount of information required, and therefore, a change in syllabus content. A more recent study reported similarly.[74]

Curriculum maps can be shown to pupils at the beginning of a course or a section of a course and used by them to check their understanding of the framework or scaffold in which their learning is taking place. Such maps should help them distinguish between fact, concept and principle. And for this purpose they should be used by test designers and examiners to design tests and examinations that require the development of higher order thinking skills that demand an understanding of principles rather than the rote-memorisation of facts.

Implications for curriculum and instructional leaders

The illustrations given above suggest there is level at which teachers of different subjects can discuss the teaching of concepts and principles and obtain insights that may be of benefit to them. "Assumptional-dialogues" about the teaching and learning of concepts and principles come within the general context of learning for higher order thinking. Beginning teachers need to realise that hurrying through course content may inhibit the understanding of concepts. They also need to appreciate that student understanding needs to be checked regularly. Instructional leaders who mentor beginning teachers can offer advice and guidance on these matters.

More generally the case needs to be made to teachers that much can be done within the framework of a curriculum they perceived to be overloaded. If students understand the key concepts they have a support for memory and a base for the transfer of learning, and therefore the potential to learn by ones-self. But the advantages from slowing down the pace of information transmission cannot be over emphasised. Therefore, instructional and curriculum leaders have a "political" duty to persuade policy makers that curriculum and assessment design needs to be revolutionised.

Notes and references

[1] Saupé, J. (1961). Learning in P. Dressel (ed). *Evaluation in Higher Education*. Houghton Mifflin, Boston.
[2] *ibid*
[3] Ausubel, D. P. (1968) *Educational Psychology: A Cognitive View*. Holt, Rinehart and Winston, New York.
[4] Clarke, B., Clarke, D., and P. Sullivan (1996). The mathematics teacher and curriculum development in A. J. Bishop et al (eds). *International Handbook of Mathematics* Education Part 2. Kluwer, Dordrecht. They cited Shulman, L. S. (1986) Those who understand knowledge growth in teaching. *Educational Researcher* 15, 4 – 14. And Brophy, J. E (1991) Conclusion to advances in research in teaching. In J. Brophy Ed. *Advances in Research on Teaching: Teachers' Subject-Matter Knowledge and Classroom Instruction* Vol 2. JAI Press, Greenwich, CT.
[5] For example Gage, N. L. and D. C. Berliner (1984) *Educational Psychology* (3rd ed). Houghton Mifflin, Boston. Prawat, R. S. (1989). Teaching for understanding: three key attributes. *Teaching and Teacher Education*, 5, 315 – 328. Tennyson, R. D. and M. J. Cocchiarella (1986) An empricially based instructional design theory for teaching concepts. *Review of Educational Research*, 56, 40 –71.

[6] For example Bellon, J., Bellon, E. C., and M. A. Blank (1992). *Teaching from a Research Knowledge Base. A development and Renewal Process*. (1992). Merrill (Macmillan), New York. Gunter, M. A., Estes, T. H., and J. Schwab (1999) *Instruction. A Models Approach*. 3rd ed. Allyn and Bacon, Boston.

[7] Erickson, H. Lynn (1998) *Concept-Based Curriculum and Instruction. Teaching Beyond the Facts*, Corwin, Thousand Oaks, CA.

[8] Based on the evaluation of graduate student teachers attitudes during their training but supported in the USA by Erickson, H. L. *ibid*.

[9] St Thomas Aquinas

[10] Gagné, R. M. (1965). *The Conditions of Learning*. Holt, Rinehart and Winston, New York.

[11] Gagné, R. M. (1984) Learning outcomes and their effects. *American Psychologist*, 39, 377-385.

[12] See for example, Chi, M., Glaser, R and E. Rees (1982). Expertise in problem solving in *Advances in the Psychology of Human Intelligence*. Vol 1. Erlbaum, Hillsdale, NJ
Fordyce, D (1992). The nature of student learning in engineering. *International Journal of Technology and Design Education* 2, (3), 22 – 40. (Compares student concept maps with those of an expert).

[13] Clement, J (1981) Problems with formulas: some limitations. *Engineering Education*. Nov. 158 – 162.

[14] See Heywood, J (1989). *Assessment in Higher Education*. 2nd edition. Wiley, Chichester. P 166

[15] Driver, R (1983). *The Pupil as Scientist*. Open University Press, Milton Keynes.

[16] McElwee, P (1995). *Personal to Scientific Understanding*. Doctoral Thesis. 2 vols. The University of Dublin, Dublin.

[17] Shulman, L. S (1970). Psychology and mathematics Education in E. Begle (ed) *Mathematics Education*. Chicago University Press, Chicago. P51. The idea of disequilibrium comes from Piaget. In order to move from one stage to another a stage of disequilibrium has to occur.

[18] Hernstein Smith, B (2005). *Scandalous Knowledge. Science, Truth and the Human*. Edinburgh University Press, Edinburgh. Chapter 1 of this book gives a review of the history of constructivism that takes in authorities other than Piaget. In this chapter she writes " In the *Social Construction of What?* Ian Hacking observes that nominalism is a crucial conceptual commitment in the constructivist epistemology [which as it happens, he calls, 'social constructionism]. Hacking explains nominalism as the 'denial', contra realism's affirmation, that Nature is inherently structured in certain ways. Contrary to his implication, however, constructivists do not characteristically 'deny' metaphysically what realists evidently metaphysically maintain: namely, first, that Nature is structured in certain ways inherently (meaning independent of our perceptions, conceptions and descriptions) and, second, that we properly assume (Hacking says 'hope') that those ways are largely in accord with our perceptions, conceptions and descriptions of them. Rather constructivists typically decline, in their historical, sociological or psychological accounts of science and cognition, to presume either any particular way the world inherently is or such an accord. This professional ontological agnosticism is not, as realists may see it, a perverse refusal of common sense but an effort at due methodological modesty and theoretical economy" p 6. Hacking, I (1999). *The Social Construction of What?* Harvard University Press, Cambridge, MA.
For a contrasting view in which constructivism is compared with realism without a concluding commitment see Vardy, P. *The Puzzle of Ethics*. 1st edition.Fount/Harper Collins.
My own position is that of a moderate realist. There is a real world. There are universals that we continually seek and in this search we create knowledge (ideas) with the knowledge we hold and that which is available to us.

[19] Matthews, M. R. (1994). *Science Teaching. The Role of History and Philosophy of Science*. Routledge, London. p144.

[20] Hestenes, D., Wells, M., and G. Swackhamer (1992) Force Concept Inventory. *The Physics Teacher*, 141.

[21] Wittrock, M.C (1986) Students' thought processes in M. C. Wittrock (ed). *Handbook of Research on Teaching* 3rd edition. Macmillan, New York.

[22] Taraban, R et al (2007). First steps in understanding students' growth of conceptual procedural knowledge in an interactive learning context. *Journal of Engineering Education* 96, (1) 57 – 68.

[23] Fernandez Prieto, C and M. Marsh (2002) Learning through texts. Spanish CALL courses in Heywood, J. Sharp, J. M. and M. T. Hides (eds). *Improving Teaching in Higher Education*.. University of Salford, Salford (ISBN 0-902896-28-8). P 211. See also Windeatt, S (1986) Observing

CALL in action in Leech, G and C. N. Candlin (eds) *Computers in English Language Teaching and Research*. Longman, London.
[24] Cowan, J (1998). *On Becoming an Innovative University Teacher. Reflection in Action*. SRHE/Open University, Buckingham
[25] Skemp, R. R (1979). *Intelligence, Learning, and Action*. Wiley, Chichester, see Ch 9.
[26] *ibid*
[27] *loc cit* ref 24. P2
[28] de Cecco, J. P and W. R. Crawford (1974) *The Psychology of Learning and Instruction*. Prentice Hall, Englewood Cliffs, NJ.
[29] Driver, R and V. Oldham (1986). A constructivist approach to curriculum development in science. *Studies in Science Education* 13, 105 – 122. Cited by Matthews ref 10.. Matthews points out that constructivists do not deal with the issue as to what happens if the students view continues to differs from the view the teacher wishes to project.
[30] loc.cit de Cecco and Crawford cite Archer, J (1966) The psychological nature of concepts in H. J. Klausmeir and C. W. Harris (eds). *Analyses of Concept Learning*. Academic Press, New York
[31] This comment came from a graduate student teacher Michael Ashcroft who made his lesson plan publicly available.
[32] Culture is not the only factor. Spatial ability is likely to be important
[33] Point made by a graduate student teacher.
[34] Cited by de Cecco and Crawford
[35] Nuthall, G and A. Alton Lee (1992). Understanding how students learn in classrooms in M. Pressley, K. R. Harris and J. T. Guthrie (eds). *Promoting Academic Competence and Literacy in School* Academic Press, New York.
[36] Reports from my graduate student teachers suggest that this is quite normal behaviour. One of the few memories I have of primary education is of playing the piano (as it were) on my desk top while looking out of the window onto lush playing fields during the reading of *Wind in the Willows* by the teacher
[37] Miller, N. E. (1935) The influence of past experience upon the transfer of subsequent training. Doctoral dissertation. Yale University, Newhaven. Conn. Cited by de Cecco and Crawford.
[38] Luria, A. R. and I. Yudovitch (1971). *Speech. The Development of Mental Processes in the Child*. Translated by J. Britton. Penguin, Harmondsworth
[39] *loc.cit* (1965)
[40] One or two in each cohort who undertook the concept learning exercise reported difficulty with the readings they were given.
[41] Stern, C (1965) Labelling and variety in concept identification by young children. *Journal of Educational Psychology*, 56, 235 – 240. Cited by de Cecco and Crawford *loc. cit*.
[42] Keogh, B., Naylor, S., and C. Wilson (1998). Concept cartoons. A new concept in Physics education. *Physics Education* 33, (4) 219 –225
[43] Segall, A (2002). Science fiction in the engineering classroom to help teach basic concepts and promote the profession. *Journal of Engineering Education*, 91, (4), 419 – 424.
[44] Crynes, B. Greene, B and C. Dillon (2000) Lectrons or lectures-which is best for whom. *Proceedings Frontiers in Education Conference* 3, S2D- 21 to 24 IEEE, New York
[45] Writing about the teaching of the separable verb in German a graduate student teacher wrote "*I found that there was still a great deal of confusion regarding regular verb endings which meant that I had to reinforce them before I could continue. I had also assumed that the meaning of terms such as 'prefix' and 'noun' were familiar to them. This was not the case, and further time was needed to explain these*"
[46] Some reports refer to positive and negative examples
[47] One year group (N=73) were asked the question "Having done the experiment which one of the traditional approaches are you likely to use?" 59% said they would used positive and negative examples, of these 32% said they would use positive examples first and negative example second, while 19% said that they would alternate between positive and negative examples. !8% were undecided. The majority found the exercise useful
[48] 64% said that they had not considered the issues surrounding the teaching of concepts before, and 60% said they had been cause to revise their approach to teaching as a result of the exercise. Similar percentages were obtained from graduate student teachers in the year that followed
[49] McDonald, F (1968) *Educational Psychology*. Wadsworth, Belmont, CA.

[50] *loc.cit* 9
[51] Yudin, L and S. L. Kates (1963). Concept attainment and adolescent development. *Journal of Educational Psychology*, 54, 177 – 182.
[52] Brayley, L (1963) Strategy selection and negative instances in concept learning. *Journal of Educational Psychology*, 54, 154 – 159. Compared the merits of teaching an easy concept with all negative examples and a difficult concept with all positive examples. The difficult concept was learnt more quickly than the easy concept in these circumstances.
[53] Buss, A. H (1950) A study of concept formation as a function of reinforcement and stimulus generalization. *Journal of Experimental Psychology*, 40, 494 – 503.
[54] One graduate student teacher who taught metaphor to twelve to thirteen year old students found that those who performed best were those who were able to define and recognise the metaphor and were also able to explain why a particular class of stimuli made up the concept.
[55] One graduate student teacher found that pupils obtained a better test result when positive only examples were used. But the idea that some of the students might not have understood led her to test the students for their ability to discriminate between examples and non-examples. She found that the higher ability students were better at discriminating than the lower ability students.
[56] Howard, R. W. (1987). *Concepts and Schemata. An Introduction.* Cassell, London.
[57] Dunleavy, P (1986). *Studying for a Degree in the Humanities and Social Sciences.* MacMillan Education, London.
[58] *ibid*.
[59] *ibid*.
[60] *ibid*.
[61] *loc. cit.*
[62] Bruner, J (1966). *Toward a Theory of Instruction.* Harvard University Preston, Cambridge, MA
[63] See Howard ref 56 who cites Rosch, E (1973). On the internal structure of perceptual and semantic categories in T. E. Moor (ed) *Cognitive Development and the Acquisition of Language.* Academic Press, New York.
[64] As described by Howard ref 56 chapter 6 from Tennyson, R. D and O. Park (1980) The teaching of concepts. A review of instructional design literature. *Review of Educational Research*, 50, 55 – 70. See alo Tennyson, R. D. and M. J. Cocchiarella (1986) An empirically based instructional design theory for reaching concepts. *Review of Educational Research* 56, 40 – 71.
[65] By a graduate teacher
[66] cited by Howard ref 56 p164.
[67] *ibid*.
[68] Novak, J. D., Godwin, D. B and G. Johnson (1983). The use of concept mapping in knowledge with junior high school science students. Science Education, 67, 625 – 645.
[69] Heimlich, J. E. and S. D. Pittelman (1986) *Semantic mapping. Classroom Applications.* International Reading Association, Newark.
[70] Taba, H (1962) *Curriculum Development. Theory and Practice.* Harcourt Brace, New York.
[71] Blyth, W. A. L. et al (1972). *Place, Time and Society 8 -13. An Introduction.* Collins, Bristol. Also small brochure from the University of Liverpool. For examples of concept maps appropriate for the age range 16 plus see Donald, J. G. (1982). Knowing structures for exploring course content. *Journal of Higher Education*, 54, 31 – 41.
[72] See ref 7 p vii.
[73] Heywood, J (1978) *Examining in Second Level Education.* Association of Secondary Teachers Ireland, Dublin.
[74] Heywood, J and M. Murray (2005). Curriculum-Led Staff development. Towards curriculum and Instructional Leadership in Ireland. *Bulletins of the EFEA (European Forum on Educational Administration* No 4, 3 – 90.

7
LEARNING FROM THE OUTSIDE-LEARNING FROM THE INSIDE.

Summary

This chapter continues the discussion on the teaching of concepts begun in Chapter 6.

One of the arguments in the nineteen fifties and sixties advocated that concepts and principles are better understood and affirmed if they are "discovered" by the learner and discovery or inquiry learning became a vogue. It is said to have failed in the sciences.[1] Discovery learning is also associated with the progressive education advocated by John Dewey [2] who argued that children learn best when they discover for themselves the verities of life. In England, it became polarised with traditional methods of education when the government decided to take over responsibility for a national curriculum, and teaching methods became part of a national debate. Thus traditionalists said that "find out methods" used in primary education must give way to structured teaching toward the end of the primary school curriculum.[3] The term 'progressive' was used to describe any method of teaching that departed from the traditional. In Ireland the Department of Education and Science is committed to guided discovery teaching at the primary (elementary) level.

The problem is that debate quickly becomes polarised and one method is expected to solve all problems in one go. Thus inquiry learning was intended to solve all the problems of science and mathematics learning, but it did not. The trouble is that it was never seen as one of a number of techniques available for the achievement of the various objectives of education, a point elegantly argued by Shulman.[4] One reason for this is that teachers do not seem to be motivated by theories of instruction other than by their own beliefs and prejudices. Rigour has not been a characteristic of teaching. There have not been the curriculum and instructional leaders available either to inform and help teachers evaluate the range of options available to them, or to persuade policy makers and journalists that there is more to teaching than the simplistic notions they promote.

In 1994 in a book that consisted of a number of articles showing the relation *between cognitive science and educational practice Hunt and Minstrel described a method of inquiry learning in physics. The teaching technique and the theory attempted to bridge the gap between "students' physics and scientists' physics." In other words it was particularly concerned with students misconceptions, It is briefly described. It is preceded by a summary of Bruner's views on discovery as he is widely regarded as the father of the modern discovery movement. His theory of instruction is stated.*

The attitudes of Ausubel, Bruner and Gagné to discovery teaching are contrasted and it is noted that a guided discovery approach may be applied to Gagné's hierarchical model.

Problems in defining discovery are considered. The remainder of the chapter is devoted to a discussion of student teacher investigations of the relative merits of expository and inquiry based learning. Guided discovery worked in a large number of cases, and it seems that depending on the level of control many pupils found it demanding. Of some significance is the fact that it was often reported that even when there was little difference between the scores obtained the discovery mode motivated the students more.

Many of these student teachers reported that they had learned a new technique that they could add to their repertoire of strategies. Experienced teachers asked to undertake the same experiment in a professional development programme came to a similar perspective.

Many reports allude to the fact that in the discovery mode pupils were forced 'to think'. Several of the reports took into account the issue of 'transfer' in the design of their tests. For many pupils the discovery strategy was a different mode of teaching. Like all the methods reported in these chapters, if they are to help children learn and find and utilise their own learning styles, they need to be regularly included in their programmes. This is a matter for school policy so that each subject does what it does best in determining its goals. As Shulman said, if he "had to identify a single dimension most critical as a determinant of an instructional strategy, it would be the objectives sought", and that has profound implications for the planning implementation and evaluation of a course of lessons.

The discovery/expository debate could provide the basis of an "assumptional-dialogue" within the framework of teaching and learning for higher order thinking. A curriculum and instructional leader can create the culture for an inquiry school where teachers necessarily require a theory of instruction.

Jerome Bruner

Although the discovery movement had begun before Jerome Bruner wrote an article entitled *"The Act of Discovery."*[5] Through *The Process of Education* he gave it great impetus.[6] According to Shulman he *"more than any one man, managed to capture its spirit, provide it with a theoretical foundation and disseminate it[...] he is its prophet."*[7] Later on in 1966, and also in a general book published in 1971, Bruner published comments that were intended to correct the misuse of discovery.[8] They will be discussed below.

During the same period he developed a theory of instruction that was published in 1966.[9] Bruner's view was that *"developmental psychology without a theory of pedagogy is an empty enterprise as is a theory of pedagogy that ignored the nature of growth."*[10] (See chapter 13). The four axioms of Bruner's theory of instruction are:

*"1. Predisposition to learn. A theory of instruction must be conceived with experiences and contexts that will tend to make the child willing and able to learn when the child enters school.
2. Structure of knowledge. A theory of instruction must specify the ways in which a body of knowledge should be structured so that it can be most readily grasped by the learner.
3. Sequence. A theory of instruction should specify the most effective sequences in which to present the materials.
4. Reinforcement. A theory of instruction should specify the nature and pacing of rewards, moving from extrinsic rewards to intrinsic ones."*

These have to take into account the differences between pupils at a given age level, developmental growth, and the structure of the field or fields of knowledge. In relation to the latter Bruner argued, you can teach anything to anyone in a language appropriate to the level of development of that person. Hence the interest that some scientists have in explaining theories such as Einstein's to children[11] It is a different view of "readiness" to that expressed by Piaget. Piaget held that if there is a large gap between the structure of matter to be learned and the present state of the child's cognitive structure then the child was not be "ready" to learn until the child's cognitive structure had been developed and the mismatch reduced. Bruner however did not believe in waiting and held that the child could be "taught" readiness. The teacher can reduce the gap.

In Bruner's view the child constructs the world which is "represented" through media. that develop. These representations are the *enactive*, the *ikonic*, and the *symbolic*. These are developed in order with age. Representations are systems of rules that a person conserves for future use. The three modes of representation follow in sequence. The enactive stage is learning through action without words. Bruner notes that conditioning and stimulus-response learning are appropriate to this mode. The second stage *ikonic* is one of mental representation. *Ikonic* is taken from the Greek word *ikon*. In this stage the child uses concrete visual imagery. It may be related to Gestalt psychology. The final representation the *symbolic* occurs when children are able to translate experience into language and think with language. Then they are able to develop abstract images. As indicated above Bruner believes that children can be helped to learn at the level of the most advanced kind of thinking in which they engage. That is, a teacher can help a child develop more sophisticated kinds of thought process. For this reason Bruner advocated that we should teach readiness and not wait for it to occur.

Student teachers have found the idea of applying the representations to lesson planning useful as the example in exhibit 7.1 shows.

The idea of the "spiral" curriculum should also be apparent, for the structure of the disciplines are developed through these representations and have therefore to be repeated in the form appropriate to the representation and developmental level of the child. It seems that this approach might lead to too much "review" of what has gone before and this might inhibit new learning, so care needs to be taken in structuring the spiral.

Bruner and discovery (inquiry) learning

Discovery learning has also been called inquiry learning Although it has been much criticised it continues to have its proponents.[12] However, Bruner used the term discovery. That said, while there may be some difficulty in defining discovery it is axiomatic that much of the learning that is done outside of school is in the discovery mode even if it is only trial and error. Given that this is the case then the purpose of discovery in the classroom is the formal exploration of ideas, the intention of which is to discover new models (frames of reference) for internalisation in our thought structures. To put it in a another way it is to discover principles and the principles of transfer to unsolved problems and issues. Ultimately it is to formalise it in everyday life for that is the ultimate goal of education. A good example is the mode of learning we bring to the reading of textbooks. It can be either discovery or expository. Reigeluth[13] believed that a greater depth of learning would be achieved if the reading is approached in a discovery mode He edited his book on the planning and implementation of lessons with this in mind (see exhibit 7.2).

At issue is the best way of doing this in classrooms. From the perspective of experiential learning discovery or inquiry learning would seem to be the appropriate way forward since it is simply a formalised development, in the sense that correctives are or should be built in to the procedure of our normal learning. To that extent it might be argued that school learning is contrived or artificial. Thus, it is the case for schooling that has to be made rather than the case for discovery or inquiry for the latter is what we do all the time.

Unfortunately, however the experience of inquiry leaning in the sciences in the fifties and sixties rather points in the opposite direction. Moreover, Bruner had to issue his own corrective statement in the middle nineteen-sixties and repeated in *"The Relevance of Education."*

Objectives of a lesson
(i) Pupils will be able to identify and describe various emotions as reflected by facial expressions and general body language. This includes discriminations between and generalisations about the various emotions.
(ii) To carry out a challenging pupil-centred problem-solving exercise related to the concept which requires them to communicate effectively in the target language (i.e. make themselves understood to their peers).
The target language German.

Presentation of the lesson through Bruner's representations.
(i) **Enactive stage**. Pose the question to pupils of how they interpret how another person is feeling,- do they find it easy e.g. to interpret someone's emotion by means of their facial expression. What are the most obvious facial expressions which portray a particular emotion and also the less obvious?
(ii) **Ikonic stage**. Pupils at this stage will manipulate the words associated with particular emotions raised, learning their pronunciation and spelling (by means of blackboard presentation). Pupils will thus associate the word with the relevant facial expression.
(iii) **Symbolic stage**. Introduce and distribute among pupils a set of different pictures (one per pupil) Instruct pupils not to reveal their picture to others for the purposes of the game. Concentrating on their own individual picture pupils are given. 8 minutes to reflect on the mood portrayed by the person in question, why they think the individual is either happy, sad, angry...etc...Other revealing details in L2 like clothes, physical appearance, should also be taken into account. Pupils should also make an educated guess at the nationality of the child in question (as pictures portray a wide cross-section of nationalities mainly Asian, African and South American. This is to go beyond the typical physical features and dress of modern western society.

From the evaluation.
Partly as a result of the enthusiastic pupil response to Stage 1, I feel that I introduced the pupils to too many new words in the ikonic stage. Because pupils felt that words like frustration and confusion were easily portrayed by means of body language (and provided this by miming them). I felt obliged to supply them with these words which I instinctively felt were too abstract to be dealt with at this level –until of course I remembered that Bruner tells us we can teach anything at any stage provided we adapt it to the pupils needs!

Exhibit 7.1 From a Graduate Student teacher's report on the use of Bruner's representations in the planning and implementation of a lesson.

Discovery reading as it may be applied to Reigeluth's book on the planning of lessons.
1. Read the portion of the lesson that corresponds to the first numbered comment.
2. Try to guess what the comment says, based on the chapter introduction or your own intuition.
3. Look at the numbered comment to see how close you were.
4. Continue this process for each remaining numbered comment.

Expository reading as it may be applied to Reigeluth's book.
1. Read the portion of the lesson that corresponds to the first numbered comment. While reading keep a finger on the comments section so that you can easily flip to the numbered comment as the number is encountered in the lesson.
2. Read the numbered comment, while keeping a finger in the lesson section so that you can easily flip back to it.
3. Return to the lesson to see each aspect of it that the comment identified
4. Continue this process for each remaining numbered comment.

Exhibit 7. 2. Reigeluth's advise to student-teachers reading the book he edited about the planning and implementation of instruction

Bruner was very cautious about the role of discovery in education. He wrote, *"I am not quite sure I understand what discovery is and I don't think it matters very much. But a few things can be said about how people can be helped to discover things for themselves."*[14] This is to take away the chance element in everyday life and to formalise the method by which we acquire information and, in particular concepts and principles. *"Education must programme their development of skills and provide them with models, if you will, of the envi-*

ronment. All of these things bring into serious question whether discovery is a principal way in which the individual finds out about his environment". When for example a parent helps a child to learn grammar, the parent takes the child's utterances and helps the child bring them into conformity with adult grammar. The child is not allowed to discover haphazardly, but is provided with a model. Children have to be constantly provided with models. *"The constant provision of a model, the constant response to the individual's response after response, back and forth between two people, constitute 'invention' learning guided by an accessible model".* Thus, discovery learning is not the haphazard approach that some teachers consider it to be. Children have to be given models, and through these models invent *"certain patterns that probably come out of deep grooved characteristics of the human nervous system".* Much of the shaping of this learning is done by adults. In these circumstances it is not possible to argue that *"discovery is a principal means of educating the young. Yet, the one thing that is apparent is there seems to be a necessary component in human learning that is like discovery, namely the opportunity to go about exploring the situation".* Therefore the critical thing is to teach children something they will know how to use in problem solving. Thus the central issue is how do you arrange for children to recognise they can go beyond the information given, for children who do not believe this will inevitably not be able to solve problems. And, that is the central problem of teaching in an inclusive classroom.

Bruner considered there were six aspects of learning that will help students develop skill in transferability. These are:

1. The organization of learning so that the child recognises that he/she can go beyond the information he/she already has (the attitude problem).
2. The organization of new materials so that the child is able to fit it into his/her own frames of reference (the compatability problem).
3. The organization of the problem so that the child can perceive it to be within his/her own capacity to solve successfully.
4. The provision of training in the skills of information acquisition and problem solving, more especially in relation to the heuristics of the subject being studied.
5. Aiding the child who can do things but who cannot convert what he/she does into a compact notion in his/her mind- Bruner calls this the self loop problem.
6. Helping the child learn skills for information handling.

Models are related to discovery thus: *"Discovery teaching generally involves not so much the process of leading students to discover what is 'out there', but rather their discovery of what is in their own heads. It involves encouraging them to say, 'let me stop and think about; let me use my head, let me have some vicarious trial-and-error. There is a vast amount more in most heads (children's heads included) than we are usually aware of, or that we are willing to try to use. You have got to convince students (or exemplify for them, which is a much better way of putting it) of the fact that there are explicit models in their heads which are useful"*[15]

It is a view that is in the Platonic tradition. It might also be said that the function of teacher in this tradition is to assist, guide, facilitate (whatever term you will) the learner to find these models. In achieving this goal, Bruner's illustration of the development of skill in transfer shows that questioning and the sequencing of questions have a powerful role to play. Through them children learn to re-arrange the information given and learn to invent hypotheses, even though at an early stage they may not have the skill to test them. So what if any are the relative merits of discovery and expository teaching. To try and answer this question two studies will be considered.

Clarifying concepts

The first study begins with the problem of learning concepts, and in particular avoiding misperceptions that was the subject of the last chapter. In the United States Hunt and Minstrell described an approach to the teaching of introductory physics to high school students that utilised a form of discovery learning.[16] Based on di Sessa's[17] concept of "knowledge in pieces" they see the teacher as helping students to bring the pieces of knowledge that the student has into a synthesis (*'coherent whole'*) based on more abstract principles than would normally be considered by the students. To achieve that goal, the teacher has to operationalize the representations of the ideas the student already has and this is achieved by organizing *facets* into clusters of domain specific knowledge.

"A facet is a convenient unit of thought, an understanding or reasoning, a piece of content knowledge or a strategy seemingly used by the student in making sense of a particular situation"[18] and paraphrased into simple statements. Such statements may relate to a specific situation or to more strategic reasoning in the understanding of principles (e.g. "the average velocity can be determined by adding the initial and the final velocities and dividing by two). If they are made recognisable in the actions (writing, speaking, reading) of the learners then the learner will be able to use them at a more abstract level. The task of the teacher is to learn to recognize the *facets* and when students use them. In the language of perceptual learning these *facets* would be the *schema* that the learners already have. The facets are used to focus instruction.

"Consider one commonly encountered situation, in which students believe 'active objects [like hands] can exert forces', but many also believe ' passive objects [like tables] cannot exert forces'. Students who appear to hold these two facets can be guided, through activities and discussion, to believe that consistent explanations for the 'at rest' condition of an object, would also involve believing that both active and passive objects can exert forces."[19] Hunt and Minstrell point out that physics texts rarely make the distinction between active and passive force. The distinction is not necessary for the physicist but students find it useful. *It is a distinction students want to make, and it can be put to use later in energy related discussions such as which object is doing the work, and which object is 'losing' energy in an interaction."* [20]

It follows that a guided discovery approach should be used and Hunt and Minstrell developed such an approach that would encourage students to subject their *facets* to open examination through exposure to questions and situations which would lead them to a better understanding of the concepts of physics. Instruction is carried on in a discussion that is supported by a computer. The *facets* are established with the aid of a pre-instruction quiz. This is designed to help the students become more aware of the content and issues to be dealt with in the forthcoming study as well as to provide the teacher with information about the *facets*. The quiz described by them is not set in multiple-choice form but through short answers seeks to find out the student's understanding. The example given concludes with *"Briefly explain how you decided"*. Open-ended questions enable *facets* to emerge that may not have been previously considered.

Based on analysis of a pre-test the teacher selects a 'benchmark problem'. It is intended to become a 'memorable' liaison for subsequent discussion that enables the students to discuss their *facets*. The teacher tries to remain neutral until such time as an experiment is done after which he/she initiates a discussion on the interpretation of results. The session is brought to a conclusion through questions like *'What of the original answers can be excluded?'* *'What ideas can we conclude do not apply?'* and, of course *'what do we include?'*[21] This approach lays the foundation for subsequent lessons, experiments and discussions.

During these subsequent lessons the students test themselves through computer designed assessments. A programme called Diagnoser based on the same units as those of the lessons is used. The questions are organized around five hypercard screens. The first asks a *'what if?* Question, the second asks the students to rate the confidence level they have in their answer, the third asks *'what reasoning best justifies the answer you chose?'* The fourth is arranged to respond to the answers the students have given. It is intended to encourage those who have given the correct answer, and should provide students who have given consistent reasoning but not in accord with the principles of physics further situations to explore. When there are inconsistencies in the students reasoning these are pointed out. Students can write notes to their instructor.

When the lessons have been completed there is a post-instruction examination. Hunt and Minstrell report a comparative study between two schools in upper-middle class areas in which it is shown that those students taught by conventional methods did less well than those taught by this method. (A covariant comparison of mechanics in a national examination was made with a mathematics achievement test).

In the school where the new methods were used, four different teachers were coached and all saw improvements in their student's performance.

The reader will appreciate that such an approach takes up an immense of time. Hunt and Minstrell say that it is not possible to cover the one-year physics course with their method but they believe it is more important to provide firm rather than a fuzzy foundation in physics. The same is true of the experimental examinations designed by teachers for the research unit of the Committee on the Intermediate Certificate Examination in Ireland. Unfortunately the research unit was not allowed to do a study of the syllabus content as a function of the instructional procedures required to achieve the goals.[22] In that case the development of higher-order thinking skills. But it was clear that there would be less time available to cover the whole syllabus.

Gagné and guided expository teaching

Gagné whose hierarchies of learning began chapter 6 believed that learning resulted from the cumulative effects of experience and for this reason instruction should be arranged to add and accumulate. "Readiness" is a function of the child's previous experience. His approach might be called guided expository teaching although he is not averse to using the term "discovery". Writing about a rule he says that there is a certain class of numbers whose only divisor is the number itself. *"The learner may be able to "see" this rule immediately. If not, he may be led to its discovery by a series of communications in the form of questions [...] These communications and others like them may be said to have the function of "learning guidance." Notice they do not tell the learner the answer. Rather, they suggest the line of thought which will presumably lead to a desired 'combining' of subordinate concepts and rules to form the new to be learned rule."*[23] We may deduce that the amount of guidance is a function of what is to be learnt.

As is evident the term "guided discovery" is sometimes used instead of "guided expository." Whether or not they are intended to mean the same thing is a matter of conjecture. They certainly imply different connotations in so far as the role of the teacher in learning is concerned. Some authorities have been concerned about the lack of control that the advocacy of discovery learning caused. In Ireland an official committee writing the *Handbook of the Primary Curriculum* said that it wished *"to affirm the value of directed discovery methods in teaching and learning. In this regard we feel that a revision of the Handbook should differentiate between free and directed styles. In practice the value of discovery methods will depend on a variety of factors including (i) the type of learning objective (ii) the age and background of the pupils, (iii) the pedagogic preferences of the teacher, and (iv) the constraints in the classroom. However, rather than seeing discovery methods as experience that involve the teacher only minimally, the Review Body sees such learning as requiring a high level of teacher skill and preparation"* [...] the Review Body's recommendations in relation to the value of activity methods are similar to those for guided discovery learning. *"The empirical evidence in this area has shown that directed activity enhances learning especially the understanding of central concepts in mathematics and science."*[24]

We shall return in a later section to the problem of defining discovery learning.

Ausubel contrasted with, Bruner and Gagné

Another major psychologist of the sixties and seventies was Ausubel. Reference has already been made to his advocacy of advanced organizers and verbal mediators. The advanced organizer was predicated on the principle that what has to be learned should be presented in its final form. *"The entire content of what is to be learned is presented to the learner in final form. The learning task does not involve any independent discovery on his part. He is required only to internalise or incorporate the material [...] so that it is available or reproducible at some future date."*[25] Taken together with his assertion that the *"most important single factor influencing learning is what the learner already knows"* the significance of advanced organizers and verbal mediators is immediately apparent. While it gives clear support to expository teaching the construction of advanced organizers can be difficult and teaching has to be carefully planned. It is not a support for that kind of traditional teaching that encourages rote learning.

It will be seen that Ausubel's approach is to work from the relative abstraction of the advanced organizer in which the whole task is presented briefly to a detailed and more concrete study of what is to be learnt. In contrast Gagné's approach is to work from the particular or less abstract to the rule or the more abstract.

In contrast to Bruner and Gagné who believed that intellectual skills are transferred Ausubel believed that it was the subject matter that was transferred. What mattered to Bruner and Gagné was that students should understand how they learn. That is meta-cognition and for many educators that is the most important aim of education. Perhaps a midway position is the view that a person's problem solving skills (critical thinking) would be improved if they worked with a model of critical thinking. In either case it seems that the characteristics of knowledge that are sought differ as between the protagonists.

It is contended here that a person judged by their pupils to be a good teacher and by his/her peers to be effective will be eclectic and draw on all these theories. Moreover how they are used in the design of instruction will be determined by the nature of the objectives to be sought. This is in keeping with the finding of Shulman after his search for a definition of discovery in a review of theory and practice relating to discovery and more generally instruction.[26]

Expository versus Discovery in the classroom

The second study reported here is from the same groups of graduate student teachers who undertook evaluations of their teaching and as based on an archival study of their reports together with a detailed analysis that was made of particular year groups whose work was described in chapter 6. As with the concept learning exercise the students were asked to read and summarise specified articles. The major study was Shulman's 1970 article in the yearbook of the

LEARNING FROM THE OUTSIDE-LEARNING FROM THE INSIDE

National Society for the Study of Education on Psychology and Mathematics Education. Although this article relates specifically to mathematics his study of Ausubel, Bruner and Gagné (as well as many others) is perfectly generalizable. Moreover, it is as pertinent today as when it was written.

The second study was a chapter in a book by McDonald.[27] The third publication was a very short article by Boffy. It was hoped that his description of the differences to teaching of the design and manufacture of a tool box broadly resembled expository and discovery approaches

"1. Trainee A is told exactly what tools to use, how to use them, is given pre-formed parts to assemble, told how to assemble them, and is closely checked and corrected by the tutor during the assembly stage. In this case the trainee is little more than an adjunct to the tutor and it is questionable whether he really 'made' it at all. The range of core skills being used is very small-interpreting spoken instructions; adopting safe working practices; manipulating materials, and operating tools.
2. Trainee B is asked to consider various designs for toolboxes and to decide which one is the most suitable for the purpose; to select the appropriate tools and materials, to assemble the toolbox according to the chosen design specifications and to refer to the tutor for advice and guidance when problems occur. The tutor's response typically is to encourage the trainee to think of solutions to problems and to come up with alternative strategies for solving them. Only then, if necessary, does he provide the answer."[28]

If nothing else they are illustrative of the point made in an earlier paragraph that the knowledge acquired from the two methods will be different (see Suchman below).

Within the chapter of McDonald's book experiments by Kersh[29] and Suchman[30] were recorded. In 1969 sometime after these and other experiments Craig[31] had concluded that discovery techniques had not been adequately tested. Unfortunately the design and experimental procedures of the different studies differed. Suchman's attempt to train students in scientific inquiry illustrates the different kinds of knowledge that are learnt. The training sessions (experimental group) were conducted once or twice a week outside of classroom time. Each session began with a short film or demonstration. They ended with the key question. The students then discussed the answer. The teacher responded to the questions with 'yes', 'no', 'maybe'. The teacher helped students who were in difficulty by making the nature of the difficulty apparent. At the end of the session the teacher reviewed the exercise so as to show the students the inquiry strategies used.

No differences were found between the experimental and control groups in respect of the products of inquiry i.e the learning of the underlying principles, knowledge of the parameters of the problem. However the experimental group did better than the control group in respect of knowledge content for which they had no prior training. It was found that the students who had been trained asked 50% more questions, many of which were higher-order and focused.

In my study the graduate-student-teachers were asked to set up an experiment that would enable them to evaluate the relative merits of expository and discovery teaching. It was suggested that they use Wittrock's classification that was cited in Shulman.[32] Shulman was critical of Wittrock's classification because it did not take into problems that were not formulated by the teacher in items (2) and (3) of the classification (see exhibit 7.3). Nevertheless many of the graduate students did use the table and found it helpful. One student for example replicated part of Kersh's experiment. Some examples from their reports are shown in exhibit 7.4.

The second example is illustrative of a common practice in schools namely a simple investigation or extended project where the students have to formulate the problem and then follow it through. Exhibit 7.5 gives the regulations for experimental investigations and projects in an advanced level examination in England that seem to fall into the discovery mode. The examiners thought this to be the case.[33]

Type of guidance	Rule	Solution
1. Expository teaching	Given	Given
2. Guided Discovery (deductive)	Given	Not given
3. Guided Discovery (Inductive)	Not Given	Given
4. Discovery	Not Given	Not Given

Exhibit 7.3 Wittorck's classification of the different types of instruction

In extreme cases a small number of graduate student teachers interpreted the term expository to mean continuous talking at the class, with little or no interaction between themselves and the class. No wonder they reported that the students found the classes "boring." It does raise the question as to when an ordinary class is expository and when it is guided. If questioning helps a student to discover then there must be an element of discovery, at least for the student concerned. But if only that student 'discovers' then, the class can hardly be called discovery. Similarly some of those describing deductive guided discovery left one wondering if the lesson was not expository. Again when work sheets are used it seems that some can be designed to elicit a discovery mode of thought while others are simply designed for the student to acquire and memorise more information. In two successive years when questionnaires were used to obtain opinions from these graduates it was found that 26% and 20% respectively used brainstorming to begin their expository lessons, and a very small percentage used group work. Around half in both years reported that they had based their expository lessons on Gagné's hierarchical model.

Spanish
Expository. To conjugate the verb 'tener' on the board and ask the pupils to repeat and then question different 'persons on the verb.
Deductive Guided Discovery. Give students the rule: tener que = the infinitve = to have to do something, and ask the pupils for examples.
Inductive Guided Discovery. Give the students several sentences involving 'ser' and 'estar' which both mean 'to be' and ask students to induct when they use one or the other.
Discovery. Ask the students to work out the meaning of a new Spanish word in a sentence without using a dictionary.

History for a Junior class.
Expository. Presentation (lecture /paper) on the interpretation of archaeological remains, illustrated with examples of finds/evidence from simple house site and the interpretation of individual pieces of evidence.
*Both rule (evidence) and solution (interpretation) given.
Deductive Guided Discovery. A number of finds and details of features from a simple house site are presented. Pupils are told that conclusions can be drawn and guided by questions. What shape was the house? Where was the fire? What food did the people eat?
*Rule (evidence) given but solution (interpretation) not.
Inductive Guided Discovery. Descriptive account (or mock archaeological synthesis report) of a simple house site with various conclusions – size, plan of house, position of fire, diet of inhabitants. Pupils to suggest how the archaeologists knew?
*Rule (evidence) not given, solution (interpretation) given.
Discovery. Pupils to research life in medieval or pre-medieval Ireland (e.g someone living in a simple house in Viking Dublin). Direct pupils towards books, the national Museum for sources.
*Rule (evidence) not given, Solution not given.

English
One simple set of examples to illustrate this table could be given using the learning aim of "pronouns take the place of nouns in a sentence". The table would then be as follows.
Expository. I would tell the pupils that pronouns replace nouns and subsequently offer examples, demonstrating the rule at work. Probably a series of positive and negative examples would be most useful, as in concept teaching previously. Moreover, throughout the class, instructions would be teacher oriented, as I would be the person giving the pupils both the "rule" of pronouns and the "solution" of examples of the usage. The pupils do not "solve" the examples for themselves, largely, although this could still be part of expository teaching, which is not synonymous with rote learning.
Deductive Guided Discovery. In this situation, I would again give the pupils the rule about pronouns replacing nouns and then let pupils "solve" the "problem", without telling them the "solution" mutually. Thus, the pupils would have to use deductive reasoning, working from a series of examples and learning to identify examples of pronouns, knowing only that they replace nouns. This is a common teaching method and is certainly not synonymous with leaving children alone to work out everything with the teacher not offering assistance or help.
Inductive Guided Discovery. In this method, the pupils would again be given an initial "help," and left to work in some measure by themselves. In this particular situation, I would present a series of examples to the pupils, with how words replacing nouns (the "solution") and then ask the pupils to use inductive reasoning to define "pronoun" – thus working out the "rule" for themselves: with limited guidance from me.
Discovery. I would tell the pupils what a "pronoun" is or does, but rather let them work with words and examples until they could identify a particular type or word which was acting in a certain way. Only after they had "solved" the problem for themselves and realised the "rule" would I volunteer the word "pronoun" and refine the definition they had discovered through the "solutions".

Exhibit 7. 4. Graduate student teacher examples of Wittrock's categories of instruction.

If by 'discovery' we mean an internal mental development (move) from notional to real assent of an axiom or opinion, any mode of instruction has within it the potential to assist such a jump. The question is whether the chosen mode will create a lasting affirmation. So there will always be an element of discovery inherent in expository teaching and the argument about the different methods will resolve around (1) facts and understanding of concepts and principles, and (2) the degree of control exercised by the teacher over content and through method. Nevertheless Wittrock's categorisation provides a useful mechanism for evaluating the extent to which the lessons were governed by the expository mode although some had difficulties with the categorisation (see exhibit 7. 6). A typical lesson plan is shown in exhibit 7.7.

It was impossible in some cases to determine if there were real differences between the techniques used. It seemed that some student teachers were frightened to lose control. Some students evidently have to be helped to take risks with their teaching particularly if they want to be more diverse. Equally some students teachers have to be persuaded that diversity may be necessary as the findings presented in the next chapter will show.[35] Safety (security) may have caused many of the student teachers to have preferred deductive guided discovery to inductive guided discovery. At that time the effects of the examination system on teaching were such that, because the syllabus (required content) had to be covered it was believed that this could only be done by a more or less rote expository teaching. Many pupils come to believe that this is the only way of teaching and they may react against alternative methods of teaching that they may not consider helps them pass the examination (see exhibit7.8). Some student teachers deliberately chose the expository method for weaker students. At the same time few of these student teachers advocated that low achievers should only be exposed to expository teaching. These are clearly problems for instructional leaders.

Controlled assignment. Traditional laboratory experiment. Rules and solution given.

Experimental investigation. Problem chosen by the students within the syllabus content rules. Is an open-ended investigation in which students are to develop their own lines of inquiry. It is intended to encourage students to devise experimental procedures, to select appropriate apparatus, occasionally to adapt pieces of equipment to new purposes, to perform experiments and to analyse results. It poses an engineering or scientific problem and involves the student in an analysis of the situation and an appropriate selection of the procedures and techniques for solution. The end point of the particular investigation may or may not be known, but the means for its achievement are comparatively discretionary" (N.B experimental investigations can be simulated by computers).

Project. The project is a substantial exercise that involves the design, manufacture and evaluation of an artefact in 50 hours of laboratory time. The topic is chosen by the student.

Exhibit 7.5. The components of coursework in the Joint Matriculation Board's examination in Engineering Science at 'A' Level. (In both the experimental investigations and projects there are substantial elements of discovery, although advice is available and careful planning required. An important facet of the regulations is the requirement that students possess copies of the assessment schedules).[34]

These graduate student teachers used a variety of techniques to compare the two methods and this confounds analysis to some extent. As mentioned above some were forced to achieve the goals of the study by comparing a weak achievement group with a middle-to-high achievement group. Those who split the classes or compared different classes usually tried to match the pupils for achievement level. By far the larger number divided the class into two and taught the same lesson twice.

> "Expository teaching is where one gives the students everything: facts, concepts, principles, rules etc. Discovery teaching is where one sets them a problem to solve, perhaps, and gives them no help towards finding the solution. In guided discovery, one sets them a problem but guides their efforts along a certain channel which one hopes will help them to discover the solution.
> I chose guided discovery as a method because my experience with students in my teaching practice has been that they rarely arrive where one wants them to be without a considerable amount of help. It has been my practice to refrain as much as possible from telling them what they will find in a particular experiment, in order to provide an element of discovery and the unknown for them. In these situations it is usual for me to have to give considerable guidance in the interpretation of their results, as they are frequently unable to interpret them for themselves.
> In the present instance where the content matter involved the lever, my expository group were led up the hierarchy of prerequisites through the concept of the lever, fulcrum, perpendicular distance, moment of force, clockwise and anti-clockwise moments, equilibrium and the law of the lever. All this was given.
> For a pure discovery group, I would have given the weights and suspended metre sticks, and directed them to see if they could discover any pattern when the stick was balanced with the weights in different positions to be chosen by themselves.
> Using the guided discovery approach, I stacked the odds in may favour by directing them to place the weights on one side of the metre stick at specific points. I hoped through this method to have the simple numerical values they would find so obviously related that the law would be apparent after a few examples of equilibrium. Using only two weights, one of which was twice the size of the other, was an attempt to simplify things and stack the odds in my favour.
> I confess to finding it difficult to distinguish between the discovery and guided discovery approach. Although the former is supposed to involve no help from the teacher, by his setting up of the problem in the first place, he is guiding the learners in a certain direction. If one simply left a metre stick, a piece of string, a retort stand and some weights on the bench and told students to find 'a law connected with balancing stick', it is unlikely that they would get very far. One has to guide them to some extent, even if it is only in terms of the hidden guidance involved in how you present the problem to them. For this reason, I would prefer to look at discovery methods as a spectrum running from more to less guidance, rather than from a guided/unguided point of view. (The description of Kersh's work recognises this fact by talking of strong and weak discovery conditions)".

Exhibit .7 6. From a Graduate-Student teacher's report illustrating the difficulty he had with defining discovery.

Given all these variations, is it possible to draw any conclusions from analysis of the content of these reports? Many of the student teachers recognised that their data was weak. Earlier a few results from questionnaires given to the graduate student teachers in two successive years were reported. Their reports were also subject to holistic and semi-criterion analysis when they were graded for their course work. These reports were also subjected to marking by a second grader (after the coursework marks had been returned) after the first grader had interpreted the data for the purpose of a research report. An extensive report was a prepared together with a paper for publication.[36] They included a summary of the different techniques used and the student's analyses and evaluations. They inferred from the data that guided discovery was statistically better than expository in test results but not all the differences were substantial. Of more interest was the suggestion from the data that on the whole guided discovery produces a lower standard deviation even when the difference in mean marks was small.

It seems that many pupils found the discovery mode demanding but the teachers reported that the students were more motivated in this mode. This was regarded as the major advantage by many of the student teachers.

In general, good examples of discovery and expository teaching were found in all subjects and at all age levels. Success seemed to depend on the particular concepts, principles and ideas chosen, rather than any inherent difficulty in the subject matter. As indicated above there were problems of definition of which the students were not always aware. Thus, expository was interpreted in different ways. Some went so far as to allow no interaction between themselves and their students. About half the students used the Gagné model in an expository mode. In contrast some students who chose the deductive mode of guided discovery restricted the amount of interaction to such an extent that it was difficult to determine the difference between their approach and what might be termed expository. What seemed to matter was that the teachers perceived themselves to be functioning in a different mode and this was the basis of judgements they made about their teaching. Some student teachers found that it was this exercise which brought home to them the value of variety in teaching.

These trends were consistent over the years. During the last two years of the program, that is two years after the report given above was presented, the exercise was extended so as to bring it into line with the experiments done by some of the investigators whose work the student teachers had to read. In those investigations a test had been completed several weeks after the activity. The students were now asked to set an additional test between three and four weeks after the exercise. In the second test, 54% (N=73) of the student teachers reported that the group taught by guided discovery performed better than the group taught by expository. In contrast 22% reported that the group taught by an expository method did best. As might have been predicted marks decreased in the second test but perhaps, not as drastically as might have been anticipated. Large decreases (up to 10%) in the average marks were recorded by 36% of the student teachers for the groups taught by expository methods, and 24% for the groups taught in a discovery mode. Small decreases (of up to 5%) were recorded by 29% of the expository groups and 36% of the discovery groups.

It seems that there is a slight tendency for the discovery groups' second test marks to hold up when compared with the expository mark. However, there were variations in treatment since in some cases the pupils were warned that they would have a test. In other cases they were not. These results were obtained in the context of wide variations in the techniques employed in the discovery mode as well as the expository but the student teachers clearly believed that what they did was in keeping with the literature. There were similar variations in test design. The same applied to all the years in which the student teachers participated in this exercise.

The reports showed that student teachers perform better in smaller classes. While this had much to say about their training needs it may also have something to say about the conditions for effective learning.

Aims/objectives	Lesson phase and strategy	Content	Questioning
Aim/non-behavioural objective. To develop pupils knowledge and understanding of the water cycle.	Introduction. Expository	(a) Entry. arrange seats in groups of 5. (b) Divide pupils into 5 groups of 5. © Tell each group to take out a sheet of paper and appoint a scribe.	
Behavioural objective Pupils will be able to draw and label a diagram of the water cycle.	Presentation Guided discovery (group discussions)	(a) Ask each group in turn "where does the water in rivers or the ground come from?" Tell them to write the answer on the bottom of the paper. (b) Check each groups answer ('rain') and ask each group the next question- © Repeat the process in (b)- (d) ask groups to connect each element with arrows (they should perceive a cycle at this stage.	Where does rain come from? Where do clouds come from? Where does water vapour (evaporation) come from? Where does water in seas/lakes come from? Where do rivers/ground water come from?
Behavioural objective Pupils will be able to describe in their own words what happens in the water cycle; in particular, they will be able to explain why it is a cycle.	Application Guided discovery (reinforcement by written activity)	(a) Label each group an element from the cycle; I am 'water'. Go from group to group (by asking class) to illustrate the cycle. (b) Tell pupils to draw the cycle. (c). Show water cycle on overhead projector. Explain the terms	
	Conclusion	Collect/return any copybooks.	

(a) discovery lesson.

Lesson phases	Lesson Strategies	Content	Questioning
Introduction	Expository	(a)Entry (a) Return or collect copy books	
Presentation	Expository	(a)Introduce water cycle by writing title on board. (a) Explain the cycle. Write each element on the board and connect them with arrows (c) any questions from pupils	
Application	Expository	(a) Display water Cycle diagram on overhead projector. (b) Tell class to copy Diagram in their notebooks.	
Conclusion	Expository	Return to topic begun in previous lesson (Pressure, wind etc) (if time)	

(b) Expository lesson. Same objectives as for the guided discovery lesson

Exhibit 7. 7. From Donovan, I (1992) Part II of The Training of Students in Discovery methods of Instruction and Learning.Monograph 1/92. Department of Teacher Education, University of Dublin.

> **Example (a).**
> " I have found it quite difficult to engage them for any length of time in communicative games or imaginative play or in placing their language learning (German) in a meaningful cultural context. Usually, they would give me to understand that what they really wanted to do was follow the course book chapter by chapter and make sure that at the end they had condensed the content into frames and boxes that would record grammar points and set phrases in easily accessible way. This is the mental disposition of most of the pupils in that class – a disposition that is cultivated by their highly results-oriented school, as well as the national examination system".
>
> **Example (b)**
> "The class was a bit put off when I asked them to find a definition (in science) themselves and there was a lot of looking around to each other to see what to do, or whether to take instruction. The suggestion that they should come up with a definition was apparently absurd –that's what the textbooks are for and our role is to learn from the books. Thinking isn't popular with this class. I gave everyone a half-metre stick to experiment with, about half the students never really started, they seemed intimidated by their task and, in their charming ways, suggested that I was and idiot to come up with a conclusion".

Exhibit 7. 8. Two examples of pupil resistance to different approaches to teaching reported by Graduate Student Teachers

In these circumstances can any generalisations be made? In answering these questions it is important to remember that they were about 'live' classroom practice. Moreover, the applications of the models and the subsequent evaluations made were fairly rigorous. There was a relatively high level of consistency in the responses over the years. Given these points it cannot be concluded that expository teaching is to be preferred. Guided discovery worked in a large number of cases and it seems that depending on the level of control many pupils found it demanding. Of some significance is the fact that it was often reported that even when there was little difference between the scores obtained that the discovery mode motivated the students more. Evidence from other sources supports the view that when students become involved in their learning motivation is enhanced. Project work is known to enthuse pupils: Its weakness as with any 'pure' or near 'pure' discovery approach is that the pupil understanding of concepts and principles may be wrong. Therefore it has to be properly assessed and feedback given that is reinforced. Nevertheless given the 'instant' society in which we live and the ease with which children become bored this finding is equally significant. A class that is motivated is likely to be disciplined and that is likely to enhance the teacher's motivation.

Many of these student teachers reported that they had learned a new technique that they could add to their repertoire of strategies. Experienced teachers asked to undertake the same experiment in a professional development programme came to a similar perspective.

Many reports allude to the fact that in the discovery mode they found the pupils were forced 'to think' (see exhibit 7.8). The student-teachers were not asked to consider this aspect of teaching and given the need to develop higher order thinking skills the role of discovery modes in learning may be somewhat more important than these results suggest. Several of the reports took into account the issue of 'transfer' in the design of their tests. For many pupils the discovery strategy was a different mode of teaching. Like all the methods reported in these chapters if they are to help children learn and find and utilise their own learning styles methods such as these need to be regularly included in their programmes. This is a matter for school policy in order that each subject does what it does best in determining its goals. As Shulman said, if he "*had to identify a single dimension most critical as a determinant of an instructional strategy, it would be the objectives sought*", and that has profound implications for the planning implementation and evaluation of a course of lessons.

Implications for curriculum and instructional leaders.

The implications are very similar to those for chapter 6. The discovery v expository teaching debate is an issue that can provide the basis for an "assumptional-dialogue" within the framework of the development of higher order thinking. It is important to note that discovery methods take up more time than expository methods and may be accompanied by increased motivation. Instructional and curriculum leaders need to be able to argue that educational theories should not be dismissed out of hand without an understanding of the evidence or evaluation in practice.

Notes and references

[1] Matthews, M. R. (1994) *Science Teaching. The Role of History and Philosophy of Science.* Routledge, London.
[2] Dewey, J (1897). My pedagogic creed. *School Journal* 54, 77-80
[3] Hill, G (1988) Lessons for Life on two views of structured teaching. *The Times*
[4] Shulman, L. S. (1970) Psychology and mathematics education in E. Begle (ed). *Mathematics Education.* 69th yearbook of the National Society for the Study of Education. University of Chicago Press, Chicago.
[5] Cited by C. H. Patterson (1977). *Foundations for a Theory of Instruction and Educational Psychology.* Harper and Row, New York p 162.
[6] Bruner, J. S (1963). *The Process of Education.* Harvard U.P. Cambridge MA
[7] Shulman, L. S (1970) *loc.cit.*
[8] Bruner, J. S (1971). *The Relevance of Education.* Norton, New York. Published as a Penguin paperback 1974
[9] Bruner, J. S (1966). *Toward a Theory of Instruction.* Harvard U. P. Cambridge, Mass.
[10] *loc.cit* ref ref 4.
[11] e.g Stannard, R. (1992) *Black Holes and Uncle Albert.* Faber and Faber, London.
[12] Landa, L. V (1987) A fragment of a lesson based on algo-heuristic theory of instruction in C. M. Reigeluth (ed). *Instructional Theories in Action.* Erlbaum, Hillsdale, NJ. And Skolnik, S (1995). Launching interest in chemistry. *Educational Leadership,* 53, (1), 34 – 35. National Research Council (1994). *National Science Education Standards "Headline" Summary.* National Committee on Science Education Standards and Assessment. National Research Council, Washington, DC
[13] Reigeluth, C. M. (ed) *Instructional Theories in Action.* Erlbaum, Hillsadale, NJ.
[14] quotations are from *The Relevance of Education* and also ref 4.
[15] *loc. cit* ref 4.
[16] Hunt, E and J. Minstrell (1994) A cognitive approach to the teaching of physics in K. McGilly (ed). *Classroom Lessons. Integrating Cognitive Theory and Classroom Practice.* The MIT Press, Cambridge, MA.
[17] Di Sessa, A (1988) Knowledge in pieces in G. Forman and E. Pufall *Constructivism in the Computer Age.* Erlbaum, Hillsdale, NJ
[18] *loc.cit* ref 16 p52
[19] *loc.cit* ref 16 p53.

[20] *loc.cit* ref 16
[21] *loc cit* ref 16 p 55.
[22] Heywood, J., McGuinness, S and D. E. Murphy (1980). *Final Report of the Public Examinations Evaluation Project*. University of Dublin, School of Education, Dublin.
[23] Gagné, R. M., Briggs, L. J. and W. W. Wager (1992). *Principles of Instructional Design*. 4th edition. Harcourt, Brace and Jovanovich, Orlando, FL
[24] Department of Education (1990). *Report of a Review Body on the Primary Curriculum*. National Council for Curriculum and Assessment/Department of Education. Dublin.
[25] Ausubel, D. P. (1960) The use of advaced organizers in the learning and retention of meaningful verbal material. *Journal of Educational Psychology*, 51, 267 – 272. Ausubel, D. P., Novak, J. S and H. Hanesiam (1978*). Educational Psychology. A Cognitive View*. 2nd edition. Holt, Rinehart and Winston. New York.
[26] Shulman *loc cit* ref 4.
[27] McDonald, F (1969*). Educational Psychology*. Wadsworth, Belmont, CA
[28] Boffy, R (1985). YTS core skills and participative learning. *NATFHE Journal* 20 – 23.
[29] Kersh, B. Y (1962). The motivating effect of learning by direct discovery. *Educational Psychology*, 53, 65. Kersh (cited by McDonald) compared three groups. The first received 'no help' in solving mathematical problems. The second group (direct reference) was given some direction in the form of visual aids and verbal instructions directed at these aids while the third group (rule given) were given the rules and practice in their applications but they were not helped to understand the mathematical relationships involved. They learnt mechanically by rote. The direct reference group understood the relationship involved better than the other groups although the "no help" group did better than the group given the rules. Kersh reported that the "no help" group had greater intrinsic motivation than either of the other two groups and were prepared to work at problems. This also true of project work in engineering science (see ref 34). In the second experiment the "no help" group was replaced by a group who were taught the generalizations and had them explained. Each group was subdivided into three sub-groups of ten each. These sub-groups took the test at 3 days, 2 weeks and 6 weeks respectively and the test was designed to assess the recall of generalizations and their application to new problems. The students were also asked to report on the frequency of use of the generalizations in between the teaching and the test. In this way it was hoped to eliminate practice effects. The rote learning group proved to be better than those who had been given an explanation. This is important since we all too often assume that students will learn if the explanations are good. Hence the value of advanced organizers. It also shows that discovery methods do not necessarily promote retention. Finally when students are actively involved in their learning they are more motivated.
[30] Suchman, J. R (1961). Inquiry training. Building skills for autonomous discovery. *Merrill Palmer Quarterly of Behaviour Development*, 7, 147 – 169.
[31] Craig, R. C (1969) Recent research on discovery. *Educational Leadership*. 26, 501 – 508.
[32] *loc.cit* ref 4
[33] Heywood, J (1976) Discovery methods in engineering science at 'A' level. *International Journal of Mechanical Engineering Education*, 4, (2), 97 – 107.
[34] Carter, G., Heywood, J and D. T. Kelly (1986). *A Case Study in Curriculum Assessment. GCE Engineering Science Advanced*. Roundthorn, Manchester. The assessment schedules will also be found in Heywood, J. (2000). *Assessment in Higher Education*. Jessica Kingsley, London.
[35] It was found that 28% and 38% of these teachers experienced "a little apprehension" in implementing these lessons
[36] (a) Heywood, J and S. Heywood (1992) *The Training of Student Teachers in Discovery Methods of Instruction and Learning*. Monographs of the Department of Teacher Education, No 1/92. University of Dublin. (b) Heywood, J. and S. Heywood (1992). The Training of Student teachers in Discovery Methods of Instruction and Learning in Anna Lisa Leino, et al (eds). *Integration of Technology and Reflection in Teaching. A Challenge for European Teacher Education*. Association of Teacher Educators in Europe, Brussels and University of Helsinki, Helsinki pp 158 – 172.

8
LEARNING STYLES AND STRATEGIES

Summary

One of the least discussed topics in education, be it in the teachers' common room, or the classroom is learning. Yet it is the purpose of education that students should learn subject matter and cognitive skills so that they can solve previously unseen problems and bring critical thought to bear on daily events. Yet how students learn is the subject of many assumptions by them as well as their teachers. Many of these assumptions are open to challenge. For that reason issues surrounding learning are an ideal topic for instructional and curriculum leader facilitated dialogue.

A question that should create critical dialogue is "What more, if anything, should we know about how our students learn?" This chapter focuses on the question "Will a knowledge of students learning styles and strategies of learning help to make my teaching more effective?" Learning (cognitive) Styles are dispositions that students bring with them; strategies are approaches they learn as a result of their attempts to learn and to adapt to the learning environment.

Issues that an "assumptional-dialogue" would seek to answer are- first does the teacher agree with the hypothesis that we have pre-dispositions for learning? Assuming that there are these dispositions the second question is how important are they anyway? Do pupils respond to different kinds of instruction, as some theorists would suggest? The third question is-. Do we agree that we can and should cause students to adopt certain strategies toward learning? Do we agree with the dichotomy that distinguishes deep from surface learning? Do we expect learners to approach our subject in depth and what do we do to help them facilitate this goal? Fourth, how much do we need to know about our students? Is it sufficient to base our planning on prior test results? If the results are similar to those obtained previously is it enough to say OK or should we be trying to do something about the low achievers? Can student learning styles help us to a better understanding of our students?

One way to answer these questions is to use a learning style inventory with one's self and students. In this chapter a variety of learning styles and strategies are summarised and details of learning style evaluations conducted by graduate student teachers are reported. It is concluded that understanding the learning styles of students is of value to teachers.

The studies reported here show that the type of assessment and instruction given can have a profound effect on learning. They strongly support the need for variety in teaching and assessments that are carefully designed to match the objectives of that instruction. This has implications for the design of the curriculum.

The implications for educational and instructional and curriculum leaders are considered.

Introduction

We all have preferred ways of organizing what we see and think about[1] or different styles of conceptualisation and patterning of activities. Styles are dispositions that students bring with them; strategies are approaches they learn as a result of their attempts to learn and to adapt to the learning environment. They may be the most important characteristics of an individual in respect of learning.[2] These cognitive or, as they are more commonly called learning styles have been shown to be related to learning and studying. Although numerous learning styles have been proposed[3] only a few will be considered in this chapter, the purpose of which is to consider if an appreciation of the learning styles of students and their teachers can be used to enhance the design of learning environments and, therefore, learning. The bearing of answers to these questions on instructional and educational leadership should be evident.

Grasha who has made extensive reviews of the literature on learning styles found that the factors said to contribute to learning styles could be grouped into five categories.[4] These are:

Cognitive   *relating to the acquisition, retention and retrieval of information*
Sensory   *relating to the acquisition of information via the senses*
Interpersonal   *relating to the acquisition of information within social groupings and groups, influenced therefore by roles and role expectations, group norms, leadership and discourse (occasions of formal and informal learning)*
Intrapersonal   *relating to the influence of the individual on him/herself. Needs and motives and especially the thinking needed for self-control*
Environmental   *relating to the physical environment in which we learn and the resources provided.*

Many theories have been offered to describe the way in which learning is influenced by style; in consequence there are many styles. Just as there are many theories so there are many instruments designed to measure these styles. These instruments, suggests Grasha[5] should

- show high internal consistency and test-retest reliability.
- exhibit construct and predictive validity.
- produce data that can influence instructional practice.
- produce high degrees of satisfaction from these instructional practices.
- assist learners to better develop their cognitive abilities to acquire and use the content with which they are presented.

He concludes that an instrument should *'perform its magic in ways that are clearly superior to those possible without it'*.

It may be argued, however, that a teacher might apply a theory without the use of instruments, for all that is required is that in its application the 'magic' which Grasha seeks is produced. Of course if one knows what learning styles one's students have, this is an undoubted advantage.

Based on the view that no one theory embraces everything Grasha takes an eclectic view and considers that all theories should be examined for their potential in teaching. This is the approach taken in this book. Teachers have to search for what works for them, and it has to be a continuing search and evaluation of theories as they are generated. But their assumptions have to be defensible. So what are these theories and how may they be of use to teachers?

Convergent and divergent thinking styles (and creativity)

The best known cognitive styles are probably those described at either end of the continuum of convergent-divergent thinking. Divergent thinkers are commonly described as creative. These two dimensions originated with Guilford's study of the intellect. The Guilford model assumed that creativity and intelligence are different things and that creativity is as important as intelligence. Convergent thinkers tend to concentrate on test questions that require a single answer, whereas divergent thinkers do not like the confines of conventional tests; they are more at home when generating many solutions. It is said that they perform well in activities like brainstorming. Divergence is associated with creativity. For some teachers the behaviours of divergent thinkers can be contentious.

Hudson[6] used tests for convergent and divergent thinking in the UK, and found that those who studied arts (humanities) subjects were much more creative than those who studied science. One of the problems with the tests used by Hudson was that they were of the pencil and paper variety. It was argued that scientific creativity was difficult to measure with such tests.[7] Guilford considered that effective thinking resulted from the sequential use of convergent and divergent processes.⁸ In general, it is held that there has to be a balance between convergent and divergent thinking. This point is reinforced by another study of engineers that showed a marked tendency for the best performers to record central scores on both co-ordinates. The poorer students tended to perform high on one co-ordinate and low on the other.⁹

An American study of school children that was much discussed showed that intelligence in the normal range was sufficient for high level creativity but that above an IQ of 120, creativity and intelligence were not correlated.¹⁰ Other studies have confirmed this view.

At school level much has been written about the tendency of teachers to encourage convergent thinking at the expense of divergent thinking. It was also argued that examinations reinforced this situation and one of the reasons given by teachers for more assessed coursework was that it would encourage creativity. But it was also reported that teachers felt they might lose control if they allowed children to be to creative.¹¹ Borich writing of American classrooms said that the predominant form of questioning was convergent and much of it was about the recall of facts. He pointed out that higher order thinking does require factual knowledge and thought that this may have something to do with the predominance of such questions. He also noted that more instructional time was required for higher order questioning.¹² It seems to be generally accepted that creative thinking consists of combinations and patterns of the same processes that are used in ordinary pursuits.¹³

Holistic and Serialist Learning

These terms are now part of common usage and originate with Gordon Pask and his colleagues. During the nineteen sixties he, Brian Lewis and Bernard Scott had suggested that learning strategies, teaching strategies and plans of action can be differentiated by type.¹⁴ Their concept of style is based on what they call conversation theory. Conversations are behaviours that may be observed in the form of understandings. Within conversation theory, understanding includes the relationship between the topics discussed but also the ability to apply that relationship to new situations. We may have conversations with ourselves and they can be in the form of gestures or mediated through a computer interface. A style is a disposition to adopt one class of learning strategy or one class of teaching strategy in conversations. Such conversations are usually verbal.

Pask and Scott¹⁵ distinguished between two kinds of learning strategy that they called holist and serialist. They are mirrored by similar teaching strategies. Holists prefer global predicates and relations of topics whereas serialists prefer step by step approaches to learning. Teaching preferences along these lines are readily identifiable. They suggest strongly that strategic mismatches between learning styles and teaching strategy can impede learning. Later studies suggested that matched performance is better than mismatched performance. Also revealed were different types of serialists and holists. There are those serialists who move step by step; they do not proceed to the next thing to be learnt until they have mastered the present. There are also serialists who learn by rote; they follow a well-defined and narrow route and may do well in examinations that demand memory skills.

They distinguished between redundant and irredundant holists. Both focus on global, predicate rules but the redundant holist learns better with minimally specified rules. Some holists prefer analogies and generalisations that provide contrasts and similarities within the material. But there is another type of holist who likes to discover or invent these analogies and generalisations between the topics. Pask argues that while this is one of the most productive ways of learning neither the serialist or holist is at an advantage since learning involves both discovery and invention as well as, integration of both local and global rules. Pask noted that whatever the problem some persons use the same strategies which if they are holist would be mismatched in academic environments where a serialist style is the dominant approach. This would seem to be similar to set mechanisation in problem solving (see Ch 9). However, he also reported that some persons are more flexible and versatile than others in their response to changing contexts, a fact which relates to that aim of education that persons should learn to be adaptable in life's situations.

Pask used the terms- improvidence and globe trotting to describe learners who relied on one process at the expense of the other. Serialists show improvident behaviour because they are likely to miss important relationships between ideas whereas globe trotters rely on holism and build up views quickly that do not contain the evidence to support the conclusions reached.[16]

Studies of reading have found the three styles of global, analytic and synthetic learner. In a global approach reliance is placed on prior contextual knowledge. An analytic reader is oriented to the detail of word identification and meaning thus relying on the information in the material rather than on prior knowledge. The synthetic style integrates in progression the other two strategies. Kirby describes the sequence as (a) general orientation to the task, (b) learning of the specific skills required for the task and finally (c) the integration of the two.[17] Kirby suggested that children with reading difficulties approach reading in a global manner and this is a source of their disability.

At the same time people generally are able to switch between styles as a function of the situation in which they find themselves. For example academics who are skilled readers are unlikely to engage in the global style of processing but to quote *"if [they] were assessed on the basis of their performance in situations related to problems with their automobile or with their home life, much more global processing would be observed."* Directly related to these ideas of holistic and serial learning, are the concepts of field dependence and field independence.

Field-dependence and Field-independence[18]

Many factors come together to influence our perception. Cognitive or learning styles may be described as the particular mode of perception that an individual brings to the understanding of his or her world. In the United States Witkin and his co-workers suggested that individual dispositions toward the perception of their environment lie on a continuum. Its polar ends are called field-dependent and field-independent.[19] Individuals who are field-dependent look at the world in a global way, while those who are field-independent would see it analytically. The reactions of the field-dependent to people, places and events are undifferentiated and complex. In contrast, the events (objects) in the environment are not associated with the background of that environment by a person who is field-independent. The relationship between these ideas and those that have just been described will be self-evident.

The embedded-figures test is an inventory for the evaluation of these particular learning styles that does not depend on verbal statements.

Several investigators using this inventory have claimed that an individual's location on the continuum between the two poles contributes to academic choice, success and vocational preference. Field-dependent persons require their learning to have more structure, direction and feedback than field-independent ones, who tend to dislike collaborative learning. This would explain the everyday experience of teachers who find that some students who do not like group work are nevertheless good at academically analytical work. Tyler has pointed out that the same may apply to teachers in higher education, and this would account for the liking that some teachers have for lectures and others for group discussion.[20]

The field-dependence-independence dimension has a slight relationship to verbal skills. But it has not been related to overall academic achievement. Choice of academic study does, however, appear to be related to cognitive style, especially in mathematics and the sciences.[21]

In the academic situation how does what we perceive "study to be" affect our approach to study? Does it make us adopt particular strategies toward learning or, do these and possibly other learning styles have a greater influence on the approach we adopt to learning?

Depth and Surface Approaches to Learning

Although the investigations that distinguished between depth and surface approaches to learning were undertaken with students in higher education the findings are of some significance to primary and post-primary education.[22] Cowan associates deep learning with reflective learning, and university teachers often talk about learning in depth.[23] Such learning is a search for understanding. It is, therefore, related to higher order thinking.

Marton and Säljö who started it all off asked students to read a text. Then the students were asked to recount it, answer questions on the content, describe how they had read it, and how they went about remembering its content. On a second occasion they were asked to recall as much as they could of the text. On the first occasion one half were given questions in advance on particular points in the text, the other half received no guidance. For the second occasion half the group were given instruction as to how they should read while the others were given no instructions. A free recall was requested, and questions were asked about the text immediately after reading and after 65 and 85 days. Marton and Säljö distinguished between *"the students who did get 'the point' and those who did not"*. They argued that those who did not did so because they were not looking for it. *"The main difference which was found was whether the students focused on the text itself or on what the text was about; the author's intention, the main point, the conclusion to be drawn."*

Marton suggests that the strategies they found, apart from anything else, are indicative of different perceptions of what is wanted in learning in higher education. For some, *"learning is through the discourse and for others learning is the discourse'"* Those who adopt the former strategy get involved in the activity while those who take the latter view allow learning to 'happen' to them. It is this group who are *surface* learners who pay but superficial attention to the text, who are passive, who do not reflect and who do not appreciate that understanding involves effort.

In Australia studies among senior-year students have suggested that deep-level students were more likely to perceive their course as encouraging independence in both attitudes and approach to learning and as not being overburdening.[24] Clearly a question for high schools is whether or not the curriculum encourages depth learning. And should it?

During the late 1970s Entwistle[25] began an extensive program to extend the work he had begun on motivation. He and his colleagues wished to confirm Marton's conclusion that the approach to learning was related to the outcome of learning. In their factorial analysis they found two factors were related to deep approaches to study. One described a student who would concentrate on relating ideas without examining the evidence in detail. In the other reliance was placed on factual detail but was not accompanied by a clear overview. Few students it seemed were capable of undertaking all the processes demanded by a fully deep approach. Entwistle in other studies found students who adopted a 'strategic' approach in which they *"try to manipulate the assessment procedures to their own advantage by a careful marrying of their efforts to the reward system as they perceive it.'"* These different orientations to study have some similarity with Bey's[26] distinction between students who are intellectually oriented (study for its own sake); those who are academically oriented (i.e. concerned with passing examinations), and those who are socially oriented (i.e., concerned more with what college has to offer their social life).

Entwistle's study led him to produce three orientations. These he called meaning, reproducing and achieving. Related to these are three motives-personal interest, fear of failure and need for achievement. Need for achievement is linked to strategic approaches to learning and is accompanied by organized study methods and positive approaches to learning; fear of failure is linked to surface approaches and extrinsic motivation; and, personal interest is linked to intrinsic motivation and deep approaches to learning. Entwistle considered that the deep approach included not only the learning process involved in the study but the intention to reach personal understanding.

Entwistle believes that the way instructions are interpreted is an important factor in determining the approach adopted. They create an intention to learn in a certain way that determines the level of processing. His colleague, Wilson[27] queried this emphasis on intention, and argued that it is the conception of what learning involves which is one of the most important factors affecting the approach the student adopts. Either way these interpretations lent support to those who in the nineteen-sixties had introduced new approaches to assessment with a view to positively influencing learning. At the same time they are a reminder of the care with which examination questions and instructions must be designed. This applies equally to second level education as it does to higher education. Entwistle is also known for his development of the 'approaches' to study questionnaires.[28]

The approach learners' adopt will depend upon several factors: First is likely to be the difficulty of the subject matter: some texts can be skimmed over while others can only be understood by systematically setting out the arguments, evidence and conclusions. Second is the interest and importance of the text: a 'set' book will receive a closer look than supplementary reading, but especially if its' subject matter appeals to the student. Third may be the student's natural preference for reading in a particular way. The studies so far reported have not really clarified whether there are in fact basic differences in approach or whether the approaches actually used reflect the fourth factor, viz. the student's conception of what it takes to learn complex subject matter.

Ramsden argues that it is clear that individual students display variability in their approaches to learning.[29] He had previously reported that students could adopt both surface and depth approaches. Student expectations are a powerful influence on the style they adopt. Thus, the perceptions that students have of assessment even at the end of an exercise will dictate their approach even if that is not the approach that is called for. Ramsden considers that the evidence for consistency in approach over time is persuasive.[30] However, he argues that consistency is not the same as fixity, and orientations to study may be changed in response to teaching, assessment and the curriculum.

The implications for the type of instruction are as great as they are for assessment and the two have to be designed literally together. Moreover, the same applies to schools. Courses have to be planned as a whole; random changes to try and meet these criteria are unlikely to suffice

Departments also, and institutions in general convey images to students not only of what is expected of them but of what they can expect of their tutors. These pictures are not always happy ones.

The learning-in-context theory affirms the findings of perceptual learning theory that learning outcomes are dependent in no small way on the learner's perceptions and previous experience. Some persons appear to be able to adapt and others find it difficult but it is a capacity that can be partly learnt.[31] For which reason students need to learn a variety of strategies and they might be helped with context related "learning how to learn" programmes. As indicated above there is a message for teachers in that they too can begin to help by designing courses that demand some variability of approach.[32] This was done by some of the teachers in a transition year project that developed a course on learning how to learn.

In his attempt to draw conclusions from these various studies of deep and surface learning Schmeck draws attention to a number of points that have a bearing on school education. First (my ordering), is Marton's finding that university students in physics and economics can pass in economics and science and yet have no basic understanding of the concepts and principles of these subjects. They acquire large bodies of knowledge without acquiring the understanding required by these concepts and principles (see also chapter 6 on concept learning). At the same time "*we have adults who do not see it as their function to reflect, form opinions, evaluate, disagree, oppose, challenge, conceptualise, or integrate information in meaningful ways. We have adults who plod along without thought until, at roughly 10 year intervals, they have what has come to be popularly known as the 'mid-life crisis*" - permitting themselves for one brief period to ask "*what does it all mean?*" Schmeck's solution lies primarily in the design of examinations and classroom tests. Questions should be set which integrate knowledge. One has to get the students to make a perceptual shift.

Taken together all of this work leads to the view that such learning begins in elementary school for it seems that by the time students reach high school the semblance of deep and surface approaches have emerged. In systems where there are public examinations students may adopt a reproducing style. The evidence from Irish studies suggests teachers believe this to be case. Accordingly they adopt teaching strategies they believe will help their pupils reproduce.[33] This situation reflects badly on teacher training for it suggests that student teachers have not been encouraged to vary their approaches or design lessons and instruction to help students acquire 'intrinsic motivation' and deep approaches to learning. Equally it reflects badly on the examination designers.

If Bennett[34] is correct and an unreflective approach to learning is fostered in primary schools then pupils will be directed away from deep learning toward surface approaches that foster the acquisition of knowledge at the expense of other skills. During secondary school the concern with the acquisition of knowledge will reinforce the surface approach. There are therefore, signs that orientations have emerged in high school which would influence student expectations of what to expect from university that will not easily be changed especially by simple short how to study courses.[35]

Schmeck[36] considers that cognitive style may have its origins explained by the possibility that some children have to 'prove' themselves if their self-esteem is inadequate. In order to establish conditional worth within the classroom context of achievement and competition they learn to 'crack the code' with analytic skills. If a student clings to this way of doing things then they will continue to approach things in this way and develop a high level of analytic skill and not move beyond this to thinking in synthesis.

In contrast a person who does not crack the code will be left at the global stage, become field dependent and continue to be child like and undirected and within the context of study have low esteem reinforced. Schmeck relates this to parenting and not merely schools. Early parenting can influence the dependence/independence continuum as well as the locus of control.[37] Thus, teachers should encourage creative self-expression and help students to realise that self-expression has to precede self-improvement on the grounds that *"you can't change who you are if you don't know who you are*!" In many respects many of the student teachers whose work is quoted in this book, have arrived at this conclusion by different routes. The course from which most of the examples were taken had as one of its aims the understanding of need for variety not merely as a stimulus for intrinsic motivation but for the development of versatility in cognitive functioning. Much of this can be accompanied by relatively simple changes in teaching.

The Dunn and Dunn Learning Styles Model[38]

This model arose from an attempt sponsored by the New York State Department of Education to increase the achievement of educationally disadvantaged children. In their evaluation of previous research Dunn and Dunn identified twelve variables which differentiated students. Subsequently they found a further six and had begun to incorporate hemisphere preference and global analytic inclinations in their framework. Dunn and Dunn's learning styles model is based on these two dimensions that is the left/right brain theory and cognitive style theory. They had found that when students are taught through their identified learning style preferences that their achievement level was increased. Moreover, as has been found for imagery, student discipline improved. Because they held that teachers cannot identify all the elements of a student's learning they set out to develop learning style inventories that could be used with elementary and high school children.[39]

The twenty-one elements when categorised revealed five fundamental dimensions. These are:
1. Immediate Environment
2. Emotionality
3. Sociological preference in learning
4. Physiological differences
5. Processing limitations

The influence of the emotions on performance as well physiological differences relating to energy levels at given times of day have been widely discussed. It comes, therefore, as no particular surprise to find that food and drink are one of the parameters. Processing is the term used for the limitations on learning imposed by cognitive style. Their research has led them to the view that instructional environments, resources, and approaches respond to diverse learning style strengths. They found among other things that global-analytic children have different environmental and physiological needs. Thus, analytics prefer a formal setting that is quiet and well lit. "*They rarely eat, drink, smoke, chew, or bite on objects while learning.*" Those (of whom many are known to us) who like having music as a background, take some form of food or drink and are rather more casual in their seating approach tend to be globals.[40] Globals may work on several tasks at once and sometimes prefer learning with their peers. Of course there may be mixes. Very high achievers (gifted children in the US context) tend to be global as do underachievers which seems surprising given the previous discussion.[41]

Dunn and Dunn argue that globals require new and difficult information for it to be interesting. They also take the view that no learning style is better or worse than any other and that each style encompasses similar intelligence ranges. They hold that students do better when they are taught through their learning style preferences. There are three aspects of Dunn and Dunn's work which are of particular interest. These are:
1. It is practically oriented and aims to help practice at kindergarten, elementary and secondary levels.
2. It highlights the importance of the teaching environment.
3. It led to the development of instruments to detect learning styles for K-12 elementary and secondary levels.[42]

From the point of view of the management of learning whether it be the teacher or the school managers the reminder of the old tag "*no more Latin, no more French, no more sitting on the hard old bench*" is important. It is a reminder that sitting for four hours or more does create stress and young children are often told off for fidgeting when they cannot help trying to obtain relief. Seating they argue can be arranged to suit learning styles and when it is test scores have been found to improve.

At the K-2 stage Dunn suggests that classrooms should be redesigned *"with cardboard boxes and other usable items placed perpendicular to the walls to allow quiet, well-lit areas and, simultaneously, sections for controlled interaction and soft lighting. Permit children who want to do so to work in chairs, on carpeting, bean bags, or cushions; and/or seated against the walls - as long as they pay attention, and perform as well as or better than they had previously. Turn the lights off and read in natural daylight with underachievers or whenever the class becomes restless. Establish rules for classroom decorum as you feel comfortable - for example, no feet on desks, no shoes on chairs, do not distract anyone else from learning. You may not require test performance and behaviour. You will be surprised at the positive results."* For many teachers that is likely to be an understatement, our views of classroom behaviour are deeply embedded.

Environmental arguments support those who timetable secondary students to move from room to room during the school day. Less attention has been paid to the design of rooms in universities yet it is evident that many lecture theatres and rooms are not conducive to learning. My students often have to learn in seminars where there is no daylight and poor ventilation. In spite of criticism of the tests, Dunn and Dunn's work has proved attractive to many school teachers.[43]

The implications of the studies reported so far are that teachers should recognise that they often create a gulf between themselves and their students in so far as the academic goals of education are concerned by the techniques of teaching and assessment they use. It may be argued that teachers should take into account the learning styles and orientations of their students in their teaching. At a more general level it might also be argued that teaching styles should be matched to learning styles. However, the foregoing literature on learning styles, as for example that of Pask[44] and Kirby[45] suggests that students ought to be aware of other styles and in the case of Kirby that they should be able to move from the global to the analytic to the synthetic. It will also be evident that there are differences in interpretation of global and analytic thinkers as between the authorities. Dunn and Dunn for example appear to distinguish sharply between analytic and global whereas Kirby sees global as being a first stage from which the learner has to move.

Kolb's learning theory and Learning Styles Inventory.

In 1984 Kolb[46] proposed an experiential theory of learning that has proved popular in management and higher education. It is with its application to school teaching that this section is concerned. The theory is illustrated in figure 8.1. At the centre the student is a receiver but as the student moves between the stages on the perimeter, he/ she is an actor.[47] The theory proposes that all learning is cyclic. Each cycle involves four processes. First comes a specific experience that causes the learner to want to know more about that experience. For that to happen, the learner has to reflect on that experience from as many viewpoints as possible. From this reflection the learner draws conclusions and uses them finally to influence decision-making or take action. A different style of learning is required for each activity. It will be apparent, for example, that the cycle draws the learner into a form of reflective practice.[48] The axes represent the available information or abstraction contained in the experience (y-axes) and, the processing of information through reflection or action on the conclusions drawn (x-axes).

Since the theory holds that we have a predisposition to think in a style associated with one of these activities in any group of people one is likely to find persons with different learning dispositions or styles. If correct the implications for teaching and learning are profound. It is argued that different types of learner require different treatments. Thus if a teacher wishes to teach a concept or a principle he/she should teach it in four different ways even though he/she has a preference for one style. This means they will have to be cognisant with a whole range of instructional strategies.[49] This proposition is consistent with all the research on learning styles and strategies previously reported. The theory also proposes that learners should learn to learn in each of the other three styles.

Figure 8.2 shows the generalizability of the model to any subject. It is an adaption by Todd[52] of Svinicki and Dixon's model of the teaching strategies relevant to each stage of the modle that takes into account the questions that McCarthy used in her development of the Kolb model. McCarthy[53] developed a learning type measure based on the Kolb theory. She called the learning styles Types. In terms of the questions asked she described the types as- Type 1, divergers who ask "why" questions. Type 2- assimilators who ask "what" questions, Type 3, convergers who ask "how" questions, and type 4 accommodators who ask "what if" questions. It followers from this theory that students need to be able to learn all four styles in order to answer and pose questions in all four categories.

McCarthy showed that her model could be used for systems design in teaching. Each quadrant can be divided into principal, teacher and student perspectives. Quadrant one is devoted to the question "what?" Quadrant two becomes "why?" Quadrant three becomes "how" and Quadrant four "if". These questions are addressed to the principal, the teacher and the student in turn and their roles change as a function of the question type. For example in Quadrant three the student is a user of content and skill, the teacher becomes the coach and the principal the facilitator of resources.

Perhaps the most important feature of the system is that the students can be taught to use the system for themselves. Thus Weber and Weber[54] used McCarthy's 4 Mat wheel to show students how to write their oral reports. It is interesting to note that the students generated a model very similar to those generated by Svnicki and Dixon who described the instructional activities which might relate to each quadrant

INSTRUCTIONAL AND CURRICULUM LEADERSHIP

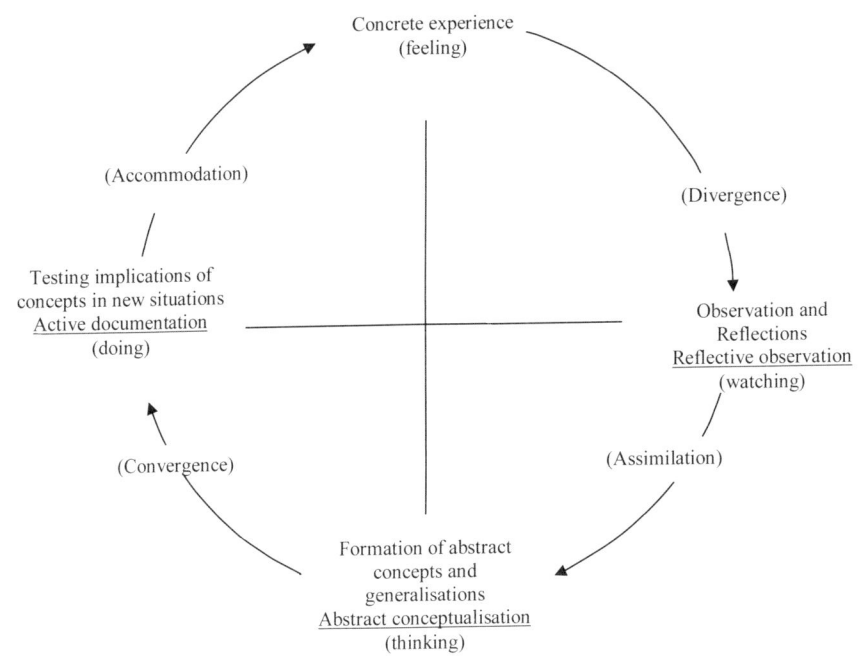

```
                    Concrete experience
                         (feeling)


  (Accommodation)                           (Divergence)

Testing implications of
concepts in new situations          Observation and
 Active documentation                  Reflections
       (doing)                    Reflective observation
                                        (watching)


  (Convergence)                            (Assimilation)

                  Formation of abstract
                      concepts and
                      generalisations
                  Abstract conceptualisation
                         (thinking)
```

Figure 8.1. An adaptation of Kolb's experiential learning model based on Fitzgibbon[50] and Stice.[51]

In quadrant one, activating knowledge, the students wanted to get others interested. Therefore, they suggested brainstorming, hook questions, show pictures, demonstrations, mind maps, make a logo and imagery. In the second quadrant they need lots of detail so the teaching of factual information is important. Thus lectures, charts, pictures, examples etc are used. Then in the third quadrant the students learn by practice through a variety of methods ranging from hands on activities through worksheets to reading specific materials. Finally the students have to do something personal like having to apply it in real life to drawing and writing.

Following FitzGibbon[55] the four styles of the Kolb model are:
(1)   Convergers: Their dominant learning styles are abstract conceptualization and active experimentation. It is the mode of learning that has often been associated with the classroom and caused by traditional assessment. People with this style do best in tests where the problems require single solutions. Not very emotional, they tend to prefer things to people. Convergence relates to that part of problem solving which is related to the selection of a solution and the evaluation of the consequences of the solution.

(2) Divergers: These are the opposite of convergers. Both terms come from the early research in creativity, and Kolb cites Hudson's study in particular. Divergers are best in the situation of concrete experience and reflective observation. They like to 'imagine' and generate ideas. They are emotional and relate well to people, and do not perform as well in tests which demand single solutions. Divergence relates to that part of the problem-solving process that identifies differences (problems) and compares goals with reality.

(3) Assimilators: Their dominant learning skills are abstract conceptualization and reflective observation. They are not so much concerned with people as with abstract concepts. They are interested in the precise and logical development of theory rather than with its application. Kolb describes them as pure rather than applied scientists. Assimilation relates to the solution of problems and the considerations of alternative solutions in the problem-solving process.

(4) Accommodators: These are the opposite of the assimilators. Their dominant learning strengths are concrete experience and active experimentation. They like doing things and want to devise and implement experiments. Such individuals take more risks than those with the other learning styles. Kolb says 'we have labeled this style "accommodator" because he tends to excel in those situations where he must adapt himself to specific immediate circumstances'. Such individuals are at ease with people, although they are relatively impatient. Accommodation relates to the choice of goal(s) and the execution of solutions in problem-solving.

In Kolb's theory problem-solving requires the use of all four skills. An interesting feature of research in problem solving is the fact reported by several authorities that, once taught a method of problem solving, many students use the same technique to solve all others. This 'problem set', as Luchins[56] calls it, is extremely limiting and can prevent effective transfer (see chapter 9). The same may be true of learning styles and learning strategies.[57] Kolb's theory suggests that over use of one dominant style can be a serious impediment to learning.

Kolb and his colleagues devised a self-assessment inventory to measure the preferred learning styles of individuals (The Learning Styles Inventory), which has been substantially revised.[58] Using the original version they found from undergraduate data that those who had studied business were accommodators. Nursing and Engineering undergraduates were convergers, History, Political Science, English and Psychology students were divergers, and those studying economics, mathematics, sociology, chemistry and physics were assimilators. He came to the conclusion that different subjects required or encouraged/developed different styles of learning as indicated above. Svinicki and Dixon have shown how this might be translated into practice.[59] Kolb argued that undergraduate education was a major factor influencing style while at the same time recognizing that his results might be due to the academic process of selection. Our interest here is that divergers and accommodators could be disadvantaged by some techniques of assessment and teaching.

INSTRUCTIONAL AND CURRICULUM LEADERSHIP

The Learning Styles Inventory has been used in teacher and higher education as part of a self-assessment process designed to help students learn how to learn.[60] Loacker[61] and her colleagues report on the Alverno experience with Kolb's LSI thus:

"The identification of experiential validation of knowledge and theory as a significant cause of learning relates to the student's awareness of learning as a process of experiencing, reflecting, forming new concepts, and testing one's judgements and abilities in action .... At entrance students showed a marked preference for 'concrete experience' over abstract conceptualization' and for 'reflective observation' over 'active experimentation'. Eventually students showed that they had come to rely equally on concrete and abstract models and to use a similar flexibility in choosing either reflective or active approaches".

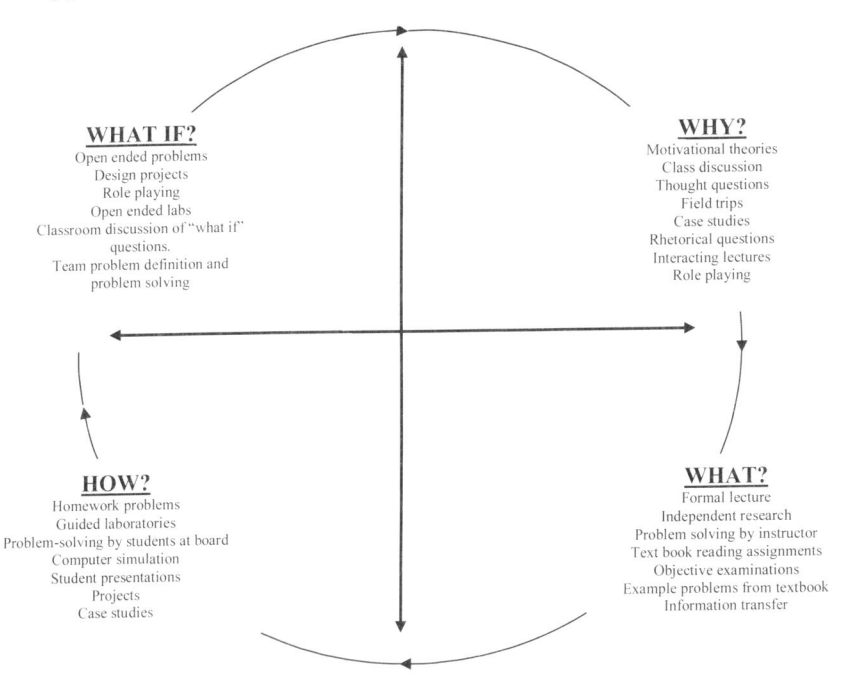

WHAT IF?
Open ended problems
Design projects
Role playing
Open ended labs
Classroom discussion of "what if" questions.
Team problem definition and problem solving

WHY?
Motivational theories
Class discussion
Thought questions
Field trips
Case studies
Rhetorical questions
Interacting lectures
Role playing

HOW?
Homework problems
Guided laboratories
Problem-solving by students at board
Computer simulation
Student presentations
Projects
Case studies

WHAT?
Formal lecture
Independent research
Problem solving by instructor
Text book reading assignments
Objective examinations
Example problems from textbook
Information transfer

Figure 8.2. Todd's (1991) adaptation of Svinicki and Dixon's (1987) application of the Kolb model to teaching, showing the 4-Mat questions

Nevertheless, as the studies by Loacker and FitzGibbon show, independently of what it actually measures this inventory can be used by teachers to better understand their students and to design their courses. This latter point is particularly well illustrated by Svinicki and Dixon[62] who related the many different types of instructional activity to the components of the cycle most likely to support that method (for example, concrete experienced-fieldwork; reflective observation-discussion; abstract conceptualization-papers; active experimentation-homework-[see above]). They agree with Kolb that there are fundamental differences in the nature of the disciplines, and because of these differences the discipline itself can circumscribe an instructor's choice of learning activities. More generally high psychometric reliability and validity are not necessarily required to illuminate the problems that the teacher has in the classroom. It was with that spirit in mind that the groups of graduate student teachers who participated in the concept learning and discovery exercises described in chapters 6 and 7 were also asked to evaluate the use of the Learning Styles Inventory in their classrooms.

Teaching with the aid of the Learning Styles Inventory.

The first judgement a teacher (particularly someone in pre-service training) has to make is whether or not they agree with the hypothesis that we have predispositions for learning. This can be accomplished at a face validity level by inspection of the descriptions that accompany the different models, as for example Honey and Mumford's[63] or Kolb's as described by Fitzgibbon above. Do we recognize ourselves in these descriptions? It is unlikely that we would agree with everything we read about ourselves: that suggests that some aspects of the other styles enter into our pictures of ourselves

And, if on reflection we cannot write a description of ourselves what does this have to say about our self-awareness and ability to reflect?

The second judgement we have to make, assuming that we accept the idea that there are these dispositions, is to answer the question how important are they anyway? Do pupils respond to different kinds of instruction, as some theorists would suggest? If the theorists do not agree about anything else, they do agree that different styles merit different treatments? Since these treatments often require a change in the role of teacher do they merit the effort required to make this change? The third judgement relates to strategy and orientation. Do we agree that we can and should cause students to adopt certain strategies toward learning? Do we agree with the dichotomy that distinguishes deep from surface learning? Do we expect learners to approach our subject in depth and what do we do to help them facilitate this goal? Fourth, how much do we need to know about our students? Is it sufficient to base our planning on prior test results? If the results are similar to those obtained previously is it enough to say OK or should we be trying to do something about the low achievers? Can student learning styles help us to a better understanding of our students?

To answer this question we asked a group of our post-graduate student teachers to familiarise themselves with Kolb's theory through lectures and the papers by Grasha[64] and Svinicki and Dixon[65] They were asked to devise a lesson plan that would take their pupils through each quadrant of the cycle. In order for them to devise a test it was suggested that rather than teach a concept in different ways in the four phases of the learning cycle they should advance the lesson through the stages of the cycle.[66] In that way they would be able to test each quadrant. They would also be able to get some idea if there was a correlation between style and performance in the different quadrants (i.e. do the divergers do best in the divergent part of the test, the assimilators in the assimilator part of the test and so forth?). A week after the lesson was completed the test was to be set. These graduate student teachers were then given additional literature to enable them to discuss the question - Should learning styles be matched to teaching styles (their response to take into account their own learning styles as assessed in another part of their training programme)? To achieve these goals the students had to administer the Learning Styles Inventory to their students.[67] In addition to the reports many of students voluntarily completed a questionnaire designed to elicit their opinions about certain dimensions of the exercise and simplify the analysis of the reports.[68]

In the discussion that follows the data obtained from two groups of graduate student teachers separated by 5 years are presented.[69] It was found that the comments and responses of the students cover the same issues in each of the intervening years. The examples, except for the lesson plans, are taken from another year to illustrate and support this contention. The first group used the Kolb inventory and the second group assigned their own descriptions as indicated below . Example lesson schemes are shown in exhibits 8.1, 8.2 and 8.3.

Most of the students tried to design a lesson in which they could cover the whole of the cycle but there were a few who took two lessons and one or two took three or four, each lesson being devoted to one style. One of these is shown in exhibit 8.1. Since it was published with the student's (Paula Carroll) permission it is appropriate to build the discussion around that report as it raises most of the issues.[70] It is of some significance to note that half of the student teachers found it difficult to cover the cycle within a single lesson. No reason was found to suggest that the cycle should not take more than a lesson.

Related to this is the question of entry into the cycle. One or two students started at different points such as beginning with a theory. Cowan[71] supports an approach that allows entry at other appropriate points – that is, appropriate to the objectives to be achieved.

First, Carroll reported an 8% improvement overall between pre and post-test scores. In a graded public examination system this is a matter of a difference of a grade for many students. While the material was not totally new to the students Carroll was of the opinion that this was no bad thing because repetition does not mean assimilation and the lesson may have helped assimilation. However, she had set a test at the end of each lesson and had expected there to be an improvement in scores as between the first and last tests. But that had not happened. She put this down to the fact that test 1 was easier than the other tests. She felt that it was notoriously difficult for a novice to design 4 tests of equal difficulty. She does not comment on the validity of the tests for testing the particular style. Many of the student teachers found test design difficult and this has implications for their training.

Second, Carroll raised the question of the validity of the Kolb Inventory. So did many other student teachers especially with younger children (12-13 years of age) they found they had to explain some of the items/words in the inventory. Carroll pointed out that the students were, according to Piaget, just coming out of the stage of concrete operations and they would have a first preference for 'action' oriented options. But this assumes that children are not capable of critical thought (see chapter 9). One student teacher who questioned the validity of the inventory administered the test twice to her students with a space between. One third of the twenty-one tested changed their styles. *"Inspection of the results suggests that there was a general movement toward the centre of the axes"* which was not accounted for in her comments. But when she came to evaluate her work she concluded that although there was no evidence to support the view that students learn best in the phase which corresponds to their own

Lesson phases	Content	Learning strategies
Introduction: (Day 1: 1class period 1) Students are reminded of Learning Styles Inventory (rationale has been explained) and told they are to have a lesson divided into 4 parts based on LS theory with a short test after each part. 2) Students divided into 5 groups and told each group will interview the 5 German exchange students present in the school. 3) Groups prepare (in German) batteries of questions to ask. Group work.	3) Questions prepared are based on topics in course (e.g. age hobbies, school etc. Students are focussed on 1st + 2nd person singular verb forms.	1) Expository 3) Brainstorming. Some guidance from teacher mainly grammar in question preparation
Phase 1: Concrete Experience (Day 2: 1 class period. 1) The 5 German students are interviewed, one at a time by each group-such that the group carries out 5 interviews, one with each German student. 2) Students write down information about each German. 3) Students then given a short verb test.	1) Questions prepared above in German are used. When exhausted the students switch to English to ask anything of interest to them. 3) See test after phase 1	1) Group work (minimal interference from teacher). 3) Individual written work.
Phase 2: Reflective Observation (Day 3: ¼ of double class period). 1) Discussion/reflection on what students learned from the interviews (in English). 2) Short verb test given. Same format as for phase 1.	1) Some leading questions from teacher in order to direct discussion: *What did you learn about the German students/ Anything unusual? *What did you find out about Germany? *Did meeting the people make you interested in the place? *What verbs are you using? In what way did you use them? (focus on verb form + pronoun for 2nd person singular) *What verbs did the German use in answering? The same ones? How did they use them? (focus on verb form + pronoun for first person singular) 2) See test after phase 2..	1) Brainstorming. Large group discussion. Guided discovery when focussing on verbs year. 2) Individual work.

Continues over

Phase 3: Abstract Conceptualization (Day 3: 1/3 double class) 1) Students given written script of an interview with 1st, 2nd, 3rd person singular verb forms in it. 2) They study it & try to work out rules governing use of verbs. 3) Short verb test given. Same format as in other phases.	1) See sheet for phase 3 in attached samples of student work. On it are instructions which guide students in their attempt to work out rules.	1) Guided discovery. Individual or pair work (students choose how they want to work).
Phase 4. Active experimentation, (Day 3: 1/3 of double class). 1) Students write up report on any one of the Germans they interviewed. 2) Short verb test given. Same format as in other phases.	1) Here 3rd person singular is used	1) Individual written work
Conclusion: (Day 3: Final 10 minutes of double class) 1) Students asked to reflect on lesson. 2) Given questionnaire on how they felt about the lesson		1) Individual written work 2) Individual written work.

Exhibit 8. 1. Extract from a lesson plan for 12 to 13 year olds in German. The non-behavioural objective was to reinforce use of the present tense (1st, 2nd, 3rd person singular) of common German verbs (both strong and weak). This to be achieved by means of a four phase lesson, , each phase of which corresponds to a quadrant of the Kolb learning cycle.

learning style, nevertheless teaching a lesson that passes through the Kolb cycle improves learning. This was also the view that Carroll took. She made the point that while students might enter school as concrete thinkers they might leave secondary education as convergers. This suggests that the type of instruction given might influence the styles of some of the students and supports the point made by Loacker above.

As for this group of graduate student teachers' 84% would examine the learning styles of their pupils again. 63% would in the future teach their students about learning styles again. 77% thought Pupils' needed training in learning styles.[72] Five years later 56% of the group said they intended to use the Kolb theory again and interestingly 29% said they would use a learning style inventory. One at least suggested the need for a variety of measures including student perceptions of themselves (see exhibit 8.4 (a)). Another suggested that the examination process should be adjusted to take the different styles into account. This she thought would enable the teachers to *"feel free to use all styles with confidence and without the threat of being charged willing his/her class with irrelevance"*.

Third, Carroll found that while there was no relation between learning style and the phase in which best score was achieved there was a relation between learning style and preferred phase of lesson.[73]

Fourth, Carroll related her experience of designing lessons and implementing them to the Kolb cycle thus: CE –Reading material on a particular learning theory. R.O. Reflection on material. Discussion in lectures. Generation of ideas. AC – formulating hypotheses on the particular learning theory. AE-Design and implementation of experiment to test hypotheses. She liked reading about the material and reflecting on it the most enjoyable. The most difficult was devising a lesson to test the hypotheses. *"yet I feel the discipline was good for me."* The Kolb cycle may also be applied to the supervision of teaching (see below).

Subsequently two modifications were made to the exercise. First, in the years that followed instead of administering the inventory the student teachers were asked on the basis of their experience of their pupils to that date to assign them learning styles on the basis of the Kolb descriptors (see exhibit 8.2 example d). We hoped that by causing them to think about their students in this way they would obtain a better understanding of them within the context of their teaching. The test data would be related to these descriptions. Second, because the six exercises represent a huge workload and sometimes created conflict with the demands of other subjects we asked a later group to include an imagery exercise (see chapter 4) within the learning styles exercise. (Exhibits 8.3 and 8.4) It was recommended that it should provide the concrete experience for the first stage. A few students used it to cover the whole cycle, which was permissible.

This approach illustrates the use of inventories as "operators" regardless of what they actually measure. They are also useful for "framing" discussions. Many student teachers learnt that some of their pupils had different styles to their own (exhibits 8.2(b) and 8.2 (c)). Many of the student teachers found the exercise of assigning styles to their students difficult. Exhibit 8.2 (d) illustrates what this exercise entailed. Some involved their pupils in the activity (exhibit 8.2 (e)). Those teachers who involved their students in the activity were careful to point out that the styles were not rigid categories.

The limited evidence available suggested that the number of instructional methods adopted by student teachers could be restricted by their own needs, preferences, and prior-experience. This limitation may have been reinforced by their previous experience of education at school and university that emphasises content regurgitation at the expense of conceptualization, understanding and application. This view is supported by the extensive information given in the student teacher's educational autobiographies, journals and reports of these investigations. It is clear that these investigations have caused very many students to broaden their repertoire of instructional techniques.

INSTRUCTIONAL AND CURRICULUM LEADERSHIP

> "In future to determine students learning styles I would ask the students to write a self report, as Sternberg suggests, specifically in relation to geography. I would make known to the students that what they would write would be treated with the utmost confidentiality, and that its intention was to help students in their learning and they would therefore take it seriously (and admit, for example, the extent to which they are competitive). I would also take students performance into account (as I did in this exercise) as this is the sole evidence of the areas which a student found easiest to learn.
>
> In addition I would use a learning style inventory such as David Kolb's. The questionnaire might identify some additional credentials. I would also take into account my observations of the students and the types of instructional and assessment activities which a student prefers. In summary, therefore, I would use a variety of instruments to assess students learning styles as the more information that can be gathered on each student the more likely the teacher will be correct in assessing the students learning styles.
> **Example (a). Intention. The need for variety in assessment.**
>
> Perhaps the greatest single lesson I will take away from this assignment is that a class is not a single unit but rather a collection of individuals. The way that I learnt best (assimilator/converger) is not necessarily going to be the way that each student in my class learns best.
> I found that the pupils in this particular class tend to lean towards active experimentation more than I had realized. I feel that this question (no 4 in his test) might have been the most difficult yet 50% of the pupils decided to answer. This indicates a strong experimental emphasis in this class that I had not recognised until recently.
> **Example (b). Reflection.**
>
> From the experience of this lesson plan it has become clear to me that the learning styles of my pupils are very varied and that each of them required different teaching methods. I have now found that my students enjoy learning in different ways and that they benefit from the style that suits them. I had a fairly good idea of the learning styles of each student but now I am more certain and as a teacher, I can try to meet their classroom needs and demands.
> In a science class it is noticeable that pupils prefer different activities some like discussion, some problem solving and others experiments. But up until now I was not fully aware that these preferred activities relate directly to the pupils learning styles. Since this research I have learnt that I need to look closely at my teaching methods for all classes and try to match teaching styles to learning styles.
> **Example (c). Reflection**
>
> Clare. She is very good at making decisions and being practical about how to apply ideas in class. When she is working she likes to organize her notes and apply herself to finding the answer. She feels uncomfortable talking about feelings and emotions and is really happier dealing with tasks than people. (converger)
> Deirdre. She is very imaginative and loves doing and experiencing things. Deidre is happy watching and reflecting on problems because she always likes working out alternative answers. She is very interested in people and in touch with her feelings (Diverger).
> Amy: Amy likes observing and thinking about ideas but she has to work in a logical way and is very precise. She really enjoys bringing in different information to her projects but is more comfortable with ideas than people. (Assimilator)
> Annabel: She is the opposite of Amy and loves doing and experimenting and new experiences. She is very adaptable and intuitive and good at working by trial and error (Accommodator).
> **Example (d). Describing students the learning style way.**
>
> I explained my own learning style (assimilator) to the students. I told them that my preferred style of learning was by watching and thinking, that is, I grasp and experience by comprehension and transform it into knowledge by watching (reflection) rather than by doing. I informed them all people differ in their way of thinking of learning. I gave the students some examples i.e. some like to deal with concrete things and actively work with them whereas some like to reflect on the concrete experience rather than apply it to some new experiences. I then gave the students the terms of the different [modes of learning]. The students immediately wanted to pick their own style of learning there and then. I thought this was a good idea and let them pick the one they felt they were and I promised them at the end of the project we should have a better idea if they were right or wrong. They thought that this was great fun and were instantly motivated and wanted to get started right away.
> **Example (e). letting the students choose their styles.**

Exhibit 8.2. Extracts from reports of the graduate student teachers.

Some students made use of the experience of this exercise in the design of their other lessons. One student related his choice of groups for the expository/discovery experiment to their learning styles. A sociogram of his class is shown in figure 8.3. However, this did not deter from the attempt to evaluate the merits of following a lesson designed to meet the requirements of the Kolb cycle. In sum, these student teachers could draw conclusions about the general value of Kolb's theory in lesson design but not necessarily about the relationship between learning style and performance.

The indications are that over the years when the student teachers were asked to undertake the task of assigning skills to their students that two thirds or more in each year reported they had learnt that learning styles were important. Most of them suggested that teachers must accommodate to all styles. The exercise caused half of them to learn more about the way they taught and about a quarter reported that the teaching they offered was limited. Well over half had to revise their judgements about their students as a result of the exercise.

Lesson Phases	Content	Methods of Instruction	Imagery and test questions
Concrete Experience **Terminal objectives.** By the end of the lesson the students will be able to have experienced the concept of hope/wishing via guided imagery. Write a personal response to this imagery. Discuss poet's responses to related themes. Compare and contrast these notes. Analyse the structure and imagery within the poem. Write their own descriptive passage or poem using the concept of "hope".	Preparation for imaginary exercise. Guided Cognitive imagery Reading of Poem	Individualised work. Each student imagines and listens **Intention of test question.** "Will give direct feedback on the experience of the imagery component and test its effectiveness in relation to the studied poem. As it refers to actual (concrete) experience of the imagery and poem, it should be most suited to DIVERGERS.	Spoken words to accompany imagery. "You are on a country road. You're walking slowly. It's raining heavily. How do you feel? Imagine your self as a still picture. What do look like? You resume walking and start day-dreaming to distract yourself from the weather. Where would you like to be? Picture the place. What would you like to be doing there? Imagine the possibility that you may eventually get there. How does this feel? What is your mood? Keep in mind your imagined place as your destination and continue your journey. How do you now feel? Has your mood changed? As a still picture do you look any differently to the earlier one? What are your feelings? **Test question.** (1) What effect did the imagery exercise have on you? Did it influence your thoughts when you first heard Colum's poem?
Reflective Observation	Invite students to write notes describing atmosphere and their feelings during the imagery exercise. They write brief notes on their initial reaction to feelings presented in the poem. In pairs, compare and contrast their responses. Invite comments on the effect of the imagery component.	Individualised Writing. Discussion in pairs. (I will assist and monitor pair work as required)	**Test Question** (2). Describe the overall theme of Colum's poem. (Requires a general description and is inherently reflective. It should be most suited to ASSIMILATORS.)
Abstract conceptualization	In stanza order I will take students through the poem. The imagery and variations of tone and mood will be related via an expository style. Invite students comment on the poet's approach to the concept of "hope".	Expository method [teacher] Reading and analysis [students].	**Test question** (3) How does the poet convey the overall them of the poem? (Requires a theoretical approach and conclusions must be drawn from the poem's structure. It should be most suited to CONVERGERS)

Continues over

Active experimentation.	Students write their own descriptive passage or poem illustrating the theme of "hope".	Individualized work. Application of knowledge learned to create a new experience. Copies to be collected at the end of the class for review.	**Test question** (4). Write a descriptive passage or poem of your own based on the concept of hope. *(involves using everything learned in the lesson and applying it to create something new. It should be most suited to ACCOMMODATORS).*

Exhibit 8.3. Lesson plan in English for 15 to 16 year olds in which the Graduate student teacher hoped that the students would learn the value of guided cognitive imagery as an aid to learning, and come to an understanding of "hope" and its literary expression. (Edited from the original to include the terminal objectives, the written text of the imagery and the four test questions). The poem read was *An Old Woman of the Roads* by Padraig Colum.

Contrary to the view that pupils might not like changes in teaching nearly four fifths of the student teachers reported that their pupils like to be presented with new ways of learning and that they like a variety of teaching methods. This is consistent with the "instant" society in which we live. More than that it is consistent with theories of brain-based learning[74] that show that the brain needs to be continually challenged if it is to be enriched. Variety in teaching can help with those challenges.

Supervision of teaching practice

Kolb's model can be applied to the supervision of classroom practice as has been shown by FitzGibbon.[75] The model was derived from the post graduate course referred to above. During the year the course is divided more or less equally between classroom practice that is undertaken throughout the whole of the school year and study in college. The graduate student teachers are seen on five occasions during their teaching practice. Each of these is assessed: by a supervisor. After the lesson there is a conference between the supervisor and the student. A written evaluation of the supervision of teaching practice using Kolb's model would have had, as FitzGibbon suggested, considerable advantages to both the teacher and student. The concrete experience is the students teaching. Reflective observation takes with the supervisor after the lesson is taught during which time abstract conceptualization generalizes from specific instances to be followed by active experimentation by the student teacher. Exhibit 8.5 relates to assessment and shows the strengths and weaknesses of each type. It might be assumed from this model that there would be personal growth during the year, in which case the five assessments should not be given equal weight.

LEARNING STYLES AND STRATEGIES

Lesson phases	Content	Learning strategies	Imagery
Introduction	Explain to students about there being four types of learning and that today's class is investigating that theory		
Concrete experience. **Aims** (1) To extend students' understanding of area. (2) To introduce the four different learning and hence teaching styles. **Non-behavioural objectives.** (1) To introduce the concept of Simpson's rule. (2) To illustrate the use of guided imagery in mathematics. **Behavioural objectives.** By the end of the lesson the students should be able to: (1) Describe in their own words, what is meant by area? (2) State the purpose of Simpson's rule. (3) Give examples of where Simpson's rule can be applied. (4) Apply Simpson's rule mathematically.	Guided cognitive imagery. Students take part in this exercise on the area of shape with irregular boundaries. (see next section)	Students participate individually. Speaking to entire class.	Initially five minutes was taken to get them to sit back and relax using the method involving awareness of surroundings and self. "I then invited them to imagine an unevenly shaped field/piece of land/island (or whatever came to mind) I then asked them questions about its colour, scent, were there any flowers? Animals? They were then invited to get into a helicopter and fly all along the outside/periphery of the field and to examine what was around it.- Was it fenced off, an island etc. the students were asked to picture the boundaries of the field and to imagine flying the exact path of the boundary-twisting and turning along, inspecting every section of the boundary. Time was given throughout to allow thought and imagination."
Reflective Observation	Students asked to write down what shapes they saw etc as a result of imagery exercise. Discuss in groups of 2/3 what each person experienced.- Discuss in same groups of why they think, in everyday life, it would be necessary to know the area of such shapes and where it would be useful. Group opinions are written down on to OHP	Accommodators and divergers should benefit greatly from group work Convergers should gain from written exercise.	
Abstract conceptualisation	Draw shape with irregular boundary on board-Divide into strips of equal width and assign y, etc to lengths. -Give formula for Simpson's rule.-Explain basis of formula.-Give easy method for remembering formula -Sample problems solved on board and then by individuals.	Students work individually and are given time to ask questions Should appeal to convergers	

Continues over

Active experimentation.	Students asked to recall the shape they pictured in the imagery exercise. Each asked to make that shape with a piece of cardbosrd.-Students asked to predict area of shape it most resembles.-then divide into strips and apply Simpson's rule.-compare result with estimate.-ensure all using correct units of measurement.	Students work individually on making own model and applying Simpson's rule. Expect assimilators to gain most.	
Conclusion	Reinforcement of lesson using questions to test behavioural objectives. Collect written descriptions and cardboard shapes	Questioning	

Exhibit 8.4 A mathematics lesson for 15 – 16 year old students (girls) by a graduate Student teacher. (Edited to show imagery and objectives).

Concrete experience in the supervised class	Concrete experience in the supervisory conference
Accommodation S. Writes lesson plans incorporating desired skills and class needs, teaches lessons adapting plan as required; takes appropriate risks. E. Over plans, fits class or content to suit skills. D. Cannot use points elucidated in supervisory conference in plans, cannot adapt plan to suit class.	**Accommodation** S. Invites student to set own goals for teaching and development; challenges student to take risks; affirm student in own decisions. E. Be totally directive. D. Be totally non-directive.
Convergence S. Able to select skill needing improvement, able to test hypotheses, prioritise. E. Premature closure, excessive focusing on small area. D. Unable to select priority areas, unable to focus attention.	**Convergence** S. Stimulates student to think through implications of theory in relation to practice; helps student to prioritize. E. Forces premature closure; avoids interpersonal issues. D. Allows student to float in an undifferentiated mass of theories: fails to focus student.
Divergence S. Generates data from observations and subsequent reflection, analyses causes of actions and incidents. E. Produces too much data to manage, creation of sense of hopelessness. D. Inability to recognize problems/opportunities, rationalization of difficulties.	**Divergence** S. Identifies and exposes the 'here-and-now' situations; allows ambiguity and variety in interpretation; invites different perspectives on data. E. Invades privacy of student; dominates; too many points made. D. Ignores opportunities of 'here-and-now' situations; alternatives not suggested nor allowed.
Assimilation S. Identifies theory underlying actions, defines problems, suggests conceptual basis. E. Sees theories everywhere; attempts total integration of difficulties. D. Not able to identify theoretical basis of actions, unable to learn from successes or mistakes.	**Assimilation** S. Helps in relating of data observed to current theories; creates models; integrates points. E. Suggests too many theories; ignores practicalities in evaluating ideas. D. Allows student's statements to stand outside of theoretical body of knowledge.

Exhibit 8. 5. Kolb's model adapted by FitzGibbon to show how it can be applied to the observation and supervision of student teaching showing the strengths and weaknesses of each learning type. S = Strength; E = Excess; D = Deficiency.

Other models

Finally there are a group of typologies that derive from the Jungian concepts of extraversion and introversion. These require formal training in their administration interpretation. The results with university students have considerable implications for the design of assessment. In the UK and in the US in the nineteen sixties studies showed that student performance was related to the bi-polar dimension of introversion-extraversion. Furneaux[76] who studied personality in relation to examination performance classified students on two dimensions of stability; stable - unstable/neurotic with extraversion and introversion. He found, in his particular sample, that the stable extraverts were most likely to fail university examinations. They were followed by the neurotic-extravert. The neurotic introverts did best. He explained these results in terms of the drive level of the different personality types. Persons who easily enter into states of high drive are likely to score highly on neuroticism. In this way a high drive person can compensate for relatively poor intellectual qualities. In contrast good intellectual qualities can compensate for extraversion. These results had implications for assessment and teaching because the 'types' respond differently to the techniques applied. Work with students who were having psychological difficulties also showed that any system of examining was likely to produce its own "flock of casualties"[77] Thus variety and flexibility was required and this supported the idea of multiple strategy examining[78] whereby the techniques chosen are used to asses the objectives for which they were most appropriate.. This was the idea that was the basis for the experimental examinations developed for the Intermediate Certificate Committee in Ireland.[79]

Since then there have been many studies and the emergence of the Eysenck personality inventory which evaluates introversion-extraversion and neuroticism and is now widely used.[80] There is a junior version of the Eysenck test. The general ideas of introversion and extraversion are now part of everyday parlance. Simply put the introvert is bookish, takes care with study and does not like broad generalities. All are characteristics that academic study likes to foster. In contrast the extravert likes being with people, likes variety and action and tends to dislike complicated details and so on. Put simply an extravert may well be unhappy with academic study unless s/he is highly intelligent. However, the extravert is likely to do well in primary school where they can obtain stimulus from a noisy, lively environment.

There is however, much more to Jungian Typology than this. As early as 1962 Briggs and Myers had published a test for 15 year olds and above. It attempted to classify individuals into Jung's four functional types of sensing, perception, thinking and intuition. It did this by pairing the perception and thinking functions into four types. The best introduction to this work is by Kiersey and Bates in their book *"Please Understand me."*[81] The MBTI inventory has proved popular among teachers and for personnel testing. Although its' psychometric properties[82] are questionable it has proved useful as an instructional aid in higher education.[83]

Implications for curriculum and instructional leaders

To summarise: First, whatever about the psychometric properties of these instruments and whatever they actually measure as indicators they illustrate the enormous variability among individuals, their learning preferences and the strategies they use. Clearly knowledge of this variability and how teachers respond to that variability is of enormous consequence to effective teaching. Moreover, schools and higher education institutions should be concerned that their students are able to function in all domains.

Second, there is a voluminous literature on learning styles, and very many styles have been described. Some relate to abilities and one of these "spatial ability" has been found to be of considerable importance in the facilitation of learning although it is comparatively neglected in curriculum design.[84]

Third, the use of an inventory or descriptors developed on the basis of the styles described by the various theories gives insights into pupil performance that otherwise might not found in the arbitrariness of experience. Having to describe students in these terms is a valuable aid to assessment and a check on first impressions.

Fourth, in so far as beginning teachers are concerned they are brought to an understanding of how their teaching styles impact on pupils learning in their classes.

Fifth, pupils can learn about their own learning through participation in similar types of exercise.

Sixth, research on learning styles clearly illustrates the need for multiple strategy approaches to curriculum and assessment.

Dialogue about the nature of learning seldom takes place in schools. Yet as the findings of these case studies show teachers and pupils have much to gain from participation in such exercises. It has been shown elsewhere how discussion of learning styles can be used as the focus in courses on Learning-how-to-Learn for senior high school classes. But this study also showed the need for such experiments to be supported by a whole school policy.[85] It is for the educational leader assisted by the instructional and curriculum leader(s) to implement such a policy. No better way of achieving this is for the instructional and curriculum leaders to begin a dialogue that tests the assumptions underlying teacher knowledge of their pupil's learning by asking what do we know and what should we know about the way pupils in groups and as individuals learn. Clearly the understanding of learning caused by the study of learning styles has implications for the curriculum and therefore for those who design the curriculum and assessment strategies. Instructional and curriculum leaders have at level four an obligation to see that policy makers are aware of and make sensible responses to educational research.

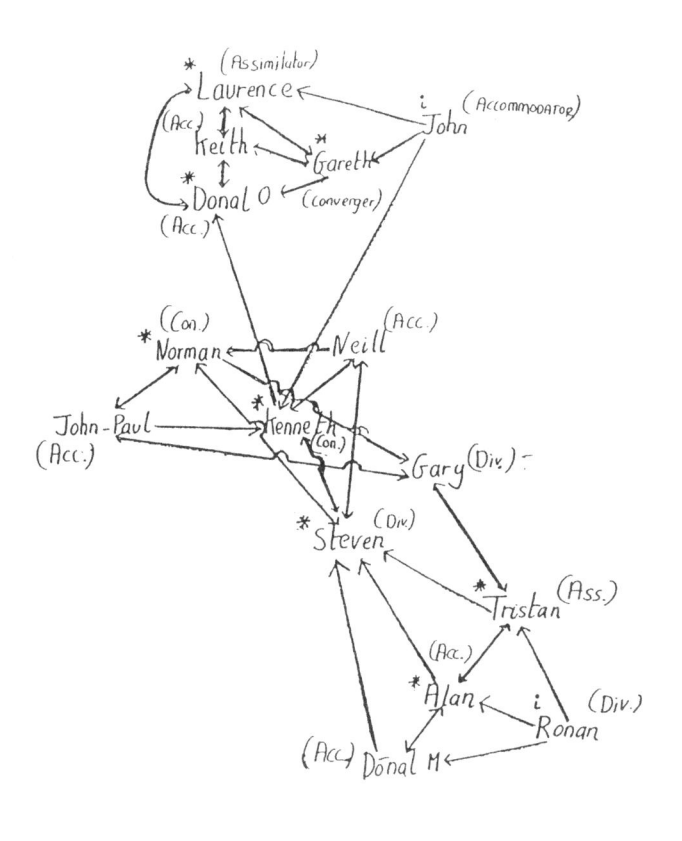

Figure 8.3. Sociogram of a class sketched in a report from a graduate student teacher that relates to the groupings in his class to their learning styles.

Notes and references

[1] Messick, S and associates (1976) *Individuality in Learning. Implications of Cognitive Styles and Creativity for Human Development.* Jossey Bass, San Fransisco.
[2] Tyler, L. E (1978) *Individuality: Human Possibilities and Personal Choice in the Psychological Development of Men and Women.* Jossey Bass, San Fransisco.
[3] Grasha, A. F (1984) Learning styles: The journey from Greenwich Observatory (1796) to the college classroom. *Improving College and University Teaching* 32, (1), 46 – 53.

⁴ *ibid.*
⁵ *ibid.*
⁶ Hudson (1966) *Contrary Imaginations*. Methuen, London.
⁷ Hudson's report led to a furore at the 'political level' because lack of divergence among scientists might have been a contributory factor to Britain's poor performance. It caused an investigation into the problem by the Council of Engineering Institutions and a resulting conference reported in Gregory, S. A.(1972). *Creativity and Innovation in Engineering*. Butterworth, London.
⁸ This point was illustrated for engineering by Whitfield, P. R. (1975) *Creativity and Industry* Penguin, Harmondsworth. Freeman, J., McComiskey J. G. and D. Buttle (1968) found that balance between convergence and divergence was an important predictor of academic performance among students of electrical engineering in the UK. Research into Divergent and Convergent Thinking. *International Journal of Electrical Engineering Education*. 6, 99 – 108.
⁹ Carter, G and T. A. Jordan (1986). *Student Centred Learning in Engineering. Enhancement in Higher Education. Problems and Prospects*. Monograph. University of Salford, Salford, UK
¹⁰ Getzels, J and P. Jackson (1962) *Creativity and Intelligence. Explorations with Gifted Students*, Wiley, New York.
¹¹ *ibid*
¹² Borich, G. D (1992) *Effective Teaching Methods*. Merrill/Macmillan.
¹³ For a recent review although primarily American see Dacey, J. S and K. H. Lennon (!998). *Understanding Creativity. The Interplay of Biological, Psychological and Social Factors*. Jossey Bass, San Fransisco.
¹⁴ Pask, G (1988). Learning strategies, teaching strategies and conceptual or learning style in R. R. Schmeck (ed) *Learning Strategies and Learning Styles*. Plenum Press, new York. Styles
¹⁵ *ibid*
¹⁶ For variations on these ideas see Marton, F (1988) Describing and improving learning in R. R. Schmeck (ed). *Learning Strategies and Learning Styles*. Plenum Press, New York and Svensson, L (1976). *Study Skill and Learning*. ACTA Universities Gothoburgensis, Goteborg
¹⁷ Kirby, J. R. (1988) Style, strategy and skill in reading in R. R. Schmeck (ed). *Learning Strategies and Learning Styles*. Plenum Press, New York
¹⁸ Elsewhere I have linked discussion of field dependence and independence to spatial ability. (e,g Heywood, J (2005) *Engineering Education. Research and Development in Curriculum and Instruction*. IEEE/Wiley, New York. Irrespective of any link spatial ability is a key skill and many years ago MacFarlane-Smith showed that the curriculum tended to ignore those subjects that could develop spatial ability. At the time he argued that this was one of the reasons why students did not go into science and technology. (MacFarlane Smith, I (1964). *Spatial Ability*. University of London Press.
¹⁹ Witkin, H. A (1976). Cognitive styles in academic performance and in teacher student relations in Messick, S and associates (1976) *Individuality in Learning. Implications of Cognitive Styles and Creativity for Human Development*. Jossey Bass, San Fransisco
²⁰ *loc cit* ref 2.
²¹ Witkin, H. A, Moore, C. A., Oltman, P. K., Goodenough, D. R., Friedman, F., and D. R. Owen (1977). *A Longitudinal Study of the Role of Cognitive Styles in Academic Evaluation in College Years*. GRE Research Report CRES 76-10R. Educational Testing Service, Princeton, NJ.
²² Marton, F and R. Saljö (1976). On qualitative 1. Outcomes and processes 2. Outcomes as a function of the learner's conception of task. *British Journal of Educational Psychology* 46, 4 – 11 and 46, 115 – 127. Entwistle, N. J. and P. Ramsden (1983). *Understanding Student Learning*. Croom Helm, London
²³ Cowan, J. (2006) *On Becoming an Innovative University Teacher. Reflection in Action*. SRHE/Open University Press, Maidenhead
²⁴ Watkins, D (1981). Identifying the study process dimensions of Australian University students. *Australian Journal of Education*, 26, (1), 76 – 85.
²⁵ Entwistle, N. J (1988) Motivational factors in students' approaches to learning. In R. R. Schmeck (ed) *Learning Strategies and Learning Styles*. Plenum, New York.
²⁶ Bey, C (1961) A Social theory of intellectual development in N. Sanford (ed). *The American College*. Wiley, New York
²⁷ Wilson, J. D (1981). *Student Learning in Higher Education*. Croom Helm, London
²⁸ The Lancaster Approaches to Studying and Course Perceptions Questionnaire. It has been

revised. The questionnaire derives from an attempt to describe the development of the student in terms of how different levels of question are answered. These levels are:
1. Pre-structural: in relationship to the prerequisites given in the question, the answers are denying, tautological and transductive. Bound to specifics.
2. Uni-structural: the answers contain generalizations only in terms of one aspect.
3. Multi-structural: the answers reveal generalizations only in terms of a few limited and independent aspects.
4. Relational: characterised by induction, and generalizations within a given or experienced context using related aspects.
5. Extended abstract: deduction and induction. Generalisations to situations not experienced or given in the pre-requisites to a question

[29] Ramsden, P (1988) Context and strategy. Situational influences on learning in Schmeck, R. R. (ed). *Learning Strategies and Learning Styles*. Plenum, New York.
[30] *ibid*
[31] Heywood, J (1989). *Learning, Adaptability and Change*. Paul Chapman, London.
[32] Ramsden (*ibid*) takes up the issue of strategies versus style and points out that they have been confused in summaries of research on deep and surface learning. Styles are bipolar but each has positive aspects as the Pask and Witkin models illustrate and if used can help the individual adapt to different situations. The approaches are unipolar and are necessary. Following Messick's definition, styles are stable and persistent characteristics of the individual. But approaches can change. So how does one help students learn strategies within the confinements of their style? Ramsden answers this question by reference to Pask's learning style model. Pask had suggested that the bipolar characteristics were comprehensive and operation learning. Because these can be conceptualised as contextually dependent then depending on the circumstances learners would use differing mixtures of comprehension and operation learning. Thus, one may have a dual conception of these types of learning as being consistent and variable. Thus Ramsden argues that both styles and strategies (approaches) 'need to be seen as consistent and context dependent'
[33] On the 17th May 2006 BBC Radio 4 carried a criticism of examinations in England and Wales for doing just this.
[34] Bennett, C. K., Desforges, C., Cockburn, A., and B. Wilkinson (1984). *The Quality of Pupil Learning Experiences*. Erlbaum, NJ
[35] Selmes, I. P. (1965). Approaches to learning at secondary school. Their identification and facilitation. Ph. D Thesis. University of Edinburgh, Edinburgh
[36] *loc.cit* to Chapter in Schmeck ref 14
[37] This is supported by Elkind, D (1988) *The Hurried Child. Growing up too Fast too Soon*. Addison-Wesley, Reading MA, and more recently by Rutter, M and D. J. Smith (1995) (eds). *Psychosocial Disorders in Young People*. Wiley, Chichester.
[38] Dunn, R and K. Dunn (1992a). *Teaching Elementary Students through Their Individual Learning Styles*. Allyn and Bacon, Boston. (1992b) *Teaching Secondary Students through Their Individual Learning Styles*. Allyn and Bacon, Boxton.
[39] *ibid*
[40] Cody, C (1983). Learning styles including hemisphericity. A comparative study of average, gifted, and highly gifted students in grades 5 through 12. Temple University. *Dissertation Abstracts International*. 44, 1631, A.
[41] *ibid*
[42] Dunn, R., Dunn, K. and G. E. Price (1989). *Learning Style Inventory*. Price systems, Lawrence, KA.
[43] *ibid*
[44] *loc.cit*. Ref 14
[45] *loc.cit*. Ref 17
[46] Kolb, D (1984). *Experiential Learning. Experience as a source of Learning and Development*. Prentice Hall, Englewood Cliffs, NJ.
[47] Svinicki, M. D. and N. M. Dixon (1987) The Kolb model modified for classroom activities. *College Education*, 35, (4), 141 – 146.
[48] For a practical example see Cowan (1998). *loc.cit*. Ref 63
[49] *loc.cit*. Svinicki and Dixon. Ref 43
[50] FitzGibbon, A (1987) Kolb's experiential learning model as a model for the supervision of class-

room teaching. *European Journal of Teacher Education*,10, (2), 163 – 178.

[51] Stice, J. E. (1987) Using Kolb's cycle to improve student learning. *Engineering Education.* 77, (5), 291 –296.

[52] Todd, R. H. (1991). Teaching an introductory course in manufacturing processes. *Engineering Education*, 81, (5), 484 –485.

[53] MacCarthy, B (1986). The 4 MAT System. *Teaching to Learning Styles with Right-left Mode Techniques.* Excel Inc. Barrington, Il

[54] Weber, P and F. Weber (1990) Using 4MAT to improve student performance. *Educational Leadership* 48, (2),41 – 46.

[55] *loc.cit*

[56] Also called 'set mechanisation'. Luchins, A. S. (1942). Mechanisation in problem solving: the effect of 'einstellung' *Psychological Monographs* No 248

[57] Thomas, P. R and J. D. Bain (1982) Consistency in learning strategies. *Higher Education* 11, (3), 249 – 259.

[58] Kolb modified the first editions of his inventory because of evaluation research which proved to be non-supportive. The second instrument has also been criticized for lack of reliability and stability Sims et al., 1986,The reliability and classification stability of the Learning Style Inventory. *Educational and Psychological Measurement*, 46, (3), 753 –760. Highhouse, S and D.Doverspike (1987-The validity of the Learning Style Inventory and occupational preference. *Educational and Psychological Measurement* 47, (3), 749 –753.) tested its construct validity by correlating it with field-independence field-dependence and the Vocational Preference inventory (Holland, J. L. 1978- *Manual for the Vocational Preference Inventory*. Consulting Psychologists Press, Palo Alto). They concluded that it measured preferences rather more than cognitive style.

[59] *loc.cit*. Ref 47

[60] FitzGibbon, A (1994). Self evaluation exercises in initial teacher education. *Irish Educational Studies*, 13, 145 – 164.

[61] Loacker, G et al (1984). *Analysis and Communication. An approach to Critical Thinking.* Alverno Publications, Milwaukee, WI

[62] *loc. cit* ref 47

[63] In the UK Honey and Mumford (1992) have also developed a model (and inventory) that has many similarities with Kolb. They call their styles Activists, Reflectors, Theorists and Pragmatists. Here is their description of the Activist.
"Activists involve themselves fully and without bias in new experiences. They enjoy the here and now and are happy to be dominated by immediate experiences. They are open-minded, not sceptical, and this tends to make them enthusiasts about anything new. Their philosophy is: I'll try anything once". Their days are filled with activity. They tackle problems by brainstorming. As soon as the excitement from one activity has died down they are busy looking for the next. They tend to thrive on the challenge of new experiences but are bored with implementation and longer term consolidation. They are gregarious people constantly involving themselves with others but, in doing so, they seek to centre all activities around themselves".

[64] *loc.cit* ref 3

[65] *loc.cit* ref 47

[66] In the theory, by contrast, a concept or principle would be taught in each of the styles but this would make it extremely difficult if not impossible to test differences in performance arising from the different methods of teaching. It was appreciated that in any event test design would be most difficult and this was taken into account in the assessment of the reports.

[67] The aim of this particular experiment on learning styles was to help graduate student teachers to
(a) improve the quality of the judgements they make about their students, and
(b) acquire variety in their teaching styles, and
(c) further their understanding of student learning, and
(d) evaluate the merits of Kolb's theory of learning and its application to classroom practice.

[68] A complete description of the exercise and analysis of the questionnaires is given in FitzGibbon, A., Heywood, J., and L. Cameron (1991) *The Matching of Teaching to Learning Styles during Teacher Education*. Monographs of the Department of Teacher Education No 1/91. University of Dublin, Dublin. Part II of the monograph contains the complete report of one of the student teachers Charlotte O'Callaghan.

[69] Group 1. 1991. 85 reports and 57 questionnaires. Group 2. 1996. 107 reports and 79 inventories (rating scale). Examples in text from 1995 reports apart from lesson plans.
[70] Carroll, P (1991) Researching instruction while student teaching .II. Research in Teacher Education Monographs, No 2/91. Department of Teacher Education, University of Dublin, Dublin
[71] *loc.cit*. Ref 23
[72] Unfortunately this was not followed up.
[73] 11 of 14 usable cases..
[74] Jensen, E (1998). *Teaching with the Brain in Mind*. Association for Supervision and Curriculum Development, Alexandria, VA.
[75] FitzGibbon, A (1987) Kolb's experiential learning model as a model for supervision of classroom teaching for student teachers. *European Journal of Teacher Education*, 10, (2), 163 – 178.
[76] Furneaux, W. D (1962). The psychologist and the university. *Universities Quarterly* 17, 33.
[77] Ryle, A (1969). *Student Casualties*. Allen Lane, London.
[78] First called multiple objective examining in Heywood, J (1979) *Assessment in Higher Education*, Wiley, Chichester. Subsequently multiple strategy in Heywood, J (2000) *Assessment in Higher Education. Student learning, Teaching, Programmes and Institutions*. Jessica Kingsley, London.
[79] Heywood, J (1978). *Examining in Second Level Education*. Association of Secondary Teachers Ireland, Dublin.
[80] For a technical review of the Eysenck Personality Questionnaire see Kline, P (2000). *Handbook of Psychological Testing*. Routledge, London. The test is suitable for those of 16 years and above.
[81] See Kiersey, D and M. Bates (1984). *Please Understand Me. An Essay in Temperament Styles*. Oxford Psychologists Press, Oxford
[82] *loc.cit* ref 80 Kline.
[83] See for example Rutsohn, J (1978). Understanding personality types. Does it matter? *Improving College and University Teaching*, 26, (4), 249 – 254. For a more detailed argument see Silver, H. F and R. J. Hanson (1995). *Learning Styles and Strategies*. The Thoughtful Education Press, Princeton, NJ
[84] McFarlane Smith, I (1964). *Spatial Ability*. University of London Press, London.
[85] Heywood, J and M. Murray (2005). Curriculum-Led Staff Development. Towards Curriculum and Instructional Leadership in Ireland. *Bulletins of the EFEA* (European Forum on Educational Administration) No 4. P54 summarises an evaluation of this course by Keane, D (1999) *A study of a Learning to Learn Module in a Community School*. MSt. Thesis. University of Dublin. Details of the implementation the course are in an assignment by Mairin Wilson (1993). The syllabus outline is given on pp 77 and 78.
[86] *loc.cit* ref 68

9
PROBLEM SOLVING, DECISION MAKING AND HEURISTICS

Abstract

A major criticism of much teaching is that it concentrates on the lower order skills of knowledge acquisition and comprehension at the expense of the development of the higher order skills of problem finding and solving and critical thinking. In countries where there are public examinations teachers often say that the questions set in examinations together with the quantity of knowledge required by the syllabus requires them to cover militates against the use of teaching strategies that would develop these skills. When put to the test, as the examples given in these chapters show, there is little evidence to support that view although assessment practices and type of content are restrictive.

If the key aim of education is to help students develop the capacity to transfer their learning to the solution of previously unseen problems, that is 'to think for themselves,' then the task of the instructional and curriculum leader is to persuade, and help when necessary, teachers to implement learning strategies that will achieve that goal.

The purpose of this chapter is to demonstrate the validity of this argument. It is achieved by illustrations from exercises done by graduate student teachers to evaluate the merits of teaching problem solving heuristics.

The learning of many pupils was enhanced. Many low achieving students benefited from the structure provided by the heuristic although some high achieving students wanted to solve problems in their own way. These graduates responded positively to the experience and many said they had learnt about their own decision-making processes as a result. A large number thought it was valuable for their teaching, and most of them thought the exercise had helped their pupils develop decision-making skills. Even at this age pupils might benefit from some explanation of metacognition. The factors contributing to effective problem solving are discussed.

At the 'political' level instructional and curriculum leaders need to persuade policy makers that the development of higher order thinking may require subsyamtial changes in assessment and curriculum.

At the school level teachers together with the educational leader need to establish whole school policies for the achievement of these goals. An 'assumptional-dialogue' is well suited to bringing about this objective.

Introduction

A graduate student teacher wrote that *"the first year history programme exposes the children to so many new concepts that quite a lot of expository teaching has to be engaged in. In teaching a concept like 'renaissance' or revolution' my teaching is mainly expository. At other times I set up problem situations, e.g. 'When the Third estate arrived at the Estates General meeting place they found the doors locked. They did not go home but went to a tennis court close by and resolved not to disband until a constitution was written and they got their demands'. In a problem situation like this I ask the children to identify the problem, to analyse it, to make hypotheses and to find possible solutions."*[1]
Teachers of any subject can relate approaches to teaching similar to this. Take away the arrows and script from the diagram in figure 9.1 and ask any group of student teachers to outline a model of problem solving using the squares. The chances are that irrespective of subject, they will come up with more or less the same headings, although the terminology may differ. Invariably many miss out the feed-back loop. Substitute decision making for problem solving and a repeat of the exercise will get almost the same answers for problem solving and decision making depend on the same skills.[2] In this sense learning and decision making are the same thing. McDonald used this model to describe the teacher at work. He saw the planning of instruction and its implementation as activities involving decision making.[3]

Some of these teachers may miss out problem formulation and not see it as a distinct activity. The view taken here is that it is and that evidence can be found in the difficulties that pupils have, for example, in deciding the title for a project, dissertation or other piece of work that requires them to decide what and how to do it. It requires an ability to focus. Pupils may not understand the problem sufficiently for them to be able to formulate it in a way that will develop learning.

The process, therefore, involves the collecting and comprehension of information, its application, analysis and synthesis in bringing everything together in order to make a judgement. Clearly the categories of the *Taxonomy of Educational Objectives* (see Chapter 10) describe key skills in problem solving and decision making processes. Indeed its authors claimed that all the categories would engage a pupil in problem solving. But Prince and Hoyt[4] make a distinction between introductory problem solving in which knowledge, comprehension and application come into play, intermediate problem solving involving analysis, and advanced problem solving involving synthesis and evaluation. They make the point that 'traditional' courses in science and technology rely heavily on textbook problems that do not require problem solving skills. They were exercises that tested the material in the chapter involved. *"That is not "problem solving" in any real sense*" and some of those who could solve such problems might not be able to apply the concepts to real life problems. Another way of expressing this criticism is to say that whereas students are encouraged to solve well-defined problems they are not helped to solve ill-structured problems.[5] Text-book problems are closed requiring a single correct solution. Open-ended questions are more often than not, those that are not amenable to such solutions.

This is a serious problem in countries like Ireland where there is a system of public examinations because the textbooks become all important, and they reinforce the examination system. Thus changes in examinations to test Higher Order Thinking Skills (HOTS) as the higher levels of the *Taxonomy* are sometimes called also require changes in textbooks.

By the early nineteen nineties a voluminous literature on problem solving and critical thinking had emerged.[6] Much of it was in response to the view that at school level instruction for the curriculum emphasises the transmission of information and that assessments and tests encouraged the recall of that

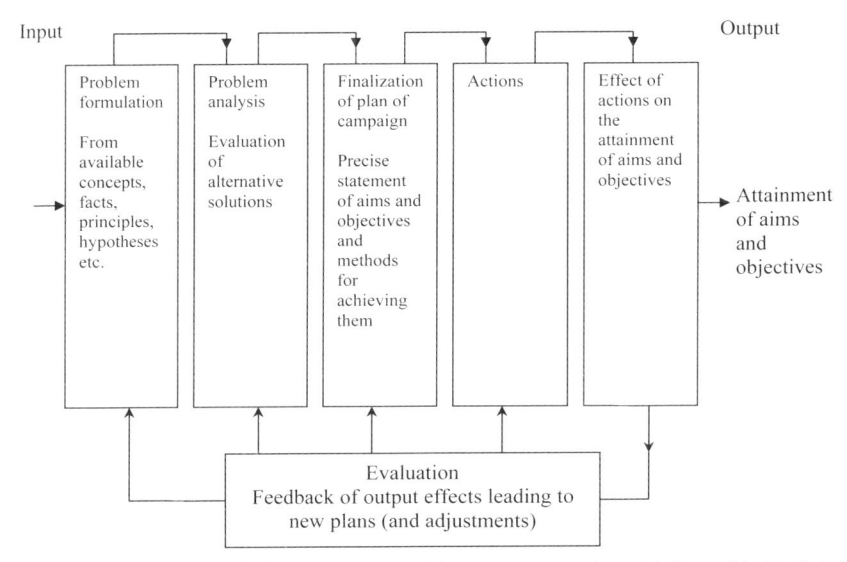

Input					Output
Problem formulation From available concepts, facts, principles, hypotheses etc.	Problem analysis Evaluation of alternative solutions	Finalization of plan of campaign Precise statement of aims and objectives and methods for achieving them	Actions	Effect of actions on the attainment of aims and objectives	Attainment of aims and objectives
		Evaluation Feedback of output effects leading to new plans (and adjustments)			

Figure 9.1. A model of the decision making process (after McDonald, F. J (1969). Educational Psychology. Wadsworth, Belmont, CA).

information which is another way of saying that the curriculum concentrated on the lower orders of *the Taxonomy*. This was how it was expressed in terms of the Leaving Certificate examination in Ireland by the distinguished American educator George Madaus.[7] This same criticism has been made of the gold standard 'A' level examinations by no less a person than the British Prime Minister Mr Blair. In 2007 he called for the design of questions to be changed.

But as the literature shows the higher order categories of *the Taxonomy* did not satisfy some educators and broad categories of problem solving, critical thinking, decision making and creativity were introduced. But first some remarks that apply generally although they were highlighted in the debate about critical thinking, and they relate to whether or not critical thinking (and for that matter problem solving) is a generalizable skill, or whether it is a skill specific to subjects only.

According to Norris[8] debate about this issue has catalysed some of the most significant advances in the understanding of critical thinking. Two approaches to teaching had emerged. One was by infusion and the other by immersion. Ennis[9] who made this distinction meant by infusion the specific attempt to help students to think critically in subject matter teaching "*in which general principles of critical thinking dispositions and abilities are made explicit*". McPeck[10] took an alternative view for he argued that one learns to think critically if one becomes immersed in the subject, therefore, there is no need to make the principles of critical thinking explicit. Many school teachers would be of this view. For example teachers of mathematics in the Public Examinations Evaluation Project in Ireland wanted to design an improved public examination that would include a sub-paper in problem solving. However, when they administered this test within a multiple strategy examination it gave the poorest results. It was found that they had given no specific teaching in problem solving. This is a case where teaching to the test would have given beneficial results.

Related to this is the issue of transfer. How, for example, do I learn skills that will enable me to think critically about the situations I face in every day life? Substitute problem solving for critical thinking and the same question applies. Are these skills something I learn independently of education? Would infusion (specific training) help? Does it occur because of immersion in a subject(s)? Or, more probably, is it a combination of all three?

One way of approaching this issue is to look at it from the perspective of learning and to ask if by using an infusion approach to critical thinking, problem solving and decision-making learning is enhanced. Such an approach embraces critical thinking, problem solving and decision making as being the same thing-at least in the sense outlined above. It sees the issue as being in part semantic for sometimes those teaching in the humanities regard themselves as critical thinkers whereas engineers and the like regard themselves as problem solvers. Both use similar heuristics (see figure 9.2) and these heuristics differ little from those of problem solving. Similarly with decision making but the heuristic is "action oriented". Which ever one is used teachers also use the term "reasoning" to describe them and this term has now reappeared in the textbooks of educational psychology. At the practical level in the United States a recent issue of *Educational Leadership* (February 2008) is titled "Teaching Students to Think."

A model of how a scientist solves problems. (From J Heywood and H Montagu-Pollock (1976) *Science for Art Students: A Case Study in Curriculum Development* Guildford, Society for Research into Higher Education

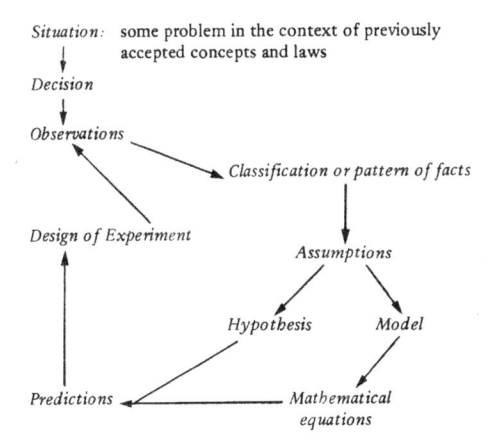

```
Situation: some problem in the context of previously
   |        accepted concepts and laws
Decision
   |
Observations
          ↘       ↙ Classification or pattern of facts
                            |
Design of Experiment        ↓
   ↑                    Assumptions
                        ↙         ↘
                  Hypothesis      Model
                      ↙             ↘
Predictions ←─────────────── Mathematical
                                equations
```

After a number of cycles there may emerge new *concepts, laws,* or *practical applications* of this knowledge.

Figure 9.2. Solving a problem in science (from Heywood, J and H. Montagu Pollock, (1977). *Science for Arts Students. A Case Study in Curriculum Design* Society for Research into Higher Education, London)

It is unlikely that the issue is as polarised as presented. Training is likely to be valuable but how can one solve problems without becoming immersed in the subject. If that immersion is accompanied by meta-cognition then it is impossible to believe that no skill development takes place.

In this chapter the focus is on the value of teaching a heuristic to enhance learning or in the practical jargon of the moment "thinking." But first some general remarks about problem solving.

Problem Solving

It is probably a truism that we cannot help solving problems whether we like it or not. It is very difficult for a day to go by without our having to solve problems. Some of these problems are very small and to all intent and purpose are solved automatically. They are routines. At the other end of the spectrum are problems that require a lot of thought and may be very difficult. One classification of the levels of difficulty is shown exhibit 9.1. It is probably the understanding that many problems are 'routines' that leads teachers to think they can all be solved by osmosis. Thus attempts to develop problem solving skills can all too easily become focused on the project method and the big problem, a disposition that is reinforced by the ease with which projects can be assessed (see the discussion below on Polya). But many of the problems we have to solve have to be solved in short periods of time and are not routines. The argument is simply that to learn to solve such problems requires some training and that training might take the form of training in heuristics or strategies as Woods[11] prefers to call them.

Level.	Description.
1. Automatic.	Performance of task without thinking.
2. Skill exercise	Consciously involved but minimal challenge using specific knowledge.
3. Problem Solving	Challenging, but possible with current knowledge and skills through a strong problem solving approach.
4. Research	Requires additional knowledge that currently does not exist within a learning effort to effectively accomplish the task.
5. Overwhelming	Cannot be accomplished without a significant increase in capacity, most likely by bringing in additional expertise.

Exhibit 9.1. Levels of difficulty in problem solving situations due to Apple et al[12]

A first step is an awareness of one's own approach towards problem solving and the extent to which it is limited by "set mechanisation" (sometimes called set induction).

Set mechanisation (induction)

Sometimes the problem solver is limited by "set mechanisation" It does not imply that the problem solver will not be able to solve the problem: it does imply that he/she might make the process more difficult than it might be. The idea is due to Luchens[13] who asked pupils to obtain specific amounts of water from three jars filled to three different levels (capacity). He showed them first how to do two problems that involved all three jars. In a further nine problems, the subjects mainly used the three jar solution to solve the problem even when two jar solutions were possible. The 'set' interfered with their problem solving. Subsequently Luchins divided another group into two sub-groups. The first sub-group worked through the problem in the usual way, using the three-jar solution. The second group were told to think more carefully about how to solve the problems. Given that instruction the majority of students in the second sub-group moved to the more simple solution of using two jars.

Wittrock[14] has suggested that 'sets' can also assist learning. He cites research on advance organisers to this effect. But the point is that we too easily accept 'sets' and follow a particular approach to solving problems. Moreover, teaching and examinations can induce sets. My first introduction to set in problem solving was in a paper by W. D. Furneaux.[15] In a factor analysis of engineering examinations at a British university he showed that each examination (whether it was mathematics, aerodynamics or electricity and magnetism) tested the same 'thing'. He called it examination-passing ability. But there was another interpretation. The questions were closed requiring single solutions that depended on the application of a limited range of mathematical techniques. The papers were all testing a particular kind of analysis. They were not testing the wide range of skills necessary for the practice of engineering. More generally teachers tend to teach, when they are not giving information, in an analytic and convergent mode. Question spotting is a form of 'set' and pupils require their teachers to spot questions and help them remember the answers. It is for this reason that there is so much criticism of public examinations. The art of examination design is to use a number of strategies that test for different skills. In the sense of 'set' pupils need to recognise the limitations of 'set' and acquire a range of 'sets'. In this sense teaching to the test is legitimate. It was for this reason that the teachers who participated in the Public Examinations Evaluation Project in Ireland designed multiple strategy experimental examinations in history and mathematics.[16]

Familiarity increases the likelihood of a 'set' becoming a controlling influence. Thus, teachers should try to design problems for which there are several different methods for obtaining solutions so that students become aware that most complex solutions and indeed many simple ones can be solved in a number of ways, some of which are likely to be more simple than others. 'Sets' may have an inhibiting or enhancing effect on learning and the more we know about how we learn the more likely they are to have an enhancing effect. A graduate student teacher's ideas of 'set' induction are shown in exhibit 9.2.

More generally it seems from cognitive science that general strategies as well as domain specific ones are required to solve classroom problems.[17] Reed[18] is of the opinion that it might be beneficial to teach problem solving strategies through diagrams and other strategies like looking for an inductive argument, arguing by contradiction, formulating a simpler problem, and establishing sub-goals. He reported one research that showed that a group taught the strategies did better than a control group that were not.

Given the time required for such interventions those responsible for syllabus content would have to look again at its requirements, and again such revision would have to be looked at in the light of a whole school, and or system policy

> "Working with a number series in my own class I tried using discovery techniques. The class were given the number series and asked to complete them without any help which most managed. When they were given a second number series there were more problems. The vast majority attempted to apply the same type of rule which had solved the first problem for them only to find that it did not work. They had as such become 'set' in their thinking"
>
> First series n   2 4 6 8 10 12
>
> Second series (more difficult) n   2 4 6 12 18 36
>
> **Example (a)**
>
> In comprehension problems in English from my experience children are largely incapable of deducing from a fairly long passage the essential points. In second language teaching the subjects find a common word in the question and in the comprehension passage and copy large sections of irrelevant material rather than analysing the situation. Students are also disinclined to use fresh approaches in the use of words in certain 'sets' rather than applying them to new situations.
>
> **Example (b)**

Exhibit 9.2. 4 Graduate student teachers' ideas of 'set' induction[19]

Using heuristics to enhance learning

The argument for teaching heuristics is based on the principle that if the learner knows the steps involved in problem solving the learner's performance in problem solving will be improved. Saupé[20] suggested the following steps:

1. Ability to recognize the existence of a problem.
2. Ability to define the problem.
3. Ability to select information pertinent to the problem.
4. Ability to recognize assumptions bearing on the problem.
5. Ability to make relevant hypotheses.
6. Ability to draw conclusions validly from assumptions, hypotheses and pertinent information.
7. Ability to judge the validity of the processes leading to the conclusion.
8. Ability to evaluate a conclusion in terms of its assessment.

Each of the steps in this model represents a different kind of ability, and help can be given to learners to develop these abilities. Among the simplest heuristics are those used in decision making when we have to make a choice.

The same groups of graduate student teachers whose work was described in chapters 6, 7 and 8 were asked to evaluate the teaching of a problem solving or decision making heuristic in their classes. They could not evaluate whether it had improved their pupils' skill in decision making for the reason that they had no prior measure of what that level of skill might be. Given that in a sense the processes of decision making and learning are similar (see above) then the use of a heuristic might enhance learning.

As in previous exercises (chapters 6, 7 and 8) the students were provided with literature that would enable them to undertake the exercise. Although they were directed to consider two particular heuristics (those of Polya and Wales and Stager) a number of decision-making models were discussed as a pre-requisite.[21] The discussion was built around *compensatory, additive-difference* and *elimination by aspects models*.

We are likely to recognise *Compensatory models* in our own decision making. For example when we choose a car we do so against a real or imagined list of attributes and values (e.g petrol consumption, comfort, colour, performance). Different purchasers will have different priorities. Positive attributes in such models compensate for negative attributes. They can be ranked and rated. In this example scores can be given for the price of Car A versus Car B and so for each attribute. The one that gains the most points will be the most appropriate choice for us. We can do this exercise for the purchase of most goods. House purchase is often cited in textbooks to illustrate the *additive model*.

A variation of this model is the *additive-difference model*. This simply totals the differences between the attribute of two alternatives. It comes up with the same answer as the additive model. Its value lies in the fact that it compares the differences between each attribute whereas the *additive model* gives the sum of the attributes.

It will be appreciated that such models are easy to teach in class and have relevance to more than one subject. They convey a degree of rationality that is seldom observed in practice. Take the car. Long lists of attributes are published but it is only the very meticulous who use them. By contrast at work we may have to be very meticulous particularly if we are doing research. But in every day life we all choose differently for different reasons.

Tversky[22] goes along with this view to some extent. His elimination by aspects model assumes we approach choice by eliminating less attractive options by assigning criteria to each option and have a minimum criteria below which we will not go. As Reed[23] says it has the advantage for many people that it does not require calculation. A variant of this model, the conjunctive requires that minimum criteria are assigned to each attribute of the option. That option remains an option only so long as the minimum criteria are reached and then from the reduced list in a narrow band (for each criterion) we choose according to our criterion and these might be emotional. Estate agents (realtors) tell us that a women knows within fifteen seconds of entering a house whether or not they would wish to live in it!

Simon is probably more realistic. He argues that most people do not have the capability to handle many alternatives so they settle for one that *satisfices* all the minimum criteria. He calls this "*satisficing research.*[24]

In the process of making a choice other restraints enter the equation and available time often conditions choice such as when we are purchasing a home. Television programmes that show people searching for houses also illustrate the problem of 'set' in that purchasers often have fixed values and attributes from which they are unwilling to depart. But this is not always the case.

Perhaps the best known heuristic is due to Polya. He wrote a book "*How To Solve It*" on its use in mathematics.[25] The four stages of his model are understand, plan, carry out, and look back. His book begins with a basic list of injunctions one of which highlights the value of analogy. "*If you cannot solve the problem try to find some related problem that is related to the auxiliary problem, which we consider not for its own sake, but because we hope that its consideration may help us solve another problem or original problem. This does rely on past experience, albeit implicitly*".

The Polya model or modifications of it have been used successfully, that is to improve performance, in engineering[26] as well as in training in problem solving.[27] Students in the year of the study reported were allowed to use the Polya model if they so wished. However, pressure was put on them to evaluate a model that had been forward by Wales and Stager.[28] Although concerned to help students learn engineering design Wales and Stager claimed that it was generalizable to all subjects. I wanted, apart from helping the student teachers to see from their results if this was the case.

The Wales and Stager heuristic.

The Wales and Stager[29] heuristic was originally used to teach engineering students engineering design. (It was called guided design). It is worth noting that one of the most important books on education of the eighties considered "*Knowledge as Design*"[30]. Together with Nardi they applied the heuristic to courses other than engineering. As a result they argued that the heuristic was a generic strategy.[31] They claimed support for their approach which was now directed at thinking skills in general in a report from the National Research Council[32] from which they cited the following: "*from kindergarten on and in every subject matter. Training in general skills must be supplemented and supported by application throughout the curriculum. Various subject matters in the school program should be taught with an eye to developing the powerful thinking methods used by experts in those disciplines. Students must come to think of themselves as able and obligated to engage in critical analysis and problem solving through schooling.*"

"*Thinking skills tend to be driven out of the curriculum by ever growing demands for teaching larger and larger bodies of knowledge. The idea that knowledge must be acquired first and that its application to reasoning and problem solving can be delayed is a persistent one in educational thinking*".

The report makes the important point that reading and writing are as much problem solving activities as mathematics. Unskilled writers think that composition is simply writing down. Research, they argue, showed that students can become good writers without engaging in complex problem solving processes. The report also noted that in a university where a freshmen course in thinking was introduced students obtained above average scores, moreover the students persisted (as opposed to dropping out) throughout the four years of the course.

Wales and Stager argued that because *"Guided design is part system, part attitude"*, it is important to pay attention to the needs of students. In their theory these needs are perceived to be hierarchical and ordered as in Maslow's model.

The course *"is based on the conviction that the student who works through an ascending order of well designed problems, who is actively seeking solutions to problems rather than passively assimilating knowledge, will emerge not only better educated but far stronger intellectually"*. (From d'Amour and Wales[33] - who used the guided design approach to structure a course on the Nature of Evidence)

During the course the students" *work in small groups (and) attack open ended problems rather than masses of information"*. The course is structured so that each problem creates the need for subject matter that has to be learned independently by the student out of class time. Its purpose is to show that in decision making, knowledge of concepts, principles, and values is necessary. The teacher is a facilitator who in part listens and encourages the students to participate in the decision making process in part by asking them leading questions. They learn from the decision model with which they are presented. The problems are chosen to be relevant and interdisciplinary.

Wales, Nardi and Stager said their research into decision making processes led them to the view that experienced decision takers first defined the situation and then used four operations to arrive at a decision. The heuristic that describes this process is:

1. Define the situation.
2. State the goal
3. Generate ideas.
4. Prepare a plan.
5. Take action.

Each of these three modes of thinking is combined with the operations of analysis, synthesis and evaluation. Thus, each step results in an action which these writers called evaluation: ideas have to be selected after they have been generated, a plan has to be selected from the available options, and once action has been taken the next action has to be selected. In their adaptation of the model Eck and Wilhelm[34] listed the steps of the model in this way 1) Problem identification. 2) Information gathering. 3) Statement of objectives. 4) Identification of constraints and assumptions. 5) Generation of solutions. 6) Analysis. 7) Synthesis. 8) Evaluation of alternatives. They would seem to place analysis and synthesis as separate categories in a linear process, but that is hardly likely to be the case in complex processes. Nevertheless their separation should help students understand the differences between them.

In a particular set of publications, Wales, Nardi and Stager presented a series of Sherlock Holmes stories for solution. In these situations the decision maker, (we might call him/her the detective), had to ask when defining the situation who is involved? (the actors). What things are involved? The props). What happened? (actions). When did it happen? (scene). Where did it happen? (scene). Why did it happen? (cause). How serious is its effect? (effect). These are of course questions that help the decision maker 'learn' about the situation, and in this sense this decision making model is also a model of learning. Thus, we might conclude that if students use such a model in problem solving they are likely to enhance their learning. As indicated Wales and his colleagues also claimed that the model is generalizable; that is, it can be used in any subject. They published examples in nursing, mathematics, [35]research and practice, and the humanities supported by terminology appropriate to those subjects to argue their case.[36]

Clearly in approaches such as this the role of knowledge in learning changes since its purpose is now its use in problem solving. Moreover, the role of the teacher changes to that of facilitator. The combined result is to influence the design of the course.

What then did the teachers make of the guided design exercise?

Generally over the years the reports of these graduate student teachers sustain the claim made by Wales and Stager that their model is generalizable to the subjects of the curriculum. Examples of lesson plans are given in exhibits 9.3, and 9.4. They have been chosen to illustrate the generality of the model as its value in science and technology is fairly well established. In the geography lesson for 12 to 13 year olds a handout was used (exhibit 9.5) which showed how the teacher incorporated the additive model in the lesson. That decisions involving values will have to be made is apparent. Most important is the test he set which is shown in exhibit 9.6. It should cause transfer of skill since the pupil is asked questions about a new map. He reported that the students achieved high scores and that most of them enjoyed the exercise. The test might be criticised in that it did not directly address the issue of pupil's ability to apply the heuristic.

In this particular year[37] when some pressure was exerted to get them to follow the Wales and Stager model 33 of the 97 students who participated used that model, others adapted the model, and 10 used the Polya model. 60 responded to a questionnaire. In the lesson the student teachers were expected to take their pupils through a heuristic related to the subject material they were studying, and at a week distant to test the students on the knowledge of that class and their understanding of the heuristic. Most of the studies were done with students in the age range 12-14. Irrespective of the model presented 27 were sceptical about the exercise before it began but on completion this number had been reduced to eight but two who had not been sceptical before it began became sceptical as a result of the exercise. Some were quite surprised at what happened.[38] Some foreign language teachers accustomed to the communicative approach regretted they had to use so much English in their classes. Others did manage to function in the target language (see exhibit 9.7) 37 claimed that they were made aware of their own decision processes as a result of the exercise.

" I never knew there were methods to approach decision making. I feel the various models provide very helpful guidance".

"I am more aware of the various ways which one may make a decision".

"Before doing this lesson plan I had not thought about how to go about making a decision".

Such remarks have some thing to say not only about school education but university education as well. At the same time they are a base for metacognition and it may be argued that more should have been done, perhaps by inclusion of additional literature to explain metacognition and argue for its merits.

The heuristic -outline of instruction (handout provided)	The test
1. Define the situation. Given a set of poems of varying lengths of which one could be a Shakespearean sonnet. What features are involved? List the features.	
2. State the goal What do I have to do? i.e find out if these poems are Shakespearean sonnets.	
3. Generate ideas Consider different ways you can achieve your goal. Will you count the lines/ Will you go by the technical characteristics of a Shakespearean sonnet? Are they all important?	

Continues over

PROBLEM SOLVING, DECISION MAKING AND HEURISTICS

4. Prepare a plan. How are you going to decide? Suggestion: Consider the features which a Shakespearean sonnet must have. List them. Match your two poems against these features. Give +3 if totally agrees, and –3 if totally disagrees with the feature. Compromise with values between +3 and –3 if it half-agrees or disagrees. Add up the scores and see which is the greatest value. Poem with the greatest value is a sonnet. Or, use a process by elimination by aspects. Have the minimum criteria which the poem must have in order to be a Shakespearean sonnet. Put these attributes in order of importance. Check attributes against each possibility and eliminate where the poem does not meet the criteria.	Test 1. List the 5 steps we can take when we want to solve the "problem" of approaching a poetry question. (20 marks) 2. Briefly discuss what each step involves. (20 marks) 3. Using the 5 step strategy and illustrating reasons for your choices, write your approach to the following question: What is the salient theme of Dickinson's poem *Because I Could Not Stop for Death*. (60 marks) *(The pupils were provided with the poem)*
5. Take action. Make your decision. Is this a Shakespearean sonnet?	

Exhibit 9. 3. The teaching of a heuristic in English for 15 to 16 year olds by a graduate student teacher.

Problem solving using a cloze test in German.

Step 1 What is the problem? What is involved.
I must fill in the German sentences with the correct German word. I must choose the correct word for each gap.

Step 2. State the goal.
By the end of the six step approach I will have chosen between a range of options to fill in each gap in the above exercise.

Step 3. Generate ideas.
Using the non-compensatory elimination by aspects model. Those aspects which prove to be unsuitable will be disregarded and those proven to be suitable possibilities must satisfy the requirements set out by the questions posed in the step.
A. What is missing from the above sentence?
B. What does the above sentence mean as it stands.
C. What is given in the above sentence?
D. If the verb is missing (1) What are the possible verbs that make sense here?
                      (2) Who is the subject of the sentence?
                      (3) What are the endings for this verb?
                          Is it regular or irregular?
                      (4) What tense is the most appropriate?

Step 4 prepare a plan.

Organise the above questions in order of importance whereby when I answer the last question I will have to answer I need to fill the gap.
e.g. C.B.A.D. 1.2.3.4

Continues over

Step 5. Take action
Place the correct word in the sentence and read the complete sentence.

Step 6. Look back
Am I happy with this choice? Are there any alternatives which I feel would be better suited to the sentence?

N.B This is the second part of the lesson plan. In the first part the heuristic was illustrated by the question "I do not know whether to choose science or home economics next year". The teacher hoped the test would encourage reflective thinking because the pupils should reflect on the alternatives. While the teacher explored different strategies in the lesson she did not give the pupils their descriptor titles as she did not want to prohibit comprehension of the models.

Exhibit 9. 4. An approach to the teaching of a heuristic for use by 12 to 13 year olds in German.

Lesson plan handout
Solving a Location Problem in Geography

A When we want to solve a problem and make a decision, we can take a step-by-step approach. What are these steps?
1. **Define the situation** (What is the problem? What things are involved?)
2. **State the Goal.** (What do you have to do to solve the problem?)
3. **Generate ideas** (How many ways can you think of to solve the problem?
4. **Prepare a plan** (How do you rate the different answers to the problem?)
5. **Take action.** (Which answers are you going to choose?)
6. **Look back** (Is your decision a good one? Is their a better answer?)

B When we want to choose a location for something in geography, we can use this model. How can we use this model?
1. Define the situation
   The problem is we have to find somewhere to put a new school. The following things are involved.
   Relief: Mountains, valleys, hills etc.
   River. Is there a river? Will it affect the choice of location?
   Road. Is there a road? Is it important for the location?
   Resource. Does our chosen location need to be near any local resources?
   Population. Are there any people involved? Will they be affected by your choice of location?

2. **State the goal.** We want to find the best place to build a new school.

3. **Generate ideas.** Look at the map. What information does it give you? Choose at least two locations for the school.

Continues over

PROBLEM SOLVING, DECISION MAKING AND HEURISTICS

4. **Prepare the plan**
   You can only choose one location. Which one will it be? There is a helpful way to do this, it is shown on the next page

   To make your decision write down in columns, the five things involved in the situation. then make two new columns for each of the two locations, just like this

Factors.	**Location A.**	**Location B.**
Relief		
River		
Road		
Resource		
Population.		

   Next you pick a range of values for each factor. Try –3 (terrible) up to +3 (excellent). Now, if the relief of location A is good, you might like to give it a +2. If relief at location B is not as good for school, and the ground has to be levelled, then you might give it –3.
   I will do one more for you, then you can finish the rest. If you need a river close by the school, and location A is further away from the river than location B, then, for location B give it, lets suppose, +2 (very good), and give location A-3. Now you can finish the rest of the columns.

5. **Take action.** Now that you have compared one location to another, how will you finally pick the location for your school. Easy as pie! Add up your two columns (don't ignore the minus signs!) and whichever one has the highest score then that's the place to put the school.

6. **Look back**. Ah! but is it the best place to put the school? Perhaps you want to rethink the values you gave to the 4RP factors? Look back and see if you are happy with your decision.

Exhibit 9. 5. Handout for a Lesson in Geography

Decision Making Test

1. When we want to solve a problem, there are six steps we can take. What are these steps and what do they involve?

2. Look at the map provided. Imagine you are a planning officer and you have to decide where to locate an industrial estate. Write down five questions you should ask yourself in trying to decide on a location.

3. You have now chosen your locations, however you can only build one estate. Fill out the model below and choose one location.

4. Please write your reasons for choosing that location and say whether or not you are happy with it. Would you like to change your mind?

Continues over

5. Please say whether you like or disliked being taught decision making in Geography. Don't be afraid to say you disliked it if that is the case?

Exhibit 9.6. A test set after the lesson in exhibit 9.5.

"I feel that the exercise was an interesting one and worthy of spending time on. The pupils enjoyed it and were motivated by it., but then generally pupils are, when something new is done in class. Compared to other experiments I've carried out, I didn't find this one too consuming on the time in preparation and teaching that was spent on it. However, if I am honest with myself, how many times will I use such a device in a language class in the future? If pupils are to become critical thinkers and problem solvers it certainly will not happen as the result of just one lesson. They need continual practice in the area, and considering how much of the lesson would then be spent in talking in English as opposed to the target language, I could not justify incorporating such learning in a language class. Howver, this is not to say, that I believe they should not be taught at all- quite the contrary, but in a subject area of their own in the curriculum.
Example (a)

Frome previous lessons I knew that the majority of the class had not grasped the concept of the dative and accusative cases. They would either guess the ending or leave it in the nominative case with which they were familiar. Before the lesson began I decided to confront them with this issue to see if I could get any insights from their position. Most of them, as I had thought found the grammar very difficult and confusing at the best of times. I then explained the Wales, Stager and Nardi decision making and problem solving model. They were very interested. I began the lesson explaining the step by step heuristic and the benefits in knowing such a model, not just for German, but with problems in other subjects too. The pupils soon got the hang of what was involved and what steps they had to take. I gave them a few example questions to work on, so that they could adjust to this new system. They were kept very busy and seemed to work well in pairs, helping each other out. Even the weaker pupils grasped the concept quite easily. Because each question was different a variety of problems existed which kept the class motivated. Since the class was such a success I'm keen to employ this heuristic in other aspects of German grammar which prove to be of difficulty to some students.
Example (b)

Exhibit 9.7. The response of two graduate student teachers of modern languages to teaching the heuristic

Achievement level	The least benefit	The Most benefit
Low	21	24
Middle	5	17
High	25	14

Table 9.1. Students who benefited from the decision making exercise

In this particular year only four student teachers said that the exercise demanded of them a considerable change in attitude. This is in contrast to two other years in which a questionnaire was administered. Around thirty percent[39] of those year groups said that it demanded a considerable change in their attitude which suggests that the first group may not have been particularly representative.[40] Over 90% in each of the three years said that the exercise was a valuable aid to their teaching, and that they would try it again in different circumstances and with different classes.

While it is not possible to say if the students' decision making skills were improved as a result of the exercise there was evidence of an improvement in average test performance especially among average and weaker students. This is consistent with the view that some students will enhance their learning by using this or similar methods. Nevertheless 80% of the student teachers believed that the exercise had been successful in developing decision-making skills. 18 (of 60) felt that all their students benefited but 39 believed that only some students benefited. It might be thought that the most able students would benefit but there was no general support for this view as Table 9. 1 shows:

In the previous years the students felt that low achieving students benefited from the exercise.[41] They thought it helped them to better retain concepts and that their self-esteem was enhanced through their participation (see exhibit 9. 8). One reason for this might be that the weak pupils benefit from the structure imposed on the lesson by the heuristic, although not every student liked the planning. For these students it might induce 'set mechanisation' but it could be argued that it is better that they try to solve problems rather than give up. The examples show difficulties that weaker students have with learning that are well understood as for example, the ability to formulate a problem or plan, the ability to distinguish between relevant and irrelevant information. Occasionally pupils in the class came to the rescue (exhibit 9.9)

Evidently the situation in mixed ability classes is very complex and demands a wide range of teaching skills. Forty four percent of the comparison group thought that it was the middle range of achievement that the exercise helped to retain concepts. Some also suggested that the middle group had their self-esteem enhanced.[42] In so far as the bright students are concerned another teacher of French offered the view that the decision making process clashed with their own decision making processes. But there is an alternative hypothesis and that is that the problems were not difficult enough for them. Perhaps even at this age they would benefit from some explanation through action of the basic idea of metacognition.

"Set mechanisation" was not discussed by most of these student teachers. One teacher of 16 year olds in Business Studies did. She argued that some problems would not be best solved by the Wales and Stager approach and she gave an example of a problem where there could only be one right answer for which a compensatory approach would be more appropriate. She went on to say that *"the importance of "set" is that the teacher should try to design problems which have several different methods or solutions so that the student becomes aware that the most complex problems and indeed the most simple ones can be solved in different ways. If they become familiar with this when facing new problems they will realise there may be more than one way to solve it"*. Just how difficult this may be, is illustrated by another teacher of business studies to the same age group. She reported that *"even though the students responded positively to the teaching of the decision making heuristic and were able to recall various stages, when it came to actually attempting the second game, the heuristic was abandoned...They didn't use the systematic approach, reverting instead to their basic instincts*" (see exhibit 9.12). As Lydon put it "*the knowledge they acquired is by no means permanently in their heads. Only by continued exposure to this type of exercise, or better still, this method of teaching will the pupils be able to become critical thinkers, or at the very least effective decision makers*".

"It was the weaker pupils who worked most diligently and appeared to enjoy filling out each section based on the Wales and Stager five step decision making scheme. Brighter pupils, however, seemed to find the steps unnecessary and frustrating even. They showed a marked tendency towards side stepping stages 3 and 4 ("generate ideas and prepare a plan"). Instead they jumped ahead to the final stage to take action. This leads me to speculate that the brighter pupils may already be quite skilled at decision making and do not need to verbalise their ideas or plan before solving a problem"
Example (a) relates to a group of 12 year olds learning French

"One of my students Sean, has very weak writing skills in English and is diagnosed dyslexic but is nevertheless bright and good at mathematics. In this exercise Sean was particularly enthusiastic and came up with good ideas and finished before everyone else"
Example (b) relating to a pupil with dyslexia.

" 'Weak' students are very weak at science and in particular at any aspect of the course that required problem solving abilities. They have trouble identifying and understanding the problem, they often go off at a tangent or make no attempt at all solve the task set. I would suggest from the class performance that they have great difficulty in assessing a situation and drawing from it the desired information. They appear unsure and are easily distracted"
Example (c) relating to science and weak students.

"I did notice that the weaker students performed poorly in step 1 which I would have presumed to be easier than the other steps. As a result of this their chances of doing well in the rest of the questions were minimised. I think this type of question is demanding for weaker students' as it requires them to summarise and highlight the important points. They seem unable to recognise what is relevant and what is irrelevant. This probably relates in some way to the way they process information"
Example (d) relating to the difficulties faced by weaker students.

"I didn't really like it cause it was too much planned"…"The weaker students perceived it as an added complication, and had particular difficulty with step 3 which involved coming up with alternative ideas and writing them down. Phrasing these ideas proved to be a problem, and was I feel viewed by them as compounding the difficulty of the problem"
Example (e) example of resistance to planning

"Although the pupils were uneasy with this approach to begin with, many particularly the weaker pupils took it on board and saw themselves as "real scientists" to quote one of the boys. It was interesting to see the pupils who normally perform practical work well having some difficulties adjusting their approach. It gave those pupils who can appear to be in difficulties all the time a chance to shine. It was therefore a good exercise in morale boosting for these pupils and a humbling experience for those who have become complacent where practical work is concerned…..The weaker students were definitely more motivated and as a consequence were happier at the task….whether this translates into understanding concepts is another matter".
Example (f) relating to practical work in science.

Exhibit 9.8. Problems in teaching a heuristic

PROBLEM SOLVING, DECISION MAKING AND HEURISTICS

> Throughout the class I felt they were a little confused as the relevance of the heuristic and model- they wondered what it was leading to. However, by the end of the class most of them seemed to have understood the content and relevance. One of the students explained it to the rest of the class as follows "When you're doing an essay its hard to know what you are going to say. There's a lot of things that come into your head but you don't know how to write all down, or what to leave out. We have to write and essay about a person we like. Its really hard to find the right ideas and words. So we start with a list of good and bad things about people. We have to decide which of the good things are important to us- so we use the additive model to help. That makes the decision easy" ".
> **Example (a) of a pupil coming to the rescue**.
>
> Taking things step by step I introduced the six steps involved in decision making, following with an example each time. The weaker students were slightly confused while the average and above average students paid great attention to what I was saying, asking questions at every opportunity once I began to explain the stages. Having recapped on the process once again with more input from the class the majority of students were fairly enlightened once they could place the steps into context using an example they could relate to. Clearly the information had become meaningful to the majority. I was delighted when one above average student pointed out how it was necessary to look at all the available options before deciding what actions to follow enabling me again to emphasise the elimination by aspects model of decision making. Moving a step further I asked the class if they thought they could only apply the model to a science problem and was pleased at how many of them related the use of the model to other subjects, with two students actually providing examples for use in other subjects".
> **Example (b) of students helping the teacher**.

Exhibit 9.9. Studnts helping the teacher

The heuristics and assessment

Heuristics very often indicate the type of assessment that should be used. For example Red gave instructions to his students for the planning stage of his modification of the Polya heuristic to

"Write down the equations from which the unknowns can be found using the given information. These equations are the connection between the given data and unknowns. Then
1. Carry out the plan to apply the equations.
2. Check each step.
3. Underline or block in each answer so that it is easily identified.
4. Make sure that each answer meets with common sense i.e is it realistic? Then make sure each answer satisfies the assumptions and conditions stated for the problem."[43]

These statements and ones like them can easily be turned into questions for a rubric. In Exhibit 9.11 rubrics are shown for analysis and synthesis and evaluation. These can be used to help students to think about the skill they have to develop and they can be used for something as small as a written test and something as large as a project. Notice how they also describe executive skills required for most kind of managerial tasks either at a high or low level. These particular rubrics were designed by history teachers to test small-scale project work in history. A scheme for assessing essays is shown in exhibit 9.12. Evaluation is a form of self-assessment and it is an important activity in metacognition. As Loacker of Alverno College points out self-assessment and reflective capability go hand in hand. The one informs the other and vice-versa.[44]

The Alverno interpretive framework is a heuristic. Loacker writes *"we have identified four components or skills inherent in self-assessment: observing, interpreting/analyzing, judging, and planning. Although these components are not absolutely sequential-particularly in their development, which is an ongoing zig-zag- we encourage students to form the habit of observing carefully and interpreting or analyzing their observations before they leap to judging.* [This was the intention of the two evaluations required of our student teachers when implementing their lessons]. *Planning seems to follow organically from the other components, yet a student might intuitively recognize the worth of some aspects of her work and continue to refine them without really understanding or even carefully observing them. She would then at least partially be meeting the criteria for planning as a beginning self-assessor (i.e., identifies aspects to maintain for performance and/or the process of producing a performance" and "identifies aspects to develop further and suggest approaches for performance and/or the process of producing performance")."*

" Although judging seems to be the core of self assessment, we consider it important to separate out the interpreting/analyzing as a component that emphasizes the reflective nature of self assessment. We encourage students to probe the meaning of their actions- the sources; the role of intuition, emotion and attitude; and the process by which they came to understanding or failed to come to it. Doing so, we find, enables them, to make more informed judgements, to take a process perspective by connecting the current performance to past ones, and to develop understanding that assists improvement. The planning component is meant to extend the process forward." [45]

She had done more "problem solving with the girls. I found five girls that by the third problem they were looking at the heuristic as a set of rules. Their vision had been tunnelled yet again by the format. They were not letting themselves think freely by trying to answer problem according to a set of rules".
Example (a). relating to a maths class of 15 – 16 year olds.

"Brian claimed that we automatically pick on the best solution first and that any subsequent ideas generated are bound to be lest robust than the original. I discussed this point with him for sometime, advocating the benefits of "brainstorming" and pointed out to him, that his best solution was in fact faulty on many grounds"
Example (b) relating to a science class of 15 to 16 year olds.

Exhibit 9. 10. Relating to set mechanisation (induction)

A group of first year university students[46] who reflected on their experience suggested the following factors contributed to problem solving:

1. There must be a problem or an awareness that a problem exists.
2. Six prerequisite skills and attitudes are essential. These are:
    (i) The basic knowledge pertinent to the problem(s).
    (ii) The learning skills necessary to obtain the information necessary to solve the problem.
    (iii) The motivation to want to solve the problem.
    (iv) The memorized experience factors that provide order of magnitude "feelings" as to what assumptions can be made and how reasonable the answer is.
  The ability to communicate the answer; and perhaps
    (v) Group skills if the problem must be solved by a group of people. [47]
3. An overall organized strategy is required.
4. For specific steps in the strategy there are well-known alternatives.
5. A problem solver uses four abilities time and time again. These are, to create, analyze, generalize and simplify.
6. Sets of "good hints" or "heuristics" have been developed about what to do next.

We should add that a good problem solver will have a developed reflective capability demonstrated through skill in self assessment.

Looking backward

This chapter ends this block of chapters (5 – 9) on instruction. It also ends the focus provided by archival analysis of the graduate student teacher reports of the classroom investigations they had undertaken. Some 7000 investigations were undertaken during the twelve-year period of the programme. Although each one of them was a *singularity* taken as group, there are important findings of general relevance. First there are good and poor examples of each of the investigations in all the main subjects of the second-level curriculum including music. They are therefore of general interest. Together they provide a possible framework (there are others) for the development of thinking. The last exercise is reminder that 'thinking' has to be done in every subject of the curriculum. Thus each subject can contribute to the development of problem solving and critical thinking skills. As the title of one recent article states "Thinking is Literacy. Literacy is Thinking."[48]

Second, the investigations put substantial stress on the student teachers because of the work they demanded. This was much larger than would be expected in the every day work of a teacher primarily because of the review of the literature and the design of the lesson not only to fit the normal programme but, to test a hypotheses about the instructional technique used.

Third, many of these student teachers gained considerable insight into their work which they would not otherwise have gained in traditional student teaching. Thus these research exercises were of value and have the potential to influence teaching for the better. They clearly validate the model of teaching as research.

Fourth, it is clear from the reports that pupils are motivated when they experience variety and are challenged. But many have to be persuaded that such variety is in their interests and will better help them pass their examinations. Whether or not it is a function of the fact that it was the first activity or not these student teachers did not like the exercise on concept learning, yet learning concepts and principles is probably the most important thing we do. Overall the teachers found that in class the exercises were time consuming. To put it in another way the evidence shows that very often pupils only learn when they have substantial exposure to a concept/issue/skill. While teachers may well understand this they are unlikely to change their stance and provide the time for reflection that pupils need unless they are encouraged to do so by the authorities. And this may well mean changes in the length of syllabuses and the techniques of assessment in state mandated assessments, tests and examinations. Unless such changes are made the ability of teachers to help students to think critically will be limited.

Fifth, it is well established that pupils respond favourably to teachers who show they are well prepared. During this period it is clear that the "backwash" effect of public examinations influenced student attitudes toward learning and the approaches used by teachers in their instruction. There is no evidence that examinations were designed to enhance learning. Examination design is difficult and seems to be underrated. Even the design of classroom tests was found to be difficult by some students. Good teaching cannot be divorced from good examining (assessment).

The studies reported in this chapter indicated that appropriate to age, and level of cognitive development it is possible to help pupils develop skill in metacognition. There is plenty of evidence in the reports to show that pupils require time to learn and that this time is often not given. This is a key issue for curriculum designers.

Although the student teachers were asked to write behavioural objectives for their lessons they were not asked to write them to fit the categories of *The Taxonomy of Educational Objectives*. Some of the questions that the student teachers asked clearly tested higher order thinking. The decision making/problem solving exercise is only one aspect of critical thinking. While it is controversial *The Taxonomy of Educational Objectives* is one of the conceptual ideas that has caused educators to distinguish between higher order thinking skills and basic knowledge (see chapter 10).

Implications for curriculum and instructional leaders

Many of these student teachers commented that doing once off exercises was not particularly helpful to their pupils. For pupils to benefit they have to be exposed on more than one occasion to the different strategies so that they become part of the repertoire of learning. In another study a principal suggested that innovations in teaching can easily be undermined when teachers of other classes do not support an innovation. That principal said that if the learning styles exercise was to be successful then every teacher should be aware of learning styles and be prepared to engage with pupils in discussions about how they learn.[50] In this way teachers using them to design their lessons are supported. To achieve such a goal demands a 'team'/whole school approach to instruction and that would be a radical change.

Such change is about changing attitudes. In this case it is toward developing and participating in an inquiry oriented school. It is not that everybody should engage in 'research' activities of this kind all the time but that the participants should have a positive disposition to such research. This can be achieved in part by accepting the proposition on accountability put at the beginning of this text. This was that professionalism requires personal accountability and that requires a willingness to continually evaluate (assess) ones own instruction through the utilisation of the many simple techniques open to us for this purpose. That was called level 1 of instructional and curriculum leadership. It also implies a willingness to participate in whole school policy making in curriculum and instruction.

It was suggested that 'assumptional-dialogues' of the kind proposed by Cohn and Kottkamp[51] could be an effective vehicle for the development of whole school policy. Several were suggested in the preceding chapters. In this case the arguments surrounding the teaching of higher order thinking skills provide ample scope for such a dialogue. For such dialogues to be successful they have to be initiated by the educational leader at the policy level. In some instances the instructional and curriculum leader may have to persuade the educational leader that this or that policy should be pursued on a whole school basis. In other instances they will be the resource with the detailed knowledge and the skill (courage!) to persuade their colleagues to contribute to the dialogue and to assist them accomplish whatever developments emerge from the dialogue.

At the political level instructional and curriculum leaders need to persuade policy makers to encourage the development of higher order thinking skills and to take whatever steps are necessary to induce appropriate teaching through changes in syllabus and assessment. Policy makers need to be persuaded that covering a large syllabus may not be accomplished with understanding. Time is required to learn key concepts.

INSTRUCTIONAL AND CURRICULUM LEADERSHIP

Analysis and Synthesis. (Analysis is a preliminary step to arranging the material collected in a coherent patters. It involves the selection of the most important and relevant points from the information assembled. Synthesis is the expression of the pattern that emerges from the analysis of subject matter).

1. This candidate
   - made no attempt at analysis
   - fails to distinguish relevant from irrelevant material and issues and important unimportant material and issues.
   - Distinguishes some important issues arising from his topic.
   - Has isolated the important issues, factors or questions arising from his topic.

2. This candidate
   - shows little attempt to organize the material collected
   - has organized his material into a coherent pattern.
   - Has organized his material to answer questions or to describe issues, or to explain factors involved in the material.

Evaluation (the student applies standard reasoning and judgement which leads him to assess causes and consequences and to distinguish between fact and opinion; history and legend. The project should have some form of conclusion in which the candidate is expected to explain his/her findings and/or opinions, having taken into account different viewpoints and values)

1. This candidate
   - made no attempt to distinguish fact from opinion; history from legend; causes from consequences.
   - fails to distinguish fact from opinion; history from legend; causes from consequences.
   - shows some ability to distinguish fact from opinion; history from legend; causes from consequences.
   - assess causes and consequences; distinguishes fact from opinion and history from legend.

2. This candidate
   - made no attempt to draw a conclusion.
   - fails to come to any conclusion or judgement
   - accepts received opinion and judgement without comment.
   - critically examines (questions) received opinions and judgements and forms his own independent judgement.

Exhibit 9. 11 Part of a teacher designed assessment schedule in history[49]

In your work	In assessing someone else' work (especially when acting as an adviser, assessor or in a debate)
Outlining the argument List the premises (hypotheses/propositions) which you wish to demonstrate or prove. State the conclusion(s) List the reasons for the conclusions.	**Outlining the argument** Identify the premises (hypotheses) and conclusions. Establish which sentences do not add to the argument. List the reasons for the conclusion

Continues over

Examining the argument for clarity	Examining the argument for clarity
Check the key terms (concepts/ principles are stated clearly. Do not attempt to fudge the issue. NB An argument whose key concepts and principles are not clear, or which contains ambiguities is not a good argument. A good argument should be brief and the point.	When any terms and phrases are unclear ask for clarification in a live argument. In an examination write a note at the side of the script to check you have not misperceived what is being said. Look out for fudging.
Asserting and checking the truth of premises	**Asserting and checking the truth of premises**
You must be able to stand over each premise you use, and, where necessary cite supporting evidence and its course. Don't throw false premises into an argument, because they are easily spotted	Any questionable premises must be defended by another argument. In an examination answer look for false premises as a foundation for your own assessment. List the reasons which make you think that the proposition is false (see last section below)
Ensuring that the premises are necessary and relevant to the argument.	**Ensuring that the premises are necessary and relevant to the argument.**
Check that each premise is both necessary and relevant to the argument. Eliminate premises which are not. NB Any person involved in a disputation must have sure grounds for the claims that are made.	In debate the person offering the argument must be able to show the necessity and relevance of each answer. In scripts look out for circular argument and tautologies.
Testing the strength of an argument	**Testing the strength of and argument.**
Predict the counter argument and test your conclusion for validity against the alternative. If the alternative view has strong merits then your conclusion may be wrong.	In debate and examination scripts look for weaknesses in the logic of the argument, and the data used to support the conclusion.

Exhibit 9. 12. Evaluating arguments in essays. Adapted from FitzGibbons, R. E. (1981) *Educational Decisions. An Introduction to the Philosophy of Education.* Harcourt, Brace Jovanovitch, New York. See Heywood, J (1989) *Assessment in Higher Education* 2nd edition, Wiley, Chichester for an extended discussion in the context of essay writing.

Notes and references

[1] Cited in Heywood, J (1982). *Pitfalls and Planning in Student Teaching.* Kogan Page, London. p49.
[2] I have done this exercise on several occasions with the same results.
[3] McDonald, F. J (1969). *Educational Psychology.* Wadsworth, Belmont, CA.
[4] Prince,M., and B. Hoyt (2002). Helping students make the transition from novice to expert problem solvers. *Proceeding Frontiers in Education Conference.* 2, F2A 7 to 11. They were speaking of engineering in particular but their argument applies more generally to the spectrum of subjects.
[5] Kahney, H (1986). *Problem Solving. A Common Sense Approach.* Open University Press, Milton Keynes(cited by Bolton, J and S. Ross (1997) Developing students' physics problem solving skills. *Physics Education.* 32, (3), 176 – 185.
[6] (1993). Teaching for Higher Order Thinking. All of issue no2 Vol 32 of *Theory into Practice.* Guest editor D. Petersen.
[7] Madaus, G Educational Research Centre, Drumcondra, Dublin, 1974.
[8] Norris, S. P (ed) (1992). *The Generalizability of Critical Thinking. Multiple Perspectives on an Educational Ideal.,* Teachers College Press, New York.
[9] Ennis, R. H. (1991) *Critical Thinking.* Prentice Hall, Englewood Cliffs, NJ and in Norris *loc. cit.*
[10] McPeck, J (1981). *Critical Thinking in Education.* St Martins Press, New York.
[11] Woods, D. R. et al (1997) Developing problem solving skills: the McMaster Problem Solving program. *Journal of Engineering Education* 86, (2), 75 - 79

[12] Apple, D. K., Nygren, K. P., Williams, M. W. and D. M. Litynski (2002). Distinguishing and elevating levels of learning in engineering and technology instruction. *Proceedings Frontiers in Education Conference*, 1, T4B – 7 to 11.
[13] Luchins, A. S. (1942) Mechanisation in problem solving: the effect of 'Einstellung'. *Psychological Monograps* No 248. Cited by McDonald, F. J. ref 2.
[14] Wittrock, M. C (1963). Effect of certain sets on complex verbal learning. *Journal of Educational Psycholgy*, 54, 85 –88.
[15] Furneaux, W. D (1962). The psychologist and the university. *Universities Quarterly*, 17, 33 - 47
[16] Heywood, J., McGuinness, S., and D. E. Murphy (1980). Final report of the Public Examinations Project. University of Dublin, School of Education, Dublin. The model was based on that of engineering science at 'A' level developed in England. Carter, G., Heywood, J and D. T. Kelly (1986). *A Case Study in Curriculum Assessment. Engineering Science Advanced*. Roundthorn, Manchester.
[17] Reed, S. K. (1988). *Cognition Tehiry and Applications*. 2nd edition, Brooks/ Cole, Pacific Grove, CA.
[18] *ibid*
[19] Cited in Heywood, J (1982*). Pitfalls and Planning in Student teaching*, Kogan Page, London p 125
[20] Saupé, J (1961) Chapter on Learning in P. Dressel (ed). *Evaluation in Higher Education*. Houghton Mifflin, Boston, MA
[21] The text used was that of Reed *loc. cit.*
[22] Tversky, A (192). Elimination by aspects: a theory of choice. *Psychological Review* 80, 352 – 373. Cited by Reed *loc cit.* Ref 17
[23] *loc.cit.*
[24] Simon, H. A. (1957). *Models of Man*. Wiley, New York.
[25] Polya, G (1957). *How to Solve It*. 2nd edition. Anchor Doubleday, Garden City.
[26] Red, W. E. (1981). Problem solving and beginning engineering students. *Engineering Education*, 72, (2), 167 – 170. Rosati, P. A (1987). Practising a problem-solving strategy with computer tutorials. *International Journal of Applied Engineering Education*, 3, (1), 49 – 53.
[27] *loc.cit* Woods
[28] Data was available from other years when no such pressure was exerted.
[29] Wales, C. E and R. A. Stager (1986). Series of papers on guided design in issues 5, 6, 7, and 8 of *Engineering Education*. Vol 62.
[30] Perkins, D. N (1986). *Knowledge as Design*. Lawrence Erlbaum, Hillsdale, NJ.
[31] Wales, C. E., Nardi, A.H and R. A. Stager (1976). *Professional Decision Making*. Center for Guided Design. University of West Virginia, Morganstown, WV.
[32] Resnick, L. B (1987) *Education and Learning to Think*. National Academy Press, Washington, DC For a recent papers of practical work in schools see *Educational Leadership*, 86, issue 6, 2008 which is devoted to Teaching Students to Thiml.
[33] D'Amour, G and C. E. Wales (1977) Improving problem solving skills through a course in guided design. *Engineering Education*. February 381 – 384.
[34] Eck, R. W and W.J. Wilhelm (1979) Guided design an approach to education for practice in engineering. *Engineering Education*. November 191 - 198.
[35] Wales, C. A and R. A. Stager (1990). *Thinking with Equations. Problem Solving in Math and Science*. Center for Guided Design, West Virginia University, Morganstown, WV.
[36] Wales, C. E. Nardi, A. H and R. A. Stager (1990) Research or Practice. The debate goes on. *International Journal of Technology and Design Education*, 1, (1), 40 – 47.
[37] The instructions changed during the eight years the exercise was run. At first the students were asked to teach a problem solving skill. Subsequently it became a problem solving heuristic, then it became a decision making heuristic.
[38] Similar responses were obtained in a previous year when 16 said they were sceptical. 48 were either not so sceptical or open minded.
[39] 22 of N = 64 and 25 of N = 70 respectively. A third of the first group said they underwent a permanent change as a teacher
[40] Age might be a factor since there was more than an average number of mature students in the group
[41] 78% and 80% respectively
[42] 15

[43] loc *cit* Red

[44] Loacker, G (ed) (2000) *Self Assessment at Alverno* College. Alverno College Institute, Milwaukee, WI

[45] *ibid* pp 3 & 4.

[46] Leibold, B. G. et al (1976). Problem solving: a freshman experience. *Engineering Education*, 67, (2), 172 – 176.

[47] It will be noticed that apart from the sixth skill, quite independently, and during much of the same period those responsible for the JMB Engineering Science had made the same assumptions. Thus, while the assessment schedule focused on the skills of the chosen heuristic the moderators of the project necessarily took into account the correctness of, and the available knowledge that the student had.

[48] Roberts, T and L. Billingsm (2008). Thinking is Literacy, Literacy is Thinking. *Educational Leadership* 65, (5), 32 –36.

[49] Full schedule is given in Heywood, J (1978). *Examining in Second Level Education*. Association of Secondary Teachers Ireland.

[50] cited in Heywood, J and M. Murray (2005). Curriculum-led staff development. Towards curriculum and instructional leadership in Ireland. *Bulletins of the EFEA No 4*. (European Foundation on Educational Administration).

[51] Cohn, M. M and R. B. Kottkamp (1993). Teachers the Missing Voice in Education. State University of New York Press, Albany, NY.

Part IV
Curriculum:
theory and practice

10
AIMS, OBJECTIVES AND OUTCOMES

Summary and introduction

It is a matter of confusion, if not regret, that the educational fraternity cannot agree common definitions for the terms used in the study of the curriculum and its application to practice. A task of the curriculum leader is to clarify the issues raised. This chapter is concerned with the purposes of education as evidenced in mission statements, the specific curriculum, general instruction in particular, and specifically with the derivation of aims and objectives at the level of curriculum. It is approached from an historical perspective beginning with Tyler's first question governing the design of the curriculum namely, its objectives. The Taxonomy with which he was associated was introduced in chapter 5. The key questions for curriculum and instructional designers were also listed in the first section of that chapter.

The Taxonomy of Educational Objectives[1] became one of the most widely read works in the educational literature, and it had a world-wide influence. For example, the Joint Matriculation Board in the UK used it to define the outcomes of their examinations for the General Certificate of Education. The Intermediate Certificate Committee in Ireland wanted the examination to test the higher order skills of the Taxonomy. Some teachers continue to use it to this day even though it has been substantially criticised.[2] Its purpose was to provide a common framework for testing. Its authors proposed that there was, beyond knowledge, a hierarchy of skills involved in all learning. They were application, analysis, synthesis, and evaluation. It can contribute to the design of a curriculum programme, a subject curriculum, or a unit of that curriculum. The authors recognised that it could not apply exactly to every subject and that other categories might have to be defined. A curriculum development in the UK based in part on the idea of The Taxonomy promoted the concept of multiple strategy assessment and instruction.

Against the idea inherent in The Taxonomy were those who argued that all education should not proceed from pre-formulated goals. Teachers, Elliot Eisner argued, should be able to plan for the expressive in the curriculum.[3] But this is to all intent and purpose an objective and if this view is accepted it broadens what is understood by objectives. As indicated in chapter 2 just such a broad view is taken here although it is predicated on the principle that teachers should be able to declare where they are going in order that they may evaluate (assess) that they have arrived.

One danger has been that teachers see The Taxonomy as the sole source of objectives when there are many others. For example other information in the literature of education can inform aims, curriculum structure and teaching practice. It is the task of curriculum and instructional leaders to place before teachers the case for and against objectives and to indicate the many sources of objectives including The Taxonomy.

There is a danger that policy makers see the objectives approach as justification for the demand that schools demonstrate their accountability by achieving large numbers of outcomes or standards as they are known in the United States (see also chapter 12). There is a further difficulty that they may associate the attainment of these outcomes with a transmission model of the curriculum when in fact the attainment of some of the outcomes may best be obtained by methods other than transmission. It is easy for policy makers to persuade the public that transmission approaches are best. For this reason, curriculum leaders need to enter into such debates and bring the authority of knowledge, experience and research that is lacking and when necessary emphasise the need for independent evaluation. It is also clear that if the public and parents are not to be led by the over simplifications of policy makers that curriculum leaders and the teaching profession have to engage the community in rational and not emotional dialogue.

The same group of educators produced a Taxonomy of Educational Objectives for the affective domain in 1964. Affect is about feelings (emotions), attitudes, beliefs, values, ethics and morals. Combinations of these factors affect the way we approach change, whether we embrace it or resist it irrespective of its merit or otherwise. More generally the importance of the affective domain has been consistently neglected in the planning of curricula. Both student and teacher attitudes and beliefs have an impact on what is learnt and how it is taught.

Mention is made of taxonomies for the psychomotor and experiential domains, and some other approaches to the classification and derivation of objectives are discussed. The chapter begins with a comment on mission statements and the importance of aims.

The general principles described in this and the previous chapter 2 apply as much to the design implementation and evaluation of instruction as they do to the curriculum It should be clear that neither the design of the curriculum or instruction is a simple matter. The internal role of the curriculum leader is to help teachers to work together in curriculum design. Externally it is to ensure that policy makers and the public that changing the curriculum is complex and not a simple issue. The chapter begins with the problem of clarifying aims.

Mission statement, aims and goals

Unfortunately there is no agreed terminology about the use of these terms and they are often used interchangeably. Even the term objective may be used. Those who use them seem to be agreed that they are fairly general and to be used to provide a focus for where an institution or a department should go (or be going). Some authorities, especially religious orders have talked about the vision that educational institutions should have. Vision and Mission would appear to be the same thing. Both indicate something to be aimed at – a path along which the school should be led. Leaders are expected to have vision.

A mission statement should be the emotional hook on which a school should derive its energy. The trouble is that very often mission statements lack substance, a consequence of which is their disregard by both teachers and students.[4] The linkage between them and the reality of the institution is broken. Sometimes they are simply expressions of hope. Through an "assumptional-dialogue" curriculum leaders should be able to ensure that a mission statement necessarily informs the practice of curriculum and instruction.

One of the reasons that the so-called 'objectives movement' emerged was that many of the statements of aims became a pious list of platitudes that teachers used when they had to defend what they did. They had no means in fact of judging whether, in fact, what they did was achieving the goals they believed in. Therefore, if we were to establish what teachers achieved in their teaching it would be necessary to have some criteria against which the performance of students could be judged. In consequence assessments of student's performance would have to be designed to meet these criteria.

Today the term *outcome* is preferred to objectives. Some writers infer differences between objectives and outcomes that were not in the minds of those with whom the so-called *'objectives movement'* is associated. In any event the terminology has become thoroughly confused.[5] There is no consistency in usage. For example Yokomoto and Bostwick's criticism of the usage of objectives in engineering could be applied to any other subject or curriculum. They wrote:

"Dissimilar words are used as synonyms, such as "outcomes", "attributes", and "competencies to describe what students must demonstrate" [6]

Sometimes the term "performance outcome" is used.

Nevertheless, discussion about aims and objectives has been very restricted to the developments associated with Tyler and his colleagues. It tends to ignore content in favour of learning skills in the cognitive, affective and psychomotor domains, yet the understanding of a key concept is as much a learning objective as are the development of skills in analysis and synthesis (see chapter 6).

AIMS, OBJECTIVES AND OUTCOMES

The trouble is that like all movements there was a danger of throwing the baby out with the bath water. In this case, the move to 'objectivity' carried with it the danger that it removed the emotional props that supported teachers in their everyday work.[7] The language of school education is a language of aims and goals, not a language of objectives and outcomes however useful they may be. The role of objectives and outcomes is in the interpretation of aims into practice. Therefore, discussion of aims is important because of its link to teacher motivation, and several seminal texts on the aims of education continue to be relevant.[8]

Origins of the objectives movement

Although the idea that schools should declare their objectives has a long history (e.g. Bobbitt, cited by Jackson[9]) the starting point for this section is based on Ralph Tyler's (1949) *Basic Principles of the Curriculum and Instruction*.[10] As we saw in Chapter 2 he proposed that the curriculum designer and/or teacher should begin the exercise by declaring the aims and objectives to be achieved. Tyler took part in a number of conferences with a group of educators between 1949 and 1953 to develop a taxonomy that would help educators *"evaluate the learning of students systematically."*[11] It was aimed at college and university examiners although it would apply at school level. This group believed, *"that some common framework used by all college and university examiners could do much to promote the exchange of test materials and ideas for testing [....] After considerable discussion there was agreement that the framework might be best obtained through a system of classifying goals of the educational process using objectives."*[12]

As this group developed the taxonomy they became aware, *"that too much emphasis was being placed on the lowest level of the taxonomy-'knowledge'. Frequently as much as 90% of instructional time was spent at this level, with very little time spent on the higher mental processes that would enable students to apply their knowledge creatively"*.

As result the group paid considerable attention to what some now call Higher Order Thinking Skills (HOTS). The cognitive domain of *The Taxonomy* was finally published in 1956 and the principal categories are shown in exhibit 5.7. It has had a profound influence on many educators and educational practices both at school and post-school levels in many countries.[13] Some teachers (world-wide) have used it for planning their assessment, courses, and lessons, and continue to use it in its original form. Others have adapted the idea while others have rejected it. Some want to change the vocabulary and add to the confusion that already exists.

There is little doubt that the so-called 'outcomes movement' has its origins in the *Taxonomy of Educational Objectives* (see below). An understanding of its development may help resolve some of the terminological in-exactitudes that Yokomoto and Bostwick described.[14]

The idea of the *Taxonomy of Educational Objectives*.

The group had the intention of developing taxonomies in the affective, cognitive and psychomotor domains. While they achieved separate volumes on the affective and cognitive domains it was left to Harrow[15] to describe a taxonomy for the psychomotor domain. Subsequently, Steinaker and Bell[16] described a taxonomy for experiential education. The first volume to be produced was on the cognitive domain, and is commonly known as the *"Bloom Taxonomy"* after the lead editor.[17] It was this volume that created the stir.

To be a taxonomy the categories have to be hierarchically ordered and independent of each other yet build on each other. One way of understanding the intention *of The Taxonomy* in the cognitive domain is to imagine the mental processes that one goes through when reading an editorial in a quality newspaper. That activity faces one with having to make a judgement about the validity of the article. Clearly it is impossible to be critical unless one has knowledge of the subject with which to comprehend the article. It is also clear that one cannot criticise without comprehension, and in that sense, our thinking is hierarchical. Analysis and synthesis follow. One cannot synthesise without analysing, and we cannot judge without analysing and synthesising.

Each of the sub-sections in *The Taxonomy* was described in great detail and examples of test questions provided. These were intended to describe what a person would be "able to do" in terms of a particular category. What one does as a result of teaching is an "outcome". The sub-categories of knowledge are shown in exhibit 10.1. The beginning of the category of comprehension is shown in exhibit 10.2. The preface of the category of Synthesis is shown in exhibit 10.3.

Several British philosophers argued that the *Taxonomy* was based on an inadequate epistemology, and Furst[18] admitted that the committee paid little attention to the philosophic dimension. *"Instead they placed much of the burden of defining educational goals and cognitive levels on test items, the correct response to which was taken as necessary evidence of the attainment at issue. Thus the authors took as the only viable alternative the operational definition in which the intended student behaviour was implicit. They did recognise, however, that the operational definition was not sufficient; one also had to know or assume the nature of the students' educational experience."* [19]

AIMS, OBJECTIVES AND OUTCOMES

> **Knowledge.**
>
> **Knowledge of;**
> Specifics,
> Terminology,
> Specific facts,
> Ways and means of dealing with specifics,
> Conventions,
> Trends and sequences,
> Classifications of categories,
> Criteria,
> Methodology,
> Universals and abstractions in a field,
> Principles and generalizations,
> Theories and structures.

Exhibit 10.1. The sub-categories of knowledge in *The Taxonomy of Educational Objectives*.

> **Definition of the Comprehension Category.**
> This category represents the lowest level of understanding, where the pupil knows and can make use of the material communicated without necessarily relating it to other material or seeing in it all its implications. It includes the ability to recognise freshly presented pieces of information as illustrations of particular generalisations, the ability to recognise the essential elements of information presented, to relate them to one another and to obtain some total ordered view of the information as a whole. Comprehension behaviours can be subdivided into three types that are hierarchical in nature.
>
> (a)   **Translation**- which requires the individual to transform a communication into another language, into other terms, or into another form of communication.
>
> (b)   **Interpretation**- the ability to sift the important factors from the less important ones i.e. to show judgement.
>
> (c)   **Extrapolation**-the ability to perceive the underlying relationship governing a relationship

Exhibit 10.2. More detailed explanation of the category of Comprehension in *The Taxonomy*.

> **Definition of Synthesis.**
>
> Having analysed a problem the student may be required to reconstruct its elements in an entirely new structure which was not clearly visible before, as in designing an experiment to solve a certain problem or to present conclusions with logically organised supporting evidence. This ability is called synthesis and tests creativity and originality.
>
> Synthesis divides into three main sub-categories:-
> Production of a unique communication.
> Production of a plan or Proposed set of operations.
> Derivation of a set of abstract relations.

Exhibit 10.3. More detailed explanation of the category of synthesis in *The Taxonomy*.

The problem arose from the fact that the committee had chosen Ralph Tyler's definition of an educational objective. For him, an educational objective represented a change in behaviour in ways of acting, thinking and feeling. *"A behavioural objective expresses what a person will be able to do. It is action oriented. At the end of a class or course a student will be able to define..., discriminate between..., identify..., etc."* (See exhibit 5.7)

As we saw in chapter 5, in lesson planning Cohen and Mannion.[20] distinguish between, aim, non-behavioural objective and behavioural objective). Some examples by student teachers were shown in exhibit 5.5. The last behavioural objective of example c is clearly a behavioural objective since it requires a measurable response from students even though it is unusual to include it in such a statement. Teachers evidently think that lessons can be designed to cover all the dimensions of the *Taxonomy* as the examples in exhibits 10.4 and 10.5 show.

The committee used the term behavioural in a broad sense. It is, wrote Furst, a broad concept rather than the usual (overt) behavioural one, because it includes covert as well as overt states.[21] It is this which creates the philosophical difficulty because tests only measure something that is overt, hence the need to know or assume the nature of the students' educational experience. Many other criticisms of the *Taxonomy* were made on behaviourist grounds. There was an unwillingness to accept the broad use intended by the group. Had the authors been behaviourist then the *Taxonomy* would have produced a curriculum based on drill and practice. An important criticism made by a mathematics educator in England was that some of the demands for knowledge were more complex than those demands for analysis and evaluation.[22]

As indicated the authors foreshadowed what has come to be known as outcomes based assessment since they declared that, *"The Taxonomy is designed to be a classification of the student behaviours which represent the* **intended outcomes** *of the educational process. It is assumed that essentially the same classes of behaviour may be observed in the usual range of subject-matter content of different levels of education (elementary, high school, college). Thus a single set of classifications should be applicable in all these circumstances."*

"What we are classifying is the intended behaviours of students- the ways in which individuals are to think, act or feel, as a result of participating in some unit of instruction. (Only such of those intended behaviours as are related to mental acts of thinking are included in the part of The Taxonomy developed in the handbook for the cognitive domain)".

"It is recognized that **actual behaviours** *of the students after they have completed a unit of instruction may differ in degree as well as kind from the intended behaviour specified by the objectives. That is, the effects of instruction may be such that students do not learn a skill to any given degree."*

There is still much confusion about outcomes. For example, one assessment specialist went so far as to propose that objectives were used by course designers whereas specifications of learning outcomes were made by teachers.[23] It is, however, difficult to see what the differences between objectives and outcomes are when they are statements of what it is expected that students will be able to do as a result of this or that learning activity.

Yokomoto and Bostwick said that, *"Secondary meanings of some words are sometimes used, such as using the term "criteria" to describe the level of performance that students must achieve and "outcomes" to describe the learning behaviours students must demonstrate. A more common definition of "outcome" is "result" or consequence", and anyone attaching meaning to the word will surely become confused in a discussion on writing measurable outcomes".*[24]

To illustrate just how confused things are consider the example of the Irish primary (elementary) curriculum. Its rubrics distinguish between general aims and specific aims and general objectives and specific objectives. These aims and objectives supposedly take into account the stage of development of the children, differences between children due to variations in intellectual and physical ability, personality etc., and the particular circumstances of the school.

The handbook says that objectives are generally seen as being more detailed, more precise and more complete statement of aims. If couched in behavioural terms, they attempt to describe what the pupil will be able to feel, to know or to do after learning has occurred. They tend to reflect curriculum content more accurately than aims and may contain references to materials and methodology.

A reasonable summary of the terminological debate would seem to be that educational objectives indicate the changes to be expected of students as a result of their participation in specific educational experiences. These changes are in knowledge, understanding, skills, abilities and affective characteristics.

Behavioural objectives are educational objectives stated in sufficiently specific terms for two inter-related goals to be achieved. These are the planning of educational experiences that can proceed directly from the statement, and the assessment of the individual in attaining the specified behaviour through some form of observation. This statement is the *anticipated* or *specified* outcome. Such statements are also statements of standards. If a significant behaviour is being observed it is likely that there will also be *unanticipated* outcomes some of which may be important. There is, therefore, a need for evaluation since both the *intended* and *unintended* outcomes may enhance or inhibit learning.

A curriculum, course, or lessons are designed for *intended* outcomes. It is not proposed here that a teacher should hold steadfastly to the plan indicated by the outcomes. Neither is it expected that objectives should always be declared. It is suggested that they are a powerful aid to planning, and that they have the advantage of showing how students should be tested. It is suggested that students respond well to teachers who plan their work and who demonstrate knowledge of their subject. Sometimes digressions enhance motivation and learning but achieve different outcomes that, nevertheless, may be considered important.

Advantages and disadvantages of using objectives

Stice reports the findings of a colleague[25] who had consulted faculty members about the value of objectives. She listed the disadvantages as follows,

- *Discourages creativity on the part of the teacher and learner.*
- *Takes the 'challenge out' of studying.*
- *Is not worth the amount of time and effort required.*
- *Leads to concentration on the specific details of a subject, 'while the big picture' is missed by students.*
- *Insults the students' intelligence.*
- *Seems mechanistic and dehumanizing.*

But this need not be the case. The success of programmes written by objectives will depend on the significance of the objectives chosen, and the way they are used for learning. To take the issue of the 'big picture', Stice wrote, *"When I wrote my first set of instructional objectives it was for a course I had taught eight or ten times by the lecture (transmission) method. It took considerably longer than I had expected, and I spent two days of concentrated effort going through the textbook to decide what topics were of paramount importance and what topics were 'nice to know' but not essential. When I finished, I was not very well satisfied with the results and laid them aside. About a week later I hauled them out again and worked on them some more. Finally obtaining a list of objectives I thought I could live with, I was a little surprised at the results. Several topics were omitted that I had always spent time on before, but which were not prerequisite information for the following course in the sequence[ ] the omission of 'nice to know' material and the irrelevant yarns yielded about three weeks of extra time, which I was able to use in covering material that was important and prerequisite for the following course, but which I had never had time to cover in the past."*[26]

The advantages of using objectives were found to be,

- *"• Forces an instructor to critically evaluate the relative importance of topics and the allocation of instructional time.*
- *Can contribute to more open and candid classroom atmosphere, and more positive and honest teacher and student relationships.*
- *Focuses the students' attention on learning tasks rather than on 'psyching out' the instructor.*
- *May promote rather than discourage creativity through the reduction of anxiety about tests and grades.*

- *Causes the teacher to appreciate and make good use of individual differences in teaching and learning styles. It specifies the product and allows intelligent choice of the process by which an individual teacher or learner progresses toward the goal"* [27]

Other problems with the *Taxonomy*.

Some investigators have found that the *Taxonomy* is not hierarchical. Mention has already been made of the Ormell's assertion that the demands of the knowledge category are often greater than those for the categories embracing higher order thinking.[28] Moreover the categories do not cover every subject as the authors recognised. An example of the need to provide additional categories is given by Geometrical and Engineering Drawing which required categories for technique and visualisation (exhibit 10.4) as well as knowledge, application and synthesis. Similarly in Engineering Science at the Advanced Level of the General Certificate of Education practical work also required a category for technique. Those who designed this frame work (shown in exhibit 10.5) did not believe that synthesis covered originality. However, inspection of the sub-categories shows them to come from the categories of the *Taxonomy*, which suggests that the sub-categories are not absolutes and by implication that **the** *Taxonomy* is not hierarchically ordered.

The multiple strategy approach to assessment and instruction had as its first principle the enhancement of learning. It accepted that teachers taught to the test; therefore, assessment and examining should aim to enhance learning through instruction. It accepted that there were categories that could be defined and that for the most part they would be like those in *The Taxonomy*. It also assumed that education was something more than tests in the cognitive domain and that attitudes could be influenced by appropriately designed coursework. It also held that coursework could be assessed but it did not believe that everything should be done by coursework. Rather coursework should be designed to assess skills that could not be tested easily or at all in written examinations. It also held that coursework should consist of projects and practical work and should not be a replica of essays set in examinations. In that case the same qualities would be tested. It held that specific sub-tests should be designed to test the qualities sought in particular subjects. Knowledge could be examined by objective tests but other qualities such as those of analysis and creativity (originality) should be assessed in specific sub-tests designed for that purpose. In this way it believed that instruction would be influenced for the better. It accepted that much more attention should be paid to the design of the tests and that question design was difficult, and it accepted that textbooks would have to be redesigned. These views were based on evaluations of several experimental examinations.[29]

The titles of categories can produce very emotional responses and it may be better to work within the framework of the "language" of the subject taught. Even then there can be fierce debates that need to be undertaken at the level of an "assumptional dialogue." Nevertheless in engineering and medicine where it might be thought that categories of "diagnosis" and "communication" might have been considered necessary some teachers in these subjects have been perfectly happy to use *The Taxonomy* as given.

It has also been argued that it is not possible to make the sharp distinction between the cognitive and the affective that the authors of the two taxonomies make. Paul Dressel who was vociferous in his criticism of *The Taxonomy* felt that it completely underestimated the role of values in human behaviour. An education which ignores the affective dimension at the expense of the cognitive fails.[30]

However, this is no reason for not stating objectives if by this we mean a full awareness of our own position and the goals we hope to achieve. When subject specialists seek to clarify their own position and methods they necessarily make statements from which definitions of the skills required for the pursuit of understanding in their particular subject can be derived. That values are inherent in the objectives for history shown in exhibit 10.6 should be self-evident, as they should be in the student teacher designed programme for religious studies shown in exhibit 10.7.[31]

(a)   *Technique.* The ways and means of using drawing instruments to achieve good draughtsmanship, well-proportioned sketches as well as constructional accuracy. (Example. Ability to construct an accurate funicular polygon).

(b)   *Visualization and interpretation.* The demonstration of basic form and function from verbal or graphical information; translation of written information into drawings and vice-versa; recognition of functional and dimensional requirements. (Examples. (a) Ability to construct a cam profile from a descriptive specification. (b) Ability to explain the functioning of a valve from its assembly drawing).

Exhibit 10.4. The technique and visualization categories to be tested in Geometrical and Engineering Drawing at the Advanced level of the General Certificate of Education, Joint Matriculation Board (complete statement will be found in Heywood, 1984[32])

If nothing else happened, the publication of the *Taxonomy* created a climate in which many teachers were forced to think about what it was they were trying to do, and some found great stimulation from trying to achieve their aims through its application to their courses. It is clear that while it is an important source of objectives, it is not the only one. For example, Eisner who was one of its critics distinguished between three kinds of objectives, behavioural, problem solving and expressive (see below). But first the objections to *The Taxonomy* from the critical thinking lobby.

Critical thinking and *The Taxonomy*

This section is complementary to the commentary in chapter 9. Cuban argued that the area of thinking skills, reasoning and problem solving was a conceptual swamp. Ten years later Lewis and Smith[33] reported that little progress had been made in clearing up this 'conceptual swamp.' Given that educators seldom agree categories, there is no reason to suppose they will in the future. Definitions will give rise to more study.

Therefore what is of importance is the effect that these different approaches have had on the curriculum and instruction and their implications for the future. More recently the term 'thinking' seems to be used as the equivalent of critical thinking.[34]

1.	Technique.	(a) the development of the facility for making accurate observations and the ability to make reasonable estimates of the errors incurred in making such observations. (b) familiarisation with and facility in the use of scientific apparatus and equipment.
2.	Originality.	The development of the ability to (c) formulate hypotheses from given sets of observations. (d) formulate experiments to test hypotheses. (e) devise and improve upon experimental procedures. (f) appreciate the relative importance of errors in differing situations.
3.	Analysis	The development of the ability to: (g) discriminate between possible alternatives. (h) formulate problems in a form appropriate for investigation. (i) recognise assumptions made and assess their importance.. (j) extrapolate.
4.	Synthesis	The development of the ability to: (k) produce a unique communication. (l) produce a plan or proposed set of abstract relations. (m) derive a set of abstract relations. (n) design and evaluate.

Exhibit 10. 5 The objectives of coursework in Engineering Science at the Advanced level of the General Certificate of Education).

There is probably one axiom over which there will be no disagreement and that is that all disciplines involve both higher and lower level thinking. Lewis and Smith took the view that higher order thinking is demonstrated by the fact that it adds to the store of knowledge.[35] Another way of looking at the problem is to recognise that we often scan information without understanding it in (what we call) "depth". Indeed, sometimes when we find study difficult we give up because we feel we don't have the mental capacity to go into it in "depth". We may put this down to any number of reasons, ranging from lack of interest to lack of ability. We observe, of both ourselves and others, that outside our spheres of competence few of us are very good at reasoning.

Even in our areas of competence we often appear to lose arguments because we have not thought things through. At the very least, we can see value in training in reasoning or logic. Thus, analysis of the components of reasoning that is higher order thinking, as a study within the curriculum would seem to make eminent sense. Ennis[36] one of the major contributors to this view about critical thinking while agreeing that *The Taxonomy of Educational Objectives* is a useful point of entry into the field criticised it because it was not strictly hierarchical, and because it was too vague. He gives the question- *"what do you assess when you test the ability to analyse?"* as an example. This criticism seems to be unfair, since the authors elaborated the broad categories with the aid of sub-categories. However, he argued that the analysis of a political situation and the analysis of a chemical substance do not have anything in common. But is that so? Aren't the authors arguing that the same mental processes are undergone when anything is subject to their definition of analysis? It seems to me that the examples the test questions they give are quite specific. A more significant criticism is that the categories do not fit our understanding of creative learning by which I mean the ability to do things that we have not learned. Thus, to say that we are developing problem solving, critical thinking (reasoning, if you like), and creative skills accords more with what we want to do.

---

1. The Aims and objectives of Intermediate Certificate History.

Knowledge and comprehension
Pupils should be able to recall, recognize and understand the principal events and issues of periods of history set out in the syllabus. They should have some understanding of the evolution of the world in which they live.

Skills.
Pupils should be able to practise, at a level suitable to their stage of development, the skills used in history; more particularly:
(1)   The ability to locate, understand and record historical information;
(2)   The ability to examine critically and discuss statements on historical matters encountered in their textbooks and everyday life.

Attitudes
Students should feel a responsibility:
(1)   To be objective in interpreting historical material.
(2)   To find rational explanations for historical events and developments.
(3)   To respect the right of others to be different and to hold different points of view.

2. Possible relationship between the cognitive and the affective in the above

To be objective in interpreting Historical material	=	The ability to examine critically.
To respect the right of others to be different and to hold different points of view.	=	The ability to evaluate the merits of Different interpretations of historical phenomena. or The ability to evaluate different points of view.

Exhibit 10.6. The Aims and Objectives of the Irish Intermediate Certificate syllabus in History together with an example of the relationship between the cognitive and affective domains.

Knowledge and comprehension
1. The students should have a clear knowledge of many aspects of Christianity: the life and teaching of Jesus, the history of the Bible and of Christianity, the different branches of Christianity.
2. The students should have a clear knowledge of the key concepts of other world religions.
3. The student should understand the key concepts of religion in general.

Skills
1. The student should be able to evaluate and comprehend any set of religious data according to the key concepts that have been learned.
2. The student should be able to apply knowledge about religions to other fields.
3. The student should be able to interpret and weigh any evangelisation directed at him or her.

Attitudes
1. The student should know and be able to articulate his/her own stance to religion.
2. The student should know and be able to articulate his/her own stance on moral issues.
3. The student should develop an attitude or informed respect and tolerance to other religious traditions.
4. The student should be curious about philosophical questions dealt with in religion

Exhibit 10.7 A Statement of aims and objectives by a graduate student teacher. [31]

Even so there is an obligation on us to say what we mean by these skills. All too often in teaching we say we are developing problem solving or critical thinking skills without defining what we mean, and face-validity inspection of students work associated with our teaching may well suggest that we have not moved far from information giving.

Numerous lists of critical thinking skills have been published. Gubbins[37] identified as many 60, but the danger of such lists is that they become a teacher's check-list. There are some broad categories that are helpful and Ennis provides one such list. It is

1. Judge the credibility of sources.
2. Identify conclusions, reasons and assumptions.
3. Judge the quality of an argument, including the acceptability of its reasons, assumptions and evidence.
4. Develop and defend a position on an issue.
5. Ask appropriate clarifying questions.
6. Plan experiments and judge experimental designs.
7. Define terms in a way appropriate for the context.
8. Be open-minded.
9. Try to be well informed.
10. Draw conclusions when warranted, but with caution.

They derived from the view that *"critical thinking is reasonable reflective thinking focussed on deciding what to do."* Ennis admitted that this was vague and Johnson wondered how the definition, which he thought equated with rational thinking, led to the list.[38] It involves action. A psychologist might respond but, surely, that is decision-making. Ennis did not consider this proposition but argued that his definition did not exclude creative thinking. At the same time, while problem solving is not explicitly admitted, the usual steps in problem solving as creative acts are incorporated. His list is his view of what a person needs to be able to do to think critically.

It seems to me that most of the items in Ennis's list will be found in one guise or another in *The Taxonomy* but in different categories. Its authors would assume 8 and 9 and would not consider it necessary to state them even though it is clear they are necessary condition of being able to think critically. Otherwise they are a list that might be acceptable to many people as skills of critical thinking, and in this sense, they would seem to be more helpful in the design of instruction than *The Taxonomy*. Cowan suggested that an eleventh item might be "to notice what is not there."[39] Ennis suggested that while the elaborations of which this list is an abridgement are more thorough, in its simplicity it can be useful. I think this is born out by the rubrics for the assessment of project work (see chapter 9).

A teacher may want to do one of two things with these lists. One is to compile his/her own list. For example, Underbakke, Borg and Petersen[40] were concerned to evaluate the research that could form a knowledge base for teaching higher order thinking. As a start, they began with a definition of higher order (as opposed to critical) thinking, based on Halpern's view that it manipulates information so as to produce certain outcomes. Thus "*higher order thinking, accordingly, consists of ways of handling content: to learn to think more effectively is to learn more effective ways of dealing with information*". Therefore they say in the classroom, provision has to be made for the following types of experience:

1. Hypothesizing and testing. Conceiving connections among variables of a problem, and formulating and verifying connections.
2. Assessing arguments: identifying and solving problems that require evaluation of arguments.
3. Solving interpersonal problems. Analysing issues and interpersonal problems and engaging in discussions leading to their satisfactory resolution.
4. Problematic thinking: resolving uncertainties when information is only partial.
5. Developing and maintaining flexibility and student awareness: Keeping options open, evolving novel approaches to problem solution, and becoming aware of procedures and thought processes involved in solving problems.

A second way in which these lists might be used is to construct profiles of critical thinking, creative thinking and problem solving suitable for the content and age of the group to be taught. For example, exhibit 10.8 shows three of nine profiles designed by Murphy within the context of Irish post-primary education. It will be evident that pedagogical principles are easily derived from these. Notice that he thought it necessary to include separate profiles for problem finding and transfer, since at that time research suggested they were skills insufficiently understood by teachers. There is no recent evidence to the contrary.

To offset the problem that critical thinking has remained in the domain of the philosophers and teachers in the humanities and social science, Lewis and Smith argued that higher order thinking may be preferred as it is an all embracing term. It relates to the *"thinking that occurs when a person takes new information and information stored in the memory and interrelates and or rearranges and extends this information to achieve a purpose or find possible answers in perplexing situations"*. One might say that that is learning!

While there may be confusion about the definition of critical thinking it is quite clear that philosophers and teachers have derived a list of skills (abilities) that contribute to the idea of critical thinking about which many of us could agree. Moreover they seem to have caused important pedagogical innovations (see chapter 13)

Expressive outcomes

Unlike the authors of the *Taxonomy* Eisner also made a distinction between behavioural objectives and problem solving.[41] The authors of the *Taxonomy* believed that problem solving was involved in each of the categories described. Eisner conceded that it was an objective but when he used it, he did so to distinguish between pre-formulated goals and what actually happened. He argued that while there was a case for pre-formulated goals there were many teaching activities for which we did not pre-formulate specific goals (painting a picture in art). We undertook them in anticipation that something would happen, even though we could not specify what (as for example in business games and case studies). We do not think much beyond the data, even though we could predict from the ample criteria at our disposal. What we do is to evaluate retrospectively what happened against these criteria. From this he deduced that teachers should be able to plan activities which do not have any specific objectives. This leads him to express the view of many educators who would say with him that *"expressive activities precede rather than follow expressive outcomes. The tack to be taken with respect to the generation of expressive outcomes is to create activities which are seminal; what one is seeking is to have the students engage in activities that are sufficiently rich to allow for a wide, productive range of valuable outcomes. If behavioural objectives constitute the algorithms of the curriculum, expressive activities and outcomes constitute their heuristics."*[42]

Problem finding ability is necessary when the pupil is expected to examine critically data presented to her/him i.e. an historical account or description **Negative** This pupil cannot see various contradictions in a text or narrative. He accepts what is written on the external authority of the author alone without looking for an intrinsic logic and consistency in the passage or account.	Positive This pupil reasonably demanding and critical of what is given by the teacher and of what is written in various textbooks. He is sensitive to what may be propagandistic approaches in history or literature and is quick to realise an instance in which there is illogicality or intrinsic contradiction in the material he has to study.
Problem solving is concerned with the pupil's ability and skill in using information. **Negative** The pupil does not fully realise the implications of the data which he collects. He is unable to interpret the unexpected result which he may often ignore, and his thinking tends to be rigid and unimaginative and impedes his recognition of associated problems. His general shortcomings- rigidity of thought and lack of capacity to be flexible or to diverge when thinking over a particular problem have an inhibitive effect this effectiveness.	Positive. The pupil realises the importance of unexpected findings and seeks to interpret them. He understands the nature of probability and uses this to assist his decision making. He takes all data into account before making a decsion. He thinks effectively-he has the capacity to range flexibly, or 'diverge', in the search for relevant factors in connection with the problem in hand, and he has also the capacity to focus, or 'converge' his thinking on whatever factors have been decided on as relevant.
Transfer of learning. Application of knowledge and problem solving developed in the classroom in one subject to other subjects or extra-curricular activities, such as the various school clubs or societies to which hay belong. **Negative.** The pupil is concerned with gaining knowledge and problems solving ability in the classrooms but does not seem to see this as relevant to his other activities outside class. Seems unable to hold a serious or reasonable conversation. There is little or no evidence that his classroom experience influences his behaviour.	Positive The pupil without obviously trying to impress, shows signs that the knowledge he gains in the classroom and the problems solving experience he gains there overflows into his extra-curricular activities. His conversation is reasonable and interesting. His general behaviour is consistent with his classroom disposition.
Originality and creativity. Every pupil has something special of herself or himself to bring to a subject which he/she is studying. A feature perhaps which is not always appreciated or understood and difficult to assess by means of any kind of general or objective test. **Negative.** This pupil will be slow or unwilling to come forward with any ideas that he/she has not seen in a book or been given by the teacher. He/she will stick slavishly to repeating what he/she feels will please the teacher. He/she shows little imagination and he/she reveals little of himself in work presented or in his response to class.	Positive. This pupil is bright and courageous in drawing and presenting his/her own reasonable conclusions about material concerning the subject being taught. Is imaginative in his/her presentation of work or in his/her general response in class. Is concerned with the truth as he understands it and is able to present and interesting perspective on this truth.

Exhibit 10.8. A profile developed for pupils in the age range 12 – 15 by D. Murphy. The concept was based on a profile for general practitioners in medicine.[43] Murphy suggested that it might be accompanied by a twelve point scale that went from Poor to Excellent through Marginal and Good.[44]

There seem to be two difficulties with this view. The first, you might argue, is a quibble. It is that even to establish a strategy that will allow things to emerge is to formulate a goal in the expressive domain in-which the cognitive and affective are merged. This will happen, for example, if cooperative learning is introduced for the purpose of developing both cognitive and social skills. The second objection is that all too often such statements can be used as an excuse for not planning teaching. A great deal of research has been done which shows that students rate many lectures, (transmission methods of teaching and learning), poorly.[45] Often this weakness is related to poor planning and a lack of understanding of student learning. To follow Eisner properly demands both an understanding of how students learn, and how to plan classroom activities.

Nevertheless, Eisner is right to remind us of the expressive dimension in education; for all teaching, and therefore, all attempts to achieve objectives are informed by our affective dispositions. (See below).

Mager whose work on preparing instructional objectives has been cited by many educators wrote that- *"an objective is an intent communicated by a statement describing a proposed change in the learner-a statement of what the learner is to be like when he has successfully completed a learning experience."*[46] Thus an instructional objective must describe (i) what the learner will be doing when demonstrating that he has reached the objective, (ii) the conditions under which the learner will demonstrate his or her competence, and (iii) show how an acceptable performance will be assessed. As Stice says it causes an instructor to ask, *"Where am I going? How shall I get there? How will I know I have arrived?".*[47] It is possible to describe course objectives without reference to the *Taxonomy*. However, it is not possible to escape from the need to declare objectives, if teaching is to be made more effective.[48]

Unmerited spin-off

One of the major purposes of the previous section has been to show that the choice and selection of objectives for a curriculum is not a simple task. Unfortunately, the idea of objectives that are declarations of what a person is able to do, as a result of participating in the educational process can be trivialised by the development of ultra long lists of outcomes. This is what happened with Standards in the United States (see chapter 12). Moreover, the effective attainment of such lists is often associated with the transmission model of learning. These take away a large element of teacher professionalism. Teachers teach to get the student through the listed outcomes. Yet it should be evident from all that has been said in these chapters that some objectives particularly in the realm of higher order thinking skills will not be achieved by such a model. Some activity-based learning is likely to be essential. Thus it is essential to emphasise key outcomes and to design instruction so that they are met.

One problem is that policy makers are likely to be able to persuade the public and more especially what they advocate is right. There is therefore a need for curriculum leaders and the teaching profession to involve the community in a continuing dialogue about *"education so that government policies are the result of meaningful consideration and not simply a reaction to a previous approach."*[49] This implies that teachers are cognisant of research and evaluation and do not simply oppose for the sake of opposing.

The Affective domain

Inspection of the *Taxonomy of Educational Objectives in the Affective Domain* which was edited by David Krathwohl, and published in 1964 (exhibit 10.9), is not very explicit about what the affective domain is.[50] In this context it is taken to mean not only the value disposition we hold but, the behaviours we adopt and especially those enacted in relation to other people. It is a domain that is about *feeling(emotions), attitudes, beliefs, values, ethics and moral, and these can be shared*. Combinations of these factors affect the way we approach change, whether we embrace it or resist it irrespective of its merit or otherwise. Kaplan showed how the affective domain of *The Taxonomy* applied to classrooms (exhibit 10.10).[51]

For many years educators took very little notice of this domain and concentrated on the cognitive domain; however, it is not possible to separate the two in this way. The two domains depend on each other. Try to assess teaching practice without taking into account both domains or for that matter your pupils! The same applies in Law, Medicine and Engineering. A good example of the mixing of the two domains is to be found in the aims and objectives stated in 1976 for the Irish Intermediate Certificate examination in History shown in exhibit 10.6. These objectives are for an examination that was set at the end of a three-year cycle for pupils of between 15 and 16 years of age. It has the merit of simplicity but it requires a multiple strategy approach to assessment and instruction. A similar statement for a curriculum in religious studies was shown in exhibit 10.7.

But these do not take into account the emotional commitment that students have to give to the subjects they have to learn. Whether we like it or not, irrational though it may seem students do have fears. Fear of mathematics or certain topics in mathematics is common although some students can be afraid and yet do well.

Frustration can impede or enhance student performance in problem solving. Golden wrote of mathematics that *"the student's "cognitive" belief in her high likelihood of success, her confidence that mathematics yields insightful processes, along with the high personal value she places on meeting challenges may contribute to her feeling quite positive about the frustration [...]"* [53]

1. *Awareness.* e.g. Listens to advice....recognises own bias......aware of feelings of others.

2. *Willingness to receive.* e.g. seeks agreement from another...asks another to examine aesthetic value in the classroom...inquires how another feels about event or subject.

3. *Responding.* e.g., complies with existing regulations....responds to a question....takes responsibility when offered.

4. *Preference for a value.*
   e.g. seeks the value of another....defends own value....agrees with the value of another.

5. *Conceptualization of a value.* e.g. makes judgements (implies evaluation)....compares own value to that of another...

6. *Organization of a value system.* e.g. shows relationship of one value to another....synthesises two or more values into one value....

7. *Characterization by a value or value complex. Generalized set.* e.g. revises judgement based on evidence....makes judgements in light of situational context.

8. *Characterization.* e.g. develops consistent mode of behaviour. Continually re-evaluates own mode of behaviour..

Exhibit 10. 9. Summary of the Principal Categories of the Affective Domain of the *Taxonomy of Educational Objectives* in the Affective Domain (Krathwohl et al, 1964). [52]

Neither do taxonomies or curriculum rubrics take into account the beliefs of teachers or students about subjects in general and specific topics in particular. For example "*Lloyd described how materials designed to encourage student cooperation and exploration were used by two high school teachers. One of the teachers viewed the curriculum's problems as open-ended and challenging for students; the other teacher claimed the same problems were overly structured. The two teachers' classroom decisions reflected these contrasting perspectives. As Lloyd stated, "curriculum implementation consists of a dynamic relation between teachers and particular curricular features. This notion is consistent with warnings that reform recommendations and associated curriculum materials cannot and do not bring about recommendations and associated curriculum materials cannot and do not bring about change alone- educational change is a complex human endeavour.*"[54] Differences among teachers about the materials and content of teaching affect teaching in all subjects and condition curriculum debates hence the importance of "assumptiona-dialogues " among subject teachers either within the school or in networks. Curriculum leaders can act as facilitators and commentators and 'encouragers' in such dialogues.

Related to affective learning is the concept of experiential learning, and Steinaker and Bell[55] produced a taxonomy of experiential learning. This had categories for *exposure* (seeing, hearing, reacting, recognizing), *participation*, *identification* (classifying, explaining, experimenting, writing, drawing), *internalization* (generalising, comparing, contrasting, and transferring), and *dissemination*. Cooperative learning is a learning method that is designed to achieve several important skills in the affective domain. An attempt to relate teaching methods to the three domains (cognitive, affective, psychomotor) was made by Weston and Cranton.[57] It is shown in exhibit 10.11.

1.	Awareness	
1.	Listens to others.	6. Acknowledges some aesthetic factor in the classroom (clothing, furniture, design, arrangement, art)
2.	Receives others as co-workers	
3	Listens to advice	7. Aware of feelings of others (introvert, extravert, anxiety, hostility, sensitivity)
4.	Verbally pays attention to alternative Points of view on a given issue.	
5.	Refers to subgroup(s) (social, intellectual sex, race etc).	8. Recognizes own bias as bias. 9. Recognizes other bias as bias.
1.20.	Willingness to Receive.	
10.	Seeks agreement from another.	14. Seeks materials.
11.	Seeks responsibility.	15. Asks another to examine aesthetic factor in classroom.
12.	Seeks information from another.	16. Inquiries how another feels about An event or subject.
13.	Pursues another way of doing something.	
2.0.	Responding.	
2.10	Acquiescence in Responding	
17.	Complies with existing regulations(rules).	21. Responds to a question.
18.	Complies to a suggestion or directive.	22. Takes responsibility when offered.
19.	Offers materials on request.	23. Remains passive when a response is indicated.
20.	Gives opinion when requested.	24. Actively rejects direction(s) or suggestion(s).
3.0	Valuing	
3.10	Preference for a value	
25.	Seeks the value of another.	29. Openly defends the right of another to possess value.
26.	Defends value of another.	30. Tries to convince another to accept a value.
27.	Clearly expresses a value.	31. Agrees with value of another.
28.	Defends own value.	32. Disagrees with the value of another.
4.0.	Organization	
4.10.	Conceptualization of value	
33.	Makes deductions from abstractions.	35. Compares own value to that of another.
34.	Makes judgements (implies evaluation).	36. Attempts to identify the characteristics of a value or value system.
4.20.	Organizatiuon of value system	
37.	Compares and weighs alternatives.	39. Ties a specific value into a system of values
38.	Shows relationship of one value to another.	40. Synthesizes two or more values into one value.
5.00	Characterization by a value of value complex	
5.10	Generalized set	
41.	Reviews judgements based on evidence.	43. Makes judgements in light of situational context.
42.	Bases judgements on consideration of more Than one proposal.	
5.20	Characterization	

Exhibit 10.10. Kaplan's (1978) expansion of the taxonomy of affective behaviour for the classroom.

Other approaches to the classification and derivation of objectives

Without wishing to draw causal or linear historical relationships, it is useful to note that some members of the critical thinking movement began to develop their own taxonomies. There is little doubt that they were strongly influenced by *The Taxonomy*. However, in addition to adding items, they apparently also disagreed with its classes. A distinction came to be made between knowledge and comprehension and Higher Order Thinking Skills (HOTS). Imrie's RECAP model[57] followed this pattern. He divided his taxonomy into two tiers. At the first level, objectives state the minimum essentials which students should achieve. This level of objective may be tested by short answer and/or multiple-choice questions. Students can be tested for mastery. A second level comprises analysis, synthesis, and evaluation. These objectives focus on skills of problem-solving. They can be tested by essays, case study questions, and use

Domain and level.	Method.
Cognitive domain	
Knowledge	Lecture, CAI, drill and practice.
Comprehension	Lecture, modularized instruction, CAI.
Application.	Discussion, simulations and games CAI, modularized instruction, field experience, laboratory.
Analysis	Discussion, independent/group projects, simulations Field experience, role-playing, laboratory.
Synthesis	Independent/group projects, field experience, role-playing, laboratory.
Evaluation	Independent/group projects, field experience, laboratory.
Affective domain	
Receiving.	Lecture, discussion, modularized instruction, field experience
Responding	Discussion, simulations, modularized instruction, role-playing, field experience.
Value	Discussion, independent/group projects, simulations, Role-playing, field experience.
Organization	Discussion, independent/group projects, field experience.
Characteriuzation by value	Independent projects, field experience
Psychomotor domain	
Perception	Demonstration (lecture), drill and practice.
Set	Demonstration (lecture), drill and practice.
Guided response	Peer teaching, games, role playing, field experience, Drill and practice.
Mechanism.	Games, role-playing, field experience, drill and practice.
Complex overt response.	Games, field experience.
Adaptation	Independent projects, games, field experience.
Organization	Independent projects, games, field experience.

Exhibit 10.11. Matching objective, domain and level of learning to appropriate methods of instruction(from Weston and Cranton). CAI has been substituted for programmed learning which appeared in the original.

of norm referenced assessments. One problem with the use of the term problem solving skill is that some cognitive development theorists hold that problem-solving skills are Piagetian skills and not the highest level that can be obtained (i.e. reflective judgement). Crooks cited by Imrie[58] also uses the term critical thinking to encompass these skills.

The SOLO Taxonomy due to Biggs and Collis[59] attempts to link the forms of knowledge with development. There are five modes of learning that have many similarities with the Piagetian development stages. These are sensori-motor, ikonic, concrete-symbolic, formal and post-formal. The forms of knowledge related to these are tacit, intuitive, declarative, theoretical and meta-theoretical. There are five structural levels (hierarchically ordered) in a learning cycle that is repeated in each form. Both Gibbs[60] and Ramsden[61] have described these levels in terms of the type of answers a person might give to a question. Following Gibbs description the levels are:

1. Pre-structural. A stage of ignorance where the learner has no knowledge of the question.
2. Unistructural. Where the learner is able to give an answer that contains one correct feature.
3. Multistructural. Where the answer contains a check list of items.
4. Relational. The answer integrates the items into an integrated whole.
5. Extended abstract. The answer is related to the more general body of knowledge.

The SOLO taxonomy is also of interest because there is a conceptual over lap with the deep and surface learning strategies discussed in chapter 8. Level 3 may correspond to surface learning, and levels 4 and 5 to deep learning.

To return to the problem of categories, Collier[62] suggested the list of categories for theology shown in exhibit 10.12. These categories could apply to almost any subject. His short text explains how they relate to teaching methods, learning and assessment, and is as good an introduction to teaching and learning as any irrespective of the fact that it was written for higher education.

Although the studies described in this section originated in higher education they are clearly relevant to the senior cycle of education as are those taxonomies that derive from the analysis of jobs that people have to do. And such analyses are not only relevant to the so-called practical curriculum but to the academic as well.[64]

Objectives of higher education.
1. Basic knowledge.
2. Comprehension of subject discipline.
3. Self directed learning.
4. Communication skills.
5. Application to new situations.
6. Invention.
7. Assessing Quality.

Exhibit 10.12. Collier's principal objectives for higher education

Developing aims and objectives: implications for the curriculum leader

It should be clear that determining mission statements, aims and objectives is not any easy task. For mission statements to be meaningful the members of the institution have to have a commitment to the institution and be clear as to how the statement will influence their performance. The curriculum as a whole has to be seen to be contributing to that goal. There has to be a clear link with aims just as there has to be a clear link with the aims and objectives of the individual knowledge (subject) areas. In the classroom what matters is that teachers should be able to clearly state, in whatever language they care to use, where they are going and what they intend students should be able to do as a result of their arrangements for instruction/learning. Moreover they should be prepared to regularly assess they are achieving these goals.

In spite of the fact that using aims and objectives should help teachers determine what is absolutely essential in their subjects there is a tendency for those responsible for the design of the curriculum to require content and skill coverage that is too large. This is particularly true of policy makers who are solely concerned with the outcomes of the educational process and require hundreds of outcomes or standards to be declared. It cannot be emphasised too much that this is likely to lead to surface learning. For this reason it is necessary to focus on a few significant aims and outcomes. Emphasising domains and giving the teachers freedom to design their own instruction for those domains is more likely to have the better pay off. It allows for the unintended as well as the intended to happen and it allows for reconciliation between activity based and transmission based learning.

To obtain these domains it is necessary to screen these lists using philosophy, sociology and the psychology of learning. Hence the need for curriculum leaders to have defensible theories in the philosophy, psychology and sociology of education. As a result of screening new aims and objectives, alternative approaches to the declaration of aims and objectives may emerge. In the activity of determining aims it will become clear whether or not a different curriculum model of the type to be described in the next chapter is required.

Teachers also assume that if objectives are made known to students that students will necessarily have the same perceptions of what is asked of them as the teachers. My colleagues and I found that this was not true of some of the assessment objectives in engineering science and we had to change them. We found this out by asking a sample of students to write down what they thought they had to do too meet each objective. One cannot be sanguine about the effect of rubrics on student perceptions. Curriculum leaders should be in a position to establish what the perceptions of the students are independently of their subject teachers.

Not only in respect of mission statements but in individual subject areas we are likely to have views that differ from those in our group. It may take some time to obtain agreement about the principle categories (domains) that should cover the subject to be taught. At all these levels resolution of differing perceptions is likely to best achieved through "assumptional dialogues" facilitated by a curriculum leader who is able to service the dialogue with wide ranging information about research, development and practice. It is also clear that if the public and parents are not to be led by the over simplifications of policy makers that curriculum leaders and the teaching profession have to engage the community in rational and not emotional dialogue. But this will require a better educated teaching profession. The development of curriculum leadership will be a step in that direction.

Notes and references

[1] Bloom, B et al (eds). *Taxonomy of Educational Objectives. The Classification of Educational Goals. Volume 1 The Cognitive Domain*. David Mackay/Longman, New York.
[2] Anderson, L. W. and L. A. Sosniak (1994). *Bloom's Taxonomy. A Forty Year Retrospective*. 93rd Yearbook of the National Society for the Study of Education. Chicago University Press, Chicago.
[3] Eisner, E. (1979). *The Educational Imagination. On the Design and Evaluation of School Programs*. MacMillan, New York.
[4] See Heywood, J. (2000). *Assessment in Higher Education. Student learning, Teaching, Programmes and Institutions*. Jessica Kingsley, London.
[5] *ibid*
[6] Yokomoto, C.F. and W. D. Bostwick (1999). Modelling the process of writing measurable outcomes for Ec 2000. *Proceedings Frontiers in Education Conference*, 2, 11b1- pp 18 to 22. IEEE, New York.
[7] See Heywood, J. (1977). *Assessment in Higher Education*. 1st Edition. Wiley, Chichester.
[8] Cardinal Newman's *Idea of University* is very relevant to this debate. Students who attended the Catholic University in Dublin did so from the age of sixteen. For another example see A. N. Whiteheads's *The Aims of Education*. Benn, London.
[9] Bobbitt, F. J. (1924). *How to Make a Curriculum*. Houghton Mifflin, Boston. Jackson, P. W. (1992). *Handbook of Research on Curriculum*. AERA. Macmillan, New York.
[10] Tyler, R. W. (1949). *The Principles of Curriculum and Instruction*. University of Chicago Press, Chicago
[11] Bloom, B. (1994). Reflections on the development and use of The Taxonomy in L. W. Anderson and L. A. Sosniak (eds). *Bloom's Taxonomy : A Forty Year Retrospective*. 73rd Yearbook of the National Society for the Study of Education. Chicago University Press, Chicago..
[12] *ibid*
[13] For example, in Ireland, a Government Committee on the Form and Function of the Intermediate Certificate Examination wanted its research unit to devise "*examinations which will demand higher-level skills than are at present exercised in the Intermediate Certificate Examination*" By this it meant the higher order skills of *The Taxonomy*. (The Intermediate Examination was replaced by the Junior Certificate Examination in 1990). The Committee clearly had in mind the Bloom Taxonomy. It believed that the questions in the examination primarily tested knowledge. *The ICE Report. Report of the Committee on the Form and Function of the Intermediate Certificate Examination*. (1974). Government Publications, Dublin.
[14] *loc.cit*
[15] Harrow, A. J. (1972). A Taxonomy of the psychomotor domain. In *A Guide for Developing Behavioural Objectives*. MacKay. New York.
[16] Steinaker, N and M. R. Bell (1969). *An Experiential Taxonomy*. Academic Press, New York.
[17] *loc. cit.*
[18] Furst, E. J (1994). Bloom's Taxonomy. philosophical and educational Issues in L. W. Anderson and L. A. Sosniak (eds*)*. *Bloom's Taxonomy. A Forty Year Retrospective*. 73rd Yearbook of the National Society for the Study of Education. Chicago University Press, Chicago.

[19] For a detailed review of these criticisms see Anderson, L.W. and L.A. Sosniak (1994) (eds). *Bloom's Taxonomy. A Forty-year Retrospective*. And in particular the chapter by E.J. Furst. 93rd Yearbook of the National Society for the Study of Education. University of Chicago Press, Chicago. A summary of this contained in Heywood (2000)
[20] Cohen L and L. Mannion (1977) *A Guide To Teaching Practice*. 1st and subsequent editions. Methuen, London.
[21] *loc.cit..* Ref 3.
[22] Ormell, C. P. (1974). Bloom's Taxonomy and the objectives of education. *Educational Research*, 17, (1), 3-15.
[22] *loc.cit..* note 1.
[23] Otter, S (1991). *What can Graduates Do? A Consultative Document*. Unit for the Development of Continuing Adult Education (HMSO). Employment Department Sheffield.
[24] *loc..cit*
[25] Susan Hereford quoted in Stice, J. E (1976). A first step toward improved teaching. *Engineering Education*. 66, (5), 394-398.
[26] *ibid*
[27] *ibid*
[28] *loc.cit.*
[29] Engineering Science at A level in the UK and History and mathematics for the Intermediate Certicfiate in Ireland. The approach is developed in Heywood, J (1978) *Examining in Second Level Education*. Association of Secondary Teachers Ireland and, Heywood, J (2000). *Assessment in Higher Education. Student learning, Teaching, Programmes and Institutions*. Jessica Kingsley, London.
[30] Dressel, P.L. (1971). Values, cognitive and affective. *Journal of Higher Education*, 42, (5), 400.
[31] Nancy Bates whose complete curriculum appears in Heywood, J (1984).*Considering the Curriculum During Student Teaching*. Kogan Page, London.
[32] *ibid* Heywood.
[33] Lewis, A and D. Smith (1993). Defining higher order thinking. *Theory into Practice* 32, (2), 131 – 137.
[34] Glatthorn, A. A., Boschee, F., and B. M. Whitehead (2006) *Curriculum Leadership. Development and Implementation*. Sage, Thousand Oaks, CA see pages 361 – 363.
[35] *loc. cit.*
[36] Ennis, R. H (1981). Eight fallacies in Bloom's taxonomy in C. J. B. Macmillan (ed*) Philosophy of Education pp* 269 – 273. Philosophy of Education Society, Bloomington, Il. And (b) (1993) Critical thinking assessment. *Theory into Practice* 32, (3), 179 – 186.
[37] Cited by Sternberg, R. H. in an article in *Educational Leadership*.
[38] Johnson, R. H (1992). The problem of defining critical thinking in S. Norris (ed). *The Generalizability of Critical Thinking*. Teachers College Press, New York.
[39] Private communication
[40] Underbakke, M. Borg, J. M., and D. Petersen (1993) Researching and developing the knowledge base for teaching higher order thinking. *Theory into Practice*, 32, (3), 138 –146.
[41] Eisner, E.W (1979). *The Educational Imagination. On the Design and Evaluation of School Programs*. New York, Macmillan.
[42] *loc.cit.*
[43] Freeman, J and P. S. Byrne (1976). *Assessment of Post-Graduate Training in General Practice*. Society for research into Higher Education, London
[44] Murphy, D. D. E. (1974) in Heywood, J (ed). *Assessment in History. Twelve to Fifteen*. School of Education, University of Dublin, Dublin
[45] Bligh, D (1999). *What's the use of Lectures?* Harmonsdworth, Penguin.
[46] Mager, R. F (1962). *Preparing Instructional Objectives*. Fearon Publishers
[47] *loc.cit.*
[48] See Stice, J. E, and Svinicki, M.D. (1976). The test: uses, construction and evaluation. *Engineering Education*, 66, (5), 408-411.
[49] This quotation is from Clarke, B, Clarke D and P. Sullivan (2003) the mathematics teacher and curriculum development in A. J. Bishop et al (eds*)*. *International Handbook of Mathematics Education*. Part 2. Kluwer, Dordrecht. One of the examples they give to support this contention relates to curriculum in Australia. For a long period of time Australian teachers were encouraged

to be responsible for their own curricula. Then in response to the ideas of total quality management politicians demanded that curricula should measure outcomes or competencies. They cite the experience of the State of Victoria. The difficulty with their summary is that no evaluative evidence is provided to support one side or the other.

[50] Krathwohl, D. R., Bloom, B and B. Masia (1964). *The Taxonomy of Educational Objectives. Volume 2. The Affective Domain.* New York, Longman.

[51] Kaplan, L (1978). *Developing Objectives in the Affective Domain.* College Publishing, San Diego, CA.,

[52] *loc.cit*

[53] Golden, G. A (2002) Affect, Meta-Affect, and mathematical belief structures in Leder, G. C. et al (eds) Beliefs: A hidden Variable in Mathematics Education? Kluwer Dordrecht p 63. As a basic study several authors in the field of mathematics education refer to McLeod, D. B. (1992) Research on affect in mathematics education; a reconceptualization in D. Grouws (ed). Handbook of Research on Mathematics Teaching and Learning. Macmillan, New York.

[54] cited by Wilson, M and T. Cooney (2002) Mathematics teacher change and development in Leder, G. C (eds). Beliefs: A Hideen Variable in Mathematics Education? Kluwer, Dordrecht. G. M. Lloyd who is the research worker cited also has an article in this book.

[55] Steinaker, N. and M. R. Bell (1969). *An Experiential Taxonomy.* Academic Press, New York,

[56] Weston, C. A and P. A. Cranton (1986). Selecting instructional strategies. *Journal of Higher Education*, 57, (3), 259-288.

[57] Imrie, B. W. (1995). Assessment for learning: quality and taxonomies. *Assessment and Evaluation in Higher Education*, 20, (2), 175-189.

[58] *ibid*. Crooks, T. J. (1988). Assessing Student Performance. Green Guide 8. Higher Education Research and Development Society of Australia, Sydney.

[59] Biggs, J. B. and K. F. Collis (1982). *Evaluating the Quality of Learning. The SOLO Taxonomy.* Academic Press, New York.

[60] Gibbs, G (1992). Improving the quality of student learning through course design in R. Barnett (ed) *Learning to Effect.* Buckingham, Society for Research into Higher Education/ Open University Press.

[61] Ramsden, P (1992). *Learning and Teaching in Higher Education.* Routledge, London.

[62] Collier, G (1994). *A New Teaching. A New Learning.* SPCK, London.

11
Concepts of the Curriculum: The Curriculum Leaders Knowledge Base

Abstract

The study now turns from instruction to the curriculum. The purpose of this chapter is to consider in more detail the scope of knowledge required by curriculum leaders from a review of the curriculum process. Given the definition of the curriculum as the "formal mechanism through which educational aims are intended to be achieved", it follows, that a curriculum leader is one who is able to integrate the components of the curriculum in such a way as to bring about the learning necessary to achieve the declared goals. As such a curriculum leader will necessarily have to have an epistemological position as well as a defensible theory of learning. But additionally in the determination of aims a curriculum leader will have a value position, and an understanding of the culture in which these aims are determined. It is argued that it is an ethical requirement that teachers have an explicit involvement with the underlying assumptions of the education, teaching and learning they implement for children. This has profound implications for the education, training, and professional development of teachers. These points are illustrated by reference to several paradigms of the curriculum. It is noted that the traditional or received curriculum persists but within that curriculum there is a continuous flow of small changes. Occasionally major reforms are introduced. The sociology of knowledge has led to the development of other models of the curriculum. It is likely that an effective curriculum will make use of more than one model.

The need to screen the aims of education to eliminate contradictions and to focus on what is essential is discussed and the kind of questions that need to be asked illustrated. The importance of "assumptional-dialogues" in screening should be self-evident.

In some controlled curricula some freedom is given to the teacher for curriculum making. That is, teachers exercise subsidiarity. This encourages the professionalism of teachers. This point is illustrated by reference to the Irish Transition Year Programme. Substantial training is required for teachers to embark on curriculum making of this kind.

The view taken here is that a curriculum leader is concerned with the potential that curriculum practice might be improved and, therefore, with the idea that the curriculum is open to change. Therefore, the knowledge required by a curriculum leader comprises a detailed understanding of the curriculum process and the factors involved in the design or improvement of the curriculum as well as of the change process itself. The chapter concludes with a discussion of the curriculum process.

The formal, informal and hidden curricula

The formal curriculum is the mechanism by which educational goals are delivered. It is normally associated with the subjects or subject areas that are prescribed for students to learn. In either case it is written and designed to ensure that the goals of the system or subject are being achieved.[1] Associated with this curriculum is an informal or extra curriculum that provides such things as sports, clubs- ranging from debating to canoeing and the like, and religious activities for which the institution takes responsibility. They are "extra" because they provide an additional learning experience[2] and may make a significant contribution to the learner as well as to the institution's mission. The achievement of these goals is in no small way a function of what has been called the hidden curriculum. That curriculum embraces all the learning that takes place outside of the formal learning in the class- room, in the institution, and more generally in society at large. It is a function of the micro-culture of the school and the cultural norms of society.[3] Too a large extent it governs the attitudes and values that shape our response to formal learning. It is therefore of considerable importance.[4] At this stage it is only necessary to remind the reader of the powerful influences of the family, peer group, television and the World Wide Web on learning as well as their potential to influence values.

It is important to appreciate that the focus of this chapter is on what Cuban calls the "intended curriculum" and not the curriculum that teacher's teach, or the one that students learn.[5] Glatthorn and his colleagues have pointed out that the intended curriculum is influenced by the *supported curriculum*. That is, the resources made available for its implementation. It is also influenced by the *taught curriculum*, that is, what the teachers teach (*operational curriculum*); the tested curriculum, that is, what examinations and assessments actually test; and the learned curriculum, that is what the students learn (*experiental curriculum*).[6] The curriculum leader's task is the reconciliation of these different curricular in the achievement of the goals of the formal or written curriculum. The terms in brackets are due to Goodlad who also described a *perceived curriculum*, which is what teachers, parents and others think the curriculum to be.[7]

In countries (States) where there is time for the school to develop its own curriculum such as the Transition Year programme in Ireland the curriculum leader would have responsibility for its development. But he/she would be dependent on other teachers to participate in curriculum making and so enhance their professionalism. This would be an *ideological curriculum* (as defined by Goodlad[8]) constructed by the teachers in the school.

The need for a philosophy of education

The organization of the curricula will be a function of its goals. Therefore, the determination of goals is the first task of curriculum design irrespective of the curriculum paradigm that is used. This is because beliefs about the purposes of education, and because it is generally accepted that education is about learning, and beliefs about how it is that individuals learn, are fundamental to the determination of those goals. Statements about what should be, and how it should be learnt are consequences of these beliefs. Often, depending on the perspectives of their advocates the aims proposed by them will be in contradiction of each other. Therefore, the curriculum designer will require a defensible philosophy that, on the one hand has an epistemological base, and on the other hand a value position.

It is regrettable that in the UK and certain of the American States that philosophy has more or less disappeared from the teacher training curriculum.[9] It has, however, remained a requirement for the recognition of courses for post-primary teaching in Ireland.[10] This is not to say that John Dewey goes by unnoticed in the US. Far from it! Recently the curriculum especially in the sciences has been greatly influenced by an uncritical acceptance of constructivism.[11]

In the 1970's and 1980's much attention was paid to the critical thinking movement in which the philosopher Robert Ennis played a leading role. The vestiges of this movement remain in what has been called teaching for thinking (see chapters 9 and 10).[12] In the same period in the United States (Phenix)[13] and the UK (Hirst)[14] there was much discussion about the nature of meaning, the nature of knowledge and what might be called theories of the disciplines. The significance of such debates cannot be underestimated.

It is important to distinguish between epistemology and pedagogy. Epistemology considers the grounds, varieties and validity of knowledge whereas pedagogy is the art and science of teaching.[15] Although epistemology and pedagogy are intimately related, they are clearly different dimensions of learning and understanding. Epistemology is the view of the nature of the subject we teach.[16] It is concerned with truth, meaning and certainty. That it is important can be illustrated by mathematics where it might be thought that answers to such issues are agreed. Not so! Sierpinska and Lerman analysed the implications of nine epistemologies for mathematics education. Among their findings were that "*constructivist, socio-cultural, interactionist, and anthropological approaches (to mathematics education) are founded on different epistemologies of knowledge.*"[17] It is at that level of discussion that the curriculum leader has to have a defensible theory. But Sierpinska and Lerman also argue "*that an explicit engagement with the underlying assumptions of education, mathematics*" (or whatever subject), *"teaching, learning and the child is an ethical requirement of the researcher, the teacher and others involved in education."* The implications for the education, training, and the professional development of teachers are profound.[18]

There is no better display of the value of philosophy in screening the aims of an institutions curriculum than in *Understanding Educational Aims* by Colin Wringe.[19] If the broadly stated, and commonly quoted aim of education is that it " *is about developing the whole person"*, exploration of what this means in practice will necessarily involve those parts of psychology that concern themselves with human development and the way individuals learn. Therefore, curriculum leaders and teachers should possess defensible theories of learning and human development.[20]

The influence of culture on the aims of education

Because formal education is a social artefact, and governments, in theory, democratically organise it on behalf of society, government's may also determine the goals of the curriculum. Very often the interpretation of the curriculum by governments can be at odds with what philosophers and teachers consider the aims of education to be. Thus, in the British and Irish systems there is often conflict between educators who see the purpose of education as the development of the whole person, and legislators who believe that the goal of education is socio-economic who, therefore, try to steer the curriculum in the direction of preparing students for work. Whether or not there need be any conflict between the two will be discussed in the next chapter.

In the United States one hears less about this debate. There is more concern with socialization into democracy, even if it is not carried out in the way John Dewey recommended[21] than with direct preparation for work. In the nineteen nineties this position changed slightly with the publication of the SCANS report.[22] The SCANS report seemed to go someway toward resolving these conflicting positions (see next chapter).

More generally, following McClelland's theory of achievement motivation and his view that some societies have high levels of achievement and others low[23] it has been argued that societies such as England where achievement motivation has been low will not produce large numbers of persons with an entrepreneurial outlook. Therefore, school curricula that focus on enterprise and entrepreneurship have an 'attitudinal disposition' to over come.[24]

Images of the curriculum

Among educators there are many views as to what the curriculum should be. Schubert suggested eight images or major conceptions of the curriculum in 1986.[25] I have added two because of developments since then. They are shown in brackets. As you will see later one follows from the Transition Year idea or the Leaving

Certificate Applied in Ireland or the SCANS curriculum in the United States, and in part the other arises from the demand for accountability. These images are:
Curriculum as content or subject matter.
Curriculum as a programme of planned activities.
Curriculum as intended learning outcomes.
(Curriculum as Standards)
Curriculum as cultural reproduction.
Curriculum as experience.
Curriculum as discrete tasks and concepts.
Curriculum as agenda for social reconstruction.
(Curriculum as preparation for work).
Curriculum as "currere".

"Currere" refers to the running of a race. It relates to the meaning that people (students) seek of themselves as they go through life, and is a social process because it necessarily involves understanding others. It comes from a group of sociologists working with critical praxis as a mode of curriculum enquiry. They are called "reconceptualists."[26] Schubert gives this example of it in practice. *"Students write autobiographical accounts that focus on striving to know who, how, and why they have developed as they have. Teachers and or/other students respond through written and oral comment on the writing. Dialogue ensues and creates reconceived visions of self, others and the world, through mutual reconceptualization."*[27] This leads students to free themselves from the constraints of convention that bind them and seek new directions. It seems to be a form of blogging! Schubert calls the paradigm within which the reconceptualists work "Critical Praxis". Perhaps the best known exponent of this thinking is Freire whose work has been studied world wide.[28]

I have continued the discussion of the critical praxis paradigm in a later section. I make these points at this stage to draw attention to the fact that curricula are the product of the culture and the ideas and values of the culture in which they are embedded. It is for this reason that it is difficult to transplant the educational practices of one country to another, and this applies as much to the countries of the European Union as it does to any other grouping of countries. For example, the German "dual" system of education and training admired by some experts in Britain and Ireland could not be transported to those systems even if it were deemed desirable because of the attitudes of industry toward training. These attitudes were embedded in the culture during the industrial revolution and have proved exceptionally difficult to change. If it were, then much more notice would have been taken of the works of Correlli Barnett.[29]

Within cultures values are ascribed to subjects and examinations. Thus, in Britain and Ireland there is a contradiction between the desires of parents for children to receive what they deem to be the whole person approach to education, and the pressure they put on their children to pass examinations in order to go to university and get good jobs. These parents know that there is an established correlation between level of earnings and qualification and if truth would have it they are little concerned with a rounded education. They believe it is better to have a degree than not to have a one. They also know that within society some jobs are valued more highly than others' and they will direct their children in the direction of those jobs. Even in this respect there are differences between cultures. For example engineers are valued much more highly in Germany and the United States than in Britain.

But the "whole person" view of parents also raises questions about the purposes of schooling, and in this respect there is a powerful hidden agenda, and that is the assignment to the school of considerable *in loco parentis* responsibilities while parents go out to work. This has had the effect of changing the role of the teacher. It cannot be said that teacher training has kept up with the new demands that are being placed on teachers in main stream classes.

Traditional approaches to the curriculum, and the received paradigm of the curriculum

At school level the curriculum is likely to be organized around what are believed to be the disciplines of knowledge, and justification for this arrangement can be found in the philosophical work of Hirst[30] in the UK, and Phenix[31] in the United States. It can also be found in the work of the psychologist Bruner.[32] Such a curriculum is of a traditional kind. Eggleston[33] suggested that such curricula belong to the *"received paradigm"* of curriculum organization because those responsible for the curriculum accept that there is a *"received body of understanding that is 'given', even ascribed, and is predominantly non-negotiable"*.

Although the epistemologies of Hirst, Phenix, and Bruner differ considerably Eggleston had no difficulty in grouping them together within the received paradigm. These educators believe- *"there are established and knowable structures of knowledge that exist independently of teachers or indeed of any other individuals"; (they are not necessarily the subjects of the curriculum as we understand them), that these patterns may be discovered, clarified and comprehended, and that adherence to them is either necessary or at least highly desirable if curriculum is to be meaningful and learning experience successful."*[34]

It will be understood that a philosophy of this kind supplies the rationale for a common core curriculum. In the United States there was concern that the curriculum in too many schools consists of disconnected, fragmented, incoherent - collection of information and skills programs, courses and so on. In 1995 a group of US educators sought to examine the question *"In what ways is the present curriculum incoherent?"* And to suggest how the curriculum might become coherent. It was concluded that there was no recipe or packaged program that would solve the problem. However the question of how to achieve a coherent curriculum could form the basis for curriculum conversations that were desperately needed.[35] Never were such conversations or assumptional-dialogues more necessary than at present. Policy makers continue to require schools to offer more and more programmes in addition to the 'normal' curriculum. They hope that these additions will solve the ills of society. The need for a coherent programme at post-primary level is matched by the need for coherent programmes in higher education. [36]

Eggleston's received paradigm would seem to include the traditional and discipline approaches described by Posner.[37] Perhaps this is because the former has looked at the curriculum from an English perspective whereas the latter considered it from the American experience.

In Posner's view the traditional approach is about the transmission of cultural heritage of western civilisation, and this applies to the liberal education offered in higher education as Bloom (Alan)[38] made clear. Perhaps the best known exponent of this view, through his book on *"Cultural Literacy"* is E. D. Hirsch jr. Posner selects this quotation from that book to illustrate this philosophy.

"The basic goal of education in a human community is acculturation, the transmission to children of the specific information shared by adults of the group or polis" [39]

And

"only by piling up communally shared information can children participate in complex cooperative activities with other members of the community". [40]

When Posner explained the origins of this classical liberal arts movement he did so by reference to the work of William Harris. Harris had said, that he believed *"the teacher, using the lecture-recitation method, would be the driving force in the process and would be responsible for getting students to think about what they read. Examinations would monitor and classify the students as they progressed through a graded educational system"* (p48).

Perhaps the most powerful case for the classical curriculum based on the 'great books' came from Mortimer J. Adler in the *Paidea Proposal*.[41] He argued that the that study of the perennial questions that arise time and again in literature and philosophy help develop reason, logic and imagination. Schubert calls this paradigm the intellectual traditionalist, and he associates *The Paidea Proposal* with the neo-Thomism[42] that emphasizes reason as an absolute object of study.

In Britain there would be many among the public who would agree with this view but they would also hold that this goal is achieved by the disciplines taught in school. How far this view can be maintained in the modern world is debatable. However, there is clearly a view among governments in the western world that education also has to have economic goals, and as such there are basic skills in literacy and numeracy that need to be developed. Therefore, they specify the curriculum in these areas which the teachers are expected to transmit. Schubert calls this curriculum – *"Cultural Reproduction."*[43] The fact that there are major debates about what should be in the history curriculum, and in English speaking countries the content and purpose of English suggests that the common body of knowledge to be transmitted is less embracing than would otherwise seem to be the case. Nowhere is this more so than, surprisingly, mathematics. There have been longstanding debates about the merits of pure versus applied mathematics as well as "realism" in the teaching of its curriculum.[44] There has also been considerable discussion about mathematical literacy just as there has been about literacy itself.[45] Jablonka argues that mathematical literacy cannot be conceived without implicitly or explicitly promoting a particular social practice as for example the development of human capital, or the promotion of cultural identity, or social change. So much for a value-free subject![46]. Evidently that there is some body of received wisdom is an idea that is somewhat less sacrosanct than many of us might believe and in most subject areas difficulties of the kind experienced by the mathematicians are also prominent. At the same time just as in mathematics there are a commonality of trends in its current development so to there are in other subjects.[47]

The content of the particular subjects of the curriculum does change over time even if only in small increments.[48] Then there has been the possibility of new subjects with combinations of 'old' and 'new' material, as for example, the world-wide interest in the introduction of technology, (not information technology), into the school curriculum. In the United States standards for technological literacy have been declared.[49] In England Design Technology is a subject in the national curriculum. It is now to have an examination in the Leaving Certificate in Ireland. But technical subjects have not had in the past the same status as others in the curriculum.

The fact that the received curriculum changes over time, is supportive of Bruner's notion of the curriculum that it is dynamic and evolving.[50] Bruner's idea of the enquiring mind and evolving curriculum lead to a metaphor of the *"the student as neophyte scientist."* The curriculum evolves through a process of discovery learning, reinforced by a spiral curriculum in which basic concepts are discussed at increasing levels of depth in different contexts as the curriculum progresses.

This view only fits a notion of a received curriculum that is structured by disciplines. It does not fit the notion of a received curriculum to be delivered through 'traditional' methods of teaching. Indeed Eggleston included Bruner in this paradigm to avoid using the received label to describe a range of reactionary or even traditional orientations of the curriculum. The second meaning that I have given does just this. The general experience is that the curriculum is subject to continuing changes, small though they may be, at times they are the subject of substantial reform. It is then that the problems of change have to be faced both by those responsible for the change and those who have to respond to it. It is found that teachers who participate in reforms can change their positions when they are given opportunities to consider and challenge their prevailing beliefs.[51]

Sociologists and the theory of knowledge

When sociologists analyse the curriculum they often do so from the perspective of the control of knowledge. In this context the received curriculum is seen as preserving the *status quo* and it is not questioned. From this perspective it is apparent that an alternative paradigm to the received paradigm will emerge. This paradigm is based on the epistemological view that knowledge is socially constructed. Eggleston gave the name *reflexive* to this paradigm.

In Britain sociologists such as Young[52] asked such questions as why it was that the curriculum that was provided caused many students from the working class to fail their examinations at the end of schooling, or to 'drop out' mentally and/ or physically before those examinations? He and sociologists like him believed that this was due to the received curriculum that is perpetuated *"through the day-to-day activities of teachers and even of pupils."*[53] These questions apply at all levels to the education of minorities. Moreover, they are not as has been found out in England necessarily solved by the imposition of a common curriculum.

Young is a British author who worked within the paradigm of critical praxis. His book was much discussed in Britain, and it brought home the idea that 'knowledge is control'. In whatever walk of life, to be without knowledge is to be dispossessed. Therefore, it is important to study the curriculum from the perspective of the control that it exerts, through questions of the kind asked in the preceding paragraph. It is important to realise that the instigators of a curriculum may not be conscious of its controlling effects. I say this to avoid the notion that a curriculum is a conspiracy to control even if it turns out that it is. On the other hand some of those responsible for the curriculum do control it in order to achieve goals that are acceptable to the public, as for example, the attempts in England and Texas to raise standards of literacy and numeracy.

Schubert[54] lists the questions asked by the critical praxis movement as follows.
1. *"How is knowledge reproduced in schools?*
2. *What are the sources of knowledge that students acquire in schools?*
3. *How do students and teachers resist or contest that which is conveyed through lived experience in schools?*
4. *What do students and teachers realise from their school experiences? In other words, what impact does school have on their outlook?*
5. *Whose interests are served by outlooks and skills fostered by schooling?*
6. *When served, do these interests move more in the direction of emancipation, equity and social justice, or do they move in the opposite direction?*
7. *How can students be moved toward greater liberation, equity, and social justice?"*

For sociologists working in the critical praxis paradigm the received curriculum was divisive. It separated the working class from the middle and upper classes the working class had to take subjects that were regarded as low status because they found it difficult to do mathematics, science, and English which were and are subjects that have high status. The working class had to take practical subjects like woodwork and metalwork, and because of this English culture engineering became applied science in order to gain status. School technology, (however much technological literacy may be important), is a low status subject. The same is true of the industrial arts in the United States.

Resistance to changing the curriculum

The English sociologists argued that the epistemology of the received curriculum was at fault. Knowledge was socially constructed and, therefore, relative. They made this case long before the constructivism associated with Piaget became influential in science teaching. But they found that the received curriculum persists. As Eggleston pointed out, (following Kuhn), it is very difficult to be deviant, and this applies as much to university teachers as it does to schoolteachers' *"For many teachers in universities the constraints are not ones of which they are sharply aware. Their internalisation of the received perspective that surrounds their work is sufficient to ensure that they are only infrequently conscious of their constraints. And most teachers do not need reminding that their own authority and role also spring from the existing social order,"* (i.e. their profession); *"that to challenge the system is to challenge their own present position."*[55]

As Cuban pointed out *"the goals and functions of schooling, working in concert with school and curriculum structures are potent influences in maintaining curricular continuity"*[56] and preventing change.

That is why change is so difficult. Nevertheless, change does take place but usually like the changes in the design of an automobile, in small increments.[57] Such changes have been called first-order changes. First-order changes are best understood as the next most obvious step to take in a subject curriculum or school development.[58] Sometimes there are spurts and substantial changes occur. But more often than not these are due to external forces, as for example, government pressure in England for university teachers to be trained in teaching, or the introduction of the Leaving Certificate Applied in Ireland. Revamping the curriculum requires significant changes in attitudes, goals, curriculum content and teaching methods. And that may not be palatable to many teachers. Such changes are second-order because they involve dramatic departures from the expected *"both in defining the problem and in finding a solution.* Marzano and his colleagues call these changes " *deep changes*". They alter *"the system in fundamental ways, offering a dramatic shift in direction and requiring new ways of thinking and acting."*[59] Of such would be a move to a "critical thinking curriculum" or a school where the first level of learning (obtaining information) is based on computer aided instruction. Marzano and his colleagues believe that one of the reasons that major educational innovations have not been sustained is that the innovators have used change processes that are appropriate for first-order change when in fact they were of the second order and required a reconceptualization of the problem. This is the problem of experience referred to in earlier chapters. New mental maps are required to cope with such change.[60]

Marzano and his colleagues believe that one of the reasons why educational innovations are not sustained is that the innovators have not sufficiently understood that type 1 processes are inadequate to the task of acquiring that deep understanding of ideas that will lead to sustained action. It is for example possible to work within a new curriculum without understanding the philosophy inherent in its construction.

All change depends on a deep understanding of the ideas on which it is based. To achieve this ideas have to be developed and circulated until the time is ripe and they appeal, even though the idea that is adopted may not have all the characteristics of the original idea.

"Let one such idea get possession of the popular mind, or the mind of any set of persons, and it is not difficult to understand the effects that will ensue. New lights will be brought upon the original idea, aspects will multiply, and judgements will accumulate. There will be a time of confusion; and it is uncertain whether anything is to come of the idea at all, or which view of it is to get the start of others. After a while some definite form of doctrine emerges; and, as time proceeds, one view of it will be modified or expanded by another, and then combined with a third, till the idea in which they centre will be to each mind separately what at first it was only to all together." [61]

One thing is certain models of the curriculum that see the teacher as irrelevant, even as inhibitors of change, and most do, will not accomplish change. The evidence is that teachers will respond to change if they become involved in activities that challenge their beliefs.[62] Very often consultation is token and teachers do not really participate in the curriculum making process. If they are not involved in the process they are de-professionalised. Professionalization demands that teachers should become curriculum makers.[63] And some would argue that in making the curriculum they should involve their students in the process.

Ideas emerging from constructivism

In this respect two important ideas have emerged from the phenomenological approach of constructivism to the curriculum. The first is that of negotiation. The reality of a social system is, in this theory, an artefact. Common-sense knowledge is socially constructed, and, therefore, relative. The participants in a classroom take part in defining the reality of the classroom (i.e. its culture). In this situation teachers and pupils should define a curriculum which is real to them in a social context. In this sense the curriculum is negotiable, negotiation having the purpose of meeting the needs of individual students.

The trouble is that negotiate and negotiable are open to several interpretations. Negotiation can be limited or all embracing.

Boomer, an Australian, wrote *"negotiating the curriculum means deliberately planning to invite students to contribute to, and to modify, the educational program, so that they will have a real investment both in the learning journey and in the outcomes"*. But he adds the caveat that, *"negotiation also means making explicit, and then confronting the constraints of the learning context and the non-negotiable requirements that apply."* [64]

In the same text, Cook stated the motivational principle that serves the theory. He wrote that, *"the key to negotiation, both in theory and in practice, lies in the ownership principle: people tend to strive hardest for the things they wish to own, or to keep and enhance things they already own. The inverse is just as true and observable all around us: people find it difficult to give commitment to the property and ideas of others."* [65]

In any subject the idea of negotiation is present when students are given the facility to choose their own projects. They may have to negotiate the project with their tutor if only to make sure that the project can be completed in the appropriate time, that they have the appropriate resources available, and the tutor perceives it to be within the competence of the student. The ownership of the idea is, nevertheless, that of the student. This is quite different from being told what project or what investigation to do, or even to select a project from a list of topics. It is quite clear which approach is more likely to develop independence in learning and independence in design, yet the issue of who should choose a project causes much debate. Many teachers are afraid to give students the opportunity of choice.

The Transition year provides an admirable opportunity to negotiate parts of the curriculum. Anne-Marie Clarke a Transition year co-ordinator reported that *"negotiable parts of the curriculum include what we call "module time"*. Modules[66] usually take 3-6 weeks to cover. A list is drawn up from student ideas and discussion follows. Examples of past choices made by the students would be car maintenance; horse riding; self-defence; grooming/hairdressing; and golf. The idea *"was specifically to give ownership to the students on the assumption that they will attend 100%, co-operate 100%, and, therefore, learn the skills of the activity. I might add that the objective behind the modules is to develop/ broaden knowledge, experience and confidence."*

"Similarly- ownership of learning also specifically takes place within the Mini Company programme. While the structure of the programme is clearly set out- the choice of the Company and Product is negotiated by each group of students. The teacher is present in an advisory capacity".

"The P.E. teacher also negotiates with the students at the start of the programmes regarding activities and the order of them e.g. swimming, soccer, badminton".

"The results of the negotiating have been highly successful. The students complete evaluations at the end of the modules, programmes etc. The feedback is positive and students report that they feel valued, motivated and appreciate their involvement in negotiations. Even the less mature student benefits from this practice." [67]

Teachers in the transition year have the opportunity to make the curriculum provided they meet the aims set out in exhibit 11.1. Curriculum making of this kind can enhance their professionalism. But they require considerable training to be able to make the most of what is on offer.

- Have been exposed to a broad, varied and integrated curriculum and have developed an informed sense of his/her own talents and preferences in general educational and vocational matters (*transition skills*).

- Have developed significantly the basic skills of literacy, numeracy, oracy (It is assumed that most students will have developed these skills before the end of the junior cycle, but specific reinforcement may be needed for some through TYO (*literacy, numeracy skills*).

- Have developed confidence in the unrehearsed application of these skills in a variety of common social situations (*adaptability*).

- Have experienced, as an individual or as part of a group, a range of activities which involve formal and informal contacts with adults outside the school context (*social skills*).

- Have developed a range of transferable thinking skills, study skills and other vocational skills (*learning skills*).

- Have developed confidence in the process of decision-making including the ability to seek out sources of support and aid in specific areas (*decision-making*).

- Have experienced a range of activities for which the student was primarily responsible in terms of planning, implementation, accountability and evaluation, either as an individual or part of a group (*problem-solving*).

- Have developed appropriate physical and manipulative skills in work and leisure contexts (*physical*).

- Have been helped to foster sensitivity and tolerance to the needs of others and to develop personal relationships (*interpersonal/caring*).

- Have been enabled to develop an appropriate set of spiritual, social and moral values (*faith: morals*).

- Have had opportunities to develop creativity and appreciation of creativity in others (*aesthetic*).

- Have developed responsibility for maintaining a healthy life style, both physical and mental (*health*).

- Have developed an appreciation of the physical and technological environments and their relationship to human needs in general (*environment*).

- Have been given an understanding of the nature and discipline of science and its application to technology through the processes of design and production (*science/technology*).

- Have been introduced to the implications and applications of information technology to society (*information technology*).

Exhibit 11.1. The aims of the transition year in Ireland expressed in terms of skills and competencies (1986) *Planning and Developing Transition Year Programmes. Guidelines for Schools.* Interim Board for Curriculum and Examinations (CEB). Dublin.

In Civic, Social and Political Education students are required to undertake an action project. The report for this project accounts for 60% of the total marks awarded. Maria Fitzmaurice reported that in her school where the focus of the school is on the environment an Action project was negotiated with the class group.[68]

"The first year class were concerned by the amount of litter in the school building and grounds. They undertook a series of hands on activities to reduce the litter, as for example, litter picking, bringing home own waste in lunch boxes, recycling, bird tables (fir food scraps) inviting speakers to talk to the general school body on the topic of waste management."

"The result was that the school was awarded a Green Flag (equal to the Blue Flags awarded for clean beaches) by the Federation for Environmental Education in Europe. The students had a great sense of achievement and pride. They had been empowered to make a difference to their school environment."

Related to the idea of choosing one's own project is the idea of independent study where the course and associated studies are chosen by the student, subject to the university's capability to advise and assess the student's performance. One of the problems that students experience in the transition from school to college is the fact that they become immediately responsible for themselves and their learning. Could, for example, a component of the transition year be made available for them to choose whatever it is they want to study formally and how it will be assessed, and would this prepare them for such learning? [69]

Eggleston's view was that since the received and reflexive paradigms were related modes of understanding both the realities of knowledge in the school curriculum and the possibilities of change therein they would 'merge' (my word not his) and form a restructuring perspective. The reality is that as our understanding of teaching and learning develops no one model of the curriculum is likely to attain all the aims we would wish to achieve.

Screening the aims of education

The purpose of the preceding paragraphs has been to demonstrate the significance of philosophy and sociology in the determination of aims, and thus, their importance in curriculum leadership. They also illustrate that different theories stem from different aims. Furst pointed out that *"some of these goals will be more important than others; and some will be inconsistent in the sense that they call for contradictory patterns of behaviour. Clearly the school must choose a small number of important and consistent goals that can be attained in the time available."* [70]

He also argued that in order to choose these domains the lists that are developed have to be screened for consistency and significance. He argued that the educational and social philosophy to which the school (department- institution) is committed should provide the first screen. His examples of such questions relate very much to those used to illustrate the critical praxis paradigm. They were-

Should the school prepare young people to accept the present social order?

Should different social groups or classes receive different kinds of education?

Should the school try to make people alike or should it cultivate idiosyncracy?

Should the school emphasise general education or should it aim at specific vocational education?

Furst's point is that the education that will be provided will be a function of the stance taken on such issues. He points out that if a school prepares students for the present social order, the received or cultural heritage paradigm will apply and it will emphasise conformity, and the mastery of fairly stable and well-organised bodies of knowledge. Such a curriculum would be politically neutral. Whereas if a school wants to encourage students to improve society it will emphasise sensitivity to social problems, skills in analysing problems and proposing solutions. It is unlikely to be politically neutral.

Answers to these questions have to be consistent and not contradictory. In Ireland where the examination syllabus dictates learning in post-primary education, the introduction of action projects in Civic, Social and Political Education (CSPE) could be said to meet such goals. And, this is within a curriculum that is essentially academic. There are many examples of such hybrids in other parts of the world. However, the full benefit would only accrue if it were to be carried through into the senior cycle of secondary education (15/16 – 18 years)[71] and used to facilitate the development of critical thinking appropriate to the age group.

This applies at all levels of the educational process be it at the level of policy or the level of the curriculum. Helsby, for example has shown how government policies to school education in the UK have been contradictory.[72]

Furst also argued that the psychology of learning and human development can serve as a second screen for selecting and eliminating goals. As with philosophy he offers a series of questions that might be asked. Three of them follow-

At what levels of maturity are particular objectives obtained?

What is the optimum growth which may be expected of different kinds of students with respect to the objectives?

What is the transfer value of different kinds of outcomes?

Questions such as these can be used to screen courses like the Transition year programme. Exhibit 11.1 above shows the aims of the transition year in Ireland expressed in terms of skills and competencies. As mentioned in earlier chapters it functions as a moratorium on a univocal focus on academics and academic study and it gives teachers the opportunity for substantive curriculum making within the frame work of the aims of the curriculum set out in the aims in exhibit 11.1. Some years ago in a policy discussion paper the Department of Education suggested that it might continue as it is. That is for a whole year between the age of fifteen and sixteen or immediately after students had taken the Junior Certificate Examination. It also suggested an alternative whereby the equivalent period would be taken over a period of three years. This is the equivalent of about one-day per week during the three years of the Senior Cycle. Inspection of the intentions described in exhibit 11.1. suggest that the second option would be much better since it would allow for development during one of the most difficult phases of one's life (see chapter 13). A strong argument can be made that at the age of fifteen students are not mature enough to benefit from schemes that are designed to achieve these goals. Others would argue that it is good to be free of examination pressure for a whole year.

A husband and wife who teach in post-primary and primary respectively point out that *"The protocol underpinning this programme* [transition year] *seems to be that by allowing a "free" year the maturation within this process will enable the students to be more focused and better able to withstand the pressures of the Leaving Certificate Programme. It is also suggested that even if only subliminally that the work carried out in the Leaving Certificate years is by its nature stressful and onerous and a body of work that is unrewarding."* [73]

Given that this is the case they point out that the two programmes require different teaching and learning styles and that this can create difficulty for senior students as they try to adjust to the Leaving Certificate programme. Maturation does not only take place in the Transition year but throughout life. Therefore, account needs to be taken of it in 5th and 6th years. They argue that the body of knowledge undertaken in 5th and 6th years has inherent value and interest and, *"that this knowledge acquisition paralleling the maturation process can present a positive, challenging and satisfying experience"*. On this basis they argue for one continuous three-year cycle with the personal development dimension of the Transition year incorporated throughout the programme.[74] We shall return to this point in chapter 13. In opposition to this it is argued that the time available in the present Transition Year for work experience and community service activities makes it much more worthwhile. But there has been no national debate about these issues. Clearly such a debate could be facilitated by curriculum leaders in schools.

It is not the purpose here to argue the merits one way or another but simply to point out the importance of using psychology to screen the aims, and to note there are no criterion statements against which the issue can be analysed. And, also, to note that some of the points raised are contentious and open to formal research and evaluation. Which is also to emphasise the importance of evaluation in the curriculum process. As the recommendations are written it would be possible to provide a rather trivial or a rather deep education. Given that the age is fifteen it might be argued that this curriculum should be the beginning of a spiral curriculum. If it is, then how does the learner advance along the spiral?

There is a more profound question related to this issue. It is the fact that there is no curriculum continuity between primary and post-primary education as there is in other countries. Does this have particular merits?

Consider the case of the SCOOPE project that was run by The Tipperary Leader Group. It ran over a three-year period with the purpose of developing enterprise among primary school children of all ages, although the majority of the pupils were in the later years of their primary (elementary) schooling. In brief the pupils set up their own companies and made things that there were sold. It was very much like a mini-company but the teachers were asked to encourage the children to develop skills in a heuristic that included planning, making, selling, and working in teams. In one or two small schools every pupil was involved. There is no doubt that the project was very motivational, and among its outcomes it is clear that the children learnt the importance of working in teams, and the importance of communication skills.

One may question whether or not such values should be inculcated at school, and this is an example of screening with philosophy. But there is a curriculum issue. Given that such project is considered to be worth while then, would it not be better done in the transition year? The Tipperary Leader Group argued that by the time children reached the transition year it was to late, and some teachers who participated, and who had children in the transition year, thought that the project was a more valuable experience than obtained in the transition year. However, if it is to be worthwhile then the evaluation report suggests that this new learning should be followed up. In the report an example is given of where pupils had asked the business studies teacher in their local post-primary school to be allowed to initiate such a project and had been denied.[75]

Decisions about the curriculum are not a matter for pragmatism but for thorough ongoing screening. It is evident from the foregoing, and as at least one illustration of its use shows, that screening is by no means an easy task[76]

The need to screen aims and objectives provides the rationale for including the study of appropriate philosophy, psychology and sociology in the student teacher's curriculum. Curriculum leaders need to be conversant in all these areas and to be aware of the history that has brought the curriculum to where it is. The importance of "assumptional-dialogues in screening should be self-evident.

Curriculum design

Schubert considers that the dominant curriculum paradigm is due to Ralph Tyler. Tyler argued that the four questions that should govern the design of the curriculum are:

1. What educational purposes should the school seek to obtain?
2. What educational experiences can be provided which are likely to attain these purposes?

3. How can these educational experiences be effectively organised?
4. How can we determine whether these purposes are being attained?

In his discussion of the first point he introduces the term "educational objectives" which we were discussed chapters 5 and 10. A variety of diagrams have been published to illustrate the curriculum process that follows from trying to answer Tyler's questions (See chapter 5). The approach taken to the study of the curriculum in this study is in the same *genre*. *That model can be placed within a model that shows the effect of society* (see for example figure 11.1).

Tyler's book *The Basic Principles of Curriculum and Instruction* published in 1949[77] has been described by Jackson) as the Bible of the curriculum.[78] Tyler took the designer away from listing content in the first instance. He proposed that the curriculum designer had to begin, not by listing content, but by declaring the objectives to be achieved. This might lead to a discipline-based curriculum or for example an integrated curriculum. Once these were understood it would be possible to determine the instructional methods that would create the learning that would achieve those aims and objectives. As was demonstrated in chapters 7 through 9 the implication of these models is that instruction should be designed to achieve specified aims and objects, and that different methods of instruction are more likely to obtain some objectives than other instructional strategies. In systems of public examining the models also show the integral relationship that assessment has with instruction. Such curricula are assessment led and the design of assessment can either inhibit or hinder learning. (See chapter 12).

The curriculum process in action (see figures 5.1 and 5.2)

Models like the one in figure 5.2 are unusual and differ from Tyler's in that they incorporate the syllabus (content). They are intended to illustrate the syllabus (curriculum content) as being the outcome of a complex design activity involving the declaration of objectives and the simultaneous design of assessment and instruction procedures that will cause those objectives to be obtained.

The process may be illustrated by consideration of the student complaint that courses are overloaded. By this they mean that the syllabuses are so detailed that they cannot be covered adequately by the teacher or the students in the time allowed. This does not, however, mean that they would want the course lengthened. It does mean that they consider that too many topics are covered at to great a speed the consequence of which should be to reduce the number of topics.

A major problem arises from the conflict between teaching facts and developing cognitive skills. The learning of a cognitive skill often takes a long time. Consider the problem of helping students to evaluate historical documents. This takes time. Students will have to be shown examples and practice with case study material. In a subject that may only be time tabled for two sessions per week then time given to teaching a higher order skill of this type may be at the expense of important facts.[79]

It is this writer's experience that those concerned with the design of new courses tend to overload them with content and subsequently face the task of reducing them. He has been found guilty of this offence. It is only by following the design procedures outlined below that a satisfactory teaching-learning syllabus can be defined within the time constraints available. It is also his experience that policy makers allow too little time for curriculum development and this is evidently the experience of others.[80]

To determine whether or not a course would be overloaded the estimates of times taken for each instructional procedure are summed, and if they come to more than the time allowed for the course, then the course is overloaded. This is irrespective of any overloading caused by home study requirements.

Mansfield writing about the design of mini-courses said, *"try to be as realistic as possible, total up the times for all activities on your mini-course outline. Adjust any item to meet the overall goal within the allotted time trading, deleting activities or even reducing the number of realisable objectives. Alternatively, consider providing more total time for the course...be brutally honest in your time estimates."*[81] This is why the syllabus (content) has been put at the centre of these models because it is the outcome of the design process and not its beginning. It is also the reason why the key concepts to be considered are as much a component of the objectives as are the statement of skills that have come to be associated with objectives (e.g. problem solving, critical thinking). Transfer of learning will not be obtained without an understanding of the appropriate principles and concepts. For this reason a teacher should concentrate on ensuring that these concepts and principles are understood even if that means that some parts of the course cannot be covered (see chapter 7). The determination of key concepts (and principles) is a critical stage in the process of curriculum design, as is the evaluation of whether or not they have been learnt.

Implications for curriculum leadership

For a given area of knowledge curriculum (instructional) design, assessment and evaluation begin at the same point. That is the understanding and expression of what it is we are trying to do.

(1) For each general objective there will be an appropriate method of testing. Allowance for expressive outcomes should be made, and the key concepts of the programme determined.
(2) Specific learning strategies will be required if the objectives are to be successfully obtained.
(3) A multiple strategy approach to teaching, learning and assessment will be required since some methods of testing will be appropriate or inappropriate for the domain objectives to be obtained (see p 239)
(4) The combination of all these elements may lead to a substantial reorganization of the syllabus.
(5) Some models of the curriculum may be more appropriate for the attainment of the stated objectives than others. A mix of models will be more likely required.

(6) Teachers will have to be versatile in that the role of the teacher may change as the model used changes.

From this we may deduce that a single class or series of classes should be planned in the same way as the curriculum. They will have a focus point, generally expressed in simple objectives, a learning strategy that is specifically designed to meet the objective, and a strategy for assessment that enables the evaluation of both student and teacher performance. It is the ability to make such assessments, and to reflect on their outcomes, that characterises the level 1 instructional/curriculum leader.

But freedom to design courses is limited in programmes that are controlled in one way or the other by the state. When it is allowed or encouraged curriculum making enhances teacher professionalism. But teachers need substantial training to make the curriculum.

An integrated approach to curriculum making of this kind demands a considerable change on the part of the teacher to the planning and implementation of the curriculum. While curriculum leadership requires knowledge of philosophy, sociology, and psychology as they are applied to education, change is unlikely to be accomplished, unless it is shown to follow from those notional aims to which teachers are emotionally attached. Understanding teacher beliefs is the beginning of the change process. What is certain is that curriculum design is a complex process. If curriculum change is carried out *in situ* it is also likely to be a messy business as the study of innovations in the transition year by Heywood and Murray shows.[82] Not withstanding it has to begin with the determination of aims and objectives and that as we have seen (chapter 10) is not a simple activity.

At the other end of the spectrum of curriculum leadership (level 4) is the ability to participate in policy debates about the nature of the curriculum as a whole (i.e. the areas of knowledge/disciplines). Policy makers can sometimes introduce policies that are contradictory or inhibit effective teaching and learning. Worse policy makers can easily rally public support. It is incumbent on curriculum leaders to persuade the community that what they say is rational, practical and likely to produce results. Of such are debates about the aims and mission of education. They have profound consequences for learning and instruction.

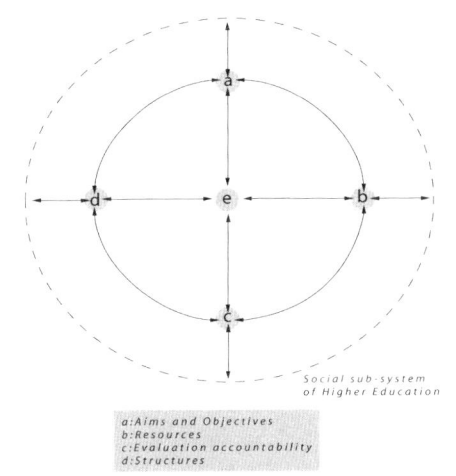

Figure 11.1 A Model of the institutional evaluation process. Substitute evaluation and accountability at the centre with curriculum/instructional model shown in chapter 5 to show the place of the subject curriculum within the sub-system of the institution and the wider social system.

a: Aims and Objectives
b: Resources
c: Evaluation accountability
d: Structures

Notes and references

[1] In the US Glatthorn, A. A., Boschee, F., and B. M. Whitehead (2006) *Curriculum Leadership. Development and Implementation*. Sage (Thousand Oaks CA) and his colleagues make a distinction between the recommended curriculum that is due to reports of commissions, or the policies of State and Federal Government and the written curriculum which they liken to Goodlad's formal curriculum. This is the sense in which it is used here. See Goodlad, J and associates. *Curriculum Inquiry. The Study of Curriculum Practice*. McGraw Hill, New York.
[2] See Otto, L. B. (1982). Extra curricular activities. In H. J. Walberg (ed). *Improving Educational Standards and Productivity. The Research Basis for Productivity*.. McCutchan, Berkeley, CA
[3] See Heywood, J. (1984). *Considering the Curriculum during Student Teaching*. London, Kogan Page. The term hidden curriculum is due to Jackson, P. W (1968). *Life in Classrooms*. Holt, Rinehart and Winston. New York.
[4] For an example of a detailed analysis of the hidden curriculum and some of its effects see Lynch, K. (1989) *The Hidden Curriculum*. Falmer Press, London, For a brief discussion of the effect of social values on attitudes to achievement see Heywood, J (1984) *loc.cit* ch 3, and in particular McClelland, D. C. (1961). *The Achieving Society*. Free Press, New York
[5] Cuban, L (1992) Curriculum Stability and Change in P.W. Jackson (ed) *Handbook of Research on the Curriculum*. MacMillan, New York.
[6] *loc cit* ref 1 ch.1.
[7] *loc.cit* ref 1.
[8] *loc cit* Goodlad ref 1.
[9] There is no mention of philosophy in Glatthorn et al
[10] J. V. Rice built up a substantial programme on Bernard Lonergan in the Trinity College Master's programme but it remains unpublished
[11] See Heywood, J (2005) *Engineering Education. Research and Development in Curriculum and Instruction*. IEEE/Wiley, New York for a critique of constructivism pp 57 – 62. See Steffe, L. D. and J. Gale (1995) (eds). *Constructivism in Education*. Lawrence Erlbaum, Hillsdale, NJ
[12] For a review including a paper by Ennis see Norris, S. P (1992) (ed). *The Generalizability of Critical Thinking. Multiple Perspectives on an Educational Ideal*. Teachers College Press, New York.
[13] Phenix, P. H (1964) *Realms of Meaning*. McGraw Hill, New York.
[14] Hirst, P. H. (1975). *Knowledge and the Curriculum. A Collection of Philosophical Papers.*

Routledge, London.

[15] As defined in *The New Shorter Oxford English Dictionary* (1993). For a brief discussion of the importance of epistemology in teaching see p 204 of Matthews, M. R (1994). *Science Teaching The Role of the History and Philosophy of Science*. London, Routledge.

[16] *ibid*

[17] Sierpinska, A and S. Lerman (2003). Epistemologies of mathematics and of mathematics education in A. J. Bishop et al (eds). *International Handbook on Mathematics Education*. Kluwer, Dordrecht.

[18] *ibid*.

[19] Wringe, C (1988). *Understanding Educational Aims*. Unwin Hyman, London

[20] E. J. Furst made this point in *Constructing Evaluation Instruments* (1960). David Mackay, New York.

[21] Dewey, J (1916). *Democracy and Education*. Macmillan, New York.

[22] SCANS (1992). *Learning a Living. A Blueprint for High Performance*. US Department of Labor. Washington, DC.

[23] McCllelland, D. C. (1969) The role of achievement motivation in the transfer of technology in D. C. Gruber and D. B. Marquis (eds).*Factors in the Transfer of Technology*. MIT Press, Cambridge, MA.

[24] *loc.cit* ch 3 of Heywood, ref 3.

[25] Schubert, W. H. (1986). *Curriculum. Perspective, Paradigm, Possibility*. Prentice Hall, 1997 printing, Upper Saddle River, NJ.

[26] For a brief account of reconceptualism see Pinar, W. F. (1997). Reconceptualization of curriculum studies. In Flinders, D. J. and S. J. Thornton (eds). The Curriculum Studies Reader. Routledge, New York,. Pinar writes *"Apple and the Marxists and Neo Marxists go further and accept a teleological view of historical movement, allying themselves with the lower classes, whose final emergence from oppression is seen to be inevitable. A number of reconceptualists while not Marxists nonetheless accept some variation of this teleological view of history.....Nearly all accept that a political dimension is inherent in any intellectual activity"*. It is this political emphasis that distinguishes the work of Apple and others from the conceptual empiricists. (pp126, 127). One of M. W. Apple's contributions will be found in this same volume headed- Is there a curriculum to reclaim. (Ch. 29).

[27] *ibid* p33

[28] Freire, P.(1970). *The Pedagogy of the Oppressed*. Seabury, New York.

[29] e.g. Barnett, C (1995). *The Lost Victory, British Dreams, British Realities 1945-1950*. London, Macmillan.

[30] Hirst, P. (1975). *Knowledge and the Curriculum*. Routledge, London.

[31] Phenix, P. H. (1964). *Realms of Meaning:. A Philosophy of the Curriculum for General Education*. McGraw Hill, New York.

[32] Bruner, J.S (1960). *The Process of Education*. Vintage, New York, and (1966). *Toward a Theory of Instruction*. Harvard University Press, Cambridge MA. See also Posner, G (1992). *Analyzing the Curriculum. New Curriculum Inquiry*, 13, (3), 239-265 McGraw Hill, New York.

[33] Eggleston, J. (1977). *Sociology of the School Curriculum*. Routledge, . London,

[34] *ibid*

[35] *Toward A Coherent Curriculum. The 1995 ASCD Yearbook*. Association for Supervision and Curriculum Development, Alexandria, VA

[36] Knight, P. T (2001). Complexity and Curriculum: a process approach to curriculum-making. *Teaching in Higher Education*, 6, (3), 279 – 381.

[37] Posner, G. J. (1992). *Analyzing the Curriculum*. McGraw Hill, New York.

[38] Bloom, A (1987). *The Closing of the American Mind*. Simon and Schuster, New York.

[39] Hirsch, E. D. (1987). *Cultural Literacy. What Every American Needs to Know*.Vintage/Random House, New York.

[40] *ibid*

[41] M. J. Adler (1982). *The Paidea Proposal: An Educational Manifesto.*, Macmillan, New York

[42] *ibid* p 129. Neo-Thomistic writers in the United States include Mortimore Adler and Robert Hutchins, and in Europe Jacques Maritain.

[43] *loc.cit* ref 25

44 see for example de Lange, J (1996). Using and applying mathematics in education in A. J. Bishop

et al (eds) *International Handbook on Mathematics Education*. Part 1. Kluwer, Dordrecht.
⁴⁵ Jablonka, E (2003) Mathematical literacy in A. J. Bishop et al (eds) *Second International Handbook of Mathematics Education* Part 1. Kluwer, Dordrecht.
⁴⁶ *ibid*.
⁴⁷ See for example Clarke, B., Clarke, D and P. Sullivan (1996). The mathematics teacher and Curriculum Development in A. J. Bishop et al (eds) *International Handbook of Mathematics Education* Part 1. Kluwer, Dordrecht.
⁴⁸ *loc.cit* ref 3. Heywood
⁴⁹ International Technology Education Association (2000) Reston, VA
⁵⁰ Bruner, J (1960). *The Process of Education*. Vintage Books, New York.
⁵¹ Wilson, S and T. Cooney (2002) Mathematics teacher change and teacher development in G. C. Leder et al (eds) *Beliefs: A Hidden Variable in Mathematics Education/* Kluwer, Dordrecht. They cited research by Wood, T and P. Sellers (1997) Deepening the analysis: longitudinal assessment of a problem-centred mathematics program. *Journal of Research in Mathematics Education* 15, 146 – 149 in support of this argument.
⁵² Young, M. F. D. (1971) (ed) *Knowledge and Control*. Collier Macmillan, London,.
⁵³ *loc.cit* Eggleston p 68.
⁵⁴ *loc.cit*.
⁵⁵ *loc.cit* Eggleston p 70
⁵⁶ *ibid*. p238
⁵⁷ *loc. cit* Heywood
⁵⁸ Marzano, R. J., Waters and B. A. McNulty (2005) *School Leadership that Works. From Research to Results*. ASCD, Alexandria, VA. they were speaking of change at school and district level in the US but it applies equally to the subject and the curriculum overall.
⁵⁹ *ibid* p 66.
⁶⁰ Marzano et al cite Argyris, C and D. Schön (1974) *Organizational Learning: A Theory of Action Perspective*. Addison Wesley, Reading, MA. They distinguished between single and double looped learning. The first is when the organization approaches the problem using strategies from the past. Double loop learning is when no existing strategy suffices in which case the problem must be reconceptualised and new mental maps acquired. They cite Fritz, R (1984) *The Path of Least Resistance: Learning to become a Creative Force in your own Life*. Fawcett Columbine, New York.
⁶¹ Newman, J. (1845). *An Essay on the Development of Christian Doctrine*. P98 of the Penguin edition (1974). Harmondsworth, Middx. Newman defines and idea as follows. "*It is a characteristic of our minds to be ever engaged in passing judgements on things which come before them. No sooner do we learn, but we judge; we allow nothing to stand by itself; we compare, contrast, abstract, generalize, adjust, classify; and we view all our knowledge in the associations with which these processes have invested in it. Of the judgements thus exercised, some are mere opinions, which come and go, or remain with us only till an accidents displaces them, whatever influence they may exert meanwhile. Others are firmly fixed in our minds and have a hold over us, whether they are principles of conduct, or are views of life and the world, or fall under the general head of belief. These habitual judgements often go by the name of ideas, and shall be called so here.*"
⁶² *loc.cit*. ref 51
⁶³ *ibid*. They cite Clandinin, D. J and F. M. Connelly (1992). Teacher as curriculum maker in P. W. Jackson (ed) *Handbook of Research on Curriculum*. Macmillan, New York.
⁶⁴ Boomer, G. (1992). Negotiating; the curriculum reformulated in G. Boomer et al (eds) *Negotiating the Curriculum. Educating for the 21st Century*. Falmer Press, London,
⁶⁵ Cook, J (1992). Negotiating the curriculum: Programming for learning in G. Boomer et al (eds) *Negotiating the Curriculum. Educating for the 21st Century*. Falmer, London.
⁶⁶ The term module is used in a variety of ways as is the term course. In pursuit a European Credit Transfer System universities have modularised their courses. The hours per module relate to teacher contact and independent study by the students. Many universities in the UK have introduced the semester system and as in America a module describes a full course taken within a semester. The hours can be split over two semesters i.e. as a long thin module. Can be thought of as an adaptation of the American semester system. A course is a coherent subject within a module or used to describe the whole programme that a student pursues. Prior to that courses ran throughout the year or for shorter periods during the year. There was no systematization.
⁶⁷ Clarke, A-M (2005) An Evaluation of a Portfolio System in Transition Year. Mst Thesis,

University of Dublin, Dublin.
[68] Reported during an in-career development programme on instructional leadership, University of Dublin.
[69] Something more academic, that is, the examples chosen by the students in Anne-Marie Clarkes school.
[70] Furst, E. J (1960). *Constructing Evaluation Instruments*. David MacKay, New York. P 39. The term screening comes from R.W. Tyler see ref 35
[71] Post primary education is 11/12 to 18. Sometimes divided into junior cycle up to 15/16 years and senior cycle. There is often a public examination at the end of the junior cycle. In the case of England it is the General Certificate of Secondary Education (GCSE). In Ireland it is the Junior Certificate. Adolescents may leave school at the end of the Junior Cycle either for further/technical/vocational education or for work. These examinations are set in each of the subjects for that a student is entered. The Leaving Certificate is set at two levels Honours and ordinary. It is used for university matriculation. It is also a leaving certificate or exit qualification.. It has the same function as the GCE 'A' level examination in England.
[72] Helsby, G. (1999). *Changing Teachers Work*, Buckingham, Open University Press.
[73] Private communication from Paul and Frances Cooke expanding on points made in an in-career programme when Frances Cook took part in a discussion of this issue
[74] They also recommended that the programme should *"include a week away together in the 4th year, work experience and project work but to have the work load of the Leaving certificate programme started and to integrate this work with the personal development areas. To allow extra time to the subject areas so as to reduce the build up of pressure which is automatic in a programme as deep and diverse as the Leaving Certificate. To factor in time for experimentation with the offered curriculum particularly in the 4th year, so as to encourage research and development among the teaching body. To continue the work of the CSPE programme in a less formal or structured way and to incorporate the goals of RE Departments. To invest in helping students understand their study patterns and to match these patters with post Leaving certificate expectations (points). To help students develop study patterns which help them achieve their 3rd level targets. Finally that students could sit the Leaving Ccertificate in a calmer more prepared manner after three years preparation having developed important life skills simultaneously".*
[75] SCOOPE. Evaluation for the Tipperary Leader Group. Tipperary, 2001.
[76] Heywood, J (1981). Acadaemic versus practical debate. A case study in screening. *Institution of Electrical Engineers Proceedings* 128, Pt A 7, 511-519.
[77] Tyler, R. W. (1949) *The Basic Principles of Curriculum and Instruction*. Chicago University Press, Chicago.
[78] Jackson, P. W.(1992). *Handbook of Research on Curriculum*. Ch 1 Conceptions of curriculum and 79 Curriculum specialists. AERA/Macmillan, New York.
[79] Heywood, J (1977). *Examining in Second Level Education*. Association of Secondary Teachers of Ireland, Dublin
[80] *loc. cit* ref 51.
[81] Mansfield, G (1979). Designing your own mini-course. *Engineering Education* 70, (2), 205-207.
[82] Heywood, J and M. Murray (2005)Curriculum –Led Staff Development. Towards Curriculum and Instructional Leadership in Ireland. *Bulletins of the European Forum on Educational Administration* (EFEA), No 4,.pp 3 – 96. Sheffield Hallam University, Dept of Education for EFEA

12
Operational Models of the Curriculum and other Issues.

Abstract

The purposes of this chapter are to examine the origins of and developments in assessment led curricula. Criticisms of traditional examining and testing led to the development of multiple strategy assessment and teaching. Two approaches to the design of such curricular, one from the US and one from England are described. The American model (Alverno College) is continuous and requires substantial self-assessment by the students. There was only a limited amount of self-assessment in the English model that was designed for a terminal public examination accompanied by coursework. Candidates were required to evaluate their coursework. Its multiple strategy approach to assessment approximates to a balanced system of assessment as defined by the US Committee on Foundations of Assessment (National Research Council). In the Alverno model all subjects are required to assist the students acquire skill in eight generic abilities. The Alverno College scheme is a major challenge to traditional modes of assessment and teaching.

The influence of the universities on syllabus content and the subjects taken is discussed. The value of equivalents to the Scholastic Aptitude Test is discussed in relation to the separation of leaving certificate (exit) examinations from university entrance requirements. The development of Standards in the US and their relation to assessment is considered.

The role of interdisciplinary and integrated studies is considered in the light of the explosion of knowledge and the fact that very many life problems require knowledge from more than one discipline. Various models of integration are described including project and problem based. A theory of interdisciplinarity within the curriculum based on Whitehead's rhythmic theory of learning development is presented.

Integrated skill curricula are discussed in relation to education and work. It is argued that studies of the needs of industry show a demand for basic literacy and numeracy among school leavers and from those coming from higher education-personal transferable skills. It is argued that contrary to commonly held views those curricula that incorporate personal transferable skills can meet the goals of liberal education.

The design of school curricula that prepare pupils for work and life are considered together with approaches to assessment.

It may be argued that an appropriately designed general education (balanced curriculum) will provide the basic skills necessary for work and life and hopefully dissolve the academic versus practical (vocational) dichotomy in education.

Assessment led curricular (Curriculum integrated assessment)

It has been well established that examinations and assessments influence learning. Teachers help students to spot questions in essay-type public examination papers. Questions are rotated through the years and not much consideration is given to their design. If the answers to questions can be memorised a premium is placed on memory and teaching is expected to support memorisation. In the 1970's it was shown that students taking examinations in higher education adopted either a 'surface' or 'deep' approach to learning and examinations as a function of what they perceived the questions to require of their answers. It might be said that examinations had a negative effect on learning. In the 1970's the public examinations in England and Wales whose prime purpose was to matriculate students for university admission were organised by Matriculation Boards. A principle of this examining was that Boards did not make any input into teaching. How a syllabus was taught was a matter for the teachers not for the Board. The Boards function was to set the syllabus and set the examination. Teaching was not their business. However, in the late nineteen sixties The Joint Matriculation Board introduced a new syllabus in engineering Science and an examination was set that deliberately set out to influence teaching so that learning would be enhanced. It used a multiple strategy approach in which there were separate sub-tests for knowledge (using objective questions), comprehension (questions set on the reading of a journal article, project planning and evaluation (for the testing of what Sternberg would call executive skills)[1] and analysis and problem solving.[2] Twenty percent of the marks were allocated for the assessment of coursework that comprised laboratory investigations and a project for testing practical skills and higher order thinking related to the design and implementation of experiments and projects and their evaluation. The assessment schedules were published for the coursework with the intention of influencing the approach students took to learning. As indicated earlier the Public Examinations Evaluation Project[3] in Ireland used this model to design experimental multiple strategy examinations in history and mathematics for the Intermediate Certificate Examination. A multiple-strategy approach should provide a balanced form of assessment

The criteria for balanced assessment were defined in the United States by the Committee on the Foundations of Assessment (National Research Council).[4] It called for a balance between classroom and large-scale assessment of the kind offered by the ACT and SAT. A balanced system of assessment would exhibit the three properties of *comprehensiveness*, *coherence* and *continuity*. By comprehensive is meant that a variety of techniques would be used because no one form assessment can serve all the purposes an examination is supposed to serve. One dimension of *coherence* is that the "*conceptual base or models of student learning underlying the various external and classroom assessments within a system should be compatible*". Another was that curriculum, instruction and assessment should be aligned. Continuity requires that student progress should be measured overtime –"*akin to a videotape record than to snapshots.*" The committee argued that " *no existing assessment systems meet all three criteria […] but some "represent steps towards these goals*". In particular it cited as an example of a comprehensive examination an 'A' level examination in physics. The progenitor of this model was the 'A' level examination in engineering Science that was developed by the Joint Matriculation Board in the 1960s and 1970s. It is argued elsewhere that the engineering science examination goes a long way to meeting the Committee's criteria.

Since the engineering science examination was developed in England there have been massive changes in the structure of 'A' level examinations. When it was developed, the content of the course (syllabus) was given during a period of two years, at the end of which the examination was taken. The investigations and project work were negotiated and were also undertaken during this two years. Recent changes to the 'A' level have included modularisation of the components of courses so that each module is assessed separately. It is difficult to see how a multiple strategy approach to assessment and teaching could be used within modules (units) that require separate assessment. The 'A' level exams have come in for criticism recently from the British Prime Minister who said that the questions set were too easy. Yet if he and politicians like him want to give back credibility to the 'A' level they should look to multiple strategy approaches like those of engineering science for a solution.

The examinations for both the Leaving and Intermediate Certificate (now Junior Certificate) are taken at the end of three year cycles in Ireland. The teachers have control of the teaching of content and there are no controls over them in that pursuit other than the questions set in the examinations. This is in contrast to the curriculum introduced in England in 1989 where there is much more control. As exhibit 12.1 shows it was organised around four key stages. During these stages a number of standard assessment tasks (SATS) have to be completed. The examination for the General Certificate of School Education (GCSE) is taken at 16 years of age. There is much more control over the teaching and there is a great deal of assessment.

The contrast between the conduct of the programmes in England and Ireland is stark. The former is highly controlled and standards are set for all levels. In Ireland, however, the only means of control are the examinations set at the end of the Junior and Senior cycles. Another difference is that in Ireland there is not a continuous curriculum from Junior infants to year 11 (i.e, K-12). The primary curriculum is separate to the secondary curriculum. There are no national selection examinations for entry to post primary education although some post primary schools might set such examinations. There are no league tables. In Britain the newspapers publish with the aid of official data rankings of schools in order of their performance in 'A' level and GCSE examinations. In Ireland the teachers unions as well as the Department of Education and Science are opposed to such rankings (league tables). Some newspapers have tried to circumvent this prohibition. Yet, as far as one can make out, the relative performance of students in the two countries differs by very little. The case for a comparative study of the two systems in terms of relative achievement is profound. In both countries the universities exert enormous influence over the school system through their entrance requirements and the demands that they make on the content of school subjects and the subjects that are acceptable. They in turn are under pressure to broaden the basis of their entry and increase their numbers. Arguments that schools should be able to offer specialist programmes so that parents have choice and can choose the school that is apparently most suited to their child's potential have always to be conditioned by the social aim they have for their child. Many will have university in mind. In the case of engineering science it was in competition with physics since it had to demonstrate that students could do physics because the subject claimed to be equivalent to physics. There was fierce competition between engineering science and physics that the engineering educators eventually lost. It became an alternative as Physics B.[5]

The Structure of the National Curriculum
The national curriculum applies to pupils of compulsory school age in maintained schools, in grant-maintained and grant-maintained special schools. It is organised on the basis of four key stages which are broadly as follows.

	Pupils' ages	Year group
Key stage 1	5 - 7	1 - 2
Key stage 2	7 -11	3 - 6
Key Stage 3	11 - 14	7 - 9
Key Stage 4	14 – 18	10 -11

In England the following subjects are included in the national Curriculum at the key stages shown

Key stages 1 and 2-	English, mathematics, science, technology (design and technology and information technology), history, geography, art, music, and physical education.
Key stage 3.	As at Key Stages 1 and 2, plus a modern foreign language.
Key Stage 4.	English, mathematics, science, technology (design and technology, information technology) and a modern foreign language.

For each subject and for each key stage, programmes of study set out what pupils should be taught and attainment targets set out the expected standards of pupils' performance.

At the end of Key stages 1, 2, and 3, standards of pupils' performance are set out in 8 level descriptions of increasing difficulty, with an additional description above level 8 to help teachers differentiate exceptional performance.*

At Key Stage 4 public examinations (GCSE) are the main means of assessing attainment in the National Curriculum.

Exhibit 12.1 The General Requirements for the National Curriculum.(Adapted from *The National Curriculum*. Department for Education, London (1995)

Recently there have been complaints from universities, science departments in particular, that A level is no longer a preparation for first year study. It is this that the British Prime Minister had in mind when he criticised the questions set in 'A' level examinations.[6] In the past the universities were able to run three year degree programmes because the three or four A level subjects that students took were set at a standard equivalent to first year work in many universities world wide, the United States included. They are still required to run three year programmes in spite of a perceived fall in the standards of 'A' level. By contrast, in the case of the Irish Leaving Certificate and the Scottish Higher Certificate where the students take more subjects in their final school leaving examination than those taking A level, the Scottish universities and the University of Dublin required most students to undertake four year programmes. In the National University where there were three-year programmes the end of first year examinations acted as a selector to courses of much higher standards. The need for four-year programmes in Ireland was reinforced by the fact that in the past many students entered university at the age of seventeen.

The point to be made about the system in England is that the linkage between study at school and study at university meant that university beliefs about school education pervaded the school system and to some extent this meant the students had to make a career choice early on. A differentiation had to be made between the 'Arts' and the 'Sciences' at about 14 years of age in order to choose their 'A' level subjects. Since then this formula has broken down as the range of subject possibilities has widened. It is not without significance that the numbers of students applying to do science and engineering students has fallen considerably. The effect of universities using the 'A' and 'O' levels for matriculation instead of having to pass a separate matriculation examination is that the final school examinations are not true leaving certificates. This applies as much to the Irish and Scottish examinations as it does to the English.

When the link between content learnt at school and content to be learnt is weak there is a strong case for an examination like the Scholastic Aptitude Test (SAT) used in the United States to be used for admission. In the nineteen sixties the universities in England did experiment with a Test of Academic Aptitude (TAA) which could have performed that service. There is no tradition in the UK or Ireland of using high school grades in the selection process. The grades in the public examination take their place and high school predictions would be considered unreliable. Yet in the United States the ACT assessment (similar to the SAT) is a weaker predictor of undergraduate academic success than high school grades, academic skills and self confidence.[7] But, such an approach would free schools to offer different types of curriculum. The same applies in Ireland where a points system operates. Points are collected per subject and summed. The subjects (disciplines) in the universities for which there is most demand, ask for the highest points. Again, a separate entrance test would release schools from the need to offer a traditional curriculum and allow the Leaving Certificate to be an exit examination. In the UK a private foundation that investigates these problems has advocated an SAT type test for a number of years. At the present time government policy is to introduce diplomas one of purposes of which is to bridge the academic-vocational divide. It seems they may cause the eventual demise of the A level system.

The pressure of the universities is not it seems a purely Anglo-Irish problem for Eisner has argued that student concentration on learning to pass the Scholastic Aptitude Test (SAT) in the US harms their learning in schools.[8] But of more significance is the development by professional associations following the lead of the National Association of Teachers of Mathematics to develop Standards. Although Glatthorn and his colleagues say that standards are not a national curriculum apart from Iowa the States require standards to be declared for each subject.[9] Standards are in essence 'outcomes.'

Glatthorn and his colleagues listed the following points about standards.

- *Standards are an attempt to define what students should be able to know and do.*
- *The standards are informed by the latest theory and research regarding the various curricula.*
- *Standards are field based; they build on past successes of teachers and students.*
- *Standards are met through a variety of teaching styles and strategies.*
- *The standards project emphasizes that all students can learn and achieve at high levels if their background needs, and interest are considered.*
- *Standards should be a source of professional conversation and critique about what to do and how to do it.*
- *Teachers are members of a professional community, and a variety of professional organizations are available to support teacher growth.*
- *The literacy demands of the 21st century will require students to construct meaning with a variety of tools and texts.* [10]

Glatthorn and his colleagues quote Marzano who found that it would take 23 years of schooling to cover all the benchmarks. *"Teachers can't possibly teach it all… and kids couldn't possibly learn it all"*. That is the problem, it is objectives taken to an extreme. It is not clear that assessments and standards are always aligned. If they are not, the pupil's will follow the test. They quote Potter to the effect that *" as things are, state standards are developed without reference to college standards."* [11] Is that a good thing or a bad thing, given the previous remarks?

It is clear that combinations of written examinations (tests) and practical work can be designed to enhance learning and as argued in earlier chapters multiple strategy approaches are consistent with the needs of students as determined by research on student health.[12] While assessment (examination) designers should concentrate on selecting a few key domains for assessment they should not fill them up with large numbers of sub-objectives. That is the lesson of the work with history, mathematics and engineering science. Those descriptors should be ones that help the students learn the meaning of the skill represented by the domain. Moreover, cognitive skill development is likely to be of more value to the student in the pursuit of university education.

The major innovation in assessment during the last thirty or more years has been the development of the assessment led curricular at Alverno College in Milwaukee. It was an attempt to bring a *"fundamentally new approach to the age old task of liberal education"*[13] Their starting point was that *"if a student is required to develop abilities, she will need to know how well she is doing, all along the way as well as at end points."* [14]

The college began with the idea that working women, required as part of their liberal education a number of generic abilities. These are shown in exhibit 12.2. Once they had identified these abilities they asked the question: "How can we tell how far along a student is to developing these abilities? The answer to this question led them to assessment. In its turn that led them to a new approach to assessment quite unlike anything they had done before. Each subject was required to contribute to the students' development in the abilities as well as to teach the knowledge component of that subject. Since they are committed to assessment outside of the classroom an Assessment Center administers faculty designed assessments that are broader than single course ones. It is supported by full-time staff and several hundred trained volunteer assessors from the outside community, including industry and commerce. They provide "interpretative feedback' to the students throughout each year. At the same time the classroom teacher is considered to be the most important assessor of the student's development. *"If learning is to be **integrative/experiential**, assessment must judge **performance**. If learning is to be characterised by **self-awareness**, assessment must include **self-assessment** as well as **expected outcomes** and **developmental criteria** that are public. If learning is to be **active/interactive**, assessment must include **feedback** and elements of **externality** as well as **performance**. If learning is to be **developmental**, assessment must be **cumulative** and **expansive**. Finally, if learning is to be **transferable**, assessment must be **multiple in mode and context**"* [15]

By *integration* is meant the ability '*to continually create new wholes out of multiple parts*'. It would differ from *synthesis* in The Taxonomy of Educational Objectives in so far as *synthesis* is confined to a single subject. Integration brings knowledge from a variety of different perspectives. *Feedback* is considered to be important and provides the matter for reflection and growth. It is related to *externality* in that if the abilities are to be *transferable* some assessment must be made at a distance from the classroom. Hence the need for an assessment centre. Within this concept of *externality* they attach considerable importance to self-assessment. *Cumulative assessment* shows how the students progress or regress and student portfolios are used to plot this journey.

At the college all the students are required to develop skill in each of the domains. These were first called competencies but they changed the term to abilities to avoid comparison with teacher education competencies as listed in the 1970's which they perceived to be narrow and inhibitive of learning. Each subject area is required to support the development of these skills so that the student is assessed in both knowledge and ability (as defined here). Each of the abilities is divided into six levels along which the student has to develop (exhibit 12.3). Students are required to develop to level 4 in each of the abilities during their first two years (if in full-time study), and in their major studies in the years that follow to level 6. An important goal of this curriculum is that the students should be able to integrate these abilities when solving practical problems. This is because the solutions to life's problems are unlikely to depend on the application of a single ability. The college has conducted an extensive evaluation of its programme that suggests it has had considerable success in meeting these goals.[16] The programme is a major challenge to traditional notions of teaching. It serves the needs of work, society and the individual through a fundamental understanding of how students learn that is driven by assessment to achieve that learning. Taken as a framework for evaluation the assessment led curricular of public examinations and standards are found to be wanting.

Interdisciplinary and Integrated studies

The idea of interdisciplinarity has been around for a long time. In the first place the case for interdisciplinarity rests on the argument that most of life's problems require for their solution knowledge and skills from more than one subject. This need can be seen to be met in many projects that pupils' conduct within the framework of a science or technological subject. Interdisciplinary studies have also been seen as a means of grouping some subjects together to make a space in the curriculum for additional study, and at the same time contribute to solving the problem of the 'explosion' of knowledge. Integration implies the merging of subjects to the extent they lose their identity.

OPERATIONAL MODELS OF THE CURRICULUM AND OTHER ISSUES

Ability 1. Communication
The competent communicator habitually makes meaningful connections between herself and her audience, with well chosen words and with or without the aid of graphics, electronic media and computers.

Ability 2. Analysis
The competent analyzer is a clear thinker and a critical thinker. She fuses experience, reason and training into considered judgement.

Ability 3. Problem solving
The competent problem solver gets done what needs to be done. The ability overlaps with and uses all other abilities.

Ability 4. Valuing and decision making.
The responsible decision maker is reflective and empathic in approaching the value issues in her life. She habitually seeks to understand the moral dimensions of her decisions and accepts responsibility for the consequences of actions taken in all facets of her life. She understands and is sensitive to a variety of perspectives and experiences in making her own decisions.

Ability 5. Social interaction
The competent interactor knows how to get things done in committees, task forces, team projects and other group efforts. She elicits the view of others and helps reach conclusions.

Ability 6. Global perspectives.
The person who takes multiple perspectives articulates interconnections between and among diverse opinions, ideas and beliefs about global issues. She makes informed judgements and tests out her own position.

Ability 7. Effective citizenship.
The effective citizen develops informed choices and strategies for collaborative involvement in community issues.

Ability 8. Aesthetic response.
The aesthetically responsive person articulates an informed response to artistic works which is grounded in knowledge of multiple frameworks and exposure to a variety of artistic forms. She is able to make meaning out of aesthetic experiences and to articulate reasons for her choice of aesthetic expression.

Exhibit 12.2 Summary profiles of the eight Alverno abilities.

1. A long time ago the OECD found that *"by interdisciplinarity people understood very different and sometimes contradictory activities. In particular the degree of cooperation between the disciplines may have led to the supposition of total integration within a new and more complex discipline"*. The OECD provided the following definitions;

2. *Pluridisciplinarity is a grouping of various disciplines assumed to be more or less related, for example, Mathematics and Physics, or French, Latin and Greek, classical humanities etc.*

3. *Interdisciplinarity is a close interaction among two or more different disciplines. This interaction may range from simple communication of ideas to the mutual integration of organising concepts, methodology, procedures, epistemology, terminology, data and organization or research and education in a fairly large field.*

4. *Transdisciplinarity establishes a common system of axioms for a set of disciplines and we propose as an example anthropology considered as science of man and his accomplishments according to L'Enfant's definition.*[17]

Ability Domain 1. Develop communication ability (effectively) send and respond to communications for varied audiences and purposes.

Level 1- Identify own strengths and weaknesses as a communicator.
Level 2 -Show analytic approach to effective communicating.
Level 3- Communicate effectively.
Level 4- Communicate effectively making relationships out of explicit frameworks from at least 3 major areas of knowledge.
Level 5- Communicate effectively with application of communication theory.
Level 6- Communicate with habitual effectiveness and application of theory, through coordinated use of different media that represent contemporary technological advancement in communication field.

These to be developed in writing, speaking, listening, using media quantified data, and the computer.

Ability Domain 2. Develop analytical capabilities.

Level 1- Show observational skills.
Level 2- Draw reasonable inferences from observations.
Level 3- Perceive and make relationships.
Level 4- Analyze structure and organization.
Level 5- Establish ability to employ frameworks from area of concentration or support area discipline in order to analyze.
Level 6- Master ability to employ independently the frameworks from area of concentration or support area discipline in order to analyze.

Ability Domain 3. Develop workable problem solving skills.

Level 1- Identify the process, assumptions, and limitations involved in problem solving approaches.
Level 2- Recognize, analyze and state a problem to be solved.
Level 3- Apply a problem solving process to a problem.
Level 4- Compare processes and evaluate own approach in solving problems.
Level 5- Design and implement a process for resolving a problem which requires collaboration with others.
Level 6- Demonstrate facility in solving problems in a variety of situations.

Ability Domain 4. Develop facility in making value judgements and independent decisions.

Level 1- Identify own values.
Level 2- Infer and analyze values in artistic and humanistic works.
Level 3- Relate values to scientific and technological Developments
Level 4- Engage in valuing and decision making in multiple Contexts.
Level 5- Analyze and formulate the value foundation/framework of a specific area of knowledge, in its theory and practice.
Level 6- Apply own theory of value and the value foundation of an area of knowledge in a professional context.

Ability Domain 5. Developing facility for social interaction.

Level 1- Identify own interaction behaviours utilized in group problem solving situation.
level 2- Analyze behaviour of others within two theoretical frameworks.
Level 3- Evaluate behaviour of self within two theoretical frameworks.
Level 4- Demonstrate effective social interaction behaviour in a variety of situations and circumstances.
Level 5- Demonstrate effective interpersonal and intergroup behaviours in cross-cultural interactions.
Level 6- Facilitate interpersonal and inter group relationships in one's professional situation

Ability Domain 6. Developing responsibility for the environment.

Level 1- Perceive and describe the complex relationships within the environment.
Level 2- Observe and explain how the behaviour of individuals and groups has impacted on the environment.
Level 3- Observe and explain how the environment has an impact on the behaviour of individuals and groups.
Level 4- Respond holistically to environmental issues and evaluate the response of others.
Level 5- Identify a researchable environmental problem and independently develop responsible alternative solutions.
Level 6- Select and rigorously support a responsible solution to an environmental problem with an implementation strategy.

Continues over

Ability Domain 7. Develop awareness and understanding of the world in which the individual lives.	Ability Domain 8. Develop aesthetic responsiveness to the arts.
Level 1- Demonstrate awareness, perception and knowledge of observable event in the contemporary world Level 2- Analyze contemporary events in their historical context. Level 3- Analyze inter relationships of contemporary events and conditions. Level 4- Demonstrate understanding of the world as a global unit by analysis of the impact of events of one society upon another. Level 5- Demonstrate understanding of professional responsibility in the contemporary world. Level 6- Take personal position regarding implications of contemporary events.	Level 1- Express response to selected arts in terms of their formal elements and personal background. Level 2- Distinguish among artistic forms in terms of their elements and personal response to selected works of art. Level 3- Relate artistic works to the contexts from which they emerge. Level 4- Make and defend judgements about the quality of selected artistic expressions. Level 5- Choose and discuss artistic works which reflect personal vision of what it means to be human. Level 6 - Demonstrate the impact of the arts on your life to this point and project their role in personal future.

Exhibit 12.3. The Eight Alverno Ability Domains showing the six levels. The college continually reviews these abilities from time to time they are the subject to minor changes.

There are several subjects made up of a number of disparate subjects that may or may not be integrated. Education and management are such subjects. Projects undertaken in primary schools often explore a theme. They are interdisciplinary. Commonly schools undertake projects on such issues as the environment and poverty in the developing world. Project work is almost by definition interdisciplinary and when it is thematic, transdisciplinary

The OECD described thematic approaches as follows

- *A single complex problem*
- *Disciplines noteworthy for their viewpoint*
    (a) The variety of their viewpoints
    (b) The possibility that the fields involved overlap.
    (c) The fact that no single discipline covers the entire problem.
- *Different solutions all of which are necessarily complete depending on the view point of each discipline.*
- *A Synthesis*
- *A single solution.*[18]

Engineers may not like the idea of a single solution if it is unique. They might not even like the term 'optimum'. Such an approach has been characterised as transdisciplinary, as for example, when the behavioural sciences and humanities are brought together in a common framework as an introduction for engineering students to their role in industry and society.[19]

At school level in Ireland science is taught in the junior cycle. It combines elements of biology, chemistry and physics. The creation of linkages between them will in turn depend on the teacher who in turn will be influenced by the public examination in that subject.

In one course in the US the students among other things learn the relationship between climate, plant type, stream flow and aquatic habitat and establish how this knowledge might be applied to a greenbelt area.[20]

Models of this kind have been called "nested" because they take advantage of natural combinations as for example a study of systems. Fogarty's example is of a unit on photosynthesis which simultaneously targets consensus making (social skill), sequencing (thinking skill), and plant life cycle (science content).[21] The problem with nesting is that students could become confused and fail to grasp the principles of the disciplines involved. Among Fogarty's ten ways of integration is a "threaded curriculum". In such a curriculum a theme is pursued across disciplines. The development of multiple intelligences in a curriculum leads to a threaded curriculum. In such a curriculum thinking skills, social skills and study skills can be interwoven in different subjects.[22] This approach would appear to have many similarities with a thematic curriculum or a curriculum constructed around key concepts that span a number of disciplines. Fogarty's key concept example is "Prediction". Similarly the concepts that contribute to a key concept when mapped from what Fogarty calls a web. He gives the example of "conflict". The geography, history and social science curriculum developed at the University of Liverpool by Blyth and his colleagues is clearly an integrated course (see exhibit 6. 15). Fogarty also gives the example of invention. Its study can lead to the study of simple machines in science, and to reading and writing about inventors, to practical inventing by pupils in any part of curriculum.

Teachers who want to develop integrated studies have to learn to work in teams and need training not only to work in teams but in the principles of design of integrated curricula.

Problem and project based learning

Projects, case studies, clinical encounters, trouble shooting, small group work when student centred are all examples which require problem based solving and learning if they are not teacher directed. Our work with projects in engineering science and history comes within the category of problem based learning as does the guided design heuristic when it is problem based rather than teacher directed (see chapter 9). While the idea of problem based learning is not new, it came to prominence with the development of a complete undergraduate programme in medicine at McMaster University[23] based on problems. Now it is widely practised in medicine but not necessarily as a whole programme.[24]

A considerable amount of research has been done on problem based learning in medical education.[25] It is found that it can foster self-directed learning, increase retention of knowledge, and increase interest in clinical subject matter. It can help students develop inquiry skills. Some courses proceed from teacher centred to student centred learning over a fairly lengthy period of time. In this way students can overcome their fears of non-traditional approaches to learning and fear is considered to be a major impediment to student adaptation to problem based learning.[26] As has been said students can be resistant to change especially if they feel their examination results will suffer.

An important finding of the research and this is found with other changes in curriculum and instruction is that the outcomes of problem based learning are different to those obtained from traditional courses.

Problem based learning uses a variety of familiar techniques. It is the context that influences how they are handled. The design of instruction is just as complex for problem based learning, as it should be for traditional teaching, as previous chapters should have demonstrated. For example it has been shown that the experience of problem based learning in small groups may not be enhanced if the experience is too short. In one-day formats interventions may be inadequate, discussion unfocussed, and there may not be time for the group to cohere.[27] More generally several reports suggest that students are more motivated when working in problem based small groups. This is consistent with the findings of many of the graduate student teachers whose investigations were reported in earlier chapters.

It is important that students should evaluate their work in terms of the contribution that it makes to their conceptual framework. One of the objections to project based learning is that since it leads to study in depth in a particular area it may only lead to a limited contribution to the student's knowledge. Moreover because it motivates students they may spend more time on the project at the expense of the acquisition of knowledge. It may be objected that students are learning other skills that could not otherwise be learnt in traditional teaching. Unless a student attempts to incorporate that scaffold then the project will not have been as efficient as it might have been in terms of student learning.

At school level Savoie and Hughes[28] in the United States introduced a problem-based study within the normal programme of a course unit on "Tradition and Change". The theme was the "family". The problem in a classroom edition of the *Wall Street Journal* was about a family experiencing marital problems. It was chosen because it was directly related to the issues in the course and it addressed a social issue of contemporary importance. The teachers did not want it to be constructed as group counselling or therapy. The class was divided into seven groups from between two to four members. At the end of the first class period the students compiled a list of questions they would like to ask the married couple. They had to be justified in the next session. Then a three-step problem solving process was introduced in order to provide an instructional scaffold and help the students' separate facts from values. Subsequently a psychologist and a counsellor were invited to discuss their jobs. The students (9th graders) had to demonstrate their learning either by writing a letter to the married couple offering advice or individual students could role play a counsellor in a meeting with the couple. The pupils had to show what they had learned about the changing nature of family life.

Savoie and Hughes considered the approach to have been successful. They made the following points: first, very little time was allowed for the activity that was carried out in normal class time. Second, the teachers found the structure of the school day was inhibitive. A day of six or seven 45-minute sessions, which is common in many countries, is not conducive to in-depth discussion. This is true of many activities designed to develop high level cognitive skills but little attention is paid to this factor. School timetables seem to be sacrosanct. Finally it demanded great skill in asking questions and probing students responses.

One theoretical model that might help reorient thinking about the structure of the curriculum is due to Whitehead. The great British mathematician Albert North Whitehead who in later life became Professor of Philosophy at Harvard published in1932 a set of essays with the *title The Aims of Education.*[29] The first section of the book describes a rhythmic theory of mental growth. In relation to the curriculum the principles are:

Principle: That different subjects and modes of study should be undertaken by pupils at fitting times when they have reached the proper mental development.

Subsidiary. The principle of the necessary antecedence of subjects is only true if you give an artificial limitation to the subjects of study.

These in turn derive from the principle underlying the theory that is, that just as life is essentially periodic so there are *"subtler periods of mental growth"*. Whitehead considers that cycles of mental growth take place in three stages. These are Romance, Precision (or Grammar) and Generalisation that Whitehead says is Hegel's synthesis. *"Life is essentially periodic. There are also subtler periods of mental growth with their cyclic recurrences, yet always different as we pass from cycle to cycle, though each of the subordinate stages are reproduced in each cycle. That is why I have chosen rhythmic as meaning essentially the conveyance of difference within a framework of repetition"*.

The stages are

Stage 1. Romance. The stage of first apprehension (a stage of ferment). Education must essentially be a setting in order of a ferment already stirring in the mind: you cannot educate the mind in a vacuum. In our conception of education we tend to confine it to the second stage of the cycle namely to precision.

Stage 2. Precision. The stage of grammar. Width of relationship is subordinated to exactness of formulation.

Stage 3. Generalisation: Hegel's stage of synthesis. A return to romanticism with its added advantage of classified ideas and relevant technique.

All learning begins with romance for it is the interest and curiosity that drives learning forward. The subject matter is novel and holds within itself unexplored connections with possibilities half-disclosed by glimpses and half concealed by a wealth of material. In this stage knowledge is not dominated by systematic procedure. Whitehead concludes that such a system must be treated piecemeal. Teaching is like that and if each year brings a new class maybe that is how the romance of teaching is maintained, why many happily see out a lifetime of teaching.

We continually enter into cycles of romance and sometimes we pursue them through to generalization.. In this theory the subject disciplines belong to the stage of precision. We have to have a grammar and poorly designed interdiscplinary work will not provided the precision grammar that is required for future study. The stages of romance and generalisation clearly benefit from an integrated approach to knowledge even when it is on a limited scale as is evident from Whitehead's treatment of mathematics. Students who take subjects for the first time whether at school or university will find them difficult if they are not first introduced to the romance of the subject. These rhythmic cycles are a matter of every day experience and it is the speed with which the stages are passed in learning that differentiates the adult from the child as well as the adult's ability to be selective.

At the macroscopic level we may conceive of primary (elementary) education as being a stage primarily of romance accompanied by some precision which increases in the last year or so. Post-primary (high school) may be conceived as primarily a stage of precision during which the grammar of the subjects is learnt, and higher education as a continuation of precision with increasing generalisation. Today "area of knowledge" might be a better alternative to 'subject'.

At the microscopic level we can view any learning as moving through these three stages and can plan lessons accordingly.

The criticism of educational systems and those who govern their policy is that they become obsessed with precision. Accompanying this view they insist on the acquisition of large quantities of Whitehead called "*inert*" knowledge. Students do not reach the stage of generalisation and in consequence never receive a complete education. Immediate questions hang over the structure of the curriculum: They are neither, posed or answered.

In many systems modes of study that are likely to encourage curiosity are discouraged and those thought to encourage precision encouraged. There is a demand in late secondary education and higher education for the development of generic core and personal transferable skills yet traditional teaching methods are inimical to their acquisition. The methods used in primary (elementary) project and group work are more likely to foster their development and increasing use of them is to be found in higher education. Indeed some engineering educators have suggested that their colleagues should look at what goes on in primary education and take lessons from it.[30]

It is clear that in order to help children to be curious or should we say retain their curiosity that they are allowed to range across the subjects. Interdisciplinarity is then a formal structure and precision is elucidated in terms of fundamental concepts and principles. Accompanying such interdisciplinarity might be an emphasis on projects that allow children to create knowledge about a particular theme. The precision would lie in the evaluation of the project, and the attempt to draw from the children the concepts and principles learnt. And, then to show how they might be applied to other areas in practice (which is to give a whole new meaning to "application" in the Bloom *Taxonomy* since the high level skill of transfer is involved).

I am not advocating that a child's work should be based on projects. Far from it! There are places for traditional learning, and as was shown in an earlier chapter, many children value the structure it affords. Unfortunately, if there is too much grammar children may not only become demotivated but, come to believe that this is the only way to learn. Reflection on how we learn and develop is unlikely if our cycles depart radically from those suggested by Whitehead. As such his theory provides framework for curriculum design and the design of instruction.

Integrated skill curricula and the aims of education (education and work)

The Alverno College curriculum is one that integrates skills across the curriculum. Moreover the college argues that such a liberal arts education prepares students for both life and work. On the other side of the Atlantic it is clear that a major reason, if not the major reason supporting education, especially higher education is the economic well being of society. That a higher education for its own sake might also be for the good of the social well being of a nation is not considered. The result of this kind of thinking permeates through to school education. Governments listen to industrialists and very often their views take precedence over the view offered by those in the education system at all levels. Thus in respect of jobs done by school leavers it is a regular complaint of industrialists that school leavers are neither sufficiently numerate, or literate. But exactly what this means in terms of content and skill is entirely unclear. It is clear that many students fail mathematics (or do not do sufficiently well). It is also clear that there are relatively high levels of illiteracy. But it is not clear what employers would do with everyone if they were all highly literate and numerate. Evidence from England suggests that employers have varying levels of commitment to training and providing career paths for the school leavers. Firms undoubtedly cherry pick the best students. Employers' immediate interests dominate how they use school leavers and those from government and training schemes. This places huge responsibilities on the education system for its fundamental purpose, and from this there can be no escape, is to prepare its pupils for life and that implies the socio-economic system not the economic system alone.

Pragmatic decision-making has overridden debates about purpose and in consequence traditions within a culture persist. One of these traditions is the belief that only some persons have an aptitude for the academic therefore the others must have an aptitude for the practical or the vocational. Simon Jenkins a former editor of *The Times* and formidable critic of developments in education in the 1990's, (i.e., the national curriculum) wrote that *"the greatest irony was that a curriculum justified on economic and vocational grounds should turn out so traditional and unvocational in content."*[31]

It seems unequivocally clear that most people will require some degree of IT literacy and that for this they will require to have a basic literacy. It is not clear what kind of numeracy they will require to support their use of IT or dealings in life. On the one hand it is possible to argue "not much", but on the other hand it is equally possible that they need to have a much better understanding of "risk" than is apparent in society at the present time. It is not the purpose of this section to pursue these arguments. It is to utter a word of caution about employer comments on what is required apart from an ability to be adaptable and flexible in the light of current employment conditions. It is also to argue that employers may not know how to employ a well-educated work force effectively. This view applies as much to employer views about higher education as it does to school education. One interesting feature of complaints by employers on both sides of the Atlantic is that they are concerned with the failure of educational institutions to produce graduates who have high level of interpersonal skill. The results of one US survey suggested that they were *"indicative of mounting evidence that employers, especially those that are joining or that have joined the quality revolution, are desperate for people who do not have to learn on the job how to fit into a team-centred culture where, communication, interpersonal skills, and professionalism, are as important as technical skills."*[32]

During the same period employers persuaded the British government that this was the case for all graduates irrespective of subject. One novel investigation also supported that view. 10,000 job advertisements for graduates in the British quality newspapers were analysed for the skills sought. 59% contained explicit reference to the personal skills required for performance in the job. Of the remainder, a further 15% could be inferred to require such characteristics. Of the 32 significant characteristics that were isolated 20 were considered to be genuine transferable skills. They collated into the four generic categories of communication; teamwork; problem solving (creativity); and management and organizing and numerous sub-skills.[33] The unit at Sheffield University that supported this investigation also showed how through active learning strategies within the subjects that students were learning they could develop what came to be known as personal transferable skills.

The effect of this kind of information (and pressure from industrialists) on the British Government was that through the Department of Employment a five year project was established, to develop the skills of what was called *enterprise learn-*

ing across the university curriculum. The majority of universities participated in the initiative. The Committee that advised this Enterprise in Higher Education initiative listed the areas that every student should experience. These are shown in exhibit 12.4. The Department believed that these could be developed, that is integrated, within subjects. They thought that there was no need for bolt on subjects but the author of one of their reports challenged this view on the grounds that understanding human and organizational behaviour required a theoretical framework on which to judge experience. The same author argued strongly that the areas of experience listed in exhibit 12. 4 reflect a need for a broadly based liberal education. Some quite profound developments were encouraged by this initiative such as the complete reorganisation of the philosophy programme at the University of Leeds. But it was an initiative that was not sustained. It proposed radical changes the implications of which were not thought through.

The same thing happened to an earlier Employment Department initiative in schools, The Technical Vocational Initiative (TVEI) which was very much concerned with the development of skills highlighted in the model. This same idea of integration through the type of teaching offered was inherent in the TVEI programme. TVEI was concerned with *"developing active teaching and learning strategies designed to complement existing practice in schools and colleges. Thus, in addition to promoting technology, business studies and personal and social education and so forth. TVEI has become synonymous with equal opportunities, mixed ability, profiling, guidance counselling, accreditation, improved school/college collaboration, modular development, staff development and a host of other activities."* [34]

Cognitive knowledge and skills
(1) **Knowledge**:- Key concepts of enterprise learning (accounting, economics, organisational behaviour, inter and intra-personal behaviour.
(2) **Skills**:-The ability to handle information, evaluate evidence, think critically, think systemically (in terms of systems), solve problems, argue rationally, and think creatively.

Social Skills, as for example the ability to communicate, and to work with others in a variety of roles both as leader and team member.

Managing one's self, as for example, to be able to take initiative, to act independently, to take reasoned risks, to want to achieve, to be willing to change, to be able to adapt, to be able to know one's self and one's values, and to be able to assess one's actions.

Learning to learn. To understand how one learns and solves problems in different contexts and to be able to apply the styles learnt appropriately in the solution of problems.

Exhibit 12.4 The four broad areas of learning together with the elements they comprise that are important for equipping students for their working lives, as defined by the REAL working group of the Employment Department.[35]

The irony of TVEI was that because it did not have the status of an examined subject(s) it remained a distinct stream for average and low achieving students. If the criticisms of industrialists are to be believed then high achieving students would have benefited from the acquisition of the personal transferable skills that was part of its aim. In any event it was child of the Employment Department and not the Department of Education and it was doomed to fail when the latter brought in the national curriculum.

The story is a little different in Ireland where in the middle 1970's a few schools were selected to pilot the Transition year (TYO) that has already been discussed in chapter 11. One of the aims of this TYO was to give students a break from the cycle of examinations. Thus at 15 after Intermediate Certificate (now Junior Certificate) the students would pursue a year in which there would be only limited traditional study. Otherwise it would be devoted to a range of activities like community service, work experience and studies that would be useful to students throughout their lives. Once the year was completed they would pursue a two-year programme for the Leaving Certificate Examination. The control of the programme and thus the design of the curriculum is for the most part, in the hands of the school with a minimum of central direction and control. The broad requirements were shown in exhibit 11.1. Not every student was selected for the programme and among high achieving pupils and their parents it got the name of a 'doss year'. However, over a thirty-year period it has with curriculum support from Education Centres, particularly in the 1990's, gained a substantial reputation and research has suggested that those who do the Transition Year are likely to gain more points than those who do not. It is an excellent example of school based curriculum development (and subsidiarity) but as other research shows had the teachers been trained to design, implement and evaluate curricula it might have been even better than it is now.[36] This is supported by a study in which teachers were trained to design and evaluate courses in management studies and learning how to learn.[37]

When it began it was a firm intention that it should not be assessed some like the present author argued that is should be for social as well as educational reasons. The social reason was that without assessment it would not have status. So now it is being assessed and a variety of measures including portfolios are being used.[38] There is a group of students who stay in secondary education beyond the Junior Certificate for whom studies for the Leaving Certificate examination are not appropriate. A Leaving Certificate Applied (LCA) has been developed for them. It has many of the features of TVEI and unusually for Ireland it is primarily coursework assessed. A Leaving Certificate for Vocational Practice (LCVP) has also been developed.

One lesson of the TYO is that innovations of this kind take a long time to become embedded. They belong to level 2 change and require a different approach to development if they are to be sustained.[39] The TYO achieved what the TVEI did not which in the words of Gleeson was to engage with the school and the teaching profession in a meaningful reform.[40] In respect of TVEI there was as Jamieson in the UK pointed out no curriculum framework for handling work.[41] Just such a framework has been provided by the US Department of Labor and it is based on the integration of skills across the curriculum. It has many similarities with the Alverno Curriculum. It is the work of the SCANS Commission.[42]

The Commission's starting position was that, " *the time when a high school diploma was a sure ticket to a job is within the memory of workers who have not yet retired: yet in many places today a high school diploma is little more than a certificate of attendance. As a result, employees discount the value of all diplomas, and many students do not work hard in school*".

When it wrote this the Commission had already discovered to its satisfaction what skills and competencies were associated with high wage jobs. These are shown in exhibit 12.5. They argued that all Americans should be entitled to multiple opportunities to learn the SCANS know-how well enough to earn a decent living. They argued that every employer in America should create its own strategic vision around the principles of the high performance work place. They believed that this task would require *"the reinvention of elementary and secondary education"*. The Commission believed that the competencies should be integrated into core subjects such as English and Mathematics, which theoretically, leaves the integrity of the individual disciplines in tact. The example of how the commission thought this might happen is shown in exhibit 12.6. It differed from the TVEI project in that it was aimed at the core curriculum whereas the TVEI was run in parallel with academic curriculum. The SCANS commission wanted the competencies to be integrated into the national standards and assessments then being developed.

Christiano and Ramirez argued that there was a need to improve the match between what industry expects and what students are taught. *"This means that the "how" of education can be just as important as the "what". The SCANS classroom, developed in Fort Worth public schools, is one possible way to change the "how" of education [...].In the SCANS classroom, there is often more than one viable solution to problems, and students work with peers and teachers to negotiate classroom activities and solve problems. Students often assess themselves (self-calibration of goals) in addition to external review and lessons are interdisciplinary in nature. Listening and speaking are fundamental to the learning process."*[43] Christiano and Ramirez cited a document from Fort Worth Public schools that compared the conventional classroom from the SCANS classroom. This is shown in exhibit 12. 7.[44]

The American College Testing Program (ACT) developed a test for assessing the competencies identified by SCANS. It is a test that is intimately related to the curriculum and not independent of it. It offers work place assessments in reading for information; applied mathematics; listening and writing; teamwork; locating information; applied technology; motivation; observing; and speaking and learning. The assessments are offered at five levels and are criterion referenced. The idea is that jobs should be profiled. In this way the job profile can be compared with the individual's performance profile so that it may be used for selection and diagnosis at work. High schools can use job profiling in consultation with employers to establish the levels of competency that students should have in order for them to obtain jobs.

Individuals are provided with portfolios. The information provided may include self-assessments of the examinee's perspective of work place skill attainment, instructor-guided information including grades, project results, training evaluations, or curriculum embedded activity. It may also include outside examiner data as for example the work keys scores and other pertinent test information. The work keys assessment tests are each of one hour's duration. The results that are sent to the candidate explain the scores obtained and give quite detailed instructions on how that individual might improve his/her scores. The adoption of a SCANS like curriculum in schools would have implications for the design of third level curricula both in terms of content and instruction. However, like the TVEI initiative that was sponsored by the Employment Department in the UK the SCANS programme recommended by its American equivalent (Department of Labor) has had little impact on the school system. Nevertheless it is an important curriculum model and many teachers practice in the way the classroom model suggests.

Work place Competencies	Effective workers can productively use
1. Resources	They know how to allocate time, money, materials, space and staff.
2. Interpersonal skills.	They can work in teams, teach others, serve customers, lead, negotiate and work well with people from culturally diverse backgrounds.
3. Information	They can acquire and evaluate data, organize and maintain files, interpret and communicate, and use computers to process information.
4. Systems	They understand social, organizational, and technological systems; they can monitor and correct performance, and they can design or improve systems.
5. Technology.	They can select equipment and tools, apply technology to specific tasks and maintain and troubleshoot equipment.
Foundation Skills	**Competent workers in a high performance workplace need**
1 Basic skills	Reading, writing, arithmetic and mathematics, speaking and listening.
2. Thinking skills	The ability to learn, to reason, to think creatively, to make decisions, and to solve problems
3. Personal qualities	Individual responsibility, self-esteem and self-management, sociability and integrity.

Exhibit 12.5. The SCANS Competencies

In the early 1990's there were also ideas in the US for academies. These were schools within schools that were occupationally focussed. *"Typically, four teachers collaborate: one in math, one in English, one in science, and one in the vocational subject that is the core of the academy (e.g., electronics, computers, health, business, finance). The students take all four subjects from these teachers who remain with them for two years."* They take other subjects in the 'regular' high school. There were other schools that emphasised preparation for clusters of occupations. One school integrated specific academic subjects with vocational coursework. *"For example the English sequence emphasises com-*

munications skills necessary for the workplace; maths course incorporates technical math; the science sequence includes principles of technology, an applied physics course, as well as more conventional courses; the social studies curriculum stresses the historical influences of work and technological advances, as well as ability skills".[45] In these schools teachers are attached to career paths and academic departments. It is argued that these approaches bring coherence to the curriculum.[46] It would seem that there are many similarities with the City Colleges of Technology that were developed in England during the 1980's. These are schools for children from the age of eleven with a strong vocational interest. They received substantial funding from industry. The SCANS commission believed that the competencies could be achieved through each of the subjects of the normal curriculum. It is this model that makes it unique and it is one that those who wish to preserve a curriculum and resist additions to it favour. The same arguments have been used to resist arguments for the inclusion of such subjects as industrial studies or sociology and psychology, and the study of man in the curriculum. The weakness of the SCANS curriculum is that it pays little attention to the domains of the practical (art, craft, music) but that is easily remedied.

Independent testing

Teachers in the British Isles are not used to testing the curriculum with standardised tests that are in a sense independent of the curriculum. The American College Testing Program (ACT) had experience of developing a group of tests called the "College Outcome Measures Program[47] (COMP)." The idea was to help institutions evaluate the relevance and usefulness of their general education programs. It is of interest as it is of relevance to the last two years of schooling, and in Ireland to study that is undertaken for the Post-Leaving Certificate. It is inevitable that the outcomes selected by the test agency shown in exhibits 12. 9. and 12. 10 will influence teaching and therefore the taught curriculum.

Two kinds of assessment are used. The comprehensive measures comprise an objective test and an activity inventory. The former has as its goal the estimation of a group's ability to apply general education skills and knowledge to problems and issues commonly confronted by adults: the latter assesses the quality and quantity of involvement in key out-of-class activities in the six key outcome areas. It is a self-report inventory in multiple choice format: it may be completed at home or in groups. ACT believes that it can help determine if a non-traditional student could earn their credits through portfolio assessment.

The other measures are called authentic. There are four all of which may administered individually or to groups. They are the composite examination, assessment of reasoning and communication, speaking assessment and writing assessment. The composite examination questions are based on television documentaries, recent magazine articles, ads, short stories, art prints, music, discussions and newscasts that are presented in a variety of formats. The responses range through short and long answers to audio-taped oral responses and what ACT regarded as innovative multiple choice questions. (The Southern Regional Examinations Board in England used a specially designed newspaper [real articles] to examine General Studies in the 1970's) in the Certificate of Secondary Education.

A recent development in programme assessment in the United States is the Collegiate Learning Assessment (CLA) Project. This has been developed by the Council for Aid to Education and the Rand Corporation. Its purpose is to assess an institution's contribution to student learning. The tests are designed to elicit written responses to the analysis of complex material. They are set to samples of freshmen during the Fall and Seniors in the Spring. Two kinds of instrument are used in the testing of critical thinking, analytic reasoning and written communication. They are performance tasks in which students must complete a "real life" activity such as preparing a memo or a policy recommendation and writing prompts that evaluate students' ability to articulate complex ideas.[48]

ACT research found that scores on the COMP tests correlated strongly with instruments such as indicators of effective functioning as a job supervisor and socio-economic status of job function. Their results suggested that the COMP tests are valid in so far as they are representative of potential performance in adult functions. Another finding of some interest was that persistence in college was related to perceived relevance and practical skill building within the structure of the education programme.[49]

Altogether it might be argued that an appropriately designed general education (balanced curriculum) will provide the basic skills necessary for work and life and hopefully dissolve the academic versus practical (vocational) debate.

Competency	English/Writing	Mathematics	Science	Social studies/Geography
Resources	Write a proposal for an after-school career lecture series that schedules speakers, coordinates audio-visual aids, and estimates costs.	Develop a monthly family budget, taking into account family expenses and revenues using information from the budget plan. Schedule a vacation trip that stays within the resources available.	Plan the material and time requirements for a chemistry experiment to be performed over a two-day period that demonstrates a natural growth process in terms of resource needs.	Design a chart of resource needs for a community of African Zulus. Analyze why three major cities grew to their current size.
Interpersonal	Discuss the pros and cons of the argument that Shakespeare's *Merchant of Venice* is a 'racist' play and should be banned from the school curriculum.	Present the results of a survey to the class, and justify the use of specific statistics to analyze and represent the data.	Work in a group to design an experiment to analyze content in the schools water. Teach the results to an elementary class.	Debate the issue of withdrawing US military support from Japan in front of a peer panel. Engage in a mock urban planning exercise for Paris.
Information	Identify and abstract passages from a novel to support an assertion about the values of a key character.	Design and carry out a survey and analyze the data in a spread sheet using algebraic formulas. Develop a table and a graphic display to communicate results.	In an entrepreneurship project present statistical data pertaining to a high tech company's production and sales. Use a computer to develop statistical charts.	Using numerical data and charts, develop and present conclusions about the effects of economic conditions on the quality of life in several countries.
Systems	Develop a computer model that analyzes the motivation of Shakespeare's *Hamlet*. Plot the events that increase or decrease Hamlet's motivation to avenge the death of his father.	Develop a system to monitor and correct the heating/cooling process in a computer laboratory using principles of statistical process control.	Build a model of human population growth that includes the impact of the amount of food available, on birth and death rates etc. Do the same for a growth model for insects.	Analyze the accumulation of capital in industrialized nations in systems terms (as a reinforcing process with stocks and flows).
Technology	Write an article showing the relationship between technology and the environment. Use word processing to write and edit papers after receiving teacher feedback.	Read manuals for several data-processing programs and write a memo recommending the best programs to handle a series of mathematical situations.	Calibrate a scale to weight accurate proportions of chemicals for an experiment. Trace the development of this technology from earliest uses to today.	Research and report on the development and functions of the seismography and its role in earthquake prediction and detection.

Exhibit 12.6 The SCANS Competencies integrated into the curriculum as illustrated in the report.

From the Conventional Classroom	The SCANS Classroom
Teacher knows answer	More than one solution may be viable and teacher may not have it in advance.
Students routinely work alone	Students routinely work with teachers, peers, and community members
Teacher plans all activities	Students and teachers plan and negotiate activities
Teacher makes all assessments. Information is organized, evaluated, interpreted and communicated to students by teacher	Students routinely assess themselves. Information is acquired, evaluated, organized, interpreted, and communicated by students to appropriate audiences.
Organizing system of the classroom is simple, one teacher teaches 30 students.	Organizing systems are complex: teacher and students both reach out beyond school for additional information.
Reading, writing and math are treated as separate disciplines; listening and speaking often are missing from the curriculum.	Disciplines needed for problem solving are integrated; listening and speaking are fundamental parts of learning.
Thinking is usually "theoretical" and "academic"	Thinking involves problem solving, reasoning and decision making.
Students are expected to conform to teacher's behavioral expectations; integrity and honesty are monitored by teacher; students' self-esteem is often poor.	Students are expected to be responsible, sociable, self-managing, and resourceful; integrity and honesty are monitored within the social context of the classroom; students' self-esteem is high because they are in charge of own leaving.

Exhibit 12.7 The Conventional Classroom compared with the SCANS Classroom Cited by Christiano and Ramirez4[40] from Fort Worth Public Schools

---

Social activities and institutions: government, *economic system, religion, marriage, family, job, civic organization, politics, recreation, home management, child care education.*

Scientific and technological Activities and Products. *Transportation, housing, energy, processed food, clothing, health maintenance, national defence, communication, data processing, farming, household appliances.*

Artistic activities and products. *Reading, writing, speaking, listening, observing, using media, using body gestures, using graphs, using numbers.*

Problem solving activities. *Analyzing scientific, social, or personal problems, implementing solutions, selecting or creating solutions to problems, implementing solutions to problems, evaluating the way problems are solved.*

Value clarifying activities. *Identifying one's own values, identifying values of other people, learning how values develop and change, analyzing the implications of decisions.*

Exhibit 12.8 Categories of critical issues and activities included in the six COMP outcome areas.

Process Areas	Content Areas
Communicating Ability to send and receive information - In a variety of modes: written, graphic, oral, numeric, Symbolic. - In a variety of settings one-to-one, small group, large group. - for a variety of purposes: to inform, to understand, to persuade, to analyze.	**Functioning within social institutions** - Ability to identify activities and institutions that constitute the social aspects of a culture. - Ability to understand the impact that social institutions have on individuals in a culture. - Ability to analyze one's own and other's personal functioning within social institutions.
Solving problems - Ability to analyze a variety of problems scientific, social, personal. - Ability to select or create solutions to problems. - Ability to implement solutions.	**Using science and technology.** - Ability to identify activities and products - that constitute the scientific and technological aspects of culture. - Ability to understand the impact of scientific and technological activities and products on individuals and the physical environment in a culture. - Ability to analyze the uses of technological products in a culture, including one's personal use of such products.
Clarifying values - Ability to identify one's personal values and the personal values of other individuals. - Ability to understand how personal values develop. - Ability to analyze the implications of decisions made on the basis of personally held values.	**Using the arts** - Ability to identify activities and products that constitute the artistic aspects of culture. - Ability to understand the impact that art, in its various forms, has on individuals in a culture. - Ability to analyze the uses of works of art within a culture and one's personal use of art.

Exhibit 12.9 The COMP outcome areas

Notes and references

[1] Sternberg, R. S (1985). *Beyond IQ. A Triarchic Theory of Intelligence.* Cambridge University Press, Cambridge.
[2] Carter, G., Heywood, J., and D. T. Kelly (1986).*A Case Study in Curriculum Assessment. GCE Engineering Science A Level.* Roundthorn, Manchester.
[3] Heywood, J., McGuiness, S., and D. E. Murphy (1980). *The Final Report of the Public Examinations Evaluation Project.* School of Education, University of Dublin, Dublin
[4] Pellegrino, J. W. et al (2001) *Knowing What Students Know. The Science and Design of Educational Assessment.* National Research Council, National Academy Press, Washington, DC
[5] *ibid*. p254 illustrates one of the physics syllabuses.
[6] Report in *The Times* Dec 1 2006. P 13.
[7] Lotkowski, V Robbins, S and R. Noeth (2004). *The Role of Academic and Non-Academic Factors in Improving College Retention.* ACT Policy Report, ACT, Iowa.
[8] Eisner, E (1979). *The Educational Imagination. On the Design and Evaluation of School Programs.* Collier Macmillan, New York
[9] Glatthorn, A. A. Boschee, F., and B. M. Whitehead (2006) *Curriculum Leadership. Development and Implementation.* Sage, Thousand Oaks, CA. Pp 8 and 57 – 58. Cite Jones, R (2000) Making standards work: Researchers report effective strategies for implementing standards. *American School Board Journal.* 187, (9), 27 –31.
[10] *ibid* p 8.Wilhelm, J. D. (1996). *Standards in Practice, Grades 6 – 87.* National Council of Teachers of English, Urbana, Il is cited in support of the last statement

[11] Potter, W (2003, May 2). Report seeks to align state standards of high schools and colleges *Chronicle of Higher Education* 49, (34), A31

[12] Ryle, A (1969*). Student Casualties*. Allen, Lane, London. See also Heywood, J (2000) *Assessment in Higher Education, Student Learning, Teaching Programmes and Institutions*. Jessica Kingsley, London.

[13] Alverno College. *Student Assessment as Learning at Alverno College*. Alverno College, Milwaukee, WI

[14] *ibid*

[15] *ibid*

[16] Mentkowski, M and associates (2000). *Learning that Lasts*. Jossey Bass, San Fransisco.

[17] Berger, G (1975). *Interdisciplinarity*. Report of a European Symposium. Society for Research into Higher Education, London. The example given is of an Institute for Sociology and Politics of Work to establish a single theory of work at the conceptual level and to bring together as much sociological, economic, psychological information as possible at the data level.

[18] *ibid*

[19] Heywood, J (1973) American and English influences on the development of a transdisciplinary course on the technologist and society. *Proceedings of the Educational Research and Methods Division*. American Society of Engineering Education, Annual conference.

[20] Crane, S (1991). Integrated science in a restructured high school. *Educational Leadership* 49, (1), 39 – 46.

[21] Fogarty, R (1993) Ten Ways to Integrate curriculum in R. Fogarty (ed) *Integrating the Curricula. A Collection*. IRI/Skylight Publishing, Palatine, Il

[22] Fogarty, R. (1991) *Educational Leadership*, 49, (2), 61 –65.

[23] Barrows, H and R. Tamblyn (1980). *Problem Based Learning: An Approach to Medical Education*. Springer, New York

[24] Gijselaers, W. G. and H. G. Schmidt (1990) Development and evaluation of a causal model of problem based learning in Z. M. Noonam et al (eds). *Innovation in Medical Education. An Evaluation of its Present Status*. Springer, New York.

[25] Norman, G. R. and H. G. Schmidt (1992). The psychological basis of problem based learning: a review of evidence. *Academic Medicine*, 67, 557 – 565. See also Nooman, Z. M, Schmidt, H. G and E. S. Ezzat (eds). *Innovation in Medical Education*. Springer, New York.

[26] McKenzie, L (1985). Teaching clinical reasoning in Orthoptics: students using problem based learning in J. Higgs and M. Jones (eds) *Clinical Reasoning in the Health Profession*. Butterworth/Heinemann, Oxford. See also Woods, D. R (1994) *Problem Based Learning. How to get the most from Problem Based Learning*. McMaster University Bookstore, Hamilton, Ontario.

[27] Davis, D., Lindsay, E and P. Maxmanian (1994) the effectiveness of CME interventions in D. A. Davis and R. D. Fox(eds). *The Physician as Learner. Linking Research to Practice*. American Medical Association, Chicago, Il.

[28] Savoie, J. M. and A. S. Hughes (1994). Problem based learning as classroom solution. *Educational Leadership*. 52, (3), 54 –57.

[29] Whitehead, A. N. (1932) *The Aims Of Education and other Essays*. Benn, London

[30] Crynes, B and D. A. Crynes (1997). They already do it. Common practices in primary education that engineering education should use. *Proceedings Frontiers in Education Conference*, 3, 12 – 19. IEEE, New York.

[31] Jenkins, S (1995) *Accountable to None. The Tory Nationalization of Britain*. Hamish Hamilton, London.

[32] Evans, D. L et al (1993)Attributes of engineering graduates and their impact on curriculum design. *Journal of Engineering Education*, 82, (4), 203 –211.

[33] Green, S (1990) *Analysis of Personal Transferable Skills of Employees in Graduate Recruitment Advertisements in June 1989*. Sheffield Personal Skills Unit, University of Sheffield, Sheffield UK

[34] Gleeson, D (1989). *The Paradox of Training. Making Progress out of Crisis*. Open University Press, Milton Keynes

[35] Heywood, J (1994). *Enterprise Learning and its Assessment in Higher Education*. Technical report No 20. Learning Methods Branch, Employment Department, Sheffield.

[36] Heywood, J and M. Murray (2005). Curriculum-Led Staff Development: Towards Curriculum and Instructional Leadership in Ireland. *Bulletins of the European Foundation on Educational Administration* No 4 pp 3 to 97 ISBN 1 84357 121 4. This text includes a summary of research

completed on the TYO mostly in theses.

[37] *ibid*.

[38] Clarke, A-M. R., (2005). *An Evaluation of Portfolio Asssessment in Transition Year*. MSt Thesis. Education Department, University of Dublin, Dublin. See also Department of Education and Science (1994) *Transition Year Programmes. Guidelines 1995 –1995*. Department of Education and Science, Dublin

[39] See Marzano, R. J., Waters, T and B. A. McNulty (2005). *School Leadership that Works. From Research to Results*. Association for Supervision and Curriculum Development, Alexandria, VA

[40] Gleeson, D and M. McLean (1994). Whatever happened to TVEI? TVEI, Curriculum and Schooling. *Journal of Education Policy*, 9, (3), 223 – 244.

[41] Jamieson, I (1993). TVEI and the work related curriculum. *Evaluation and Research in Education*. 7, (2), 52 – 64.

[42] SCANS (1992). *Learning a Living: A Blueprint for High Performance*. US Department of Labor: Washington, DC.

[43] Christiano, S. J. E and M. Ramirez (1993). Creativity in the classroom: special concerns and insights. *Proceedings Frontiers in Education Conference*, 209 – 212. IEEE, New York

[44] see also Wright, A. T. (1993). Engineering education starts early. *Proceeding Frontiers in Education Conference*,(IEEE) 523 – 527

[45] Grubb, W. N (1992). Giving high schools an occupational focus. *Educational Leadership*, 49, (6), 36 – 43.

[46] Stasz, C., McArthur, D., Lewis, M. and K. Ramsey (1990) *Teaching and Learning Generic Skills for the Work Place*. The RAND Corporation and National Center for Research in Vocational Education. Report R-4004-NCRVE/UCB

[47] ACT (1992) COMP Technical report 1976 – 81. *Defining and Measuring General Education*. And, ACT (1992) Comp Technical Report 1982- 1991. *Clarifying and Assessing General Education*. American College Testing Program, Iowa.

[48] Council for Aid to Education. www.cae.org/default.asp. 20:03:2007.

[49] Forrest, A (1985). Creating conditions for student and institutional success in L. Noel and D. Saluri (eds*) Increasing Student Retention*.. Jossey Bass, San Fransisco. For a recent review of ACT assessment generally see Lotkowski, V Robbins, S and R. Noeth (2004). *The Role of Academic and Non-Academic Factors in Improving College Retention*. ACT Policy Report, ACT, Iowa. Notes ACT assessment is a weaker predictor of academic success than high school grades, academic skills and self-confidence.

13
Toward Intelligent Behaviour, Human Growth, and Moral Development

Summary

The aims of education too which most of us acquiesce are often so vague and ambiguous that they have no consequence for what we do. Many teachers have an emotional commitment to educating for the "whole person" or for "life" but a balanced curriculum is not provided that would provide such an education. That is a curriculum that has breadth and pays as much attention to development in the affective domain (inter and intra personal skills) as it does to higher order thinking in the cognitive domain.

We frequently use such phrases when administrators and politicians suggest that business should become more involved in education and contribute their views on the curriculum. Business is seen as being narrow whereas education is seen as giving a preparation for life. Put this to the test and question how exactly persons are prepared for life by the subjects of the traditional curriculum and it will be found that answers are difficult to come by. In determining what we do very little connection exists between the aims, the syllabuses we invoke and the learning strategies we demand. It can hardly be said that the curriculum helps to develop intelligent behaviour or equips students with a philosophical disposition that will help them tackle the moral issues that impinge on many of life's problems.

If there is then the "transfer" potential to "real life" of what is taught and how it is learnt it is hidden. The most hidden aspect of the curriculum from the students, is any instruction on learning or human development. At a more immediate level is the fact that many university students have not reached a level of cognitive development that helps them cope with the abstractions of much university study. While university teachers may complain about this they have some responsibility in that they have more power than most to cause change in the school curriculum.. But they show little or no interest in the problem. The argument to be presented is that the better preparation of students for university should also be a better preparation for life. The curriculum has to help students to grow. To achieve this goal requires an understanding of reasoning (higher order thinking), human development and how the developmental stage persons are at can be influenced by the instruction they receive. It is considered that critical or reflective thinking is a fundamental skill required for handling life's situations and how this might be developed is the purpose of much of this chapter.

But the curriculum also has to serve the end of adaptability for throughout life, and increasingly so, a person has to adapt, select, and shape real-world environments relevant to one's life. And those actions have to be purposive. They depend on practical and reflective intelligence and a significant question is whether or not such intelligence can be taught. The chapter begins with a discussion of the balanced-curriculum and how it relates to these intelligences and social and emotional intelligence.

Two theories of development that have been used to describe the process of higher education are discussed. They focus on the role of higher order thinking and the development of reflective judgement. Their relevance to schooling and the design of curriculum and instruction is considered and the idea of philosophy for children considered. Development takes place throughout life and as such primary education cannot be divorced from post primary education and vice versa.

This section is followed by a brief discussion of religious and moral development.

The chapter concludes with the view that success with curriculum and instructional projects in school provides examples of the strategies that can be used in whole school improvement. The role of curriculum and instructional leaders is self-evident.

Toward a balanced curriculum

The last chapter ended with the view that an appropriately designed general education will provide the basic skills and knowledge necessary for work and life. It expressed the hope that this would dissolve the academic versus practical debate that is endemic in the British Isles and other countries and a cause of the lack of status that practical subjects have. To put it in another way a balanced education is not a liberal education unless it embraces the practical. By practical is meant the range of subjects from crafts to technology in which there is a substantial input from science. At the same time the reader could be forgiven for understanding that this view was based on a rather narrow view of liberal education that was dependent on breadth of content rather than anything else. Nevertheless there is support from the Alverno College studies for the view that breadth can prepare students for " *and orient them toward engaging in and learning from a wide range of civic, personal, social and intellectual activities and that these were the cause of their sustained learning.*"[1] Unfortunately, as will be evident from the discussion in chapter 11, Alverno College is a unique institution. It has a unique organization and degree structure that benefits from a culture that is committed to the design of a curriculum that has as its purpose the promotion of liberal education and high levels of competence in the workplace. The Alverno College experience illustrates the point that an appropriate curriculum may well not look like a traditional broad curriculum. Again colleges as opposed to high schools have environments that can encourage breadth through the interaction of student with student. Indeed Newman felt that such extra classroom activity was as important if not more important than classroom study which suggests that there is something more to liberal education than the acquisition of knowledge. It is that something that has been called the "education of the whole-person". A curriculum that achieves this goal might be called a "balanced curriculum".

At school level, criticism of the imbalance in the curriculum taught in schools in England came from a psychometrician MacFarlane Smith. He showed long ago in the nineteen sixties that the school curriculum tended to favour the verbal/numerical at the expense of the spatial /mechanical. Children were encouraged to do "academic" subjects at the expense of "practical" subjects in spite of the contribution they might make to the development of mathematical (as opposed to numerical) and scientific development.[2] MacFarlane Smith went so far as to argue that the lack of spatial ability was a major reason why Britain was short of qualified scientists and technologists in the nineteen sixties. While recent developments in neuro-science have shown that the wiring in the brain is more complex than MacFarlane Smith envisaged the general point that the mind was not being fully exploited remains.

In the 1980's support for this view came from a critic of traditional approaches to intelligence (IQ), intelligence testing and the effect that it had had on educational thinking and practice. Howard Gardner's proposals provided a valuable theory for those concerned to provide an inclusive education.[3] He argued that the emphasis on the skills associated with traditional IQ caused people with other "intelligences" to be neglected. His view is that *"if we are to encompass adequately the realm of human cognition, it is necessary to include a far wider and more universal set of competences than has ordinarily been considered. And it is necessary to remain open to the possibility that many- if not most – of these competences do not lend themselves to measurement by standard verbal methods, which rely heavily on a blend of logical and linguistic abilities."* The fascination of this theory for teachers dealing with children of relatively poor academic aptitude and other learning disabilities will be self-evident. Some of those youngsters are good at sport and look to role models in sport: others are good at pop music. Neither of these have great status in the academic world. Gardener's theory recognizes such talent. In the first instance Gardener proposed there were seven such competences (which he called intelligences) with which we were variously endowed.[4] Schools should cater for all these intelligences and not simply those associated with traditional academic study. There have been several published reports of attempts to develop a curriculum based on multiple intelligences in elementary schools in the United States.[5] Curriculum development to design programmes that develop all these intelligences has been done in other countries including Ireland. It will be noticed that two of his intelligences are linked to the affective domain. These are the inter-personal, and the intra- personal. The former relates to the understanding we have of other people and one's self in relation to the other, and the latter is the skill involved in understanding one's self.

In a comparative study of the views that specialists and lay people had of intelligence Sternberg and colleagues[6] found that whereas the experts thought that motivation was an important component of academic intelligence, lay people placed much greater stress on the socio-cultural aspects of behaviour. That is interpersonal competence in a social context. Exhibit 13.1 shows the three factors and associated descriptions that came from the analysis of 170 items listed as characteristics of intelligence. Clearly attainment in these areas requires higher order thinking of both the problem solving and critical thinking kind. They resemble "the reasoning abilities traditionally identified as central to higher education". Each of these factors is "action" or to use a term from the Alverno study "performance" oriented.[7] To perform well is necessarily to perform well in a social context. It may be argued that social competence depends on a moral imperative. This study reinforces the findings of the Sheffield study reported in chapter 12 that showed that employers considered that graduates required but had poor personal transferable skills. These two studies provide a check- list for a balanced education that integrates the liberal with the vocational although it may be objected that it would not cover the philosophical and moral dimensions of such a curriculum as would be required for the development of the "whole-person."

It would be true to say that in the past that neither schools nor higher education institutions have done very much in these domains. A balanced education is not balanced if it does not cater for the development of skill and understanding in these domains. Within second level schooling co-operative learning can be used to assist the development of inter-personal skills. But as another intervention in the field of intelligence suggests that may be far from enough.

Three factors (accounting for 50% of the variance) that contribute to intelligence from a study by Sternberg

1. "Practical problem-solving ability: reasons logically and well, identifies connections among ideas, sees all aspects of a problem, keeps an open mind, responds thoughtfully to others' ideas, sizes up situations well, gets to the heart of the problems, interprets information accurately, makes good decisions, goes to original source of basic information, poses problems in an optimal way, is a good source of ideas, perceives implied assumptions and conclusions, listens to all sides of an argument, and deals with problems resourcefully".

2. "Verbal ability: speaks clearly and articulately, is verbally fluent, converses well, is knowledgeable about a particular field, studies hard, reads with high comprehension, reads widely, deals effectively with people, writes without difficulty, sets time aside for reading, displays a good vocabulary, accepts social norms, and tries new things".

3. "Social competence: accepts others for what they are, admits mistakes, displays interest in the world at large, is on time for appointments, has social conscience, thinks before speaking and doing, displays curiosity, does not make snap judgments, makes fair judgments, assesses well the relevance of information to a problem at hand, is sensitive to other people's needs and desires, is frank and honest with self and others, and displays interest in the immediate environment".

Exhibit 13.1

Emotional intelligence

In 1995 Goleman published a book on emotional intelligence that was an immediate best seller.[8] In it he asked, *"What factors are at play, for example, when people of high IQ flounder and those of modest IQ do surprisingly well?"* He went on to argue, *"that the difference quite often lies in the abilities called here emotional intelligence, which include self-control, zeal and persistence, and the ability to motivate oneself. And these skills [...] can be taught to children giving them a better chance to use whatever intellectual potential the genetic lottery may have given them."*

Studies of the effect of temperament on learning and performance have a long history. It is clear that the emotions influence our response to learning and intelligence in the same way they influence our response to others. We have also learnt that we need to be able to govern (control) our emotions, and the ability to do this is sometimes called emotional (and/or social) intelligence.

The subjects of emotional and social intelligence have been studied during most of the last century. That has been irrespective of whether they are the same construct or different constructs. Taken together, they may be considered as ways of *"understanding individual personality and social behaviour."*[9] There are non-traditional intelligences' such as *"practical intelligence"* that seem to overlap with them, and part of Sternberg's recent work has been to consider whether they are distinct or overlapping constructs.[10] Bar-On and Parker[11] brought together the body of American literature on this topic in a Handbook that reviewed the controversies surrounding the concept. It also evaluated methods that attempted to assess social intelligence, as for example Bar-On's[12] Emotional Quotient Inventory.

Emotional Intelligence has been seen both as a personality construct, and a mental ability.[13] It is for this reason that much that has, for example, been done in Britain and elsewhere has been developed within the framework of traditional thinking about personality and intelligence, and the cognitive and affective domains of educational thinking.

Not withstanding the debate about whether the traits that comprise emotional intelligence are personality traits or mental abilities for which adequate measures already exist it is quite clear that we all need to possess "emotional intelligence" in our dealings with people. We need to behave competently and intelligently. For this reason it clearly has a claim on the curriculum.

Some schools in the United States have promoted content for the development of emotional intelligence. Culver[14] quoted a list of the components that make up emotional intelligence from the "self-science" curriculum used by Nueva School in California.[15] The components of this curriculum follow (adapted)-

Self-awareness: observing yourself and recognising your feelings with a view to action or trying to change action in specified circumstances. This can include mode of study, reactions to people etc.

Personal decision-making: examining one's actions and predicting the consequences. Knowing the basis of the decision i.e. cognition or feeling. This covers the gamut of small and large decisions that relate to everyday actions.

Managing Feelings: requires self-awareness in order to be able to handle anxieties, anger, insults, put-downs, and sadness.

Handling stress: use of imagery and other methods of evaluation.

Empathy: understanding how people feel and appreciating that in the learning situation students can become stressed, and that such stress can be reduced by the mode of instruction (eg. the use of imagery).

Communications: Becoming a good listener and question-asker; distinguishing between what someone does or says and your own reactions about it; sending "I" messages instead of blame.

Self-disclosure: building trust in relationships and knowing when one can be open.

Insight: This is different to cognitive insight referred to previously. It is about understanding one's emotional life and being able to recognise similar patterns in others so as to better handle relationships.

Self-acceptance: being able to acknowledge strengths and weaknesses, and being able to adapt where necessary.

Personal responsibility: being able to take responsibility for one's own actions. This relates to personal decision making. Learning not to try and pass the buck when the buck really rests with one's self.

Assertiveness: the ability to be able to take a controlled stand i.e. neither with anger or meekness. This is particularly important in decisions involving moral issues in areas of work in which the professional ethic demands that a stand should be made.

Behaviour in groups. Knowing when to participate, lead and follow.

Conflict resolution: using the win/win model to negotiate compromise. This is particularly important in industrial relations, and it applies to both partners in managerial conflicts.

In the Nueva components *Behaviour in Groups* is called group dynamics but this is in some respects misleading because group dynamics is the interaction between the various members of the group or, the study of these interactions.

There might be some debate as to whether these skills, taken as a whole, are representative of emotional intelligence. Equally it might be objected that the Nueva skills are not a distinct social or emotional intelligence but rather a set of personality traits, in which case, they are better called personal transferable skills. One way of looking at emotional intelligence is to consider it to be the interplay between the cognitive and the affective domains in the conduct of living, if you accept that living is problem solving that embraces critical thinking. But, as Hedlund and Sternberg[16] pointed out, the competencies required to solve a problem will be a function of the type of problem faced.

In the UK, a substantial programme for the development of personal skills in relevant areas of the elementary and secondary school curriculum was designed by Hopson and Scally.[17] Inspection of what it is hoped the transition year will accomplish in Ireland shows that several of the constructs of emotional and social intelligence are accommodated. There is a vast popular literature on acquiring these skills, and there is a specialised literature on its role in management.

Emotional, social and practical intelligence

Sternberg also described practical intelligence. It *"involves a number of skills as applied to shaping of and selection of environments,* (which is what Sternberg argued intelligent people do). *These skills include among others, (1) recognizing problems, (2) defining problems, (3) allocating resources to solving problems, (4) mentally representing problems, (5) formulating strategies for solving problems, (6) monitoring solutions of problems, and (7) evaluating solutions of problems."*[18]

Hedlund and Sternberg[19] considered that what differentiates emotional from social and practical intelligence is "tacit knowledge". That is, the knowledge that is not taught but acquired as part of everyday living. The idea is vividly captured in Yorkshire dialect by the term "nouse!" The categories of tacit knowledge are managing self, managing others, and managing tasks. It will be understood that management education is about trying to influence these three types of knowledge. Such knowledge is procedural in the sense that it is associated with particular situations, and is transferred to similar situations, and this is why the content of knowledge and the type of problem solved differentiate between the three constructs of knowledge.

"The ability to acquire knowledge, whether it pertains to managing oneself, managing others, or managing tasks, can be characterized appropriately as an aspect of intelligence. It requires cognitive processes such as encoding essential

information from the environment and recognizing associations between new information and existing knowledge. The decision to call this aspect of intelligence social, emotional, or practical intelligence will depend on one's perspective and one's purpose." Whatever about the decision, it is clear that an education that does not provide for development in this area is unbalanced. Clearly this is a matter for the policy of the whole school in which curriculum leadership has a major role to play.

Sternberg believes that "intelligence" should be taught in American schools. In 1984 in an edition of *Educational Leadership* which included articles by de Bono, Lipman, Paul and Perkins, he recommended, while pointing out their weaknesses, the Chicago Masters Learning Programme, Instrumental Enrichment (Feuerstein) and, Philosophy for Children (Lipman). More recently he has collaborated with Gardner to merge their theories with the objective of producing a school curriculum.[20] Part of the curriculum was piloted in schools after the teachers had received in service training. It focused on the two theories of intelligence. The students received further support during the progress of the course. It was conducted with 7th grade reading classes and included a control group who took the normal course. Two tests of study skills and Sternberg's test of intelligence were administered before and after the course. The experimental group showed significant gains on all three measures over the control group.

The practical intelligence curriculum for schools covers the following areas:
1. Managing Yourself (a). overview of managing yourself. (b).learning styles. (c). improving your learning.
2. Managing Tasks. (a) overview of solving problems. (b). specific school problems
3. Cooperating with others. (a.) communication. (b). fitting into school.

Reflective intelligence

Perkins[21] in his criticism of Sternberg's model would say that it had failed to take into account reflective intelligence. Reflective intelligence contributes knowledge, understanding and attitudes about how to use our minds for intelligent behaviour- in other words the contribution of mindware. He considers that reflective intelligence is the control system for the resources afforded by neural and experiential intelligence. The neural dimension is strongly influenced by genetics and physical maturation. The experiential dimension contributes context -specific knowledge to intelligent behaviour and is learnable. He argues that the cultivation of intelligence can be achieved by concentrating on higher order learning skills eg problem solving and decision making). He also considers "remembering" to be a challenge. Therefore, opportunities for mental self-monitoring (self-awareness) and management should be provided within the formal system of education. The cultivation of such skills has become important in higher education because they are thought to encourage independent learning.

The Sheffield study reported in chapter 12, found that students showed marked individual differences in their ability to self-reflect. Variations in this ability were related to the discipline studied. Thus, students in the health sciences were quite happy talking about their feelings whereas engineers were not. *"They were not used to talking in terms of feelings, nor could they see the relevance of such reflection to learning about engineering problems"*.

Notwithstanding the problem of individual differences and the fact that some of these may be a function of deeply embedded dispositions there is surely an onus on the school system to help develop this skill of self-reflection. Various studies have shown that self-reflection has a role in the development of higher order thinking. It may be argued that skill in self-reflection in the learning context requires that the person thinks about his or her learning.[22] Whereas much has been written about the need for curriculum continuity between primary and post-primary education little has been written about such continuity between post-primary and higher education. Yet it is an assumption of all teachers that students will be able to "develop" as a result of their teaching. Education implies learning, learning implies acquisition and acquisition implies growth. There is therefore a necessary relationship between school and higher education. Currently there are theories of development pertaining to higher education and theories that apply to school education both sides need to be aware of them. Because they are seldom discussed the relevance of one to the other is in consequence ignored. In the sections that follow two theories of development are discussed. The scene is set by brief reference to the work of Piaget that has had such an influence on school education.

Piaget is best known for a three-stage theory of human development. The stages are invariant: the movement from one stage to the next brings about a change in the capacity for thought The first stage of development is from birth to one and half years. The second stage is called the period of representative intelligence and concrete operations which takes the child up to eleven or twelve years of age. It divides into two sub-phases known as the pre-operational phase which lasts from about two to seven years. The final period when the child moves from middle childhood to adolescence is that of formal operations. Now the child is able to undertake abstract thinking, to hypothesize and deduct, experiment and theorize. It is the stage of in-built maturity. It is, therefore, the stage of higher order thinking.[23]

Not much credence is given to these stages these days. But the concepts of concrete and formal operations are still valuable. In any event a number of investigations in the United States suggested that many students entering university in the sciences were not at the stage of formal operations. Even if the stages are accepted the work by Perry[24] and others shows that development continues into adulthood.

Post-formal reasoning

Broadly speaking, according to Perry's theory, the attitudes we hold and the concepts and values with which they are associated depend on the stage of development we are at. There are nine stages (see exhibit 13.2). They relate to curriculum and instruction in so far as together they either reinforce the stage we are at, or help us to move forward to another stage. Perry argued that much teaching tends to reinforce the earlier stages.

In the first stages the students come to the university expecting to be told the truth, that is, what is right and what is wrong. Subject-based knowledge is absolute. Things are right or wrong, or true or false. This is how teaching and often the system of public assessment causes students to think. They bring the attitudes they develop in school with them to their classes in university. Thus, in stage 1 all problems are seen to have right answers and authority must be followed. For this group those whom they rate as the best teachers provide the right answers. By stage 3 it is apparent that authority is *"seeking the right answers"* and only in the future will we know the right answer. Perry calls these first three stages 'dualism'. From dualism the student moves into a phase of scepticism, for now it is clear that not only does the authority not have the right answers but everyone, including the student, has the right to hold his or her own opinions, and some of these can be supported by evidence. Thus, by stage 5, some answers are found to be better than others, and knowledge has to be considered in its context. It is a stage of relativism. Marra and Palmer pointed out that the move from stage 4 to stage 5 is a significant transition because the students now *accept "knowledge as, for the most part, transient and contextual".... "Students now accept themselves as one among many legitimate sources of knowledge and often forego their former view of instructors as absolute authorities."*[25] At this stage the student begins to perceive that good choices are possible and that commitments have to be entered into. By stage 9 (acting on commitment) decisions are made with relative ease, a sense of identity and a personal style is obtained, and one is now able to take responsibility for one's own actions.

A problem for some people with this scheme is that in this process of development some students are faced with finding out for the first time that much knowledge is relative, and for some of them this may cause considerable dissonance. For others it seems, as one former student at the Colorado School of Mines put it, that *"they, Culver, Woods and Fitch, state that to become intellectually mature, you need to believe in a relativistic world and that if you believe in absolute authority, you are intellectually immature. These statements say a great deal about their own world views and nothing about the intellectual maturity of students."*[26]

> **Positions 1 and 2: Dualism**
> All knowledge is known, and it is a collection of information. Right and wrong answers exist for everything. Teachers are responsible for giving information, students are responsible for producing it.
>
> **Position 3: Early multiplicity.**
> Knowledge includes methods for solving problems. There may be more than one right answer. Teachers help students learn how to learn, students are responsible for understanding and applying knowledge.
>
> **Position 4: Late multiplicity.**
> Uncertainty with respect to knowledge and diversity of opinion become legitimate. Teachers require evidence to support opinions and design choices, students learn how to think and analyze.
>
> **Position 5: Relativism.**
> All knowledge must be viewed in context. Teachers are consultants, students can synthesize and evaluate perspectives from different contexts.
>
> **Positions 6 – 9: Commitment within Relativism.**
> For life to have meaning, commitments must be made, taking into account that the world is a changing, relativistic place.

Exhibit 13.2. The Perry positions or stages after Culver, Woods, and Fitch[27]

Philosophically they have a case to defend because as Jordan argued, *"many engineering students are philosophically unsophisticated, this amounts to an indoctrination of students by faculty"*. Not withstanding the distinguished British philosopher of education G. H. Bantock[28] who argued that all education is indoctrination, the point is whether Perry meant to imply that all knowledge is relative. It may be argued that he did not, since in the final stage, a student makes a commitment within a relativistic world, and whether we like it or not, that is how we find the world. An alternative explanation is that there are very few absolutes and that as the range of knowledge increases so we have to adapt.

As any one with strongly held religious beliefs would affirm, this does not mean that those beliefs are renounced. Indeed, it might be argued that they may have been only weak, and at the level of notional assent.[29] Jordan would probably be more satisfied with the Reflective Judgement Model, which seems to get over his difficulty. Irrespective of that model it is clear that schools should be leading students away from black and white teaching if students are to develop skill in critical thinking.

Reflective Judgement

The differences between King and Kitchener's model and Perry's model are seen immediately by comparing the stages of each model as shown in exhibits 13.2 and 13.3. Clearly the earlier stages owe much to Perry. Some critics think that the first three stages are the same as Perry's. The idea of *"reflective judgement"* was influenced by Dewey. *"We now think of reflective judgements as beginning with an awareness of uncertainty. Such judgements involve integration and evaluating data, relating those data theory and well-informed opinions, and ultimately creating a solution to the problem that can be defended as reasonable and plausible."*[30]

King and Kitchener noted that their investigations were related to what other researchers were doing in the areas of critical thinking and intelligence, and they found that while some aspects of the definitions overlapped, other aspects were quite distinct.[31]

Like Perry, the model assumes that as individuals develop, so they become more able to evaluate the claims of knowledge, and both models advocate and support their points of view about controversial issues. *"The ability to make reflective judgements is the ultimate outcome of this progression."* To arrive at this destination the learner passes through seven stages, each of which has its own assumptions and logic. The stages develop from the relatively simple to the relatively complex, each with a different strategy for solving ill-structured problems. Thus each stage has its own view of knowledge and concept justification. Reflective thinking takes place in stages 6 and 7. *"True reflective thinking pre-supposes that individuals hold epistemic assumptions that allow them to understand and accept real uncertainty"*. It is only when they engage in ill-structured or novel problems that they engage in reflective thinking as defined by King and Kitchener They found that their model complemented another model due to Fischer.[32]

Individuals will only operate at their optimal levels when they practice skills in familiar domains and receive environmental support for high level performance. There will be lots of 'Eureka' moments en-route. Unlike stage theory, which holds that all children pass through the same stages of development Fischer's skill theory argues that the steps which individuals take to attain a skill vary considerably as between one individual and the next, as a function of the environment and the individual. Because of these variations it will be difficult to find any two children who spontaneously follow the same steps in any domain. At the same time the theory states that irrespective of the path taken all skills pass through the same developmental levels. All skill acquisitions involve the same group of transformation rules. The position taken by Fischer and his colleagues is similar to that taken by information-processing theorists namely that the *"same fundamental acquisition processes occur in development, learning and problem solving at all ages"*. Instruction and assessment should, therefore, be designed to take account of these different needs. This theory has considerable implications for the design of modular (credit-unit) curriculum systems and the pacing of assessment and learning within them.

In the Reflective Judgement model a spurt marks the emergence of a new stage. The skill levels in the Fischer model correspond directly to the stages of the Reflective Judgement Model. King and Kitchener argued that the decisions students make when they are in relativistic frames of reference should reflect a level of cognitive development beyond relativism. In the Perry model, the student remains within the relativistic frame and has to make an act of faith in reaching a commitment. The purpose of the Reflective Judgement model is to deal with the form and nature of judgements made in the relativistic framework. Individuals, it is held, hold epistemological positions beyond relativism. Whatever else one may say, such a position would seem to be more satisfying than Perry's.

King and Kitchener, had much to say about teaching in higher education and they take a broad of view of who may be a teacher and what teaching is. According to the Reflective Judgement Interview, first year students in the United States lie in the range stage 3 to stage 4. Seniors were found to be around stage 5. They argue that many seniors are at a loss when they are asked to defend their answers to ill-structured problems. Therefore, if reflective thinking is to be developed, teachers should:

- Show respect for students regardless of the developmental levels they may exhibit.
- Understand that students differ in the assumptions they make about knowledge.
- Familiarize students with ill-structured problems within the teacher's area of expertise.
- Create multiple opportunities for students to examine different points of view.
- Informally assess (i.e. from student journals, assignments etc) assumptions about knowledge and how beliefs may be justified.
- Acknowledge that students work within a developmental range of stages and set expectations accordingly; and challenge students to engage in new ways of thinking while providing them with support; and recognize that students differ both in their perceptions of ill-structured problems and their responses to particular learning environments.
- Share with one another what they do and what they expect to achieve.

King and Kitchener do not, however, believe there is one best way of teaching reflective thinking.

The differences between stage 3 and stage 6 from a teaching perspective are shown in exhibit 13.4. It will be appreciated that since these descriptions could apply at any level of education they would have to be developed to describe the requirements of a particular level (e.g. year on course, course level). It is clear that if students in schools are to develop critical thinking they will have to tackle ill-structured problems, and this has implications for assessment.

Stage	Description
Stage 1	Knowing is limited to single concrete observations. What a person observes is true.
Stage 2.	Two categories for knowing; right answers and wrong answers. Good authorities have knowledge; bad authorities lack knowledge.
Stage 3.	In some areas, knowledge is certain and authorities that have that knowledge. In other areas, knowledge is temporarily uncertain. Only personal beliefs can be known.
Stage 4.	Concept that knowledge is unknown in several specific cases leads to the abstract generalization that knowledge is uncertain.
Stage 5.	Knowledge is uncertain and must be understood within a context; thus justification is context specific.
Stage 6.	Knowledge is uncertain but constructed by comparing evidence and opinion of different sides of an issue or across contexts.
Stage 7.	Knowledge is the outcome of a process of reasonable inquiry. This view is equivalent to a general principle that is consistent across domains.

Exhibit 13.3 Stages of the King and Kitchener Reflective Judgement Model (adapted)

Stage 3.
Characteristic assumptions of stage 3. Reasoning. **Knowledge is absolutely certain in some areas and temporarily uncertain in other areas.** **Beliefs are justified according to the word of an authority in areas of certainty and according to what "feels right" in areas of uncertainty.** **Evidence can neither be evaluated nor used to reason to conclusions.** **Opinions and beliefs cannot be distinguished from factual evidence.** Instructional goals for students. **Learn to use evidence in reasoning to a point of view.** **Learn to view their own experience as one potential source of information but not as the only valid source of information.**
Stage 6. Promoting reflective thinking Characteristic assumptions of Stage 6. reasoning. **Knowledge is uncertain and must be understood in relationship to context and evidence.** **Some points of view may be tentatively judged as better than others.** **Evidence on different points of view can be compared and evaluated as a basis for justification.** Instructional goals for students. **Learn to construct one's own point of view and to see that point of view as open to re-evaluation and revision in the light of new evidence.** **Learn that though knowledge must be constructed, strong conclusions are epistemologically justified.**

Exhibit 13.4. Promoting reflective thinking in the King and Kitchener model –stages 3 and 6.Reasoning.(Adapted from King and Kitchener, 1994. In their description (pp250-254) they also give for each stage a list of difficult tasks from the perspective of the particular stage, a sample of developmental assignments, and suggestions for developmental support for instructional goals).

King and Kitchener designed an instrument called *The Reflective Judgement Interview* (RJI to detect the stage at which a student is. The interview is structured with standard probe questions, each with a specific purpose. Thus, two questions, that will clearly elicit a level of development that are of direct relevance to today's media governed society are (1) how is it possible that experts in the field have such different views about the subject? And, (2) how is it possible that experts in the field should disagree about the subject?

While it is not the intention to examine the psychometric properties of this instrument it is of some interest since the questions may help with the design of assessment. There is also one important comment from one of the analysts to the effect that differences between the samples were more pronounced at lower levels of educational attainment than at the higher levels. Wood who undertook this analysis thought that this was consistent with the view that performance on the RJI is dependent on verbal ability (which is a necessary, but not sufficient condition for high scores).[33] Once again the need for a high level of verbal ability to think critically or reflectively is highlighted.

In an earlier paper Kitchener had pointed out that no single instructional or curricular experience over a limited period is likely to have an impact on development that a carefully constructed set of cumulative experiences over a long period of time is likely to have. The implication for teachers is that in planning the curriculum they have to work as a team and share with one another what they do and what they expect to achieve. There is unlikely to be one best way of teaching reflective thinking.[34] But there is a more profound implication for the system. If reflective thinking is to be developed and pupils are to be prepared for life and work in which higher education is included then the cumulative experiences should extend from primary through post-primary to third level. What better than a programme of the type developed by Lipman.

Olds in a private communication to Tsang[35] described the Reflection Rubric that is shown in exhibit 13.5. Its purpose is to document the stages of development of a student according to the Reflective Judgement Model. Thus in the diagram, in evaluative thinking the progress of a student from reliance on authority to being able to evaluate the information presented is shown. (It will be noticed that there can be confusion between what has in the past been considered to be evaluation and what now is called reflection).

There is a danger that self-reflection (reflective judgement) is taken to be the key to personal growth. Clearly it is important but as Mentowski and her associates point out our reasoning, performance and development are equally important.[36]

"It is a characteristic of Man" writes the Scottish philosopher John MacMurray *"that he solves his practical problems by taking thought; and all his theoretical activities have their origins at least, in his practical requirements […] they also find their meaning and their significance in the practical field"* […]."*Activities of ours which are purely theoretical, if this means they have no reference to our practical life must be purely imaginary"* […].[37] Necessarily our actions contrib-

ute significantly to our growth. It would seem that Mentkowski and her associates would associate this with "performance". They define "performance" as the *"extension of experience into an envisioned future.. The performer envisions and acts in the face of contingency and actively revises his or her actions in the light of their consequences."*[38] If we take "performance" for what it is it involves not only cognition but the affective emotions and dispositions and involves the performer in integrating the interpersonal with the cognitive. It involves self-reflection and higher order thinking. In Mentkowski's theory higher order thinking is associated with reasoning. Thus reasoning is an important domain of growth.

EVALUATIVE THINKING	Unable to evaluate information presented: relies primarily on unexamined prior beliefs.	Presents information to support previously held beliefs; superficial understanding of information; acknowledges need to gather more information.	Uses information to establish well-supported argument for achieving goals; indicates need to gather more information to further support assertions.	Uses information to establish well supported argument for achieving goals; suggests viable strategies for addressing self-identified limitations.
DIVERGENT THINKING	Does not make connections among relevant information.	Presents holistic self-assessment; limited breakdown and focus on achievement of individual goals.	Organizes available information into viable framework for exploring complexities of achieving goals.	Organizes and prioritizes available information appropriate for the task of self-assessing achievement.
CONVERGENT THINKING	Presents information but does not attempt to interpret or analyze.	Provides limited interpretation or analysis of how well goals were met.	Presents interpretation and analysis from multiple perspectives of how well goals were met.	Presents interpretation and analysis from multiple perspectives of how well goals were met; also includes analysis of how to continue to attempt to achieve goals.
COGNITIVE MEMORY	Asserts that goals were met; relies on external authority (moderators) for evaluations.	Uses limited information but acknowledges at least the possibility of uncertainty.	Uses range of carefully evaluated relevant information during self-assessment.	Uses range of carefully evaluated relevant information during self-assessment; suggests viable strategies for obtaining new information to address limitations.

Exhibit 13.5. Barbara Olds Reflective Assessment Rubic based on the Reflective Judgement Model.

Mentkowski and her colleagues *"believe it (reasoning) is also linked to underlying dispositions to pursue thinking with intellectual rigor."* Their view of reasoning seems to be very similar to that traditionally associated with intelligence (IQ). They describe it as *"the manipulation of ideas and abstractions"*. Indeed in primary (elementary) education children are faced with *"reasoning tests."*[39] They affirm the value of discourse in learning to reason and implicitly, therefore, the merits of cooopertive learning. *"Reasoning involves [...] the tasks of describing, explaining, predicting, arguing, critiquing, explicating and defining"*. They cite Arendt who emphasises that thinking takes nothing for granted.

As such the ability to recognize the "assumptions made" is critical in reasoning and it will be recalled from an earlier chapter that great store was set on the ability to check the assumptions made in the solution of problems in engineering science but more especially in those held by schools and teachers.

Many educators, whether in school or higher education, see the central goal of education as development in terms of one or other of the theories expressed above. Such development reconciles within the person the cognitive with what has been loosely called the affective in these chapters. That is the domains that Gardener calls the interpersonal and intrapersonal. Mentkowski writes *"development extends immediate experience into broader purposes, meaning, and commitments. As such, it can lead toward synthesis as the learner becomes increasingly able to unify capacities and awareness into a sense of personal mission, imbuing even mundane actions with a whole philosophy of life."*[40] This seems to differ little from what Newman expected of higher education. *"A general culture of mind is the best aid to professional and scientific study."*[41] It carries with it the perfection of the intellect. And with this enlargement comes *"a philosophical cast of thought, or comprehensive mind, or wisdom in conduct of policy, implies a connected view of the old with the new; an insight into the bearing and influence of each part upon every other; without which there is no whole, and could be no centre. It is the knowledge, not only of things, but of their mutual relations, It is organised and therefore living knowledge."*[42] Newman's philosophy was not about a system but a "cast of thought", a mode of thinking that he thought all should possess if they were to develop to their full potential and contribute to society.

The illustrations in the above paragraphs show that teaching plays an important role in growth by the way it is organized to encourage learning. It is also evident that theories of development have implications for the design of the curriculum. Take as an example that of the Transition Year in Ireland. At the moment it is a full year between the ages of fifteen and sixteen. As we have seen it hopes that high level skills that contribute to the development of the whole person will be developed during that year. It makes no concession to the fact that adolescents are going through an important developmental phase and may require much more time to assimilate an understanding of their own growth. For this reason it might be better to spread the programme over the three years of the senior cycle of secondary education. It is a case that merits examination and who better for this than curriculum and instructional leaders.

The question to be answered is whether or not schools can involve the students in understanding the possibilities of self-reflection. The evidence from the philosophy for young children projects suggests they can.

Philosophy for young children

In the 1970's Matthews[43] worried about how to teach introductory courses to college students who believed that philosophy was not a "natural" activity On reflection he came to the view that just as we are all learners from the time of birth, so too we are all philosophers. To put it in another way- from birth we try to solve puzzles and we ask adults to help us solve rather difficult and abstruse problems and often these questions baffle parents. Matthews point is that these questions are, while in the language of the child, the fundamental questions that philosophers set and seek to answer. Children are being philosophers. Matthews book is therefore built around questions and statements of a philosophical nature asked by children. Here are two from the first chapter.

"One day John Edgar (four years), who had often seen airplanes take off, rise and gradually disappear into the distance, took his first plane ride. When the plane stopped ascending and the seat belt sign went out, John Edgar turned to his father and said in a rather relieved, but still puzzled tone of voice, "Things don't really get smaller up here....Jordan (five years), going to bed at eight one evening, asked "If I go to bed at eight and get up at seven in the morning, how do I really know that the little hand of the clock has gone round only once? Do I have to stay up all night to watch it? If I look away even for a short time, maybe the small hand will go round twice". Several of the examples come from Piaget's[44] writing and that of Susan Isaacs.[45] Others, need one say, are *Alice in Wonderland* and *Winnie the Pooh*. More recently John Williams has written about *Pooh and the Philosophers*[46] and research in Ireland has yielded similar stories.[47]

Matthews takes issue with Piaget and says that all the concepts Piaget claims to have found in young children invite philosophical reflection. He believes Piaget is immune to philosophical puzzlement. For people like that, there is so much to learn about the world, but nothing to puzzle about. Children's remarks, argues Matthews, can lead to colloquia in which they can reason themselves out of the puzzles. Since philosophy can begin in such simple ways, why shouldn't philosophy be taught to young children so that thinking skills may be developed? This had already happened for at Mont Clair State University in New Jerrsey. Lipman and his colleagues had developed programmes and materials in philosophy for young children.[48]

The features which the programmes claim to be unusual are
1. Children look at the logic embedded in the language they use in everyday life.
2. Provision of experiences and exercises based on concepts that children love to talk about e.g friendship, fairness, reality, truth, being a person and goodness.
3. A foundation for developing thinking skills in discussion.[49]

In the programme, children read and discuss novels that have been specially written for the course. Ideally, the course designers expect the teachers who have been certificated to teach the course to cover half of each programme in a year at three hours per week. During these periods the children read a chapter aloud, they construct a discussion agenda, discuss selected items and undertake items in the course manual.

The role of the teacher is in some ways similar to that proposed by Stenhouse. He/she is expected to be *"a co-participant in a community of inquiry"*. Their role is to facilitate discussions in order to help students *"internalize the discussion process in the form of thinking"*. Pupils learn to reason together.

Apart from the programmes about thinking, reasoning, reasoning in ethics, there are also courses for reasoning about nature (K - 5), language arts (8 – 11), and social studies (9 – 12). These are intended as additions to the curriculum. A BBC documentary of this work showed children discussing moral issues and, with the exception of course material, would be similar to what some teachers of religious education in Ireland would do in their classes.

Thinking classes have been held in Irish Schools and have been the subject of evaluation. One shows the importance of oral language but at the same time they warn that centrally set curricular might operate against the development of thinking skills. Donnelly wrote *"The fundamental difficulty I have is its (oral language curriculum) implied Piagetian stages of thinking. The use of the word 'simple' in reference to the early years classes, junior and senior infants needs to be questioned. "Discuss simple solutions to simple problems," it ordains. Simple for whom? I ask. One can only interpret this approach as implying that young children are incapable of abstract thinking or asking complex questions. I would suggest that thinking in the abstract is an integral part of acquiring and refining language"* She notes that in another part of the syllabus where a list of questions that can be put to children is given that almost all of them are closed-questions that require 'right' answers.[50]

Lipman considers that in higher order thinking there is fusion of both critical and creative thinking and both lead to judgement. However, critical thinking is self-corrective, whereas in creative thinking there is something similar, but not identical to, self correction. *"I think that when an artist is in the process of composition or construction of a painting, or a dance, or a film, or a poem, then, if the artist decides 'this isn't right' and erases a word or a piece of painting and replaces it with something else... that is not the same as when you find you made a mistake in addition and you go back and correct it."*[51]

I would take the view that both involve 'review' and that is what is important. Clearly we must correct something that is wrong but, in the artistic sense, we correct what is right for us. The emotions enter into one and not the other and surely viewed in this way are self-correcting. No wonder there is a debate about the similarities and differences between problem solving, critical thinking and decision making.

Johnson[52] who considers that *"Lipman's account comes perhaps the closest to bringing out the sense in which critical thinking is 'critica,l'* "nevertheless finds the idea of critical thinking as self-corrective problematic. He argues that the danger with this definition is that it may place too much emphasis on the individual at the expense of the community and this reflects much current thinking in political philosophy at the present time (e.g., Etzioni in the USA and Selbourne in the UK). Johnson wanted a more pragmatic definition. What matters, however, is how the definition leads to curriculum and instruction. It would seem to me that the communitarian dimension is easily embraced within curricula that follow the Lipman model should that be desired.

While Johnson makes other criticisms of Lipman's model there is one that should be noted, and that is that Lipman considers critical thinking to be good thinking, whereas McPeck considers that there can be bad critical thinking. So Johnson asks *"Is critical thinking by definition something good? Can there be bad critical thinking? Is critical thinking like virtue (necessarily good), or rather luck (possibly good, possibly bad?"* One might respond that critical thinking is a skill that enables us to make decisions. In this sense it is neutral because it utilizes available knowledge to make decisions: it contributes to the goodness or badness of the decisions, which brings us full circle to the issue should critical thinking, problem solving and decision making be taught? If, as seems to be the case, most teachers believe that these skills are acquired by immersion, and teachers of mathematics and science specifically teach problem solving, then is there any need to take further action? The answer would seem to be, at least on the basis of the investigations of my student teachers and the work of experienced teachers in a mathematics project, yes. They are not learnt initially by immersion. That has to come after (and with) training and experience suggests that it is an essential feature of development

There are problems because training implies that the skills learnt will be transferable especially to "life situations" for which there has been no prior learning. Recent developments in neuropsychology suggest that each unique cognitive domain will require similar progression toward logical transformations that will be dependent on the nature of the subject. In other words development may be subject specific. Or, is development in particular subjects a second order effect that contributes to our overall development?

Matthews view is that children are not as inept as we may be led to think they are. Much would seem to depend on the expectations teachers and the curriculum and assessment systems within which they work. Clearly "assumptional-dialogues" on the teaching of higher order thinking and the attainment of a balanced curriculum should be informed about the work of Lipman and others in that field as well as with post-formal theories of development. However the development of the whole-person presupposes acquisition of behaviours based on a moral disposition. In this respect Kohlberg's theory of moral development could be the basis of an "assumptional-dialogue.

Moral development

So far the models described hear have focused on the cognitive. There would seem to be an assumption that emotional development takes place at the same rate. Yet schools are expected to cope with children's emotional problems. Every time there is public outcry as there is in Ireland at the present time when the law is not seen to protect children in their teens from sexual predators, the schools are told that they are not providing the proper sex education. Schools are also expected to provide programmes in moral development. Society finds it easier to dispossess parents of their obligations and place the responsibility on schools rather than promote and help parents to exercise that responsibility. The issues raised by Elkind[53] twenty years ago would seem to continue to be relevant. Elkind who works in the tradition of Piaget pointed out the ever-increasing tendency to hurry the child toward adulthood. He concluded that many of the ills that are besetting American society arose from the pressures on young children from adults and argued that time needs to be allowed for the emotional development of the child. Thus while he would frown upon pre-school education society has come to regard this as a right.

The introspection demanded by Elkind may be almost impossible. It is important in these circumstances that societies should be aware of the limits of what schools can achieve. Too often, too much is expected of them. This brings us inevitably to morality and the role that schools in the development of morality. Should schools and teachers play an active role in the moral development of their pupils? If the answer is 'yes' then what are the implications for the curriculum?

Kohlberg's theory of moral development

Piaget's work was not confined to cognitive development. He also proposed that moral development took place in two stages. The age division was put between ten and eleven years. In the first stage children believe that rules are handed down whereas in the second stage children become more relativistic in their approach. They begin to base their judgement on intentions. Kohlberg[54] developed Piaget's theory. In the first place he was interested to know if children continued to develop morally. To this end 72 children and adolescents were interviewed about their attitudes to moral dilemmas and he analyzed the reasoning that led to their answers. The responses were classified into stages. The inter-reliability between the judges was found to be high.

As a result of the study he concluded that there were six levels of moral development within three broad categories. In his earliest formulation of the theory stage 0 (pre-moral stage) was listed as the first of four levels. As with Piaget at the first stage the individual thinks that right is what they are told is right. At the next level they begin to conform to the norms of society and in the final category they begin to think about what is good for society and their guiding principles are those of social justice.

Kohlberg did not believe that his stages were either the product of maturation or of socialisation. Rather they arose from the child's thinking about moral problems. Our ideas change and develop as they come to be challenged by those with whom we interact. From the educational point of view we can arrange role playing opportunities that help children see one another's point of view.[55]

Like Piaget, Kohlberg believed that the levels were invariant. They always unfolded in sequence. Moreover, the levels are general patterns of thought; at the same time they were hierarchically integrated by which Kohlberg meant that the insights of earlier stages were not lost as the individual moved through the stages. Finally, this stage sequence is universal; it applies in any culture independently of the specific beliefs of the culture, a view that brought some criticism.[56]

The theory is concerned with moral thinking not moral action although Kohlberg believed there should be some correlation between the two and, that at the higher stages of development behaviour is more predictable and consistent.

(1) Education for moral development
Blatt led discussion groups in which cognitive conflict was introduced. He reported that the persons who were most interested in the discussions made the greatest amount of change.[57] There is some evidence that those who are most challenged are those who then move forward.[58] However, it has to be remembered that where personal values are at stake dissonance can reaffirm the value system especially when beliefs are strongly held as for example, in politics and religion [59].

Kohlberg also advocated a just community approach. He and his colleagues set up a high school to be run on democratic lines. It seems the group norms advanced from stage 2 to stage 3 over a period of a year.[60] One of the criticisms of this approach was that the adults in the programme stated their positions and this was thought by some investigators to contain elements of indoctrination, although they were assured that it did not.

It seems that the most appropriate way of promoting moral development in individuals may be via the discussion method, and this is often done although the questions (dilemmas) discussed will be key.

(2) Criticisms
As might be expected in an age of moral relativism the theory was the subject of much criticism for at stage 4.5 as Kohlberg calls it the individual is in a relativist state without commitment. There were two kinds of substantive criticism that have considerable substance. The first relates to the view that young childrens' opinions of morality are determined by reward and punishment. It is argued that children have a more profound understanding of morality than they can articulate. This seems to be analogous with Bruner's view that children can understand in a medium appropriate to their development. The way they answer

and judgements they may have have to be considered with that understanding in mind.[61] moreover, young children do recognise moral issues as may be demonstrated by their reactions to school discipline procedures.[62] Children it is argued will say that it is wrong to hit or steal in the absence of rules. This points to the fact that morality and social convention thinking are separate conceptual systems. These criticisms would seem to be supported by Matthews[63] and those who support the teaching of philosophy to young children.

The other quite distinctive criticism came from Gilligan.[64] She pointed out that Kohlberg's stages were derived from interviews with males and that this introduced a male orientation. Gilligan and also Lyons[65] argued that in contrast to man's notion of morality as 'having a reason,' the woman's sense of morality is a type of 'consciousness' which produces sensitivity towards others. Caring predominates. These distinctive ways of making moral choice lie in a continuum and are not dichotomous. It might be expected that if there are differences between the sexes that women would score differently to men and that in this case their scores would be lower, as was the case. Rest[66] however, believes the extent of the difference has been overstated but this would not null the general hypothesis.[67]

Both Kohlberg[68] and Gilligan[69] have begun to consider post-adolescent moral development (see below). Crain[70] envisages the possibility that there are two lines of moral thought, one focussing on logic, justice and social organization, and the other on care that could become integrated within adult years. One could also envisage the possibility that people will switch between the two as a function of the situation in which they find themselves.

It may be objected that there is no necessary relationship between moral development and moral behaviour. Kohlberg[71] thought there was and other research has supported this view.[72]

The stages of moral development do not answer the question "Why be moral?" This can only be resolved at a more comprehensive level of morality involving the whole of ones ethical-ontological orientation. Kohlberg believed that the only level which can help persons answer the question "why be just in an unjust world?" is cosmic, and therefore relies on transcendental or mystical experience. In one of his last publications he described a 7th stage. There is, however, no psychometric evidence that adults live in post-conventional stages of 5 and 6.[73]

For those who have a faith such arguments are not very attractive. They, and in particular Christians, are likely to find Moran's views more to the point.

Moral development and religion

Moran[74] argues that moral development (and thus religious development) does not just end in a stage. It must continue throughout life, otherwise atrophy will occur. The educational journey does not end until death. Moran points out that moral reasoning and moral development are not the same thing. Neither are school and education equivalent. School teachers can help students develop the life of the mind. He argues that Kohlberg reinforces Piaget's dismissal of morality in the pre-operational child. This he says goes against common sense. We should be very hesitant to say that children up to six are "pre-moral". *"If our moral system has nothing to say about younger children, then we may have to examine the adequacy of our system"*.

Moran's theory of religious education development has had an immense influence of religious education especially among Catholics. The first of his three stages, which he calls simply- 'religious,' describes the early education of the child. *"Up to the age of reflective self-consciousness the child's education and religious education are not distinguishable"*. Thus *"whatever contributes to the child's education also provides the necessary foundation for a more complex form of religious education in later life."* It is a stage that seems to be akin to Whitehead's stage of romance[75] for *"it deals with fundamental orientation to life and death, ultimate mysteries and visions of unity."* His second level is called intermediary with the sub-title Christian, Jewish or Muslim. Again it is similar to Whitehead's stage of precision; children should have the chance to understand the nature and influence of religion on their lives. *"If and when religion is taught in the school it needs more, not less, intellectual substance than it has had in most of its educational history."*

The final stage called Religiously Christian (Jewish, Muslim) is also in many respects similar to Whitehead's stage of synthesis. With the advent of self-reflective consciousness, childhood's naiveté is forever lost. Adolescence pushes aside the magical, superstitious, and religious in favour of calculative and instrumental rationality. The adolescent is looking for measurable things and reasonable explanations. Adulthood is the discovery that childhood was not all in error and that rational control needs a religious context of mystery and wonder. The *"second naivete of adulthood is a complex phase in which the simple genius of childhood reappears in chastened form."*

It is not too far-fetched to say that politicians, schools and teachers take little interest in these issues. Yet, politicians are all too ready to place the blame for society's ills on schools. The emphasis they place on the pursuit of standards in the academic subjects relegates these issues to the sidelines. There is an urgent need to face up to these issues if only to provide a framework for making the ethical decisions required by advances in technology. In such situations where emotions can easily override reason the question put at the end of the section on emotional intelligence has also to be asked- "what attention should schools pay to the development of emotional intelligence?"

Schooling, development and the curriculum

The idea that the dimensions of human behaviour discussed in this chapter are important in education is one that receives notional rather than real assent. Those of us who have been engaged in education during the last fifty years have witnessed many organizational and structural changes in response to prevailing political theories. We have also noticed radical changes in the behaviour of students that have left some of us bemused. We know that more and more we are expected to deal with severe behavioural problems for which we have not been trained. All that is available for our use is the knowledge of the shared pedagogy of experience. We have not been encouraged to engage in "assumptional-dialogues" about that experience or to examine the theories put before us such as those discussed in chapters 3 and 4. In these circumstances the first step that has to be made is for all to recognize that put against a whole variety of measures most education systems do not provide an education for the whole person. It is a pretence for them to say that they do. Knowledge based programmes in sex and civics are no answer for what is at issue is the ability of students to think. It is what John Cowan calls "reflection for action" and the acquisition of what Newman calls a philosophical habit of mind. These are not qualities that can be completed in schooling but schooling has the purpose of preparing students for their lifelong development. It seems clear that how we organise schooling outside of the classroom is as important as how we organize learning within the classroom. Our remit, however, is the classroom and the curriculum. How can the changes required be brought about?

From subject based curriculum development to whole school development

Some years ago Michael Murray evaluated an experimental programme (an introduction to management studies) in the Irish Transition year.[76] He was a participant observer. Later he developed a theory of whole school development based on his study of this subject-based curriculum.[77] He presented a model of the ideal (renewing) school. His starting point was with the aims that the teachers set themselves. These required them to move from an academic subject-centred curriculum to a more needs-based approach sensitive to the changing demands of the individual, society, and the economy. They had to change from being traditional teachers to, facilitators and evaluators. Murray argued that this experience of change within a classroom and a subject would provide the insights and skills necessary for school renewal.

Murray constructed a model of the renewing school the terminology of which was based on that used in religious institutions. The first part of any renewal process (analysis-design-implementation-evaluation) is to return to the founding vision. This has to take into account the wider community in which the institution resides. In the language of the models of this text it is a return to the educational and social aims of the school. They have to be interpreted in terms of the curriculum and its implementation. Any renewal is an emotional exercise that involves the affective domain. The renewing school has to respond to needs for affiliation (n-Aff), power (n-Pow), and achievement (N- ach). *"As in the case of the ideal business, the corporate goal of the ideal school community it to provide each member within it, with a sense of belonging, power and achievement."*[78] Murray points out that at the cognitive level questions about the identity of the institution have to be answered. *"What business are we in? Whom do we serve? What service do we offer?"* He argues *"that the mutuality between the individual and corporate goals helps the individual to internalise goals and become engaged in the learning experiences which affect character change"*. Thus Murray would understand a school to be a learning organisation. In terms of organizational theory it would be open and organic.[79] Organizations *"in which individuals understand their role in terms of the general aims of the organisation so that everyone contributes to the common goal and the head is not omnipresent."*[80] By identifying the learning styles of the school the leader can direct them to the appropriate phases of the innovation cycle and by repeated involvement in the cycle the school community is more able to participate in the innovation (renewal) cycle. The models are shown in figures 13. 1 ,13.2 and 13.3.

The programme that Murray had investigated was found to have emphasized the development of people in the belief that it is their creativity that makes a difference to organizational effectiveness. While a certain minimal level of resources were required, of of itself it could not produce any significant differences in student performance. *"Freed from the constraints of externally imposed courses, the teachers were able to internalise goals. By analogy, it pointed to the possibility that a whole school staff could exercise greater autonomy in the curriculum they offered. They could adopt a set of corporate goals more compatible with the goals of individual teachers than those dictated by a national education authority. Because the internalisation of goals is better facilitated in such circumstances, the probability of organizational renewal is enhanced."* Which is some challenge to the general community.

It has to be appreciated that the teachers in this small project acquired substantial training both formally and informally on their own part. Murray's point is that experience of micro-projects of this kind provide the experience necessary for whole school renewal, and can provide the motivation and encouragement for the larger activity. All this is to suggest that schools should engage in micro-projects and this they will not be able to do unless they have the knowledge based resource of curriculum and instructional leaders.

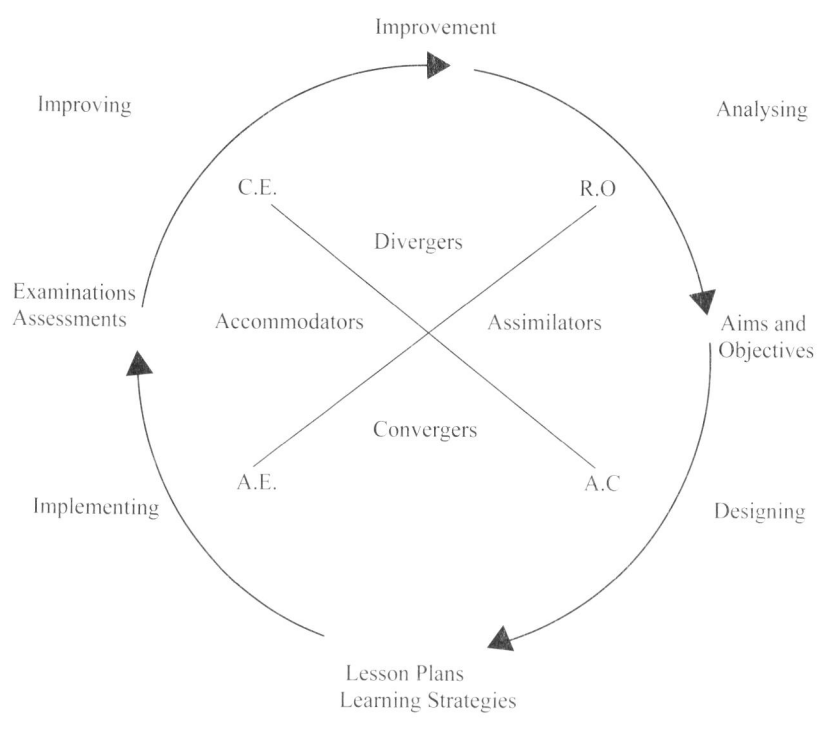

```
                    Improvement
   Improving                              Analysing

              C.E.              R.O
                    Divergers

  Examinations
  Assessments   Accommodators  Assimilators   Aims and
                                              Objectives
                    Convergers
              A.E.              A.C

   Implementing                             Designing

                    Lesson Plans
                    Learning Strategies
```

Key to Diagram

- C.E.   Concrete Experience
- R.O   Reflective Observation
- A.C.   Abstract Conceptualisation
- A.E.   Active Experimentation

Fig 13.1. The Cycle of renewal in Murray's model of the renewing school (Given in a paper to the Society for Management in Education in Ireland and subsequently revised and published in 1994 as "From Subject Based Curriculum Development to Whole School Improvement. *Educational Management and Administration*. 22, (2), 160 – 167)

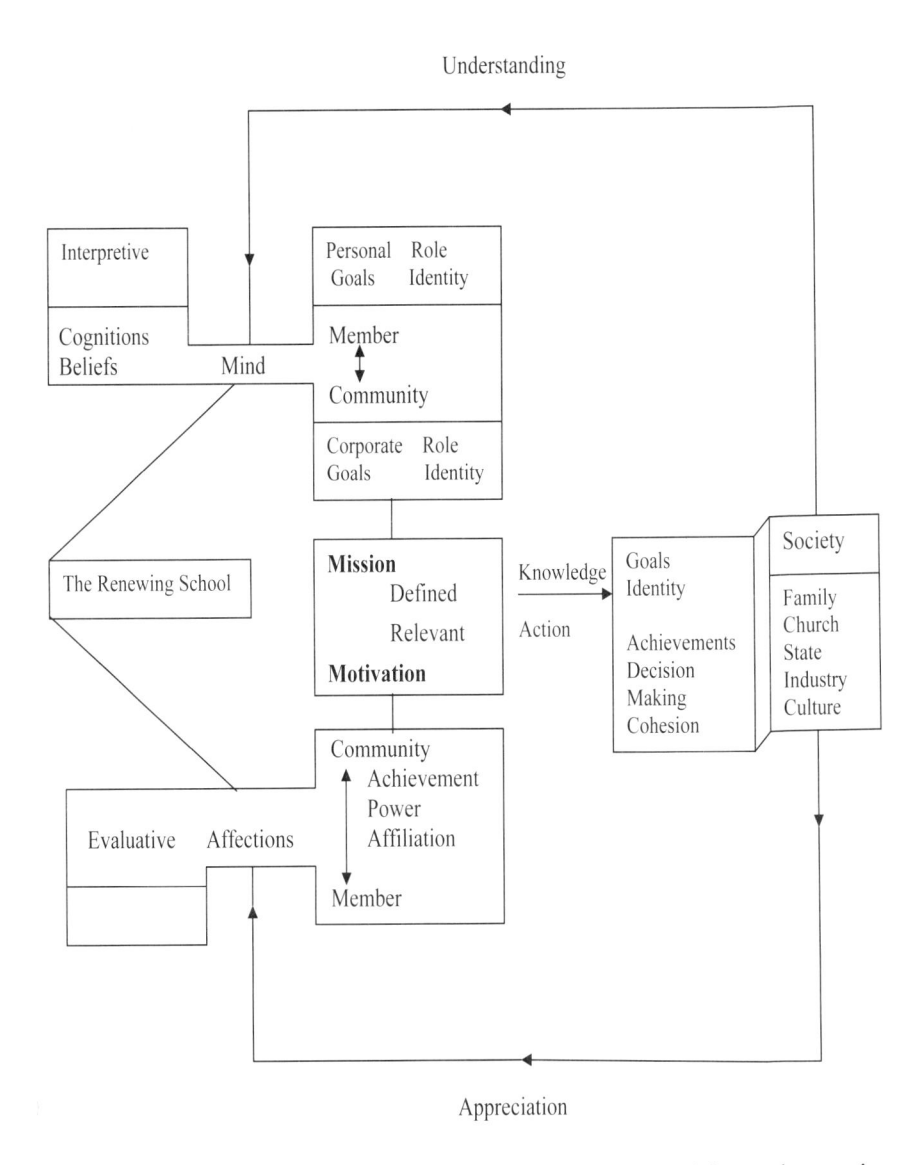

Fig 13. 2. Murray's application of the experiential learning model to the curriculum design process (Given in a paper to the Society for Management in Education in Ireland and subsequently revised and published in 1994 as "From Subject Based Curriculum Development to Whole School Improvement. *Educational Management and Administration.* 22, (2), 160 – 167)

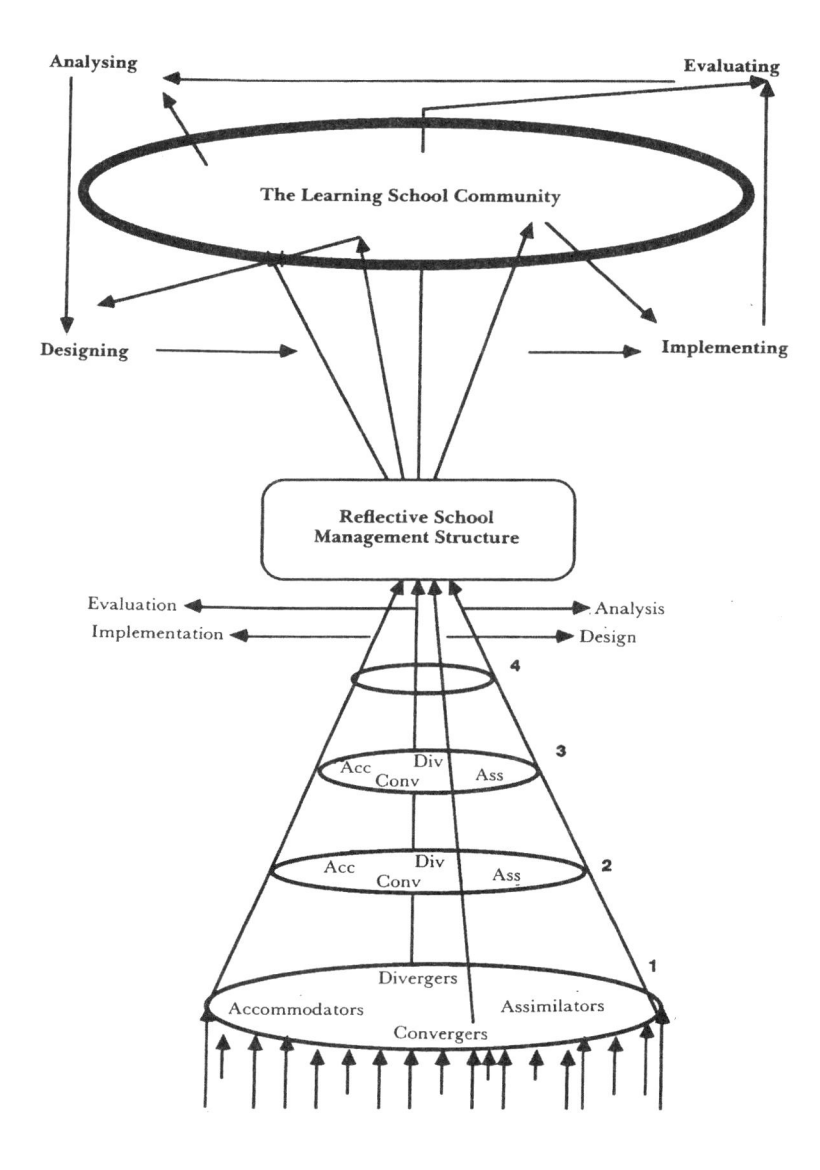

Fig 13.3. Murray's illustration of how the individual learning styles are harnessed by the initiative and are directed by school management towards the development of a learning/problem solving school (Given in a paper to the Society for Management in Education in Ireland and subsequently revised and published in 1994 as "From Subject Based Curriculum Development to Whole School Improvement. *Educational Management and Administration.* 22, (2), 160 – 167)

INSTRUCTIONAL AND CURRICULUM LEADERSHIP

Notes and references

[1] Mentkowski, M and associates (2000). *Learning that Lasts. Integrating Learning, Development, and Performance in College and Beyond.* Jossey Bass, San Fransisco p 138.

[2] MacFarlane Smith, I (1964). *Spatial Ability.* University of London Press, London

[3] Gardner, H (1985*). Frames of Mind.* Basic Books, New York.

[4] 1. Linguistic Intelligence. All the skills involved in writing, reading, talking and listening. Everyone is endowed with potential in this area. (It is not an auditory-oral form of intelligence because the deaf have the ability to acquire natural language and are able to master other systems of communication)
2. Musical Intelligence. A talent which emerges early but for the majority ceases to develop after school years begin.
3. Logical-Mathematical Intelligence. Is involved in mathematical and scientific thinking and numerical computation. More generally in the solving of logical problems.
4. Spatial Intelligence. An intelligence which draws together a number of loosely connected abilities related to the forming of spatial relationships.
5. Bodily-Kinesthetic Intelligence. Completes the trio of object related intelligences. This intelligence is exercised in the control of one's body. Involved in acting, athletics, dancing and making things (eg as in metal work and surgery). Such activities are problem solving activities.
6. Interpersonal Intelligence. Involved in the understanding of other people and one's self in relation to other.
7. Intrapersonal Intelligence. The skill involved in understanding one's self.
Later, he suggested two more intelligences (Gardner, 1995). These were the naturalist and he spiritual which latterly was called the existential. The naturalist is the capacity we have for interaction and affinity with nature and the environment. The existential relates to intuition and awareness of the future and past.

[5] Armstrong, T (2003). *The Multiple Intelligences of Reading and Writing. Making the Words Come Alive.* Association for Supervision and Curriculum Development, Alexandria VA
Campbell, L and B. Campbell (1999) *Multiple Intelligences and Student Achievement. Success Stories from Six Schools.* Association for Supervision and Curriculum Development, Alexandria, VA

[6] Sternberg, R. J (1985) *Beyond IQ. A Triarchic Theory of Human Intelligence.* Cambridge University Press, Cambridge

[7] *loc. cit* ref 1

[8] Goleman, D (1995). *Emotional Intelligence.* Bantam Books, New York

[9] Zirkl, S (2000) Social intelligence: the development and maintence of purposive behavioir. Ch 1 in R. Bar-On and J. D. E. Parker (eds). *The Handbook of Emotional Intelligence.* Jossey-Bass, San Fransisco.

[10] Hedlund, J and R. J. Sternberg (2000) Too many intelligences? Integrating social, emotional and practical intelligence. In I. R. Bar – On and J. D. E. Parker. *The Handbook of Emotional Intelligence.* Jossey-Bass, San Fransisco

[11] Bar – On, I. R. and J. D. E. Parker. *The Handbook of Emotional Intelligence.* Jossey-Bass, San Fransisco

[12] Bar-On, I. R (2000). Emotional and social intelligence. Insights from the Emotional Quotient Inventory in I. R. Bar On and J. D. E. Parker (eds) *The Handbook of Emotional Intelligence.* Jossey-Bass, San Fransisco.

[13] Mayer, J. D., Salovey, P., and D. R. Caruso (2000) Emotional intelligence as zeitgeist, as personality and mental ability. Ch 5 of I. R. Bar – On and J. D. E. Parker (eds) *The Handbook of Emotional Intelligence.* Jossey-Bass, San Fransisco.

[14] Culver, R. S. (1998). A review of emotional intelligence by Daniel Goldman. Implications for technical education. *Proceedings Frontiers in Education Conference (IEEE)* 855 –860.

[15] Stone, K. F. and H. Q. Dillehunt (1978) *Self Science. The Subject in Me.* Goodyear Publications, Santa Monica, CA

[16] *loc.cit*

[17] Hopson, B and M. Scally (1981). *Lifeskills Teaching.* McGraw Hill, London

[18] Sternberg, R. J and E. L. Grigorenko (2000) Practical intelligence and its development in chapter 10 R. Bar – On and J. D. E. Parker (eds) *The Handbook of Emotional Intelligence.* Jossey-Bass, San Fransisco

[19] *loc.cit*

[20] Sternberg, R. J., Okagaki, L and A. S. Jackson (1990). Practical intelligence for success in school. *Educational Leadership,* September, 35 – 39.

[21] Perkins, D (2003). *King Arthur's Round Table. How Collaborative Conversations create Smart Organizations.* Wiley, New York. p73

[22] *loc.cit* ref 1

[23] This is of course a very simplified view of Piaget's theory. It is expressed in this way to indicate the period of higher order thinking. The theory of psychological development depends on biological maturation; experience with the physical environment; experience with the social environment and equilibration. It is the latter that is unique to his theory. There are schemes or structure which enables the child to *assimilate* the external environment. But the *assimilation* of new information also requires that there should be a change in the existing structures so that there is a congruence between external reality and the child's mental structures. This process is called accommodation. *Equiliberation* is the adjustive process required for *assimilation* and *accommodation*.

[24] Perry, W. G. (1970). *Intellectual and Ethical Development in College years. A Scheme*. Holt, Rinehart and Winston, New York.

[25] Marra, R and B. Palmer (1999) Encouraging intellectual growth: senior engineering profiles. *Proceedings Frontiers in Education Conference*, 2, 12c1-1 to 6.

[26] Jordan, W. M. (1990) Letter. *Engineering Education*. 80 (April) 359 – 360.

[27] Culver, R. S., Woods, D., and P. Fitch (1990). Gaining professional expertise through design activities. *Engineering Education*, 80, (5), 533 –536.

[28] Bantock, G. H. *Freedom and Authority in Education*. Faber and Faber, London.

[29] Newman, J. H. (1870). *Essay in Aid of a Grammar of Assent*. Longmans, London.

[30] King, P. M and K. S. Kitchener (1994). *Developing Reflective Judgement*. Jossey –Bass, San Fransisco. P xvi

[31] Their book contains a useful summary of the different theories of critical thinking

[32] Fischer's skill theory is an attempt to resolve the paradox of investigations that show that most adults cannot perform complex tasks, yet common experience suggests they can think in sophisticated ways about abstract concepts. Fischer argued that these contradictory findings may be explained by a theory that considers cognitive development to be a function of the collaboration that a person has with his/her environment. Fischer calls this collaborative framework "skill theory". The contradictory findings of research are explained by the systematic variations in an individual's levels of performance. Individuals routinely function below their highest capacity in ordinary environmental conditions, but in environments that optimize performance they demonstrate high levels of performance (Fischer, Kenny and Pipp, 1990). New levels of competence which enable adolescents and young adults to understand abstract concepts are acquired yet most of their behaviour does not suggest they have made cognitive advances. One criterion that suggests a change in cognitive developmental level is a sudden alteration in performance during a limited age period. Fischer calls this a "spurt". The change from one cognitive level to another is characterised by a cluster of "spurts" in performance. The spurts do not occur at exactly the same age, nor do they take exactly the same form. Adolescents do not suddenly metamorphose on their fifteenth birthday. Instead, the change is relatively rapid, occupying a small interval of time. (Fischer, K. W., Kenny, S. L. and S. L. Pipp, 1990) . How cognitive processes and environmental conditions organize discontinuities in the development of abstractions. In C. N. Alexander and E. J. Langer (eds). *Higher Stages of Human Development*. Oxford University Press).

[33] Wood, P. K (1997). A secondary analysis of claims regarding the reflective judgement interview. Internal consistency, sequentiality and intra-individual differences in ill-structured problem solving in J. Smart (ed) *Higher Education. Handbook of Theory and Research*. Agathon Press, New York.

[34] They provided a list of resources ranging across the arts and sciences (King, 1992).

[35] Tsang, E (2002). Use assessment to develop service learning reflection courses. *Proceedings Frontiers in Education Conferences*,(IEEE) 2, F2A- 15 to 19.

[36] *loc.cit* ref 1

[37] Macmurray, J (1956). *The Self as Agent*. Faber and Faber, London. p 21

[38] *ibid* p185

[39] *loc.cit* ref 1

[40] *ibid* p185

[41] McGrath, F (1961). *The Consecration of Learning*. Gill, Dublin p128.

[42] Newman, J. H. (1947 edition ed Harrold). *The Idea of a University*. Longmans, London. Sixth Discourse pp 118 –119. For a detailed critical commentary see McGrath *loc cit*. McGrath pp 94 and 95 points out that Newman uses the term "philosophy" or a "philosophical knowledge" not in the traditional but in an analogous sense…"*Philosophy, then is Reason exercised upon knowledge; or the knowledge not merely of things in general but of things in relations to one another. It is the power of referring everything to its true place in the universal system […]*"

[43] Matthews, G. B (1980). *Philosophy and the Young Child*. Harvard University Press, Boston, MA

[44] Piaget, J (1951). *Play, Dreams and Imitation in Childhood*. Norton, New York

[45] Isaacs, S (1930) *Intellectual Growth in Young Children*. Routledge and Kegan Paul, London

[46] Williams, J. T (1995). *Pooh and the Philosophers*. Dutton, New York.
[47] Donnely, P (2003). *Wondering and the World and the Universe: Philosophy on the Early Classroom Years*. Eriugena Lecture Series, Lecture 1. St Patrick's College, Drumcondra
[48] Lipman, M (a) (1988). *Philosphy goes to School*. Temple University Press, Philadelphia. (b) (1988) Critical thinking. What can it be? *Analytic Teaching* 8, 5 – 12.
[49] Lipman, M., Sharp, A. M. and F. Oscanyon (1980) *Philosophy in the Classroom*. Temple University Press, Philadelphia
[50] *loc.cit* Donnelly
[51] ICPIC (1991) Philosophy for children and the opportunity for thinking in education. An interview with Matthew Lipman by Z. Carneiro de Maura. *Bulletin of the International Council for Philosophical Inquiry with Children*. 6, (2), 3 – 7.
[52] Johnson, R. H. (1992). The problem of defining critical thinking in S. Norris (ed). *The Generalizability of Critical Thinking*. Teachers College Press, New York
[53] Elkind, D (1988) *The Hurried Child. Growing up too Fast too Soon*. Addison Wesley, Reading MA
[54] Kohlberg, L (1963) The development of children's orientations toward moral order. 1 Sequence in the development of moral thought. *Human Development*, 6, 11 – 33.
[55] Kohlberg, L. (1975) with D. Ellenbein. The devlopment of moral judgements concerning capital punishment. *American Journal of Orthopsychiatry* 45, 615 – 640 and (1975b) with Kaufman, K., Scharf, P., and J. Hickey. The Just Community approach to corrections. A theory. *Journal of Moral Education*, 4, 243 –260.
[56] Baumrind, D (1978) A dialectical materialist's perspective on knowing and social reality in W. Damon (ed). *New Directions in Child Development Moral Development*. Jossey – Bass, San Fransisco, CA
[57] Blatt, M. M., and L. Kohlberg (1975). The effects of classroom moral discussion upon children's level of moral development. *Journal of Moral Education* 4,129 –161.
[58] Berkowitz, M. W and J. C. Gibbs (1985).The process of moral conflict resolution and moral development in M. W. Berkowitz (ed) *Peer Conflict and Psychological Growth*. Jossey Bass, San Fransisco.
[59] Marshall, S (1980). Cognitive affective dissonance in the classroom. *Teaching Political Science*, 8, 111 –117.
[60] Power, F. C., Higgins, A., and L. Kohlberg (1989) *Lawrence Kohlberg's Approach to Moral Education*. Columbia University Press, New York.
[61] Schweder, R., Turiel, E., and N. Much (1986). The moral intuitions of the child in J. H. Flavell and L. Ross (eds*) Social Cognitive Development. Frontiers and Possible Futures*. Cambridge University Press, New York.
[62] Weston, D and E. Turiel (1980) Act role relations: children's concepts of social rules. *Developmental Psychology*, 16, 417 – 424.
[63] *loc.cit*
[64] Gilligan, C (1982). *A Different Voice: Psychological Theory and Women's Development*. Harvard UP, Cambridge, MA
[65] Lyons, N. P. (1983). Two perspectives on self, relationships and morality. .*Harvard Educational Review*, 53, (2), 125 – 145.
[66] Rest, J (1973) The hierarchical nature of moral judgement. The study of patterns of preference and comprehension of moral judgements made by others. *Journal of Personality*, 41, 86 – 209.
[67] see (a) Walker, L. J (1984). Sex differences in the development of moral reasoning: A critical review. *Child Development* 55, 677 – 691 and (b) Rest, J. R., Narvaez, D. F., Bebau, M. J., and S. J. Thoma (1999). *Post Conventional Moral Thinking: A Neo-Kohlbergian Approach*. Erlbaum, Hillsdale, NJ.
[68] Kohlberg, L (1990) with R. A. Ryncarz. Beyond justice reasoning. Moral development and consideration of the seventh stage in C. N. Alexander and E. J. Langer (eds). *Higher Stages of Human Development. Perspectives on Adult growth*. Oxford University Press, New York
[69] Gilligan, C., Murphy, J. M., and M. B. Tappan (1990). Moral development beyond adolescence in C. N. Alexander and E. J. Langer (eds*). Higher Stages of Human Development. Perspectives on Adult Growth*. Oxford University Press, New York.
[70] *loc.cit*
[71] Kohlberg, L (1984). Essays on Moral development. Vol 2. *The Psychology of Moral Development*. Harper and Row, New York
[72] (a) Blasi, A (1980). Bridging moral cognition and moral action: A critical review of the literature. *Psychological Bulletin*, 88, (1), 1 –45. (b) Thoma, S (1994). Moral judgements and moral action in J. R. Rest and D. Narváez (eds). *Moral Development in the Professions. Psychology and Applied Ethics*. Erlbaum, Hillsdale, NJ.

(b) *loc. cit* ref 68. See also 67(b)

[73] *ibid*

[74] Moran, G (1984). *Religious Education Development. Images for the Future*. Winston Press, Minneapolis

[75] Whitehead, A. N. (1930). *The Aims of Education*. Benn, London.

[76] Murray, M (1992) *An Evaluation of an Introductory Programme in Management Studies for Schools*. Doctoral Dissertation. University of Dublin, Dublin

[77] Murray, M. F (1994). From subject based curriculum development to whole school improvement. *Educational Management and Administration*, 22, (3), 160 – 167.

[78] These come from McCllelland, D. C. (1961). *The Achieving Society*. Van Nostrand, New York.

[79] He cites Burns, T and G. Stalker (1961) *The Management of Innovation*. Tavistock, London.

[80] He cites p 74 of Heywood, J (1989). *Learning, Adaptability and Change*, Chapman, London.

Retrospect and prospect

Retrospect

The over-arching objective of this text has been to map the knowledge base required by instructional and curriculum leaders. Curriculum was defined as the formal mechanism through which educational aims are (intended to be) achieved. As such, it embraces content, assessment and evaluation, instruction and learning. It relates to the collective programme, that is the combination of all the subjects (disciplines) offered, or to the subjects (discipline) themselves, or to interdisciplinary areas of knowledge. Curriculum leadership is a sub-set of educational leadership and relates specifically to the curriculum. In the same way instructional leadership is both a sub-set of educational and curriculum leadership that relates specifically to instruction.

Four levels of curriculum and instructional leadership were described. A teacher who practices classroom assessment procedures[1] and in so doing, practices self-accountability describes the first level. A second level is reached when a teacher tries to learn through more formal research into his/her own classroom practices. The four chapters on instruction (6 through 9) illustrated such research with investigations carried out by student teachers into their own instruction. This second level requires more knowledge than the first. It requires a technical pedagogy, and these chapters illustrated some of the technical components of that pedagogy. It was argued that teachers who, in an ethos that values experience above research, spend time on classroom assessment strategies and classroom research are leading themselves, and by example others. Schools need teachers who have not only the knowledge but the skills to be able lead others. Leadership here is taken to include advice and help. This is a third level of leadership and embraces the curriculum as well as instruction. At this level a teacher is able to participate in curriculum making. A knowledge base for curriculum making was presented in chapters 9 – 13. A fourth level is reached when the teacher is prepared to engage in 'political' discussions in the public arena about the nature of the curriculum and instruction. Persons who function at this level do not accept the *status quo*.

For effective self-assessment a teacher has to develop the skills of reflective practice. Thus effective performance at level 1 is indicative of a reflective practitioner. It is also indicative of an "extended" professional. Those who function at levels 1 and 2 will be comfortable with subject review and whole school inspection.[2] Teachers who have the opportunity to participate in curriculum making are likely to increase their professionalism. They become engaged in the scholarship of teaching. There is therefore a need for greater subsidiarity.

Schools are being challenged to make learning more meaningful and this will mean both curriculum and instructional change some of it driven by technological innovation. Schools will have to become "inquiry oriented" and this will mean a new role for principals. But while it is necessary for principals to understand the tasks of curriculum and instructional leadership they may well have to delegate the actual task to their middle management. Both Principals' and their curriculum leaders will need to be schooled in the art of change and in this respect "assumptional-dialogues" have a major role to play.

Through discussion and inference the second intention of this text was to outline the principles of curriculum and instructional design. The model of the process that was presented described a system in which assessment, instruction and learning were integrated so as to achieve specified aims and objectives. *The Taxonomy of Educational Objectives* and its significance for curriculum and assessment development was discussed. The concepts of multiple-strategy assessment and balanced systems of assessment were presented.

While *The Taxonomy* remains an extremely valuable tool, it is not the only source of objectives neither is it the only grouping of sub-objectives in the domains. The importance of general statements of aims cannot be understated. They are the emotional pegs that support a teacher's motivation. When a new curriculum is proposed or an existing curriculum revised or redeveloped the starting point is the declaration of aims.

The task of deriving aims and objectives and ensuring they are complementary and not contradictory depends on a substantial knowledge of philosophy, psychology, sociology and history as applied to education. Thus curriculum leaders require defensible theories of epistemology, learning and instruction. Therefore, a third intention of this text has been to demonstrate the relevance of philosophy, psychology, sociology and history to the design of curriculum and instruction. The view taken in this text is that there is no general theory of the curriculum. Most theories give some insight, if only small, into human behaviour. Some theories are attractive to teachers while others are not. Those that are acceptable indicate the possible, and curriculum design is in part the art of the possible. Curriculum leaders have to be eclectic in their approach. It is hoped that the principles set out in the text provide a base for consideration of issues not discussed in this text.

A fourth intention was to demonstrate from the investigations reported by post graduate student teachers that pupils like variety in teaching, and that is apart from the need to understand and respond to student learning styles. Many of these students were challenged by the experience of having to utilise unfamiliar methods of teaching and found that they often had to change their roles. These studies supported the view that instructional strategies have to be designed to the meet the objectives that have been declared. As diSessa[3] writes *"an excellent learning environment is a melding of many short and long term goals, a complex negotiation of many overlapping contexts."* The problem is teachers are not trained to understand the complexity of learning or, if they are they are not encouraged or shown how to relate this to practice. Moreover, this is often reinforced by poor systems of assessment and examining. There are few examples of balanced systems of assessessment. A curriculum and instructional leader should be the focus for advice on these matters in a school. These studies also suggested that in some areas of instruction there need to be whole school policies, that apply across the disciplines or areas of knowledge. Strategies of teaching and learning that are thought to produce good results can be over utilised. Instruction has to be balanced within subjects and across the curriculum (see below).

It is clear that to some extent in addition to offering advice and practical help a curriculum leader may have to be an agent of change. Curriculum leaders need to understand that changes are of two kinds. First order changes belong to those that are considered to be incremental and a logical next step. Helping a teacher to move toward level 1 of curriculum and instructional leadership is an example of first order change. Several ideas about what a curriculum leader can do to bring about first order change were given in the text. By contrast second order change is a departure from the expected, as for example the development of a new transition year programme or whole school policies on instruction. *"Incremental change fine-tunes the system through a series of small steps that do not depart radically from the past"* for the majority of individuals involved. *"Deep change alters the system in fundamental ways, offering a dramatic shift in direction requiring new ways of thinking and acting."*[4] Strategies for first order change are unlikely to bring about second order change.

The text did not focus on a number of issues or areas that are the province of curriculum leadership. The first, while noting its significance, the hidden curriculum was not considered in detail. There is much that could have been said about educational institutions as socio-technical systems or, the influence of peer groups or gender (in particular women's ways of knowing) or the media and violence or family insecurity, or the culture- in particular as it relates to achievement. Similarly little or no attention was paid to language because the text has focussed on post-primary (11 years to 18 years) education. This is not the case in the US where writing courses continue through to higher education. Research in the United States has shown that writing can contribute to the development of problem solving skills.[5] Very often there is collaboration between writing specialists and subject teachers[6] and it is argued that it may help reflective practice. The more extensive one's vocabulary, the more one has the capability for reflective and critical thought.
Given the ideology of inclusion and the mainstreaming of students with disabilities[8] as well as the increasing diversity to be found in classrooms there is now

considerable interest in the curriculum and teaching for such diversity[9] which today is something more than mixed ability teaching. Unfortunately the capacity for academic activity is not evenly distributed. In any case there might be too much emphasis on academic development at the expense of the development of other talents that pupil's may have. This point is underlined by Gardener's theory of multiple intelligences which might be regarded as a theory of multiple talents. The need for a "balanced curriculum" is apparent and this was discussed chapters 12 and 13.

They serve to remind us that statements about education being for the "whole person" are somewhat platitudinous. The education system expects this development to happen mostly by osmosis. Indeed because assistance in these areas depends in no small measure on non-traditional modes of teaching which are likely to be condemned out of hand, positive developments in these areas are unlikely to happen, unless there is a radical change in thinking. It is a paradox that governments should worry about the social behaviour of children and adolescents, ask the schools to do something about it, but fail to recognise that there is little they can do within the constraints of an academic curriculum that has been granted pre-eminence.

Detailed consideration was not given to the content of subject disciplines and their role in developing cognitive skills and value acquisition. Several subject associations across the world have made major contributions to the development of their subjects (e.g. societies associated with mathematics, science and technology education) and more generally to our understanding of learning. There have been controversies in both the US and UK about English and History. Perhaps the subject that has received most attention is mathematics. Children simply do not like mathematics. President Bush has just created a national panel to consider how to improve the effectiveness of mathematics education in the US.[10] But the principle of curriculum design within the disciplines is no different to that for the curriculum as a whole or the design of instructional procedures.

Prospect

During the last half of the twentieth century and continuing to the present the teaching profession has become de-professionalised. Some would question if it was ever professionalied. Nevertheless it is clear that governments have increased, in varying degrees, some to the extent of micro-management, their control over teaching and teaching practices. Many of these controls have been implemented as a result of opinion, prejudice and ideology. Few of them are "evidence based." Moreover, they encourage restricted professionalism. Yet teachers are as much to blame for this state of affairs as anyone else. They have allowed the socialisation process into teaching to limit their horizons. They have not wanted to exercise subsidiarity. And, therein lies the possibility of change if instruction is to be as effective as it should be. Policy makers have to realise that micro-management ultimately limits the effectiveness of the teacher. Teachers have to realise that there is much more to instruction than the limited knowledge derived from experience. They have to respond to theories that are evidence based, be prepared to evaluate and research their own work, and acquire theories of epistemology and learning brought together in a defensible philosophy of education. Programmes for the education and training of teachers are not exempt from criticism. They have to acquire a language that will encourage teachers in that theory-practice endeavour and not be seen to be producers of the irrelevant.

The investigations reported in this text show that students like variety of instruction. They respond well to instructional situations that give them ownership of their learning. At the same time they want that instruction to be well organized whether it is teacher centred or student centered. They want, as society does, schools and teachers to learn how to deal with intransigent students. But students and teachers expect policy makers to understand that many of these problems lie deep in the mores of society, a mores that are created as much by society as by policy makers. Society and its policy makers have to listen to teachers when they comment from an evidence base.

But what of the immediate can there be school and teacher driven change within existing systems. The answer offered in this text is yes. First, teachers can learn to be more effective assessors than they are. That is a problem for training which cannot be superficial and has to go beyond test and measurement to the more general understanding of student behaviour. Second, if higher order thinking skills are to be developed public systems of examining and assessment will have to be changed. The more teachers become involved in these systems the more likely such skills are to be developed. This text did not discuss models for the organization of assessment and examining that involved some school-based activity but there have been experiments and they can be effective.[11]

More immediately Principals can do two things. First, they can embrace the idea of an inquiry-oriented school, or if they do not like that term, the idea of the school as a learning system and a system for learners. Second in order to do this they will need to embrace and encourage the idea of curriculum and instructional leadership in their schools. Looked at from this perspective there is much that can be done in schools to improve instruction and make the curriculum more effective.

Notes and references

[1] Procedures of the kind defined by Angelo, T and K. P. Cross (1993). *Classroom Assessment Techniques.* 2nd Edition. Jossey Bass, San Fransisco

[2] As practised in Ireland subject review is the inspection of teaching in post-primary education. Whole school inspection like the title implies relates to the whole school rather than to subjects, although it may include visits to classrooms.

[3] DiSessa A. A. (1998). What do "just plain folk" know about physics. In D. R. Olson and N. Torrance (eds). *The Handbook of Education and Human Development..* Blackwell, Oxford.

[4] Marzano, R. J., Waters, T and B. McNulty (2005). *School Leadership that Works. From Research to Results.*

Association for Supervision and Curriculum Development, Alexandria, VA. Ch 5.

[5] Brent, R and R. M. Felder (1992) Writing assignments. Pathways to connections, clarity, creativity. *College Teaching*, 40 (2), 43 – 47.. Also Kloss, R. J (1996) Writing things down versus writing things up: Are research papers valid? *College Teaching*, 44, (1), 3 – 7. Also Wolfe, P (2001) *Brain Matters. Translating Research into Classroom Practice*. Association for Supervision and Curriculum Development, Alexandria, VA

[6] Walvoord, B. E. and L. P. McCarthy (1990). *Thinking and Writing in College. A Naturalistic Study of Students in Four Discipline.*. National Council of Teachers of English, Urbana, IL

Rubin, D (1992). *Teaching Reading and Study Skills in the Content Areas*. 2nd edition. Allyn and Bacon, Boston

[7] Kramp, M. K. and W. L. Humphreys (1993). Narrative self-assessment and the reflective learner. *College Teaching*, 41, (3), 83 – 88

[8] McLeskey, J and N. L. Waldron (2002) School change and inclusive schools: lessons learned from practice. *Phi Delta Kappan* 84, (1), 65 – 72.

[9] *ibid*

[10] From ASEE International Engineering Education Digest, May 2006 p 6.

[11] See for example Appendix c of Heywood, J and M. Murray (2005). Curriculum-Led Staff Development. Towards Curriculum and Instructional Leadership in Ireland. *Bulletins of the EFEA (European Forum on Educational Administration)* No 4. Pp 90 –95. Sheffield Hallam University, School of Education/EFEA.

Subject Index

Academic self-image scale, 117
Academic versus Practical, 350
Accountability (self), 16, 17, 18, 27, 28 30
Accountability, 7ff, 16
Achievement, 240
-motivation, 65, 66, 300
Action research. 27, 4245
Advanced Organizers. 55, 97 ff
Affective domain, 273, 288 ff
Aims (see also objectives, screening), 125, 132, 133, 349
- conflicts about, 300
- and culture, 300, 301
'A' level (GCE) examinations
Alverno College. 43, 326, 329, 330, 336, 350
- curriculum, 327
- self assessment, 260
American College testing program (ACT), 322
- College Outcome Measures Program, 340, 342 ff
- and SCANS, 340 ff
Assessment (see also classroom, evaluation), 2, 17
- Alverno College, 327
- authentic, 147, 148
- balanced system of, 322
- classroom. 27
- as evaluation., 28
- learning strategies, 213, 215
- led curriculum, 321, 322
- multiple strategy, 2492, 355
- Portfolio, 72
- of reflective judgement, 364
- Rote meorization, 104
- university influence on, 326
Assumptional dialogues 3, 19, 21, 22, 30, 36, 46, 45, 54, 57, 70, 104, 155, 182, 204, 206, 240, 262, 286, 365
Attribution theory, 63
Attention, 68
Ausubel's theory of instruction, 196
Authentik, 94
Autocratic teacher, 81, 82
Autonomy, 74
Autotelic (motivation) 74

Balanced system of assessment, 323
Balanced curriculum, 350 ff., 380, 385
Behaviour (see discipline)
- disruptive, 54, 62
Benchmarks (see standards), 326
Bloom Taxonomy (see taxonomies), 67
Bruner's theories of learning and instruction, 189
- discovery learning 190 ff.
- transfer, 193

Change (change agents), 11
- first/second order, 306, 307
- resistance to change, 307, 308, 384
- pupil resistance to - 104
Children (attitudes to discipline), 62
Civic, social and political education., 309, 311
City Colleges of Technology, 342
Classroom assessment, 17, 382
Classroom
-affective behaviour in, 93
-culture 350
- extra activity, 350
- size, 202, 204
Classroom research. 17, 18, 42, 45 ff.
Classroom statistics/tests 135 ff
Classrooms (design of), 217, 218
Cognition (theory of Ausubel), 157
Cognitive dissonance, 66
Cognitive organizsation, 103, 104
Cognitive structures. 55,
- of reluctant learners, 104
Cognitive style (see learning styles) (ch 8)
Co-learners . 42
College Learning Assessment Project, 343
College Outcomes Measures Program, 345, 346
- portfolio assessment, 341, 342
- socio-economic status, 338
Comprehension, 92 ff
Committee on Form and function of the Intermediate Certificate Examination, 182, 196, 273, 297
Concept mapping. 27, 174 ff
Concepts
- characteristics of, 167 ff

- and curriculum content, 157, 158, 178
- complex (ity), 176 ff
- fuzzy (see complex)
(see also misunderstandings/misconceptions of)
- as objectives, 126
- problems in teaching (166 ff)
- types of (167 ff)
Concept teaching/learning
- analogy/metaphor, 176, 177
- best example, 177
- with cartoons, 170
- coping with complexity (see complex),176 ff
- de Cecco and Crawford model, 166 ff, 175
- use of examples in, 171 ff
- lesson plan for, 173
- metaphor, 176
- (see also verbal and visual mediation)
Concrete operations, 357
Conservation, 104
Constructivism, 157, 163, 164, 299, 306 ff
- negotiated curriculum, 308
- and teaching, 165
Content (syllabus), 126, 157
Convergent thinking, 209
Cooperative learning, 109 ff, 119, 289
- evaluation of, 113 ff
- group processing, 116, 117
- rewards in 116
- and social skills, 119
- versus small groups, 110, 111
Council of Aid to Education (US), 343
Coursework. 301
Critical thinking. 243, 280, 281 283 286
- definition of, 284
- immersion/infusion, 243
- profile of 286
- and the Taxonomy, 284
Culture, 10, 16, 22
- of classroom, 134
- of collaboration, 21
- extra curricular activity, 350
- influence on aims, 300
- in staffroom, 127
Cultural literacy, 304
Cumulative frequency, 146
Curriculum, 2, 6, 7, 23, 293 (chapters 11 and 12- see also hidden curriculum)
- adaptability, 349

- assessment led, 321, 322
- balanced, 350
- coherent, 302
- critical praxis, 301, 305
- cultural heritage, 303, 304
- culture, 300, 301, 350
- currere, 301
- definition of, 297
- design of (Making),124, 125, 178 ff, 182, 313 ff
- development 6, 7
- evidence based, 385
- hidden, 298
- hybrids, 310, 311
- ideological, 299
- images of, 301
- independent study, 308
- informal curriculum, 298
- key concepts for design of, 171 ff
- making, 8, 9, 10
- mini courses, 315
- models of (process) 124 ff
- multiple strategy, 32, 232
- national, 324
- negotiated, 308
- operational, 308
- ownership of, 308
- for practical intelligence, 355
- perceived, 298
- received, 6, 302 ff
- reconceptualisation of, 318
- reflexive, 305
- resistance to change,307
- restructuring
- skills based, 23
- spiral, 316
- structure of, 308
- taught, 298
- and teaching, 6
- Tyler's model of, 314
- and thinking skills, 261
- working class, 305
Curriculum development, 6, 7
- school based, 8
Curriculum integrated assessment, 322
Curriculum reform projects, 22
Curriculum leader (see also Instructional and curriculum leadership- chapter 2), 3
- knowledge base of, 22, 297, 316
- in policy making, 21, 293, 294
- role of, 272, 294, 374

Curriculum specialists. 15

Decision making (learning for) 240, 241, 242, 258
(see also heuristics and problems solving)
- in mixed ability teaching, 257
- model of, 242
- types of, 248
Defining Issues Matrix. 43
Delphi technique. 28
Democratic teacher, 82, 83
Department of Education and Science, 324
Design technology, 304
Development (human) See Chapter 13)
- hurried child, 369
- levels of moral, 369
- in reasoning, 364
- school curriculum, 374
- Piagetian stages of, 357
- criticisms of, 366
- Perry's model of, 358 ff
- King and Kitchener model, 362 ff
- by osmosis, 385
Development (subject specific)
Dictionaries (study skill-use of), 95
Discipline (behaviour). 54, 62
-assertive, 70 ff
- and cognitive dissonance, 66
-and cognitive organization, 104
- learning, 54, 567, 87
- criteria for
- and parents, 58, 62
- the Principal, 57
Discovery learning (chapter 7) 187
- and Bruner, 190 ff
- definition of, 190, 198
- versus expository, 196 ff
- motivation, 200, 202
- and readiness, 189
- and teaching, 201
Divergent thinking, 209

Education (remedial), 106, 107
Education system (Ireland) 320
Educational connoisseurship, 7, 8, 30 ff, 35
Educational criticism. 27, 30, 35 ff
Educational leader (ship), 2, 8, 9, 10ff, 21
Educational Testing Service, 136
Effective teaching, 76
Employers (attitudes to graduates) 337

Employment department (UK), 341
Emotional intelligence, 353 ff
- transition year 355
Engineering Science (A level) 31, 140, 279, 281, 322, 323
Engineers (task analysis of, 3, 9
English (remedial), 105
Enterprise in Higher Education Initiative, 338
Enterprise learning, 338
Epistemology /pedagogy, 298
Essays, 135, 141, 264, 265
- grading, 140, 141
Evaluation, formative, 131
Evaluation (illuminative). 42, 50
Evaluation see assessment
Examinations
- design of, 26, 34, 326
- learning 127
- model answers and grading, 140, 141
- university influence on performance, 108, 238
- skills tested by, 246
Examination questions (see also questions), 102
Expectancy (expectations), 63 ff
- study approach, 214
Experience 9effect on management) 69
Experiential domain, 271, 274, 289
- taxonomy of, 289
Expert versus novice, 159
Expressive outcomes, 270, 285, 287
Expository teaching (see chapter 7) 188, 195
- versus guided, 107 ff
Extraversion. 233

Facts (learning of), 157
Feelings (expression of), 105
Fischer's skill model, 360, 379
Flow, 75
Formal operations, 357
Formative assessment, 131

Gagné's theory of instruction
General Certificate of Education (A level). 48, 241
General certificate of Secondary Education, 326
Geometrical and Engineering drawing at 'A'level, 279, 280

Growth in reasoning, 364
Guided discovery (see discovery)
- knowledge in pieces, 193, 194

Handbook of the Primary Curriculum (Ireland), 195
Heuristic(s) (See chapter 9), 238, 241, 243, 245, 247
- assessment, 259, 260
- in teaching English, 253
- in teaching geography, 254, 255
- in teaching German, 253
- Polya's, 248
- problems in teaching, 256
Wales and Stager's, 249 ff
Hidden curriculum, 298
Hierarchy of needs (Maslow), 77
Higher Diploma in Education, 5
Higher Order Thinking Skills (HOTS), 132, 134, 273, 291, 349
- definition, 284
- self-reflection, 359,
- the Taxonomy, 262
Holistic learning, 210, 21i
Homework, 88 ff
Honey and Mumford Learning Styles, 223, 238

Ideas (and the curriculum) 319
Informal curriculum, 298
Imagery. 55, 88, 104 ff
- and adults, 108
- types of 106
Independent testing, 342
Independent study, 308, 309
Inquiry learning (see discovery)
Inquiry oriented (centred) school(s), 3, 20, 35, 46, 56
Instruction (see chapters 5-9).
- evidence based (see chapters 6-9), 385
- multiple strategy, 234
- Principal's role in 386
- style of, 383
- Wittrock's classification, 198
- variety in, 386
Instructional /Curriculum leaders/ leadership,
- defined, 12, 13, 16 ff, 57, 382
- discipline, 58, 61
- and inquiry oriented school, 263
- levels of, 2, 16 ff, 27ff, 45, 148, 232, 382

- knowledge base for, 9, 123, 316, 383
- mentoring, 123, 155
- as missionary 22
- and policy making, 21, 155, 205, 240, 263, 318
- role of, 12 ff, 57, 87, 117, 240
- role of principal in. 47, 58
- and teachers, 16
- Wittrocks classification of, 198
Inquiry learning (see discovery)
Instructional theories, 127
- Gagné, 159 ff
Integrated study, 322, 328, 329
-integration of skills (curricula), 317, 330, 336 ff
Intellect (growth of), 365
Intelligence, 351, 352
- reflective, 356
- teaching for 356
Interdisciplinary study, 328, 332
Interdisciplinarity,
- types of, 331, 332
Intermediate Certificate Examination. 43, 181, 322, 323
- Committee on Form and Function of, 181
Interpersonal skills, 351
Intra-personal skills, 351
Intrinsic motivation, 73, 74
Introversion, 233
Ireland (phases of school curriculum) 25
Item analysis, 139, 143

Joint Matriculation Board. 32, 200, 270, 322, 323
Junior Certificate Examination, 312, 323

Key concepts, 178, 181
- and curriculum design, 134, 135, 182
Knowledge (theories of)
- as control, 305
- tacit, 355
Kowledge-in-pieces, 194
Kohlberg's theory of moral development (see development)

Leadership (leader) 2 ff, 101ff
League tables, 324
Learned capabilities, 161
Learning

- acquisition of information, 68
- approaches to 214
- attribution, 61, 68
- concepts (see concepts)
- contracts, 62
- in context theory, 215
- curriculum design, 155
- discipline. 54, 56
- definition of, 155
- difficulties, 91 ff
- and elementary schools, 215
- formal education, 63
- and experience (and experiential), 3, 4, 289
- holistic, 106
- imagery, 106
- liberal education, 73
- motivation. (see chapter 3)
- organization for, 16 ff
- outside of school, 90
- perception, 66, 67
- principles of 158 ff
- problem(project) based, 332
- scaffold, 102
- self-study plans, 90
- to teach, 4 ff
- transmission model of, 287
- trial and check, 69
-single/double loop. 49
- spatial orientation, 108
- strategies (see below)
- transfer of, 91
-whole school policies for 234
Learning-how-to-Learn module, 19, 215
Learning organization, 16 ff
Learning Style Inventories, 219 ff
- Characteristics of, 209
- Dunn and Dunn, 216, 217
- Honey and Mumford
- Kolb, 218 ff, 238
- as operators, 227
Learning strategies, 126
- depth/surface, 212 ff
Learning styles
- classroom design, 217, 218
- convergent/divergent, 209
- defined, 208
- factors contributing to, 208
- field dependent/independent, 212
- globe trotting, 211
- holistic, 210

- instruction, 209, 219 ff
-matching with teaching, 211, 212, 218
- self-assessment, 221, 382
- self esteem, 216
- serialist, 210
-versus strategies, 126
Leaving Certificate Applied, 19, 26, 306, 339
Leaving Certificate Examination, 107, 242, 304, 312, 323, 339
Lessons
- content of, 127
- phases of, 127
Lesson planning (see chapter 5). 32 ff, 56, 124 ff
- examples of 129, 130, 223, 224, 227 ff, 250 ff
- use of objectives in 132, 133
- and reflection, 35
Liberal education, 73, 340
Libraries (use of), 96
Locus of control, 214

Managers
- behaviour of, 61
Management, 10, 11, 69
- evidence based, 388
- micro management, 381
- theories of, 58 ff.
Masterful teaching. 57, 75 ff
Mathematics, 108, 113, 115
- epistemologies of, 299
- imagery, 108
McMaster University, 332
Mediating response, 101, 102
Mean mark, 144
Median, 145
Memory 107, 158
Mentor (see instructional leadership)
Meta-cognition (knowing how we learn, 252, 263
Micro projects, 314
Minute paper, 17
Misdemeanours, 86
Misperceptions (see concepts
–misunderstandings of), 162 ff, 170, 178
Mission statement, 272, 293
Mixed ability teaching (see also cooperative learning), 257
Module (definition) 319
Moral development (chapter 13)

- Kohlberg's theory of 369 ff.
- and religion, 371
Motivation (learning and management- see chapter 3), 55, 58, 64, 308
- achievement, 64, 65
- authentic, 75
- autotelic, 74
- in discovery learning (see discovery)
-Extrinsic, 55, 57, 73 ff
- Flow, 74
- Intrinsic, 55, 57, 73 ff
- learning styles, 213
- punishments, 71 ff
- rewards, 71 ff
- self esteem, 74, 77
-Theory X and Theory Y, 59 ff
Music (practice for), 90
Multiple intelligences, 351
Multiple strategy assessment (see assessment), 322

National Association of Principals and deputies (NAPD), 12
National Association of Teachers of Mathematics (US), 326
National Curriculum (England), 324, 337
National Research Council, 249, 322
National University of Ireland , 325
Negotiated curriculum (see also independent study), 308
- transition year, 309
Nominal Group Technique. 45
Non Assertive Motivation Effectiveness (NAME), 75 ff.
Note-taking, 91

Objectives (see also aims, outcomes) (chapter 10), 125, 126, 128, 133,
- Advantages/disadvantages, 95, 278
- behavioural, 276
- curriculum design, 132
- expressive. 270, 285
- non-behavioural, 128, 129
- for history, 282, 288
- and instruction, 95, 205, 291
- lesson planning, 132
- and outcomes, 276
- for religious education
- sources of, 271
- terminology, 272
Objective tests, 137 ff

- advantages/disadvantages, 137, 138
- guessing in, 138
- item (question types), 139, 188
- item analysis, 138 ff
Objectives movement, 273
Operational curriculum, 298
Outcomes (see objectives), 272 ff
- intended/unintended, 276, 277
- terminology, 272

Paedia proposal, 303
Parents,
- the curriculum, 301
- homework, 89
Pedagogy
- epistemology. 299
Performance
- interpersonal problems, 69
- outcomes, 271
Perceptual learning theory (perception). 31, 68, 69
Perry model of development, 323
Personal Transferable Skills, 351, 352
Piaget, J
- stages of development, 357
- criticisms of, 366
Philosophy for children, 356, 365 ff
Philosophy of education, 299
Physics, 323
Pluridisciplinarity, 329
Polya's heuristic, 248, 252
- modified, 259
Portfolio (teaching), 127
Post-leaving Certificate, 342
Practical intelligence, 356
Praise (administration of), 80
Précis (study skill), 93
Principal(s) (see also curriculum and instructional leadership) 4,
-as change agents, 11, 12
-as instructional leaders, 10 ff
- responsibilities of 13, 14, 18
- role of, 9, 10, 57
- teacher expectations of, 10
- in Texas, 11, 18
Principles of learning, 158 ff
Prior knowledge, 124
- test of, 99, 100, 101
Private talk, 169
Problem-based learning, 332, 333
- example of 333

Problem formulation, 241
Problem solving
- levels of difficulty, 245
- processes of 165, 384
- reflective thinking, 260, 261
- role of knowledge, 251
- in science, 241, 244
- steps in 247
- strategies for teaching, 165, 246
- types of, 241
- writing composition, 250
Professional responsibility. 28 ff, 263
Professionals (Professionalism), 7 ff, 16, 18, 22, 263
- curriculum design
- and culture 18
- extended, 7, 19, 28
- restricted, 7
Project(s), 88, 102, 200, 331
Project based learning, 323
Protocols (talk aloud). 27
Psychomotor domain (skills), 106, 271, 272, 274
Public Examinations Evaluation Project, 20, 30, 31, 43, 48, 243, 322

Questions (questioning), 126, 127, 131 ff
- analysis, 145
- higher order, 134
- key concepts, 134
- life skill, 134, 135
- short answer, 140
- spotting for examinations, 246

Rand Corporation, 343
Reading (prior), 103
Readiness, 98, 190
Reasoning (thinking), 213, 284, 358
Received curriculum, 6, 302 ff.
Receiving, 68
Reflection (structured) 35
Reflection (types of), 28, 30, 31
Reflection for action, 373
Reflective journal. 33, 34
Reflective Judgement. 27, 28
Reflective Judgement Interview, 362, 363
Reflective Judgement Model, 359 ff
- teaching, 362
Reflective intelligence, 356, 357
Reflective practice, 7, 16, 28 ff, 34
Reflexive curriculum, 305

Reliability (statistical), 55, 135, 136
Religious education and development, 372
-Moran's model, 372, 373
Remedial education, 103, 106, 107
Renewing school, 373 ff
Representations (Bruner), 189, 190, 191
Revision, 91
Rewards, 71 ff
- attitudes of students, 73
Rubrics (for analysis and synthesis) 264

Satisficing research, 248
SCANS curriculum, 300, 340, 341, 344, 345
Scholastic Aptitude Test, 322, 325
School climate (environmental) 79,
School (s), 2
- climate, 60, 61
- inquiry oriented, 2, 20, 35, 47, 56
- micro culture, 298
- as learning organizations 20
School effectiveness, 18, 24, 25
School leadership, 61
School policy
- discipline/homework, 91
- for learning, 86, 119
SCOOPE project, 307
Screening, 293, 298, 300, 310 ff
- and psychology, 311, 312
Self assessment/reflection, 260, 357, 382
Self-esteem, 74, 77, 87, 113
Set , 63
Set (mechanization), 245, 246, 257, 260
Sheffield University, 337
Sociogram of lass, 228, 235
Southern Regional Examinations Board. 94, 343
Spatial ability, 351
Spiral curriculum, 304
Spiritual (imagery), 107
Standards, 181 287, 326
Standardized test, 150
Statistics (descriptive- see chapter 5). 56
- significance (in classroom testing), 147
- standard deviation, 145, 149
Streaming, 109, 111
Stress (reduction of), 105
Students
- entering characteristics of, 124 ff
- helping the teacher, 259
- high/low achieving, 111

- knowledge about, 207
- resistance to instruction, 204
- rewards (chapter 3), 71 ff
- variety of instruction, 262

Study discipline/skills (teaching of) 87 ff
Subject based development, 374
Subsidiarity, 9, 21, 22

Taxonomies (see also objectives, outcomes- Chapters 5 and 10)
- of Educational Objectives, 128, 181, 262, 270, 271, 274 ff, 383
- categories of, 275
- criticisms of, 272, 274, 279
- Cognitive v affective, 280
- Collier's model 292
- critical thinking/problem solving, 280
- Affective domain (see above,
- Psychomotor domain (see above)
- of engineering objectives, 10
- Imries RECAP model, 291
- the SOLO model, 292
- teacher beliefs about, 293
- terminology, 277

Teacher
- beginning, 16, 17, 36
- evaluation. 37, 38

Teacher leaders, 12 ff

Teacher training.
- Kolbs theory applied to, 230, 232

Teachers
- attitudes to instruction(beginning) 17, 18
- education of, 292
- expectations of pupils, 66
- and experience, 3
- gender of pupils, 65
- influence of past experience on, 321
- out of school learning, 88 ff

Teaching (see chapters 5 – 9). 31
- and examining, 262
- attitudes to instruction
- of intelligence, 356
- language of 273
- practice, 230, 232
-problem solving, 165
-as research (chapters 6 – 9), 17, 18, 27, 30 ff, 38 ff, 45 ff, 155, 198 ff. 263
-socialization into 5 ff
-for thinking, 301

Technical pedagogy 2, 6, 12, 21
Technical, Vocational, Education Initiative (TVEI), 338 ff

Test of Academic Aptitude, 325
Test(ing). 28. 72
Text books design of, 94
The johns Hopkins University, 109
Theology, 296
Theory (and practice). 42
Theory (ies) in use, 22
Theory Y, 47, 60
Theory X, 57, 59
Thinking classes, 280, 367
Tipperary Leader Group, 313
Total Quality Management (TQM), 46
Transdisciplinarity, 329
Transfer (see learning/skill). 40, 91, 155, 157, 160, 193, 251, 349
Transition Year (Ireland) 19, 25, 47, 215, 308, 309, 312, 320, 339
- assessment in, 339
Transition,
-primary to post primary, 9
Trinity College Dublin, 94

Understanding, 159, 281
University of Dublin (Trinity College) 325
University of Leeds, 341
University of Liverpool, 181
University of Minnesota, 109
US Department of Education, 109
US Department of Labor. 341

Valence, 64
Validity. 56, 136
-types of, 136
Verbal mediation, 170
Verbal protocols, 162, 165
Vision, 275
Visual mediation, 169, 170

Wales and Stager heuristic, 250
Wallace Foundation, 20
Whitehead's theory of education, 334, 335
- Murray's model, 373 ff
Whole school evaluation, 9, 44, 46
Whole school planning (see also school policies), 86, 87, 263
Working class, 305

Name Index

Adelman, C. 122
Adler, M. J. 306, 3021
Alexander, C. N. 383
Allport, F. H.64, 84, 85
Alton-Lee, A. 170, 186
Anderson, L. W. 297
Anderson, L. W. 13, 25
Andrich, D. 151
Angelo, T. 18, 25, 38, 36, 44, 49, 390
Antaki, C. 84
Apple, D. K. 246, 267
Apple, M. W. 321
Aquinas, St Thomas. 185.
Archer, J. 186
Argyris, C. 26, 37, 85, 322
Armstrong, T. 381
Aronson, E. 85
Arter, J. E. 150
Ashcroft, M. 186
Astin, A. W. 122
Austin, G. A .85
Ausubel, D. P. 98 ff, 120, 158, 184, 189, 197, 207
Aylwin, G. 121
.
Badger, B. 84
Bain, D.140
Bain, J. D. 239
Ball, T. 84
Bantock, G. H. 362, 382
Barnett, C. 304, 321
Barnes, C. H. 50
Bar-On, J. R. 356, 381
Barrows, H. 350
Batanov, D. M.133, 150
Bates, M. 234, 240
Bates, N. 298
Baumrind, D. 383
Bebau, M. I. 383
Beckman, M. 121
Begle, E. 150, 185, 206
Bell, M. R.277,292, 297, 299
Bellon, E.C. 50, 120, 150. 184
Bellon, J.J 50,, 91, 120, 150. 184
Bennett, C. K. 217, 238

Berger, G. 350
Berkowitz, M. W. 383
Berliner, D. C. 120, 184
Bey, C. 237
Biggs, J. B. 295, 299
Billingham, L. 268
Bishop, A. J. 50 85, 184, 298 321, 322
Blair, A. 243
Blake, R. R. 85
Blank, M. A 50. 120, 150, 184
Blasi, A. 383
Blatt, M. M. 373, 383
Bligh, D. 298
Blomfield, D .84
Bloom, A. 306, 321
Bloom, B. 68, 150, 299, 297
.Blum, R. E. 150
Blyth, W. A. L 24, 187, 235
Bobbit, F. J. 150, 276, 297
Bolton, J.
Boomer, G. 311, 322
Borg, J. M 287, 298
Borich, G. D. 150, 211, 237
Boschee, F. 298, 320, 349
Bostwick, W. D. 275, 297, 280
Boyle, T.73, 85, 120
Brayley, L 187.
Breen, C.51
Brent, R. 390
Briggs, K. C. 234
Briggs, L. J. 207
Brookfield, D. 30, 34. 36, 49
Brophy, J. E. 73, 84, 85, 158, 184
Brown, A. L. 121
Brown, G. 84
Bruner, J. S. 75, 85, 120, 178, 187, 189 ff, 197, 206, 305, 307, 321, 373
Buffy, R. 198, 207
Bullock, D. L.120
Burns, T. 384
Burridge, E. 25
Bush, G. W. 388
Buss, A. H. 187
Buttle, D. 237

NAME INDEX

Caine, G .85
Caine, R. N. 85
Cambell, L. 381
Cameron, L. 239
Campbell, B. 381
Campione, J. C. 121
Candlin, C. N. 186
Canter, L.70, 71, 72, 85
Carpenter, T. P 120
Carr, K. 18, 26
Carroll, P. 225 ff
Carter, G. 120, 151, 207, 237, 267, 249
Caruso, D. R. 381
Chi, M. 103, 121, 185
Chookittikul, W.133
Chritiano, S. J. E, 3423,348, 351.
Clandinin, D, 7, 23, 322
Clarke, A. R 150
Clarke, A-M. 322, 311, 351
Clarke, B. 50,158, 184, 298 322
Clarke, D. 50, 158, 184, 298 322
Clement, J. 163, 185
Cocchiarella, M. J. 184, 187
Cockburn, A. 238
Cody, C. 238
Cohen, L.50, 84, 128, 150,279,298
Cohn, M. M. 6ff, 20, 23, 26,33, 37, 51, 70, 264, 268
Coleman, J. S. 25
Collier, G. 295, 299
Collis, K. F. 295, 299
Combs, A. W. 85
Cone, W. F. 151
Connelly, F. M.
Connelly, F. M. 7, 23, 322
Cook, F. 322
Cook, J. 311, 322
Cook, P. 322
Cooney, T299, 322.
Corno, L. 120, 121
Coulby, D 84
Cowan, J.18, 26, 31, 49, 167, 186, 213, 237, 287, 376
Cowie, H. 85
Craig, R. C.198, 207
Crane, S. 350
Cranton, P. A. 293, 294, 299
Crawford, 64, 84
Crawford, K. R.
Crawford, W. R. 135, 167ff, 186
Cromwell, L. 44

Cronbach, L. 125
Crooks, T. J. 295, 299
Cross, K. P. 18. 25, 28, 36, 42 ff, 49,156, 390
Crutchfield, R. S. 85
Crynes, B. 187, 350
Crynes, D. A. 187, 350
Crynes, D. A. 187
Csikszentmihaly, I 120
Csikszentmihalyi, M. 74. 86 120
Cuban, L.301,309,320
Culver, R. 18, 356, 361, 381, 382
Curwin, R. L. 105
Cuttance, P. 84

Dacey, J. S 237
D'Amour, G. 251, 267
Daley, J. S.
Dalin, P. 24.
Damon, W. 383
Davies, B. M. 151
Davies, D. 85
Davis, D. 350
Dawson, S. 51
Day, J.C.121
e Bono, E. 359
de Cecco, J. P. 64, 84, 135, 167 ff 186
de Lange, J. 321
de Maura, Z. 383
Deci, E. L. 73, 86
Desgorges, C. 238
Dewey, J. 188, 206, 302, 303, 362
di Sessa, A. 194, 206, 387, 390
Dillehunt, H. Q.381
Dillman, E.24
Dittan, C. 187
Dimmit, N. J. 133, 150
Dishon, D. 120
Dixon, M. 220, 224, 238
Donnely, P. 370, 383
Donovan, S. S. 122
Doverspike, D. 239
Dressel, P. 120, 184, 283, 298
Driver, R. 164,166, 185, 186
Duignan, P. A. 26, 49
Dunleavy, P. 172, 187
Dunn, K. 122, 217 ff, 238
Dunn, R. 122, 217 ff, 238

Eck, R. W. 252, 267
Egan, K. 104, 121

Eggleston, J. 7, 23, 84, 306 ff, 309, 322
Eisner, E. 27, 32, 41, 49, 273, 247, 288, 290, 298, 349
Elias, M. J. 120
Elkind, D. 238, 372, 383
Ellenbein, D. 383
Elliott, J. 28, 29 ff, 36, 43, 45ff, 122
Elton, Lord 84
Ennis, R. H. 244, 266, 285, 287, 298, 302, 320
Entwistle, N. J. 214, 237
Erickson, G. L. 84
Erickson, H. L. 182, 185
Estes, T. H. 50, 184
Etzioni, E. 371
Evans, D. L. 350
Eysenck, H. J. 234, 240
Ezzat, E. S. 350

Feasey, R. 24
Felder, R. 390
Fernandez, Prieta, G 185.
Festinger, L. 85
Feurestein 102, 104
Fischer, C. F. 151
Fischer, K. W. 363, 383
Fiske, K. E. 84
Fitch, P. 361, 382
FitzGibbon, A. 34, 50, 221, 223, 231, 238, 240
FitzGibbons, R. E. 260
FitzMaurice, J. 12, 25
FitzMaurice, M. 212
Flinders, D. J. 321
Fogarty, R. 335, 350
Fordyce, D. 185
Forrest, A. 351
Fox, R. D. 351
Fraser, W. J. 151
Freeman, J. 237
Freire, P. 304, 321
French, W. L. 85
Friedman, F. 237
Frieurich, L. 26
Fritz, R. 322
Furneaux, W. D. 234, 240, 247, 267
Furst, E. J 150, 277, 297 313, 314, 321.

Gage, N. L. 120, 184
Gagné, R.S. 85, 99
Gale, J. 320

Gall, J.P. 120
Gall, M. D. 120
Galloway, D. 84
Galyean, B. C. 103 ff, 121
Gardener, H. 26, 354, 359, 381, 388
Garné, R. M. 157, 169 ff, 179, 185, 189, 196, 197, 200, 207
Garry, R. F. 24
George, J. 26, 49
George, T. 18
Getzels, J. 237
Gibbs, G. 295, 299
Gibbs, J. C. 383
Gijselaers, W. G. 350
Gilbert, D. T. 84
Gillan, J. 151
Gilligan, C. 374, 383
Glaser, R. 185
Glasser, W. 71, 85
Glatthorn, A. A. 298, 320, 329, 349
Gleeson, D. 342, 350, 351
Godwin, D. B. 187
Golden, G. A. 291, 299
Goldthorpe, J. 86
Goleman, D. 122, 356, 381
Good, T. L. 84
Goodenough, D. R. 237
Goodlad, I. 25, 301, 320
Goodnow, J. J. 85
Grasha, A. J. 209, 210, 236, 224
Green, S. 340
Greene, B. 187
Greene, D. 86
Gregory, S. A. 237
Grigorenko, E. L. 381
Grimmett. P. P. 49
Gronlund, N. 141, 151
Grouws, D. 120, 299
Grubb, W. N. 351
Gruber, D. C. 321
Gubbins, P 286
Guilford, J. 210
Gunter, M. A. 95, 120, 184

Hacking, I. 185
Hake, P. 151
Hall, C. 105, 121
Hall, E, 105, 121
Halpin, A. 84
Hamblin 84
Hamilton, D. 42, 50

NAME INDEX

Hampson, P. J. 121
Hanesian, H. 207
Hanson, R. J. 240
Harper, T. 84
Harris, C. W. 186
Harris, W. 306
Harrold, C. 382
Harrow, J. 277, 297
Hart, L. 121
Harvey, J. H.
Hatch, G. 43, 51
Hedlund, J. 357, 381
Heirs, B. 33, 50
Helsby, G. 23, 314, 323
Henry, J. 120
Hereford, S. 298
Hernstein Smith, B. 164, 185
Hesseling, P. 5, 23, 68, 69,85
Hestenes, D. 185
Heywood, J. 23, 24, 51, 84, 107, 120, 150, 161, 187, 207, 237, 240, 245, 267, 283, 297, 298, 320, 349, 350, 384, 390
Heywood, S. 207
Hiebert, J. 120
Hickey, J. 383
Hides, M. T. 185
Higgins, A. 383
Higgs, J. 350
Highouse, S. 239
Hillman, J. 25
Hinde, I, 49
Hirsch, E. D. 321
Hirst, P. H. 302, 305, 320, 321
Holland, J. L. 239
Holliday, C. 71, 75, 84
Holubec, E. J. 109, 110
Honey, P. 224, 239
Hopson, B. 120, 358, 381
Howard, R. W. 177, 178, 187
Hoyle, E, 4, 8, 24
Hoyt, B. 242, 266
Hudson, L. 210, 222, 237
Hughes, A. S. 336, 350
Humphreys, W. L. 390
Hunt, E. 188, 194, 195, 206
Hunt, M. P. 50
Hutchins, R. 321
Imbrie, R. W.294, 299

Isaacs, S. 369, 382

Jablonka, E. 322
Jackson, A. S. 381
Jackson, L.51, 120
Jackson, P. W.16, 23, 52, 150, 237, 276, 279, 317, 320, 322
Jacobsen, D. R. 120
Jamieson, I 343, 350
Jaques, E. 85
Javorski, B. 51
Jencks, C. 25
Jenkins, S. 340, 350
Jensen, E. 240
Johnson, D. W. 109, 110, 112, 113 , 114, 112, 121
Johnson, G. 187
Johnson, N. A. 63, 84
Johnson, R. H. 298, 371, 383
Johnson, R. W. 109, 110, 112, 113,114, 112, 121
Johnson, S. M. 26
Jones, E. E. 84
Jones, M. 350
Jones, R. 349
Jordan, T. A. 237
Jordan, W. M. 362, 382
Joyce, B. 120
Judson, G. 104, 121, 121

Kagan, S. 116, 122
Kahney, H. 266
Kaplan, L.291,293, 299
Kast, F. E .85
Kates, S. L 186.
Kaufman, K. 383
Kazdin, A. E. 72, 85
Keane, D. 240
Keane, D.26
Kelly, D. T. 120, 151,207, 267, 349
Kenny, S. L. 382
Keogh, B. 187
Kersh, B. Y198, 199, 207
Kiersey, D. 234, 240
Kilpatrick, J. 48, 51
King, P. M. 362 ff, 382
King, R. M. 151
Kirby, J. R. 212, 219, 237
Kirk, T. 110 ff, 122
Kitchener, K. S. 362 ff, 382
Klausmier, H. J. 186
Kline, P. 240
Knight, P. T. 321

399

Kohlberg, L 372 ff, 383
Kohn, A.33, 50, 72 ff, 85
Kolb, D. 219 ff, 238
Kottkamp, R 6ff. 20, 23, 26, 27,33, 47, 51. 70, 264, 268
Kramp, M. K. 390
Krathwohl, D. R. 150, 291, 292, 299
Krech, D. 85
Kulik, J. 111, 121
Kulik, L.111, 121

LaBoskey, V. K. 30, 49
Landa, L. P. 206
Langer, E. J. 383
Leary, D. W. 86
Leder, G. C.299, 322
Leech, A. 105, 121
Leech, G. 186
Leibold, B. G. 268
Leino, A. S. 207
Leithwood, K. A. 84.
Lennon, K. H. 237
Lepper, M. 86
Lerman, S. 302, 321
Lewin, K. 51
Lewis, A. 284, 298
Lewis, B. 211
Lewts, M. 351
Lieberman, A. 26
Lindsay. E 350
Lindzey, G 84
Lipman, M.369 ff, 383
Litynski, D. M.267
Livson, N. 65
Lloyd, C. M.
Loacker, G. 126, 223, 227, 239, 260, 268
Lortie, D. 6, 23
Lotkowski, V. 349
Luchins, A. S 85,239, 246, 267
Luria, A. R. 170, 186
Lydon, J. 255 ff, 259
Lynch, K. 320
Lyons, N. P.374, 383
MacPherson,. J. S. 26, 49
MacCarthy, B. 220, 221, 239
MacFarlane Smith, I. 121, 237, 240, 354, 381
MacIntosh, H. G. 151
MacMahon, A .24
MacMillan, J. B. 298
Macmurray, J. 366, 382

Madigan, C.85
Madaus, G. 243, 266
Magee, R. P. 298
Mager, R. P.
Mannion, L. 84, 18, 150, 279, 298
Mansfield, G. 318, 322
Maritain, J. 321
Marks, D. F. 121.
Marquis, D. B.321
Marra, R. 361, 382
Marsh, M. 185
Marshall, S. 383
Marton, F. 214, 237 ,
Marzano, R. J. 15, 307, 309, 310, 322, 329, 351, 390
Masia, B. 299
Maslow, A. 73, 77
Matthews, G. B. 368, 369, 382
Matthews, M. 111, 121
Matthews, M. E.
Matthews, M. R. 165, 166, 185, 186, 206, 321
Maughan, B.
Maughan, P. 25
Maxmanian. P. 350
Mayer, J. D. 381
Mayo, K. 25
McArthur, D. 351
McBeath, J. 90, 120
McCarthy, L. P. 390
McClean, M. 351
McClelleand, D. C. 65, 66, 84, 303, 320, 321, 384
McComiskey, J. G. 237
McDonald, F. J. 102, 120, 172, 186, 198, 207, 242, 266
McElwee, P. 164, 185
McGregor, D.60, 70
McGuiness, S. 26, 42, 43, 207, 267, 349
McKenzie, L.350
McKernan, J. 49
McLeod, D. B. 299
McLeskey, J. 390
McNulty, B. A. 15, 84, 322, 351, 390
McPeck, J. 244, 266, 371
Mendler, A. N. 105, 121
Mentkowski, M. 350, 367, 368, 381
Merret, P. 84
Messick, S. 236, 238
Metcalf, L. P. 50
Miller, N. E. 170, 186

NAME INDEX

Miller, T.C.G. 113
Minstrell, J. 188, 194, 195, 206
Monk, J. D. 23, 85
Montagu Pollock, H. 50, 245
Moor, T. E 187.
Moore, C. A. 237
Moran, G. 374, 375, 384
Morrison, K. 84, 128, 150
Mortimore, P. 12, 25
Mowbray, R. M. 151
Much, N. 383
Mumford, A. 234, 249
Munro, R. G. 24
Murphy, D. E. 26, 49, 207, 267, 287, 289, 298, 349
Murphy, J. M. 383
Murray, M. 26, 51 122. 187, 240 268, 322, 350, 376 ff, 390
Myers, I. B. 234

Nakamura, J74, 86, 120.
Nardi, A. H. 250, 251, 267
Narvaez, D. F 382.
Naylor, S 187.
Nesbitt, R. E. 84
Newman, J. H. 73, 297, 322, 353, 368, 376, 382
Noel, L. 351
Noeth, R. 349
Noonam, Z. M. 350.
Norman, G. R. 350
Norris, S. 244, 266, 322
Norris, S. P.
Northfield, J. 20, 26
Novak, J. S. 187, 207
Nuthall, G. 170, 186
Nygren, K. P. 267

O'Callaghan, C. 239
Oakes, J. 104, 121
Okagaki, L. 381
Oldham, V. 166, 186
Olds, B. 367
Olson, J. M. 84
Oltman, P. K.237
O'Neil, M. J. 51
Ormell, C. P.282, 298
Ornstein, A. C. 134, 150
Orton, A. 99, 120
Ossanyon, F. 383
Otter, S. 298

Otto, L. B. 320
Ouston, T. 25
Owen, D. R. 237
Oxtoby, R. 23, 85

Palmer, B. 361, 382
Pardueci, A. 85
Park, O. 187
Parker, J. D. E. 356, 381
Parlett, M. 42, 50
Pask, G. 219, 211, 212, 219, 237
Patterson, C. H. 206
Pellagrino, J. 150, 349
Pellicer, L. O. 13, 25
Perkins, D. 50, 267, 359, 381
Perrin, J. 122
Perry, W. G. 360, 382
Peter, W. 33, 56, 58, 75 ff, 84, 86, 158
Petersen, D. 266, 287, 298
Pettitm D. 49
Phenix, P 302, 305, 320, 321
Phillips, D. K. 18, 26. 164
Piaget, J. 104, 121, 190, 360, 369, 372, 382
Pickering, D. J.
Pinar, W. F. 321
Pipp, S. W. 382
Plunkett, J. 183
Polya, G. 246, 249 250, 267
Posner, G. 306, 321
Potter, W.349, 350
Power, F. C. 383
Prawat, R. S. 102, 120, 184
Price, G. E. 238
Prince, M. 242, 266
Prior, P 45 ff
Pruitt, W.120
Ramirez, M. 343, 348, 351
Ramsden, P. 215, 238, 295, 299
Ramsey, G. B. 85
Ramsey, K. 351
Reason, G.21, 26
Reason, L 21, 26
Red, W. E.260, 267, 268
Reed, S. K 247, 267
Rees, E. 185
Reigeluth, C. H. 191, 192, 206
Rentz, D. A. 151
Resnick, L. B. 267
Rest Narvaez
Rest, J. 374, 383

401

Reynolds, D. 84
Ribbins, P. 25
Rice, J. V. 320
Richardson, J. E. 121
Riehl, G. 84
Rist, 64, 84
Ritsohn, J.
Robbins, S. 349
Roberts, R. F.39
Roberts, T 268
Robitaille, D. F. 120
Rogers, C. G. 84
Rosati, P. A. 267
Rosch, E. 187
Rosenberg, M.122
Rosenzweig, J. E. 85
Ross, M. 84
Ross, S. 266
Rowe, M. B. 134, 150
Rubin, D. 390
Rutsohn, J.240
Rutter, M. 25, 238
Ryan, A. 35, 50
Ryan, K. 120
Rycarz, R. A. 383
Ryle, A. 240, 350

Saljö, R. 214, 237
Salovey, P. 381
Saluri, D. 351
Sammons, P. 25
Sanford, N. 237
Saupé, J.L 121, 122, 157, 248, 267
Savoie, J. M. 336, 350
Scally, M, 120, 358, 381
Scandura, J. M. 99, 120
Schaaf, P. 383
Schaefer, J. 20.
Schein, E. 84, 85
Schmeck, R. R.217, 237
Schmidt, H. G. 350
Schön, D. 26, 31, 37, 85, 322
Schubert, W. H.303, 304,306 ff. 321
Schwab, J 50,120.184
Schwab, J.16, 25
Schweder, R. 383
Segall, A. 187
Selbourne, D. 371
Sellers, P. 322
Selmes, I. P. 238
Seyd, R. 84

Sharp, A. M. 383
Sharp, J. 185
Shaver, K. G. 84
Shiu, 85
Shulman, L. S.30, 120, 125, 150, 158, 164, 164, 185, 188, 190, 197, 206
Sierpinska, R. 51, 302, 321
Silver, H. F. 240
Simon, H. 249, 267
Sims, 239
Skemp, R. R. 108, 121. 167, 186
Skolnik, S. 206
Slavin, R. E. 109, 121
Smith, D. 284, 298
Smith, D. J. 238,
Smith, K,. A. 121
Snygg, D. 85
Sosniak, L. A. 297
Springer, L. 122
Stager, R. A.249, 250 ff, 267
Stalker, G. 384
Stanne, M. E. 122
Stannard, R. 206
Stanne, M. E.
Stanworth, M. 85
Stasz, C. 351
Steadman, M. 18, 26, 42, 43, 50, 156
Steffe, L. D. 320
Steinaker, N. 277, 292, 297, 299
Stern, C. 171, 186
Sternberg, R. H. 298, 325, 349, 354, 356, 357, 381
Stevenson, H. W. 50
Stice, J. E. 221, 281, 290, 298
Stigler, J. W. 50
Stone, K. F. 381
Strother, D. 120
Suchman, J. B. 198, 207
Sullivan, P. 50, 158, 164, 298, 322
Svensson, L.237
Svinicki, M. D. 220, 223, 224, 238 298
Swackhamer, G. 185
Swan, V. 25

Taba, H. 135, 150, 179, 187
Taiguri, R. 85
Tamblyn, R. 350
Tappan, M. B. 383
Taraban, R. 185
Tennyson, R. D. 184, 187
Thoma, S. J. 321,383

NAME INDEX

Thomas, B. 85
Thomas, P. R.
Thomas, S. 25
Thompson, D. J. 151
Thornton, S. J.
Thouless, R. 85
Tobin, K. 49
Todd, R. H. 220, 239
Travers, K. J. 120
Tsang, E. 366, 382
Turiel, E. 383
Tversky, A. 249, 267
Tyler, L. E. 213, 236, 273, 275, 276, 279, 297, 316, 317, 323
Tyler, R. W. 9, 19, 26, 150

Underbakke, M. 287, 298

van Helden, H. J. 40, 50
Vardy, P. 185
Vaughan, F. 121
Vonk, J. H. K. 40, 50

Wager, W. W. 207
Walberg, H. J. 320
Waldron, W. L. 390
Wales, C. E. 249, 250 ff, 267
Walsh, R. N. 121
Walvoord, B. E. 390
Wang, L. Q. 50
Waring, M. 23
Warren Piper, D. 9. 24
Waters, T. 15, 84, 322, 351, 390
Watkins, D. 237
Weary, G. 84
Weber, F. 221, 239
Weber, P. 221, 239
Weil, M. 120
Weinbaum, A. 26, 27, 156
Wells, J. M. 79, 120
Wells, M. 185
Westbury, I. 25
Weston, C. A. 293, 294, 299
Weston, D. 383
Wheldall, C. F. 84
Whitehead, A. N. 297, 337 ff, 350, 375, 384
Whitehead, B. M. 298, 320, 349
Whitfield, P. R. 237
Wilhelm, J. D.
Wilhelm, W. J. 252, 267, 349

Wilkinson, B. 238
Wilkof, N. J. 25
Williams, J. 383
Williams, M. W. 267
Willis, S. 121
Wilson, C. 187
Wilson, J. D. 237
Wilson, M. 240, 299
Wilson, S. 322
Windeatt, S, 186.
Witkin, H. A. 213, 238, 237
Wittrock, M. C. 166, 185, 199, 200, 246, 267
Wolfe, P 121, 390
Wood, P. K 366, 382.
Wood, R. 150
Wood, T. 51, 322
Woods, D. R. 246, 266, 350, 361, 382
Wright, A. T. 351
Wringe, C. 303, 321
Wynne, E. A. 120

Yokomoto, C. F. 275, 280, 297
Young, D. 113, 122
Young, M. F. D. 302, 322
Youngman, M. B. 23, 84, 151

Yudavitch, I. 170, 186.
Yudin, L. 186

Zirkl, S. 381